Praise for

BOLÍVAR

"Finally, Bolívar gets the sweeping biography he deserves. He was the greatest leader in Latin American history, and his tale is filled with lessons about leadership and passion. This book reads like a wonderful novel but is researched like a masterwork of history."

—Walter Isaacson, author of *Steve Jobs*

"This is a magnificent story. Deeply researched and written with clarity, honesty, and verve, Marie Arana's book tells the life of one of the greatest heroes and founders in world history."

—Gordon S. Wood, author of *Empire of Liberty: A History of the Early Republic, 1789–1815,* Alva O. Way University Professor and Professor of History Emeritus at Brown University

"With the eye and ear of a novelist, Marie Arana chants the epic of Bolívar with love, zest, and compelling authority."

—Walter A. McDougall, Pulitzer Prize–winning historian and Alloy-Ansin Professor of International Relations, University of Pennsylvania

"Simón Bolívar has found the perfect biographer in Marie Arana, a literary journalist, brilliant novelist of South America, and wise historian as well. Her portrait of Bolívar is human and moving; she has written a powerful and epic life and times."

—Evan Thomas, author of *Ike's Bluff: President Eisenhower's Secret Battle to Save the World*

"*Bolívar* is magisterial in scope, written with flair and an almost cinematic sense of history happening. . . . A monumental achievement."

—Joseph J. Ellis, *The Washington Post Book World*

"Wonderful. . . . In Arana's energetic and highly readable telling, Bolívar comes alive as having willed himself an epic life. . . . She brings great verve and literary flair to her biography of Bolívar."

—Hector Tobar, *Los Angeles Times*

"Arana offers a clear-eyed assessment of the ideals, alliances, and human frailties that drove Bolívar's choices and shaped the Americas."

—*The New Yorker*

"Arana's prose is often beautiful. A novelist turned historian, she tells Bolívar's story wonderfully. . . . Two centuries after his death, Bolívar inflames passions that better-known characters no longer ignite. Arana's biography explains why."

—Giles Tremlett, *The Guardian* (UK)

"Arana is an indefatigable researcher, a perceptive historian, and a luminous writer, as shown in her defining, exhilarating biography of the great South American liberator Simón Bolívar."

—*Booklist* (starred review, Top 10 Biographies of the Year)

"Reads like a novel, filled as it is with portraits, landscapes, and memorable scenes, and composed with great brio and colorful detail."

—Enrique Krauze, *The New York Review of Books*

"A fascinating biography of the charismatic military leader who sparked a revolution."

—Abbe Wright, *O Magazine*

"[A] superbly balanced, but ultimately sympathetic, biography. . . . [Arana] has an instinct for the vitalising detail."

—Nicholas Shakespeare, *The Telegraph* (UK)

"Thrilling, authoritative, and revelatory, here at last is a biography of Bolívar, the maker of South America, that catches the sheer extraordinary unique adventure and titanic scale of his life with accessible narrative and scholarly judgment."

—Simon Sebag Montefiore, author of *Jerusalem: The Biography*

"[Arana's] biography is so close to experience that we are back with Bolívar himself, 'exuberant mustache and dazzling smile,' almost feeling the wind as he passes."

—Jason Wilson, *The Independent* (UK)

"*Epic* is a word used too often to describe lesser work, but Marie Arana's marvelously readable *Bolívar: American Liberator* is a biography that earns its adjective."

—David Walton, *The Dallas Morning News*

"This well-rounded work reveals not just an accomplished military tactician but also an able statesman. . . . An important contribution to Bolivarian studies."

—*Library Journal* (starred review)

"Inspired. . . . Arana ably captures the brash brilliance of this revered and vilified leader."

—*Kirkus Reviews*

ALSO BY MARIE ARANA

BOLIVAR

BOLÍVAR

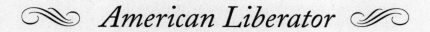

American Liberator

MARIE ARANA

SIMON & SCHUSTER PAPERBACKS
New York   London   Toronto   Sydney   New Delhi

Simon & Schuster Paperbacks
A Division of Simon & Schuster, Inc.
1230 Avenue of the Americas
New York, NY 10020

First Simon & Schuster paperback edition April 2014

SIMON & SCHUSTER PAPERBACKS and colophon are registered
trademarks of Simon & Schuster, Inc.

For information about special discounts for bulk purchases,
please contact Simon & Schuster Special Sales at
1-866-506-1949 or business@simonandschuster.com.

The Simon & Schuster Speakers Bureau can bring authors
to your live event. For more information or to book an event,
contact the Simon & Schuster Speakers Bureau at
1-866-248-3049 or visit our website at www.simonspeakers.com.

Designed by Joy O'Meara

Manufactured in the United States of America

10 9 8 7 6 5 4 3 2 1

The Library of Congress has cataloged the hardcover edition as follows:
Arana, Marie.
    Bolívar : American liberator / Marie Arana. — 1st Simon & Schuster
hardcover ed.
      p. cm.
    Includes bibliographical references and index.
1. Bolívar, Simón, 1783–1830. 2. Heads of state—South America—
Biography. 3. South America—History—Wars of Independence,
1806–1830. I. Title.
    F2235.3.A876 2013
    980'.02092—dc23
    [B]   2012034661
ISBN 978-1-4391-1019-5
ISBN 978-1-4391-1020-1 (pbk)
ISBN 978-1-4391-2495-6 (ebook)

Frontispiece drawing by José María Espinosa, Colección Fundación John
Boulton, Caracas.

For Rosa Victoria Arana and George Winston Arana,
my loyal and lifelong accomplices.

You can't speak with calm about a person who never knew calm; of Bolívar you can only speak from mountaintops, or amid thunder and lightning, or with a fistful of freedom in one hand and the corpse of tyranny at your feet.

—José Martí

Contents

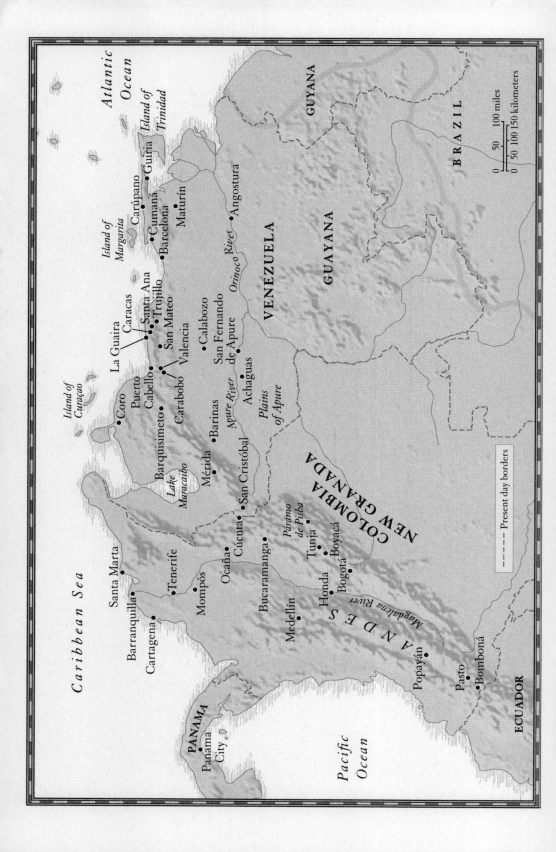

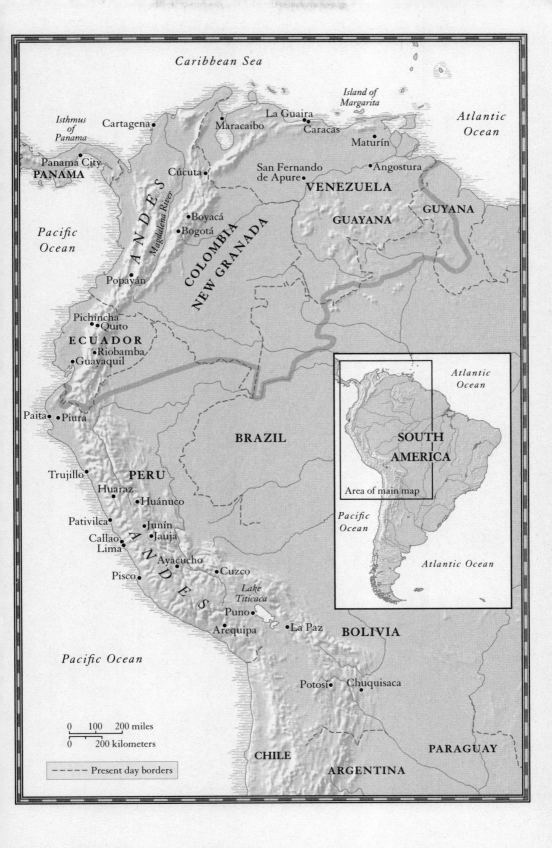

BOLÍVAR

CHAPTER I

The Road to Bogotá

We, who are as good as you, make you our lord and master.
We trust you to defend our rights and liberties.
And if not: No.

—Coronation ceremony, Spain

They heard him before they saw him: the sound of hooves striking the earth, steady as a heartbeat, urgent as a revolution. When he emerged from the sun-dappled forest, they could barely make out the figure on the magnificent horse. He was small, thin. A black cape fluttered about his shoulders.

The rebels eyed him with unease. All four had been riding north, fully expecting to come upon a royalist fleeing in the other direction, away from the battle at Boyacá. Three days before, the Spaniards had been surprised by a lightning strike of revolutionaries—barefoot, wild-eyed—swarming down over the Andes. The Spanish were running now, scattering over the landscape like a herd of frightened deer.

"Here comes one of those losing bastards," said the rebel general. Hermógenes Maza was a veteran of the wars of independence in Spanish America. He had been captured and tortured by royalists, had honed a hunger for revenge. He spurred his horse, rode forward. "Halt!" he cried out. "Who goes there?"

The rider pressed on at full gallop.

General Maza raised his lance and bellowed his warning one more time. But the stranger only advanced, ignoring him. When he got near enough to render his features sharp and unmistakable, he turned coolly to glare at the rebel general. *"¡Soy yo!"* the man shouted. "Don't be a dumb sonofabitch."

The general's jaw went slack. He lowered his lance, let the horseman pass.

So it was that Simón Bolívar rode into Santa Fe de Bogotá, the capital of the New Kingdom of Granada, on the sweltering afternoon of August 10, 1819. He had spent thirty-six days traversing the flooded plains of Venezuela; six days marching over the vertiginous snows of the Andes. By the time he reached the icy pass at thirteen thousand feet called the Páramo de Pisba, his men were barely alive, scarcely clothed, flogging themselves to revive their failing circulation. He had lost a third of them to frost or starvation, most of his weapons to rust, every last horse to hypothermia. Even so, as he and his scruffy troops staggered down the cliffs, stopping at villages along the way, he had rallied enough fresh recruits and supplies to win a resounding victory that in time would link his name to Napoleon's and Hannibal's. As news of his triumph spread, it quickened the rebels' hopes and sent a cold prick of fear through the Spaniards.

The capital of the viceroyalty was the first to react. On hearing of Bolívar's advance, agents of the crown abandoned their houses, possessions, businesses. Whole families took flight with little more than the clothes on their back. Maza and his companions could hear the deafening detonations as Spanish soldiers destroyed their own arsenals and hurried for the hills. Even the cruel and ill-tempered viceroy, Juan José de Sámano, disguised as a lowly Indian in a poncho and grimy hat, fled the city in a panic. He knew that Bolívar's retribution would be swift and severe. "War to the Death!" had been the Liberator's battle cry; after one battle, he had called for the cold-blooded execution of eight hundred Spaniards. Sámano understood that he, too, had been ruthless, ordering the torture and extermination of thousands in the name of the Spanish throne. Reprisals were sure to follow. The king's loyalists flowed out of Santa Fe, as Bogotá was then called, flooding the roads that led south, emptying Santa Fe until its streets were eerily silent and the only residents left were on the side of independence. When Bolívar got word of it, he leapt on his horse, ordered his aides-de-camp to follow, and raced ahead, virtually alone, toward the viceroy's palace.

Although Maza had fought under the Liberator years before, he hardly recognized the man passing before him now. He was gaunt, shirtless, his chest bare under the ragged blue jacket. Beneath the worn leather cap, his hair had grown long and grizzled. His skin was rough from wind, bronzed by the sun. His trousers, once a deep scarlet, had faded to a dull pink; his cape, which doubled as a bed, was stained by time and mud.

He was thirty-six years old, and, although the disease that would take his life already coiled in his veins, he seemed vibrant and strong, filled with a boundless energy. As he crossed into Santa Fe and made his way down the Calle Real, an old woman rushed toward him. "God bless you, phantom!" she called, sensing—despite his dishevelment—a singular greatness. House by house, others ventured out, at first tentatively, and then in a surging human mass that followed him all the way to the plaza. He dismounted in one agile movement and ran up the palace steps.

For all his physical slightness—five foot six inches and a scant 130 pounds—there was an undeniable intensity to the man. His eyes were a piercing black, his gaze unsettling. His forehead was deeply lined, his cheekbones high, his teeth even and white, his smile surprising and radiant. Official portraits relay a less than imposing man: the meager chest, the impossibly thin legs, the hands as small and beautiful as a woman's. But when Bolívar entered a room, his power was palpable. When he spoke, his voice was galvanizing. He had a magnetism that seemed to dwarf sturdier men.

He enjoyed good cuisine, but could endure days, even weeks, of punishing hunger. He spent backbreaking days on his horse: his stamina in the saddle was legendary. Even the *llaneros,* roughriders of the harsh Venezuelan plains, called him, with admiration, Iron Ass. Like those men, he preferred to spend nights in a hammock or wrapped in his cape on bare ground. But he was equally comfortable in a ballroom or at the opera. He was a superb dancer, a spirited conversationalist, a cultivated man of the world who had read widely and could quote Rousseau in French and Julius Caesar in Latin. A widower and sworn bachelor, he was also an insatiable womanizer.

By the time Bolívar mounted the stairs to the viceroy's palace on that sultry August day, his name was already known around the world. In Washington, John Quincy Adams and James Monroe agonized over whether their fledgling nation, founded on principles of liberty and freedom, should support his struggle for independence. In London, hard-bitten veterans of England's war against Napoleon signed on to fight for Bolívar's cause. In Italy, the poet Lord Byron named his boat after Bolívar and dreamed of emigrating to Venezuela with his daughter. But there would be five more years of bloodshed before Spain was thrust from Latin American shores. At the end of that savage and chastening war, one man would be credited for single-handedly conceiving, organizing, and leading the liberation of six nations: a population one and a half times that of North America, a landmass the size of modern Europe. The odds against which he fought—a formidable, established world power, vast areas of untracked wilderness, the splintered loyalties of many races—would have proved daunting for the ablest of generals with strong armies at his command. But Bolívar had never been a soldier. He had no formal military training. Yet, with little more than will and a genius for leadership, he freed much of Spanish America and laid out his dream for a unified continent.

Despite all this, he was a highly imperfect man. He could be impulsive, headstrong, filled with contradictions. He spoke eloquently about justice, but wasn't always able to mete it out in the chaos of revolution. His romantic life had a way of spilling into the public realm. He had trouble accepting criticism and had no patience for disagreements. He was singularly incapable of losing gracefully at cards. It is hardly surprising that, over the years, Latin Americans have learned to accept human imperfections in their leaders. Bolívar taught them how.

As Bolívar's fame grew, he became known as the George Washington of South America. There were good reasons why. Both came from wealthy and influential families. Both were ardent defenders of freedom. Both were heroic in war, but apprehensive about marshaling the peace. Both resisted efforts to make them kings. Both claimed to want to return to private lives, but were called instead to shape governments. Both were accused of undue ambition.

There the similarities end. Bolívar's military action lasted twice as long as Washington's. The territory he covered was seven times as large and spanned an astonishing geographic diversity: from crocodile-infested jungles to the snowcapped reaches of the Andes. Moreover, unlike Washington's war, Bolívar's could not have been won without the aid of black and Indian troops; his success in rallying all races to the patriot cause became a turning point in the war for independence. It is fair to say that he led both a revolution and a civil war.

But perhaps what distinguishes these men above all can be seen most clearly in their written work. Washington's words were measured, august, dignified—the product of a cautious and deliberate mind. Bolívar's speeches and correspondence, on the other hand, were fiery, passionate. They represent some of the greatest writing in Latin American letters. Although much was produced in haste—on battlefields, on the run—the prose is at once lyrical and stately, clever but historically grounded, electric yet deeply wise. It is no exaggeration to say that Bolívar's revolution changed the Spanish language, for his words marked the dawn of a new literary age. The old, dusty Castilian of his time, with its ornate flourishes and cumbersome locutions, in his remarkable voice and pen became another language entirely—urgent, vibrant, and young.

There is yet another important difference. Unlike Washington's glory, Bolívar's did not last unto the grave. In time, the politics in the countries Bolívar created grew ever more fractious, his detractors ever more vehement. Eventually, he came to believe that Latin Americans were not ready for a truly democratic government: abject, ignorant, suspicious, they did not understand how to govern themselves, having been systematically deprived of that experience by their Spanish oppressors. What they needed, in his eyes, was a strong hand, a strict executive. He began making unilateral decisions. He installed a dictator in Venezuela; he announced to Bolivia that it would have a president for life.

By the time he was forty-one, his wisdom began to be doubted by functionaries in every republic he had freed and founded. His deputies—jealous and wary of his extraordinary power—declared they no longer supported his dream of a unified Latin America. Regionalisms emerged, followed by border squabbles, civil wars, and, in Bolívar's own halls, cloak-and-dagger betrayals. Trumped at last, he had no choice but to renounce command. His forty-seventh—and final—year ended in poverty, illness, and exile. Having given away the sum total of his personal fortune to the revolution, he died a poor and ravaged man. Few heroes in history have been dealt so much honor, so much power— and so much ingratitude.

But on the afternoon of August 10, 1819, as he stood at the viceroy's splendid desk in the palace in Santa Fe de Bogotá, there was no limit to the possibilities of Bolívar's America. The Spanish despot had left the room in such alarm that he had neglected to take the bag of gold on his table. Indeed, as Bolívar lay claim to the hoard of pesos left behind in the viceregal treasury, he understood that the tide had finally turned: his revolution stood to inherit all the abandoned riches of a waning empire. It would also inherit a whirlwind of political and social chaos. In a matter of a few years, Spain's three-century yoke on the Americas would be sundered and the truly difficult journey toward freedom would begin.

THE JOURNEY OF SIMÓN BOLÍVAR'S life began in 1783, a year that was rife with incident. In an otherwise unremarkable building in Paris, Benjamin Franklin and John Adams signed a treaty with the king of England that effectively ended the American Revolution. In the radiant palace of Versailles, an emotionally fragile Marie Antoinette lost the much awaited child she was carrying. In an austere military academy in northeastern France, an adolescent Napoleon was developing a keen interest in war games. In the ancient city of Cuzco, the cousin of Túpac Amaru II led a violent insurrection against the Spanish, for which he was tortured, killed, and dismembered. In a drinking establishment in Manhattan, George Washington ended his command of the Continental Army by bidding a warm farewell to his officers.

But in the balmy city of Caracas, walled from the vicissitudes of the Caribbean by a string of green mountains, life was a sleepy affair. On July 24, 1783, as dawn filled the windows of the Bolívar family's stately mansion in the center of the city, the only sound was the serene trickle of drinking water filtering through rock into a pantry jar. Before long, the cock would crow, the horses neigh, and a whole bustling household complete with children and slaves would burst to noisy life as Doña María de la Concepción Palacios y Blanco went into labor.

She was a dark, wavy-haired beauty whose will and fortitude belied her twenty-three years. She had been married at fourteen to Colonel Don Juan Vicente de Bolívar, a tall, self-possessed, blond bachelor thirty-two years older, whose predatory sexual escapades had often landed him before the bishop of Caracas. Both man and wife brought long traditions of wealth and power to their marriage: their elegant manse on San Jacinto Street and the extensive properties they had inherited over the years were a measure of their station in a privileged world. On that summer's day, as they awaited the birth of their fourth child, they owned no fewer than twelve houses in Caracas and the port of La Guaira, a sprawling hacienda in the valley of Aragua, a copper mine, sugar fields, fruit orchards, a rum distillery, a textile business, cacao and indigo plantations, as well as cattle ranches, and hundreds of slaves. They were among the most prosperous families of Venezuela.

As Latin American custom has it, in a ritual that goes back five hundred years, no sooner had word of Doña Concepción's labor spread from the servants to the neighbors than friends began to gather in the house's parlor to await the birth. By the time the child was born that night, a festive crowd of well-wishers was toasting his health, among them the bishop, the judge, the velvet-sleeved patriarchs of Caracas's old families, and a rich priest who would baptize the boy and, within a matter of months, bequeath him a fortune. They stood in the great room, resting their elbows on ponderous carved mahogany chests and tables. The chairs were covered in dark upholstery; the mirrors heavy with decoration; the damask curtains a deep, gleaming purple, crowned with cornices of burnished gold. The servants offered refreshments from trays and, under the glittering chandeliers, the conversation was jovial and lighthearted. One by one, intimate family members were admitted to the chamber next to the living room, where they saw the pale mother bedecked in white lace, sitting up in bed under a brocade canopy. Beside her, in a lavish cradle, was the sleeping child.

Although she previously had borne three healthy children—María Antonia, who was then six; Juana, five; and Juan Vicente, two—Doña Concepción was well aware that she was ailing. As soon as she told

Don Juan Vicente of her pregnancy, he arranged for one of their prized female slaves to marry, conceive, and deliver a child at about the same time so that his wife could be relieved of the responsibility of nursing the newborn. It was a common enough practice at the time. The black slave Hipólita would prove to be a devoted nursemaid whose tender attentions to the boy would later be vividly remembered, even glorified, but on July 24, she had yet to give birth and had no milk to offer her master's child. For the first few weeks of the infant's life, Doña Concepción had to rely on one of her closest friends—Inés Mancebo, the Cuban wife of Fernando de Miyares, who later became governor-general of Venezuela—to do the nursing. Frail but determined, Doña Concepción was making the best of things. She did not yet evince the yellow, waxen skin that betrays the victims of tuberculosis. The small circle of intimates who gathered in her bedroom had every expectation that mother and boy would thrive.

Though Don Juan Vicente's lively blue eyes shone as he chatted with friends and relatives in the parlor, those eyes, too, were lit with his wife's fever. Consumption, as it was known, was prevalent in the world at that time, but in few places was it more rampant than in the sweltering South American tropics. The colonel was nearing sixty and looked far older than his years, yet, when the priest asked him what name he wanted to give his son, he replied with youthful energy. "Simón," he said, and pointed to the image of the man whose bold, confident face dominated the room.

THE PORTRAIT IN THE ELABORATE gold frame above Don Juan Vicente's sofa was of Simón de Bolívar, "El Viejo" ("The Old Man"), who, almost two centuries earlier, had been the first Bolívar to emigrate from Spain. The Old Man was by no means the first of the Liberator's ancestors to reach the New World. Through Doña Concepción, the newborn was also a descendant of the powerful Xedlers, a family of German nobles who had settled in Almagro, Spain, and acquired interests in the Americas. In 1528, Charles V had granted a select group of German bankers the right to conquer and exploit the northern coast of South America. Their advent marked the start of a ruthless era, dominated by the relentless pursuit of riches and, especially, the legendary El Dorado, the "lost city of gold." Another of the family's distant relatives, Lope de Aguirre—the infamous Basque conquistador also known as El Loco—had wreaked murderous havoc up and down the continent in search of the same dazzling chimeras.

But Simón de Bolívar, a Basque from the town of Marquina, had come on a very different mission. He arrived in Santo Domingo in the 1560s as a member of Spain's royal civil service, whose express purpose during those years was to impose some measure of discipline on the wild bonanza that Spanish America had become. Santo Domingo was the capital of the Caribbean island of Hispaniola—now Haiti and the Dominican Republic. As the first seat of colonial rule in the Americas, Santo Domingo was, during that period, the staging area for a new, brash initiative to tame the unruly coast of Venezuela, where hostile Indian tribes and rapacious pirates were playing havoc with Spain's efforts at colonization. Toward that purpose, in 1588, King Philip II bestowed on the island's governor, Diego Osorio, the additional responsibility of governing the province of Venezuela. Osorio decided to take de Bolívar, by then his trusted aide and scribe, to Caracas with him to carry out the king's wishes. Accompanied by his wife and son, de Bolívar set himself up handsomely in that emerging city, and went about acquiring enormous tracts of land even as he did the governor's bidding.

Under Osorio's auspices, de Bolívar became regent and procurator of Caracas and accountant general of Venezuela, and in those capacities sailed to Spain to report on the status of "Tierra Firma," as South America was known, to King Philip II himself. De Bolívar turned out to be a fairly civic-minded leader. He introduced large-scale agricultural projects—until then, unknown in that area of South America—and, with the collaboration of the Church, established a system of public education. With Osorio, he conceived and built the port of La Guaira, which would increase Venezuela's fortunes into the unbounded future. In 1592, he helped found the seminary that would eventually become the University of Caracas. De Bolívar built haciendas and created new wellsprings of commerce; he gave the city its first coat of arms. He also regulated the annual shipment of goods between Spain and the port of La Guaira, including the transport of one hundred tons of black slaves from Africa. In such ways did America's first Bolívar step into the continent's roiling history—not as an adventurer or settler, but as a high-ranking emissary of the Spanish crown.

Alongside this march of history, however, was the steady hardening of a racial hierarchy that would define South America into the modern age. It had begun when Christopher Columbus's men had landed on Hispaniola, and imposed their will over the Taíno people. At first, Queen Isabel and the Church roundly censured the capture and massacre of Indians. Columbus's men had committed harrowing atrocities, burning and destroying whole tribal villages, abducting natives as slaves, unleashing murderous plagues of syphilis and smallpox on the population. The priests who accompanied the crown's "civilizing missions" made a point of recording it all. As a result, the state tried to take a strong stance against any kind of institutionalized violence. It introduced a system of *encomiendas*, in which Spanish soldiers were assigned allotments of Indians and, in exchange for the task of instructing them in the Christian faith, were given the right to put them to work on the land or in the mines. The soldiers were often harsh and corrupt, killing natives who did not comply with their brutal demands, and, eventually, the system of encomiendas had to be abolished. But the notion of encouraging soldiers to work the land rather than live from plunder opened the way for a new era of plantation life.

Throughout, the state had a hard time enforcing laws that prohibited slavery. Even the queen had to agree that without the use of physical force, the Indians would refuse to work and the mines so necessary to Spain's economy would cease to function. There could be no gold, no silver, no sugar, without the systematic subjugation of American Indians. In 1503, a mere decade after Columbus stepped foot in America, the queen hedged on her initial disapprobation of slavery and decreed:

> Forasmuch as my Lord the King and Myself have ordered that the Indians living on the island of Hispaniola be considered free and not subject to slavery . . . I order you, Our Governor . . . to compel the Indians to cooperate with the Christian settlers on the said island, to work on their buildings, to mine and collect gold and other metals, and to work on their farms and crop fields.

In other words, killing was a Christian sin and genocide would not be tolerated, but "compelling" rebellious natives was a necessary evil. The Spanish colonizers understood the tacit approval in this. Despite the official condemnation of slavery, the state had conceded it would turn a blind eye. Indians continued to be a commodity to be owned and traded. And though Spanish sailors and Indian women had propagated freely from the start, a psychology of superiority and inferiority was established. It was best to be Spanish—unfortunate to be indigenous—in the New World that Europe had made.

The Dominican priest Bartolomé de Las Casas took issue with all this, especially the moral dithering about slaves. A former slave owner who had undergone an emphatic change of heart, he fumed about the brutalities Spaniards had visited on the Taíno people and the boatloads of indigenous slaves that Columbus was transporting regularly to Spain. "Slaves are the primary source of income for the Admiral," Las Casas wrote of Columbus. Finally, in an impassioned plea to Charles V, he argued that institutionalized barbarism had cruelly decimated the Indian population: "Spaniards are still acting like ravening beasts, killing, terrorizing, afflicting, torturing, and destroying the native peoples." In Hispaniola, they had reduced three million people to "a population of barely two hundred"; on the mainland of South America, they had stolen more than a million castellanos of gold and killed some 800,000 souls. A "Deep, Bloody American Tragedy" he called it, "choakt up with Indian Blood and Gore." To mitigate the damage—to prevent the depletion of these "humble, patient, and peaceable natives"—he advocated that Spain begin the importation of African slaves.

Eventually, Las Casas was to see the hypocrisy of that proposal, but not before the colonies had swung into a lively commerce. By the time Simón de Bolívar had made his children and grandchildren indisputably the richest landowning aristocrats of Caracas, there were ten thousand African slaves working the fields and plantations of Venezuela. The Indians, less able to toil in the sun, too easily affected by heat prostration, were sent off to work in the mines.

As soon as the crown was able to impose some semblance of control, it moved to enforce strict divisions between the races. A ruthlessly observed system of racial dominance was put in place. At the top were the Spanish-born, crown-appointed overseers, such as Simón de Bolívar; below them, the Creoles—whites, born in the colonies—such as de Bolívar's own son. After that came the *pardos*, an ever burgeoning mixed-race population that was either *mestizo*, part-white, part-Indian; or *mulatto*, a mixture of white and black; or *sambo*, a combination of black and Indian. As in most slave societies, labels were fashioned for every possible skin color: quadroons, quintroons, octoroons, moriscos, coyotes, chamisos, gíbaros, and so on. For each birth, a church registry would meticulously record the race, for there were concrete ramifications for the color of a child's skin. If he were Indian, he would be subject to the Spanish tribute, a tax imposed by the crown; if he were unable to pay, he was forced to meet his debt through hard labor. Indians were also subject to the mita, a period of compulsory toil in the mines or fields. Many of them didn't survive it. Chained, herded in gangs, separated from their families, those serving the mita would often be shipped great distances to satisfy the viceroy's demands.

Indians were also forced to buy goods according to laws of *repartimiento*. The governors would sell them food and supplies and expect them to pay with gold or silver. Often, the result was a disgraceful trafficking of sick mules, spoiled food, or faulty goods, sold at double or triple the normal prices. Sometimes these commodities were absolutely useless: Indian men who had no facial hair were made to buy razors. Women who wore tribal wraps were forced to buy silk stockings. The proceeds were gathered dutifully and sent off to the royal coffers in Madrid.

For blacks, life in Spanish America was equally punishing. Severed from family, country, language, they were brought as fishermen, pearl divers, cacao and sugar field workers. They were Bantu from Angola and the Congo, Mandingo from the Gold Coast. In the course of a little more than two hundred years, an estimated one million slaves were sold into South America by the Portuguese, Spanish, and English. Uniformly disdained as the lowest rung in the human hierarchy, they nevertheless left an indelible imprint on the culture. They worked their way from field hands to skilled craftsmen, from house slaves to beloved nursemaids, but it wasn't until after Bolívar's revolution that they were released into the mainstream of possibility.

For all of Spain's attempts to retain absolute control of its colonies, it could not prevent the interracial mixing that was inevitable in a world forged by male conquistadors. The crown quickly—and by necessity—took the attitude that marriage between races was acceptable, as long as Spanish men could persuade non-Spanish women to be baptized Christians. In truth, the Spaniards were hardly racially "pure" Europeans. After centuries of tumultuous history, the bloodline contained traces of Arab, Phoenician, African, Roman, Basque, Greek, Ligurian, Celt, German, Balkan, and Jew. But once they began mixing with Indians and blacks in the Americas, a cosmic race representative of all continents began to emerge. When Simón de Bolívar, the Spanish overlord, arrived in Venezuela in the late 1500s, the population counted 5,000 Spaniards, 10,000 Africans, and 350,000 native Indians in the country. Two hundred years later, when the Liberator was born, according to anthropologist Alexander von Humboldt, Venezuela had 800,000 inhabitants, of whom more than half were mestizo or mulatto. Today, more than two thirds of all Latin Americans are mixed-race. Nowhere else on earth has a civilization of such ethnic complexity been wrought in such a short span of time.

IN THE PATRICIAN HOUSEHOLD TO which Simón Bolívar was born, race was hardly a preoccupation. Marriages had long been arranged in order to ensure future generations all the privileges an aristocratic bloodline could afford. But in 1792, when Doña Concepción decided to seek official approval for a title of nobility her father-in-law had bought sixty years earlier, Spain's rigorous wheels of justice went into motion and secret doubts about the family's racial purity began.

For Creoles like the Bolívars, a title of nobility was an enormously valuable asset. In spite of the wealth and comfort they enjoyed, Creoles were second-class citizens, barred from the government's most powerful positions. Many of them yearned for the singular advantages—the opportunity to hold office, the possibility of higher income, the ability to hand down hereditary rights—a marquisate or baronetcy might bring. When the Liberator's grandfather Juan de Bolívar learned in 1728 that King Philip V had donated a marquisate to a Spanish monastery in order to raise money for the monks, he bought the title outright. It cost him 22,000 ducats. In such ways were noblemen made.

Juan Vicente de Bolívar, his son, had every right to use that title and call himself the Marquis of San Luis, but he didn't. For him, it was enough to be a Bolívar, the descendant of so many rich and illustrious Bolívars before him; it was enough to lord over the vast holdings he had inherited. But when Juan Vicente died and Doña Concepción decided to try to make the marquisate official for her sons, she learned that the Bolívar family tree wasn't so pristine, after all.

It turned out that Juan de Bolívar's grandmother had been the illegitimate daughter of a liaison between his great-grandfather, Francisco Marín de Narváez, and a chambermaid. Whether the servant was white or brown or black was uncertain—no one was able to say. But Spain's strict laws of succession did not allow for such aberrations, quite apart from the prickly question of race. The title remained in official limbo, unavailable to Juan Vicente de Bolívar's sons. They hardly seemed to care. In time, they would drop the "de" from the Bolívar surname, ignoring that last marker of peerage.

Bolívar's racial makeup has been a subject of endless fascination for generations of historians, but ultimately the debate comes down to the color of this one servant and, in the end, it is a matter of conjecture. Some claim that the personal chambermaid of a rich seventeenth-century Caracas matriarch would most likely be white; others say that she was bound to be mulatta or mestiza. One thing is sure: no mention of race is made in the family's papers or letters. And more: upon the illegitimate child's seventh birthday, she inherited much of her father's vast estate. Whatever her mother's skin color might have been, when little Josefa Marín de Narváez reached fourteen, she became a highly marriageable young woman.

Historians are not the only ones who argue over the "knot of Josefa Marín." Simón Bolívar's political boosters and detractors alike have used it to support opposing points of view. For some, Josefa's mother was an Indian from Aroa; for others, she was a black slave from Caracas. Bolívar's critics have often raised the question of race to impute a character flaw. His disciples see it as a way to identify an ethnic group with greatness. But if Bolívar had African blood in his veins, it very well might have been in the family before his Spanish ancestors ever set foot in America. If he had traces of Indian blood, he was probably no different from many Latin Americans who have it, yet consider themselves pristinely white. In the end, the question of Josefa's race serves more as a mirror on history's polemicists than as any possible insight into the man. For all the ink that has been expended on the subject, "the knot of Josefa Marín" is little more than unsubstantiated gossip.

There was, however, very real reason for gossip in the house where Don Juan Vicente presided over guests and Doña Concepcion cooed over their newborn baby. Little Simón's great-great-great-grandfather hadn't been the only one in the family to exercise his *droit de seigneur* over the female servants. His father, Don Juan Vicente, had been doing it for years.

Don Juan Vicente de Bolívar y Ponte had been born into a considerable fortune, the careful accrual of many generations of Creole wealth. He had inherited the splendid house on San Jacinto Street and the lucrative cacao plantations from none other than Josefa; a side chapel in the Cathedral of Caracas from his great-grandfather Ponte; and the sprawling sugar estate in San Mateo from a legacy that dated all the way back to the original Simón de Bolívar. As a youth, he had trained in the military arts and, at the age of sixteen, served the Spanish king by defending Venezuela's ports against marauding British invaders. At twenty-one, he was appointed procurator of Caracas and was held in such high esteem by Spanish authorities that he was called to the Court of Madrid for five years. He returned to Venezuela in 1758 an educated, sophisticated man, and so was rewarded with even more prominent responsibilities. By the age of thirty-two, he had become a veritable institution.

He had also become something of a sexual profligate. He came home to his bachelor's empire flush with a sense of license. He began to molest his female servants, demand that they surrender physical favors. He singled out the most attractive and sent their husbands on faraway expeditions. He waylaid the women in bedrooms, boudoirs—in the secluded alcoves of his capacious house. The transgressions were so flagrant, so persistent—verging on outright rape—that his victims could no longer remain silent. When the bishop of Caracas made a pastoral visit to the plantation of San Mateo in 1765, he began to hear a litany of complaints from Don Juan Vicente's housemaids as well as from the wives of male employees.

One claimed she had been forced to be his love slave for three years—to be at his beck and call whenever he fancied her. She testified that there were at least two other servants he was abusing similarly at the same time; he would choose among them at whim, summon the unfortunate woman to his bedroom, then lock the door and defile her. Another witness named Margarita claimed he had assaulted her in a corridor and was in the process of dragging her into his room, but when he was told a visitor was on the way, he thought better of it. Even though she had been spared on that particular occasion, Margarita admitted that she eventually succumbed; she didn't dare lock her room against him, "fearing his power and violent temper." Margarita's sister, María Jacinta, too, wrote a petition to the bishop, begging him to intercede on her behalf against "this infernal wolf, who is trying to take me by force and consign us both to the Devil." She claimed that, for days, Don Juan Vicente had been importuning her to sin with him, going so far as to send off her husband to a remote cattle ranch so as to better carry out his designs. "Sometimes I wonder how I can defend myself against this wicked man," she told the bishop, "and sometimes I think it best for me simply to say yes to him, take a knife in with me, and kill him outright so as to liberate us all of this cruel tyrant."

The bishop was so appalled by the accusations that he was moved to address them with Don Juan Vicente himself. He suggested to the colonel that his "loose ways with women" were growing too obvious to go ignored by the Church; that it was known far and wide that he lived in "a state of moral disorder." The bishop had been careful to warn each of the witnesses that it was of utmost importance that their accounts be absolutely accurate, but as the testimonies emerged—utterly compelling, mutually corroborating—there could be no doubt: Don Juan Vicente was a moral reprobate. He had to be stopped.

But the bishop also knew that the man who stood accused was no ordinary citizen. Don Juan Vicente's station among Creoles in Venezuela had few equals; his honors and titles flowed directly from the Court of Spain. The bishop decided to recommend that the women commit themselves to prayer, avoid contact with their tormentor, and take up a strict vow of silence. To Don Juan Vicente, he intimated that he really did not believe the witnesses, but that if similar violations continued to be reported, he would be obliged to correct his lordship "by force of law." He advised him to cease all commerce with females and to contact them only through the offices of a priest. The bishop's warning had a clear and unavoidable implication: the Church would brook no more complaints. It was time for Don Juan Vicente to get married.

WHEN MARÍA DE LA CONCEPCIÓN Palacios y Blanco married Don Juan Vicente at the age of fourteen, she was no younger than other brides of her class in Venezuela: American aristocrats were known to marry off daughters as early as twelve. A girl might be sent to the convent at four and then emerge eight years later to exchange lifelong vows with a boy of sixteen.

These were the Mantuanos, the highest class of Creoles to which the Bolívars and Palacios belonged. Wealthy, white, and exceptionally favored, they were the backbone of Spain's empire in Venezuela, and oversaw all of the colony's assets, commanded all the colony's troops. In Caracas, their ranks were said to consist of nine families. The Mantuanos displayed their coats of arms, carved into great slabs of stone, over their doorways. They wore fancy hats and carried canes. Their wives were the only women permitted to wear mantillas or *mantuas*, veils that marked their status as they rode through the city on elaborate, gilded litters, borne by black slaves. Wherever they walked, tiny bells sewn into their skirts announced their approach.

We will never know with any certainty how Concepción's parents managed to arrange her marriage to the prominent, powerful, forty-six-year-old roué that was Don Juan Vicente, except that there was one strategic advantage: they were his neighbors. The Palacios lived just behind the Bolívars, on the corner of Traposos Street—only a few meters away. The city of Caracas was small, no longer than fourteen blocks in one direction and twelve in the other. In the tiny quadrant the Palacios and Bolívars inhabited, the elite were close acquaintances, often related to one another through generations of intermarriage. It is safe to assume that, in the close, insular world of eighteenth-century Caracas life, Don Juan Vicente learned on his return from Madrid that a baby had just been born to the Palacios family. The father was a mere four years younger, after all, and a fellow military man. Both were eminent

Mantuanos, active in the public life of Caracas. Having so much in common with the father, Don Juan Vicente certainly had opportunities to glimpse the daughter. As years passed and Concepción grew to puberty, Don Juan Vicente noticed that she was a lively and beautiful child.

However the subject of marriage materialized, nuptial agreements were made, two influential families were joined, and Don Juan Vicente settled down to a quiet, even sedate connubial life. Doña Concepción proceeded to dedicate herself to wifely duties. As someone who had grown up in a bustling household with ten siblings, she must have found the Bolívar house, for all its handsome rooms, a dour place, as dark and forbidding as a tomb. She opened the doors to its patios and brightened its halls with light. She decorated the heavy sideboards with an abundance of flowers. She filled the air with music. By the time she was eighteen, she began to populate the many rooms with children. María Antonia, the first, was most like her—petite, brunette, and determined. Three more followed quickly thereafter: Juana, a languid, fair-haired girl, who more resembled her father; Juan Vicente, a sweet, blond boy with blue eyes; and, last, Simón, the scamp with curly black hair.

For all the differences, Doña Concepción had one characteristic in common with her husband. Her ancestry was as renowned and illustrious as his. Her mother, Francisca Blanco Herrera, was a descendant of medieval kings and princes. Her father, Feliciano Palacios y Sojo, came from a family with a pronounced intellectual bent. From her uncle Pedro Palacios y Sojo, a celebrated priest, musician, and founder of the Caracas School of Music, she learned she had a natural gift for music. She was skilled at the harp, which was her preferred instrument, but she also loved to sing, play the guitar, and dance. Although fate would allow Simón Bolívar only a fleeting time with his mother, there were two traits he would inherit from her: a vibrant, affirmative energy and a hearty passion for dance.

AS DON JUAN VICENTE SETTLED into his new life, he began to be alarmed by Spain's dominion over it. For fifty years he had been a loyal subject of the king, a trusted judge, governor, and military commander, but by 1776, just as the British colonies declared their independence, Don Juan, too, was dreaming of insurrection. He had good reason to. Spain's Bourbon regime, which had high ambitions, had decided to impose a strict rule over its colonies. It put into place a number of anti-Creole laws that had a direct effect on Don Juan Vicente's businesses. First, Venezuela was separated from the viceroyalty of New Granada, a sprawling region that originally reached from the Pacific to the Atlantic over the northern territories of South America; next, an intendant was installed in Caracas to administer economic affairs, and a captain-general to rule over political and military matters. With a direct umbilical to Madrid now, Venezuela began to suffer tighter restrictions on its ranches, mines, and plantations. The Council of the Indies, which governed the Americas from Madrid and Seville, strengthened its hold. Taxes were increased. A ubiquitous imperial presence was felt in all transactions. The Guipuzcoana Company, a powerful Basque corporation that monopolized imports and exports, was reaping great profits on every sale.

If Don Juan Vicente feared the impact of these new regulations, he saw that the blow would be more than financial. Creoles were being squeezed out of government roles. Throughout the Spanish Americas, from California to Buenos Aires, Spain began appointing only *peninsulares*—those born in Spain or the Canary Islands—to offices that decided important affairs. This was a sweeping, ultimately radicalizing change, reversing a culture of trust between Creoles and Spaniards that had been nurtured for more than two hundred years. In Italy, an exiled Peruvian Jesuit priest, Juan Pablo Viscardo y Guzmán, wrote angrily that it was tantamount to declaring Americans "incapable of filling, even in our own countries, places which, in the strictest right, belong to us."

The most infuriating aspect of this for Creoles such as Don Juan Vicente was that the peninsulares being assigned the highest positions were often inferior in education and pedigree. This was similar to a sentiment held for years in British America. Both George Washington and Benjamin Franklin had registered strong objections to preferences given to British-born subjects when it was clear that the American-born were far more skilled. In the Spanish colonies, the new emissaries of the crown were largely members of Spain's middle class: merchants or mid-level functionaries with little sophistication. As they took over the most coveted seats of power, their inadequacies were not lost on Creoles who now had to step aside. In Spain, not everyone was blind to the implications. A Bourbon minister mused that colonial subjects in the Indies might have learned to live without freedoms, but once they acquired them as a right, they weren't going to stand by idly as they were taken away. Whether or not the court in Madrid understood the ramifications, Spain had drawn a line in the sand. Its colonial strategy shifted from consensus to confrontation, from collaboration to coercion; and to ensure its grip on the enormous wealth that America represented, it put a firm clamp on its laws.

Don Juan Vicente and his fellow Mantuanos may not have been fully aware of it, but their disgruntlement was part of a rebellious spirit sweeping the world. It was called the Enlightenment. Its seeds had been planted much earlier by the scientific revolution in Europe, which had challenged laws, authority, even faith itself. But by the time Don Juan Vicente and Doña Concepción began having children, the wheels of an extended American revolution—north and south—were already in motion. Adam Smith had published his *Wealth of Nations*, which advocated tearing down artificially imposed economic controls and freeing people to build stronger societies. Thomas Paine, in *Common Sense*, had posited that monarchies in Europe had done little more than lay "the world in blood and ashes." In France, Jean-Jacques Rousseau and Voltaire argued eloquently for freedom, equality, and the will of the people. In his *Spirit of the Laws*, Montesquieu had anticipated Don Juan Vicente's resentment: "The Indies and Spain are two powers under the same master; but the Indies are the principal, while Spain is only an accessory." It made no sense for political forces to try to shackle a principal to an accessory, he argued. The colonies were now inherently the more powerful of the two.

On February 24, 1782, a year and a half before the birth of the child who would bring luster to his family name, Don Juan Vicente met with two fellow Mantuanos, composed a letter proposing revolution, and sent it off to Francisco de Miranda, a Venezuelan colonel and dissident who had been bold enough to say publicly that his homeland should shuck its allegiance to the crown. Miranda had fought in a Spanish regiment in the Battle of Pensacola, been reprimanded by his superiors for exceeding his mandate, and had since turned against Spain, making no secret of his rancor. The letter addressed to him by the elder Bolívar reported that the noblemen of Caracas were exasperated with the insults heaped on them by Spanish authorities. The new intendant and captain-general were "treating all Americans, no matter what class, rank or circumstance, as if they were vile slaves." The three Mantuanos urged Miranda to take up their cause of rebellion, but went on to express a certain trepidation, given Spain's ruthless quashing of rebels elsewhere: "We want to take no steps, nor shall we take any without your advice, for in your prudence have we set all our hopes."

So it was prudence, not valor, that was the animating spirit behind this sedition. The Mantuanos were not ready to topple their world.

DON JUAN VICENTE WOULD NEVER have imagined that the child in the cradle under his own roof would be the one to wrest independence from the colonizers, not for Venezuela alone, but for much of Spanish America. What he did know by the time his son reached a mere one and a half was that even if the family estate crumbled the boy would grow up to be a rich man. A priest had ordained it. Juan Félix Jerez de Aristiguieta, who had baptized the boy, was, like many powerful clerics of the day, a wealthy landowner with valuable properties. He was also Don Juan Vicente's nephew. When he died in 1785 with no direct heirs, he surprised everyone by leaving the diminutive Simón his entire fortune, including a magnificent house next to the cathedral, three plantations, a total of 95,000 cacao trees, and all his slaves.

The following year, Don Juan Vicente, too, would die. The tuberculosis that had fevered him for years finally took him one warm January night in 1786 as he lay in the house on San Jacinto Street. He was not yet sixty. His son Simón was not yet three. His wife was pregnant with a fifth child, who would not see much light of day.

Don Juan Vicente's will and testament, which he had the presence of mind to prepare even as he lay dying, was a model of diligence. In it, he reported that he owed money to no one. He laid out his ancestry and described the lofty positions he had held during his long and illustrious career. Despite his brief, halfhearted flirtation with rebellion, he insisted that his remains be buried in the family chapel in the Cathedral of Caracas, "decorated with my military insignia and interred with the privileges which I enjoy under military law." He distributed his holdings evenly among his five children (including the one unborn), gave power of attorney to his wife and father-in-law, and added a special clause that required Doña Concepción "to carry out what I have imparted to her in order to relieve my conscience." The phrase could only mean one thing: he had arranged for her to distribute money to his illegitimate children. The will went on to specify how many priests and friars were to accompany his coffin to its final resting place and how many fervent Masses were to be said for his soul as it approached reckoning day. Clearly, he died a worried man.

His departure might have thrown the household into turmoil had his wife not had a practical and business-minded nature. Doña Concepción buried her husband, carried her pregnancy to term, lost the baby girl a few days later, and then set about putting the family properties in order. Relying on her father and brothers to help her manage what had become a veritable conglomerate of businesses, she tried to impose some order in her children's lives.

Simón, in particular, was an unruly child. He had been raised by his wet nurse, the black slave Hipólita, whom he would later credit as the woman "whose milk sustained my life" as well as "the only father I have ever known." She was adoring and infinitely patient with the little boy, but she could hardly control him. Willful, irascible, in obvious need of a stern hand, he became progressively ungovernable. As much as his mother tried to enjoin the male members of her family to help discipline him, the men found his impudence perversely funny. No one scolded him, much less punished him. Eventually, she found support in none other than the Royal Audiencia, Spain's high court in Caracas, which monitored all legal affairs. Since the boy had inherited such a large estate, and since his father was dead and unable to supervise it, the Audiencia appointed an eminent jurist to oversee the progress of young Simón. His name was José Miguel Sanz.

Sanz was the brilliant dean of the college of lawyers, known for his progressive views on education. An avid reader and writer, he had labored for years to persuade colonial authorities to allow him to import the first printing press to the colony. He was never able to accomplish it. Nevertheless, Sanz was highly respected by Spaniards, admired by fellow Creoles—what's more, at age thirty-six, he was the very model of a conscientious young father. It would have been difficult to find a better surrogate for the boy. As administrator of Simón Bolívar's fortune, Sanz had dutifully visited his young ward and seen for himself the extent of the boy's cockiness. But before Simón turned six, Sanz decided to take fuller responsibility and brought him to live under his own roof.

Blind in one eye, grim in demeanor, Sanz could be an intimidating presence, even to his own wife and children, but not to Simón, who is said to have issued many a brazen response to his demands. "You're a walking powder keg, boy!" Sanz warned him after one of Simón's more blatant insubordinations. "Better run, then," the six-year-old told him, "or I'll burn you."

As punishment for his many transgressions, Sanz locked Simón in a room on the second floor of his house and instructed his wife to leave him there while he went off to see about his many court cases. Bored, exasperated, the boy yelled and made his fury known, and Sanz's wife, taking pity, tied sweets and freshly baked breads to a long pole and passed them to him through an open window. She swore Simón to secrecy, making him promise not to reveal her disobedience. Every afternoon when the lawyer returned and asked how he had behaved, she simply smiled and said the child had been the essence of tranquillity.

Eventually, Sanz hired a learned Capuchin monk, Padre Francisco de Andújar, to come to his house and give Simón a moral education. The mathematician priest, hoping to ingratiate himself with his student, tempered instruction with a liberal dose of entertaining stories, but no amount of patience or charm could budge the boy from what he was: a joker, a prankster, a pampered child. It's not clear how long Simón remained under Sanz's care or whether he actually spent nights under his roof, but certainly before his eighth birthday he was back in the house on San Jacinto Street. By then, his mother's health was failing and she was finding it difficult to focus on the management of her family, much less the comportment of her younger son. Worried that she might infect her children with her disease, she quarantined herself on the sugar plantation at San Mateo and left them and the servants to their own devices. Simón spent his days cavorting with the slaves' children, running wild.

If Doña Concepción had one driving ambition during her swift decline, it was to secure for her older son, Juan Vicente, the marquisate that her father-in-law had purchased so many years before. The Palacios family, unlike the Bolívars, had always attached great importance to prestige and nobility, and when Don Juan Vicente de Bolívar had died, making the title potentially available to her sons, Doña Concepción had sent her brother Esteban to Spain to hurry along the enterprise. When Esteban reported that the proceedings had come to a halt because of Josefa Marín de Narváez's questionable lineage, Don Feliciano Palacios called off the venture, unwilling to press a case that could reveal unwanted blood in the Bolívars and potentially smear them all. To be sure, managing the Bolívar fortunes had become a cash cow for the Palacios. The income from the properties that stood to be inherited by Juan Vicente and Simón was supporting their mother's siblings. The in-laws had been living on Bolívar assets for years.

On one of her long, recuperative visits to San Mateo, Doña Concepción stayed into the rainy season, and her affliction took a grave turn for the worse. She returned to Caracas and died of acute tuberculosis on July 6, 1792, leaving her four children in her elderly father's care. Not entirely well himself, Don Feliciano Palacios took up his pen and wrote to Esteban in Madrid, delivering the news with admirable equanimity: "Concepción decided to lay her illness to rest and she expelled a great deal of blood through her mouth, continuing her deterioration until this morning at eleven thirty, at which point God took it upon Himself to claim her." It had been a long and grueling death: she had bled for seven days.

Once his daughter was interred in the Bolívar family chapel, Don Feliciano dedicated himself to arranging the marriages of his orphaned granddaughters. Within two months, he married fifteen-year-old María Antonia to her distant cousin Pablo Clemente Francia. Three months after that, he wed Juana, who was only thirteen, to her uncle Dionisio Palacios. As for his grandsons, Don Feliciano decided to leave Simón and Juan Vicente—then nine and eleven, respectively—in the house on San Jacinto Street, under the supervision of the Bolívar family servants. He had a connecting passageway built from that house to his own, so that the boys could spend days with him and then retire to their old, familiar beds at night. It seemed a rational enough solution, comforting the children with an illusion of permanence and stability. That flimsy solace did not last long, however. Don Feliciano Palacios died the following year, leaving his grandsons to face yet another loss in their waning family universe.

The boys were immensely wealthy, with a net worth equivalent today to at least $40 million, and because of it, they would never go ignored. But money had bought them little happiness. Within the first decade of life, Simón had lost his father, mother, grandparents, a sister, and most of his aunts and uncles on the Bolívar side. That so few Bolívars had survived to lay claim to the family fortune convinced the Palacios it was theirs to take. So confident was Don Feliciano Palacios of this rightful heritage that he took care before his death to make sure that all the wealth eventually flowed to his own children. He drew up a will, making his sons legal guardians of the Bolívar boys. Twelve-year-old Juan Vicente was put in the custody of his uncle Juan Félix Palacios and transferred to a hacienda fifty miles away. Ten-year-old Simón was entrusted to his uncle Carlos, an ill-humored, lazy, and grasping bachelor who lived with his sisters in Don Feliciano's house—at the other end of the passageway.

So busy did Carlos become in the venture of squandering Bolívar profits that he had little time for his impressionable young charge. He relegated the boy's welfare to his sisters and servants. Ever headstrong, Simón began to spend time in the company of street boys, neglecting everything his tutors had tried to teach him, learning the vulgar language of the time. Whenever he could, he headed for the back alleys of Caracas, or took a horse from the family corral and rode out into the surrounding countryside. He avoided his studies and turned his attention instead to the highly imperfect world around him, a world that Spain had made. He would not understand much of what he saw until later, until he had crisscrossed the continent as a full-grown man. But it was an education that would serve him for the rest of his life.

FOR TWO HUNDRED YEARS, FROM the mid-1500s through the mid-1700s, the world that Spain had made had struggled against fiscal failure. The empire whose motto had once been a rousing *Plus Ultra!* had glutted world markets with silver, thwarted the economic growth of its colonies, and brought itself more than once to the brink of financial ruin. Nowhere was Spain's misguided fiscal strategy more evident than in the streets of Caracas in the late 1700s, where a deep rage against the *madre patria* was on the rise.

The case of the Spanish American colonies had no precedent in modern history: a vital colonial economy was being forced, at times by violent means, to kowtow to an underdeveloped mother country. The principal—as Montesquieu had predicted a half century before—was now slave to the accessory. Even as England burst into the industrial age, Spain made no attempt to develop factories; it ignored the road to modernization and stuck stubbornly to its primitive, agricultural roots. But the Bourbon kings and their courts could not ignore the pressures of the day: Spain's population was burgeoning; its infrastructure, tottering; there was a pressing need to increase the imperial revenue. Rather than try something new, the Spanish kings decided to hold on firmly to what they had.

At midnight on April 1, 1767, all Jesuit priests were expelled from Spanish America. Five thousand clerics, most of them American-born, were marched to the coast, put on ships, and deported to Europe, giving the crown unfettered reign over education as well as over the widespread property of the Church's missions. King Carlos IV made it very clear that he did not consider learning advisable for America: Spain would be better off, and its subjects easier to manage, if it kept its colonies in ignorance.

Absolute rule had always been the hallmark of Spanish colonialism. From the outset, each viceroy and captain-general had reported directly to the Spanish court, making the king the supreme overseer of American resources. Under his auspices, Spain had wrung vast quantities of gold and silver from the New World and sold them in Europe as raw material. It controlled the entire world supply of cocoa and rerouted it to points around the globe from storehouses in Cádiz. It had done much the same with copper, indigo, sugar, pearls, emeralds, cotton, wool, tomatoes, potatoes, and leather. To prevent the colonies from trading these goods themselves, it imposed an onerous system of domination. All foreign contact was forbidden. Contraband was punishable by death. Movement between the colonies was closely monitored. But as the years of colonial rule wore on, oversight had grown lax. The war that had flared between Britain and Spain in 1779 had crippled Spanish commerce, prompting a lively contraband trade. A traffic of forbidden books flourished. It was said that all Caracas was awash in smuggled goods. To put a stop to this, Spain moved to overhaul its laws, impose harsher ones, and forbid Americans even the most basic freedoms.

The Tribunal of the Inquisition, imposed in 1480 by Ferdinand and Isabel to keep a firm hold on empire, was given more power. Its laws, which called for penalties of death or torture, were diligently enforced. Books or newspapers could not be published or sold without the permission of Spain's Council of the Indies. Colonials were barred from owning printing presses. The implementation of every document, the approval of every venture, the mailing of every letter was a long, costly affair that required government approval. No foreigners, not even Spaniards, could visit the colonies without permission from the king. All non-Spanish ships in American waters were deemed enemy craft and attacked.

Spain also fiercely suppressed American entrepreneurship. Only the Spanish-born were allowed to own stores or sell goods in the streets. No American was permitted to plant grapes, own vineyards, grow tobacco, make spirits, or propagate olive trees—Spain brooked no competition. It earned $60 million a year, after all (the equivalent of almost a billion today), by selling goods back to its colonies.

But, in a bizarre act of self-immolation, Spain enforced strict regulations on its colonies' productivity and initiative. Creoles were subject to punishing taxes; Indians or mestizos could labor only in menial trades; black slaves could work only in the fields, or as domestics in houses. No American was allowed to own a mine; nor could he work a vein of ore without reporting it to colonial authorities. Factories were forbidden, unless they were registered sugar mills. Basque businesses controlled all the shipping. Manufacturing was rigorously banned, although Spain had no competing manufacturing industry. Most galling of all, the revenue raised from the new, exorbitantly high taxes—a profit of $46 million a year—was not used to improve conditions in the colonies. The money was shipped back, in its entirety, to Spain.

Americans balked at this. "Nature has separated us from Spain by immense seas," exiled Peruvian Jesuit Viscardo y Guzmán wrote in 1791. "A son who found himself at such a distance would be a fool, if, in managing his own affairs, he constantly awaited the decision of his father." It was as potent a commentary on the inherent flaws of colonialism as Thomas Jefferson's "A Summary View of the Rights of British America."

A rich orphan boy wandering the streets of Caracas would not have understood the economic tumult that churned about him, but the human tumult he could not fail to see. Everywhere he looked, the streets were teeming with blacks and mulattos. The colony was overwhelmingly populated by pardos, the mixed-race descendants of black slaves. European slave ships had just sold 26,000 Africans into Caracas—the largest infusion of slaves the colony would ever experience. One out of ten Venezuelans was a black slave; half of the population was slaves' descendants. Though Spain had prohibited race mixing, the evidence that those laws had been flouted was all about him. Caracas's population had grown by more than a third in the course of Simón Bolívar's young life, and its ranks swarmed, as never before, with a veritable spectrum of color. There were mestizos, mixed-race offspring of whites and Indians, almost always the product of illegitimate births. There were also pure-blood Indians, although they were few, their communities reduced to a third of their original numbers. Those who weren't killed off by disease were pushed deep into the countryside, where they subsisted as marginal tribes. Whites, on the other hand, were a full quarter of the population, but the great majority of these were either poor Canary Islanders, whom the Creoles considered racially tainted and markedly inferior to themselves, or light-skinned mestizos who passed themselves off as white. Even a child, kicking stones in the back alleys of this crowded city, could see that a precise, color-coded hierarchy was at work.

The question of race had always been problematic in Spanish America. The laws that forced Indians to pay tribute to the crown, either through forced labor or taxation, had provoked violent race hatreds. As centuries passed and colored populations grew, the system for determining "whiteness" became ever more corrupt, generating more hostility. Spain began selling Cédulas de Gracias al Sacar, certificates that granted a light-skinned colored person the rights every white automatically had: the right to be educated, to be hired into better jobs, to serve in the priesthood, to hold public office, to marry whites, to inherit wealth. The sale of Cédulas created new income for Madrid; but it was also a canny social strategy. From Spain's point of view, the ability to buy "whiteness" would raise colored hopes and keep Creole masters from getting cocky. The result, however, was very different. Race in Spanish America became an ever-greater obsession.

By the time of Bolívar's birth, a number of race rebellions had erupted in the colonies. The trouble began in Peru in 1781, when a man who called himself Túpac Amaru II and claimed to be a direct descendant of the last ruling Inca kidnapped a Spanish governor, had him publicly executed, and marched on Cuzco with six thousand Indians, killing Spaniards along the way. Diplomacy hadn't worked. Túpac Amaru II had first written to the crown's envoy, imploring him to abolish the cruelties of Indian tribute. When his letters went ignored, he gathered a vast army and issued a warning to the Creoles:

I have decided to shake off the unbearable weight and rid this bad government of its leaders. . . . If you elect to support me, you will suffer no ill consequences, not in your lives or on your plantations, but if you reject this warning, you will face ruin and reap the fury of my legions, which will reduce your city to ashes. . . . I have seventy thousand men at my command.

In the end, the royalist armies crushed the rebellion, costing the Indians some 100,000 lives. Túpac Amaru II was captured and brought to the main square of Cuzco, where the Spanish visitador asked him for the names of his accomplices. "I only know of two," the prisoner replied, "and they are you and I: You as the oppressor of my country, and I because I wish to rescue it from your tyrannies." Infuriated by the impudence, the Spaniard ordered his men to cut out the Indian's tongue and draw and quarter him on the spot. But the four horses to which they tied his wrists and ankles would not comply. The soldiers slit Túpac Amaru's throat instead; cut off his head, hands, and feet; and displayed these on stakes at various crossroads in the city. The torture and execution were repeated throughout the day until all members of his family were killed. Seeing his mother's tongue ripped from her head, Túpac Amaru's youngest child issued a piercing shriek. Legend has it that the sound of that cry was so heartrending, so unforgettable, that it signaled the end of Spanish dominion in America.

Word of Túpac Amaru II's fate reverberated throughout the colonies, inflaming and terrifying all who would contemplate a similar rebellion. For blacks, for whom slavery's depredations were ever more untenable, the urge for an uprising only grew; they had nothing to lose. But for Creoles, the thought of insurgency now spurred a fear that revenge would come not only from Spain but from a massive colored population. Those fears were tested in New Granada months later, when a Creole-led army of twenty thousand marched against the viceroyalty in Bogotá to protest high taxes. One of the leaders, José Antonio Galán, swept by the fever of the moment, proclaimed the black slaves free and urged them to turn their machetes against their masters. Galán was executed—shot and hanged—as were his collaborators, and, for the moment at least, Spain succeeded in quashing the malcontents with a brutal hand.

But Spain could hardly quash the eloquent calls for liberty that were issuing from the European Enlightenment and traveling, despite all injunctions against foreign literature, to the colonies. In 1789, the "Declaration of the Rights of Man" was published in France. Five years later, one of the leading intellectuals in the viceroyalty of New Granada, Antonio Nariño, secretly translated it along with the American Declaration of Independence and smuggled the documents to like-minded Creoles throughout the continent. *"L'injustice à la fin produit l'indépendance!"* was the rallying cry—Injustice gives rise to independence!—a line from Voltaire's *Tancrède*. Nariño was arrested and sent to the dungeons of Africa. But in the interim, as French republicans stormed the Bastille and guillotined the royal family, as Marie Antoinette's severed head was held high for all Paris to see, a bloody echo resounded on the streets of Santo Domingo, and Venezuelans, too, took up the battle cry.

It wasn't the stately ascent to independence that intellectuals like Nariño had envisioned. It was an insurrection led by the son of slaves. José Leonardo Chirino—half black, half Indian—had traveled from Venezuela to Santo Domingo and seen firsthand how the slave revolt there had virtually exterminated the island's whites and transformed that colony—once the most productive in the New World—into the black Republic of Haiti. He returned to Venezuela in 1795 and raised a revolutionary force of three hundred blacks, who plundered the haciendas, killed white landowners, and terrorized the city of Coro. But it didn't take long for the Spanish to subdue them. Chirino was chased down and decapitated, his head displayed in an iron cage on the road between Coro and Caracas, his hands sent to two different towns due west. There was a crystal-clear lesson in this for the disgruntled Mantuanos: those willing to lay down their lives for liberty might also want equality. A revolution could truly turn.

Simón Bolívar doubtless heard news of these events in the street, in the stables, in the kitchen, as he listened to the frightened servants. He was all of twelve years old.

CHAPTER 2

Rites of Passage

A child learns more in one split second, carving a little stick,
than in whole days, listening to a teacher.

—Simón Rodríguez

Simón's irritable uncle and guardian, Carlos Palacios, had no patience
for children. He left his nephew for months at a time as he traveled
the colony, visiting the Bolívar family haciendas. He sent Simón to an
elementary school run by Don Feliciano's former secretary, the eccentric
young Simón Rodríguez. It was a shabby little institution, plagued by
truancies, one teacher for 114 students, and barely any supplies, but it
was a salve of conscience for Don Carlos, who, with a bachelor's logic,
decided that a schoolroom was the perfect remedy for a restless boy.

In June of 1795, as the black revolutionary Chirino fled through Venezuela's forests, evading his angry pursuers, Simón, too, decided to run.
His uncle had been away from Caracas for two and a half months. Simón
gathered a few of his things and headed across town, seeking refuge in
the house of his sister María Antonia, where his old wet nurse, Hipólita,
worked. María Antonia and her husband, Pablo Clemente, happily took
him in, registered his change of address with the courts, and made a
formal request that the Palacios family—who, after all, were living on
Simón's inheritance—contribute financial support for the boy.

Eight days later, Carlos Palacios was in court, trying to win back custody. On July 31, he filed a lawsuit against María Antonia and her husband, insisting that Simón be returned to his house, even if it had to be done by force. Pablo Clemente argued that if the child were returned to Carlos's house, his lively mind would only continue to go ignored. "We've already warned his guardian about this neglect," Clemente fumed. "The child is always wandering the streets alone—by foot as well as on horseback. What's worse is that he's always in the company of boys who are not of his class. The whole city has taken notice."

Despite those pleas, the courts of the Audiencia ordered the Clementes to return the boy to his legal guardian. Simón refused to go. No matter how much the magistrates tried to persuade him to rejoin his uncle or how much the Clementes, who ultimately didn't want to disobey the law, urged him to go, the twelve-year-old stood his ground. "Slaves have more rights than this!" he insisted. "The courts have every right to dispose of property and do whatever they want with a person's things, but not with the person himself . . . you cannot refuse someone the right to live in whatever house he pleases."

Peeved by the rejection, Don Carlos decided to send the boy to live with Simón Rodríguez, the public school teacher. Don Carlos assured the Audiencia that since Rodríguez was "a highly respected and capable individual, someone whose business it is to teach children, he will provide for the boy's education and keep him in sight at all times in his very own house, which is spacious and comfortable."

The Audiencia readily agreed. But Simón still stubbornly refused to leave his sister's house. Even his uncle Feliciano Palacios, whom he liked better than Carlos, was unable to budge him and ended by punching the boy's chest in frustration. The family was in such an uproar over that assault that Pablo Clemente threatened to draw his sword. Finally, a strong black slave dragged Simón, kicking and howling, to Rodríguez's house. On August 1, 1795, the Audiencia's records show, the child became a ward of his twenty-five-year-old teacher.

Rodríguez's house was neither spacious nor comfortable, nor could the teacher possibly have kept Simón in sight at all times. The place was, in sum, unremitting bedlam. For ten days, Simón complained bitterly, begging his sister and brother-in-law to rescue him. Finally, the Clementes filed another petition on Simón's behalf, prompting an investigation. A court-ordered inspection of Rodríguez's house revealed that its five bedrooms were home to nineteen people: the teacher; his wife; the teacher's brother, sister-in-law, and their newborn baby; a boarder and his nephew; five male students entrusted to Rodríguez's care; two of Rodríguez's wife's siblings; three servants; and two black slaves. The conditions were shabby, the disorder constant, the fare necessarily meager. In order to humor his new ward's tastes, Rodríguez arranged for Simón's every meal to be delivered from Don Carlos's kitchen. All the same, the boy was inconsolable.

Three days later, Rodríguez reported to the Audiencia that Simón had disappeared. A search team was organized, but before it could set out into the streets of Caracas, a priest appeared with the boy in tow. It seemed Simón had run off to argue his case with the archbishop: a letter from the eminence himself requested clemency for the child.

Within two months, the misery of being separated from his childhood surroundings radically changed Simón's mind. On October 14, 1795, he retracted all the negative things he had said about his uncle Carlos. Through his sister, he requested that the Audiencia return him to "the harbor" of the Palacios house, where he pledged to behave and focus on his studies. The Audiencia agreed, with a stipulation—since the uncle was often away from Caracas—that Don Carlos "hire a respectable teacher, if possible a priest, who can be a constant companion to the boy and give him the best education possible." Within three days, Simón Rodríguez had quit his post to be Bolívar's tutor.

Simón Bolívar would hardly be the model student—he was too fond of games, too fidgety a boy for desks and pencils—but for the next three years, he managed to receive a largely private education under the tutelage of some formidably bright minds. Rodríguez was in charge of reading and grammar. Andrés Bello, who later became a towering figure in Latin American letters, tutored him in literature and geography. Padre Francisco de Andújar, the priest who had taught him in Sanz's house— a scholar praised by no less than the great naturalist Alexander von Humboldt—taught him mathematics and science. He is said to have studied history, religion, and Latin with a number of other esteemed Caracans of the day. But for all the claims some breathless biographers have made about his early brilliance and education, Simón Bolívar was well past childhood before his thirst for learning was awakened. It was his irrepressible instinct for adventure—his highly developed sense of curiosity—that taught him most during those stormy years.

THE TEACHER WHO MOST UNDERSTOOD that irrepressible nature was Simón Rodríguez. He was not a particularly skilled pedagogue, and too many writers—including Bolívar himself—have exaggerated his abilities. But Rodríguez had a broad and agile mind, as well as a keen instinct for adventure. His most important contribution to the education of Simón Bolívar was that he understood the boy's eccentricities and allowed him to be himself.

Rodríguez certainly didn't broadcast it openly at the time—the penalties for advocating liberty and egalitarianism were too severe—but he was a keen admirer of Rousseau, Locke, Voltaire, and Montesquieu. Which is to say he was a staunch supporter of Enlightenment notions of self-determination. Not for him the paralyzing strictures of the Spanish church and colonial law; he subscribed instead to a very modern wave of French encyclopedism. He was a believer in science as opposed to religion, the individual as opposed to the state.

He had been born in Caracas in 1771, birthed in secret and disposed of in secret by parents who very well may have been Mantuanos. The note they tucked into the infant's blanket when they left him to fate and a doorstep said he was a bastard son of whites. He was adopted by Doña Rosalia Rodríguez and later by the priest Don Alejandro Carreño. From these two benefactors he took his name, Rodríguez Carreño; eventually, however, in a fit of pique against the Church, he dropped Carreño altogether.

Indeed, most of Rodríguez's life tended toward fits of pique. He was irascible, libidinous, unpredictable, peripatetic—a compulsive talker whose basic teaching method was to impart his private passions. Coarse in manner, slight in frame, he was hardly an attractive man. His features were grotesquely out of proportion: ears too big, nose too hooked, mouth a grim line when it wasn't in motion. He was the antithesis of Andrés Bello, the fair-faced scholar—barely two years older than Bolívar—who was hired to expose the boy to good literature.

Whereas Bello was reserved, cool-headed, and grasped immediately that he would never be able to win Simón to a formal education, Rodríguez took the opposite tack. He showed genuine interest in the boy's caprices; he encouraged his adventuresome spirit, taught him outdoors, on horseback, in the wild. Much is made of the fact that Rodríguez's bible was Rousseau's *Émile*, the story of an orphan whose classroom is the natural world. More of a treatise on education than a true work of fiction, Rousseau's novel describes the ideal teacher as one who allows the child to imagine himself as master, while guiding his physical and mental progress with a firm hand. Rodríguez's freewheeling, exaggerated approach—his ability to make learning come alive—was precisely what an overactive boy needed. For the first time, a teacher was communicating something Bolívar understood. He may not have learned to spell as well as he should have, or write with true proficiency, but Rodríguez helped the boy lay a foundation for his love of ideas. A lifelong pursuit of liberty would take root in it.

If young Simón did not immediately understand how Rousseau's, Locke's, and Voltaire's ideas on liberty worked in the world, he soon got a notion of it in 1797, when another bold bid for independence was attempted in Venezuela, this time by established whites. The movement had begun in Madrid as a coup against the king, organized by Freemasons. A Spanish writer and educator, Juan Bautista Picornell, was charged, arrested, and sentenced to prison in the Venezuelan port of La Guaira. There, in shackles, he made contact with two dissident Creoles: retired military captain Manuel Gual, whose father had once fought alongside Colonel Juan Vicente de Bolívar; and José María España, a landowner and local magistrate in the seaside town of Macuto.

Gual and España's carefully planned plot against the Spanish overlords in Caracas was eventually betrayed to authorities and the two fled for their lives through a number of ports in the Caribbean. When the courts went through their papers, they learned what their revolution had in mind: total control of the army and government, the freedom to grow and sell tobacco, elimination of the sales tax, free trade with foreign powers, the end of gold and silver exports, the freedom to establish an army, absolute equality between people of all colors, eradication of the Indian tribute, and the abolition of slavery.

As the colonial government went about rounding up anyone—barbers, priests, doctors, soldiers, farmers—who had the slightest involvement in that brash conspiracy, it came upon evidence that implicated Simón Rodríguez. It isn't clear whether Rodríguez had told his pupil that he was colluding with Gual and España, but it is very probable that the fourteen-year-old Bolívar attended Rodríguez's trial, since his childhood mentor, the lawyer José Miguel Sanz, argued the teacher's defense. With Sanz's help, Rodríguez escaped conviction, but the court ruled that it would drop charges only if he would leave the colonies forever.

Rodríguez set sail for Jamaica without so much as a goodbye to his wife, his brother, his former associates, or to his impressionable pupil. In Jamaica, he adopted the name Samuel Robinson, then went on to the United States and, eventually, Europe, where many years later he would meet Simón Bolívar again. The boy was left to slog ahead with tutors who were far less interesting to him. But Carlos Palacios had his own ideas of what his nephew now needed to do. In order to satisfy the conditions of his inheritance, Don Carlos enrolled Simón as a cadet in the elite militia corps, the White Volunteers of the Valley of Aragua, which Simón's grandfather Juan de Bolívar had founded and his father, Don Juan Vicente, had commanded. Simón spent a year in "military" training—an obligatory rite of passage for Mantuano boys—during which he studied topography, physics, and doubtless learned very little about martial arts. Nevertheless, he was promoted to second lieutenant and, in the process, admitted to a coveted inner circle.

"I keep worrying about the boys," Esteban Palacios wrote Carlos from Spain, "especially Simón." Once Simón turned fifteen, the two uncles decided they should round out his education with a period of study in Madrid, under Esteban's supervision. Don Juan Vicente de Bolívar had always wanted it; Doña Concepción, too; it was simply Simón's grandfather's stubbornness—and perhaps his unwillingness to part with money—that had kept the two brothers at home. In January of 1799, Simón sailed for Cádiz with the understanding that his brother, Juan Vicente, would follow. All too mindful that the boy's vast inheritance might slip through the family's fingers, Carlos wrote to Esteban, "Keep a good eye on him, as I have said before, first because he will spend money without discipline or wisdom, and second because he is not as rich as he thinks. . . . Talk to him firmly or put him in a strict school if he does not behave with the requisite judgment."

As Simón was boarding the ship *San Ildefonso* in La Guaira, José María España—one of the Gual-España co-conspirators—was making his way back to Venezuela in a canoe, secretly reentering the colony after almost two years in flight. España managed to dodge the authorities for months, slipping from village to village, until he finally took shelter with a black family. Simón was halfway across the Atlantic when Spanish troops surprised España in his hiding place, arrested him, and then convicted him of high treason. He was tied to the tail of a mule and dragged to the main square of Caracas. There he was hanged, dismembered, his head and limbs taken to far corners of the colony. Once again, people were made to witness the iron cages, the vile putrefaction of flesh, the ravening vultures, in the event they needed to be reminded: Spain had no patience for revolutionaries. Within a year, Spanish spies tracked down Manuel Gual on the island of Trinidad. A vial of poison handily dispatched him.

FOR AS LONG AS HE could remember, Simón had begged his uncles to send him to Spain, so he boarded the *San Ildefonso* on January 19, 1799, in high spirits, anticipating his life adventure. His cabin mate was Esteban Escobar, an exceptionally bright thirteen-year-old who was headed to Spain on a scholarship to study at the military college in Segovia. Having grown up with similar backgrounds, the two boys became friends.

Their ship was a fleet, agile man-o'-war, built in the port city of Cartagena. It was originally part of a flotilla of six that had fought in many a Caribbean and Atlantic skirmish and would meet a bitter fate five years later at the Battle of Trafalgar. With seventy-four cannon and the capacity to transport six hundred, it was one of the finest battleships in the service of the Spanish crown. But traveling the seas in a ship built for combat was a perilous business. The last time the *San Ildefonso* had taken passengers from America to Cádiz, its twenty-six-ship convoy had run up against the English in the Battle of Cape St. Vincent. It was a measure of Spain's ruined economy that warships were now being employed to haul passengers and goods.

The *San Ildefonso* was far from comfortable—the accommodations were cramped, the food substandard, the company rough and rude—but the boys were given special quarters and privileges above deck, far from the bilge and vermin. As they plied north, across the crystalline blue waters of the Caribbean, they grew accustomed to life at sea.

From the start, the ship's commander was generous to his two young passengers. It's safe to assume that they learned much under his tutelage: intelligence that Bolívar later would find vital to a revolution that spread well into the sea. But the captain's munificence could not mask the hazards of their expedition or the nervousness of the time. The *San Ildefonso* was known to carry precious metals—it had shipped mercury and silver to Cádiz before—and so it was potential prey not only to the British enemy but to pirates who had terrorized Caribbean waters for centuries.

The trip was dangerous for another reason: the fledgling United States Navy was locked in a fierce "quasi-war" with French privateers who preyed mercilessly on American trading ships. During the American Revolution, France and America had been allies, but the French Revolution and subsequent trade wars had soured the friendship. The jockeying at sea threatened to become a full-scale conflict. Indeed, allegiances were shifting constantly during this volatile period; it was hard to know whether an approaching ship was friend or foe. Spain, which only years before had allied with Portugal against France, was now allied with France against England. And, in the course of Simón Bolívar's boyhood, the United States had gone from fighting a bitter revolution to becoming England's major partner in trade.

For all the attendant peril, the *San Ildefonso* arrived as scheduled in Veracruz, Mexico, on February 2, fourteen days after its departure from La Guaira. After loading seven million silver coins into the convoy's holds, the captain had expected to lift anchor and head east for Cádiz via Havana, but he was informed that a British blockade had impeded all travel in that direction. The *San Ildefonso* remained docked in Veracruz for forty-six days.

Simón took advantage of that numbing delay to borrow 400 pesos from a local merchant and travel by stagecoach to Mexico City. His uncle Pedro, the youngest of the Palacios brothers, had furnished him with a letter of introduction from the bishop of Caracas. As he rode into that splendid city—the jewel of New Spain, the pride of the Spanish colonial empire—he was struck by the sheer opulence of the city. "The city of Mexico reminds one of Berlin," wrote Alexander von Humboldt, "but is more beautiful; its architecture is of a more restrained taste." It was a time of general abundance in that bustling capital of the viceroyalty— a golden age in which each aristocrat's palace was built to surpass its neighbor. The grand avenues, the extravagant homes, the spacious parks, the spirited commerce: these represented a pinnacle of grandeur that Mexico would never reach again, and Bolívar marveled at it.

He spent a comfortable week in the magnificent home of the Marquis of Uluapa, a stay that was arranged by Mexico City's chief justice, the oidor Don Guillermo Aguirre, a nephew of the bishop's whose letter he carried. Under Aguirre's guidance, Simón mixed with Mexico's high society and was presented to the powerful viceroy Asanza. Much has been written about Simón's conversation with the viceroy and his supposedly plucky and incendiary references to revolution, which may or may not have been made. It is hard to believe that the Mexican sovereign would have engaged in political debate with a fifteen-year-old. But there is no doubt that they did speak and that the subject of their brief exchange was the blockade that prevented the *San Ildefonso* from setting sail. For all of Spain's empire, for all the gold and silver of Mexico, the British had reduced Spanish trade to a standstill. Simón's presence alone—a direct result of the blockade—was proof of Spain's relative powerlessness. That thought cannot have been far from anyone's mind.

Along with Simón's heady introduction to the Mexican society, it is said that he had his first romance while he was there. He had been known to flirt with pretty cousins in Caracas, had learned from his musical uncle, Padre Sojo, to dance, and he had turned into something of a dandy in his frilly lace collars and handsome waistcoats. But after twenty-five days of boredom and idleness in the port city of Veracruz, Simón was given an opportunity to act on amorous impulses.

She was María Ignacia Rodríguez de Velasco y Osorio, a married woman of twenty-one. She was flaxen-haired, blue-eyed, the daughter of aristocrats, and she had been introduced to Simón by his hostess, the Marquesa of Uluapa, who was her older sister. His romance with María Ignacia was instantaneous, ephemeral, wedged into a brief eight-day dalliance, but as the two were very much at home in the marquesa's house, they managed to snatch a few private moments in a narrow staircase of an upper floor. "The blond Rodríguez," as she was called, already had quite a reputation in Mexico City. Married at fifteen, this indefatigable voluptuary would scandalize Mexico with a string of husbands and scores of lovers, among them the Mexican emperor Agustín de Iturbide and Baron Alexander von Humboldt, who proclaimed her the most beautiful woman he had ever seen. It's impossible to know whether this romantic encounter was a first for Simón Bolívar. Certainly, it was the first time he had engaged with a woman as a fully independent male, free from the oversight and encumbrances of family.

Simón finally returned to Veracruz and departed for Havana when the blockade lifted, on March 20. Soon, his ship joined an even larger convoy and headed north, making its wary way past the Bahamas toward the Chesapeake Bay. The captain of the convoy had decided to follow the North American coast until his ships were well past danger, risking a longer trip and the possibility of exhausting their supplies. In Havana, they had taken on cattle, goats, sheep, chickens—enough food and water for sixty days. The trip would take seventy-two. Caught in a violent storm as they approached Cádiz, the fleet scattered; the *San Ildefonso* tossed alongside the coast of Portugal, toward northern Spain. By the time it pulled into the Basque port of Santoña, it stank of rancid cheese and a pestilential bilge of the blood of animals. Burned by relentless sun, buffeted by angry winds, the sailors were a ragged lot. As they squinted through rain at the gray huddled houses of Santoña, they must have felt great weariness and hunger. But they had evaded war.

SPAIN HAD BEEN AT WAR for six long years, and it would be at war for twenty-six more, until its strength was sapped and its standing as one of the most powerful nations in the world was ancient memory. King Carlos IV had become a laughingstock in his own country. A man of shallow abilities and a weak will, he had relinquished all power to his prime minister, Manuel de Godoy, who had been cuckolding him for years. At seventeen, Godoy had come to the king's palace as a royal bodyguard, and, before long, his virile good looks had caught the eye of the queen. For all her plainness of face and ruined complexion, Queen María Luisa had a formidable appetite for good-looking young men. Godoy soon became her lover. The queen rewarded his sexual favors with greater titles and responsibilities, marrying him off to disguise their entanglement, persuading her dull husband to appoint him head of state in 1792. That same year, the queen gave birth to her fourteenth child, who, it was rumored throughout Europe, looked shockingly like the new prime minister. As the king whiled away the hours in his palace workshop, fiddling with furniture and polishing swords, Godoy commandeered the throne. It was Godoy who disastrously declared war on England, initiating Spain's precipitous financial decline; and it was Godoy against whom the population of Spain had turned in an avenging fury. It can't have escaped anyone's notice that the French king and queen had been marched to the guillotine just a few years earlier. Trying to regain approval, Queen María Luisa appointed a new prime minister, the physically frail Francisco Saavedra, who had been in the New World and had helped the Americans defeat the English at the Battle of Yorktown; and, ever flighty where sex was concerned, she set her sights on another man.

The new object of her concupiscence was Manuel Mallo, a strapping young bodyguard from Caracas and, as it happened, a friend and confidant of Esteban Palacios, the uncle Simón had come to see. The fifteen-year-old boy could hardly know it, but the *madre patria* was a hotbed of decadence—not the inviolable power it pretended to be. Politically, economically, morally, Spain was suffering the consequences of its own ruinous management. The upper classes could feel it in their pockets; the rabble, in their bellies. It is hardly surprising that a rich young aristocrat from the Indies was welcomed with open arms.

Simón arrived in Madrid "quite handsome," as his uncle Esteban reported. "He has absolutely no education, but he has the will and intelligence to acquire one, and, even though he spent quite a bit of money in transit, he landed here a complete mess. I've had to re-outfit him totally. I am very fond of him and, although he takes a great deal of looking after, I attend to his needs with pleasure."

Esteban had been in Madrid for more than six years, trying to confirm the title of marquis for Simón's older brother, Juan Vicente. In the process, he had expended a considerable amount of Bolívar funds and achieved very little. However charming and handsome—however engaged in swank musical circles—Esteban was inexpert at politics, unable to win the sort of influence it took to rid a family tree of its pesky defects. He had been about to abandon his efforts and return to Caracas empty-handed, when three eventualities changed his mind: he was made minister of the auditing tribunal, a distinguished if modestly paid position; he knew Saavedra, who had just been appointed prime minister; and, last, his housemate, the irresistible Manuel Mallo, had become the favorite of the queen. All Spain had heard about María Luisa's latest inamorato, and all Caracas was abuzz with rumor. Though Mallo had actually been born in New Granada, he had grown up in Caracas and was a fixture in Mantuano society. Sure that his fortunes would rise alongside his friend's, Esteban had decided to stay. He had urged his brothers in Caracas to send Juan Vicente and Simón, so that they, too, might take advantage of this new American moment. When Juan Vicente demurred and Don Carlos Palacios proposed to send Simón alone, Esteban had agreed. When the Palacios' younger brother Pedro wrote that he also wanted to come bask in Mallo's successes, Esteban had agreed to that as well.

Simón arrived in Madrid eleven days after the *San Ildefonso* had docked in Santoña; he had little baggage and almost no clothes. Days later, his uncle Pedro stumbled into the city, penniless and scruffy; his ship had been seized, first by British corsairs near Puerto Rico and then by the English navy, which had set him free. At first, Simón and Pedro moved into Esteban's rooms in the house Esteban shared with Mallo, but the crowded conditions soon made it evident that they would need to find their own quarters. The three took a modest apartment on the Calle de los Jardines and hired three manservants to attend to their needs. "We do enjoy some favor," Pedro wrote to his brother Carlos, "but it is too complicated to be explained in writing." The favor, in fact, was scant. Mallo appeared to have considerable run of the queen's boudoir, but he had little influence in her court, surely nothing approaching Godoy's power. More troubling, the war with England had thwarted the regular transport of funds, which the young Venezuelans needed desperately in order to keep up appearances. Neither of the Palacios brothers possessed anything like the fortune that belonged to their charge, Bolívar. As best he could, Esteban set about organizing Simón's education, so that the boy might shine amid society circles in Madrid.

He hired a tailor to outfit the boy in an elegant uniform, an evening tailcoat, cashmere jackets, velvet vests, silk shirts, lace collars, and capes. He arranged special tutors who could teach him proper Castilian grammar, French, mathematics, world history. But after a few months, Esteban had a better idea. He asked the Marquis of Ustáriz, a native of Caracas and an old family friend, to take on the boy's education. The marquis, then sixty-five, was a highly respected member of Spain's Supreme Council of War and in the prime of a distinguished career. But he had never had a son. He did not hesitate; he accepted the responsibility with pleasure. An erudite man who read widely and studied deeply, the marquis turned out to be an ideal teacher. He was liberal, wise, a paragon of integrity, and an ardent lover of all things Venezuelan. He and Bolívar liked one another immediately. Within days, the sixteen-year-old moved into the marquis's resplendent mansion at No. 8 Calle Atocha and began study under his direction.

The change Simón experienced under the marquis's fatherly tutelage was swift and dramatic. Until then, his schooling had been erratic. The only surviving letter written in his hand before this time—directed to his uncle Pedro—exhibits an appalling lack of knowledge for a fifteen-year-old aristocrat. He misspells the simplest words, has little grasp of good grammar. His mentor surely recognized this right away and undertook to remake the boy completely. He hired the best tutors available in Spanish literature, French and Italian languages, Enlightenment philosophy, world history. He recommended books, piqued Simón's curiosity with tales of his own experiences, looked over the boy's shoulder as Simón read and wrote. Surrounded by the marquis's books in his magnificently appointed library, Simón read avidly, applying his considerable energies to mastering the classics as well as works of contemporary European thought. He listened to Beethoven and Pleyel—composers of the day, whose works were just being introduced in Madrid's salons. He learned principles of accounting, which he would turn one day against his predatory uncle Carlos. But as cultured and academic as the program of his instruction was, it did not lack the physical. He trained in fencing and, being quick on his feet, developed a keen aptitude for it. He studied dance, a pastime that gave him enormous pleasure. Come evenings, he would engage in long philosophical conversations with the marquis, mingle with illustrious guests, or embark on a whirl of social activities with his uncles.

From time to time, the young Venezuelans would call on Mallo in the royal court, where Simón would have the opportunity to observe Queen María Luisa at first hand. He had glimpsed her before, when she had visited Mallo in the house Esteban shared with him. Disguised in a monk's cape, slipping furtively into her lover's quarters, the woman would not have inspired particular awe in a boy. But here, in the glittering halls of the royal palace, there was no question that she was a powerful presence. Surrounded by toadies, ruling her courtiers by whim, she cut a formidable figure with her grim face and flamboyant silk gowns. In a portrait painted within a year of Bolívar's arrival, Francisco de Goya captured the queen's frightening amalgam of debauchery and cunning. Even then, judging by Goya's candid and openly satirical depiction, her critics were legion. "There is no woman on earth who lies with more composure or is as treacherous," a respected diplomat in Madrid wrote. "Her simple observations become irrevocable law. She sacrifices the best interests of the crown to her low, scandalous vices." Now, with her empire beset, her lust too much in evidence, her very teeth marred by decay, the queen's corruption cannot have been lost on the young man from the Indies. He was acquiring an education befitting a Spanish nobleman, but he was also learning how fragile the construct of monarchies could be.

Henry Adams, a great chronicler of the times, described the fatuousness of the Spanish court in his *History of the United States During the Administrations of Thomas Jefferson and James Madison:*

> The Queen's favorite in the year 1800 was a certain Mallo, whom she was said to have enriched, and who, according to the women of the bed-chamber, physically beat Her Majesty as though she were any common Maritornes. One day in that year, when Godoy had come

to pay his respects to the King, and as usual was conversing with him in the Queen's presence, Charles asked him a question: "Manuel," said the King, "what is it with this Mallo? I see him with new horses and carriages every day. Where does he get so much money?" "Sire," replied Godoy, "Mallo has nothing in the world; but he is kept by an ugly old woman who robs her husband to pay her lover." The King shouted with laughter, and turning to his wife, said: "Luisa, what think you of that?" "Ah, Charles!" she replied; "don't you know that Manuel is always joking?"

One afternoon, Bolívar made a trip to the palace to visit the queen's fifteen-year-old son, Prince Ferdinand, the future king. Ferdinand had invited him to a game of badminton. In the heat of one of their volleys, Simón's shuttlecock landed on the prince's head, and the young monarch, incensed and humiliated, refused to continue. The queen, who had been watching all the while, insisted that Ferdinand go on, instructing him to comport himself like a good host. "How could Ferdinand VII possibly have known," Bolívar commented twenty-seven years later, "that the accident was an omen that some day I would wrest the most precious jewel from his crown?"

At about the same time, in February of 1800, Esteban and Pedro moved out of their apartment on Calle de los Jardines and left Madrid altogether, wanting to distance themselves from a mounting problem. It's not entirely clear why, but it is reasonable to assume that they had come under suspicion as the century turned, power shifted in court, two prime ministers came and went, and the queen's lover was taken for what he was: a simple gigolo. It might also have been due to the queen herself, who was highly jealous, inclined to suspect that Mallo was disloyal and had mistresses elsewhere. In any case, Esteban was arrested and put in prison—an unremarkable eventuality in those convoluted times—and Pedro proceeded to make himself scarce, spending much of his time in Cádiz. The Marquis of Ustáriz, a proud pillar in that increasingly venal city, became Bolívar's sole anchor.

But by then young Simón had a very pressing distraction: he had fallen in love. He had met María Teresa Rodríguez del Toro in the marquis's house and, in the course of two or three afternoon visits, expressed his affection and managed to win hers in return. She was the daughter of rich Caracans—a cousin of one of his close childhood friends, Fernando del Toro—which meant that even though she had been born in Spain, she had been raised with the American customs that Bolívar held dear. She was pale, delicate, tall, not particularly beautiful, but she had large dark eyes and an exquisite figure. Not quite nineteen, she was almost two years older, and yet she seemed pure and innocent, with a child's easy nature. As the marquis and her father bent over a chess game or discussed politics in comfortable chairs by the great, blazing fireplace, Bolívar drew María Teresa into intimate conversation. Before long, he began to dream of a lifetime at her side.

He proposed marriage to her father so soon that Don Bernardo Rodríguez del Toro was taken aback. It was an advantageous proposition for María Teresa, to be sure: the Bolívar name was persuasive in and of itself, and Simón had acquired quite a reputation for a young man, having been received at court and so obviously favored by the elegant marquis. But Don Bernardo worried about the aspirant's age. He had yet to turn seventeen. Don Bernardo decided to take María Teresa off to their summerhouse in the Basque city of Bilbao to cool the youngsters' passions as well as to test the genuineness of the boy's proposal—and patience.

In the interim, Bolívar persuaded the marquis to help him secure María Teresa's hand. He shot off a letter to his uncle Pedro, advising him of his intent to marry. He wrote a letter to his beloved, calling her the "sweet hex of my soul." Six months later, on March 20, 1801, with an official passport in hand, he left for Bilbao to join her.

There is too little evidence to know with any certainty what happened during the year that followed, but it is clear that Bolívar spent most of it in Bilbao. All spring and summer, he visited with his prospective bride and family. By August, Don Bernardo had taken María Teresa back to Madrid, but Bolívar stayed on in Bilbao. A few months later, in the beginning of 1802, he made a brief visit to Paris. Why? Some historians have suggested that he had a plan to help his uncle Esteban escape from prison. Others have said that Bolívar had become persona non grata, because Queen María Luisa believed he was carrying love letters from Mallo to someone else. Yet others say that Godoy, newly reinstalled as prime minister, despised the queen's lover along with all of his "Indian" cronies, and had intentionally blocked Bolívar's movements. Most likely, Bolívar stayed in Bilbao and traveled to Paris simply because he had made French friends in Bilbao and was trying to prove himself to his prospective father-in-law—show that he was a man of the world. Whatever the reason, shortly after Cornwallis and Napoleon signed a treaty effectively ending the war between England and France, Bolívar was granted a passport and headed back to Madrid. It was April 29, 1802. He was eighteen years old.

He applied for a marriage license immediately on arrival in Madrid, and on May 5 received it. Elated, he bought two tickets to Caracas on the *San Ildefonso,* the same ship on which he had sailed three years before. Clearly, he had already persuaded his sweetheart to return with him to his homeland, where life promised to be far less complicated and a large inheritance awaited them. One of the main stipulations of his inheritance, after all, was that he had to reside in Venezuela.

Simón and María Teresa were married with all of her father's blessings on the balmy spring day of May 26 in Madrid's Parish Church of San José, a short walk from the bride's house. The wedding, so ardently desired by the groom, was celebrated largely by the bride's family, as Esteban was still in prison and Pedro unable to travel from Cádiz. Three weeks later, the happy newlyweds departed Spain from the port of La Coruña, in a ship's cabin Bolívar had festooned with flowers.

They returned to Venezuela for what Bolívar assumed would be a comfortable landowner's life filled with the business of property, harvests, and the management of money and slaves. They spent a few carefree months in Caracas next to the cathedral, in the splendid mansion Bolívar had inherited from the priest who had baptized him—the house his uncle Carlos had coveted for years. María Teresa was welcomed warmly, not only by Simón's family, but by her own. The del Toros had had a long, illustrious history in Venezuela and her uncle, the Marquis del Toro, was an influential presence in the capital. But María Teresa had never experienced the colonies for herself and so her first sight of the tropical city with its exotic races, riotously colored birds, and rich women trailed by retinues of slaves must have made a striking impression.

Bolívar had hoped to take her to one of the family haciendas—the estate at San Mateo, perhaps—where he might show her, for a fleeting glimpse at least, his childhood idyll: the sugar fields, the orchards and gardens, the charmed country life they had so often envisioned together. But he never accomplished this. She felt too weak to travel, too frail to undertake the long carriage ride on rutted roads. There, in the city where his father had died too soon, where his mother had died young, María Teresa grew gravely ill with yellow fever. Whether she had contracted it in Caracas or in La Guaira, or even on board the *San Ildefonso,* will never be known, but there is no doubt that the disease came over her quickly, surprising her frantic husband with its virulence. Within five months of their joy-filled arrival in Venezuela, she was dead.

CHAPTER 3

The Innocent Abroad

I was suddenly made to understand that men were made for other things than love.

—Simón Bolívar

María Teresa's body, jaundiced and emaciated by disease, was laid to rest in an open coffin for all Caracas to see. She was dressed in a richly decorated gown of white silk brocade. Her head rested on a pillow that held her husband's baptismal garments; no child would ever wear them again. A cloth covered her face. When the funeral was over, the mourners gone, her casket was nailed shut and slipped into the family crypt to await eternity with the Bolívars.

Simón's grief was so extreme that, according to his brother, Juan Vicente, he veered into a kind of madness, alternating between fury and despair. Had Juan Vicente not spent each waking minute caring for him, he might have lost his will to live. "I had thought of my wife as a personification of the Divine Being," Bolívar later told one of his generals. "Heaven stole her from me, because she was never meant for this earth." Spiritually depleted, physically exhausted, he tried to manage his cacao and indigo estates, but the work failed to distract him; everywhere he looked, there were only shards of an imagined life. "May God grant me a son," he had once written to his uncle Pedro when he was seventeen and deeply in love, but he had been stripped of that dream for now, forced to rethink every ambition of his hope-filled youth. He could hardly go on living alone in his immense mansion next to the cathedral, its yawning rooms a reminder of his lost, irrecoverable bliss. He could take no comfort from the parlors of Caracas society. He could no longer look forward to a tranquil life in his haciendas with a doting wife and a spirited brood of children. As he later recounted:

> Had I not become a widower, my life might have been very different. I would never have become General Bolívar, nor the Liberator, although I have to admit that my temperament would hardly have predisposed me to become mayor of San Mateo. . . . When I was with my wife, my head was filled only with the most ardent love, not with political ideas. Those thoughts hadn't yet captured my imagination. . . . The death of my wife placed me early in the road of politics, and caused me to follow the chariot of Mars.

If Bolívar went on to develop a remarkable capacity to rebound from setbacks, it started here in his twentieth year of life. From the depths of despondency he found a survivor's grit. He became aggressive, combative, blunt. Soon he was involved in a legal dispute with Antonio Nicolás Briceño, a neighbor who, he claimed, had trespassed on one of his haciendas—building houses and planting fields on his land in the valley of Tuy. Not long after, he wrote a letter scolding his uncle Carlos Palacios for not keeping him properly informed about his finances. Eventually, he assigned the management of his properties to another person entirely, José Manuel Jaén. But none of this held his interest or counted as any kind of life for a young man. By his twentieth birthday, he was planning a return trip to Europe. He was bored beyond imagining, eager to get away.

He commissioned a ship to transport his cacao, coffee, and indigo to Spain and set sail on it from La Guaira in October of 1803. Armed with a stack of books by Plutarch, Montesquieu, Voltaire, and Rousseau, he settled down for the hard journey across the Atlantic. Two months later he arrived in Cádiz after a turbulent passage.

He stayed in that port long enough to sell his haciendas' crops and send detailed instructions to his agent Jaén. But Cádiz in January was a rainy, windy city, and he was anxious to move on. In February, he headed north to Madrid to console his father-in-law, Don Bernardo del Toro, and to give him a few melancholy keepsakes that had once belonged to María Teresa. Bolívar spent two chilly months in Madrid, a city that could only depress him, filled as it was with countless reminders of his dead wife and the evidence of a decaying empire. He was still in mourning clothes, which decency and custom demanded that he wear for a least a year. He found some comfort in weeping with Don Bernardo, but seeing old friends and trying to renew past ties proved as unbearable as it had been in Caracas. In March, when the crown issued a decree demanding that all transients evacuate the capital because of an acute bread shortage, Bolívar was almost relieved. Come April, when the violet fields bloomed, sending their sweet fragrance into the warming air of the Pyrenees, he made his way across those mountains into France with his childhood friend, Teresa's cousin Fernando del Toro.

They arrived in Paris just before the French Senate proclaimed Napoleon emperor, on May 18. The capital was filled with high spirits, trembling with possibility. It seemed there was no limit to what France could achieve. Its Enlightenment philosophers had shaped a new era; the Revolution, for all its atrocities, had reinvented a nation; and Napoleon's striking military successes in Europe and the Middle East suggested that France could become the dominant world power.

Bolívar had watched Napoleon's star rise with fascination. Now, as he walked the streets of Paris, he could not fail to see the man's accomplishments: there was a new air of prosperity that contrasted starkly with the mold and ruin of Spain. Napoleon was undertaking a redefinition of all public institutions—education, banking, civil laws, even transportation and sewage—and the improvements were bold and evident. A larger global strategy also seemed to be at work. By then, Napoleon had sold Louisiana to Thomas Jefferson; months before, he had conceded defeat in the bloody insurrection that had birthed the Republic of Haiti. But even as France appeared to be shrinking in the New World, in the Old it was emerging as a muscular nation. No ruler in the world could claim more admiration at that moment than the newly proclaimed emperor. Seeing Napoleon, in a modest coat and cap, review his splendidly arrayed troops in the court of the Tuileries, Bolívar, too, was filled with awe. "I worshiped him as the hero of the republic," Bolívar was later to say, "as the bright star of glory, the genius of liberty"—and, perhaps most of all, as a humble servant of his people. But that was soon to change.

BOLÍVAR AND FERNANDO DEL TORO found an apartment at the Hotel for Foreigners on the Rue Vivienne, only a few blocks from the Palais du Louvre. There they established a comfortable gathering place for friends, among them Carlos Montúfar of Quito and Vicente Rocafuerte of Guayaquil, young Creoles who would reappear many years later to play radically different roles in Bolívar's life. In time, Bolívar's teacher Simón Rodríguez—in exile and little more than thirty years old— joined their ranks and, in the company of these spirited men, the widower finally shed his mourning clothes and embraced all the restorative pleasures Paris could offer.

It was a sybarite's city, riotously liberal, filled with every sort of entertainment, from glittering opera houses to smoke-filled gambling halls. Theaters, which had been emptied during the Revolution, were now scenes of nightly brilliance where *tout* Paris gathered to hear Frédéric Duvernoy's virtuosic horn, or Cousineau's harp, or Kreutzer's violin. The ballet was in full flourish, dazzling audiences with performances of *La Fille mal gardée* or *Dansomanie*. In the Palais-Royal, a magnificent complex of arcades and public gardens that became one of Bolívar's favorite haunts, he frequented the Comédie-Française and a veritable profusion of restaurants and shops, bookstores and *cabinets de curiosités*, gaming houses and celebrated *maisons d'amour.* With Simón Rodríguez, he read Helvetius, Holbach, and Hume, and spent hours in smoke-choked cafés, arguing about Spinoza. By day, Paris was swarming with horse-drawn carriages—*wiskis, demifortunes, cabriolets, boguets*—clattering over the mud and ruts of the streets. The commerce of pastry vendors, cat peddlers, shoe menders filled the air with raucous cries. By night, the city was a shimmering miracle, lit by newfangled gas lamps that allowed the revelry to continue unabated until dawn.

It was in this polestar of splendid modernity that Bolívar got to know "Fanny" Denis de Trobriand, the Countess of Dervieu du Villars, one of the Parisians he had met during his visit to Bilbao. The pretty socialite hardly recognized him as the serious youngster she had known three years before, but she was delighted by what she saw. "He was another man entirely," the writer Flora Tristan later recounted. "Bolívar had grown at least four inches; he had acquired a certain grace and strength, and a lustrous black moustache that set off his brilliant white teeth, giving him a wonderfully masculine air."

Fanny was almost a decade older than Bolívar. At sixteen, she had married the Count Dervieu du Villars, the commanding general of Lyon, who was twenty-five years her senior. Legend has it that when the count was arrested by agents of the Revolution and sentenced to death, the fearless Fanny surprised the revolutionary prosecutor late one night in his quarters and, with a pistol to his head, forced him to sign her husband's pardon. Count du Villars went on to become a colonel in Napoleon's army and, once the Revolution was over, a senator in his government. By the mid-1790s, he had acquired a luxurious mansion on the Rue Basse de Saint Pierre, where Fanny established herself as one of the grandes dames of high society. The old count, preferring his country home in Lyon, often left Paris for long stretches at a time, and so his gregarious young wife was left to her own devices. She became a regular at Parisian soirees, sought after in the emperor's court, and an intimate friend of the famously beautiful Mme de Récamier.

Like many Frenchwomen who had won a different sort of liberty in that defiant age, Fanny was frankly promiscuous. Her coquettishness and vivacity led to countless romances, and she was said to have had children by at least three lovers, among them Empress Josephine's son Prince Eugène de Beauharnais, whom Napoleon later made viceroy of Italy. She was golden-haired, vivacious, with deep blue, beguiling eyes. Alabaster-skinned, fresh-faced, with a melodious voice and a languid, feline grace, she was a beautiful woman, all the more so for her sly wit and intelligence. The salon she hosted drew some of the great minds of the day, including Baron Alexander von Humboldt, the botanist Aimé Bonpland, minister of police Pierre Denis-Lagarde, the writer-philosopher Benjamin Constant, and the extravagant Mme de Staël.

Fanny welcomed Bolívar into this whirling social milieu, attracted

by the young man's cleverness and the startling change he had made
since his moody youth in Bilbao. As a contemporary noted:

> His spirit, his heart, his tastes, his character had changed completely.
> He was renting an apartment for 500 francs at the Hotel for Foreign-
> ers; he had servants in elegant uniforms, a coach, magnificent horses,
> a box at the Opera. It was known that he kept a ballerina. Finally,
> his wardrobe, which was extravagantly luxurious, contrasted sharply
> with everyone else's miserable, outdated attire.

Dancing with Fanny at one of her elegant parties, he learned that an
ancestor of hers was an Aristiguieta—a name in his own family tree,
indeed, the name of the priest who had bequeathed him a fortune—and,
although a genealogical connection was never proven, they proceeded to
call one another "cousin." The appellation had its conveniences. From
that day forward, Bolívar became one of Madame du Villars's most assiduous visitors. The old count, believing that the young Venezuelan
was his wife's relative, received him warmly. Bolívar and Fanny soon became lovers, spending long, pleasurable afternoons together at the house
on Basse de Saint Pierre, or riding horses into the nearby countryside.

But Fanny and the unnamed ballerina were by no means the only
Frenchwomen with whom Bolívar tried to erase his unhappy past. Yet
another young matron he had met in Bilbao had reemerged to help
him forget his widowhood. She was Thérèse Laisney, the common-law
wife of a retired colonel of Peruvian extraction, Mariano de Tristan y
Moscoso. Their daughter, Flora Tristan, who went on to become a renowned socialist activist and grandmother of the painter Paul Gauguin,
recorded something of her parents' relationship with Bolívar:

> Eight months after my father left Bilbao, he saw a notice in a Paris
> newspaper that said someone was trying to reach him. My father im-
> mediately went to the posted address . . . climbed to the third floor,
> and saw Bolívar lying in bed. He was emaciated, pale, and deathly
> sick. His first love, his lovely wife, had died. . . .
>
> Though he would go on to be a great warrior, a political genius,

he was virtually drowning in misery at the time and needed the lifeline of a compassionate woman's heart. For six weeks in Paris, he visited no house but ours. He spoke with no one but my mother.

Bolívar appears again in Tristan's account after Paris had applied its salve. According to her (and her chronology cannot be trusted), Bolívar left the city for a short time. When he returned, he checked into the Hotel for Foreigners, where her mother hastened to see him:

Turning onto the Rue Richelieu, my mother was almost run over by a splendid coach, whose horses were racing around the corner. She drew back against the wall, but to her surprise the coach suddenly stopped, and the rider threw open the door and flung himself on her, clasping her in his arms, practically suffocating her. "It is I! It is I! Don't you recognize me? Oh, it's probably better that you don't! It's proof that I've changed completely."

If he hadn't known it before, Bolívar learned in his scant year and a half in Paris how much—and how little—women now meant to him. For the rest of his life, he would be irresistibly attracted to them, but would find them surprisingly easy to win and discard. Bored, he would move on, far more interested in the ambit of men. And yet, he was an incurable romantic, incapable of living without female companionship. As the historian Gil Fortoul said of Bolívar's unbridled appetite, "All in all, one can say that he never lived alone." One could also say that he never again wanted a wife. Much later, Bolívar was to admit, "I loved my wife very much and at her death I took an oath never again to marry. As you can see, I have kept my word."

Paris had taught him about the consoling powers of sex. Many years later, in the fields of revolution, Bolívar would relive those heady, Parisian days with his soldiers. One of his generals, Manuel Roergas de Serviez, recalled:

With his keen appreciation for pleasure and especially for carnal pleasure, it was truly extraordinary to hear the Liberator enumerate all the female beauties he had known in France with a meticulousness and precision that gave credit to his fine memory. He would recite the puns of Brunet, sing all the songs that were in vogue at the time, and he would roar at his own past indiscretions, making fun of his naïveté.

IT MAY HAVE BEEN IN Fanny du Villar's house that Bolívar met Baron Alexander von Humboldt, for the great naturalist was said to frequent her salon. But it is equally possible that he met him through Carlos Montúfar, who had arrived in Paris as part of Humboldt's retinue. Montúfar, a botanist from Quito and a member of Bolívar's intimate circle of young Latin Americans in Paris, had accompanied Humboldt and Aimé Bonpland on the last leg of their much celebrated "New Continent" expedition. In a remarkable voyage, undertaken between 1799 and 1804, Humboldt and Bonpland traveled the length of Latin America, recording their observations and collecting plant and animal specimens from the Amazon basin to the heights of Mount Chimborazo. The trip, which Humboldt later described in thirty volumes, transformed Western science and marked the foundation of modern geography. But in the course of publishing his findings, Humboldt, a strikingly handsome man, also became enormously popular in society circles, having met many of the great eminences of his time. He had come to Paris in August 1804 almost directly from Jefferson's White House. He had advised the president on the Louisiana Purchase, conferred with him about the Lewis and Clark expedition, had his portrait painted by the artist of presidents, Charles Willson Peale. After a pleasant spring evening with Humboldt in Washington, Dolley Madison had written, "We have lately had a great treat in the company of a charming Prussian Baron. . . . All the ladies say they are in love with him."

Little wonder, then, that Humboldt was sought out in the salons of Paris and fussed over by Fanny du Villars. It may even have been Bolívar who introduced Fanny to him. In any case, Bolívar had many reasons to visit with Humboldt, having learned that, during the baron's visit to Caracas, he had met Bolívar's sisters as well as the Palacios, and even lodged with his in-laws, the del Toros. In conversation, Bolívar learned that Humboldt had great respect for the learned scholar Padre Andújar, the very priest who had taught him mathematics as a child.

So it was that Bolívar became a frequent guest at Humboldt's elegant apartments on Rue du Faubourg Saint Germain, where visitors from all over Europe gathered to inspect the baron's extraordinary collection of sixty thousand botanical specimens from subequatorial America. In his quirky jumble of languages—part Spanish, part English, part French—Humboldt praised South America's physical beauty, its people, and its promise. Bonpland, too, expressed wonder at the natural riches he had seen. Bolívar was enchanted. Although Humboldt and Bonpland cannot have been entirely convinced of the young man's seriousness, they could not doubt his energy and enthusiasm. They became friends.

On one occasion, as the three of them discussed colonial politics, Bolívar made a passionate case for a liberated continent, free from the yoke of the Spanish crown. He asked Humboldt whether he thought America had what it took to govern itself. The scientist ventured that the colonies might indeed be ready for freedom, but he added that he knew of no leader who was capable of winning it for them. Bonpland better understood the spirit of the question: a revolution *makes* its leaders, he replied.

Whether Bolívar thought of himself as that leader at that precise moment we cannot know. He was a chrysalis of what he would become, a mere twenty-one years old. But during that visit to Paris a germ of a political idea grew: a man could change the course of history. There was no better example for that than Napoleon. And South America was a land ripe with possibility; Bolívar had been told so by the greatest scientist of his time.

Bolívar's admiration for Napoleon was tested, however, when the emperor crowned himself at the Cathedral of Notre Dame later that year. It isn't clear whether Bolívar saw that spectacle on December 2, 1804, or witnessed the triumphant parade, the splendid coaches, the ermine robes, the roar of adoring multitudes. Simón Rodríguez recalls, "On that day, so notable and happy for the French, Bolívar and I decided to stay in at our hotel." According to Rodríguez, the two of them shuttered the windows and drew the drapes, stubbornly ignoring the festivities, while the rest of Paris rejoiced. American naval officer Hiram Paulding confirms this story, having heard it from Bolívar himself when he visited him twenty years later in Peru. In any case, Bolívar's aide-de-camp, Daniel O'Leary, recorded the Liberator's feelings about the coronation in strong and unequivocal terms:

> He made himself emperor, and from that day on, I looked upon him as a hypocritical tyrant, an insult to liberty and an obstacle to the progress of civilization. . . . What terrible feelings of indignation this sad spectacle produced in my soul, possessed as it was by a fanatical love of liberty and glory! From then on I could not abide Napoleon, his very glory seemed to glow from hell. France, too, surprised me: a great republic covering itself with trophies and monuments, flaunting its armies and institutions, casting aside its cap of liberty for a crown.

Bolívar was not alone in thinking Napoleon had gone too far when he took the crown from Pope Pius VII's hands and placed it on his own head. Ludwig von Beethoven, who had composed the "Eroica" in Napoleon's honor, decided to strip out the emperor's name. William Wordsworth called the coronation "a sad reverse for all mankind." For the rest of his life, however, Bolívar would prove ambivalent about Napoleon, his feelings vacillating wildly from admiration to aversion. He would say to one of his biographers:

> I regarded the crown that Napoleon placed on his head as a miserable, outdated relic. For me, his greatness was in his universal acclaim, in the interest his person could inspire. I confess that the whole thing only served to remind me of my own country's enslavement, of the glory that would accrue to him who would liberate it. But I was far from imagining that I would be that man.

By the end of 1804, Bolívar's disgust with the emperor was so intense, his nerves so ragged from too many late night dissipations, that his temper erupted at a banquet attended by a number of distinguished guests, among them senators, decorated soldiers, and a few prominent priests. He railed so vociferously against Napoleon, prompting such outrage, that the argument quickly degenerated into a shouting match. He accused Napoleon of being a traitor to liberty. He blamed the clergymen at the table of being too fanatical in Napoleon's favor. The evening ended badly, the guests scattering in a huff. The next morning, he felt obliged to write a letter to Colonel Mariano de Tristan, who had been present and later suggested that Bolívar would do well to leave the country.

Colonel, I have known you for six years, and for six years I have loved you as a true friend, have had nothing but the deepest respect for the nobility of your character and the honesty of your views. I can't tell you how deeply I regret that you were made to witness that disgraceful scene at my table caused by the fanaticism of a few intolerant clerics . . . and the shouts with which they defended Bonaparte! Like you, I admire his gifts as a soldier. But how can one fail to see his single-minded pursuit of personal power? He is turning into a despot. . . . Is it wise for the nation to entrust its fate to a single man? I'm no politician, able to hold a debate before a congress; I don't lead an army, am not expected to inspire confidence in anyone's troops; nor am I a sage who can calmly and patiently parse difficult truths. . . . I am a nobody, just a rich man, society's fluff, a mere stone in Bonaparte's dagger. . . . But I am curious to know: Is a foreigner in this republic allowed to speak out about the men who govern it, or will he be thrown out for the crime of having spoken freely?

He was not well. His untrammeled life had finally gotten the best of him. He had lost a fortune at Parisian gaming tables and had had to borrow from Fanny, a humiliation he did not want to repeat. He played one more time, repaid the debt, and swore off gambling forever. But as Europe slid into winter and the chill bore into his bones, he grew weak, unhealthy. Simón Rodríguez, seeing his former pupil on the verge of physical and nervous collapse, suggested a spring excursion. A long, leisurely amble through France and Italy in warm weather would be just the thing to revivify an exhausted young man.

BY THEN, BOLÍVAR'S SCHOOLTEACHER—THE ECCENTRIC, peripatetic Rodríguez—had been away from Venezuela for more than six years. Having fled during the Gual-España conspiracy, found safe haven in Jamaica, and changed his name to Samuel Robinson, he taught school for a while, and learned English and typography. Shortly thereafter he turned up in Baltimore and lived there for almost three years, working at a printing press. Rodríguez would come to earn his living in a myriad ways—as schoolteacher, small farmer, estate manager, soap maker, candlemaker, gunpowder merchant, journalist, writer, organizer of orphanages and old people's homes, reformer of prostitutes, avant-garde educator—but always he would be traveling, learning, living by the principles of the Enlightenment, in which a "republic of letters" transcended national borders. "I don't want to be like trees that put down roots in one place," he wrote. "I'd rather be like the wind, the water, the sun—like all those things that are forever in perpetual motion." And so he was.

In 1799, he traveled to Bayonne, where he taught Spanish, French, and English and, with the exiled Mexican priest Fray Servando Teresa de Mier, began to dream about establishing a language school in Paris. By 1801, that dream had come true. He and Mier were gainfully employed in Paris, teaching Spanish, which was in vogue, given France's new alliance with Spain. But Rodríguez's itinerant spirit soon had him yearning for the road. When Bolívar caught up with him in Paris in 1804, Rodríguez was just returning from Vienna, where—in yet another remarkable reincarnation—he had worked for a brief time in the laboratory of a noted Austrian chemist. He didn't hesitate to abandon his plans to the task of restoring his former pupil's health.

Bolívar, Rodríguez, and Fernando del Toro set out on their curative trip to Italy in April of 1805. They traveled to Lyon by public carriage, rested for a few days, then sent their luggage ahead and made their way on foot—à la Rousseau—covering short distances every day. The French countryside was glorious at that time of year: the wisteria, poppies, and irises blooming in vibrant profusion; the willows and poplars a bright new green. Bolívar had always loved nature—enjoyed travel on an open road—and, little by little, the fresh air and exercise began to animate him.

They crossed the Savoy Alps and stopped in the valley of Les Charmettes, where Rousseau purportedly had spent a few happy years in the house of his lover, the scandalous "Maman." Rodríguez delighted in recounting the details of his hero's eventful life as they visited his various hideaways. From there, they headed for Italy, increasingly aware of the triumphal arches, the monuments—even a towering pyramid—that had been erected along the way in preparation for Napoleon's Italian coronation.

The three made harmonious traveling companions. Rodríguez, the eldest at thirty-three, was jolly, earthy, irrepressible, ever the teacher and instigator. Fernando del Toro was an aristocrat and soldier—son of the Marquis del Toro, the very distinguished Mantuano with whom Humboldt had stayed in Caracas—but Fernando was also an inveterate gambler and bon vivant. Bolívar, by far the youngest, was restless, moody, already marked by life yet deeply curious. It is easy to imagine them making their way down dirt roads, singing, talking—the teacher declaiming on philosophy, the soldier recalling his exploits, the future Liberator marveling at the history around them. As they crossed into Italy, they plunged heartily into the study of Italian, reading Boccaccio, Petrarch, and Dante, writers from whom Bolívar was to acquire many a useful maxim. But they also did what any traveler would have done— buy fruit in the open markets, repose at small inns along the way, dodge mud as carriages hurtled by in the rain, fall into conversation in cafés, deliberate their route in boisterous roadside trattorias. Few South Americans traveled the countryside at that time, and so—with their eccentric manners and accents—they must have drawn attention.

By May 26, they were in Milan, watching Napoleon don the historic crown of Lombardy, said to contain one of the nails from Christ's crucifixion. "*Dieu me la donne,*" Napoleon announced as he placed it on his head—God gives me this—"woe to the man who dares lay a finger on it." Fanny was there to see it, as were her old husband and young lover Eugène de Beauharnais—and it seemed all Europe was pointing at this moment, exulting in the triumph of one man. On the fields of Montechiaro a few days later, Bolívar had the opportunity to watch Napoleon review his troops—once again, in humble clothing—and, as Bolívar told it, Napoleon stared back from his throne, training his small telescope at the South American travelers, who stood apart on a far hillock. "Perhaps he will think we are spies," one of Bolívar's companions said, and, awe turning to dread, they decided to move on.

Milan's feverish celebrations went on for days. On June 8, Napoleon made his adopted stepson, the twenty-four-year-old Eugène de

Beauharnais, viceroy of the New Kingdom of Italy. Bolívar and his friends witnessed it all from the sidelines. It was no secret that Fanny and Eugène were lovers and that she delighted in playing Josephine's son off against Bolívar. Years later, she mentioned in a letter that she and Bolívar had seen one another in Italy, but whether it was in a large gathering or alone, we do not know. In either case, it would have been an awkward encounter: Bolívar had already said goodbye.

Soon after those festivities, the travelers set out for the open road. Pointing to Rome, they made leisurely stops in Verona, Venice, Ferrara, Bologna, Padua, Florence, and Perugia. Florence is said to have delighted Bolívar with its art and history; Venice disappointed him with what he felt was insufficient grandeur; but the Eternal City of Rome filled him with a profound inspiration that would ignite his career.

By July he was there, exploring the ruins of the Colosseum, the Roman Forum, the Temple of Castor and Pollux; recalling history; reading the works of Livy; imagining the days when Julius Caesar trod that ground and framed the empire's destiny. The three friends found an apartment on the Piazza di Spagna, near the Church of Trinità dei Monti. As they roamed the streets, eager to see the city, they spoke tirelessly of ancient Rome's miseries as well as its glories—how, from a humble village, a grand republic had been made. "I found Rome brick, and left it marble," Caesar had boasted. The notion of doing the same for Venezuela filled Bolívar with purpose. There can be little doubt that it was among Caesar's ruins that he began to build hopes for America.

In Rome, Bolívar saw Alexander von Humboldt again as well as Madame de Staël, who virtually had been hounded out of Paris for her outspoken censure of Napoleon. De Staël was traveling with her usual entourage of celebrated writers and busily gathering material for what would be her most famous book, *Corinne; Or, Italy.* Humboldt, on the other hand, was visiting his brother, Wilhelm, the noted philosopher, who was Prussia's minister to the Holy See. Wilhelm von Humboldt was a favorite at the papal court and his splendid house on Monte Pincio became a gathering place for the famous. It was probably in that house—the towering Villa di Malta—that Bolívar met a number of European intellectuals who happened to be in Rome at the time and taught him much about the world.

While some have claimed that Bolívar and Alexander von Humboldt traveled to Naples together and climbed Mount Vesuvius side by side, neither Bolívar's nor Humboldt's papers mention it. More likely, Bolívar's visits with Humboldt took place entirely at Wilhelm's house, where Humboldt continued to promote his expedition and discuss the New World's natural marvels, and Bolívar tried to nudge the discussions toward America's independence from Spain. Even as the young man grew more radical in his thinking, Humboldt maintained a strict objectivity.

More than a year before, as Humboldt had traveled the heart of the American continent, he had written vividly in his journals about the injustices of colonialism. "How could a minority of European Spaniards hold on to so vast an empire for so many centuries?" he posed rhetorically. But he never did so publicly, deciding that the people of Spanish America were essentially complacent, indolent by nature, and insufficiently motivated to throw over the yoke. Almost half a century later and long after Bolívar's death, Humboldt would write apologetically to Bolívar's aide-de-camp, Daniel O'Leary:

> During my time in America, I never encountered discontent; I noticed that while there was no great love of Spain, at least there was conformity. . . . It was only later, once the struggle had begun, that I realized that they had hidden the truth from me, and that far from love there existed a deep-seated hatred. . . . But what surprised me most was the brilliant career of Bolívar, which took off so quickly after we separated. . . . I confess I was wrong back then, when I judged him a puerile man, incapable of realizing so grand an ambition.

Whoever was hiding the truth about the colonies' deep-seated hatred of Spain, Bolívar was not among them. On the contrary, he had been trying to enlighten Humboldt on this very score, but he was never able to persuade Humboldt that his visions of rebellion were anything more than the fleeting passions of a callow young man. Humboldt wrote to him much later, in the heat of the revolution, when Bolívar's name was already known to the world. They exchanged a few polite letters, but they never saw one another again.

In the elegant bustle of the Humboldt villa in Rome, however, the diplomat Wilhelm von Humboldt introduced Bolívar to Antonio Vargas Laguna, Spain's ambassador to the Holy See. Vargas would later be imprisoned for his harsh and principled views of Napoleon, but in those early and heady days of 1805, when tolerance was the rule and France was perceived to be a progressive force in the world, the candid ambassador was a highly respected presence. In a fit of generosity, he offered to take Bolívar to the Vatican to meet Pope Pius VII.

Perhaps Vargas thought he had prepared his young guest adequately when he told him that a visitor to the pope should be ready to kiss his sandal and pay deference to papal symbols. But the ambassador was rudely surprised by the scene that unfolded under his supervision. When they were ushered into the papal offices and Bolívar was expected to step forward, kneel, and kiss the cross on the pontiff's sandal, he refused to do it. Vargas was taken aback, visibly flustered. The pope, seeing the diplomat's embarrassment, tried to make light of it. "Let the young Indian do as he pleases," he murmured. He extended a hand and Bolívar took it and kissed his ring. The pope then asked him a question about the Indies and Bolívar answered it to his satisfaction, after which the audience was over and the pope moved on to someone else. As they were leaving the Vatican, Vargas scolded the young man for not following the proper etiquette, to which Bolívar had the sharp retort, "The Pope must have little respect for the highest symbol of Christianity if he wears it on his sandals, whereas the proudest kings of Christendom affix it to their crowns."

It is hard to know what was more irksome to Bolívar at that moment: being expected to kiss a shoe or being rebuked by a Spaniard. He had been away from Spain's sphere of influence for almost a year now and the distance had been clarifying. He had—as Alexander von Humboldt would come to realize many years later—a deep-seated hatred for Spain. It had started as a natural Mantuano response and had grown in the few months he had spent in Venezuela as a married landowner, struggling to manage his properties. It had grown again in France, where he had seen the exuberance of a nation rid of its Bourbon king.

On August 15—a hot, airless afternoon—Bolívar trudged up Monte Sacro with Rodríguez and del Toro, all of them glistening with sweat.

Rodríguez reminded them of the plebeians of ancient Rome, who, weary of patrician rule, had labored up that very hill in 494 B.C. to vent their fury and threaten secession from the Roman republic. By the time the three travelers reached the top, a flaming sun lingered on the horizon. They sat on a massive block of ruined marble and looked out at the city that lay before them, resplendent and golden. Bolívar seemed lost in thought, contemplating those vicissitudes of history. After a while, he rose and began to ponder aloud why Rome had been so unwilling to grant its people simple freedoms. The arrogant stubbornness of it! The political folly of it! He was pacing, agitated, as if all the tragedies of his short life had predisposed him to understand that rage. Suddenly, eyes bright with emotion, he whirled around, sank to his knees, and clasping Rodríguez's hands swore by the God of his fathers that he would liberate his country. "I will not rest until I have rid it of every last one of those bastards!" he cried. Twenty years later, he recalled the scene in a letter to his old teacher: "Do you remember when we went together to Monte Sacro to swear on that sainted ground that we would not rest until our homeland was free? Surely you haven't forgotten that day of eternal glory."

The vow on Monte Sacro was a turning point, the genuine expression of a radicalized spirit. But, ultimately, it can be seen as an extension of Bolívar's father's anger, the wrath of colonial frustration, passed down from American to American over the course of three hundred years. In 1824, when the U.S. naval officer Hiram Paulding asked Bolívar what had impelled him to undertake the liberation of America, he replied:

> From boyhood I thought of little else: I was fascinated by stories of Greek and Roman heroes. The revolution in the United States had just taken place and it, too, was an example. Washington awoke in me a desire to be just like him. . . . When I and my two companions . . . arrived in Rome, we climbed Mount Palatino [*sic*], and we all knelt down, embraced, and swore that we would liberate our country or die trying.

Bolívar left Rome shortly after the pledge on Monte Sacro and returned to France, although it isn't clear whether he arrived in Paris at the end of 1805 or at the beginning of 1806. A record in the Paris lodge of the Freemasons, the antimonarchical fraternity that was furiously recruiting young men at the time, lists him as being inducted sometime between November 1805 and February 1806. Most likely, he and his companions knew that they would do well to undertake the walk back in clement weather, arriving in Paris before the November frost. The Bolívar who returned was a different man: robust, energetic, his health renewed by exercise, he never again succumbed to a wastrel's life. He was the model revolutionary: abstemious, disciplined in his personal habits, insatiably curious. If indeed he joined the Freemasons at this time, it was certainly in order to meet other men who, like him, were keen to change the world.

It is most likely that Fanny was not in Paris when he returned, and, in any case, she was pregnant with her son Eugène. From the child's birthdate, April 23, 1806, we can deduce that he was conceived in late July of 1805, just after Fanny's lover Eugène de Beauharnais was made viceroy of Italy, about a month after Bolívar left Milan. (Beauharnais is listed on the child's birth certificate as his godfather.) Much later, when Bolívar was known as the Liberator of South America, Fanny would try to suggest that one of her children might have been his.

But he had lost all interest in Fanny. His hopes and ambitions had turned elsewhere. Perhaps it was because she was pregnant by another man; perhaps it was simply because he was bored with her. Before leaving Paris for Italy, he had given her an engraved ring as a parting bauble, and she had cried and begged him not to go. After his rise to glory, after she had fallen into debt, she would try to borrow money from him, convince him to buy her house, even offer her son in marriage to any female in his family. He ignored her grasping efforts until the very last—until after she had sent him scores of pleading letters— and then he sent a terse instruction to one of his minions traveling through Europe: Take this copy of my likeness, he wrote, and deliver it to Mme Dervieu.

EVEN AS BOLÍVAR WAS ON his knees, vowing to liberate his homeland, there was an older, worldlier Venezuelan readying himself for the task. On September 2, 1805, a graying war veteran traveling under the name of Mr. George Martin boarded the *Polly* in Gravesend, England, en route to New York to muster an army of freedom fighters. He was Francisco de Miranda, the famous rebel to whom Bolívar's father had appealed almost a quarter century before.

Miranda, at fifty-five, had led a remarkably colorful life. He had met many of the leading personages of the day, including Thomas Jefferson, Alexander Hamilton, George Washington, James Madison, Thomas Paine, Henry Knox, Catherine the Great, Maximilien de Robespierre, General Lafayette, even Joseph Haydn. He was at once a glamorous, well-traveled, sophisticated polyglot and a hapless itinerant who, during the course of his quest for liberty, would be accused variously as a smuggler, a deserter, a charlatan, and a gigolo. He had been born in Caracas in 1750, the son of a Canary Islander. His father, a prominent merchant, owned a number of businesses, including a textile factory and a bakery, but when the Spanish authorities chose him to be the leader of a new militia, the Mantuano elite rose up in fury. The very men—including Juan Vicente de Bolívar—whose signatures were on the letter begging Miranda to mount an insurgency against the Spanish had led a campaign against Miranda's father, excoriating him as "a mulatto, a government henchman, a mere shopkeeper, an upstart, and unworthy" of his honorary appointments. Miranda's father was forced into a mortifying legal battle in which he was expected to produce lengthy genealogies proving the "purity" of his blood.

Stung by that humiliation, Miranda set off for Spain in 1771 at the age of twenty. After two years of study in Madrid, he became a captain in the Spanish army, a position his father bought for him for 85,000 reales. He went on to fight in Spain's conflict against the Moors in North Africa, against the redcoats in the final stages of the American Revolution, and as a spy on British exploits in the Caribbean. In 1782, badgered by Spanish authorities for a fleeting collaboration with a British smuggler, he escaped to the hills outside Havana. Within a year—even as the infant Bolívar was coming into the world—Miranda was working his way up the east coast of the newly independent United States of America, consulting old soldiers about how to wage a revolution, consorting with rabble as well as founders, enchanting women with his manly good looks and erudition, visiting whorehouses with prominent New Englanders, reading voraciously all the while. He was an irresistibly charming man.

Eventually, Miranda left the United States and crisscrossed Europe—from Marseille to Istanbul and from Corinth to St. Petersburg—in a campaign to gain adherents to his cause. In London he was put on the prime minister's payroll as a consultant for American affairs. He gave William Pitt innumerable documents describing Spain's fortifications and outlining his plan for a unified, liberated South America: its parliamentary system would be modeled after England's; its head executive would be a descendant of the Inca. For the rest of his days, he would try to get these documents back from the English government, but his pleas would go ignored.

All the same, Miranda was a tireless diplomat for the cause. He traveled to Prussia with John Adams's soon-to-be son-in-law, William Stephens Smith; Miranda and Smith became good friends, sharing their wardrobes and carousing in bawdy houses. Miranda had fought in the French Army of the North as a field marshal, a rank he was given on the mistaken understanding that he had been a brigadier general in the American Revolution. Clearly, he was a master of exaggeration. So intimate a friend did he become of Catherine the Great that her court assumed they were ardent lovers. Miranda has "traveled to great advantage," one friendly observer was prompted to say, and "nothing has escaped his *penetration*, not even the Empress of all the Russias."

Despite his service to France, however, Miranda was caught in the web of French revolutionary intrigue and was tried for desertion and cowardice. He was declared innocent of all charges. But Robespierre, suspecting Miranda of other perfidies, sent him to prison to await the guillotine. Although Miranda survived to have his name engraved in the Arc de Triomphe as one of the Revolution's heroes, the experience made a deep and bitter impression. He had risked his life for the French, and yet all he had received in return was persecution or imprisonment. "What a country!" he exclaimed in an outraged public letter. As Gual and España conspired to overthrow Spanish rule in Venezuela in 1799, Miranda wrote to Gual, "We have before our eyes two great examples, the American and the French Revolutions. Let us prudently imitate the first and carefully shun the second." Disgusted with France, he had settled in London, where, in the wake of Gual and España's failures, he resumed his campaign to liberate his homeland.

In the fall of 1805, as the British reveled in their decisive victory over the combined French and Spanish naval forces at Trafalgar—as a starry-eyed Bolívar made his way back from Rome to Paris over roads strewn with autumn foliage—Miranda was on board the *Polly*, headed to North America after a hiatus of twenty years. He had gone, like Hannibal, from country to country, gathering support for his beleaguered people, and he had decided that it was in the United States that those people would be best understood. Five months later, on the icy wintry morning of February 2, 1806, his warship, the *Leander*, left New York harbor with 180 men on board. Among them was William Steuben Smith, ex-President John Adams's twenty-year-old grandson—the son of Miranda's old traveling companion, William Stephens Smith. By then the elder Smith had become an important official for the Port of New York and chief facilitator of the mission. The expedition, ill-prepared and badly equipped, arrived on the coast of Venezuela after six months of serial calamities at sea. Two schooners that had joined the *Leander*—the *Bee* and the *Bacchus*—had fallen into Spanish hands. When General Miranda's ragtag troops finally entered the Venezuelan city of Coro, they found no one there. Coro's priests, hearing rumors that the invaders numbered as many as four thousand, had frightened the residents away. The Spanish army dismissed Miranda as a madman, and so the would-be liberators saw little action, apart from nervously shooting at one another from opposite ends of town. Even the Creoles denounced Miranda as a fanatic, a marauder—a deserter who hadn't bothered to stand on Venezuelan soil for thirty-five years. Not one would be recruited to his cause.

Miranda and his men were in Venezuela for a total of eleven days, during which time it became all too clear that his war of independence was a rank disaster. On August 13, the frustrated general gave orders to withdraw, and his creaky ship set sail for Aruba, leaving the Venezuelans to scratch their heads and wonder just who he was. Sometime later, the Marquis del Toro, the commanding colonel charged with defending the coast, wrote into a captain's record, "On August 10th, this officer marched to Coro with his battalion . . . against the traitor Miranda." The young officer was Juan Vicente Bolívar, the older brother of Simón.

NAPOLEON'S WAR IN EUROPE HAD a dispiriting effect on Bolívar. Britain, which now ruled the seas, blockaded the entire coast of France, rendering it impossible for Bolívar to receive funds or sail home easily. He was frustrated, too, by the news of Miranda's botched expedition. He had heard of it well in advance of its ill-fated landing in Venezuela. The campaign was the talk of New York and Washington—indeed of Europe—months before it ever set sail. Writing to a friend more than a month before Miranda stepped foot on Coro, Bolívar declared that it was sure to be a blighted operation. Venezuela wasn't ready for Miranda's revolution, Bolívar complained. "He'll only do harm."

He was eager to leave Paris, anxious to go home. A friend obliged by loaning him 2,400 francs, which enabled him to travel from France to Germany and sail from a neutral port. He had a family duty to discharge: he had promised his sister María Antonia to deposit her son—his nephew Anacleto Clemente—in a private school in Philadelphia. Anacleto, a mere ten-year-old at the time, had arrived in Paris sometime before, just as the Napoleonic Wars were escalating. It was a perilous time to be young and male in France. Napoleon's Grande Armée, which numbered in the millions—ten times the size of Britain's standing army—was a ravening war machine that took recruits as young as fifteen. Surely María Antonia worried about her son's and brother's safety. Bolívar and his nephew made their way east in October of 1806, hoping to sail from Hamburg, just as Napoleon's hussars rode through the fog over the plains of Auerstadt, routed the Prussian army, and captured Berlin. Slipping into Germany through Holland in late November, Bolívar and the boy succeeded in boarding a ship bound for Charleston, South Carolina.

It was a hard winter's passage, the sea made fierce by icy gales, and when the ship finally hove into Charleston in January of 1807, Bolívar was ill with a raging fever. He was also completely out of funds. But he had established a warm friendship with one of the ship's passengers, a certain Mr. M. Cormic of Charleston, who offered Bolívar and the boy his hospitality. How long Bolívar convalesced in Cormic's home we do not know, but before long, he sailed to Philadelphia, where he finally received a shipment of money from Caracas and deposited Anacleto safely in school. Some historians have claimed that, from Philadelphia, Bolívar went on to visit Boston and New York, but there is no evidence to support it. All we know for sure is that by June he was home in Caracas.

All the same, there is much we can deduce about Bolívar's trip to North America. It was, after all, a time of great growth and ferment in the United States. He arrived in the South at the very moment when slavery was the most profitable, most deeply entrenched commercial enterprise in its economy. It is very possible that during his brief time in Charleston he visited its infamous slave market, which was only a short walk from the imposing mansions of the rich and whose clamor was all too palpable. As he looked around, he could not have failed to note that there was little evidence of the racial mixing so common in his own America: few mulattoes, almost no Indians, the differences between races extreme.

He had come, too, during a time of expansion in the newly independent nation. The population of the United States had doubled since the Revolution, a growth rate more than twice as fast as that of any country in Europe. Everywhere he walked, he could hear hammers pounding nails into new construction, carts groaning under loads of marble, the frenzied whir of a nation on the climb. In four short years, since 1803, America had pushed its boundaries west by more than a thousand miles, pressing up against the Rocky Mountains.

In Philadelphia, Bolívar saw evidence that in the scant twenty-three years since the United States had won its independence, it had become one of the most highly commercialized nations in the world. The people of the North reveled in work, and their attitude contrasted sharply with the leisurely slaveholding aristocracy Bolívar had seen in Charleston. In no country he had ever visited were business and profit more glorified. And in no country he had ever traveled were Sundays so sacrosanct—no music, no drinking, no loud, brazen conversation: the United States of

America was quickly becoming the most evangelically Christian nation in the world. Bolívar cannot have helped but be struck by what he was seeing; he knew that his own fellow Americans were nothing like their northern counterparts—racially, spiritually, historically—and he would often say as much throughout his career, but there could be no doubt that freedom had brought great prosperity and democracy: "During my short visit to the United States," he would later write, "for the first time in my life, I saw rational liberty at first hand."

What was surely most remarkable of all to Bolívar at this volatile juncture in history was the attitude North Americans held toward their southern neighbors. It was one of suspicion, and it was not without cause. The country was just emerging from the rancorous trial of William Stephens Smith, who had been charged with treason and, during the course of the proceedings, publicly thrashed for his involvement with Miranda. On the stand, Smith recounted how President Jefferson and Secretary of State Madison had dined with Miranda and openly discussed Miranda's project to liberate Venezuela. In effect, Smith swore, they had approved the Miranda plan. As a result, Smith had felt perfectly justified in supplying Miranda with men, ammunition, and a warship—actions, the prosecution contended, that were in clear violation of the Neutrality Act of 1794. By the end of the affair, which eventually became rabidly political, the real subjects under discussion were the powers of the American presidency, the authority vested in Congress to declare war, the business of supplying weapons to foreign rebels, and the courts' ability to make a punishment fit a crime. In the course of the trial, the prosecution managed to smear mud on the Adams family, Jefferson, Madison, and any future South American rebel who had the temerity to approach the United States for military support.

As Bolívar traveled the country, wherever he turned, whomever he met, whenever he identified himself as a Venezuelan, he was confronted with Miranda's fame. Despite any opinions of the man he might have had or criticisms about his timing, he had to appreciate Miranda's extraordinary access to world power. In the United States at least, among the people who counted, the name Miranda was synonymous with Spanish American independence. There was no question that any hope for American solidarity had been dealt a mighty blow.

A mere quarter century after the Declaration of Independence, Latin America had already become a shuttlecock in the larger game of United States world diplomacy. In 1786, Thomas Jefferson had suggested that the United States might want Spanish America for itself. In a letter to a friend, Jefferson confided that Spain's colonies were ripe for the plucking. "My fear," he said, "[is that Spain is] too feeble to hold them till our population can be sufficiently advanced to gain it from them piece by piece." Less than six months later, Jefferson's political rival John Adams wrote to Secretary of Foreign Affairs John Jay that London was under the illusion that a revolution in South America would be "agreeable to the United States" and that North Americans would not only refuse to prevent it but would do "whatever possible to promote it." Once he had won the presidency, however, Adams began to speak differently about the region: "You might as well talk about establishing democracies among the birds, beasts, and fishes as among the Spanish American people," he said. Adams's secretary of state, Timothy Pickering, seconded the opinion, adding his own jab: those people are "corrupt and effeminate beyond example," he said, referring perhaps to Miranda himself. Where European dreams of liberty were concerned, the founders' rhetoric was kinder. "It accords with our principles," Secretary of State Jefferson said, speaking of the new French Republic, "to acknowledge any government to be rightful which is formed by the will of the nation substantially declared."

Acknowledging a nation's desire for independence may have accorded with American principle, but a more pressing political reality was beginning to take root in the fledgling United States of America. President Jefferson moved to make that clear in a proclamation he issued just weeks before Bolívar stepped into the chill of a Philadelphia winter: any citizen conspiring to go to war against the dominion of Spain, Jefferson announced—anyone planning to rebel against Madrid's rightful power—would be vigorously prosecuted and punished. Perhaps he was trying to make a point about meddling with sovereign governments. Perhaps he was attempting to counter the stinging embarrassment of the Miranda-Smith affair. In any case, economic realities had come to rule the way North America looked—or didn't look—on its hemispheric neighbors. No one understood this better than Simón

Bolívar as he sailed his way home through the Caribbean in the spring of 1807. The United States would be the last foreign soil he would tread before undertaking the liberation of South America—he would henceforward credit it as an eye-opening experience, an undeniable inspiration. But it could not be a model. Nor was it a country on which he could rely.

~ CHAPTER 4 ~

Building a Revolution

They say grand projects need to be built with calm!
Are three hundred years of calm not enough?

—Simón Bolívar

Bolívar arrived in Caracas in June of 1807, filled with resolve. He was convinced that his America, like France and the United States, could shuck its past, shed its masters, and redefine itself. But he also knew that liberation would not be easy. War and blockades had brought trade to a standstill; Creoles were cut off from the outside, their information restricted to what Madrid and the Inquisition would allow. Yet even Madrid seemed strangely absent now, its regents in Caracas disconnected and rudderless. It was as if the whole of South America were in limbo, awaiting the *madre patria*'s next move.

As Bolívar went about managing his estates, improving the family businesses, and tending the fields alongside his slaves, he understood that many Creoles of his class, too, longed ardently for liberation. There were differing views on how it should be won. The young seemed unwilling to contemplate anything less than a revolution; their fathers were afraid of losing all in a race war. But there was no question the will to independence was there. Miranda simply hadn't cultivated it.

Little by little, Bolívar attuned himself to the temper of the times.

Even as he battled his neighbor Antonio Briceño in a land dispute that began with pitchforks and ended up in the courts, he met with like-minded republicans. They gathered, ostensibly to socialize, in sparkling salons organized by the best and brightest of the colony: Bolívar's former tutor, the writer Andrés Bello; his in-laws, brothers of the Marquis del Toro; boyhood friends Tomás and Mariano Montilla; his young uncles Pedro Palacios and José Félix Ribas. Scions of the privileged aristocracy, they were conspirators now. Their meetings masqueraded as literary events or musical recitals, even gambling affairs, and many were hosted by the Bolívar brothers, especially at their house on the River Guaire, which was surrounded by ample gardens and so was perfectly suited for clandestine conversations. As Bolívar regaled his friends with eye-opening tales of his travels in Europe or the United States, and Andrés Bello—by then a prominent official—recited his translations of Voltaire, they all spoke freely of sedition. But for all the high hopes and spirited exchange, it would take a miracle to convert rhetoric into revolutionary acts.

That miracle arrived in the form of Napoleon Bonaparte, who, in the autumn of 1807, crossed Spain under false pretenses to conquer Portugal.

The invasion of the Iberian Peninsula began simply enough, and, some might say, in response to bald invitation. It started in October, when King Carlos IV chanced upon some papers written in his son's hand that made it clear that the crown prince was planning to dethrone his father and, very possibly, poison his mother. Horrified, the king wrote to Napoleon, reporting the whole affair, denouncing his son, and suggesting that a brother of Napoleon should succeed him. Not twenty-four hours later, Prince Ferdinand, too, dashed off a letter to Napoleon, inviting the emperor to choose a bride for him from among his family and so unite the empires. It was a naked lunge for power, fresh evidence of the prince's treason. For years, Ferdinand had brooded about Godoy's sexual hold on his mother and the craven way his father had handed the cuckolder all the power. But Carlos IV proved more of a match than his son had anticipated. Goaded by the queen and prime minister, the king now began serious negotiations with France.

Napoleon took rank advantage of the family squabble by flattering the king and offering him an opportunity to expand his empire. The Treaty of Fontainebleau, put forth by Napoleon and signed by Godoy on October 27, 1807, promised Spain half of Portugal in a joint invasion—a truly perfidious arrangement, given that the king's eldest daughter, Charlotte, was Portugal's queen. Napoleon was given permission to march 25,000 troops through Spanish territory to Lisbon. When time for the invasion came, however, Napoleon sent quadruple that number, overwhelming Lisbon in a bloodless coup and securing a firm foothold in Spain. By the end of 1807, Queen Charlotte and the royal Braganza family had fled Portugal and, with ten thousand of their most loyal subjects, filled a convoy of fifty ships headed for Brazil. Four months later, in the spring of 1808, the French army slipped into Spain's most strategic fortresses and took control. King Carlos IV finally understood his predicament. Spain was under occupation. He began to consider a secret plan to escape to Mexico.

The Spanish people were outraged. They blamed Godoy for all their misfortunes and sacked his palace in a riot. In the course of that uprising, Carlos IV was forced to relinquish the crown to his son, who was now King Ferdinand VII. Napoleon managed to lure the whole royal family—mother, father, and son—to Bayonne for a conference. After a sumptuous dinner, the newly crowned King Ferdinand VII was told that Spain's Bourbon era was over. He was king no more. In response, Carlos IV tried to nullify his own abdication, but eventually agreed to cede Spain and its colonies to Napoleon for an annual salary of 1.5 million pesos. By the end of April, the Bourbons were virtual prisoners on French soil. Joseph Bonaparte—the emperor's brother—was crowned the new king of Spain, making America, from Texas to Tierra del Fuego, a cog in Napoleon's empire.

If Spain's kings had been easy to dupe, its people were not. Years later, Talleyrand would write that the invasion of Spain was more than a crime. It was a gross miscalculation—a patent stupidity—with disastrous consequences for Napoleon: the people of Spain surprised their more powerful invader by mounting a fierce guerrilla war. A virtual firestorm shook the country day and night as ordinary citizens took up arms against the French. Napoleon's generals responded by sacking Spain's cities, garroting its leaders, raping its women. But Madrid's resistance was implacable. The city would not be subdued until the French generals summoned the infamous Mameluk cavalry to trample the crowds.

Even as the *madre patria* erupted in violence, even as ruling juntas sprang up around Spain, proclaiming loyalty to King Ferdinand, her colonies lived on in languid ignorance. The English blockade had silenced communication across the Atlantic, and Thomas Jefferson's misguided Embargo Act, announced just months before, had choked all north–south trade and compounded the isolation. In Caracas, the news that Spain had been savagely overrun by France was not known until a full seven months later, in early July of 1808, when two old, dog-eared issues of the London *Times* arrived in the governor's office, sent on by a functionary in Trinidad. The publications seemed harmless enough, four-page broadsheets with real estate and shipping news. But wedged in between the notices was the remarkable revelation that the Spanish king had been deposed and Napoleon now occupied the country. Andrés Bello—then secretary to the most important Spaniard in Venezuela, Captain-General Juan de Casas—translated the notices for his boss, who simply dismissed them as English lies. The facts were confirmed days later, however, when two ships—a French brigantine and an English frigate—arrived simultaneously in La Guaira with versions of the same story. The French agents, dressed in resplendent uniforms, presented the captain-general with an official document signed by Joseph Bonaparte, announcing that Spain had capitulated to France and that the colonies were now under Napoleonic rule. The captain of the English ship, on the other hand, came huffing over the mountain from La Guaira to call the French liars and report that the Spanish people had not yielded. Indeed, according to his account, Spain had undertaken a bloody war, a junta in Seville now represented the embattled nation, and Britain had pledged its unconditional support.

This news had a profound and galvanizing effect on the colony. Dissidents like Bolívar began to wonder if it was their moment. Why didn't they form their own junta? Why should they bow to some hastily extemporized, reduced body in Seville? Hadn't they always claimed they could govern themselves? In all, one thing was sure: the Creoles would never allow Napoleon to rule Spanish America. Within days of arrival in Caracas, Joseph Bonaparte's agents met with such outright hostility and ridicule that they were forced to flee the city and skulk off into the ink of night.

The Creole movement to set up a self-governing junta was immediate. Marquis del Toro received a letter from Francisco Miranda urging the Venezuelans to wrest power while they could. The marquis was hesitant, but others on the Caracas city council were not. They made an impassioned request to the captain-general to allow them to install their own government, which, like the junta in Spain, would remain loyal to King Ferdinand. The captain-general, who had received no instructions from the king's court, feared that he had no choice but to please the clamoring masses beyond his door. Grudgingly, he agreed.

For many in Bolívar's circle, this was the moment they had prayed for—a chance to seize the reins and shape their economic destinies. They gathered eagerly to form a local junta and, at least outwardly, profess loyalty to Ferdinand. But Bolívar demurred. His convictions about independence were absolute; he had little patience for those who would take up the banner of liberty while pledging allegiance to a king. Moreover, King Ferdinand was someone he knew—an insufferable little whiner with whom he had sparred as a boy—a man for whom he had no respect. And if Bolívar despised the prince, he loathed the queen, whose lechery was notorious and whose weaknesses he knew intimately through one of her many lovers, his friend Manuel Mallo. The strongest contempt, however he reserved for Carlos IV, whose dithering and inadequacies had enslaved an empire. Bolívar had spent too much time nursing his animus to let go of it now. His abhorrence of Spain was so great, as he later wrote, that it dwarfed the sea that separated him from it. He continued to meet with his less demanding colleagues, but refused to compromise. He decided to watch and wait.

It proved a shrewd choice. On August 3, Captain-General Casas received yet another visitor from Spain, Joaquín Menéndez, the representative of the *madre patria*'s new Central Junta. To Casas's great relief, Menéndez confirmed Casas's position as the colony's ruler and ordered him to take all future commands from Seville. That was all the ammunition Casas needed. Overnight, the Creoles who were working to establish a separate, Venezuelan junta were branded outlaws. The most brazen among them, Manuel de Matos, who had tried to incite an insurrection in the city plaza by calling for the immediate expulsion of all Spaniards, was arrested and put behind bars. General Casas's son made a visit to the Bolívar brothers to warn them to stop hosting their conspiratorial meetings. "But I'm totally innocent!" Bolívar protested. Still, he made a point to leave the city for a while. As fate would have it, his lawsuit against Briceño was still in the courts and he had just been elected mayor of a town near his hacienda—which allowed him to look too busy to cause much trouble.

The captain-general's newly confirmed power over the colony launched an era of caution. Dissidents now conducted meetings in strictest confidence; only trusted friends were admitted now. These were hardly society's malcontents but men of prestige—wealthy, educated, respected—from families with long and illustrious histories. "For the first time," as royalist historian José Domingo Díaz put it, "we were seeing a revolution fomented and carried into execution by the very persons who had most to lose." The circle was composed of the Marquis del Toro and his brothers, men at the pinnacle of power for generations; the Tovars, who lived in the colony's most opulent houses; Juan Vicente and Simón Bolívar, who owned, among many valuable properties, the coveted copper mines of Aroa; the Montillas, who were considered men of fashion, well acquainted with the king's court. These were not fortune hunters, but the wellborn, the rich, who expected more from government and believed they alone could deliver it.

By then, the Bolívar brothers had grown far more radical than most of their fellow Mantuanos. When the venerable eighty-three-year-old Count of Tovar drew up a formal letter on behalf of "the most distinguished gentlemen of the city," requesting the right to assembly and identifying his fellow Creoles as "vassals of Don Fernando VII," the Bolívars staunchly refused to add their signatures. Within days of receiving the letter, Captain-General Casas rounded up the old count and his collaborators—including Bolívar's uncles, Pedro Palacios and José

Félix Ribas—and threw them all in jail. They didn't stay long. The chaos of ongoing war in Spain and the absence of any true direction from Seville were such that even the captain-general couldn't be entirely sure who his enemies really were.

It didn't matter. By May of 1809, there was a new captain-general, Field Marshal Vicente Emparan. Napoleon had recommended him long before, when France and Spain had been allies. Proving the turmoil and contradictions of the time, Emparan's appointment was blessed by Napoleon's bitterest enemy, the junta in Seville. A further irony: accompanying Emparan to Caracas was none other than Fernando del Toro, Bolívar's brother-in-law and old hiking companion in Europe, who had risen through army ranks to become Emparan's inspector general. Bolívar suddenly found himself in a strategically advantageous, if thorny, position. His in-laws, the del Toros, like many Creole families, represented a slew of conflicting allegiances. Fernando was at the very heart of the new governor's offices, but he was also the brother of a revolutionary—the Marquis del Toro. Not only that, but Fernando had been witness to an incriminating scene: he had been on Monte Sacro when Bolívar had vowed to overthrow the king.

And yet there was no king. Ferdinand VII's power had always been a figment, a fabrication. He was a prisoner languishing in Bayonne, still in Napoleon's clutches, incapable of ruling a far-flung empire. For all the hatred that Napoleon could inspire in Spanish America, for all the fierceness of his ambition, no one could deny that the French emperor's invasion had opened the door to American possibility. Creoles understood this. They knew that they were suddenly at great advantage and needed to work quickly; perhaps they also suspected that to pledge loyalty to a prisoner king was merely a political convenience, an empty gesture, a way to camouflage dissent.

But unruly times make for unruly opportunities, and although Creoles had common interests, they did not always agree. Many with close family ties to Spain were adamantly against making a clean break with the *madre patria*, arguing that they only wanted a few more rights, a bit more control over their economic aspirations. The more independent-minded insisted that severing the tie was essential, but strategies varied wildly. To complicate matters, a new social reality was at work. The revolution could not count on support from blacks, pardos, and the indigenous. Few nonwhites favored independence, fearing that, without Spain's oversight, the Creole landowners for whom they labored would grow more brutal. Eventually, those racial tensions would come to play a defining role in the wars for independence. But even now, at the dawn of that foreboding, rich Creoles began to feel that all was not right in their fields or kitchens. The more fevered the conversations in the drawing rooms, the more frequent the escapes from servant quarters, as slaves slipped away in the cover of night, seeking freedom on the open plains.

The first declaration of independence, "*el primer grito*," came in mid-1809, even as Emparan was settling into his new quarters in Caracas. It began a thousand miles away in Spain's colony of Quito, as Creoles ejected their overlords and took government into their own hands. Although those attempts were short-lived—squelched within months in a series of bloody strikes—the machinery of revolution had sputtered into uncertain motion. On Christmas Eve, the Creoles of Caracas, Bolívar among them, prepared to storm city hall, but the new captain-general was warned in advance and managed to put a stop to it. Emparan had Bolívar taken aside and told him to stop consorting with enemies of the state, but Bolívar was no longer trying to mask his politics. His response was civil but firm. The warning was clear enough, he replied calmly, but he and his revolutionary cohort had long since declared war on Spain; in time, the world would see the result.

Few who knew him would have predicted at this juncture that Bolívar would go on to play an essential role in the war for independence. The Spaniards and Creoles respected him for his pedigree, his wealth, and his obvious brilliance, but neither side imagined him as a leader. Only Juan Vicente, his brother, had any hopes in this regard. Nominating Bolívar to head the circle of conspirators as they colluded one night in their house on the Río Guaire, Juan Vicente found his proposal roundly dismissed. Simón Bolívar was too young, his fellow rebels said—too untried, too impulsive, too incendiary.

AS WAR RAVAGED THE IBERIAN Peninsula and Spain's cities fell to Napoleon one by one, the Central Junta was forced to flee Seville. Its members eventually took refuge in Cádiz. By the end of January 1810, they had reconstituted the government and named the new ruling body the Regency. Among the many changes the Regency decreed was a fundamental shift in the way Spain would treat its colonies: Spanish America would now be an integral part of the nation. Welcome as these words sounded, they turned out to be patently untrue. The finer letter of the law revealed that colonials would not be allowed to vote, nor would their districts be granted equal representation. On April 17, four months after all this was signed into law, delegates of the Regency arrived in Caracas and pronounced it a fait accompli, papering the city with posters.

One of the Regency's representatives, as it happened, was Carlos Montúfar, the young aristocrat from Quito who had accompanied Humboldt on his expedition and befriended Bolívar and del Toro in Paris. The three young men had lived together on Rue Vivienne and spent many a night in Fanny's salon, toasting the American future. Bolívar hurried down to La Guaira to meet his friend and hear the latest news. What he learned—that the Central Junta had been dissolved, that Napoleon had Spain on its knees, that the Regency was struggling to keep its hold on the colonies—was all the intelligence he needed.

Within twenty-four hours, the conspirators were planning a coup that would depose the captain-general and take control of Venezuela. Emparan had proven to be a weak governor, a master of ambiguities, indecisive at every turn—friendly, possibly, to France because of his previous service to Napoleon. Friendly, even, to certain outspoken rebels: to Fernando del Toro's family, for instance, and to Simón Bolívar himself. He was clearly a soft mark, and the Creoles were confident they could achieve his ouster without bloodshed. They met at three in the morning on Maundy Thursday—April 19, 1810—at the house of José Angel Alamo. According to one witness, there were nearly one hundred of them. Whether Bolívar was there that day is a point of much debate. Some historians—present in Caracas at the time—have claimed that he was, although his name appears on no documents. Others say that Emparan had warned him to make himself scarce or be subject to imprisonment or exile. Still others claim that Bolívar recused himself from that final meeting, because by then he knew it would be dominated by those who were not true seekers of independence but crypto-royalists willing to make concessions.

In any case, after a spirited discussion that lasted until dawn, the Creoles proceeded to city hall. Along the way, they called citizens to gather on the main plaza. In a rush of confidence, they summoned the captain-general to an extraordinary meeting of the city council—which was clearly beyond their power to do—but Emparan took the bait. He appeared within the hour and, seeing a large crowd of activists in long capes milling about the plaza, grew wary. No sooner had he entered his office in city hall than the Creoles began demanding the immediate formation of a local junta. The captain-general heard them out, but protested that it being a holy day—and the matter meriting serious consideration—all discussion would be postponed until after the morning Mass. He peremptorily halted the meeting and strode off to church, across the square, but got no farther than mid-plaza when the crowd began to chant, "To city hall, Governor! To city hall!" One of the Creoles took Emparan firmly by the arm in full view of a cluster of royal guards. "The people are calling you, Señor," he said. He motioned the governor to go back and finish the conversation. Such a flagrant affront to the colony's ruler should have prompted the guards to draw their swords, but Fernando del Toro, the army's inspector general, had already instructed them to stand down. Astonished, Emparan looked about anxiously, but was obliged to obey.

When the meeting resumed, the Creoles proceeded to outline their proposal for self-rule under the Spanish king. But before they were done, noise erupted in the hall, the doors of the chambers opened, and this canon of the cathedral, the imposing José Cortés de Madariaga, of the same stock as the great explorer Cortés, swept grandly into the room. The churchman took a seat and listened to the Creoles as they politely invited Emparan to lead their junta, at which point Cortés could contain himself no longer. Didn't city hall know anything about the people they represented? he thundered. Didn't they know that Venezuelans hated Emparan? Why were they prostrating themselves in front of this man? How could they invite a Spanish *governor* to lead their insurrection? If Creoles truly wanted independence, they would run him off, end Spain's dominance for good, and put all the king's men on the first ship out of La Guaira. The council broke out in an uproar—half riotous dissent, half boisterous approval. But the priest had made a point.

Emparan protested. The people, he insisted, were on his side. To prove it, he went out to his balcony and asked the mass gathered below what they thought of him. Did they approve his command? Did they appreciate the Regency's rule? Cortés, who stood just behind, gesticulated extravagantly, urging them to say no. The people took his cue. "No!" they cried. And then louder: "No! No! We don't want it!"

The captain-general was taken aback. "Then I do not want it, either," he shouted, and went back inside. It was a clear and public renunciation and it was duly recorded into the meeting's minutes. The rule of Spain was over. Within two days, Emparan and his deputies were on a ship bound for Philadelphia and a new government was in place. They called it the Supreme Junta of Caracas, Dedicated to Preserving the Rights of King Ferdinand VII. Among its most pressing declarations: The colony could engage in free trade. Indians would no longer pay punishing tributes. The slave market was a relic of the past.

That year, like bricks tumbling in a row, the colonies of Buenos Aires, Bogotá, Quito, and Mexico declared their sovereignty, established juntas, and dispatched Spain's governors to an open sea. By the end of the year, every major metropolis on the continent, except for Lima, had rid itself of its Spanish garrison. It was a strange and surreal uncoupling: King Ferdinand's American empire had declared autonomy—in his name. And yet, for all the talk about liberty, little was said about the other two pillars of democracy: fraternity and equality. The rallying cries that had guided revolutions in France and North America would be slow to catch fire in Spanish America. Class was too delicate a question; race, a virtual tinderbox; the region's ethnicities and allegiances too jumbled to parse. There was another problem. The independence movement's aristocratic origin was a liability in the eyes of the colored masses that made up the vast majority of the population. In certain areas—Coro and Maracaibo in Venezuela, Pasto in New Granada, and in all of Peru—Americans would feel more loyalty to Spain than to the land on which they stood. It would be many years before any unity of purpose was reached, and a civil war would be fought in order to reach it. The struggle for liberation had just begun.

THE FIRST ORDER OF BUSINESS for the tenuous Junta of Caracas was to create alliances as quickly as possible. Too many ill winds—war, blockade, embargo—threatened the fledgling government. A firm footing had to be established so that independent rule could take root and grow. The junta dispatched three representatives to Coro, a district of Venezuela that had always considered itself Caracas's equal, but the envoys were greeted with open contempt. In Maracaibo, they were imprisoned and deported. It became all too apparent that it would take time—perhaps even military muscle—to win over a nervous populace, and success might very well depend on recognition from world powers. By May, the junta was organizing diplomatic missions to London, Washington, and the Caribbean.

Bolívar had been surprised by the success of the April 19 coup. A resolute radical, he had no faith in restraint as a strategy against repression, and yet he had to concede that the moderates had won the day—not through belligerence but parley. He rode from his hacienda in the valley of Tuy to offer them his services. The cautious members of the city council—now rulers of the junta—were wary of Bolívar's uncompromising positions, but when he offered to pay all costs for the diplomatic mission to London, they had no choice but to accept. Their treasury was depleted—they had sent Emparan and his minions off to Philadelphia with a sizable portion of the city's funds. Reluctantly agreeing to Bolívar's conditions, they made him head of the London delegation and granted him a rank of colonel to lend his name more prestige. To balance Bolívar's relative inexperience, they insisted he be accompanied by a deputy in whom they had infinitely more confidence, the former mayor of Caracas Luis López Méndez; and, in the role of secretary, Andrés Bello. In the same spirit, the junta sent Bolívar's brother, Juan Vicente, to the United States, the flamboyant deacon Cortés to New Granada, and two delegations to the English islands of the Caribbean—Curaçao, Trinidad, and Jamaica.

Bolívar, López Méndez, and Bello set sail in early June on an English brig of war, the *General Wellington*, which had been sent expressly by Lord Admiral Cochrane for the voyage. The *Wellington* dropped anchor in Portsmouth on the 10th of July, accompanied by the Spanish battleship *Castilla*, whose captain was unaware that the vessel he was protecting carried the representatives of a rebel government. The three Caracans were promptly escorted through customs and issued passports; they arrived in London on July 13, settling into comfortable rooms at Morin's Hotel on Duke Street.

For a nation that was engaged in wars on so many fronts—France, Spain, Russia, and the Caribbean—England appeared to be thriving. Although the English king was bound to his chair, gagged, suffering debilitating bouts of insanity, his doughty empire was on the rise. In population alone, the tiny island nation was double the size of the United States, twelve times the size of Venezuela. In manufacturing and industry, it led the world. That sense of busy abundance was apparent in London, which deeply impressed the South Americans with its new breed of bankers. Its exploding commerce. Its hubbub and modernity.

Bolívar immediately set about arranging a meeting with Richard Colley, the Marquis of Wellesley, Britain's foreign minister. Indeed, Lord Wellesley had expressed considerable eagerness to meet with the Venezuelan delegation. Although he portrayed himself as a neutral party, he had every intention of using their visit in a calculated scheme to force the Spanish Regency to accept Britain's commercial demands. For decades, England had been trying to force its way into Spanish America, keenly aware of the bonanza of raw materials that it represented. But Spain held a punishing monopoly on trade in its colonies, frustrating British ambitions. In 1806 and 1807—during the prolonged war between the powers—the British had invaded Buenos Aires twice, and twice they had been repulsed. Unable to make military headway on the mainland, England set its sights on controlling trade on the high seas, particularly now that Spain was defenseless. But here, too, Napoleon turned history inside out. Britain and Spain, fierce, intractable enemies for more than two centuries, were now fast allies against France. England wanted to preserve that bond, but it also wanted to take commercial advantage of Spain's weakness. Lord Wellesley would need to tread carefully with the rebel diplomats from Venezuela.

The first meeting took place on July 16, not in the Foreign Office, since the Caracans were not agents of a recognized country, but in Wellesley's home, the magnificent Apsley House, on the edge of Hyde Park. At the appointed hour, Bolívar, López Méndez, and Bello were led through the house's immense and resplendent lobby, up the stairs, past the filigreed walls and elaborate marble mantelpieces, into the brightly lit drawing room where Wellesley and his staff awaited. The windows were open; the warm summer air wafted in from the garden. After polite introductions, during which French was established as the common tongue, the foreign minister launched in without delay. His French was superb—his wife was Parisian—and, having been ambassador to Spain, he had a rudimentary command of Spanish. Opting for bluntness, he declared straightaway that the action the Venezuelans had taken against the *madre patria* was unwise: Spain's cause was not lost. Quite the contrary. With Britain's help, Spain stood a very good chance of expelling Napoleon. He wanted to know from the outset, he said, whether the Caracas junta had sent the delegation to report abuses in the colony or whether it sought total separation from Spain. It was an arch beginning, meant to signal England's allegiances and bring his visitors to the point.

Bolívar took the lead, speaking fluently and eloquently in French. He gave Wellesley a spirited account of the events that had led to the revolution—and he called it just that, a revolution—describing the Creoles' frustrations, the befuddled captain-generals, the activists' clandestine meetings, the suppression of trade, the colonial abuses, and the final confrontation when Venezuelans refused to bow to an illegal government. The Spanish Regency, such as it was, represented an arbitrary arrangement, Bolívar explained, and Venezuelans were "eager to shake off, by whatever means possible, its intolerable yoke."

There was no question that he was making a passionate case for total liberty, although his directives from Caracas had forbidden it: he had been instructed to profess loyalty to Ferdinand VII, refuse any agreement that recognized the Spanish Regency, and make absolutely no mention of independence. Lord Wellesley listened to Bolívar with cold officiousness, his hawkish face revealing little sympathy for the appeal, and then he responded crisply that, as England was Spain's ally, he could neither sanction nor sponsor its colony's bid for independence. The conversation appeared to be at an end.

But Bolívar went on, ever more fervent in his argument. There, in the presence of one of the most powerful men in Europe, the young man employed, perhaps for the first time, the clear and resonant voice, the gift for the bold image, the extraordinary powers of persuasion that soon would become his hallmark. Black eyes flashing, forehead dug with intensity, he rushed to communicate all the dreams and hopes of a budding nation. In a burst of enthusiasm, he handed his credentials to the marquis, sure that from them Wellesley would be able to glean something of the conviction that had animated his people. Bolívar had forgotten that those papers contained his instructions, which had been laid out very carefully by the Junta in Caracas. He went on to argue that Venezuela deserved the freedom to govern itself, that there was no doubt it could do so more capably than Spain's war-torn offices or an imprisoned king. Lord Wellesley and his aides looked over the documents as Bolívar spoke, waiting to hear him out. When he was done, the minister looked up and commented drily that the ideas Bolívar had just expressed were in direct contradiction to the documents he had just been handed. Wasn't his government called "the Supreme Junta of Caracas, Dedicated to Preserving the Rights of King Ferdinand VII"? And didn't it say here, for everyone to see, that the delegation had been instructed not to bring up the subject of independence?

Bolívar was speechless. Untrained in diplomacy and its formalities, he had not inspected the documents before bringing them to the meeting. The careful preparation was in his head, where he had framed a strong argument for absolute independence. The delegates quickly took another tack. Venezuelans would rather die than be governed by an upstart, illegal government, they told Lord Wellesley. What they wanted now was Britain's cooperation in trade—an alliance that could only benefit England. Bolívar added that it was only natural for Venezuela to do this in a time of war.

For all the rigidity of his manner, Lord Wellesley understood something about the Latin temperament—perhaps because of his Irish roots, perhaps because of his tempestuous French wife, perhaps because of his diplomatic service in Seville. In any case, he was hardly as implacable as he seemed. It was well known in London that he was an incorrigible voluptuary with scandalous personal habits. He was perfectly capable of understanding passions. Wellesley found Bolívar's ardor appealing and said so, complimenting him on the zeal with which he defended his people. Bolívar shot back good-naturedly that the foreign minister had defended Spain's interests with even greater zeal. The Irishman laughed. He thanked the delegates and added that he wished them well. He escorted them out genially and invited them back to a second meeting a few days later, on July 19.

The next meeting did not accomplish much more. The foreign minister was friendly, but his gaze was firmly on the war with Napoleon and the Spanish collaboration necessary to win it. Even so, the Latin Americans took heart. They had been admitted to the highest diplomatic court in the world. They had aired their views on the aspirations of a people. As the Earl of Harrowby commented portentously, "The events in Caracas are the beginning of a great drama. The curtain has been raised sooner than we thought." The Venezuelans came away with little doubt that, despite England's immediate commitment to Spain, their long-term ambitions had been understood: the Creoles were serious about freedom.

There was another ally to be won in London—Francisco de Miranda—and, although the delegates had been instructed to avoid him, Bolívar departed once more from the script. He sought out the fabled revolutionary, whose rhetoric against the Spanish king had grown only stronger now that Spain was under Napoleon's boot. The old veteran was sixty—a grizzled version of the dashing adventurer he once had been—but he welcomed his compatriots with all the enthusiasm of a young man. "Despite his age," Andrés Bello commented, "he seemed at the peak of his youth and ideals, still working to promote the independence of Spanish America." Miranda invited them to his house at 27 Grafton Street, which for many years had served as a gathering place for Latin Americans in London. According to López Méndez, it was Miranda who eagerly undertook to make them at home in that bewildering city:

The only person with whom we consulted with any confidence—and who gave us the preparatory briefings we needed—was our country-man; he more than anyone else, with his extensive experience and travels, his long contacts with the local government, and well-known exertions on behalf of America, was in a position to give us broad and reliable advice.

It is very possible that Miranda even briefed Bolívar on how to renew talks with the British foreign minister. Miranda knew a great deal about Lord Wellesley, having been a close friend of his more fa-mous brother, the Duke of Wellington. In fact, Miranda had been on the Foreign Ministry's payroll—receiving a modest pension—for quite some time. Just two years earlier, before Napoleon changed the world order by invading Spain, the Foreign Office had been on the verge of assisting Miranda in a new liberating expedition. Wellington eventually was instructed to take Miranda for a walk on London's streets and give him the bad news that England was coming to Spain's aid, not Venezu-ela's. If anyone could prepare Bolívar for British fickleness and cunning, it was Miranda.

Bolívar and his colleagues spent much of their time in the old gen-eral's comfortable house, availing themselves of his remarkable library, which contained six thousand volumes, many of them annotated in his own hand. Miranda also took pleasure in introducing the travelers to his distinguished circle, inviting them on visits to the Duke of Gloucester; the Duke of Cumberland; the chancellor of the exchequer, Nicholas Vansittart; the abolitionist William Wilberforce; the educator John Lancaster; and John Turnbull, his personal financier. But the English sought out the Venezuelans on their own, eager to learn about the recent events in Caracas: Lord Wellesley's son Richard was a frequent visitor to Morin's Hotel, as were other members of London society. For them, and indeed for anyone who would listen, Bolívar painted a splendid picture of Spanish American independence, of how a desire for liberty had gal-vanized the continent, and of the investment opportunities in store for any who would aid the cause.

There is little doubt that he spoke of such things in gatherings of the Great American Reunion, a Masonic lodge that Miranda had founded in London for radical Spanish Americans. In general, the Masonic movement of secret societies had proved to be a singularly powerful force for revolution throughout the Atlantic world, and the society of Freemasons in Miranda's day was enormous, counting such eminences as George Washington, Benjamin Franklin, Thomas Jefferson, James Monroe, the Marquis de Lafayette, William Pitt, the Duke of Wellington, Alexander Pushkin, and Sir Walter Scott. At meetings of Miranda's Great American Reunion—held routinely at his Grafton Street house—Miranda became a mentor to many a starry-eyed young rebel. Eventually, the three preeminent figures of the Spanish American wars for independence—the Argentine liberator José de San Martín, the Chilean hero Bernardo O'Higgins, and Bolívar—sat in Miranda's library, met with his friends, and thought through their strategies for insurrection.

Miranda's lodge, like all Masonic lodges, was considered anathema by the Spanish crown and Catholic Church, which looked on revolutionary cells with alarm, and so it was spied on routinely by royalist agents. In 1811, one of those agents intercepted a letter from an Argentine "brother" to a New Granadan, revealing the names of all men who had been officially inducted into Miranda's secret society. Andrés Bello was among them, as was Luis López Méndez—Bolívar's companions on that fateful trip. Even the outspoken Caracas canon José Cortés de Madariaga was listed as having taken the vows at Grafton Street. Curiously, Bolívar is not on the list. Given his later criticisms—even prohibition—of secret societies, it is likely that he found the concept of secret brotherhoods pointless in a people's revolution. Not for him the undeclared war.

But Miranda and Bolívar could not have agreed more on central questions of independence. When they were alone, they discussed the gritty questions of founding a republic, and every particular it entailed. In countless countries Miranda had visited, he had always made a point to study its public services—to take notes on how Philadelphia or Vienna served their urban populations, and how drastically these services were neglected in Madrid. He spoke of irrigation, mines, schools, museums, penitentiaries, public health, and the fine details of administration, and Bolívar listened with fascination. They spoke, too, of the public morality essential to any democracy, and spent long hours discussing the singular example of the United States. Dazzled by the older man's worldliness and wisdom—but mostly by his record as a man of military action—Bolívar implored him to return and rejoin Venezuela's struggle for independence.

Miranda balked. He had seen Venezuelan indifference at first hand and did not believe that he would ever be welcomed as a leader. As summer grew into autumn, Bolívar used all his powers of persuasion to convince the general that he was wrong.

Those weighty conversations between Miranda and Bolívar did not always take place in Miranda's library. The two appeared everywhere together—at the opera, the theater, in Piccadilly, at the Royal Observatory, or strolling through Hyde Park or Kew Gardens—and the London papers breathlessly reported their outings. They must have made an eccentric pair, ambling through London's streets: the elegant, handsome older man with the irrepressible, highly strung youth, conversing spiritedly in Spanish, stopping to argue their points. Miranda introduced Bolívar to the portraitist Charles Gill, a student of Sir Joshua Reynolds's, and evidently to his tailor, too, for Gill's portrait of Bolívar in London depicts him in a dashing jacket with a high collar and a black cravat—the very picture of English period elegance. His hair is slicked back, his chin hard with purpose, his eyes lit with resolve.

Bolívar also managed to navigate the city on his own. Many years later, he told of a "singular adventure" at a London brothel that both amused and amazed him. In the course of negotiating his desires with one of the prostitutes, he made a request that infuriated her, and she accused him of being a homosexual. She raised such a ruckus that the entire house came running, and when he tried to calm her with a few banknotes, she threw them scornfully into the fire. She didn't speak Spanish and he didn't speak English, so there was no hope of correcting her misapprehension. As he later related to friends, he ended up exiting the house of pleasure "with far greater urgency" than he had entered it. Little could he have known that the woman probably feared for her life. Only weeks before, on July 8, the London police had raided the White Swan, a Vere Street "molly" house, as transgender clubs were then called, and arrested a group of suspects. An angry mob followed the accused homosexuals to Bow Street Station, knocking them down, pelting them with mud, and threatening far worse. The men were charged with attempted sodomy; a number of them were hanged. The prostitute clearly had England's harsh laws in mind when she voiced her objections. For Bolívar, however, that incident became a striking metaphor for the vast cultural distance that separated London from Paris. Two years before his death, he still had a vivid memory of it.

ON SEPTEMBER 22, 1810, BOLÍVAR left London for Caracas on a sleek eighteen-gun sloop, the HMS *Sapphire*. He had intended for Miranda to travel with him and indeed Miranda had his luggage and sixty-three books carried on board with that objective in mind. But Lord Wellesley thought it unwise to allow the old revolutionary to make his voyage home under a British flag. The *Sapphire* sailed without him, arriving in La Guaira on December 5 and delivering Bolívar alone. Miranda managed to book himself on a far less comfortable packet boat, and reached Venezuela on December 10. López Méndez and Bello decided to stay on in the house on Grafton Street, where they continued Miranda's diplomatic efforts and went on to play very different roles in the revolution.

Bolívar was dismayed to see what had become of Venezuela in his absence. While he had been touting unconditional independence in the drawing rooms of London, the Caracas junta had cemented its ties to Ferdinand VII, weakened its influence in the provinces, and splintered into a score of bickering factions. The jealousies between Coro, Maracaibo, and Caracas had festered and, in the opinion of one traveler, "a deadly animosity exists, for which I fear much blood will yet be shed." The junta seemed wholly unaware of the civil unrest beyond the capital. The blacks and pardos did not trust the Creole government and were saying so openly, declaring a steadfast loyalty to the Regency. The royalists were busily recruiting the lower classes to their cause. Blind to those realities, the junta had set out to mimic the government of the United States of America, although that example—born of a rare ethnic and ideological solidarity—was singularly unsuitable for a populace that had no uniformity of race, class, or experience, and so couldn't agree on much of anything.

Worried that Miranda would feel he was stepping into a quagmire, Bolívar went about trying to rally support for him. But it wasn't easy to persuade men who felt Miranda was a poseur—or, worse, a deserter— that they should bury their resentments and give the old general a hero's welcome. When Miranda arrived on December 10, Bolívar raised a good crowd to meet him at La Guaira, but the only member of the junta who was there to greet him in any official capacity was the fearless canon Cortés de Madariaga. The junta itself had decided to put the best face on an awkward state of affairs by issuing a frigid salutation.

That day, Bolívar was merely an austere figure in the milling throng. Beside him, in splendid robes, Cortés seemed to tower over him. They watched from the pier as the British brigantine *Avon* approached, ferrying the great man from Curaçao. Expecting to be greeted as the leader of the newly formed Venezuelan government, Miranda had dressed to honor the occasion. He appeared on the prow of his ship in the glorious old uniform in which he had led French troops in the battles of Maastricht and Neerwinden. The coat was sky blue, the trousers white, the vivid tricolor sash of the Great Republic across his breast. He was a barrel-chested man—full-lipped, straight-backed—but he looked a good decade older than his years. His thinning hair was powdered and pulled into a scrawny tail. In one ear, he sported a single gold ring, as was the fashion among European gentlemen of his generation.

The royalist historian José Domingo Díaz made the observation:

I saw Miranda enter in triumph, welcomed as a gift from heaven, with all the hopes of the worst rabble-rousers resting on him. He was then about sixty-five years of age, serious looking, tirelessly loquacious, altogether too friendly toward the dregs of society, and ever ready to boost their hopes. The wildest saw him as a political sage, the only one capable of heading the government; moderates with more rational minds, on the other hand, saw him as a looming danger.

So it was that the general came home after his bumbling 1806 invasion. It was soon clear to Miranda that Bolívar, the "wildest" of them all, had overestimated the enthusiasm with which his countrymen would receive him. He would come to learn that even Cortés de Madariaga—

despite his presence on the dock—had bombastically opposed his return, threatening to leave Venezuela if Miranda were allowed reentry. The priest had appeared only to deliver the junta's pointedly cold salutation. As Miranda traveled to Bolívar's house, where he would lodge for the next few days, he began to absorb the reality of his situation. For all of Bolívar's fine words, Venezuela was unprepared for drastic change. He would have to grasp the reins. They would not be handed to him.

What *was* handed to him three weeks later was a title of lieutenant general with an equivalent salary and benefits. These were hardly satisfactory, he complained, for a dignitary with his experience. Miranda insisted he be named a full general and paid commensurate wages. When his objections went ignored, he decided to mount a political campaign to rouse the public on his behalf. Such an effort might have seemed normal enough in England, but in Venezuela, emerging from the twilight of colonialism, it struck the Creoles as outlandish. Even so, with Bolívar's help, he managed to win a seat in congress as the representative of the province of Pao. Bolívar, on the other hand, made no effort to run for election or seek a government position. Indeed, in the bureaucratic shuffle, the junta had demoted him from lieutenant colonel to captain. Undaunted, he threw himself wholeheartedly into assisting Miranda. Together, they took over a party called the Patriotic Society and Miranda did what any modern politician would do in a run for election: make speeches; call on powerful people in the community; write hectoring pieces for his party's newspaper, *El Patriota de Venezuela*.

In time, Miranda took control of the *Gazeta de Caracas*, the capital's journal of record. The junta's leaders, all of whom were in their thirties, were hardly fazed. They considered him pompous, laughable, and—most damning of all—hopelessly out of step with the times. Nevertheless, Miranda's efforts began to pay off with the colored classes, a logical enough development for a candidate whose father had been forced to prove his "cleanliness of blood." In popular assemblies, the pardos gathered to flex their collective muscle and make demands. Little by little, they took positions that were formerly reserved for whites; they penetrated high posts in the military. The rich Mantuanos were aghast. In March of 1811, they responded with a large-scale reorganization of the government: thirty-one representatives, all from landed families, joined congress, the majority of them in favor of King Ferdinand's rule; in place of the junta, an executive body of three rotating presidents was put in place. By June, however, those three newly anointed officials awoke to a new reality. For all their efforts, there was little doubt who had the overwhelming support of the people. Miranda's Patriotic Society was well in the lead.

The Rise and Fall of Miranda

Liberty is a succulent food, but hard to digest.
—Jean-Jacques Rousseau

For all Miranda's and Bolívar's abounding successes, not everything was right between them. First, there was the matter of Miranda's extreme arrogance, which even the fussy Mantuanos found insufferable. He was flagrantly egotistical, a name-dropper, incapable of responding to praise with praise. The former head of the junta, Juan Germán Roscio, was aghast at his behavior at banquets given in his honor: "He listened to toasts with enormous satisfaction and then simply let them pass, as if everyone there were his inferior. The polite expressions so familiar to people of good breeding never once left his lips."

Bolívar's irritation with Miranda was compounded by the animus between him and the Marquis del Toro, one of Bolívar's oldest and dearest friends. The hostilities had begun years before, when the marquis received more than one letter from Miranda suggesting that he take advantage of Napoleon's Spanish invasion to create a local junta and break relations with the *madre patria*. The marquis would later become one of the most ardent supporters of independence, but at a time when so little was known, his first reaction was to report Miranda's letters to the presiding captain-general, who, in turn, reported them to Cádiz.

Miranda would never forget it. Difficult to forgive, too, was Bolívar's unequivocal loyalty to the marquis. Not only had the del Toros and Bolívars enjoyed a warm friendship for generations; the marquis was an uncle to María Teresa, Bolívar's dead wife.

The uneasy relations between Miranda and del Toro came to a head when the congress decided to pass over Miranda's considerable military experience and place the Marquis del Toro in command of the newly formed War Department. It was a surprising dismissal. There was simply no one in Venezuela, the proud marquis included, who could match Miranda's credentials as a warrior. Bolívar was torn, but he refused to be disloyal to his wife's uncle. And so, despite the shared dreams and ambitions, a seed of mistrust was sown. When in June congress discussed the possibility of a military assignment for young Bolívar, the old general pronounced—perhaps not unreasonably—that Bolívar was unprepared for a post of any consequence. He was too raw a soldier, Miranda sniffed, too impulsive.

This bickering was soon dwarfed by an uproar in congress, when it was discovered that one of the newly appointed members, Feliciano Montenegro y Colón, was actually an agent for the Regency and had absconded with the War Department's plans. The flagrant theft had an electrifying effect on the fledgling government. Why were Venezuelans continuing to pledge loyalty to a king who would send spies to steal precious documents? On July 1, Cristóbal Mendoza, a member of the executive triumvirate that rotated the presidency, condemned this affront publicly and announced that perhaps the moment had come to discuss total sovereignty of the nation. Hearing these words, the citizens of Caracas, who had always leaned toward total independence, stirred with excitement. The halls of congress burst to life as men, women, and children poured in to hear the arguments. One by one, representatives made their way to the podium, some cautioning prudence, others thundering their outrage against Spain and the Regency. Members of the Patriotic Society, too, clamored to make their censure known. On the night of July 4, Bolívar took the floor at a special meeting of the society, arguing in strong, unequivocal terms for absolute independence. "Let us valiantly lay the cornerstone of South American liberty!" he cried. "To hesitate is to perish!" A British traveler who was present recalled:

Among all the rest, young Bolívar stood out for his piercing voice, his agitated, imperious manner, and especially for the unforgettable fire in his eyes, which burned with all the intensity of a conquistador's or a visionary's. He was small in stature, thin, lightly tanned, with an angular brow and sunken temples, small hands and feet, and the dress of a European gentleman. . . . I listened to him speak and, although I didn't know the language perfectly, I understood him to say that he would die before he would allow his country to be a slave to Spain. He was a commanding presence in that hall and everyone seemed to know it. They told me he was a nobleman of considerable wealth, but that he was willing to give all of it for his country's freedom. It seemed to me that the young man was destined either for an early death or extraordinary heroism.

All night long, young revolutionaries, fueled by drink and fury, swarmed the streets, defacing the property of the crown. The next morning, on July 5, the halls of congress teemed with greater ferment. Miranda took the floor and gave a report on the most recent dispatches from the Spanish peninsula: the Duke of Wellington had just defeated the armies of Napoleon's greatest marshal, Masséna, for the second time. Soon Spain would be free of Napoleon, and its generals would turn their attention to subduing the colonies and unraveling all the freedoms they had put in place. If they cared about the future of Venezuela, he said bluntly, now was the time to act.

It was an irresistible appeal. That afternoon, the question of separation from Spain was put to a congressional vote; it passed with only one dissenting voice. The acting president of the triumverate, Cristóbal Mendoza, declared absolute independence and the first republic was born. Miranda triumphantly unfurled his tricolor banner—yellow, red, and blue—and Caracas went wild with jubilation. Late into the night, revelers delivered ecstatic speeches on the plaza, ripped Spanish flags to shreds, broke into private homes to destroy portraits of the king, and the royalists cringed, fearing the wrath of Cádiz and the vengeance of heaven.

For Bolívar, the joys of that seminal victory were soon tempered by sorrow. He learned that his brother, Juan Vicente, had died in a shipwreck on the way home from his diplomatic mission to the United States. It would be a while before Bolívar would know the details of his brother's demise, but eventually he would understand that not much of that trip had gone well. Luis de Onís, Spain's ambassador in Washington, had duped Juan Vicente into believing that the Regency was about to recognize the Venezuelan government, and so the gentle-hearted Juan Vicente spent the 70,000 pesos entrusted to him not for guns, but for farm equipment—not for swords, but plowshares. As his ship made its way south, it ran into a hurricane off the coast of Bermuda. Both he and his cargo were dashed into rocks by a merciless August wind.

EVEN AS THE BLOODIED HEAD of Mexico's ferocious rebel priest Miguel Hidalgo swung from a rooftop in Guanajuato so that the world could see how Spain dealt with revolutions, republican Venezuela was caught up in the euphoria of its newly declared independence. Patriot gangs in Caracas rounded up Spaniards and royalists and stripped them of all weapons. Blacks taunted the wellborn, addressing them as "citizens" and menacing them in the streets. Pardos were granted high posts in the military and welcomed at balls and celebratory dinners. Some, reported one Englishman, "carried insolence so far as to demand in marriage the daughters" of former (white) magistrates. Even so, King Ferdinand's loyalists were not easily cowed. Within days they organized a retaliatory uprising in northwest Caracas, where they gathered with cutlasses, muskets, and improvised tin shields. "Long live the king!" they cried, riding against the new masters. "Death to the traitors!"

But it was a shabby show of force and patriot troops succeeded in rounding them up quickly: sixteen prisoners were lined up against a wall and shot, then hanged, after which their heads were shoved onto stakes and displayed—Hidalgo-style—in every corner of the city. The retaliation was swift and brutal, but even the mild-mannered intellectual Juan Germán Roscio, chief architect of the new government, approved it. "Unless we spill blood, our rule will be seen as weak," he wrote his friend Andrés Bello, who was still living in Miranda's house in London.

Although the framers of the new republic claimed the establishment of a full democracy, it soon became clear that democracy would have a different face in Venezuela. Only citizens who owned property would have the right to vote; others would merely have the right to "enjoy the benefits of the law without participating in its establishment." Bolívar was dismayed. Miranda, who originally had envisioned a unified America under the rule of a hereditary Inca, was equally distressed, but their views were largely ignored as congress set out to fashion a constitution. Miranda and Bolívar may have disagreed on some points—Bolívar wanted all Spaniards expelled, while Miranda was willing to let them stay—but they agreed completely on the notion that the new republic would need, more than anything, a united purpose and a strong central government to deliver it. Congress, on the other hand, favored a loose federation of states that would preserve old ruling factions, and it set out to write a constitution that would ensure that existing class structures prevailed. The result was anything but egalitarian. The military remained segregated (even the black militias were to be headed by whites); the slave trade was suspended, but slave owners could keep the slaves they had; and although pardos were told they were now free from "civil degradation," they were given no ballot and no franchise in the future of the republic. The constitution, in short, handed all power to rich whites, and it fooled no one.

Almost immediately, Spain's agents, including the Church, moved to take advantage of the injustices. The archbishop of Caracas directed his priests to educate blacks and pardos about the racial discrimination inherent in the new laws. Royalists traveled up and down the coast trying to provoke a slave insurrection. It didn't take long for their strategy to work. Slaves, outraged that they they had been cheated of their promised freedom, rose up against their Creole masters, raiding their country estates, massacring whole families, burning fields, and demolishing property. As whites recoiled in horror, the black counterrevolutionary ranks only swelled, drunk now with newfound power.

In Maracaibo, Coro, and Guayana—a vast swath that reached from the agriculturally rich west to the eastern savannas—the poor and exploited pledged undying devotion to King Ferdinand. Cacao fields languished in the sun, mines went neglected, and the economy began a dangerous downward spiral. On July 19, 1811, a violent uprising erupted in the city of Valencia, less than a hundred miles from the capital. Congress decided to send the Marquis del Toro and his troops to quell it, but neither the congress nor del Toro himself had much faith they could accomplish their mission. Just months before, the junta had directed the marquis to put down a royalist disturbance in Coro, and the old nobleman, more comfortable in a salon than on a field of battle, had proceeded to correspond politely with the leaders of the port city he was supposed to besiege. Eventually, when diplomacy failed, he had set out over two hundred miles of desert road with defective ammunition and a few obsolete cannons, borne on the backs of slaves. Only one in ten of his soldiers carried a gun. When they arrived, the Spaniards simply sprayed them with grapeshot, and the general and his troops turned and fled for their lives.

Much the same happened in Valencia. No sooner did the marquis's army attack than the royalists countered with a superior force and the marquis lost his nerve. It became patently clear to the republicans in Caracas that the only real soldier in their midst was Miranda; they offered him the post of commander and called on him to lead a larger expedition. Miranda agreed on the bizarre condition that the eager young Bolívar, who fully expected to march at his side, be given some pretext and removed from his post as commanding officer of the militia of Aragua.

It is difficult to say what in Bolívar had irritated Miranda more—his inexperience, his brash confidence, his loyalty to the marquis, perhaps even his brilliance—but it was a firm stipulation and Miranda was in dead earnest. Members of congress were surprised, even taken aback by the general's demand. They asked why he had such a bad opinion of Bolívar, to which he replied, "Because he is a dangerous young man." In the end, they agreed to Miranda's terms. When Bolívar heard of it, he burst into their hall in a fit of rage: "How can you refuse me the chance to serve my country?" he fumed. "What will people say when my men march off and their commanding officer is kept behind? That I'm a coward! A traitor!" Bolívar's fellow Mantuanos were sympathetic, and they all agreed that Miranda was a high-handed prig, but they desperately needed his military expertise. Eventually, the Marquis del Toro, whose troops were still in the field, waiting to be joined by Miranda, took Bolívar under his command as his personal adjutant. Colonel

Bolívar distinguished himself in Valencia, driving the royalists out of the city after two battles and fighting bravely under fire.

Miranda may have been arrogant—perhaps even overly wary of Bolívar's ambitions—but he was not a malicious man. He decided that Bolívar should be the one to carry word of the republican triumph back to Caracas. Moreover, in his report to congress, he singled out Bolívar for his valor and recommended that his rank of colonel be reinstated. But privately, he was more critical. Bolívar's style was that of a guerrilla leader, not a disciplined European soldier; he was, according to Miranda, too informal, too dismissive of military ceremony, too free and friendly with his troops. Nevertheless, the victories in Valencia were a turning point for Bolívar. It was there that he established his bona fides as a warrior; and it was there, for all his disagreements with congress, that he plunged wholeheartedly into a revolution that others had made.

As Miranda's army continued to hold Valencia, word of the commanding general's arrogance began to trickle back to the capital. The Mantuanos had never liked Miranda's foreign pretensions; now the troops were complaining about his undisguised scorn. The word was that, as the ragtag, improvised force of four thousand had stood at attention for his review, he had sneered openly, "Where are the armies that a general of my standing can command without compromising his dignity and name?" He would make exasperated comments in French, baffling his soldiers; snap at officers when he wasn't paid due deference; wonder aloud when the English or North Americans would come help him make warriors out of these hopelessly inept men.

To be fair, little was going the way Miranda had imagined it when he had sat in his comfortable library on Grafton Street, nursing his dreams of liberty. The specter of civil war troubled him most. He had come to fight soldiers of the Spanish crown, not raise arms against fellow Venezuelans. He had not anticipated that his most rabid antagonists would be Canary Islanders like his father, as indeed many royalists turned out to be. Although Miranda had prevailed in that first battle at Valencia, much of what he saw about him was dispiriting. His troops were raw and unruly, unlike any he had led before; the enemy, more often than not, was better prepared and armed; and Miranda had sustained a debilitating number of dead and incapacitated—more than half out of a force of four thousand. Wanting to teach a stern lesson to anyone who would dare instigate another royalist revolt, Miranda sentenced the insurrection's leaders to be hanged in Caracas. But four months later, hemming and hawing about the rights of man, congress dismissed all the charges and sent the insurrectionists home.

EVEN HERE, IN THESE FIRST glimmers of liberty, we begin to see the character of a continent. The American-born were hungry for liberties, yet unaccustomed to freedom; resourceful, yet unacquainted with self-rule; racially mixed, yet mistrustful of whatever race they were not. For three hundred years of authoritarian reign, Spain had carefully instilled these qualities. "Divide and subjugate" had been the rule. Education had been discouraged, in many cases outlawed, and so ignorance was endemic. Colonies were forbidden from communicating with each other, and so—like spokes of a wheel—they were capable only of re-porting directly to a king. There was no collaborative spirit, no model for organization, no notion of hierarchy. It was why the people of Coro or Maracaibo or Guayana refused to obey their newly independent brothers in Caracas; given the choice, they preferred the crown. And even though Americans had been inclined to mix across racial lines from the beginning, Spain had worked hard to keep the races apart, feed their suspicions. Add to this a church that was thoroughly opposed to independence, and a picture emerges unlike any other in that age of revolutions. If Spanish America now found itself strong enough to rise up against Spain, it would never quite rid itself of the divisions that the Council of the Indies had carefully installed in the first place. Bolívar was particularly aware of this deepest of flaws, predicting a fragmenta-tion that remains prevalent to this day. It was why he was so adamantly against federation—a concept he thought far more workable in the United States, where the population was largely homogeneous and, so, inherently more governable.

The new federalist constitution with its misguided premise and un-gainly 228 articles was passed on December 21, doomed from the outset by the querulous times into which it was born. It named the new nation Colombia, after Christopher Columbus, and moved the capital deci-sively from Caracas to the newly tamed city of Valencia. But even before the start of the new government, which had been set for March 1, 1812, forces were at work to crush it.

Don Juan Manuel Cajigal, a cousin of the Spanish general under whom Miranda had fought thirty years earlier, arrived in Coro to restore Spanish rule and install a new captain-general, Fernando Miyares. Among his officers was a frigate captain, Domingo de Monteverde, whom Cajigal ordered to march south and assist a band of conspirators who had declared themselves on the side of the crown. By March 17, Monteverde held the region, but exceeding his orders, he made himself head of his own army; recruited thousands of pardos, blacks, and Canary Islanders; and began to advance against the patriot forces.

Monteverde was strategizing a raid on a number of towns between him and Caracas when, one sun-filled spring day, nature contrived to assist him. It was Thursday of Holy Week, March 26, 1812, exactly two years after Venezuela's declaration of independence. In Caracas, the sun was oppressively hot, the air stagnant and still, the sky a deep azure, bereft of even a wisp of cloud. At four in the afternoon, a company of infantrymen was making its way toward the cathedral in preparation for a procession. The churches were full of worshippers, celebrating Mass, reenacting the washing of the Apostles' feet before Christ's last supper. Seven minutes into the hour, a sprinkling of raindrops fell, inexplicably, out of that clear blue sky, and then, from the depths of the earth, came a deafening rumble. The ground began a fierce undulation, heaving and rippling, as if something enormous were squirming beneath it, and then the houses began to fall.

For a seemingly interminable two minutes, a terrible earthquake shook Caracas, its violent convulsions parting the city's walls and crumbling whole buildings. A cacophony of bells rang out as the Cathedral of the Trinity collapsed to its foundations. José Domingo Díaz, the royalist historian, was rushing to Mass when the earth began to churn beneath him. He watched the Church of San Jacinto brought to rubble in the time it took him to cross the square. Balconies crashed to his feet; roofs creaked and gave way. Terrified cries came from inside the caving houses as their inhabitants struggled to run through the confusion, find doors. When the shaking stopped, the city was little more than debris, bathed in billowing plumes of dust, locked in a sepulchral silence.

Díaz made a dazed run for the mound of ruin that had been the church. Through dark clouds of dust, he could make out the severed limbs, crushed corpses, and, here and there, the stubborn evidence of life: a flailing arm, a tangle of humanity. As he stepped through the wreckage, squinting into the haze, he chanced on a familiar face coming the other way.

> I will never forget that moment. There, at the very top, I found Simón Bolívar, who, in his shirtsleeves, was doing exactly what I was doing—moving through, trying to reckon the damage. His face was the picture of terror and despair. When he saw me, he called out, addressing me with these preposterous words: *If Nature itself decides to oppose us, we will fight and force her to obey!*

Nature had indeed opposed Caracas. Within minutes, the city was reduced to a grave site. More than ten thousand were buried by the rubble. Another six thousand, it was said, were swallowed by yawning ravines. Some, laboring in the open fields, died of shock. Half an hour didn't pass before another quake shook the city. Survivors, caked with dust and blood, staggered through streets littered with cadavers, looking for their relatives. By nightfall, it was clear that the accumulations of dead would have to be incinerated in pyres. There were far too many to bury in mass graves.

The looting began almost instantly. The poor rushed in to carry off what they could, rob gold from corpses, rip jewelry from the ears of trapped women who implored for help. Crimes went unseen, unchecked, as smoke from the fires coiled into sky and the thick, yellow dust yielded to darkness.

Bolívar's house had been seriously damaged, its floors so buckled that doors had been ripped from jambs, windows from casings, but he was more concerned about the devastation around him. He organized what slaves and friends he could and, with makeshift stretchers, went about exhuming the living and carrying off the dead. There were no tools for digging or clearing away the foul heaps, and so they dug with their bare hands. It was as he was engaged in this work, hurrying across the main plaza, that he saw a red-faced priest shout at a cowering crowd, exhorting them to repent, blaming them for the destruction. "On your knees, sinners!" the priest told them. "Now is your hour to atone. The arm of divine justice has descended on you for your insult to his Highest Majesty, that most virtuous of monarchs, King Ferdinand VII!"

If Bolívar threatened that priest with his sword—as legend has it he did—he would soon find that it was impossible to defy the entire clergy. He combed the ruins, working hard to disabuse his fellow survivors of their superstitions, but it didn't take long for the ministry of the Church to convince Caracas that the earthquake was God's angry hand, punishing them for the perfidy of insurrection. Hadn't the declaration of independence two years before been on a Maundy Thursday, too? The revolution was a sacrilege, and all its adherents, blasphemers. The people would need to atone for the sin of betraying the *madre patria*. Fearing the fate of a Sodom and Gomorrah, Venezuelans now rushed to make right with the Lord. As days and weeks went by, men of means married slaves with whom they had had sexual relations. Chastened revolutionaries fashioned colossal wooden crosses and dragged them, Christlike, through the ruined city.

The quake had coursed through the upper half of South America, its shocks proceeding in devastating opposition from the Andes to the coast. Strange natural phenomena occurred: water had burst from a chasm in the earth to form a new lake in Valecillo; the river Yurubí had dammed up to a standstill; other rivers had changed course. But it was human carnage to which the Church pointed. One traveler estimated the loss of life at 30,000; other estimates climbed as high as 120,000.

To add fuel to the clergy's condemnations, it was soon evident that the brunt of the earthquake's damage had been in republican strongholds. In the port of La Guaira, firmly controlled by the rebel government, the only house that remained standing belonged to Spain's once all-powerful Guipuzcoana Company. Hundreds of patriot soldiers had been crushed in their barracks in San Carlos and San Felipe, and in Barquisimeto twelve hundred more disappeared into a fissure in the earth. Even Cartagena, a newly independent city in faraway New Granada, reported crippling damage. In royalist outposts, on the other hand—in Coro, Maracaibo, and that hotbed of royalist sympathy, Valencia—there was hardly a brick out of place. Agents of the crown moved quickly to play up this fact and add further evidence of God's favor: the gallows to which dissident Spaniards had been sent eight months earlier, for instance, had been toppled by a single, rolling stone; the only pillar left standing in a church bore an immaculate image of the king's royal insignia. The mass hysteria increased. The Venezuelan people, terrified by these revelations and sure now that God had spoken, streamed to the royalist side. Republicans deserted to the king's army. As Spain's General Monteverde advanced swiftly toward the republic's capital, he had no trouble recruiting troops.

IF GOD HAD UNLEASHED A seismic fury on Venezuela, he had inflicted it on the whole of the Americas. For more than a year, earthquakes rocked the hemisphere. In fall of 1811, a blazing comet half again larger than the sun lit the skies over North America. The first earthquake struck on December 16, its epicenter between Memphis and St. Louis, causing the Mississippi River to churn with a fetid gas and spill its banks so that flatboats sailed into cities and coffins floated down streets. The earth was crazed by great, wide fissures; water spurted as high as trees. In February of 1812, an even more violent shock ripped through Missouri, causing a flood that carried away the town of New Madrid. By April, when news of the Caracas disaster reached Washington, many North Americans became convinced that the entire race of man needed punishing. Religious fervor reached a high pitch. The *Pittsburgh Gazette* editorialized: "The period is portentous and alarming. . . . The year past has produced a magnificent comet, earthquakes have been almost without number . . . and we constantly 'hear of wars and summons of wars.' . . . Can ye not discern the signs of the times?"

The tremors were unremitting, and those who knew to hang a ball from a string could see that the ground was in continuous motion. A week after the Pittsburgh editorial, a volcano on the Caribbean island of St. Vincent hurled a discharge of shattered rock, black smoke, and flaming lava into the vault of sky, shrouding the island in darkness. The subterranean rumblings went on for months. By December, when tectonic shifts had rattled their way north, bringing a tsunami that ravaged the coast of California, the city of Washington was too deep in preoccupation to pay much attention to calamities beyond its ambit. The nation had gone back to war with England.

The War of 1812 was the result of a series of annoyances bedeviling relations between the United States and its former colonizer. The British navy had rounded up American sailors on the high seas and pressed them into service; the British army had slipped down from Canada to help the Indian tribes resist westward expansion. Americans were weary of England's ongoing blockade, which—along with Jefferson's misguided Embargo Act—had sapped the country's economic vigor; and there were many war hawks who saw the revolution as unfinished until the United States liberated Canada and expelled the colonizer from the continent completely.

There were many reasons for the country to avoid involving itself in South America's conflagrations. But it needed to take a pragmatic view as trade in the Spanish colonies had once accounted for a full forty percent of all U.S. exports. Now, the embargo and blockade—as well as the war in Spain—had put that lucrative traffic into England's hands, giving British merchants a virtual monopoly in Latin America. When the newly independent Venezuela sent its ambassador Telesforo de Orea to Washington to establish diplomatic relations, he could hardly be ignored. President James Madison wasn't quite ready to recognize the new republic, but he needed to make some gesture of support. In the address in which he urged Congress to arm the nation against the British, the president reported "an enlightened forecast" in the "great communities" of South America. The U.S. Congress, he said, had "an obligation to take a deep interest in their destinies." The president had little support in Congress—either for his war or for his Pan American intentions. Congress issued a dry statement promising that when those "great communities" reached the status of nations, it would consider a fitting response.

The message was clear: the United States would not recognize declarations of independence as evidence of full-fledged nations, nor would it spring to assist South America in its harebrained revolutions. Indeed, when John Adams had first heard of Miranda's elaborate plan to establish a vast empire in Spanish America with an Inca at its head, he had said that he didn't know whether to laugh or cry. In as gracious a manner as he could, Secretary of State James Monroe met with Ambassador Orea to advise him of the U.S. position. Within a few months of that meeting, Great Britain and the United States—the very powers on which Miranda and Bolívar had rested their hopes—were at war on land and sea.

WITH CARACAS IN RUINS, THE republican population decimated, and Monteverde's army advancing on the new capital of Valencia, the Venezuelan congress was in a panic. Desperate to save the republic and realizing that what was needed most was a swift, unified operation, its members offered the Marquis del Toro a dictatorship. When he declined, they offered it to Miranda, who accepted.

Generalísimo Miranda began his rule by evacuating the capital. Alarmed by the reputation that preceded Monteverde's invading troops—many of them truculent plainsmen who killed and looted everything in their path—Miranda gathered his army and headed back to Caracas. On the way, he stopped at San Mateo, visited Bolívar, and appointed him to command the strategically vital port of Puerto Cabello. Bolívar accepted, but "not without misgivings." On the one hand, it was a serious political responsibility, well beyond any capacities he had ever demonstrated: the dungeons of Puerto Cabello's fort, San Felipe, held powerful enemies of the revolution; and the bulk of patriot arms and munitions were stockpiled there. On the other hand, what was offered was command of the town—not the fort. Bolívar preferred the offensive; he longed to be on the glorious front lines of war. On May 4, the day after Monteverde readily took Valencia, Bolívar rode into Puerto Cabello and had his first glimpse of the squat, gloomy bulwark in whose shadow he would brood for fifty-eight deceptively languid days.

Out on the battlefront, Miranda's officers, too, were chafing with frustration, eager to engage Monteverde in an all-out war, but Miranda restrained them, vying in skirmishes only as necessary. After every action, whether it was a victory or defeat, he ceded territory and retreated. Certainly, he had his reasons. For all the pugnacity and determination of his officers, the republican soldiers were unproven, skittish. Many were farm boys, recruited with swords to their hearts, brought to the barracks in manacles. Nonetheless, Miranda had six thousand of them; Monteverde had only fifteen hundred, and, for all their truculence, they were surrounded by republicans on every side. On June 20, Miranda withdrew to La Victoria, less than two hundred miles west of Caracas, where he succeeded in repulsing a vigorous attack by Monteverde, by far the bloodiest engagement of that war. Over the years, historians have posited that, had Miranda taken advantage of that golden moment—had he grasped the initiative and ordered a full-scale attack—he might have saved the republic. But he failed to act, and that faintheartedness worried his soldiers. Morale plunged to such an extent during those months that one disillusioned corps in all its entirety defected to the Spanish side. Even the Marquis del Toro, the former commanding general of the republican army, deserted with his wounded brother, Fernando, and sought refuge on the island of Trinidad. As Miranda continued to watch and wait, the enemy sent troops in the opposite direction, west toward Bolívar's garrison in Puerto Cabello.

Why did Miranda hesitate? Because he feared a bloody, unwinnable race war. When a massive slave insurrection erupted in the farmlands of Barlovento in June, something turned in Miranda. Just weeks before, he had urged congress to pass an act that freed slaves if they enlisted in his army; he had instructed a diplomat in Haiti to recruit blacks to their cause. Now the very people he had hoped to rally were moving through Creoles' haciendas, butchering whites and burning property. He began to be convinced that the colored population, which amounted to half the province of Caracas, would fight only for its interests, not for independence at large. In the back of his mind, too, were the vivid horrors of the Haitian revolution—the infamous 1791 Night of Fire, when two thousand whites in the colony of Santo Domingo were massacred and 180 sugar plantations burned to the ground. "As much as I desire liberty and independence for the New World, I fear anarchy," he had written a friend. "May God prevent my beautiful land from succumbing to another Santo Domingo. Better would it be for [blacks] to suffer the barbarous, imbecilic rule of Spain for another century."

But other possibilities, too, began to play on Miranda's mind. Spain had just installed the most liberal constitution the empire had ever known. In a document released by the Cádiz Regency that spring, there were hints that the colonies might be granted greater freedoms. With his eye firmly on mounting liabilities—the paralyzed economy, the earthquake's ravages, proliferating starvation, the threat of a fierce civil war—Miranda began to wonder whether trusting Spain wasn't preferable to inviting further mayhem. He was an old soldier, weary of battle, with aims that were largely idealistic, and it was difficult for him to imagine his homeland rent by his own hand.

SETTLING INTO AN AUSTERE ROOM in the municipal hall on Puerto Cabello's main plaza, Bolívar had no way of knowing he had stepped into a trap. The city was outwardly pleasant enough, filled with fragrant gardens, well-kept houses, and a charming park that looked west toward a wide expanse of sea. To the north, on a promontory overlooking the city, sat the fort of San Felipe, by far the strongest fortification in all Venezuela—a thick, solidly built bastion that lay less than a hundred miles by sea from Caracas. To the east lay the sheltered port, embraced by long, sandy beaches; behind that, the cactus-covered hills. So still was the air, so absent the wind, that the port was said to get its name, "Cabello" from the single strand of hair it took to moor a ship there.

The people of Puerto Cabello were dependent entirely on rain, situated as they were a mile from the nearest river and blocked from the rest of the country by high, forested mountains. Water was collected in cisterns, and its availability greatly valued, although the ground seemed to be perpetually damp from the mangrove swamps that blighted it. Puerto Cabello, in other words, for all its visual beauty, was an unhealthy town, and a foul, suffocating exhalation hung over it. "The graveyard of Spaniards," locals called it; and with reason, for they buried their dead from yellow fever all year round.

Bolívar had little to do in Puerto Cabello during those first muggy weeks of summer but practice his sword fighting; ride through the wide, picturesque streets; and worry about getting enough provisions to the people under his command. But all that changed on June 30, 1812, when the fort's commandant, Ramón Aymerich, left the premises to attend his own wedding. Taking advantage of his absence, his second in command, Francisco Vinoni—in a flagrant act of treason—released all the Spanish prisoners from the dungeons, raised the Spanish flag, claimed the fort for King Ferdinand, and threatened to fire on the plaza unless Bolívar surrendered it.

Bolívar refused, urging the renegades to reconsider and lay down their arms. The firing began almost immediately. Since the fort held most of the republican munitions, Bolívar was at a loss to defend the city. His soldiers had few rifles, little gunpowder, limited food, and no water. Worse still, the captain in charge of defending the main gate soon defected to the Spanish side with all 120 of his troops. Bolívar and his regiment stood their ground and held the plaza for as long as they could while heavy artillery rained on them and residents ran for their lives, scrambling over walls and out into the hills. But the odds were impossible. On July 1, even as deaths and desertions whittled his unit to a scant forty men, Bolívar was told that five hundred of Monteverde's troops were advancing on them. Desperate, he dispatched a messenger with a terse letter to Miranda, begging him to send reinforcements. But by the time his courier was able to put the missive into the generalísimo's hands four days later, Bolívar's fate was written. Miranda was sipping coffee with his officers, chatting breezily of Jefferson and Adams after a dinner marking the first anniversary of the republic, when Bolívar's letter arrived. He opened it and read:

> Generalísimo, At one o'clock this afternoon, a seditious officer with all the troops and prisoners under his command seized the fort and opened a terrible fire on this city. The fort contains 200 tons of gunpowder and almost all the artillery and munitions of Puerto Cabello; the town is in high duress, its houses in rubble, and I am trying—without arms or provisions—to defend her to the very end. The ships' sailors have all joined with the fort, making the situation even worse. I hope you will hasten to send what reserves you can, and that you will come to my aid before I am done.

For a long while, Miranda was silent. When he finally spoke to his officers, his voice was hard and grim:

You see, gentlemen. Such are the ways of the world. Just moments ago, we were safe: Now everything is uncertain, risky. Yesterday, Monteverde had no gunpowder, no lead, no guns. Today, he has it in abundance. I am being urged to attack the enemy. But the enemy already holds all the power in his hands. The postmark here says the first of July and now it is the fifth, at sundown. Let us see what happens tomorrow.

But tomorrow was too late. On the 6th of July, Bolívar and his tiny retinue of five ragged officers and three soldiers—all that was left of his troops—had no choice but to flee Puerto Cabello. They stole along the coast to the nearby harbor of Barburata and slipped aboard a ship for La Guaira. By the time Monteverde's men arrived in Puerto Cabello, the royalist army had a firm hold on the port and its immense store. Scarcely was it in their hands when a swarm of Spanish ships packed with fresh troops arrived to support them. There was every chance now that they would try to take Caracas.

Bolívar was dispirited and humiliated, fully aware that he had lost one of the most important footholds of republican power. He assumed responsibility for it. How could he have predicted that, as commandant of the town of Puerto Cabello—a duty that paled alongside that of the commandant of the fort—he would ultimately be accountable for the fort, too? He wrote two tortured letters to Miranda and a fully detailed report of the disastrous events. He was sick with misery at his own failure, disgusted, too, by his men's fickleness and inexperience. "My General," he wrote,

my spirits are so low that I do not feel I have the courage now to command a single soldier. My vanity had me believing that desire and patriotic zeal alone could offset my lack of experience. I beg you now to assign me to an officer of the lowest rank, or grant me a few days to compose myself. . . . After thirteen sleepless nights under extreme conditions, I find myself in a rare state of mental ruin. . . . I did my duty, General, and, had one of my soldiers stayed, I would have fought to the end, but they abandoned me. . . . And, alas, the nation is lost at my hands.

Indeed, even as he penned these words from the republican bastion of Caracas on July 12, events were rushing to unravel everything the revolution had accomplished. Within the few days it took Bolívar to send his report and express a profound regret that he hadn't been crushed under the ruins of Puerto Cabello, Miranda had decided to cast independence to the winds.

"VENEZUELA IS WOUNDED IN THE heart," Miranda had said when he informed his men about Puerto Cabello. Perhaps it was a genuine expression of disillusionment. Perhaps it was an excuse for what he was about to do. The next morning, before dawn pierced the skies, his officers saw him pacing the corridor outside his quarters—shaved, groomed, in dress uniform—as if he were readying himself for an important occasion. "They've probably stormed the plaza by now," he commented to them, referring to Bolívar's holdout in Puerto Cabello. "It's absolutely necessary that we take extraordinary measures to save Venezuela." By this, Miranda did not mean that they needed to infuse troops with a new vigor. Like most of his soldiers, he had long since ceased to place much hope in the foundering republic. Yet his subordinates feared his indignation and so did not dare raise the possibility of a capitulation until Miranda raised it himself in a passing exchange with the Marquis de Casa León, the newly appointed finance minister. Casa León immediately seized on Miranda's vague mention of a cease-fire and suggested that the generalísimo convene an emergency council to discuss the matter. The marquis was Spanish-born, a wealthy landowner worried about his considerable holdings, and had lost heart in the tumultuous republican venture. He wanted nothing more than a peaceful reconciliation with Spain.

That very day, Miranda called a meeting of the few leaders he could muster—among them two members of the executive body, Francisco Espejo and Juan Germán Roscio, as well as Secretary of War José de Sata y Bussy, Minister of Justice Francisco Antonio Paúl, and the Marquis de Casa León—and proposed the possibility of negotiating with the enemy. The republic was in extremis, he argued: the western regions, the banks of the Orinoco, the plains, the entire coastline were under Spanish control. In the nation's breadbasket, the fertile valleys of the southeast, slaves were slaughtering their masters in the name of King Ferdinand. Even in the streets of La Victoria, the very town in which they stood, Monteverde's soldiers had been seen racing through the alleyways. The republican ranks were being depleted daily by desertions. And now, with the loss of Puerto Cabello, they had too few weapons to prosecute a war. It was time to talk about an armistice. The men unanimously agreed. The Marquis de Casa León happily volunteered to be the intermediary.

The discussions with Monteverde began on July 12 in Valencia, just as Bolívar reached Caracas from La Guaira and wrote his first letter of abject apology to the generalísimo. To show the Spaniards a little muscle before joining them at the negotiating table, the republicans launched a modest attack. But there was no doubt in anybody's mind that what would be discussed was unequivocal surrender. As negotiations were taking place, Miranda traveled from La Victoria to La Guaira to charter a ship for his evacuation. He made sure that the Marquis de Casa León put aside 22,000 pesos for his voyage. Here, as one historian has said, is proof incontrovertible that the generalísimo had abandoned the cause of the republic for his own.

On the 25th of July, after minimal disputation, the republicans agreed to Monteverde's terms, even leaving it to him to apply all the particulars. The pact did seem to ensure the most important points: patriot lives and properties would be protected, a complete amnesty for political crimes would be granted; and passports would be available to any republican who wanted to leave the country. The agreement was signed and sealed and, although Miranda made no official announcement, word of it began to trickle back to the republican stronghold of Caracas.

Miranda immediately ordered a freeze on all movement in La Guaira so that neutral ships would be available to him and other leaders seeking to flee the crumbling republic. He made sure that even as his own soldiers were systematically stripped of their weapons, the rebellious slaves, too, were made to give up their arms. He attempted an orderly withdrawal from La Victoria, but almost half of his troops had already gone over to the Spanish side; many of the rest dispersed into the woods on the long march back to Caracas. Even as Miranda entered the capital on July 29, Monteverde's troops followed close behind, striking fear into the waiting populace. From the moment the banner of independence was lowered and King Ferdinand's flag was hoisted over the main square, a looming dread spread over the city.

That dread was followed immediately by fury. Creoles who had never liked Miranda were now outraged by his easy surrender. As far as they were concerned, the generalísimo hadn't made one vigorous attack, hadn't deployed his six thousand warriors with any verve or skill. Wasn't a fierce war to the finish preferable to this humiliation? Not one member of the Caracas government had been warned of the capitulation before the city was surrounded by Spanish soldiers. Miranda had made no effort to consult with the city's leaders; he had not confided his plans to his military officers; and, for all the service his foreign soldiers had rendered, he had made no provision in the capitulation for their safe passage. Even as defenders of the republic hastened to escape—or put themselves in positions of favor with Monteverde—few thought to defend Miranda, although it was clear he had not surrendered alone.

Bolívar was astounded by his chief's precipitous and unilateral resignation, and his surprise, too, turned to rage. What might he have accomplished in Puerto Cabello with all the guns and men under Miranda's command? And, if Miranda had felt unable to carry on, why hadn't he passed the scepter to someone who could? Instead, the generalísimo's proclamation, posted throughout Caracas, announced that the patriot army had ceased to exist: less than three hundred of Monteverde's soldiers now held dominion over a city of fourteen thousand. To Bolívar, there was only one possible reason for Miranda's reversal: it was treason of the highest order, and it demanded swift and dire retribution.

Bolívar immediately sought out fellow republicans in hopes of reconstituting the army and mounting a new front against Monteverde, but it was increasingly clear that the moment had been lost. Many of those men had gathered their families and headed for the port, frightened by the swift collapse of the republic and rumors of violence that accompanied Monteverde's arrival. But the clamor to emigrate, as Bolívar soon found when he rushed back to La Guaira to witness the situation firsthand, had been foiled by Miranda himself: for four days now, republicans had swarmed over the mountain and onto the docks, ready to board ships, only to learn that the generalísimo had ordered the port closed. Colonel Manuel María de Las Casas, the port's commandant, told them categorically that no vessel could leave until Miranda himself had sailed. Frustrated, fuming, Bolívar and his cohort awaited the generalísimo's arrival and considered how best to foil his escape.

On July 30, the evening that Miranda was to make his getaway, the dusty remains of the port of La Guaira bustled with fretful life. A suffocating heat was finally beginning to lift and, through the gaping doorways of improvised inns, one could see the gathering multitudes— pacing, nervous, eager to make their escape. The dim light of lanterns revealed the miserable lot: sailors whose ships had been grounded; soldiers stripped of their weapons; officers with no authority; worried mothers; weeping children. Out in the noisy streets, servants hauled trunks; mules stumbled through rubble; hulking stevedores offered their services. The sea, ruffled by a rising night breeze, began to grow agitated, and the ships bobbed upon it, trying the seamen's legs.

Miranda's baggage had been sent to La Guaira fifteen days before, and it awaited him now, on board the HMS *Sapphire*, the very ship that had borne Bolívar, flush with excitement, from London. Now, two years and a revolution later, the corvette's captain, Henry Haynes, was eager to board the old rebel and depart the ruins of the republic. As soon as the generalísimo arrived at the port commandant's house at seven o'clock that evening, Captain Haynes went to implore him to lift the embargo and board the ship at once. Miranda responded that he was much too exhausted to put to sea right away. Once inside Commandant Las Casas's quarters in the spacious, magnificent old Guipuzcoana building, he made himself comfortable. Las Casas invited him to stay for dinner, encouraging him to spend the night. Miranda was assured that the 22,000 pesos that had been promised were now aboard the *Sapphire*, in the hands of a British agent. All was ready for his departure, his host assured him, but there was absolutely no reason to leave before morning.

Miranda sat down to dinner with Las Casas and the governor of La Guaira, Miguel Peña. Joining them were Miranda's aide Carlos Soublette and Pedro Gual (nephew of Manuel Gual), his former secretary. They discussed the terms of the capitulation, with Gual stubbornly doubting that Spain would live up to them. Miranda rudely dismissed his concerns; Spain was too distracted by war to be able to keep a strong hold on Venezuela, he said gruffly. His hope in time was to ally with New Granada and reenter Caracas from Cartagena. With such dreams did the old generalísimo take to his bed, as Soublette lit his way and promised to wake him early in the morning.

But a nightmare of betrayals was about to descend on Miranda. Colonel Las Casas, in an attempt to ingratiate himself with his new master, had already communicated with Monteverde. The commandant knew that it would not be long before the Spanish arrived and took control of the port. He had confided as much to Governor Peña. But there were other schemes at work. Days before, Bolívar and his angry cohort had sought out Las Casas and Peña to persuade them to prevent Miranda from departing Venezuela. Now, with that deed accomplished and Miranda fast asleep in the other room, twelve conspirators—Bolívar among them—gathered in Las Casas's house to decide what to do. A passionate discussion followed, in which all the bitterness they had long harbored against Miranda was unleashed. They spoke of his contempt for his countrymen, his past service for France and England, the potential profits that awaited him on board the *Sapphire*. How was it that an English captain had emerged so conveniently out of the sea to rush Miranda to safety? How could anyone be sure that Miranda was not colluding with England and Spain now that they were allies? And why had the Marquis de Casa León (who had since become one of Monteverde's most prominent advisors) been asked to procure so hefty a monetary reward? Perhaps most puzzling of all: if Miranda trusted Monteverde to honor the terms of surrender, why was he unwilling to stay and see those terms enforced?

By three in the morning, the twelve had come to a decision. They would arrest their former leader, charge him with treason, and, with the men available to them in La Guaira, mount an attack on Monteverde. Las Casas seemed to go along with it. He put his troops on alert, soldiers surrounded the house, and one of the conspirators raced up the mountain to prepare the dungeon at the fortress of San Carlos. Bolívar and a cohort rousted Carlos Soublette from sleep and ordered him to take them to Miranda's bed. The generalísimo was in a deep slumber when Soublette rapped on the door. "Too soon!" Miranda growled, misunderstanding the aide's intent. But he quickly understood that the men at Soublette's side wanted his urgent attention. "Tell them to wait," Miranda said. Bolívar and Tomás Montilla stood by tranquilly, confident that enough guards had circled the building to secure it from any ambush. After a few minutes, the door swung open and they saw the generalísimo impeccably dressed and groomed, preternaturally calm. Without preamble or courtesies, Bolívar told him he was being taken prisoner. Miranda seized the hand in which Soublette held the lantern, and thrust it high, so as to study each of his captors' faces. "Ruffians! Ruffians!" he sighed, putting it down again. "All you know is how to make trouble." Without another word, he strolled to the front door of the Guipuzcoana building and out into the warm night, submitting easily to the guards who escorted him to the mountain fortress. It was early, July 31, before dawn.

As soon as he received confirmation that Miranda was chained to a wall in the dungeon of San Carlos, Governor Peña set out for Caracas to give Monteverde the news. But as night met the first light of day, he encountered a party of couriers in full Spanish regalia, riding in the other direction. The communiqué they carried, which the duplicitous Las Casas had been expecting, demanded a lockdown of the port. No ship, no traveler, no citizen of any nation could leave La Guaira without the express approval of Venezuela's new leader. The edict was a clear breach of the terms of surrender. They were all Monteverde's prisoners now.

Colonel Las Casas wasted no time in instructing his soldiers to lower the republican colors and raise the Spanish flag. "It's no small surprise to me," Captain Haynes snipped at Las Casas, "to see that in the course of a few hours you have changed loyalties completely." Haynes's ship, the *Sapphire*, eventually managed to slip away, along with Miranda's money. The USS *Matilda*, which had brought relief supplies after the earthquake, also made an escape, but not without vigorous rounds of cannon fire in its wake. Somehow, in the confusion, Bolívar, too, succeeded in evading capture. He hastily improvised a disguise and, in the cover of night, rode off into the trees—up, past the cliffs—toward Caracas.

Miranda was not so fortunate. After months in the impenetrable citadel of San Carlos, the visionary who had once dined with the likes of Jefferson and Washington, and romanced the empress of Russia, was taken from his vault and thrust into the dank crypts of Puerto Cabello, where he languished for another half year, contemplating the harsh mill of fortune. There, he wrote letters to everyone he could think of, railed bitterly against the perfidy of Monteverde's promises; and to get attention even claimed to be in the service of the English crown. On June 4, 1813, he was hustled onto a shabby little boat and shipped off to Morro Castle in Puerto Rico, and eventually to the dread rat-infested dungeon of La Carraca outside Cádiz, where he died three years later with an iron collar around his neck. His corpse was dumped in a mass grave, along with those of a cartload of common criminals.

THE THEME OF BETRAYAL IS never far from any story of revolution; deceit is at the very heart of radical upheaval. But history has not looked kindly on the events that unraveled on that early morning in La Guaira. For all the glory that would accrue to Bolívar, he would never be free of the stain of Miranda's fate. He had lured an old man to a revolution, and, after its failure, delivered him into enemy hands. There can be no doubt that it was a monstrous act of deception.

But there was no shortage of deceit on all sides. The patriots had been taken in by Miranda's swagger and braggadocio—had invested all their hopes in him—and they reacted now with all the fury of the betrayed. The leader they had trusted to guide them through the vicissitudes of revolution had turned out to be more comfortable with failure than with victory. Faltering and indecisive in the face of clear advantage, he always managed to be magnificent in the face of defeat. His fellow rebels believed they were seeing him now as he really was: a fraud who could only shrink from battle; a tinhorn general incapable of a strong will. Alexander Scott, a special consul from the United States, overseeing relief supplies after the earthquake, sent a report to Secretary of State James Monroe that reflected the common view: "Miranda by a shameful and treacherous capitulation surrendered the liberties of his country. Whether he was an agent of the British Government as he now states, or whether this conduct resulted from a base and cowardly heart, I cannot decide. . . . He is a brutal, capricious tyrant destitute of courage, honor, and abilities." Miranda's minions were equally scathing, labeling him an outright coward whose behavior, when not absurd, was nothing short of treasonous. To them, the secret negotiations had been unforgivable. The reward of money, obscene.

With time, historians have grown more generous toward Miranda. He is considered the "Proto-leader" or Grand Precursor—a visionary without whom Latin American dreams of independence might never have begun. Certainly, he was, as many biographers have depicted him, a master of promotion, far more skilled at plotting grand schemes than effecting their practical implementation. For him, as one biographer put it, the hatching of revolutions was a profession, and he performed it well. No one can doubt Miranda's love of country and his lifelong efforts to see it free. It is why, today, he is a beloved if complicated figure of Latin American history. His splendid memorial in the National Pantheon of Caracas is a triumph of resurrection.

But in Miranda's own time, Caracas received the news of his surrender with resounding invective; in Valencia and Coro, royalists celebrated in the streets. Bolívar, having lived and relived the anguish of his failure in Puerto Cabello, felt the general's defection all the more keenly. Had Bolívar suffered the torments of the damned—begged for an opportunity to clear his honor—only to see all hopes dashed with a craven signature? He could not forgive Miranda, and, unlike future generations of Venezuelans, he would never change his mind. To him, Miranda was "a loathsome leader, despot, arbitrary in the extreme, obsessed with his own ambitions and cravings, who either never understood the stakes or was all too happy to relinquish his country's liberty." Bolívar was so convinced that the generalísimo deserved to rot in Spain's dungeons that he never ceased to trumpet his part in the deed. Twenty years later, one of his aides, Belford H. Wilson, wrote to another aide, Daniel O'Leary: "To the last hour of his life he rejoiced of that event, which, he always asserted, was solely his own act, to punish the *treachery* and *treason* of Miranda in capitulating to an inferior force, and then intending to embark, himself knowing the capitulation would not be observed." Later, Wilson wrote again: "General Bolívar invariably added, that he wished to shoot Miranda as a traitor, but was withheld by others."

As ironic as it seems—and those days were rife with irony—when Bolívar slipped past the Spanish sentinels that night, into the heart of Caracas, he found himself seeking refuge in the house of the very man who had negotiated Miranda's surrender to Monteverde: the Marquis de Casa León. He had known the marquis and his brother since childhood and was confident he could find shelter there. He also knew that, for a leader of the republican effort, there was no safer place in all Caracas than the home of a Spaniard who had ingratiated himself with the crown.

The marquis welcomed him and immediately confided his whereabouts to a fellow Spaniard, Francisco Iturbe, who not only was an old family friend of Bolívar's, but an official of the crown and, so, on excellent terms with Monteverde. Iturbe was also a kind man with a large heart, and learning of Bolívar's predicament put all politics aside to approach the new governor and request a passport for the young lieutenant colonel. It was a bold request in a roiling time: Caracas was under siege, its houses raided for goods, its patriots snatched from their beds and marched off to prisons in chains. Conditions became so crowded in the prisons that, to make room for more, guards flung alkali against the walls, asphyxiating prisoners in their cells. The day after Miranda was taken prisoner, the proud canon Cortés de Madariaga was pulled from a fleeing boat and severely beaten. The author of the republic's constitution, Juan Germán Roscio, was bound hand and foot and thrust into stocks to be publicly humiliated. Six of the most respected republican leaders were tied to mules, dragged through the mud, and cast unceremoniously into the foul cells of La Guaira. Eventually, they were shipped to the dungeons of Cádiz along with a document that described them as "eight monsters—root and spring of all the new-fangled evils in America that have terrorized the world."

This was the Caracas through which Iturbe spirited Bolívar to a meeting with Monteverde. One thousand five hundred revolutionary leaders would be hauled off to prison in the time it would take for Spain to reestablish itself in the colony. If the earthquake had demolished the city, the reconquest would extinguish its spirit. Bolívar, too, might have been marched off to die in the dungeons of Puerto Cabello or Cádiz, but for the long and complicated relationships between his prominent family and the royalists of Caracas. As it was, Iturbe saved his life.

When Iturbe first spoke on Bolívar's behalf, offering himself as a guarantee, Monteverde waved him away, claiming to have in his hands a report that described Bolívar as a rabid patriot who had held Puerto

Cabello against Spain. But Iturbe persisted, bringing Bolívar into Monteverde's office and introducing him in the most passionate terms, "Here is the commander of Puerto Cabello, Don Simón Bolívar, for whom I have offered my personal guarantee. If he meets with any harm, I will suffer. I vouch for him with my life."

"All right," Monteverde replied, and then, eyeing Bolívar, told his secretary, "Issue this man a pass as a reward for services rendered the King when he imprisoned Miranda." Bolívar had pledged to be quiet and let Iturbe do all the talking, but he found it impossible now to hold his tongue. "I arrested Miranda because he was a traitor to his country, not in order to serve the King!" he said emphatically. Monteverde was taken aback and, in a pique, threatened to cancel the pass. But Iturbe gently insisted that the governor had already agreed to it, and then he added good-humoredly to the secretary, "Go on! Pay no attention to this scamp. Give him his passport and be done with it."

On August 27, Bolívar sailed for Curaçao on the Spanish schooner *Jesús, María y San José*, accompanied by a manservant, a few trunks, and his young uncles José Félix and Francisco Ribas. He had left all his property, or what remained of it, in the hands of his sister Juana. The royalists, drunk with success at their easy victory, rang down a final curtain on the first republic. As they applied themselves to the bloody work of purging the colony of its rebels, Monteverde had no notion that, in releasing Bolívar, he had unleashed the most dangerous rebel of all. It is said that whenever Bolívar's name was mentioned in the chaotic months that followed, the governor's face turned a deathly white.

CHAPTER 6

Glimpses of Glory

The art of victory is learned in failures.
—Simón Bolívar

Even as the troubled coast of his homeland receded in the distance, Bolívar began plotting his return. But the sea itself reminded him how tenuous his life had become: Storms bedeviled his journey, and when at last his ship dragged into the British port of Curaçao, he was met with yet more turmoil. The customs officials were singularly inhospitable; they confiscated his baggage, took his money, and held him liable for a debt owed the ship that had ferried him away from Puerto Cabello. Worse, he learned that Monteverde had violated the conditions of Miranda's surrender by appropriating all Venezuelan property owned by rebel leaders. His mines, his land, his haciendas were no longer his. Bolívar wrote to Iturbe, asking him to intercede on his behalf. He was beginning to see his straitened circumstances "with no little horror." His personal wealth had bought him a way into the revolution; he needed his properties in order to fund his way back.

Two months of enforced idleness on the dry, torrid shores of Curaçao had a profound effect on Bolívar. For the first time, he was in a foreign place that had few entertainments. In the sleepy capital of Willemstad, there were no salons with bracing conversations, no stimulat-

ing sights apart from the dazzling carmine sunsets, no men of wide
influence or matters of historical moment. Marooned with his fellow
soldiers, he had little to do but contemplate their failed attempt to defend the new republic: Why had it gone so wrong? What might have
been?

By late October, he had secured a loan from a friendly merchant
and, with his small band of warrior comrades, set sail for New Granada,
where, as they understood it, the flag of independence still waved. The
Bolívar who stepped off the boat in the port of Cartagena was an entirely different man. Tempered by war, sobered by defeat, he seemed
more deliberate, judicious, mature. It was as if all the missteps and
catastrophes of the past two years had brought the realities of liberation
into sharp relief. In light of this hard-won wisdom, he had begun to
organize his ideas and—following a rigorous discipline he would maintain for the rest of his life—set them down on paper. Along with the few
personal effects he carried onshore on that crisp November day in 1812
was the full awareness that, in the heat of a revolution, words were as
valuable as weapons.

On arrival in Cartagena, Bolívar lodged in a modest house on San
Agustín Chiquito Street. Diminutive, white, resplendent in the Caribbean sun, it was all of ten paces wide. The bedrooms and alcoves were
hung with hammocks; a tiny wood balcony opened onto the street
from one of the windows. The breeze, the blue vault of sky, the clear
nights strewn with stars, the vibrant port with its raucous comings and
goings—all served to fill the young traveler's heart with promise and
possibility.

In New Granada, the revolution was indeed alive, if chaotic—
defended by a number of vying independent governments. Granadans
wanted their freedoms, but had countless opinions on how to win them
and who should govern. The result was an unruly splintering of regions
and factions. *La patria boba*, they would come to call it, a republic of
fools. The city of Bogotá, under the government of President Antonio
Nariño, had declared itself the capital, and a loose federation had been
established at Tunja under the leadership of Camilo Torres, but the
fortified port city of Cartagena had risen against both, proclaimed its
sovereignty, and established its own constitution. Drunk on illusions

of grandeur, other communities, cities, provinces were following suit. The region had become a cauldron of discontent, a din of quibbling functionaries, a hotbed of pirates and opportunists. For all its wealth and abounding whiteness, New Granada was on the verge of a civil war. Rather than be discouraged by this ruinous state of affairs, Bolívar was eager to join it. He and his fellow Venezuelan revolutionaries—his uncle José Felix Ribas, his firebrand neighbor Antonio Nicolás Briceño, the Carabaño and Montilla brothers—assumed that their military experience would be in demand.

They were right. Bolívar and his companions were received warmly by the government of Cartagena. Its twenty-four-year-old president, Manuel Rodríguez Torices, was in urgent need of seasoned officers, not only because the Spanish army had installed itself in the nearby port of Santa Marta, but because Torices needed to temper the ravening ambitions of his own commanding general, the French pirate Pierre Labatut. He directed Labatut to appoint Bolívar and the others to prominent positions.

But General Labatut knew these men too well. Like them, he was a veteran of Miranda's revolutionary forces. He knew about Bolívar's rout at Puerto Cabello; knew about Miranda's harsh estimation of the young colonel. A sergeant in Napoleon's army before he became an adventurer on the high seas, Labatut had mediocre credentials as a soldier. But he had been a favorite of Miranda's, and had been present in La Guaira during the desperate last days of the republic. Standing on the deck of the USS *Matilda* as it pushed off from the frantic port, eluding enemy cannons, he had had plenty of opportunity to look back and contemplate the fate of Miranda. Labatut was immediately suspicious of Bolívar, and certainly he had every reason to be jealous: here was a Creole aristocrat who had managed to charm the callow president—who, it was rumored, was even writing presumptuous letters to President Antonio Nariño in Bogotá and to Camilo Torres in Tunja. Labatut was in no rush to help launch Bolívar's career. On December 1, 1812, he assigned him to the remote outpost of Barranca, an insignificant little town on the banks of the Magdalena River.

Bolívar had indeed written passionate appeals to Nariño and Torres, as well as to the congress in Tunja, but before leaving to take up his post in Barranca, he turned to animate a far more crucial audience: the ordinary Granadan citizen. Hoping to persuade the people that their struggle was intimately tied to Venezuela's—that it would take a united front of all colonies to eject Spain from America once and for all—he spent the next two weeks on a frenzy of publications. First, he published General Monteverde's official proclamations, which served as clear indictments: the Spaniard had broken every promise he had ever made. Then he arranged for the release of a testimonial he had been mulling since Curaçao. He called it *A Manifesto from the Venezuelan Colonel Simón Bolívar to the Citizens of New Granada*. It was disseminated on December 15, a few days after Bolívar's departure from the city.

The Cartagena Manifesto, as it became known, stands as one of the great documents of Latin American history. In it, Bolívar departed radically from revolutionaries before him who had echoed French or North American ideas in ponderous, stuffy prose. It is hard to overestimate the effect that his words had on the leaders of New Granada, and, as the document began traveling from hand to hand, on the region's people. Bolívar's words were muscular, direct; his manner of thinking, fresh and riveting. He made the language come alive.

"I am," it began, "a son of unhappy Caracas." With persuasive logic, he went on to analyze the loss of Venezuela, explaining why the fledgling republic had failed: it had been hopelessly fragmented by federalist divisions; ruined for lack of a strong, unified army; there was, of course, the earthquake, the obstructionist clergy, an overreliance on paper money. In the main, its leaders had grown too tolerant, sloppy, corrupt. They had never established a firm, undisputed authority. "Each conspiracy was followed by an easy acquittal followed by another conspiracy," he explained. The first sign of the republic's weakness had come early, when the original junta had failed to subdue the feisty city of Coro, from which all royalist opposition had sprung. Had the republic's leaders been truly assertive—had its institutions been unified and disciplined rather than separate and fractious—things might have turned out differently. But in New Granada, he argued, republicans now had the opportunity to set history straight: Unite, he implored; be firm. Invade Venezuela. Root out the Spaniards, who were a cancer on the Americas, who only stood to get stronger if left to their own devices.

Only then would New Granada be free: "Coro is to Caracas as Caracas is to all America," he wrote with a tidy algebraic logic. In short: do now to Venezuela what Venezuela should have done to Coro in the first place, for all South Americans are linked by a common past and a common destiny. It was a passionate appeal with the clear tenor of truth. In time, it would be recognized as the cornerstone of Bolívarian thought.

As resolute as the tree to which the poet Andrés Bello later compared him, Bolívar sent down roots, weathered storms, grew stronger. There is no question that he learned richly from his mistakes. How else does a soldier untrained in the art of war—a rebel unschooled in the rule of nations—undertake to harness a revolution? Only months before, Bolívar had been a humiliated man seeking revenge on his failed commander. Now, given this bridge to a new chance, he decided to take nothing for granted. He set out for the tiny town of Barranca—however insignificant and obscure the assignment—determined to make his mark, convinced he could turn random fortune to revolutionary advantage.

By then he had learned a great deal about New Granadans. He had walked the ancient streets of Cartagena, sat in its colorful plazas, mingled with its residents. He had established what he could about rebel movements in the countryside. He had made a point to get to know rich Creoles who owned property in strategic points along the Magdalena, and who might be helpful to a commander's cause. He had met with landowners from the Valle de Upar, who impressed him with their revolutionary ardor; they offered the young officer their support, not only moral but in livestock, mules, and supplies. It was in socializing this way that he came to know Anita Lenoit, the angelically lovely seventeen-year-old daughter of a French merchant in town. Lenoit was immediately enchanted with the wiry, electrifying young Venezuelan. She wrote a letter on his behalf to María Concepción Loperena, a wealthy widow with political clout in the provinces, and implored her to help Bolívar's cause. Legend has it that Bolívar had a brief but passionate dalliance with the comely Lenoit, and that—desperately in love—the delicate, dewy-eyed girl turned up in his military compound weeks later, having eagerly followed him upriver.

Arriving in Barranca, near where the mighty Magdalena makes its final approach to the sea, Bolívar learned from the scant seventy men under his command that enemy troops had consolidated their hold on the river; republicans on the coast had lost all communication with republicans in the interior. Bolívar immediately set about recruiting more troops. This was hardly an easy enterprise. The only men willing to be recruited came from the dregs of society: slum dwellers, runaway slaves, out-of-work peasants, near-naked tribesmen; they were untrained, undisciplined, weaponless, shoeless, with little more than a pair of tattered trousers, a flea-ridden blanket, a frayed hat. Nevertheless, Bolívar took them on, trained them, fed them; and it was with such troops that he set out against the soldiers of the crown.

His instinct was to take a bold offensive, and with rapid strategic attacks dislodge the enemy from the river. But General Labatut expressly forbade anything of the kind. Poised to lead an expedition against the Spanish in Santa Marta, the general instructed Bolívar to stay where he was and await further instruction. Bolívar had little faith in Labatut's abilities; he suspected that the former pirate simply wanted all the glory for himself. He decided to countermand him. On December 21, after building the necessary boats, Bolívar began quietly mobilizing two hundred soldiers upriver. They took off on ten *champanes* (large dugouts with straw roofs) toward Tenerife, where five hundred royalists were garrisoned. As they approached, Bolívar sent ahead one of his officers to offer the commandant a chance to surrender peacefully. When the Spaniard scoffed, Bolívar rounded the corner with all two hundred men and they leapt ashore, rifles blazing. Terrified, the royalists abandoned the fort in wild disorder, scattering into the forest. It was a stunning victory. Tenerife was a major depository of Spanish ammunition and equipment, and Bolívar appropriated every last sword and musket ball. He summoned the townspeople to the riverbank, scolded them for supporting Spaniards, and insisted they pledge allegiance to Cartagena. "Wherever the Spanish empire rules," he told them, "there rules death and desolation!" Giving them a stirring lesson in their liberties, he enlisted hundreds to the cause. The following day, fortified by superior arms and fresh troops, he headed to the next enclave on that river, the vigorously republican city of Mompox. News of Bolívar's valor preceded him. He was greeted with joy, a festive ball, and a new infusion of recruits.

Bolívar didn't linger. He had learned a lesson from Miranda's indecisions. He deployed again immediately, with an avid army of five hundred, to Guamal, Banco, Tamalameque, sweeping enemy guerrillas from the river, alarming them with surprise raids. It was no easy task. The water was infested with crocodiles, the land with snakes; the way was a tangle of green, more likely traveled by hand and ax than by foot alone. As he tramped through the grassy swamps, startling the royalists in their camps, they were so shocked by his army's ferocity and determination that they fled their garrisons, leaving behind their ships, weapons, and prisoners. Bolívar incorporated them all into a stronger war machine. In the valleys east of the river, the contacts he had made in Cartagena delivered on their promises; the widow Loperena and other wealthy landowners contributed mules, provisions, and sturdy clothing for his troops. He moved quickly, hardly stopping, and, everywhere he went, the enemy panicked at his approach. In the Cartagena Manifesto, Bolívar had written, "every defensive action only brings harm and ruin to those who wage it." Basing his strategy on a brash, unremitting offensive that was entirely new to the revolution, he moved swiftly over five hundred punishing kilometers; by January 8, 1813, he controlled the entire length of the river. The operation had taken him fifteen days. Soon after reporting this success to the congress of Cartagena, he liberated the city of Ocaña, a natural staging area for an incursion over the mountains into Venezuela.

By now Bolívar's name was known and admired throughout New Granada. "I was born in Caracas," he later noted, "but my fame was born in Mompox." As General Labatut marched into Santa Marta with his marauding troops—largely adventurers—sacking, plundering, and sending its governor running for other shores, Labatut learned he would have to share the glory. The general accused Bolívar of insubordination and called for a court-martial, even making a trip to the capital to see that it was carried out, but President Torices paid him no mind. No one could doubt Bolívar's military prowess. He had opened nearly three hundred miles of the region's main shipping route and freed the plains to its west, for which the independent governments of Cartagena, Bogotá, and Tunja could only thank him. A mere four months after he had been cast from Venezuela, wretched and humbled, he had joined another revolution, devised an audacious strategy, thwarted his commanding officer, and risen to honor and acclaim.

MEANWHILE, IN CARACAS, MONTEVERDE HAD succeeded in cowing the population with months of unbridled violence. No measure of fragility or infirmity could exempt republicans from his cruelty. From summer's swelter to winter's damp, his victims perished in dungeons, steadily making room for more. As the mill of souls ground on, Spaniards confiscated the Creoles' land and possessions and divvied them up among themselves. An official who arrived from Madrid, convinced he could eradicate the unrest by installing a new policy of tolerance, was so appalled by Monteverde's reign of terror that he gave up his mission in despair.

The *Gaceta de Caracas*, once the mouthpiece of revolution, was back in Spanish hands, and it reproached its readers roundly: "Happiness. Prosperity. Liberty. Three Hundred Years of Slavery. . . . Go on. Be honest: When were you more enslaved? More miserable? When were you more wretched, more immolated by hunger? When did you ever live with such fear, forced to flee to the hills to avoid being pressed to serve as yet one more victim in that disgraceful sacrifice? And why? And for what? For words. Empty words." A shrill propaganda machine swung into action, denouncing the patriots' "pompous and extravagant promises"—their childishly irresponsible behavior. Even worse, according to the Spanish, was that they had insulted the king by seeking help from Great Britain. To thwart all future repetition of this madness—to save the Creoles from themselves—Monteverde gave his officers full rein to mete out a crippling punishment.

Monteverde, in fact, was never meant to be the man in charge. Spain had dispatched Fernando Miyares to take over as captain-general of Caracas. But Monteverde, appointing himself "commander general of the army of pacification," had managed to scare off Miyares from the moment the captain-general had landed in Maracaibo. A coward by nature, Miyares retreated to Puerto Rico, afraid to enter the bloody fray.

Monteverde kept Miyares at bay with promises that he would hand over the command when Venezuela was fully pacified, and Miyares, happy to let someone else do the fighting, allowed himself to be duped. His more intrepid officers, Field Marshal Manuel Cajigal and Brigadier General Manuel del Fierro, could only chafe with frustration, but eventually even they were won over by Monteverde. After months of fruitless waiting, Miyares realized that he was little more than an object of ridicule, and slunk back to Spain, leaving the colony to suffer the excesses of an illegitimate regime.

Monteverde cannot take all the blame for the cruelty and rapine under his rule, but there is no doubt that he turned a blind eye to his generals' atrocities and deliberately ignored the laws of conquest spelled out by the constitution of Cádiz. There is no doubt, too, that his officers reveled in bloodlust. In the plains that surrounded Caracas, unchecked by higher power, Eusebio Antoñanzas, governor of Cumaná, had unloosed a wanton truculence, ordering his troops to sack towns, rob the innocent, kill anyone who got in their way. The terrible Antoñanzas was often the first to throw a flaming torch into an unsuspecting house, lancing the frantic family as it fled the fire. Terrible, too, were the deeds of his lieutenant Antonio Zuazola, who commanded his men to slit prisoners' throats, lop off their ears, and wear human trophies as decorations. No one could deny the chilling effect of seeing a Spanish soldier ride by with ears flapping from his hat, or the sight of a body part nailed to a patriot's door. Zuazola would order his men to sew prisoners back to back, flay the skin from their feet, then force them to hobble together over broken glass. One pregnant woman who came to beg for her husband's life was bound and beheaded; when the unborn child began to wriggle in her belly, they stopped it with a bayonet. Twelve thousand Creoles died as brutally. "If it were possible," Spanish general del Fierro wrote home from Caracas, "it would be best to exterminate every American from the face of this earth." Even Franciscan priests were seen galloping through republican neighborhoods dressed more like Tatar warriors than men of God, urging their fellow soldiers to "spare no one over the age of seven!"

If this uncurbed savagery served to boost the royalist morale, it also inflamed Americans. In outlying areas, a republican backlash gained swift momentum. But it did so in a highly fragmented manner as the struggle for independence became the work of *caudillos*, leaders who fought on the strength of their regional charisma rather than with any concept of a greater cause. In January of 1813, as Bolívar was purging the Magdalena River of royalist garrisons, Santiago Mariño, a patriot thousands of miles away, mounted a campaign to liberate eastern Venezuela. Within six months, Mariño would free the historic provinces of Barcelona and Cumaná, becoming their de facto leader. Under him were equally ambitious young warriors: the brave mulatto colonel Manuel Piar, who had won significant gains against the Spaniards; José Francisco Bermúdez and his brother Bernardo, who had shown extraordinary mettle at pivotal points of the revolution. In New Granada, too, there were many who harbored grand aspirations. Pierre Labatut would eventually break with Cartagena and declare himself president of the port city of Santa Marta. The young Torices continued to rule Cartagena by hiring pirates to fight off anyone who threatened his walled city. There was President Nariño in Bogotá, President Torres in Tunja. In Pamplona, a province that bordered on Venezuela, Colonel Manuel del Castillo—a well-born Granadan with a large ego and grand designs, had already made it abundantly clear that he answered to no one.

Colonel Castillo, along with his paltry three hundred troops, was getting ready to defend New Granada against an impending invasion by Monteverde. As soon as he learned that Bolívar had penetrated the interior as far as Ocaña, he sent a messenger asking for Bolívar's help. Bolívar demurred, replying that he needed Cartagena's approval. In truth, he was seeking approval for something else: the ability to lead his troops over the border into Venezuela. For weeks now, he had prepared his men to invade his homeland. If he was going to fight Monteverde's army, which had already spilled over into the Granadan valley of Cúcuta, he was not going to do it under someone else's command.

There were other reasons Bolívar needed to buy time. His army was experiencing rampant desertions. Many of the recruits Bolívar had gathered on his triumphant march up the Magdalena had lost their enthusiasm for warfare, either because the booty fell short of their expectations or because they had no desire to risk their lives to liberate lands beyond their own. Bolívar left his army in charge of his uncle,

José Félix Ribas, while he traveled to Mompox, appropriating munitions and recruiting fresh troops from both sides of the river. By February 9, he had increased his ranks to four hundred good men; President Torices instructed him to join them to Castillo's three hundred and march against the Spanish in Cúcuta. Only then would he be willing to listen to Bolívar's request to take his soldiers into Venezuela.

Wanting to please his benefactor, Bolívar left for Cúcuta immediately with his army, cutting a path to the high, windswept cordilleras, where desolate plateaus stretched as far as the eye could see. His soldiers carried what food they could; there were no villages along the way, nor any sign of human habitation, except for the odd hut on the mountainside. Few braved the punishing journey easily, for they were river dwellers, born and bred in the languid tropics, unprepared for the cold and vertiginous terrain. They made their way through February rain, across slippery rock, and deep into humid canyons, edging along cliffs where one false step would hurl them to sure death. In Alto de la Aguada they caught a glimpse of the royalist army, guarding a high pass as Monteverde mobilized his invasion of New Granada. Bolívar decided to send out a spy with a letter containing the lie that Castillo and his republican forces were advancing from Pamplona. The spy was captured, the letter confiscated, and the Spanish general Ramón Correa took the bait. He abandoned the pass and headed for Pamplona, thinking he would surprise Castillo en route. When Bolívar fell on his rear, the Spanish scattered in stupefied retreat. Correa limped his way back to Cúcuta to regroup his forces.

In time, Bolívar was joined by Castillo, and together they pressed ahead, until by dawn of February 28—the last Sunday of Lent—their troops crossed the Zulia River, just west of Cúcuta. General Correa was in church, attending Mass at nine in the morning, when one of his officers burst in to warn him of the approaching patriot army. Hastily, he rallied his troops and attempted to take the offensive. The Battle of Cúcuta was bloody, uneven—Correa's troops were double the force of Bolívar's—but just as the republican effort seemed all but lost, Bolívar ordered Ribas's division to make a full-bayonet, uphill charge. The bout was rabid, quick, relentless, inflicting countless casualties; in the skirmish, General Correa fell to the ground with a wound to his head. That brazen charge—a desperate act in the face of superior force—succeeded in stunning the Spaniards. They fled that border city in alarm, leaving Bolívar in control of a vast supply of food and ammunition, and a million pesos in merchandise, which the rich royalists of Maracaibo had transported to Cúcuta for safekeeping. At the cost of only two dead and fourteen wounded, Bolívar had secured New Granada's freedom.

The Granadans wasted no time in thanking him. Bolívar was lauded in Cartagena, Tunja, and Bogotá. President Torices awarded him the title of honorary citizen and he was promoted to brigadier general. The young Venezuelan had met every challenge, conquered every obstacle, including a raging fever as he had scaled the heights of the cordillera. Within a few months, in a rare show of solidarity, Camilo Torres and Antonio Nariño met in Tunja to confirm the Union of New Granada and to proclaim its independence from Spain.

Even so, Bolívar felt his work had hardly begun. Venezuela was yet to be free; Spain had yet to be ejected from the continent. Restless and anxious, he dispatched the tall, elegant Ribas to meet with Torres and Nariño, and argue the case for a Venezuelan invasion. In the interim, he rallied his soldiers, paid them with the booty he had captured, and then, superseding his command, led them across the border into Venezuela. Stopping in the rugged Andean town of San Antonio, he spoke to them of greater sacrifices. "Loyal republicans!" he appealed fervidly, "America awaits its liberty and salvation from your hands!" The fortunes of New Granada, Bolívar told them, were tied inextricably to those of its neighbor. He had believed it from the beginning and he believed it now. "If one country wears chains," he wrote days later in an impassioned letter to President Torres, "the other is equally enslaved. Spanish rule is a gangrene that starts in one place and then overwhelms everything else, unless it is hewn off like an infected limb."

But the prospect of liberating a foreign land did not sit well with all his men, most notably Colonel Castillo and his able sergeant major Francisco de Paula Santander. Although Castillo had been thrilled by Bolívar's victory at Cúcuta and said so in early reports, he was bitterly opposed to engaging Granadan soldiers in Venezuela. More, Castillo had been stung by Bolívar's promotion; he considered himself the exclusive commander of his troops, and now President Torices had named

Bolívar chief of the whole liberating expedition. A deep fissure entered Bolívar's ranks—a rancorous envy—and it would have profound implications for his future.

For two months, Castillo worked to undermine Bolívar, making no effort to mask his pique. He bickered about rank, lodged formal complaints about the new brigadier general's allocation of the Cúcuta booty, railed to anyone who would listen about his "mad undertaking" to free Venezuela. On May 7, when Bolívar finally received approval to march as far as Mérida and Trujillo, Castillo patently refused to go. An invasion of Venezuela, he argued, was anathema to his principles. Bolívar tried to calm him, sending a friendly letter as a palliative. But Castillo was determined to thwart the action. He resigned abruptly, taking one hundred of his men with him, and left the rest of his troops under the command of his junior officer Francisco Santander.

Santander, too, was a proud Granadan, put off by the brash, willful Bolívar. At first, he ignored the brigadier's order to cross into Venezuela and stood fast in defiance. An angry Bolívar confronted the mutinous officer. "March at once!" he barked. "You have no choice in the matter! March! Either you shoot me or, by God, I will certainly shoot you." Santander obeyed, but he never forgot the humiliation. A lifetime and many victories later, the insult would continue to gall him. For Bolívar, the clashes with Castillo and Santander would mark the beginning of a long struggle with his subordinates. He would learn in time that for every revolutionary brother there was a ready traitor; and for all his vision of a unified Colombia, there were small-minded obstructionists, happy to lord over their tiny turfs.

NOT ALL HIS OFFICERS WERE so perverse. For the time being at least, Bolívar could count on men like José Félix Ribas in his showy red cap, or the fearless youth Atanasio Girardot, or even his hot-tempered old neighbor Antonio Nicolás Briceño; or stalwarts like Rafael Urdaneta, who would be with him until the last and wrote him now to say, "General, if two men are enough to liberate the fatherland, I am ready to go with you." With these and a small "liberating army" of five hundred, he set out to mount a swift, decisive campaign that would surprise the enemy at every turn and spill like quicksilver toward Caracas.

Anyone with the slightest judgment would have seen how foolhardy an operation it was. As soon as he was given the approval to march, Bolívar wrote to the newly installed president of the union, Antonio Nariño, to tell him about the true condition of his troops. Many were hungry, fevered by plague, in tatters. Some had deserted. Others, in distant garrisons, hadn't been paid in weeks and had to beg handouts from the locals. Meat was rare. Rice nonexistent. Weapons faulty. The march to Trujillo promised to tax his soldiers further, Bolívar added, taking them over difficult, unyielding terrain. They could count on no food along the way: farmers, devastated by the war, had not planted; ranchers had lost their livestock to marauders. He pleaded with the president to issue him the badly needed ammunition and funds. "I will await the result of this request when I get to Trujillo," he ended confidently. "The campaign will depend on it."

But when Bolívar's army swept down from the Andes into the green vale of Mérida on May 23, they found no enemy to oppose them. The Spaniards, having heard of Bolívar's successes in New Granada and expecting a much larger force, had evacuated the city. As Bolívar entered Mérida, its residents, ardent partisans of independence, swarmed down the road to greet him, and, leading them with a broad smile, was the former president of the republic Cristóbal Mendoza. The city was hung with bright bunting, Bolívar was proclaimed "Liberator," and six hundred recruits signed on to his cause, many of them sons of the region's aristocratic families. A good number were royalist defectors, leading one Spanish commandant to posit that they had been stealth revolutionaries all along—a veritable Trojan horse.

To lead the new troops from Mérida, Bolívar installed Vicente Campo Elías, a Spaniard by birth who so loathed his native land that he had murdered some of his own relatives and vowed that when he had finished killing every last Spaniard in Venezuela, he would turn his sword on himself and end the accursed race. The wrath against the colonizer was at such an extreme within Bolívar's ranks, in fact, that for some of his officers killing Spaniards became a goal in itself. This had not occurred in a vacuum: in nearby Barinas, the king's commandant had just posted a Royal Order that called for the extermination of all avowed republicans—without exceptions. Nicolás Briceño, who had once channeled aggression into lawsuits and pitchfork assaults against his old neighbor and cousin-in-law Bolívar, now went on a fanatical rampage. He took off on a bloody campaign through the mountainous terrain with his 143 soldiers—men who had never been on a horse, never carried weapons, whose only qualification to recommend them was an all-consuming racial fury. In the town of San Cristóbal, Briceño published a broadside exhorting slaves to murder their Spanish masters, and then, to prove his point, had two quiet, unassuming Spaniards decapitated on the square. He sent one of the heads—along with a letter signed in the victim's blood—to Castillo. The other he dispatched to Bolívar.

Bolívar was horrified. He denounced it as "the work of Satan" and sent an officer to rein in Briceño. But by then Briceño was listening to no one. Like other renegade caudillos, he saw himself as the anointed liberator. "The Devil Briceño," as he subsequently became known, declared that any ordinary soldier who presented him with twenty Spanish heads would become a second lieutenant; thirty made him a lieutenant; fifty, a full-fledged captain. But two months later Briceño was overcome by royalist forces, taken prisoner along with eight other patriot leaders, and shot. The news came as a great blow to Bolívar. He had disapproved of Briceño's conduct, but no one could fault the man's patriotism and passion for liberty. He had waged an unconditional war against the Spanish and, for a while, succeeded in terrifying them. His ruthlessness made a deep and lasting impression on Bolívar. He needed to turn that angry energy into a unified war machine.

On June 14, Bolívar's army liberated the province of Trujillo much as it had liberated Mérida: he ordered his spies to penetrate the royalist camp and persuade the enemy that his troops were fierce, indestructible, and numbered in the thousands; the Spaniards fled at the prospect of his advance. At nine o'clock on that warm summer morning, the Liberator's army rode into that ancient city without so much as a sword wagged against them. The republicans received the hero with unalloyed joy, sending their pretty adolescent daughters to lay wreaths of laurel on his head.

Bolívar was well aware that he was waging psychological warfare. Surprise and deception had been his ablest adjutants, striking fear into the enemy wherever he went. His soldiers, like him, were self-taught; they had learned war as they went, in the roar and clang of battle. Some were as young as thirteen, filled with nothing so much as a child's sense of invincibility. They understood that they were inferior to their Spanish counterparts in every way—in weapons, training, and experience—but they were also discovering that, with stealth, ingenuity, and swift guerrilla strikes, they could confuse their opponents. There was another advantage: the Spanish were an imported population and, therefore, limited in number; Americans, the thinking went, were a boundless resource, and vastly more acclimated to the terrain. In the end, nothing bred confidence like victory, and rebel victories were growing exponentially, lending the sheen of indomitability to what had once seemed an impossible venture.

After an exultant arrival in Trujillo, Bolívar sat down to think through a strategy he had had in mind for some time. In Mérida, he had complained about the enemy's disdain for rules of war, railing vociferously against their summary execution of eight republican prisoners of war, including Briceño. "We've run out of goodness," he had announced, vowing to avenge those murders. "Now that the enemy has forced us to a deadly war, we will eradicate them from America, and this land will finally be purged of the monsters that infest it. Our hatred will be implacable, and our war will be to the death." It had been just another bit of battlefield rhetoric, a timely flourish, but now, on the occasion of his victory in Trujillo, he considered writing it into law. All night he pondered it, and by dawn, he had made a decision: Miranda's revolution and the first republic had failed because of a sloppy tolerance—a lack of mettle. He would not let it happen again. Before daybreak on the 15th, he called a council of war to announce his new edict. In it, all Spaniards in Venezuela would be targets in a war of extermination, unless they renounced King Ferdinand and fought on the American side. Americans who had once fought for the royals, on the other hand, would face no punishment. The language was brutally clear:

SPANIARDS AND CANARY ISLANDERS:
COUNT ON DEATH, EVEN IF YOU HAVE BEEN INDIFFERENT.
AMERICANS: COUNT ON LIFE, EVEN IF YOU HAVE BEEN GUILTY.

Not one member on his war council opposed the decree. Indeed, they all roundly approved it. Persuaded that he had found a way to unite mavericks like Briceño and harness their rage, Bolívar signed the document that very day. For all the clarity he thought it would give the war, the ultimate consequence of the decree was a storm of violence.

History has not been kind to Bolívar's decision to proclaim war to the death. Some historians have called it an outright abomination. Others have said it was a rash act, impetuous in the extreme, and unnecessary. United States politicians would later use it to decry the bloody, Jacobin nature of Bolívar's revolution, and the inherent barbarity of the Spanish American people. Still others have rushed to Bolívar's defense, claiming that his was the logical response to three hundred years of inhuman oppression and the deadly Royal Order against the patriots that Spain had just decreed. Perhaps more persuasive is the argument that Bolívar's edict tried to make clear that what was being fought was not a civil struggle but an uncompromising war against an outside invader; with it, the ejection of Spain became a manifest goal and Americans—regardless of race or ideology—were the heroes. "Either Americans allow themselves to be exterminated gradually," Bolívar argued, "or they undertake to destroy an evil race that, while it breathes, works tirelessly toward our annihilation."

The response was immediate. After Bolívar's proclamation, hundreds of royalist troops defected to the republican side; wherever the liberating army marched, it found soldiers willing to join it. Under the slack leadership of Miranda, as Bolívar knew very well, republican troops had deserted in droves, betting on the likelihood that if they defected and fought for Spain, they would be spared Spanish cruelties, and, if they were captured by lax, softhearted patriots, they would likely be pardoned. Now there was no doubt about it: Bolívar's patriots were forgiving no one. It may have been a horrifying declaration, but, for the short run, it worked: it worried the royalists and fortified the republican will. In the long run, however—as history would show all too vividly—it engulfed Venezuela in a sea of blood.

WITH HIS VICTORIES IN MÉRIDA and Trujillo, Bolívar's campaign was technically over. His bosses in New Granada had given him explicit orders to stop; he was not to proceed to Caracas. But when Bolívar learned that his fellow republican in the east Santiago Mariño was marching toward the capital with a force of five thousand, he could not restrain his impulse to best him. In a letter to Camilo Torres, he wrote with extraordinary frankness, "I worry that our illustrious brothers-in-arms will liberate our capital before we can share the glory. But we will fly, and I hope no liberator will tread the ruins of Caracas before me."

By the end of June, Bolívar and his army were on the march again, headed over a perilous mountain route toward the plains of Barinas. When Monteverde heard of it, he went south to meet them. Although the Spanish were greater in numbers and better disciplined, the republicans proved more nimble. Colonel Ribas won a decisive victory against a Spanish division on the outskirts of Niquitao, descending from glacial peaks to engage them in hand-to-hand combat. He took more than four hundred prisoners and succeeded in drafting them all to the republican cause. Only eighty miles south, Bolívar rode across the dusty plains of Barinas in a sweltering heat. He made a rapid, preemptive strike on the city of Barinas and took it on July 6, forcing the Spanish into a frenzied northern retreat. Without delay, he chased after them and, as he went, joined forces with Ribas and Girardot. The speed and audacity of republican movements confounded the enemy completely. In skirmish after skirmish, the patriots emerged victorious, so that in the course of a hundred miles, they were able to scatter two divisions and send the Spaniards flying for their lives. Within ten days, they had destroyed, imprisoned, or disbanded five thousand enemy troops.

Bolívar celebrated his thirtieth birthday in Araure, stopping briefly to raise a celebratory glass before he set out to face Monteverde. Even as he prepared to go, he learned that a fearless fourteen-year-old soldier, Gabriel Picón, had flung himself on a Spanish cannon and was in the battle hospital, fatally wounded. In a gesture Bolívar would repeat countless times as such sacrifices mounted, he paused to write to the boy's father. "The glorious hero who spilled his blood on the battlefield today is not dead, nor is it feared he will die; but if he has ceased to exist, he will live forever in the hearts of fellow patriots." Tucked into that letter was a short poem—the only verse Bolívar is known to have written.

Its closing line: "Pause now your weeping to remember/Your love of country is the primary thing."

Joined now by Urdaneta and Girardot, Bolívar's improvised legion of fifteen hundred finally met Monteverde in the grasslands outside Valencia. In every move, Monteverde had found himself doing too little too late, and this encounter would be no exception. Twelve hundred of his men lined up to defend the road to Valencia but, although they were superbly trained, they were too few—rapidly outnumbered and easily outflanked. Bolívar's infantry leapt onto his cavalry's horses and—two or more men to an animal—charged deep into enemy lines. Once inside, they sprang from the horses and attacked the regiment from within. The tactic worked. It was a long and bloody battle, but the lunge at the enemy heart inflicted punishing losses. When Bolívar's triumphant army finally entered Valencia, Monteverde had already fled, cutting a desperate path to the fortress at Puerto Cabello.

Caracas was next to fall. Four days later, the Marquis de Casa Léon—who had gone from serving Miranda to serving Monteverde when winds of war required it—now met with Bolívar to finalize the Spanish surrender. With him was Bolívar's old family friend Francisco Iturbe, the man who had negotiated Bolívar's safe passage only a year before. The ironies were rich. The marquis had harbored the once fugitive Bolívar in his house; Iturbe had saved his life. For all the blood that had been shed between republicans and royalists, certain family friendships still held. The meeting was cordial. And so, in the very halls where Miranda had submitted to the royalists, the royalists now submitted to Bolívar.

In return for the peaceful surrender of Caracas, Bolívar offered the Spaniards amnesty, repealing the harsh words of the past. He assured them their safety; granted passports to those who requested them, including soldiers; and gave them permission to emigrate with their families and possessions, even their sidearms. His motive in this, he relayed in a letter to the municipality of Caracas, was "to show the world that even in victory the noble Americans reject rancor and offer mercy." To President Camilo Torres in New Granada he wrote, "Here, your Excellency, is the fulfillment of my promise to liberate my country. We undertook no battle we could not win."

But in Caracas, there was no one to receive Casa León and Iturbe when they returned with Bolívar's promises in hand. Monteverde, who had holed up in Puerto Cabello, had delegated all power to the governor Manuel del Fierro; and Fierro, in turn, in a breathtaking act of cowardice, had abandoned the city without so much as ratifying the treaty he had personally called for. He rushed to La Guaira in a panic, as did a thundering horde of six thousand royalists. Slipping out under cover of night, Fierro embarked secretly and set sail for Curaçao. The scene at La Guaira as he departed was raucous, tumultuous: the Spanish so desperate to board ships that they elbowed their way onto canoes only to be capsized in a rough black sea. Eventually fifty ships ferried them to safety. In Caracas, where an unforgiving heat choked the city, the royalists left behind had no recourse but to abandon their possessions, cast off the clothes they had heaped on their backs, and try to make a swift passage overland to the fortress of Puerto Cabello.

Bolívar entered Caracas on August 6, 1813. An assiduous student of Julius Caesar, he knew how a conqueror should make his appearance. He arranged to be met at the gates of Caracas as Caesar's chariot had been met in Rome—by radiant girls in the flower of adolescence, dressed in white, bearing laurels, and casting garlands. In Caesar's case, the chariot had been drawn by white horses; in Bolívar's, it was drawn by the daughters of the most prominent families of Caracas. A good number of the city's thirty thousand residents were there, lining the roads in a noisy throng. The Admirable Campaign, as the past six months of war came to be called, was celebrated as heartily as a beleaguered population could manage. There were rounds of artillery, a din of cathedral bells, Te Deums to liberty, and, at the end, the title of Dictator and Liberator was bestowed on the returning hero.

No one could doubt that Bolívar's victories were astounding. He had started eight months before with fewer than five hundred men and bested Spain's formidable war machine. In contrast, Napoleon, with a colossal army of 500,000, was limping out of Spain at about the same time, on his way to losing the war in Europe. As Bolívar rode in with his exuberant mustache and dazzling smile, stepping off his cart to embrace residents of his native city, he was as loved as he ever would be. Colorful silks hung from balconies, horns blared a joyful noise, roses rained from windows, people clamored to get a glimpse of the great man and his liberating army: the roar of jubilation was heard for miles around. So glorious was the reception—so realized the dream—that Bolívar could not restrain tears of joy. An observant witness might have seen the bright-eyed dog trotting at Bolívar's side, the faithful mastiff Nevado, who had been given to him during the campaign and would accompany him for eight more years. That bystander might have noticed, too, that one of the girls in white, a nubile nineteen-year-old with lustrous hair and black eyes, was in palpable thrall to the hero she was ferrying. Bolívar himself had noted the animation in her face.

She was Josefina "Pepita" Machado, daughter of a prosperous bourgeois family in Caracas. She was not a Mantuana or a titled Spaniard—not endowed by birth to expect society's favors. She was a young woman who had come of age in a time of bewildering upheaval, who very well may have understood that, in revolution, the world was fluid, easily altered, and that the illustrious warrior in the rig behind her might offer a rare chance. We cannot know who was more avid in the pursuit, but as fireworks illuminated the summer evening—as dungeons emptied of rebel prisoners and Caracans celebrated into the night—Pepita became Bolívar's lover. She would continue to have a hold on him for six more years.

History does not call her a beauty. She had full lips, a hearty, infectious laugh, and an undeniably appealing figure; she could dance. But apart from her kittenish ways, she was ordinary of face. She was also obdurate, outspoken, feisty, and Bolívar's officers would come to detest her. With her mother and sister in tow, she followed Bolívar everywhere, even onto the battlefield when it proved necessary.

There is scant evidence of Bolívar's romantic life between his time in Paris and that August day when Caracas welcomed him as its savior, but the legend is rich and well known. He was an openly flirtatious bachelor—an enthusiastic if fickle suitor—and, in every city he liberated, there were lovely maidens to greet him and ambitious parents to spur them on. After all, not only was he a hero, he was a very rich man. We can be sure that, during those footloose years, Pepita Machado was not the only "nymph in white" to win his attentions. But in Pepita, he found a woman who was at once a revolutionary and a striver. Comfortable in his ambit of war, she was also acutely aware of the social luster that her romance with the Liberator offered. Bolívar, on the other hand, was a soldier in the flush of victory, a prodigal returned home after many a hardship, and he plunged into the affair spiritedly. Eventually, Pepita gained his trust and even participated in matters of state, to her detractors' dismay. "The most important business," one grumbled, "would end up in the hands of those who fawned over him, especially in the hands of Señorita Josefina, his infamous mistress, a conniving and vengeful woman if ever there was one. I've been in the company of that siren more than a hundred times and I have to confess I can't imagine what he saw in her."

CHAPTER 7

The Legions of Hell

All murderers shall be punished, unless of course they kill in large numbers, to the sound of trumpets.

—Voltaire

For all the happy distractions Pepita provided, there was a nation to found, order to wrest from chaos. It would not be easy. Fifteen hundred Spaniards had remained in the capital and, in the course of a full-scale evacuation, homes had been sacked, shops and warehouses looted. Bolívar secured the streets, promised a peaceful transition, installed former president Cristóbal Mendoza as governor, and invited foreigners to immigrate and help rebuild the country. But he made no effort to restore congress or hold an election. He arrogated all power to himself. He had his reasons. He would not tolerate, he said, the fractious government that had scuttled the 1810 republic in the first place. When the governor of Barinas called for the restoration of the old federalist constitution—the very document Bolívar blamed for the demise of the first republic—Bolívar balked, saying that henceforward Barinas would be ruled out of Caracas. He insisted that the new republic, later known as the "second republic," be conceived as a united whole. He argued that there were strong, unified governments in France and England; and as federalist as the United States had become, it had a centralized treasury and War Department.

It didn't stop there. Even as Santiago Mariño—liberator and supreme chief of Venezuela's eastern provinces—insisted on separate states in Barcelona and Cumaná, each with its own commander, Bolívar responded that Venezuela should be one polity with one head of state. That head, by implication, would be Simón Bolívar. Two independent authorities, he told Mariño, "will look ridiculous." He went on to say that Venezuela not only should remain one, but should unite with New Granada, thereby "forming a nation that inspires respect. How can we think of dividing anything in two?" Mariño refused to hear of it. He was not alone. As prominent republicans gathered around the country, they began to grouse about Bolívar's arbitrary authoritarianism. Home had turned out to be a devilishly unruly place.

But Bolívar was not home for long. Despite his eagerness to get on with the business of government, it soon became clear that Spain would not go so gently. Perched a little more than a hundred miles away in the fort of Puerto Cabello, General Monteverde now flatly refused to acknowledge independence. "Spain does not treat with insurgents," he responded when the treaty was delivered to him under a flag of truce, and then promptly imprisoned the priest who brought it. He rejected Bolívar's offer to exchange prisoners of war, no matter how advantageous the trade. Boosted by an infusion of twelve hundred fresh troops, Monteverde's army attacked the republicans on the plains of Valencia in late September of 1813, and was roundly pounded back. That rebel victory came at some cost. One of Bolívar's ablest officers, the valiant and much loved Granadan Atanasio Girardot, was killed by a musket ball to the forehead as he tried to plant the republican flag on high ground.

When Bolívar heard of the young colonel's valorous death, he mourned deeply. But in it he saw an opportunity to inspire men to a higher zeal; he decided to stage a funeral worthy of a great hero. He ordered Girardot's remains returned to his birthplace in Antioquia and his heart carried in an elaborate procession to Caracas. So it was that Girardot's heart was cut from his chest, placed in a gilded urn, and borne to the capital by an army chaplain. A corps of drummers led the cortège, and they rolled a slow, mournful dirge as Bolívar and three companies of mounted dragoons in full regalia rode somberly in the rear.

The theater had its effect. Patriot generals made bold by grief wasted no time in attacking the Spaniards; they succeeded in wounding Monteverde before capturing and killing his fearsome adjutant Colonel Zuazola, the butcher of human ears. But these advances only quickened the fears of blacks, who continued to be apprehensive of a white-led revolution. A counter-insurrection of slaves ripped through the countryside, surprising the patriots with its rage. On the prairies of Calabozo, rough-riding plainsmen, eager to raid the rich, declared their loyalty to Monteverde and swept into republican strongholds, plundering haciendas and massacring their residents. By November, a galvanized Bolívar was back on the battlefield, leading the troops. By then, too, his war to the death had resumed with vehemence. As a result, the entire population was swept into the business of combat: wives, children, cooks, servants, surgeons, musicians—even traveling brothels—followed soldiers to battle. Like a mighty river, the mass of humanity moved overland, pots clanging, babies screeching, laundry fluttering in the wind. Among Bolívar's retinue were Pepita, possibly her mother and sister (without whom Pepita seldom traveled), as well as his old black nursemaid, Hipólita, who cooked, tended the wounded, and ironed his clothes.

A British traveler in the service of Spain now noted a marked change in Caracas. Spaniards were being dragged to the dungeons, made to surrender their wealth to patriot coffers. The unwilling were taken to the marketplace and shot. Not outright, but limb by limb, so that onlookers could watch them wriggle as musicians struck up lively airs. These spectacles caused such merriment that the multitude, provoked to an obscene frenzy, would finally cry, "Kill him!" and the executioner would end the victim's suffering with a final bullet to the brain. A Spaniard in agony had become a source of amusement, a ready carousel of laughs.

Outside Caracas patriots hardly fared better. The "Legions of Hell"—hordes of wild and truculent plainsmen—rode out of the barren llanos to punish anyone who dared call himself a rebel. Leading these colored troops was the fearsome José Tomás Boves. A Spanish sailor from Asturias, Boves had been arrested at sea for smuggling, sent to the dungeons of Puerto Cabello, then exiled to the Venezuelan prairie, where he fell in with marauding cowboys. He was fair-haired, strong-shouldered, with an enormous head, piercing blue eyes, and a pronounced sadistic streak. Loved by his feral cohort with a passion verging on worship, he led them to unimaginable violence. As Bolívar's aide Daniel O'Leary later wrote, "Of all the monsters produced by the revolution . . . Boves was the worst." He was a barbarian of epic proportions, an Attila for the Americas. Recruited by Monteverde but beholden to no one, Boves raised a formidable army of black, pardo, and mestizo llaneros by promising them open plunder, rich booty, and a chance to exterminate the Creole class.

The llaneros were accomplished horsemen, well trained in the art of warfare. They needed few worldly goods, rode bareback, covered their nakedness with loincloths. They consumed only meat, which they strapped to their horses' flanks and cured by the sweat of the racing animals. They made tents from hides, slept on earth, reveled in hardship. They lived on the open prairie, which was parched by heat, impassable in the rains. Their weapon of choice was a long lance of alvarico palm, hardened to a sharp point in the campfire. They were accustomed to making rapid raids, swimming on horseback through rampant floods, the sum of their earthly possessions in leather pouches balanced on their heads or clenched between their teeth. They could ride at a gallop, like the armies of Genghis Khan, dangling from the side of a horse, so that their bodies were rendered invisible, untouchable, their killing lances straight and sure against a baffled enemy. In war, they had little to lose or gain, no allegiance to politics. They were rustlers and hated the ruling class, which to them meant the Creoles; they fought for the abolition of laws against their kind, which the Spaniards had promised; and they believed in the principles of harsh justice, in which a calculus of bloodshed prevailed.

At first, Bolívar easily routed Boves's undisciplined troops. On October 14, he sent his fiercest colonel, Campo Elías, and an army of twenty-five hundred men against the llaneros in Calabozo and nearly eradicated them, along with their horses. After the battle, Campo Elías took hundreds of prisoners and slaughtered them all. But Boves got away. In time, Boves formed alliances with similarly enterprising Spaniards—

Juan Yañez and Francisco Tomás Morales, a former haberdasher and a former butcher, respectively—who had scrapped their way up the royalist ranks and created marauding armies of their own. By the start of the following year, Boves and Morales had raised a formidable horde of seven thousand roughriders with machetes; Yañez, in turn, had leveled Barinas, killing every last inhabitant, branding corpses' foreheads with R for "republican," and burning the city to the ground. In the Spanish bastion of Puerto Cabello, the wounded Monteverde had been deposed, deported, and replaced by the equally ruthless Colonel Salomón. In the stronghold of Coro, Field Marshal Juan Manuel Cajigal—who would eventually be made captain-general—sent out the city's governor, José de Cevallos, to join Yañez in a full-frontal attack on Bolívar. The republicans and royalists traded one victory after another, massacring each other's ranks at every turn. Atrocities became so common on either side that no army could say it had a moral advantage.

It soon became clear to Bolívar, especially after the first pitched battle of his career at Araure on December 4, 1813, that although he might triumph—as he did, and brilliantly—his army simply couldn't recruit soldiers as quickly and effectively as the enemy. For every thrashing the republicans could deliver, the Legions of Hell would come hurtling back like the mythical Hydra, with ever more heads and a greater fury. The reason for this was obvious, although republicans were slow to see its significance: the Spanish had race on their side. The vast majority of the nation's people—black, Indian, mixed-blood—were acting on age-old democratic impulse. They were joining an effort to squelch the people of privilege, level the classes. But it was a narrow interpretation of democracy, promoted by Spanish generals, and blind to the revolutionary struggle at hand. The colored masses understood that the world was unjust, that the Creoles who lorded over them were rich and white, but they hadn't understood the true pyramid of oppression. They hadn't factored that the roots of misery were in empire, that Spain had constructed that unjust world carefully, that tyranny was rooted in the colonial, and that its system had been in place for over three hundred years.

EVEN AS DECEMBER CAME AND went—even as Spain crept out from under Napoleon and Ferdinand resumed his teetering throne—the butchery in Venezuela continued. It is altogether possible that the Spanish nation, emerging from its long night of terror, had little idea of the carnage that consumed its colonies. For Bolívar, a war to the death was a retaliatory measure; he had believed it would unite Americans against foreigners. The result was quite the opposite: Americans turned against Americans—Venezuelans took up weapons against their neighbors—and the revolution became a racial conflict, a full-fledged civil war.

On January 2, 1814, Bolívar convoked a public assembly in the ancient church of San Francisco—the church of his ancestors—so that he could address the people. He was aware of the concerns about his authoritarian ways, and could sense a need to bolster his position. "Citizens!" he began, "I am not your sovereign."

> To save you from anarchy . . . I exercised supreme power. I gave you laws; I gave you government. . . . You honor me with the illustrious title of Liberator. The officers, the soldiers of your army—*those* are your liberators, they are the ones who deserve the nation's gratitude. You know very well that they are the authors of your rebirth. . . . I beg you now to release me from a charge that is far greater than my capabilities. Elect your representatives, your magistrates, a just government, and rest secure that the forces that rescued the Republic will protect your liberty. . . . A country in which one lone person exercises all power is a country of slaves!

At the end of the address, Governor Mendoza begged him to continue as supreme commander, and the audience responded with deafening support. Bolívar argued, "There are more illustrious citizens than I!" And then, after a pause, added, "General Mariño! Liberator of the East! Now *there* is a leader worthy of directing your destinies!" But the assembly wouldn't hear of it. They insisted he retain the title of dictator. Bolívar had surrendered his power only to have it bestowed again. It was a strategy he would employ again and again during his long career as Liberator: resign a position, be implored to take it back, and, in the process, impel everyone to share in the responsibility.

Indeed, Bolívar needed all the help he could get. He had barely been able to equip his soldiers. No arms were manufactured in Venezuela and, although Bolívar was seizing lead, sulfur, and coal in order to forge bullets and make gunpowder, all guns and munitions had to be purchased from elsewhere. This was no easy venture in a world reeling from Napoleon's wars. Britain had outlawed the arms trade, and the United States—aspiring to purchase Florida from Spain—categorically refused to sell arms to Spanish American rebels. Bolívar was forced to buy illegally from merchant ships, and he welcomed Caribbean captains and businessmen to help him do it. This shortage of guns would have dire effects on the war for independence; some historians claim it was a decisive factor in the second republic's demise.

Guns alone wouldn't have fixed the problem. Boves's Legions of Hell did not depend on guns and, in any event, against an onslaught of horsemen with lances and machetes, a man with a musket didn't have a chance: rifles of the time required six complicated motions to load and, although a well-placed first round might have picked off the enemy's vanguard, by the time the patriots reloaded, the next wave of cavalry would have mowed them down.

More than horses or arms, Bolívar needed powerful partners who could help tame an unruly population. He was well aware that he could not continue to govern without a better hold on the patriot forces. Managing both a revolution and a civil war was more than he had bargained for. By the start of 1814, he was trying everything he could think of to save the effort. He offered Spanish deserters unquestioned amnesty if they would join him. He sent a diplomat to the United States to lobby for support. He wrote an impassioned letter to Lord Wellesley, congratulating him for Wellington's victory over Napoleon and beseeching him to intervene in the South American effort. He had written a number of gracious, even pleading messages to Mariño, liberator of eastern Venezuela, in a last-ditch effort to consolidate the country. Mariño, by nature, was haughty, ambitious—the privileged son of a Spanish nobleman and an Irish mother—with strong visions of his own. Daring and charismatic, he had learned soldiering in the heat of battle and, despite his twenty-six years, had risen through the command quickly. At first, he had sent one of his officers, the audacious pardo captain Manuel Piar, with a brig and five schooners, to help Bolívar mount a naval blockade at Puerto Cabello; then petulantly, and without explanation, he had ordered Piar to withdraw. By mid-January of 1814, Mariño had relented; the Liberator of the East sent the Liberator of the West a more encouraging response. He would contribute soldiers.

Even so, Mariño was slow to put words into action. On February 2, Bolívar again dispatched Campo Elías with fifteen hundred men to meet Boves, who was cutting through the country like a knife—the Legions of Hell were now a mere fifty miles south of the capital. Mariño agreed to assist Bolívar, but the Liberator of the East never showed up. The oversight had fatal consequences. Boves entered combat in a high wrath: his favorite general, Yañez, had been killed in Ospino, and when his men had gone to recover the body, they had found it dismembered, hanging in little pieces along the road. Campo Elías finally met Boves in battle at La Puerta, but for all his army's ferocity, it was no match for the thundering hordes of angry horsemen. The Legions of Hell took the republican infantry easily, leaving a thousand corpses in their wake.

Once again, brutality was met with brutality. The countryside was strewn with dead, towns razed or abandoned. Lakes delivered up carcasses. Skeletons dangled from trees. Fugitives huddled in hill and forest, fearing the rumble of hooves, the cloud of dust on the horizon. People had learned to be practical in the extreme. If it served them to say they were royalists, they said it; if it kept them alive to claim the opposite, they did that, too. Some soldiers deserted and rejoined the enemy as many as eight or ten times. One thing was clear by now: the royalists had a numerical advantage, though Bolívar was loath to admit it. In many of the ongoing conflicts, it had been boldness that counted, not size. Nevertheless, his army was so desperate for troops that José Félix Ribas was forced to recruit boys from seminaries; children as young as twelve were ordered to report for service.

Ribas and his army of youngsters were able to fend off Boves's second in command, Colonel Morales, at La Victoria, largely because Campo Elías came to the rescue, but that victory was soon offset by disaster. Bolívar had ordered Ribas to march to the nearby town of Ocumare, a republican enclave not far from Caracas, having heard that Boves was riding there with an army of a thousand slaves. But Ocumare was silent as a tomb when Ribas entered it. The city had already been ransacked. Dead women and children littered the streets. The church's floor ran with the blood of old men. In that hecatomb, Ribas found a lone priest, able to recount the atrocities. But a sack flung on the roadside would tell more. It belonged to General Morales, and had been dropped in the course of the raid and forgotten in the frenzy of massacre. Inside was a packet of correspondence that revealed a plan to incite the royalist prisoners in the dungeon of La Guaira to a violent uprising.

One of the commandants in La Guaira, Leandro Palacios, Bolívar's nephew, had already warned him of just such an eventuality. What sprang to mind now as Bolívar heard this new evidence was his own scarring experience less than two years before in Puerto Cabello—the dungeon uprising he had been powerless to contain, the one that had scuttled the revolution. Bolívar could not afford to lose La Guaira and, in so doing, risk the capital; worse, he had no troops to spare. He responded swiftly and decisively. He ordered the immediate execution of every Spanish prisoner in La Guaira and Caracas, with no mercy for the sick, the elderly, or even those who, in times of shifting loyalties, may have sheltered a patriot or two. His words were simple and to the point: "Without delay and without exception, you will put to the sword every Spaniard in dungeon or hospital." Colonel Juan Bautista Arismendi, the interim military commandant of Caracas at the time, was only too happy to comply. He fulfilled the command to the letter, and with relish. With no questions asked and no due process of law, he and his minions marched more than one thousand Spanish prisoners out into the sunlight and, over the course of four days, beheaded them all.

History would never forgive Bolívar for it. It was one thing for an untested soldier to become feral in the field; it was quite another for a liberator to exterminate a thousand chained prisoners. His war to the death had been difficult enough to justify. As time passed and the rest of the world learned of it, this mass execution would mark him as a brutal man.

EVEN SO, FOR THE MOMENT, the world had other things on its mind. By the middle of 1814, Napoleon had been reduced to a prisoner on Elba, Louis XVIII was busily restoring the French monarchy, and England was dusting itself off and looking to intensify its wan, two-year war against the United States of America. Within a few months, the British would invade Washington and set fire to the White House and U.S. Capitol, the flames of belligerence visible as far as thirty miles away. Rear Admiral George Cockburn pocketed a few knickknacks as he strolled through the deserted White House, then supped on the president's wine and dined at Dolley Madison's table before he ordered the presidential mansion torched. In Spain, King Ferdinand didn't wait until he got to Madrid to start undoing the work of the Regency. He abolished the liberal 1812 Cádiz constitution, which had established, among other things, universal suffrage, freedom of the press, and free enterprise; after that, he arrested the leaders who had written it, reinstated the Inquisition, and began an iron rule. It was a vicious time.

For Bolívar, caught in the dust of stampeding llaneros, time seemed to be running out. To make matters worse, his enemy had molted, and no longer was it an orderly column in strict service to the Spanish crown. His new foe was massive, undisciplined, lawless, with no real love for King Ferdinand and his empire, and with no apparent agenda beyond rape and despoliation. Boves's army had grown so large and fierce that his troops seemed to be everywhere at once, terrifying villages, violating women, sporting squirming babies on lances. The Spanish field marshal Manuel Cajigal, who headed the king's militias and understood rules of battle, wrote to Boves, asking him to cease unnecessary cruelty and join his command. Boves's response to Cajigal was blunt and unequivocal: he was the leader of the colored people, whose cause he championed. He had no superiors, answered to no one, and, once he was done exterminating patriots, he would come after Cajigal himself.

Although Mariño had joined Bolívar in earnest now, the two could not claim enough victories against the royalists to make significant gains. At first, there were encouraging moments—on the plains of Carabobo, for instance, when Bolívar and Ribas engaged General Cajigal's army in a long and stubborn struggle. Nature itself seemed on the side of the patriots. Gunfire set the tall grasses of the savanna ablaze and a brisk wind blew blinding smoke into the Spaniards' faces. Bolívar's troops were able to outflank them, inflict punishing losses, and emerge with four thousand of the enemy's horses. In the confusion, General Cajigal had no recourse but to flee on foot, wander the forests, eat wild fruit, and escape down the Orinoco to fight another day. What might have been luck for the patriots, however, was war as usual for Boves. The llaneros habitually used dust, wind, fire, smoke—even seasonal floods—to their advantage. They routed Bolívar decisively at La Puerta, they pushed him back until he was obliged to take refuge at his hacienda at San Mateo. And then the patriot troops seemed to vanish in insurmountable losses. The Legions of Hell took them easily at Valencia. Boves personally led the charge, storming the city at the head of his roaring horde.

When Valencia surrendered, Boves signed a treaty, even celebrated a Mass in church, assuring citizens they would be safe. The townspeople were stunned and deeply grateful. A Spanish general later recounted how, on the night of his victory, Boves invited the city's matrons to dance the *piquirico* at a celebratory ball—convincing them that by doing so they would guarantee their husbands' well-being. When they resisted, he took out his lash and made them dance by force; then, sufficiently amused, he beheaded them all. Within days, his multitudes were riding toward the capital, sending its citizens into paroxysms of fear and forcing Bolívar to contemplate a major evacuation. The Liberator called for a sweep of all the precious silver and gold objects in the city's churches, impounded the republic's treasury, put all of it in twenty-four trunks, and ordered them shipped out at once to Mariño's republican stronghold in the east. Mariño had assured Bolívar that in Barcelona, his domain on the coast, the patriots would be out of harm's way.

On the morning of Thursday, July 7, as an unrelieved rain fell from the gray expanse over Caracas, twenty thousand people—almost the entire population of the city—began a long march toward Barcelona, two hundred miles away. Led by Bolívar's army, which had dwindled to a force of twelve hundred, they waded through knee-high mud, ferrying what worldly possessions they could. They were largely members of the Creole class, aristocrats who had never had to walk to church much less trudge through swamps. As the road grew worse, the heat intolerable, the mosquitoes thick and fierce, even the strong grew weak. Soldiers took the incapacitated onto their horses, often two at a time, to cross the swollen marshlands. Soon they were in a harsher landscape, scored by high rivers and treacherous mountains—alive with snakes and jaguars—where food or rest could not be found. For twenty-three days the diminishing mass inched ahead, ragged, hungry, with no shelter from torrential rains, no mantle against the damp of night. Many died along the way, drowned in floods, killed by roving bandits, or devoured by wild animals. Many of those fortunate enough to survive died later, of cholera and yellow fever. Often they succumbed to a spiraling madness. Bolívar told of a starving mother who—in a fit of desperation—snatched the baby from her empty breast and hurled it away, to a quicker, more merciful death.

We can only imagine the horrors of this tragic exodus. His cape pulled tight against the deluge, Bolívar watched his people pass, unable to offer them much hope or comfort. He had, in three years of war, gone from pampered plutocrat to hardened soldier; from sleeping in a gilded bed to spending nights in an improvised hammock. His hair was long, his beard full; and yet, despite that hirsute guise, the dark hollows of his face were all too evident. For all the energy that fueled his purpose, he was frail in body, plagued by hemorrhoids, susceptible to fevers, delicate of stomach. But his was a single-minded vision. He could admit no pessimism. If there were moments, as there had been for Miranda, when the sight of a bloodied earth forced him to wonder whether his war of ideals was worth the soul-breaking sacrifice, Bolívar never let on. He kept his eyes firmly on the dream.

He would not allow his sisters to remain in Caracas, although María Antonia had insisted on it. Four thousand souls had stayed on in that phantom capital: some, like the Marquis de Casa León, because as Spaniards they could count on pardons; some because they were pardos; others because they were patriots who preferred to die inside their houses; still others because—as nuns, priests, or artists—they felt immune to war's prejudices. But Bolívar knew what Boves's men would do to any Creole who fell into their hands: he had seen the pyramids of skulls, heard the stories of rape and mutilation. Bolívar decided that what little family he had would travel under his protection. María Antonia, Juana, and their children, as well as his mistress, Pepita Machado, and her family, made the arduous trip at his side. Once they reached the northeastern coast of Venezuela, Pepita, who had spent a year following Bolívar from battle to battle, was shipped off to the island of St. Thomas to await her lover's instructions. Bolívar's sisters were sent on to Curaçao.

WHEN THE CARACANS FINALLY STRAGGLED into Barcelona or, farther east, to Cumaná, they realized that the safe harbor Mariño had promised was little more than a mirage. The ports were chaotic, teeming with too many patriots and too few ships to ferry them away; and to the south, heading toward them, was the royalist general Morales with a ravening army of llaneros. The war, at least from the republican side, was all defense now—precisely the kind Bolívar had struggled to avoid. To make matters worse, they were in a part of Venezuela that seemed utterly alien to Bolívar. The east was markedly different terrain, and Mariño's troops made sure he knew it.

With the Legions of Hell approaching, the patriots now struggled to rally a defense of those valuable port cities. Bolívar hastily raised an army and marched to the town of Aragua, where Mariño's second in command, Francisco Bermúdez, awaited him. The situation seemed promising: they had gathered six thousand patriot soldiers in all. But on August 17, the royalist general Morales swept into the valley of Aragua with a force of eight thousand. A savage combat began the next morning, and by late afternoon 3,700 patriots lay dead on a scorched and bloody field. Bolívar and Bermúdez had no option but to abandon the fight. As republicans scattered over the hills, Morales and his horsemen took Aragua, where they butchered three thousand townspeople, including those who had sought refuge in the church.

It was a resounding defeat. The patriot leaders could only flee now—to Cumaná and, ultimately, toward Guiria, a slender spit of land even farther east. On August 25, Bolívar arrived in Cumaná, where Mariño awaited him with the silver and gold of Caracas—it was their only hope for equipping a renewed republican offense. But, in preparation for evacuation and in the roiling confusion, Mariño had placed the treasure on board several ships belonging to an Italian captain, who now threatened to sail away with it all. Panicked, Bolívar sent Colonel Mariano Montilla to persuade the perfidious captain to return the trunks, but when Montilla went on board the captain's schooner, he was taken prisoner. Mariño then embarked to try to recoup the situation, and, when he, too, didn't emerge, Bolívar embarked as well. As the ship pulled anchor and drifted off toward the island of Margarita, the two liberators succeeded in convincing the Italian captain to return sixteen of the twenty-four containers. All would be settled amicably once they reached the island. But Mariño's man in command of Margarita—the ambitious pardo colonel Manuel Piar—wanted no part of it. When he was notified that Bolívar and Mariño were on board one of the approaching ships, Piar refused to acknowledge their authority, and gave the command to open fire. The Italian ordered his ships to wheel around and hurry back to the mainland, but there, too, they found a similar reception. This time it was Bolívar's deputy, the haughty Field Marshal José Félix Ribas, who confronted them on the pier. He accused Bolívar and Mariño of cowardice, desertion, and conspiring to steal the gold and silver for themselves. It was clear that Ribas and Piar had fed one another's suspicions and, ready to take power into their own hands, decided to depose their superiors. Eventually, Francisco Bermúdez, Mariño's trusted officer who had fought alongside Bolívar days before, began to have misgivings, too. Taken aback by this alarming turn of events, Mariño and Bolívar tried to defend their actions—explaining that they had left shore to rescue the precious relics for the republic, not to abscond with them—but mistrust and misapprehension ruled the day. Publicly stripping the two liberators of their power, Piar and Ribas declared themselves supreme commanders of east and west. With no further ado, Mariño was thrown into prison and Bolívar forced to turn over the trunks.

Bewildered, heartsick, Bolívar had no choice but to do what Ribas demanded. He was a virtual stranger in the eastern provinces, despised by Mariño's army, and now, with his own field marshal's betrayal, he had lost hold of the republic altogether. The sudden hostility from Ribas was especially galling; he was Bolívar's uncle, after all, married to his mother's sister. There was no doubt that Ribas was hotheaded, vain, and far too hungry for power—it had always been so—but he had never shown Bolívar anything but loyalty. In a strange twist that echoed the fate of Miranda, Bolívar was cast to the winds by a man he had assumed to be one of his most loyal defenders. Ribas wasted no time in ridding Venezuela of Bolívar; he yanked Mariño out of prison and exiled them both on the same ship.

So was it that the second republic crumbled as quickly as the first and the patriot leadership splintered into a host of petty, internecine squabbles. Eerily enough, Bolívar repeated the arc he had traveled almost exactly two years before. He set sail from the turbulent coast of Venezuela, hoping to start all over again on calmer shores. This time, however, instead of being accompanied by his uncle, he was in the company of a former rival, General Mariño, in a bizarre, uneasy partnership that only a cauldron of revolution could forge. It was the 8th of September, 1814. Only hours after their departure, Colonel Piar arrived from the island of Margarita with a company of two hundred riflemen, intending to shoot them both.

ENTERING THE GHOST CITY OF Caracas on July 16, 1814, Boves was greeted by white flags and a nervous archbishop. On the road, he had made it clear to Spanish general Cajigal, to whom he had already made menacing remarks, that Caracas was his to rule, not some lily-handed appointee's. Cajigal, who had been made interim captain-general of Venezuela, tried to appease Boves by promising to make him colonel, but Boves scoffed, saying that he had promoted many a colonel himself—he was nobody's officer. The insubordination was so blatant that Cajigal, red-faced and speechless, didn't know what to say. He made a quick course for the fortress at Puerto Cabello, where he sulked and sent off bitter complaints to Madrid.

In Caracas, Boves issued a proclamation promising that henceforward bygones would be bygones—all who had remained in the capital would be safe from harm. But no sooner had the Spanish archbishop of Venezuela Narciso Coll y Pratt intoned a grateful Mass for this welcome peace than the killings began. Anyone who had assisted the patriot cause was put to the lance or machete. Anyone who had remained faithful to King Ferdinand was allowed to live. In this, the people of color, especially, were rewarded: beggars were sent off to manage haciendas and produce food for the city. Pardos rose to high positions in the army.

In an irony few at the time appreciated, the royalist victory succeeded in toppling the social pyramid that Spain had been building for three hundred years. Overnight, Boves inverted the racial order: The colored, whom he perceived as loyal and trustworthy, were favored; the whites were treated as dangerous foes. To be Creole or Mantuano, for Boves, was tantamount to being a criminal. Only in Haiti had the lower classes achieved such a stunning reversal; but in Haiti the revolution—bloodily fought and won—had been undertaken in the name of freedom, not in the name of a king.

By October, Boves had moved up the coast, from Caracas to Cumaná. Here, too, he rode into a largely deserted city. The Legions of Hell, grown to more than ten thousand, now controlled the entire seaboard of Venezuela. The patriot leadership, on the other hand, had fallen into disarray. General Piar ignored Field Marshal Ribas's desperate communiqués. Ribas and Bermúdez, too, were bickering, unable to agree on how to confront Boves. They finally met him in battle on December 5 in the valley of Urica, just south of Cumaná. The royalists, with a force twice as large, crushed the patriots easily, but as the republicans fell into retreat one of their ranks managed to leap toward Boves and spear him in the heart. He died instantly.

It is difficult to overestimate the impact Boves had on Venezuelans, their revolution, the Americans they would become. It was he who first allowed blacks and Indians to imagine they could have a voice in the nation's future. The Creole revolution had begun, after all, much like its North American version: as a movement that was of, by, and for whites. Boves changed that; the irony is that Spain saw potential in his racial war, and used it. Retrieved from the battlefield, his body was given an elaborate funeral in Urica; in time, it was mourned by Spanish priests throughout the land, most elaborately by that fanatical enemy of the revolution Archbishop Coll y Pratt.

Boves's sudden death only served to whet the Legions of Hell's appetite for vengeance. General Francisco Tomás Morales took command of Boves's troops and Ribas and Bermúdez fought him a few days later outside the republican city of Maturín. There, too, the patriots lost decisively. Reduced to a tiny force now, the patriots dispersed. Ribas made a vexed escape west, through mountain and vale, and finally—exhausted and sick—took refuge in a house near Pascua. He was awakened one night by a band of angry townspeople, pro-Boves royalists who had persuaded Ribas's manservant to tell them where he was. They dragged Ribas into town, killed him, dismembered him, fried his head in a vat of bubbling oil, and transported it in an iron cage to Caracas, where it was displayed—with his customary red cap perched jauntily on top—on the road that led to La Guaira. No one was surprised.

The people had seen too much to be shocked by any one atrocity. By the end of 1814, Boves had killed eighty thousand republicans. But Bolívar's war to the death, too, had executed thousands. Bolívar didn't deny it. He openly reported that "all Europeans" he encountered in his Admirable Campaign "almost without exception were shot." This incontinent violence had not sprung spontaneously from the Venezuelan people; it was the calculated result of strategies put into place by two rival leaders who were intent on unnerving their enemies. Bolívar was not a truculent man: killing in cold blood sickened him. But he was well versed in the uses of fear. Boves, on the other hand, reveled in death. He had laughed to see an unborn child struggling for life in its dead mother's belly; he took pleasure in watching a boy witness the mutilation of his father. It is said that Boves was eager to march on Cumaná precisely because his bloodlust had grown extreme. Whatever Boves's and Bolívar's intentions, the results of their policies were one and the same: the country stank of death; hospitals were overrun with invalids; populations were displaced; women were transferred from one place to another to care for the maimed and dying. The nation was devastated beyond recognition. A Spanish official wrote of Venezuela:

> There are no more provinces left. Towns that had thousands of inhabitants are now reduced to a few hundred or even a few dozen. In some, there are only vestiges of human habitation. Roads and fields are strewn with unburied corpses; entire villages have been burnt; whole families are nothing but a memory.

By now, the republicans held only a small patch of land: the island of Margarita. As Bolívar contemplated this reduced universe from a distant shore, he must have seen what was so clearly obvious: the uprising he had helped to kindle was unlike any other he had read about in the comfortable library of his old Spanish mentor, the Marquis of Ustaríz, and certainly like no revolution since. This was no uniform group of like-minded whites united by class and faith upending an oppressor and casting out an old system: it was no France or United States of America—or Haiti, for that matter—where strong commonalities existed among the rebels. The overwhelmingly mixed-race population of Latin America existed in few other societies, and it was a population too prevalent to ignore. A revolution would never succeed without engaging it. If Miranda had taught him that Creoles were profoundly afraid to confront the perilous questions of race in Spanish America, Boves had taught him that no war could be won without doing exactly that.

The idea of recruiting black troops had occurred at about the same time to the Argentine liberator José de San Martín, as he contemplated the liberation of Chile and Peru. The notion had suggested itself, too, to Andrew Jackson, who had led two battalions of free blacks—among them Haitian refugees—to defend New Orleans against a looming British attack. Jackson would later declare himself in favor of shipping all freed slaves back to Africa, but in that fraught year of 1814, Old Hickory defended himself against his critics by arguing that blacks made first-rate soldiers. "They must be for, or against us," Jackson said, in a phrase that Bolívar himself might have spoken. "Distrust them, and you make them your enemies, place confidence in them, and you engage them by every dear and honorable tie to the interest of the country who extends to them equal rights and privileges with white men." It was no small irony that a North American was arguing this, for in Washington's halls of power, the fact that Bolívar began conscripting blacks and mulattoes to his revolution would be enough to cast suspicion on his whole enterprise. Nevertheless, for a fleeting moment in time, it seemed—at least to those three American contemporaries, Bolívar, San Martín, and Jackson—an idea whose time had come.

Bolívar's message to fellow patriots as he left his native shores in early September was repentant, but resolute. "Destiny elected me to break your chains," he wrote, "as surely as Providence charged me to be the instrument of your misfortune. Yes, I brought you peace and liberty, but those inestimable treasures were followed immediately by war and bondage." With a clear grasp that the nation needed to understand and overcome its racial divisions, he went on to say:

> The destruction of governments, the ousting of laws, the reform of customs, the reversal of opinions, and the founding, finally, of liberty in a country of slaves are goals as impossible to achieve overnight as they are beyond our power to control. . . . I swear to you that, Liberator or dead, I will strive to merit the honor you have conferred on me; there is no human power on the face of this earth that can impede the course I am determined to follow, until I have returned to liberate you by way of the west, covered in blood and laurels. . . . Do not compare your might with that of the enemy, because spirit cannot be compared to matter. You are men, they are beasts; you are free, they are slaves.

BOLÍVAR ARRIVED IN CARTAGENA, NEW Granada, on September 19, 1814. Despite his bitter failures in Venezuela, the people of Cartagena received him warmly. To them, he was the hero who had won them a republic. He installed himself in the palace of the Spanish bishop, who had evacuated the city years before, and found himself sharing that grand manse with a family he knew all too well: the mother and sisters of his fellow soldier Carlos Soublette, who had been Miranda's adjutant.

The Soublettes were distant cousins of Bolívar's and, like him, refugees from Caracas. In the fragrant, bougainvillea-hung gardens of Cartagena and on the avenues lined with stately palms, he came to spend considerable time distracting himself with lovely Isabel Soublette—sixteen years old, irresistibly flirtatious, with an abundance of pale red hair. She was nothing like the intense Pepita, who had insinuated herself into his political affairs, miffed his officers, and then fled to safety and the Caribbean. Isabel was too young and tender to be anything more than a light diversion. Eventually, she and Bolívar fell into a love affair, which they would have an opportunity to renew as the winds of revolution buffeted them from exile to exile. He would memorialize those dalliances much later with the gift of a house—on the occasion of her wedding to another man.

But romance, for Bolívar, was but a passing salve in an ongoing war, and revolution was never far from his mind. He was nervous in the extreme, in perpetual motion, lit by a preternatural energy. The bishop's house became more a nest of intrigue than a nest of love; in it, he proceeded to plot a campaign to reconstitute his revolution. But it was clear that what had happened in Venezuela was now coming to pass in New Granada. Antonio Nariño, the former president in Bogotá, was languishing in the dungeons of Cádiz, alongside Miranda. Republican governments were being threatened by royalists on all sides. In the south, the Spaniards had a firm grip on the gold mines of Popayán. In the north, they had retaken the crucial port of Santa Marta. Bolívar knew he could not rely on Cartagena alone to reignite his revolution; he needed the firm support of the confederation. Toward that end, he traveled to Tunja, where the congress gave him a rousing show of support, an army, and instructions to march immediately to subdue the unruly capital of Bogotá. The congress's president, Camilo Torres, assured him, "General, as long as your sword lives on, your country is not dead. . . . You have been an unfortunate soldier. But you are a great man."

Bolívar was not considered great by the people who ruled Bogotá. To them, he was the Man of Terror, the architect of a barbaric war. The archbishop had gone so far as to excommunicate him. In early December, as Bolívar and his army of eighteen hundred camped outside Bogotá's walls, he exhorted the city leaders to listen to him. "I give you my word of honor," he wrote one of them, "My goal is to conserve human life, and so I urge you to negotiate with me and spare your citizens the horrors of a siege and battle." The city put up a halfhearted struggle, but after two days capitulated. On December 12, Bolívar entered the city and took power, assuring the people of their rights. Not long after, the Church commuted its decree of excommunication and, reversing itself completely, celebrated a glorious Mass in his honor. The Congress of the Confederation, overjoyed with Bolívar's success, made him commander in chief of its army, and Camilo Torres's government in Tunja hastily moved to reestablish itself in Bogotá.

But the rest of New Granada would not be so easily won. Spanish generals had reconquered the inland waterways. In order to dislodge them, Bolívar needed to secure Santa Marta, the port at which the great

Magdalena rushed to sea. With congress's blessings, he marched from the mountains of Bogotá toward the coast, liberating towns along the river, much as he had done in the opposite direction two years before. But even as history repeated itself in reverse in those early months of 1815, his enemies, too, flew back to haunt him.

By the time Bolívar arrived in Mompox, his old nemesis Colonel Manuel del Castillo had seized control of Cartagena. Castillo was a dedicated republican, an ardent American, greatly favored by the people of that city, but he was virulently opposed to the Venezuelan liberator—brazenly so—and just as he had spurned Bolívar's liberating expedition a year before by refusing to march into Venezuela, he furiously rejected him now. Castillo immediately set out to blacken Bolívar's reputation, attributing the loss of Venezuela to his cowardice and ineptitude. He published broadsides against him, arrested anyone suspected of being Bolívar's supporter. He was aided in this by others as passionately jealous of Bolívar. They urged Castillo to resist Bolívar at all costs and liberate Santa Marta himself. Boosted by this vote of confidence, Castillo began a mad course toward civil war. He refused Bolívar's innumerable attempts at reconciliation. He put the city of Cartagena on high alert. He ordered his commandant of operations along the river to raise troops against Bolívar's army. Bolívar had no choice but to linger on those muggy banks for more than a month as smallpox and cholera tore through his ranks, eradicating them one by one. Castillo's efforts became so blatant, so infamous, that the Spaniards eagerly dispatched a messenger to him, offering to help squelch the Liberator for good.

It was a disastrous situation; and as it unfolded, Bolívar made a drastic miscalculation. He decided to use the same tactics he had employed in Bogotá: he would camp on the outskirts of the city, send in a few strongly worded missives, and then threaten an incursion. He moved his headquarters to the monastery of La Popa, a walled fortress on a verdant promontory overlooking Cartagena. But when he arrived he found that Castillo had poisoned its water supply. Putrefying animal corpses bobbed in the monastery's wells. To make matters worse, Cartagena's cannons were turned against him and the incoming fire was so constant that fetching fresh water from the lake was impossible. Bolívar's troops grew weak with thirst and succumbed to rampant infection. Six weeks elapsed in this mind-numbing waste of manpower and, in the interim, royalists began to sweep down the Magdalena again, taking back all the ground Bolívar had gained and opening the way for a large-scale invasion.

On March 30, Bolívar wrote to the head priest of Cartagena, imploring him to use his holy office to bring about a resolution. The notion of raising arms against a fellow republican seemed obscene. He wrote on April 12: "I have offered to withdraw. It seems to me that I've done it with more generosity of spirit than anyone might have expected. This is hardly a contrived liberality, but one that springs from my heart, which cannot abide the possibility of seeing this place despoiled by a frightening anarchy. . . . The very thought of it makes me shudder." But the priest didn't answer that letter or, for that matter, any of the letters that followed. On April 24, he sent Bolívar a terse message advising him that a mighty armada—sixty ships and more than fourteen thousand Spanish soldiers—seasoned veterans of the Napoleonic Wars, had landed in Venezuela. At its head was one of Spain's most illustrious warriors, Pablo Morillo, a general who had distinguished himself at Trafalgar and fought brilliantly at the Duke of Wellington's side.

Bolívar may well have suspected that such an expedition was inevitable, but he probably did not know the depth of Spanish conviction that animated it. King Ferdinand had expressed a mortal impatience with the tenets of democracy; in order to please him, his court had urged him to be "absolutely absolute"; mobs in the streets of Madrid had taken to yelling, "Death to the Constitution!" Spain was getting its empire in order, and it wanted its rebel colonies back.

History unfurled quickly after that. Taking advantage of the standoff between Castillo and Bolívar, the royalists sped down the Magdalena and took Mompox handily. Bolívar, agonizing over the impossibility of his situation, called a council of war and explained that the only thing left for him to do, given Castillo's obstinacy, was to resign his commission and separate himself from New Granada. His troops, which had once numbered 2,400, had been reduced to 700. He negotiated a treaty with Cartagena, insuring the safety of those few. On the 8th of May, he handed over their command to his cousin Florencio Palacios and set sail for Jamaica on board a British brig. With him were his secretary, his aide-de-camp, and a handful of loyal comrades. Santiago Mariño, Liberator of the East, followed a few days later.

By then, all indications were that the cause of independence in Spanish America could not possibly survive. The Spanish general Pablo Morillo, "Pacificator of Tierra Firma," had landed at Margarita and was working his way west. It's not difficult to imagine the impression his magnificent expedition of sixty ships must have made as it approached the tranquil shores of Margarita. Six regiments of infantry and two of cavalry—sporting splendid uniforms, shining medals, and the latest in arms—had arrived on battleships the likes of which America had never seen. It was the most expansive, organized force Spain had sent to the New World. One look at that breathtaking sight, and it didn't take long for General Juan Bautista Arismendi, governor of Margarita, to surrender. On April 7, General Morillo strode off his ship to embrace the infamous "butcher of La Guaira," recalling later: "I treated them all with respect, even Arismendi—the fierce, cruel Arismendi—who only a year before had been the instrument of death, in the most inhuman way, for eight hundred captive Spaniards." Morillo's mandate in the Americas could not have been clearer: he was to reconquer Venezuela, the most recalcitrant and rebellious of Spain's colonies, then move on to pacify New Granada and Quito. After that, he was to continue over the Andes and—with the help of loyal Peru—crush San Martín's anarchists in Argentina.

San Martín had fought valiantly in Spain, defending the *madre patria* against Napoleon, but on his return to Buenos Aires, he joined the Argentine revolution, rising to command the rebel Army of the North. Even as Morillo's ships were approaching Venezuela, San Martín was beginning to plot a bold strategy to train a more disciplined army, cross the Andes, and attack the viceroy of Lima from the sea. It was an ingenious plan, conceived almost entirely in secret and with careful, military precision. But that victory was yet to come. As far as Morillo was concerned, San Martín would be an easy conquest for Spain's seasoned troops. As would Bolívar and the rest of the unruly Americans.

By May 11, as Bolívar's ship lost sight of the Colombian coastline, Morillo and his legions swarmed ashore at La Guaira and overland to Caracas. The capital had been prepared by Captain-General Cajigal, who had published a long string of recriminations about the Liberator. According to him, Bolívar's revolutionary career was finished: he had made bitter enemies, spilled much of his country's blood, shown a patent inability to rule, pressed his own prejudices on the people, engaged in puerile self-salutes, and, in the mass evacuation of the capital, had caused unimaginable and unnecessary suffering. "Some day," the new captain-general added, "God will punish his execrable deeds."

There seemed to be little point in thrashing Bolívar. There was every reason to believe that his revolution was truly over. Morillo announced a general amnesty and declared business as usual. "The army of King Ferdinand VII has entered your country without shedding one drop of blood!" he told the people, "I trust you will now return to the peace and fidelity of former years. Prepare to tremble if you do not!" But Caracas was a fraction of its former self, its society turned upside down. Pardos ruled; whites were few. There would be no going back to the old colonial ways. Morillo, whose skills were far more acute in military matters than political, washed his hands of administrative details, reorganized his army, and in July sailed to Santa Marta with fifty-six ships and a force augmented by five thousand of Boves's finest horsemen. By August, he was planning a siege of Cartagena.

Colonel Castillo—stubbornly proud, fatally grandiose—decided to lock down the fortress of Cartagena, hold out against the inevitable. The day before the Spanish landed in Santa Marta, he took a young woman's hand in marriage and, for all the impending danger, there seemed to be a dreamy, deluded air about the man. Eventually, the city was choked by Morillo's blockade and, surrounded by an army more powerful than any Spanish America had ever known, Castillo began a suicidal effort that would be remembered as one of the grimmest moments of Colombian history. For 108 days, from September to December, he barricaded the population in that mighty stone citadel. From without, the city was virtually indestructible; from within, however, it was a different story. There was nothing to drink, nothing to eat.

Little by little, the once beautiful, prosperous city of Cartagena began to die from the inside. By the end of November, conditions were desperate. Every donkey, dog, cat, rat—even leaves off the trees, grass sprouting from walls, shoes of dead men—had been devoured and starvation was rampant; disease, endemic. The few republicans who had managed to slip into the walled city from the outside—among them, Antonio José de Sucre, Carlos Soublette, and José Francisco Bermúdez, all fugitives from Morillo's invasion—deposed Castillo and sent off a letter begging Bolívar to return, but the damage had been done. The city was in ruins, the population doomed. Half of them—more than six thousand—perished in the course of the Spanish blockade. Every day, three hundred corpses were swept off the streets in a desperate attempt to curb cannibalism. On December 5, in the pale light of a new moon, two thousand patriots, men and women, scaled the walls and stole out of the city, streaming down to shore, where corsairs awaited with promises to sail them to liberty. Many of them drowned; others were robbed or abandoned in the wild; but some who would play significant roles in Bolívar's future—Sucre, Briceño, Bermúdez, Soublette, Luis Ducoudray, and Mariano Montilla—made it to safety. When General Morillo and his troops stormed into Cartagena the next day, they found its streets abandoned, its houses silent. Cowering in a corner of one house was Manuel del Castillo. He was taken prisoner and shot.

There was little doubt that Spain was master of Tierra Firma now. By mid-1815, there were countless signs to prove it. Boves, author of one of the bloodiest hecatombs in the annals of American horrors, was honored with a lavish Mass in the Cathedral of Caracas, pronounced by the eminent Archbishop Coll y Pratt. "The throne thanks his important services," the holy man proclaimed, enshrining for all posterity the notion, so common in South American history, that power buys impunity. In Peru, the most obedient of Spanish colonies, the Inca Mateo Pumacahua, who had fought for Spain then protested against it by overtaking La Paz and Arequipa, was dogged down by the king's army, and, in a lesson to the Peruvian people, hanged, decapitated, and quartered. Thousands of miles away, on the highway from Caracas to

La Guaira, the fried head of José Félix Ribas sat in its iron cage for a thousand days, picked over by birds and flies, reminding anyone who dared pass that there was no glory in crossing Spain, no triumph in being a rebel. His widow, Josefa Palacios, the sister of Bolívar's mother, fell mute, shut herself in her room, and, for seven long years, refused to open the door.

REVOLUTION HAD BEGUN TO TAKE a physical toll on Bolívar. Everyone could see it. In Jamaica, the Duke of Manchester, governor of the island, looked across his dinner table and beheld a spent man: his guest was restless, fidgety. Seeing the black eyes glitter from an unnaturally gaunt face, the governor remarked that the oil had consumed the flame. Bolívar was thirty-two years old.

But as Bolívar would prove in harder years to come, he was far stronger than he appeared. He had a near-Herculean appetite for adversity. Challenges seemed to electrify him. Within two weeks of his arrival in Kingston, he was writing to Lord Wellesley, trying to convince the former foreign secretary that it was high time the English turned their sights on Latin American independence. "I have seen the ravening fire that devours my benighted country," Bolívar told him. "After innumerable efforts to quench it, I have come to sound an alarm, beg for help, say to Great Britain and the rest of humanity: a vast part of your species is about to expire, and the most beautiful half of this earth will soon be a desert." Britain, however, had its sights firmly fixed elsewhere. It was fighting the Battle of Waterloo. Napoleon had escaped to invade once again, and Wellesley's brother, the Duke of Wellington, would win eternal fame for crushing him. But there were other reasons for Britain's demurral. The country was entering into a treaty with the Holy Alliance—a powerful cabal that included Prussia, Austria, and Russia, and had firmly outlawed revolution—and so its only response, ironically, was to forbid its retired officers in the Caribbean from serving Bolívar's cause.

Help was forthcoming from no one. In the United States, an eighty-year-old John Adams, who perhaps had never forgotten his son-in-law's perilous friendship with Miranda, now wrote:

What could I think of revolutions and constitutions in South America? A people more ignorant, more bigoted, more superstitious, more
implicitly credulous in the sanctity of royalty, more blindly devoted to
their priests, in more awful terror of the Inquisition, than any people
in Europe, even in Spain, Portugal, or the Austrian Netherlands, and
infinitely more than in Rome itself.

On September 1, 1815, President Madison drove a final nail into
Bolívar's hopes by issuing a proclamation that prohibited United States
citizens from enlisting in military campaigns against Spain's dominions.

Bolívar's lone offer of support was from a wealthy Dutchman in
Curaçao. He was Luis Brion, a young Jewish merchant with a lust for
adventure. Brion had a Philadelphia education, multiple citizenships,
and a twenty-four-gun English brig to give away. He was one of a network of freewheeling Caribbean businessmen from whom Bolívar had
bought arms and munitions. An ardent proponent of free trade who
wanted Spain out of the Americas, Brion was keen to help Bolívar any
way he could. He offered Bolívar the battleship. Bolívar thanked him
warmly, calling him "America's best friend," and then sent one of his
trusty colonels, Miguel Carabaño, to Curaçao to urge Brion to mount an
entire expedition.

In the interim, Bolívar wrote editorials, memos, letters to anyone
he could think of, including one respectfully declining the invitation
to take up the reins in the besieged fortress of Cartagena. Little did
he know that as he penned those words, Cartagena was littered with
corpses, its scant survivors plotting a fevered getaway.

One of Bolívar's many writings during that time was an astonishingly prescient letter addressed to an Englishman in Jamaica who expressed interest in his struggle for independence. More than a friendly
missive, this was a masterful *tour d'horizon*. Clearly Bolívar meant
it to enjoy wide dissemination. Written in vibrant prose and reflect-
ing a profound grasp of the legacy of colonialism, the letter was read
at first only by the small English circle for whom it was intended. It
would take more than a dozen years to be retranslated into Spanish.
But the letter served as a blueprint for Bolívar's political thought, and

its ideas would emerge in countless documents during those formative days.

The "Letter from Jamaica" declared unequivocally that the bond between America and Spain had been severed forevermore: it could never be repaired. Although the "wicked stepmother" was laboring mightily to reapply her chains, it was too late. The colonies had tasted freedom. "Our hatred for Spain," he declared, "is vaster than the sea between us."

In turns a paean to the inexpressible beauty of the continent and a shriek of fury at its despoliation, Bolívar's letter is a brilliant distillation of Latin America's political reality. His people, he explains, are neither Indian nor pardos nor European, but an entirely new race, for which European models of government are patently unsuitable. Monarchies, to these Americans, were abhorrent by definition; and democracy— Philadelphia style—inappropriate for a population cowed and infantilized by three hundred years of slavery. "As long as we do not have the political virtues that distinguish our brothers of the north," he argued, "a democratic system, far from rescuing us, can only bring us ruin. . . . We are a region plagued by vices learned from Spain, which, through history, has been a mistress of cruelty, ambition, meanness, and greed." Most important to the welfare of these fledgling republics, Bolívar insisted, was a firm executive who employed wisdom, dispensed justice, and ruled benevolently for life. His America needed a strong, centralized government—one that addressed the people's wretched condition, not a perfectly conceptualized, theoretical model dreamed up by idealists on some far-flung shore.

But the "Letter from Jamaica" was more than mere propaganda; it was inspired prophecy. In it, Bolívar predicted that revolution-torn Mexico would opt for a temporary monarchy, which indeed it did. He pictured the loose confederation of nations that later became Central America. Given Panama's "magnificent position between two mighty seas," he imagined a canal. For Argentina, he foresaw military dictatorships; for Chile, "the blessings that flow from the just and gentle laws of a republic." For Peru, he predicted a limbo in which privileged whites would not tolerate a genuine democracy, colored masses would not tolerate a ruling aristocracy, and the constant threat of rebellion was never far from hand. All these would come to pass. In some countries, one could even say, Bolívar's visions still hold.

Reduced for the time being, however, to producing revolutionary doctrine, Bolívar was living like a pauper, using what funds he could cadge to contribute to a flurry of rebel ventures that blew in and out of Jamaica along with his erstwhile companions. Most of his financial assistance came from Maxwell Hyslop, an Englishman he had known from Caracas—a merchant who, like Brion, avidly advocated free trade. Hyslop's loans afforded him two tiny rooms, a black manservant named Pio, and a hammock. "I am," as he reported to Brion in Curaçao, "living in uncertainty and misery." Eventually he wrote Hyslop that he had lost all patience with his harridan landlady and left her house.

A few days later, on December 10, when a former paymaster in Bolívar's army, Félix Amestoy, came looking for him at that address, Bolívar was no longer there. That very day he had found new quarters. But Amestoy didn't know that. Seeing the hammock in the corner, he decided to take a nap and wait until Bolívar returned. Bolívar's manservant, Pio, too, had no idea his master had moved. In the black of night, he crept in and attacked the man in the hammock with a knife, stabbing the body several times. The killing done, Pio made a quick escape through the window, but he was drunk, loud, and, in the course of the murder, his victim had managed to cry out, "A Negro is killing me!" Shortly after, Pio was hunted down and apprehended. He admitted that foreigners had plied him with liquor and paid 2,000 pesos—an unimaginable sum—to assassinate Bolívar. The courts never determined by whose agency the murder had been contracted, or why. Within a few weeks, Pio was convicted and hanged—his head lopped off, affixed to a stake, and exhibited on Kingston's Spring-Path.

Many a legend has been made of that fatal night. Some historians claim that Bolívar was saved because he had lolled abed with Julia Cobier, a wealthy widow renowned for her beauty and brains, whom he'd been romancing. Others say he was off having dinner at Hyslop's. Rumors even had it that General Morillo himself had ordered the assassination, and that money had passed from Spanish hands to a Polish Jew in Kingston, who ended up recruiting Pio to the task. In any case, the incident was enough to unnerve Bolívar. He left Jamaica on December 18 before authorities carried out Pio's execution. Assisted by Brion and Hyslop, he sailed with food and supplies for the beleaguered city of Cartagena.

While at sea, however, Bolívar was stunned to learn from corsairs headed the other way that Cartagena had already fallen. The news shouted from bow to bow was grim: The trusty colonel sent as an intermediary—Carabaño—was dead; neither he nor Brion's battleship had ever made it to Cartagena. Half the city had perished. The unfortunates too weak to escape had been slaughtered indiscriminately. Even after the royalists had taken Cartagena, they continued to fly the rebel flag precisely in order to trap rescue operations like Bolívar's. Lastly, the patriots who had managed to escape were all headed for Haiti. Bolívar immediately ordered his ship to change course and follow.

There was every reason to choose Haiti. During his four-month stay in Jamaica, Bolívar had been introduced to Hyslop's wealthy colleague Robert Sutherland, an Englishman who ran a lucrative shipping trade there. Sutherland traded in cotton and coffee, and essentially controlled import-export traffic out of that island, operating as Haiti's de facto minister of trade and finance. But he was also a passionate liberal and an active gunrunner, selling arms and munitions to revolutionaries. With Sutherland in Haiti, Hyslop in Jamaica, and Brion in Curaçao, Bolívar soon had a solid network of some of the most influential shippers and merchants in the region. But in Sutherland he had something else: an ally who boasted a close friendship with President Alexandre Pétion, one of the heroes of the Haitian revolution. The son of a French father and an African mother, Pétion was a steadfast republican and generous soul, who had made it known throughout the Caribbean that in his country all freedom seekers were welcome. Sutherland had spoken to Bolívar of the importance of establishing a relationship with Pétion and, toward that end, urged him to visit Haiti as his personal guest.

On Christmas Eve, Bolívar landed in the port of Aux Cayes, where many of the fugitives from Cartagena had taken refuge. By New Year's Day, he was comfortably lodged in the capital of Port-au-Prince. Sutherland received him and personally escorted him to the gleaming white presidential palace to meet the great man Pétion. The Haitian president welcomed Bolívar warmly. "I was immediately drawn to him," Pétion later confided in a letter, "and I could feel his greatness." Before long, he offered the Liberator his complete support. When Bolívar said that he would repay Pétion by making him the patron of Spanish American independence, the president replied, "No, don't mention my name; my only desire is to see that those who tremble under slavery's yoke are free: Liberate my brothers, and that will be payment enough." It was a bold demand: ending slavery would alter the social fabric of South America. But Bolívar already knew that he needed to lure the colored classes to his side. He readily agreed. Within days, Bolívar was given everything he needed to mount a new invasion: one thousand guns, thirty thousand pounds of gunpowder, a fleet of seven ships, and all the captains and sailors necessary to man them. It wasn't the vast, muscular support Bolívar had hoped for from Britain or the United States, but it was enough to attempt a reentry.

Straightaway, he called a meeting with his cohort in Haiti, a motley crew of friends and rivals: Santiago Mariño, Manuel Piar, José Francisco Bermúdez, Carlos Soublette, Francisco Zea, Mariano Montilla, the French mercenary Luis Ducoudray, and the dashing Scottish colonel Gregor McGregor, who had married one of Bolívar's cousins at the start of the revolution. Among those, Luis Brion was his most steadfast supporter, and it was Brion now who proposed Bolívar as head of the expedition, but Montilla, Bermúdez, and others objected. Montilla even went so far as to challenge Bolívar to a duel; and Bermúdez continued his insubordination against Bolívar, which had begun even as they battled the Legions of Hell side by side in the waning days of the second republic. In the end, Montilla and Bermúdez were dropped from the expedition. Mariño, the Liberator of the East, was made chief of staff, with the thoroughly dyspeptic Frenchman Ducoudray as his assistant. But as plans developed, it was Bolívar who took command.

Bolívar busily prepared for the expedition, heartened by the faith of his new sponsor, Pétion; his vital network of European businessmen; and his passionate republican collaborators. All the same, in the course of those few months, he found time to renew his affair with the irresistible young Isabel Soublette, who with her brother Carlos had made the harrowing escape from Cartagena. It was a transitory romance, dashed all too soon by the winds of revolution, but like the congenial hospitality of Haiti, it gave him the fleeting illusion of home.

CHAPTER 8

A Revolution Struggles to Life

*Our people are nothing like Europeans or North Americans;
indeed, we are more a mixture of Africa and America than
we are children of Europe. . . . It is impossible to say with any
certainty to which human race we belong.*

—Simón Bolívar

Eighteen sixteen was the year without a summer. As Lord Byron put it, the bright sun had vanished and stars wandered "darkling in the eternal space." The colossal eruption of Mount Tambora in Indonesia on April 10, 1815—the largest volcanic event in recorded history—had traveled the globe to spew a fine ash over Europe and the Americas. A year later, the earth's atmosphere was so saturated with sulfur that brilliant sunsets inflamed the English skies, torrential rains washed away European crops, and a persistent gloom hung over North America. At the time, few imagined that a single geologic event in a remote location could affect the entire globe, and yet there was so much evidence of a freak imbalance: stinging frosts carpeted Pennsylvania in the middle of summer, killing the livestock; in Germany, harvests failed, causing a crippling famine; a typhus epidemic swept through the Mediterranean. There were surprising ramifications. Food riots gripped England and Ireland; Luddites torched textile factories with renewed frenzy. In a dark castle in rain-pelted Switzerland, Mary Shelley wrote the novel *Frankenstein*. In northern Europe, J. M. W. Turner was so stunned by the fiery skies that he recorded them in magnificent canvases for years to come. In France, rampant disease prompted a new age of medical discovery. And in the Caribbean, where Bolívar prepared to relaunch his revolution, a perfect calm preceded the hurricane season, which arrived a month sooner than usual, tossing the sea with singular fury.

Eighteen sixteen also became the revolution's cruelest year. There were wholesale beheadings, hangings, firing squads—all in the name of "pacification." General Morillo had installed draconian laws to rid Venezuela—Spain's most defiant colony—of revolutionaries once and for all. The royalists arrested suspects in rural backwaters and relocated them to heavily defended towns, where they could be overseen. Anyone found wandering the countryside was a candidate for the gallows. Morillo's men burned crops, purged the forests of fruit trees, killed farm animals, impounded horses, and executed any blacksmith capable of forging a lance's head or any other weapon. Royalist commanders exacted taxes and punitive fines, making themselves rich and powerful in the process. Patriots, on the other hand, were stripped of whatever property they had. In the course of a single year, Venezuela's Committee of Confiscation sold land valued at almost one million pesos, thereby funding Spain's treasury and enabling its army to secure badly needed supplies. More than two hundred haciendas were expropriated—all of them owned by the patriot leadership, including the Palacios, del Toros, and Tovars, many of whom had fled in the mass emigration to the east. But the largest and most retaliatory confiscation was reserved for Bolívar, who was divested of five estates and numerous smaller properties, valued at a staggering 200,000 pesos.

Patriots who were not given the death penalty as "traitors to the king" were condemned to heavy labor, and royalists set revolutionaries to paving roads and building bridges. Wives were chained inside houses; rebel priests, detained and exiled. But by and large, enforcing this new order was not all that difficult; Boves had done a good job of cowing the population. Morillo moved swiftly to take up the pricklier work in New Granada, where a purge of republican leaders followed. Manuel del Castillo, found quailing inside his deserted citadel of Cartagena, was dragged to the public square and shot in the back. The president of New Granada's congress, the statesman and orator Camilo Torres, tried to flee Bogotá with his wife and children, but eventually was captured and killed with a bullet to his brain. To signal the crown's displeasure, Torres's corpse was drawn and quartered—his body parts hung out for view in four corners of the city. Manuel Torices, the young president who had welcomed Bolívar so warmly in Cartagena four years before, was shot, then hanged.

But in moving so swiftly from Venezuela to New Granada, Morillo had created a strategic problem for himself: Venezuelan rebels with nothing to lose now roamed the plains, trying to reorganize their efforts, getting stronger all the while. Although the Venezuelan coast was firmly under Spanish control except for the patriot stronghold of Margarita—which Arismendi had retaken with a fierce battalion of fifty men—the vast inland wilderness posed difficulties for Spain, and Morillo knew it. The llaneros, on whom his predecessors had relied, were proving true to Boves's word: they answered to no one. Under a new leader, they gradually defected to the republican side. Morillo had other worries. A ship holding a million pesos (meant to pay his troops) had burned in port; and worse, as he had approached the island of Margarita his fleet had incurred costly casualties. These challenges would have been surmountable if Morillo had been able to secure money and reinforcements from Spain; but the Indonesian volcano had inflicted incalculable damage on Europe and the mother country. For all his pleading, Morillo got no response from Madrid. Frustrated, ill-humored, he began to fear that he wouldn't be able to fulfill the continental mandate he had been given. Even before Bolívar's return to Venezuela, the Spanish general began to imagine the worst.

Bolívar's expedition set sail from Haiti on March 31, filled to capacity with disputatious officers, querulous wives, a full complement of servants, and an army of black Haitians. They floated away from harbor only to encounter a paucity of wind. For all their eagerness to restart a revolution, they were creeping across a flat sea. Bolívar decided not to plow a direct route to Venezuela, but to make a brief stop on the island of St. Thomas—ostensibly to pick up recruits, but actually to collect his mistress Pepita Machado, with whom he had been corresponding anxiously for months. No sooner had the fleet gone 150 miles, however, than Bolívar received news from a passing vessel that Pepita had already gone from St. Thomas to Aux Cayes and was waiting for him in Haiti. The news caused great consternation. Brion argued vehemently against changing the expedition's plans for Pepita's sake. But Bolívar was adamant: Pepita and her family were probably in danger without him. He commanded all ships to drop anchor at Beata Island, and then sent Carlos Soublette back to Haiti on a schooner to fetch his mistress.

For more than two days, as the outraged French colonel Ducoudray reported, the revolution stalled as an entire squadron of ships lay anchored off the coast of Santo Domingo, waiting for a woman to arrive. On the third day, the bright-eyed Pepita appeared on the deck of Soublette's schooner with her mother and sister, and the sailors could do little but gape while a magnificently groomed Bolívar repaired to her quarters to spend another full day and night. Just as Marc Antony had infuriated his generals by holding up a war and lingering abed with Cleopatra, Bolívar now maddened his officers with his unquenchable libido. Some huffily threatened to abandon the expedition; one—Bolívar's cousin Florencio Palacios—actually managed to do just that, and disappeared over the water toward Jacmel.

It was a bad start for a year that—like the peevish weather moving through it—would grow steadily worse before it cleared. But Bolívar had always been a measured hedonist, never quite losing himself fully to the pleasures at hand. Within days, the patriots were back on the high seas. They stopped briefly to pick up cattle for provisions in St. Thomas, vegetables in Saba. It took a month to make the full crossing, but, finally, on May 2, the expedition left the roughening waters to dock at the island of Margarita. Once there, Bolívar proclaimed the dawn of the third republic, the liberation of Spanish America, and an end to his war to the death. Arismendi welcomed him warmly and Bolívar was reinstated as supreme chief of the republic. As much as was possible in that tiny patch of republican officialdom, *el jefe supremo* was brought abreast of the situation.

The news was not good. The island of Margarita was the only republican stronghold in all Venezuela, this by virtue of Governor

Arismendi's formidable tenacity and grit. The governor was tall, athletic, muscular—half Creole, half Indian—an incongruous blend of old-world hospitality and rank revolutionary. He was forty, but looked far older for the hard life he'd led and the wounds that riddled his body. His face, according to a seaman who knew him,

> exhibits a peculiar ferocity of expression, which his smile only increases. His laugh never fails to create a momentary shudder, and the dreadful distortion of the muscles which it produces, can only be compared with that of the hyena when under similar excitement. His displeasure is always signified by this demoniacal grin . . . and should the object of his rage be at these moments within its compass, death inevitably ensues.

If Spaniards feared Bolívar as the man who had declared war to the death against them, they feared Arismendi as the butcher who had delivered that war to the last letter. Arismendi had been the one, after all, to behead a thousand hapless prisoners in La Guaira. Although Bolívar's tiny expedition and Arismendi's troops were no match for Morillo's prodigious army, Spaniards trembled at the thought of so many republican champions reunited at the gates: the fearsome Mariño, the valiant Piar, the terrifying Caribbean pirate Beluche who joined them, not to mention hardened veterans from the wars in Europe. Bolívar had actively sought that fear: he had written exaggerated letters to fellow republicans, hoping that false information would leak, and he had boasted, all too publicly, that he had fourteen—not seven—warships, two thousand men, and "enough arms and munitions to make war for another ten years." Rumor had it, too, that, given the backing of a mulatto president and boatloads of Haitian warriors, Bolívar was bringing a black revolution to America. Terrorized, the royalists engaged his troops briefly along the coast, but withdrew quickly to Cumaná.

By June, as hurricanes blew record winds and a stinging rain from Tierra Firma to the coast of South Carolina, Bolívar still hadn't been able to recruit enough men or organize what men he had to make a dent on Spanish dominion. When his expedition of three hundred landed in

Carúpano and scattered inland in a desperate attempt to enlist soldiers, the army was largely made up of officers. He never increased it to more than triple that number.

But he was able to deliver on his promise to Pétion. In Carúpano on June 2, 1816, Bolívar declared absolute freedom for Spanish America's slaves. "I have come to decree, as law," he announced, "full liberty to all slaves who have trembled under the Spanish yoke for three centuries," and then he specified that they had twenty-four hours to join his revolution. It was a daring declaration and it fulfilled his obligation to Haiti, but it also risked alienating fellow Creoles, who believed that their livelihoods—if ever they were able to resume them—depended on slave labor in the fields. But Bolívar's needs were more immediate. He lacked fighters, and enlisting former slaves was a way to get them. Bolívar had learned that if people of color weren't for him, they would be against him, and he could afford that risk no longer. Without the support of blacks, his revolution was lost.

Ironically, just months before, the Spanish general José de Cevallos, interim captain-general of Caracas, had written to his superiors in Spain, complaining about the law that prohibited blacks from serving in the Spanish army. If Spain didn't support this growing population of people, he argued, "it will form a class more dangerous than the ancient Helots of Greece." As everyone knew, blacks had fought for Spain under Boves and Morales, but they had done so unofficially; generals had not given them arms, put them in uniforms, trained them as soldiers. "We all know that Venezuela has been restored to the rule of our King because of the efforts of these people," Cevallos wrote, "the armies carrying our banner have been composed almost entirely of blacks. Many have shown extraordinary valor. . . . Grant them the privileges of whiteness enjoyed by any citizen under the Constitution." But Madrid didn't listen, and it was Bolívar now who publicly took the high road.

For all Bolívar's admirable pronouncements, however, by July his military operation was in shambles. His officers were unable to coordinate their efforts; minions relayed faulty information; and all came to a disastrous head on the beach of Ocumare, where Bolívar had hoped to push his invasion inland. For that very purpose, Colonel Soublette had taken a position in Maracay, halfway between Valencia and Caracas; McGregor had marched to Choroní; Brion, whom Bolívar had promoted to admiral of the navy, had gone down the coast with the fleet. But on July 10 in Ocumare, plans went badly awry. Soublette sent his aide-de-camp to Bolívar with the news that his position was good and all was well; but the messenger, whether by malice or misunderstanding, reported something very different. He said that the royalist general Morales was approaching with a force of seven thousand men and was no more than three miles away. The same aide then returned to Soublette and reported that Bolívar had already pulled anchor and departed.

Disorder now reigned in Bolívar's expedition, and Ocumare in particular swirled in confusion. No one could be relied upon to relay a reliable fact; no one seemed to know what a reliable fact was. Bolívar instructed his captain, a Frenchman named Villaret, to load the expedition's considerable store of arms onto the one available warship, but Villaret stalled, arguing that the crew was too small to defend such a large shipment of guns. Even as they were disputing the point, a wave of panicked Frenchwomen and their slaves streamed onto the beaches, desperate to save their lives; Captain Villaret seemed more intent on rescuing his countrywomen than on saving the revolution. The situation was acute: expensive war matériel lay strewn on the beach, sailors were refusing to take it on board, and a clamoring horde threatened to bring down a tenuous military operation. At one point, two enterprising corsairs took advantage of the confusion to make off with a hefty load of arms. Making matters worse, Francisco Bermúdez, whom Bolívar had left behind because he was a deeply disruptive influence, suddenly arrived in port, threatening to sow discord. Angrily, Bolívar categorically denied him permission to disembark.

It is unclear what happened next, except that Soublette leaves us with an ambiguous phrase: "Events were clouded by love," he wrote to a friend, suggesting that an additional complicating factor may well have been Pepita. She had been traveling at Bolívar's side—as always, with her mother and sister—and they, too, needed saving. Whether Bolívar lost valuable time trying to deal with Pepita and her family we will never know. But this much is clear: as the tumult was growing ever more dire, word came that General Morales had already overrun

Ocumare. That report was untrue, but at this point no one was going to doubt it.

For all his attempts to bring matters under control, Bolívar now proved singularly incapable of imposing order on chaos. There was nothing to do but go. In a matter of hours, all of Pétion's valuable contributions to the revolution were either pilfered or abandoned for the royalists' taking. As Morales reported exultantly, "The gang of criminals that once imagined themselves masters of Venezuela has vanished like smoke"; he found Ocumare empty, the port deserted. Littering the ground were the patriots' precious supplies.

Few events in Bolívar's life have been the object of as much censure or debate as those disastrous few days in Ocumare. Even he would come to look back at the catastrophe with regret, admitting much later that perhaps this was the moment in his military career when he might have employed better judgment. In the immediate aftermath, however, he would have a string of excuses.

Taking off in a fast sloop, he tried to deliver a few arms to patriot forces farther down the coast, but found that every port he approached sported the royalist flag. Yet again, Bolívar was obliged to make a humiliating escape by sea. He sent Admiral Brion on a frantic mission to the United States to seek diplomatic recognition and whatever arms and assistance he could muster, but Brion's ship was blown off course by violent winds and wrecked off the coast of Panama. Miraculously, Brion managed to survive. Bolívar himself did not escape the raging winds of the Caribbean. After a tempestuous journey, he was finally able to deposit Pepita and her family near St. Thomas. He did not reach the eastern port of Guiria, Venezuela, until a month later—on August 16.

Bolívar looked forward to reuniting with Mariño and continuing to press the revolution toward Caracas, but he was in for a rude surprise. Upon his arrival in Guiria, Mariño received him coldly. Bermúdez, who had sailed from Ocumare to rejoin his old chief, was downright hostile. Old resentments resurfaced to destroy whatever amicable relations Bolívar had been able to craft. Now that the two easterners were back on their own territory, they wanted no part of Bolívar. To them, he was just another revolutionary—a man with a ready sword, his greatness as yet inchoate, his genius and imagination unseen. Even he had not quite understood what he needed to do in order to bring about the solidarity his revolution so desperately required. He spent a few days trying to muster support, continuing to call himself by his former titles—Liberator, chief of the Armies of Venezuela and New Granada—but before long, a coup broke out against him. On August 22, Mariño's supporters gathered in Guiria's plaza and began to shout, "Down with Bolívar! Long live Mariño and Bermúdez!" A crowd took up the cries. There was no question Bolívar was out of his element—he was far from Caracas, far from his Granadan admirers, in a remote part of Venezuela he hardly knew. There was also little question that his life was in danger. The Spanish captain-general had offered 10,000 pesos for his head. If he couldn't rely on his fellow patriots for protection, he was as good as dead.

Keen now to make a getaway, Bolívar hastened to the port. But he got no farther than the beach before Mariño's men surrounded him. They moved to take him into custody. Bolívar pushed past them, drawing his sword into the air. Suddenly Bermúdez—in an uncontrollable fit of rage—lunged at him with his saber. If it hadn't been for Bolívar's extraordinary calm and two nimble soldiers who pulled Bermúdez away, the sword would have met its mark. "Never," asserted a witness, had "Bermúdez's arm moved with more determination." Somehow in the skirmish Bolívar managed to slip away, leap onto a canoe, and make a swift course toward his waiting ship. Betrayed, humiliated, but alive, he headed back to Haiti.

IN AN IRONY NO ONE appreciated at the time, Bolívar took flight from Ocumare on the very day that Miranda took his last breath in a dank prison cell in Cádiz. History was repeating itself. Just as Bolívar had rejected Miranda's authority, Bolívar's minions had discarded him from the foray. There was no doubt the Liberator had enemies. Some of his officers were using every excuse to snatch the reins for themselves. Mariño, goaded by Bermúdez and Piar, had disagreed openly with Bolívar about strategies, goals—the very meaning of the word "republic." Luis Ducoudray, whom Bolívar had forbidden from assuming the title of field marshal, now turned the full force of his bile against him, eventually recording it for all time in his famous invective, *Memories of Simón Bolívar.* Even Arismendi, once one of Bolívar's strongest advocates, was infuriated by Bolívar's retreat from Ocumare. "Bolívar's cowardice has emerged once too often," he was heard to say. "He should be court-martialed for it and shot."

Warlords were now in charge of the revolution in Venezuela, each with his own patch of territory and band of men. Piar was fighting royalists in the wilds of Guayana. José Antonio Páez had emerged in the western plains. Mariño was in Guiria, Arismendi in Margarita, Manuel Cedeño near the Orinoco River, Pedro Zaraza in the upper plains, José Tadeo Monagas in Cumaná. The republic in disarray, the republicans had fled to far-flung corners, gathering under the most powerful chieftain they could find. Bolívar had never been inclined to be a regional warlord. He had no private army, no rooted power base—his notion of the republic was the vast canvas of America. But it was with such divisiveness and regionalism that he would have to contend.

It was early September before Bolívar arrived in Haiti. Pétion didn't hesitate to welcome him back and to offer his continued support, both moral and material. Sutherland, too, seemed willing to subsidize him again. If Bolívar's own officers doubted his ability to lead a successful revolution, these two did not. Pétion was generous in his praise, firm in the belief that Bolívar had the vision and mettle to effect a true liberation. Sutherland was more pragmatic; he understood that with Bolívar in power in Spanish America, Haiti would have a strong partner in trade.

But another option soon presented itself. While in Port-au-Prince, Bolívar received a letter from a Spanish insurrectionist, Francisco Javier Mina, who, charming his way through Boston and Baltimore, had taken up residence in New Orleans and was trying to restart the Mexican revolution. Having heard of Bolívar's valor—not only in Europe, but in Haiti, where Pétion had spoken so highly of him—Mina proposed that Bolívar join him in Mexico. Once Mexican independence was won, Mina promised, a vast army of free Mexicans would help Bolívar liberate his homeland. It was a tempting offer for a warrior who had sought aid so arduously over the years. It was also deeply impressive that Mina had actually managed to raise men and guns for Mexico in North American cities—something Bolívar had never been able to do for his cause. But no sooner had Bolívar started toying with the possibility of helping Mina than he received two letters from Venezuela. One was from Arismendi, who had come to realize the vacuum of leadership Bolívar had left behind. There was simply no commander as inspiring— or appealing—to the population at large; no one as committed to unifying an increasingly fragmented revolution. The second letter was from revolutionaries near Caracas: Come back and lead, they pleaded. Then, in full acknowledgment of Bermúdez's brazen lunge at him in Ocumare, added, "and try to forget those lamentable scenes in Guiria."

For all their lack of unity—for all the unruliness—the patriots had made heartening advances. Páez, who now commanded the plains, had achieved the remarkable feat of winning Boves's llaneros to the republican side, although Páez didn't consider himself anyone's ally. Mariño and Bermúdez had won important victories near Cumaná. All the same, petty animosities between warlords were rampant now. Arismendi openly hated Mariño. Piar and Bermúdez loathed each other. Piar, high on success, had grown jealous of his own colonels and, in a fit of pique, dispatched them to remote locations. There was little cooperation among warlords now.

This was the tumult to which Bolívar was being recalled, and these were the circumstances that would forge his greatness. For all the warlords' apparent power and standing armies, not one could match the reputation Bolívar had built beyond his shores, nor the adoration bestowed on him by the people. None had his oratory brilliance, his ease in the wider world, his understanding of history, his willingness to work with rivals, his ability to lead an army and inspire it to greater sacrifice. Although Bolívar eventually met Javier Mina in Port-au-Prince and wished him well in his Mexican expedition, he could not ignore the call of his own countrymen. Nor could he ignore Brion, who had limped into Haiti after his shipwreck and promised to raise more men, more ships, more arms.

Bolívar left Haiti for the last time on December 21. Landing on the island of Margarita a week later, he issued a proclamation urging Venezuelans to elect a congress and assemble a government. In a letter to two framers of the original 1810 declaration of independence, he wrote:

"Our arms will have destroyed tyrants in vain if we don't establish order and repair wartime ravages." In a more personal letter to Santiago Mariño, he wrote, "General, I am the best friend you have. Unfortunately, your friends are not my friends, and that is the root of the trouble we now must avoid, not only to save ourselves, but our beloved country."

Bolívar embarked on a fervent attempt to build alliances. He wrote to Piar, Monagas, Zaraza, Cedeño. He had come to realize that any gains would be impossible without their cooperation; it was they who had kept the revolution alive. The most valuable among them were also the most headstrong, peevish, wildly erratic. How to harness their energy? How to command a circle of fractious and egotistical men? He would need all his wit and wiles to enlist the warlords to his cause; and then he would need to instill in them—and in the whole revolutionary effort, for that matter—a solid discipline.

IN JANUARY OF 1817, BOLÍVAR landed in Barcelona with four hundred men, hoping to work his way southwest toward Caracas. Immediately, he set about recruiting Indians, though they were armed with little more than bows and arrows. But General Morillo had returned to tamp out the resurgence, and the route to the capital was so fortified that Bolívar could make no headway. Within weeks, an army ten times the size of his own forces headed toward Barcelona to expel Bolívar. Nevertheless, his pleas for unity had not gone ignored. Colonel Urdaneta, who had fought with Páez on the plains of Apure, now decided to make his way north to join the Liberator. Mariño, too, hearing that the Liberator was in peril, did not hesitate.

At this, Bermúdez balked and tried to argue, but Mariño interrupted him, aghast. "I hardly know you!" he scolded his second in command. "How can we possibly abandon Bolívar to certain danger? So that Arismendi and all the rest of the patriots can die with him? No, that cannot be." Somehow, Bermúdez managed to stem his ire and march to Barcelona with Mariño. And somehow, Bolívar decided to forget the scene with him on the beach at Guiria—the threats, the attempted assault, the well-aimed sword. On the afternoon of February 9, Bolívar rode out to greet him. As the proud, straight-backed Bermúdez approached over the bridge, Bolívar threw open his arms. "I've come to embrace the liberator of the Liberator!" he cried. Bermúdez was so won by Bolívar's generosity, so overcome with emotion, he could hardly speak. He finally broke the silence with a husky cry, "Long live a free America!"

Piar was not so easily won. He continued to ignore Bolívar's calls for unity. "Small divisions cannot achieve great objectives," Bolívar had written to him, instructing him to bring in his troops. But Piar paid him no mind and continued to stay right where he was, in the province of Guayana, deep in the Venezuelan interior.

For all Bolívar's increased numbers, he still was no match for the Spaniards. Mariño and Bermúdez's advance had frightened them away momentarily, but they would return to Barcelona when they realized they held the advantage. Bolívar now changed his strategy entirely. With his new reinforcements, he decided to march up the Orinoco River to the wilds of Guayana, where he would join Piar, lure the powerful Páez to his ranks, take command of the plains, and keep the Spanish from spreading their influence beyond the confines of Caracas. It was a masterful plan—designed to bleed Morillo by leading him on a costly chase through the backlands of Venezuela. Since Brion's fleet was blockading the coast, the republicans had virtual control of much of the seaboard. If Bolívar and his allied warlords could master the waterways and the interior, the result would be a pincer movement on Caracas. From land and sea, the patriots would have the advantage.

It was a fundamental shift away from Bolívar's earlier obsession with Caracas. It was also one more lesson Bolívar had learned from Boves: whoever ruled the plains stood to ride in triumph to the capital. Bolívar knew that in Páez he might have his own potential Boves—a powerful llanero who would enlist pardos and strike fear into the royalist heart. Páez had already turned the tables on the Spaniards. In mid-1814, even as Bolívar and Mariño were being run out of Venezuela, accused as scoundrels and thieves, Páez had left the royalist camp and joined the rebels on the plains of Apure. He had tormented the Spanish army ever since, raising a mighty army and recruiting hard-bitten warriors from Boves's Legions of Hell. By the start of 1817, when Bolívar was heading up the Orinoco toward Guayana, Páez had gathered a potent force of eleven hundred marauding horsemen. So terrifying were they that Spanish generals consistently overestimated their numbers.

On the vast expanse of savanna near Mucuritas, just west of where Piar had garrisoned his troops, Páez had executed a stunning victory against General Morillo on January 28 by employing what would become his signature maneuver: the harrowing "about-face." Páez's men, outnumbered three times by Morillo's, provoked the Spaniards with a flank attack, then went into immediate retreat, riding into the wind and drawing the enemy's front lines after them. Suddenly, mid-course, Páez's troops set fire to the savanna's parched grasses so that smoke spewed behind and blew into the Spaniards' faces. Minutes later Páez's horsemen turned precipitously and attacked their pursuers through the flames, skewering the vanguard on their lances and sending the rest into panicked flight.

"We had hardly advanced," reported one of the Spanish captains, "when, from a distance, we saw a forest of spears descending on us at full gallop. It was Páez with four thousand horses, and, upon them, the most audacious cavalry in the world . . . an unrestrained torrent." Páez's horsemen would effect many similar victories—never quite thrashing the royalists decisively, but inflicting heavy and dispiriting losses. Every time the royalists fled through the flaming grass, they abandoned horses, swords, guns, heavy artillery to Páez's forces; and every time a Spanish soldier fell, the bare-chested llanero who had toppled him would ride away fully outfitted in Madrid finery. Morillo later confessed, "Fourteen consecutive attacks on my tired battalions made me see that those men were not just an inconsequential gang of riffraff, as I'd been told, but organized troops that could compete with the best of His Majesty the King's."

Bolívar was thrilled when he heard of Páez's triumphs. He understood that it was in Venezuela's interior, with men such as these, that a revolution was possible. The plains had horses, mules, and the grass to keep them alive; it had livestock to feed and clothe an army; it had mounted warriors who knew the terrain and whose enormous lances rendered a Spaniard's bayonet useless. "We've just had the best news from the interior," Bolívar wrote his nephew Leandro Palacios cheerily; "when we join forces, we'll have an accumulation of more than ten thousand men, and no one will have the power to prevent us from marching to Bogotá and Peru and liberating those provinces from the yoke of tyranny." Bolívar wasted no time in sending Arismendi to meet with Páez, in hopes of persuading the llanero to join him in a unified front against the Spanish. "Destiny is calling us to the far frontiers of the American world!" he told his men.

IN THE MEANTIME, HOWEVER, IT was the pardo Piar who needed to be reined in. Since the standoff in Margarita between the liberators and their deputies, he had grown ever more stubborn and unmanageable, ignoring Bolívar's appeals and instructions at every turn. On March 25, when Bolívar set out for the interior with only fifteen officers, it was to Piar's camp that they proceeded. By the time Bolívar, Soublette, Arismendi, and Bermúdez arrived there in early May, the warlord had demonstrated his worth. Piar's ragtag army of pardos and Indians had invaded and occupied a sprawling mission on the Coroní River owned by Spanish Capuchin monks—a highly prosperous system of farms and ranches that could feed whole armies. He had gone on to win a decisive victory against the Spaniards in the fields of San Félix, near the ancient and picturesque city of Angostura. He had built fortifications along the river, planned a strategic assault on Angostura, and blockaded Guayana until the starving Spaniards had no choice but to beg for mercy. Bolívar and Piar had gone on to prepare a major offensive. To protect themselves against possible espionage, they arrested two dozen Capuchin monks suspected of being royalist agents; someone—Bolívar? Piar? the history is unclear—issued an order to march the wretched monks off to Divina Pastora. The order was taken literally. The holy men were delivered to divine pastures, that is: dispatched to their Maker—a terrible eventuality, for which Bolívar was blamed, and for which Bolívar in turn blamed Piar.

All the same, there was no doubt that great headway had been made under Piar, and Piar was puffed with the triumph of it. His troops, who were equipped with little more than spears, had fought against a vastly superior army and routed it roundly. Four hundred royalists had died in battle, three hundred had been taken prisoner and butchered, and the rest had scrambled up and down the Orinoco, running for their lives.

Bolívar was not pleased about Piar's order to kill all Spanish prisoners—he had made it clear that the war to the death was over—but he could not deny that Piar's victories had helped establish the patriot stronghold he needed in Guayana. He praised Piar, promoted him to a full general, and tried to appease him.

Piar pretended to comply with Bolívar and swore loyalty to him publicly, but he was singularly suspicious of his designs. Piar had led brilliantly, fought bravely, not for the glory of the Liberator, but for the advancement of his own burning ambitions. He resented Bolívar's assumption that the region was now his to usurp and control. Unlike Mariño in the east, or Arismendi on the island of Margarita, Piar did not have a natural territorial constituency. He had won every acre of his domain on the Orinoco by dint of furious battle. His troops were largely illiterate pardos, marginalized men who obeyed him with unconditional loyalty. Although he rarely admitted it, he himself was pardo—handsome, blue-eyed, ruddy-skinned, flamboyant, with a marked predilection for violence. And although he claimed to be descended from Portuguese nobility, he harbored deep resentments against Creole whites.

He had been born in Dutch Curaçao, the son of a merchant marine and a mulatta. Uneducated but fiercely proud, he had set out at a young age to make something of himself. He was quick, intelligent, resourceful, and proficient in a number of languages. Other than his native Dutch and Spanish, he could speak French, English, and communicate with blacks in their own languages—Papiamento, Patois, Guyanese. Above all, he was a skilled warrior who had proven his mettle under Miranda, liberated the east alongside Mariño, plotted a wider revolution with Bolívar, and distinguished himself in battles on land and sea. Time had brought him to this remote area of Venezuela, where he had raised a fearsome army of disaffected men. Having labored to dissociate himself from Bolívar and Mariño, he was now in the frustrating position of having his territory wrested from his control. For all his seeming compliance with Bolívar, Piar made no secret of his antipathy toward the man. Only three years before, he had joined Ribas in exiling the Liberator, after all; he had fired on Bolívar's ship off the coast of Margarita, had set out with a handful of soldiers to gun him down in Carúpano. It should have surprised no one that Piar now began to look for ways to undermine Bolívar's authority in Guayana. At first, he tried to foment a revolt among the indigenous people of the Caroní missions, who were under his command. Failing that, he decided to provoke a pardo uprising in Maturín: the stretch of land between Guayana and Cumaná, where the ruling governor was black.

Disobeying Bolívar's orders blatantly now, Piar announced that he was in poor health and wanted to extract himself from the battlefield to take a long needed respite. Bolívar balked at this. "The nation needs you," he replied. "If you were my chief, I wouldn't abandon you." But eventually, on June 30, he accepted Piar's request for leave and granted him a passport to travel to Curaçao.

Piar did not go home to Curaçao. He began canvassing nearby towns, trying to incite racial anger by claiming that Bolívar had discharged him because of his color. He told one of his officers: "I rose to General in Chief by dint of my sword and chance, but because I am a mulatto, I am not allowed to govern in this Republic. . . . I have resolved, on my honor, to fight for those who spill their lifeblood in battle, only to be chained more and more to a shameful slavery; I'm off to Maturín and to the ends of this earth, if necessary, to lead those who are powerless apart from their brawn." But on Piar's arrival in Maturín, the black governor, Andrés Rojas, scoffed openly at his proposition of a race rebellion.

When Bolívar heard of it, he erupted in molten anger. He refused, he told one of his officers, to be undermined again, as Castillo had undermined him in Cartagena, as Ribas and Piar had done in Carúpano, as Mariño and Bermúdez had in Guiria. "If I have been the essence of moderation until now, it has been out of prudence, not weakness. . . . As long as I breathe with a sword in hand, there will be no tyrants here, no anarchy." Getting wind of Bolívar's fury, Piar fled toward Cumaná and tried to find shelter with his old leader Mariño, with whom he had had a long and warm friendship, but there was little Mariño could do for him. On the 23rd of July, Bolívar signed the order to arrest Piar. He instructed Bermúdez, now one of his most trusted officers, to hunt him

down. Bermúdez was only too happy to comply: he had always held
Piar accountable for the death of his own brother. He rode south immediately to make the capture. General Soublette was to bring charges;
Admiral Brion was to head the court-martial. After a sleepless night,
worrying about the implications of such an action, Bolívar dictated a
manifesto to his secretary:

> I want to denounce openly the most atrocious crime a man can com-
> mit against society, government and nation. General Piar . . . has
> slandered the government, proclaimed a hateful race war, instigated
> civil disobedience, invited anarchy, encouraged assassination, plunder
> and disorder. . . . What exactly is it that General Piar actually wants
> for men of color? Equality? No: They already have it, and General
> Piar himself is irrevocable proof. . . . General Piar, with his senseless,
> abominable conspiracy has tried to inflame a war between brothers
> in which the cruel would slaughter the innocent for having been
> born with a lighter skin. . . . General Piar has broken laws, conspired
> against the system, disobeyed the government, resisted censure,
> deserted the army and fled like a coward; in such ways does he put
> himself outside the law: his destruction is a duty, and his destroyer
> will be a helping hand.

Piar was arrested and brought to Angostura. As the revolution
raged, a war council was convoked, bringing together some of the highest officers in the patriot army. When the trial opened on October 4,
Piar made no effort to defend himself, except to declare that he was innocent of all charges. Perhaps he couldn't imagine that someone of his
stature could possibly be found guilty—the room contained so many of
his friends. In any case, he left all arguments to his counsel, Fernando
Galindo—a wellborn Creole and distant relative of Bolívar's—who
spoke eloquently on his behalf:

> The accused is the same General Piar who so often has saved the life
> of the Republic, who has broken the chains of countless Venezuelans,
> who has liberated whole provinces, whose sword is more feared
> by the Spaniards than Napoleon's, and in whose presence tyrants

tremble. . . . Where are his conspiratorial plans? Where is the list of his conspirators? Where are the proclamations urging the masses to rise? Where, finally, are the preparations for such a colossal, foolish enterprise?

In the end, however, the war council found Piar guilty on all counts: insubordination, sedition, conspiracy, desertion. The verdict read out on the 15th of October was unanimous; the sentence, death. When Bolívar was presented with the results, it is said he wept. But he signed the death sentence all the same, taking care to strike the clause that stripped Piar of his rank as general.

At five o'clock on the following afternoon, General Piar was led up the hill to Angostura's main square. A crowd of townspeople awaited him, as did all the soldiers who were garrisoned there. He seemed calm, unfazed, likely believing to the end that his sentence would be commuted, that he would be exiled—that one way or the other, Bolívar would not dare to have him shot. He listened as the condemnation was read yet again, staring haughtily at the crowd, tapping his right foot impatiently. But Bolívar never appeared, nor did he send a last-minute order granting the condemned man clemency. As the men of the firing squad filed out and shouldered their muskets, Piar understood he would be shown no mercy. He refused to cover his eyes, tore the kerchief from his face twice, then, when it was applied for the third time, he flung open his cape to expose his chest and instructed his executioners to aim well. As twenty bullets ripped the air, he cried out, "Viva la Patria!"

Bolívar was in his headquarters when those shots rang out and the citizens of Angostura took up the dead man's shout: "Viva la Patria!" Tears welled in his eyes once more. But he never regretted his decision. For all Piar's bravery in battle—for all his value as a skilled general— he had traits Bolívar despised: he was a divider, a racialist, a man who prized his career above the collective good. Many years later, Bolívar would say: "The death of General Piar was a political necessity that saved the country. . . . Never was there a death more useful, more politic, and at the same time more deserved."

He set about explaining the execution to his soldiers. It was no simple matter, as there were pardos among his troops, many of them proud of Piar's victories. But, as Bolívar told them now, an army needed to be single-minded. Division was unacceptable. Race, though it had plagued the Americas through three hundred years of difficult history, was no longer a justifiable reason for discord. The power of the warlord had to yield to the power of the commander in chief; and even the most laureled general could not be above the law no matter his color. Bolívar assured his soldiers that the promises he had made were real: slaves were free, men were equal, and citizens stood to enjoy all the benefits of an orderly government. As time passed, Bolívar proved less strict with other generals—he did not punish Mariño, for instance, although Mariño had a long history of flagrant insubordination—and, as a result, some wondered why Bolívar had chosen a pardo to make his point. But there was no question that the republican military, which had been fragmented for so long, was gathering force under Bolívar. Its legions numbered almost thirteen thousand now. Bolívar, confirmed as the supreme chief of the republic, busied himself making warlords into generals. He created a general staff to oversee their operations. He established courts-martial, insisted on due process. Ever more unified, more organized— with a pay structure written into law—Bolívar's military machine, one might even say, was born with the fall of Piar.

MARIÑO'S TRESPASSES INDEED HAD BEEN grave. In late March of 1817, when Bolívar had set out for Guayana, he had ordered Mariño to march west and await further instructions. But no sooner had Bolívar vanished than Mariño sprang to assume his mantle. He went east instead—to a town near his old base in Cumaná—and there began consolidating his own power. He countermanded orders, flouted the chain of command, outraged his officers; perhaps even worse, he ignored desperate calls for help from troops Bolívar had left behind in Barcelona. As a result, more than four hundred soldiers garrisoned in the convent's Casa Fuerte, along with several hundred citizens in their charge, were brutally exterminated by the Spaniards. It was a devastating loss, with harrowing stories of valor and sacrifice. One of Bolívar's aides-de-camp, a young English captain named Chamberlain, had shot himself in the head rather than surrender to the enemy. When a Spanish officer began to paw at Chamberlain's wife and then tried to take her by force, she took out a pistol and killed him. Infuriated, the officer's men hacked her to pieces on the spot.

That butchery at Casa Fuerte would go down in more than one chronicle as an utterly deplorable, possibly avoidable moment in revolutionary history. General Mariño had not been far away; he might have come to the rescue. But Mariño never looked back. He had been willing to assist Bolívar as one commander might assist another; but serving Bolívar on terrain he considered his own was abhorrent to him. He established himself in the tiny coastal town of San Felipe de Cariaco and began spreading the rumor that Bolívar had probably been captured or killed in the crocodile-infested wilds of the Orinoco. With the support of Canon Cortés de Madariaga, who had recently escaped from a Spanish prison and returned to the Americas full of bombast and ambition, Mariño lunged now to grasp at the reins of the republic. On May 8, he called to order a congress of ten men—among them Bolívar's trusty Brion and the eloquent Francisco Antonio Zea—and announced the new government of the United States of Venezuela. Cortés de Madariaga obliged by nominating Mariño supreme chief, all voted aye, the old federalist constitution of 1811 was reinstated, open trade with the United States and Britain was declared, and Brion was made commanding admiral of its navy. But Mariño's hastily cobbled regime went totally ignored by the people of Venezuela; a regional warlord could not hope to rule a vast and chaotic republic, nor did a republic really exist, as Venezuela was slipping back into the royalist maw. By the following day, the diminutive congress had put away its gavel and dissolved in haste, since the enemy was fast approaching. By the end of May, Mariño's entire government had dispersed, Cortés had rushed to safety in Jamaica, and what was left of Mariño's army began to take a heavy pounding from Spanish forces.

If Bolívar took notice of Mariño's breathtaking treachery, he made little fuss about it.

There had been plenty to draw Bolívar's attention away from the attempted coup. Come June, Bolívar was desperately trying to consolidate forces along the Orinoco; by July 17, he had won Angostura; by

August 3, he had taken Guayana; and then, flush with victory and the conviction that only a disciplined army could carry out a revolution, he had turned the brunt of his fury on Piar.

Perhaps Bolívar suspected all along that Mariño's brazen lunge for power would come to nothing. The Liberator of the East was soon discredited, and the Liberator of the West didn't have to lift a finger to contribute to that fleet fall; thirty of Mariño's officers, disgusted with their general's perfidy, left him for Bolívar. Mariño's former deputy, Bermúdez, had already defected to Bolívar some time before. Now, General Rafael Urdaneta and Colonel Antonio José de Sucre, among many others, rushed from Mariño's camp to Guayana to place themselves under Bolívar's command. Admiral Brion, trying to put the whole sordid business behind him, drove a fleet of ships up the Orinoco in time to secure Bolívar's hold on the river. Writing to a friend, Bolívar commented that the whole enterprise had been as easy to dissolve as cassava in a boiling broth. Mariño had come apart of his own accord.

In the end, Bolívar decided to forgive Mariño. "I've resisted writing a single word or saying anything critical about that so-called federal government," he told his friend. "Here, men take charge not because they want to, but because they can." To Mariño, Bolívar was cuttingly direct, singularly chilly. "If you insist on disobedience," he warned him in a letter, "you will no longer be a citizen of Venezuela but a public enemy. If you are determined to quit serving the republic, just say so and the government will gladly issue you permission to go." That was a month before the execution of Piar. A month after it, when Mariño might have feared the same ignominious fate, he received a surprisingly different message from one of his former officers. Colonel Sucre appeared at the wayward general's door, telling him that Bolívar wanted to reenlist him. Bolívar had urged Sucre to employ all the delicacy he could muster to win back Mariño. If he resists, Bolívar instructed, then bring him by force. But "if he submits voluntarily, treat him with the utmost dignity, as you would a man who has just done his country the greatest service by refusing to stain it with civil war. To right one's wrongs can only be considered a good deed, and good deeds should be rewarded."

It took several months to bring Mariño around, but when the renegade finally agreed, Bolívar made him general in chief and placed two of the most capable generals in his service. Slowly, painstakingly, Bolívar was imposing some order over the rebellious warlords who had nettled him for so long. Now with Bermúdez and Mariño on his side—and Piar well out of the way—the east was firmly under Bolívarian rule. It was left to do the same in the west, with Páez.

CHAPTER 9

The Hard Way West

A lightning bolt doesn't fall from the sky as swiftly as General Bolívar descended on the capital.

—Francisco Santander

Bolívar received news of José de San Martín's mounting victories with a mixture of joy and alarm. The soldier who had helped rid Argentina of Spanish rule was working his way north, cutting a triumphant path for liberty. In February of 1817, just as Bolívar was struggling to raise a few hundred troops in the seaside town of Barcelona, General San Martín had surprised the Spaniards by leading an army of thousands—half of them former slaves—over the ice-capped Andes into Chile. The Spanish generals responsible for defending the region hadn't imagined such a feat was possible. By year's end, San Martín was routing them in battle after battle. That was the happy news; the unsettling part was that he was headed for the prize Bolívar had dreamed of so often with his men—the viceregal heart of Peru.

Now that Bolívar had the Venezuelan east mostly under his command, he focused on moving west, over the plains to New Granada. Eventually, with inspired strategy and a bit of luck—as he wrote in a letter to the new republican chief of state in Argentina, Juan de Pueyrredón—he might push his way south, meet San Martín's effort, and create a seamless, unified America. "An America thus united," he told Pueyrredón, "if heaven grants us this favor, will call itself the queen of nations, mother of all republics." What he needed most of all now, however, was to win over allies close by, chief among them the formidable warlord of the western plains, José Antonio Páez.

Páez's astonishing victory at the Battle of Mucuritas almost a year before had been a turning point in the war. It had been General Morillo's first defeat since he had begun his campaign of pacification. Páez had won by sheer force of will: eleven hundred plainsmen and Indians—barefoot, naked except for loincloths, armed with arrows and spears—had charged against four thousand well-equipped, handsomely uniformed veterans of the Napoleonic Wars. Using fire, dust, wind, and a terrifying ferocity, they had outsmarted the Spanish hussars, scattering them over the burning plains like a herd of sheep. It was a hallmark victory, and it made Páez famous. His ranks soon swelled with men wanting to fight under his flag and share in the Spanish booty.

At twenty-eight years of age, Páez could neither read nor write, had not learned to eat with a knife and fork, had never seen anything that resembled a big city. The child of indigent Canary Islanders, he had grown up in a small village in the backlands of Barinas. By fifteen, he had killed a man in self-defense and fled into the wilds of Casanare to avoid Spanish justice. There, in that sea of grass known as the llanos, he found work as a ranch hand for a paltry few cents a week; and in that punishing terrain he learned the skills of a horseman. His cohort were pardos, Indians, mestizos—the chaff of Venezuelan society—many of them, like him, fleeing to escape poverty or the dungeon. They called him "the fair Páez," for although his hair was brown, his skin was moon white, his cheeks pink in the relentless heat of the savanna. From rougher men, he learned how to survive the harsh land. Meat became his diet, river water his drink. His bed was a hammock of pineapple twine or a length of dried hide. By three in the morning, he would be up and out on the plains, rounding up the livestock, branding them, castrating them, moving them to pasture. Páez's overseer was a towering black slave with a long, scruffy beard named Manuelote. He was taciturn, demanding, severe; but he taught Páez the trade: how to break horses, kill crocodiles, cajole cattle into crossing rivers, flip cows by their tails. In the evenings, after a hard day's work, and as an extra dose of discipline, Manuelote would call Páez to wash his feet and swing his hammock until he nodded off to sleep.

Eventually, Manuelote took him to another ranch, and Páez, a hardworking, amiable young man, won the notice of its owner, who taught him the business and helped him establish his own herd. That is, until war intervened. By the time he was twenty-four, Páez had served in both the royalist and patriot armies and was quartered in Mérida, fighting with General Urdaneta's guerrilla forces. But he quit in disgust when one officer commanded him to give up his horse and surrender it to another officer. Páez decided to cross the Andes on foot, return to the llanos, and raise his own legion of horsemen. He undertook that arduous trip with his young wife and child, arriving on the plains of Casanare in mid-1814, just as Boves was charging into Caracas and Bolívar was decamping from the capital with twenty thousand panicked citizens. Páez was convinced he could raise a cavalry as powerful as Boves's and, although his fellow patriots laughed at the notion, he soon commanded a regiment of more than a thousand men. When Boves was killed in battle a few months later, Páez was in a position to attract the dead man's multitudes. As Páez's Army of the Apure began to gather victory after victory, that was exactly what he did.

Páez's army rode at night—sometimes sixty miles at a time—in order to avoid the scorching sun. They rode against the wind whenever possible, so that the Spaniards could not see or smell the dust of their approach. They sat on skulls of bulls, for that was their furniture; they had Spartan needs and Bedouin fortitude. Even in torrential rains, they worked, ate, slept under the open skies. When rivers flooded, they rode into the muddy waters, their worldly possessions perched on their heads. They were masters of their terrain, well accustomed to the jaguars, vultures, vampire bats, and flesh-devouring insects that terrified the more urbane soldiers of the king. Chasing Páez, Morillo's armies grew exhausted, and in the effort thousands of soldiers died. If they weren't felled by malaria, typhoid, or yellow fever, they succumbed to sunstroke, skin rot, or starvation. Páez's men, in turn, pursued Morillo like an avenging shadow, making lightning incursions into his camp by night, slaughtering all men and animals in their way, and suffering only trifling losses. Or they would strike Morillo's forces after a march, sweeping in when the Spaniards were exhausted; thundering through their camps, the llaneros would scare off the Spaniards' cattle and pack animals, leaving them with no provisions. Little by little, as Morillo later admitted, Páez began to wear him down.

Páez, known as the invincible Lion of the Apure, had never been inclined to accept another's authority. He was ambitious, inconstant, and voracious when it came to power. But he was also shrewd and capable of compromise: If it behooved him to make an alliance, he made it; if allies crossed him, he exacted a costly revenge. When Bolívar sent two colonels to suggest to Páez that he recognize Bolívar as supreme chief, Páez's antiroyalist fervor was such that he agreed. He explained to his army that Bolívar's achievements were many and known throughout the world, and that the Liberator's intellectual acuity alone entitled him to the command. He even insisted that they pledge their undying allegiance to Bolívar in a religious ceremony. In truth, Bolívar was as necessary to Páez as Páez was to Bolívar. The Liberator offered the unschooled warlord a wider knowledge of strategic possibility, a more sophisticated approach to war. There didn't appear to be a risk to allying with such a man. Bolívar may have harbored many ambitions—he, too, could be voracious when it came to power—but he could not be accused of lusting after a horseman's empire. The two simply wanted to use each other for a while.

Páez set out to meet Bolívar in January of 1818 with a company of Cunaviche Indians. On his way to San Juan de Payara, where the meeting was to take place, he decided to descend on the town of San Fernando and scare off the Spanish regiment that was occupying that crucial crossroad. Worried that whizzing musket balls would unnerve the Cunaviche, he plied the Indians with strong drink. The *aguardiente* had the desired effect. The Cunaviche, dressed in leather loincloths and brilliantly colored feathers, stormed the Spanish encampment fearlessly, piercing their tongues with their own spears and smearing the bright blood across their faces. The orderly Spaniards, as startled as they were horrified, scrambled in retreat.

On January 30, Páez finally met the supreme chief. As soon as Bolívar saw Páez approaching from the distance, he leapt on his horse and rode out to welcome him. They dismounted, embraced heartily, and greeted one another with warm compliments. Yet clearly they were from alien worlds. To Páez, Bolívar seemed the embodiment of an intellectual—refined, highly animated, with a slight frame, delicate features, and quick, luminous eyes. For Bolívar, Páez was like no general he had ever commanded: no Mariño, no Urdaneta, no Sucre or Santander—no Creole aristocrat, nor even a worldly Piar—but a burly plainsman with a coarse appearance and coarser ways. Nevertheless, Bolívar understood his kind; he had known rough Canary Island boys like Páez since his childhood in Caracas, kicked stones with them in the back alleys of town.

Páez was thirty by that time, and in the full flower of his vigor. He was not tall, but he was broad-shouldered, barrel-chested, built like a bull—the upper half of his body at odds with his spindly legs. His hair was wavy, leonine, bleached by relentless sun; his neck thick and muscular. He was robust and florid where Bolívar was thin and gaunt. He was given to epileptic fits, especially in the heat of battle when blood was flying; he would become so excited by the carnage that he would foam at the mouth and topple from his horse, flailing helplessly until his giant black manservant, "El Negro Primero," would hoist him up and ride away. Bolívar, on the other hand, was a man of consummate control; he didn't drink much, was not intrinsically violent, and uncannily managed to avoid physical injury, even when he was leading a charge. Looking upon them there as they met for the first time, a casual observer might have assumed that each would be incapable of coping in the other's domain: one had come of age playing tennis with princes; the other had come of age washing the feet of a slave. But the assumption would have been wrong. Páez may have been a rube, a ruffian, the untamed Lion of the Apure, but in time he would become a national figure, world diplomat, habitué of the salon. Bolívar, on the other hand, despite his small frame and wiry body, would go on to perform Herculean feats of physical endurance. Within a year, he would be riding longer and harder than any horseman of the Apure, so superhuman in that ability that his troops admiringly named him Iron Ass.

~

BOLÍVAR AND PÁEZ SPENT A few days together, discussing the campaign to take the revolution west. The most immediate problem was getting Bolívar's army across the Apure River. He had come to San Juan de Payara with three thousand men, a third of them on horseback. They had no boats, no wood to build them, no admiral to ferry them across this tributary of the Orinoco, which, as far as they could see, was closely guarded by four Spanish ships. On February 6, when Bolívar and Páez were surveying the river, contemplating their stalemate, Páez suddenly turned to Bolívar and told him not to worry. Start the march, he said animatedly. *He* would provide the boats. "But, hombre!" Bolívar cried in amazement, "Where from?" Páez replied that they were down on the river, right there, in full sight—the enemy ships lined up before them.

"And how do you propose to do that?" Bolívar asked.

"With my cavalry."

Bolívar was irritated. "With a sea cavalry, you mean? Because one that operates on land can't possibly perform such a miracle."

Páez called down a company of fifty men, who rode nimbly to the riverbank, their saddles uncinched. When he yelled, "Bring me those boats!" the men slid their saddles to the ground, clenched their lances between their teeth, then, with loud whoops, charged bareback into the river. The Spanish sentinels, brought to life, responded with a volley or two. But they were so panicked at the sight of that fierce horde plowing the water, startling the crocodiles, clambering onto their boats willy-nilly, that they dove into the river and made for the other shore. To Bolívar's amazement—for he had thought his men would be blown to bits—Páez's riders succeeded in taking all four craft. After that, their armies had no trouble sweeping into the encampment. By the time they were through, they had captured fourteen boats and a store of munitions. "It may appear inconceivable," a witness later reported, "that a body of cavalry with no other arms than their lances, and no other mode of conveyance across a rapid river than their horses, should attack and take a fleet of gun-boats amidst shoals of alligators; but there are many officers now in England who can testify to the truth of it."

Bolívar eventually won the respect and affection of these lawless roughriders, although one can easily imagine their initial suspicions. He was a gentleman from the city, a man who wore spotless white shirts and European cologne, even when he was out on maneuvers. He was a product of precisely the social class they most detested. But he was also a product of Simón Rodríguez's unconventional outdoor education, with all of its glorifications of the natural man. It didn't take long for Páez's horsemen to discover that their new leader was an excellent swimmer, skilled rider, tireless hiker, capable of competing with them in all the rough games they enjoyed. On a dare, he had leapt into a lake with his hands tied behind his back, swearing that even with that liability he could outswim any challenger. Seeing his aide-de-camp spring out of his saddle over his horse's head and land, incredibly, on two firm feet, he wanted to do the same, and actually managed it, although it took him several tries and a few painful misses. "I confess it was crazy of me," he later told a friend, "but in those days I didn't want anyone to say they were more agile or able than I, or that there was anything I couldn't do. . . . Don't think that sort of thing isn't useful in a leader."

Eventually, Bolívar decided to waste no more time in San Fernando, and so left Páez and his horsemen behind to lay siege and win what booty they could from the Spaniards. With four thousand men, he marched north to Calabozo, where General Morillo had just arrived with an army of 2,500. Bolívar's opening strategy was masterful. On February 12, the Liberator gave Morillo the surprise of his life, descending on his post at six in the morning and inflicting punishing losses. Once he saw he was at disadvantage, Morillo shut himself off in his headquarters, prompting Bolívar to send him a high-handed communiqué, inviting him to surrender. But this was no Admirable Campaign in which the mere mention of Bolívar's name struck fear into Spanish hearts, and Morillo was no tin-hat general. The Spaniard managed to dodge Bolívar's troops and flee into the night, on foot, with a tiny remnant of his army. Bolívar captured his arms and supplies, but he failed to pursue Morillo and force him to engage in battle. As a result, the patriot advantage was quickly lost. Frustrated and weary, Bolívar waited for Páez to bring fresh troops. His own were exhausted after the 550-mile march that had started in Angostura and lasted almost two months over that merciless terrain. "Fly, fly, join me now!" Bolívar wrote to the Lion of the Apure, "so we can seize the day."

But though the union of Páez and Bolívar was a military rock on which the republic eventually would stand, Páez was still unused to taking orders. There followed a string of loud arguments, miscommunications, and misunderstandings. Páez dragged his feet, insisted on making his own decisions. He complained that Bolívar didn't understand the plains, didn't rely enough on the wisdom of the locals. He knew, too, that his plainsmen and Indians were not keen to wander too far from their natural habitat; the big cities of Venezuela did not lure them in the least. Bolívar, on the other hand, had his own ideas. He had gone as far north as Calabozo and wanted to go farther still, toward the irresistible chimera of Caracas. It was here that his mistakes began.

In Calabozo, he had had Morillo in the palm of his hand, and might have taken him there and then; he hadn't known that Morillo had limped to Calabozo in tatters. The army of pacification had suffered great losses on the patriot island of Margarita, where Morillo—distracted from more urgent matters—had tried to square a long, bitter animosity with its governor, General Arismendi. Morillo's monthlong struggle to recapture that fevered terrain had been fruitless and damaging, costing him the lives of too many. His army, which had started out as a robust force of three thousand, had been reduced to seven hundred pathetic, diseased men. Hobbled by typhoid and yellow fever, the survivors had dragged themselves back to Caracas, where Morillo asked to be relieved of his post. When Madrid refused the request, Morillo begged abjectly for reserves. The news of Bolívar's and Páez's alliance was a further blow to the Spanish general, but when he heard that the two had attacked and laid siege to Spain's strategic river garrison at San Fernando, he hurried south to help. Had Bolívar been more assertive at Calabozo—had he prevented Morillo from slipping away, had he chased him while he was vulnerable—he might have secured his surrender. As it was, Morillo's army had been given a chance to recover.

Bolívar and Páez spent much of the next two weeks bickering: Páez wanted to continue to pressure the town of San Fernando, drive the Spaniards from Apure once and for all, and capture enough booty to remunerate his men. Bolívar wanted to keep pushing toward the capital. On March 3, the day before San Fernando finally collapsed under the weight of Páez's siege, Bolívar began a march toward Caracas. His approach caused great consternation in the city, which was now largely royalist. "In a few hours," a witness recalled, "and like a bolt of electricity, the entire population of Caracas rushed to the shores of La Guaira, and men and women of every age clamored to escape." But Bolívar never did make it to Caracas. Generals Morillo and Morales, with fortified battalions, set out to stop him. Bolívar and Morillo met at last on March 16 on the rolling plains of La Puerta, where the valleys of the Guarico River join the prairies, and where the patriots had fought Boves's legions twice and lost. The battle began at dawn between Bolívar and Morales, and Bolívar might have won, for Morales's army was half the size. But General Morillo brought fresh troops to the fray, leading the charge himself in order to animate his soldiers. Although Morillo was seriously wounded and had to be carried away in a stretcher, the royalists crushed Bolívar, pounding the patriots into retreat. The army of the Liberator was seriously crippled now: He had lost more than a thousand infantrymen, a great deal of armaments, and all his papers.

One month later, on April 17, as Bolívar was trying to rebuild his cavalry in the farmlands of the Rincón de Toros, a band of eight royalists came upon a lowly servant on Bolívar's staff who happened to be wandering the fields alone. From that hapless captive, they extracted the password of the republican camp and the exact location where Bolívar slept. That night, by the light of a waxing moon, they entered the camp, passing themselves off as patriot soldiers. Claiming to have important information, they asked to see the supreme chief. The acting chief of staff, Colonel Francisco de Paula Santander, quizzed the men until he was satisfied, then pointed to Bolívar's hammock. "General!" Santander called out, and Bolívar spun around just as the assassins' shots rang over his head. Bolívar was unhurt, but in the dark of night, and with so much confusion, the royalists managed to dart away, killing patriots as they went. The Spanish generals did not tarry in their next attack: they stormed the encampment before sunrise and sent the republicans running, undoing what little progress Bolívar had made.

Fortune itself seemed to have abandoned the army of the republic. Its greatest patron, Alexandre Pétion, had died of a raging case of typhoid fever in Port-au-Prince on March 29. In May, Páez was defeated on the plains of Cojedes. Bolívar was forced to retire from the front lines, suffering from a painful case of anthrax pustules he had probably contracted from infected horses or mules. "My lesions are getting better," he wrote one of his generals wistfully. "One has already burst and soon I'll be able to get on my horse again, although I doubt I'll be rid of these wounds in three, even four days. That said, if there's the slightest need, I'm ready to march, even if they have to carry me in a litter."

June brought news from the north that Bermúdez and Mariño had lost Cumaná and Cumanaco to the Spaniards. The two former comrades were blaming each other for their ruin. In the west, Henry C. Wilson, an unruly English colonel attached to Páez's cavalry, was mounting a campaign to persuade Páez to separate from Bolívar. No one at the time knew it, but he had been cleverly planted—along with his unwitting British soldiers—by the Spanish ambassador in London. It seemed the only region Bolívar could truly claim was the heartland of Guayana. When he finally reached its capital, Angostura, the patriot outlook seemed to change, if only by virtue of his optimism. Despite his losses and afflictions, he was stimulated by his surroundings—filled with a newfound energy. Reestablishing himself in his headquarters, he began a flurry of correspondence, ranging from matters of state to matters of the heart.

He set about finding his mistress, Pepita Machado. "They say the Machados have gone to Caracas," he wrote his nephew Leandro Palacios. "If that is true, there's nothing more to say; but if it's not, I want to ask a favor of you. Mr. José Méndez Monsanto is holding 400 pesos for that family's voyage, and I'll pay whatever it costs to bring them. . . . Try to persuade the family to travel, and tell Pepita that if she wants me to be true to her, she'd better come here."

Ensconced in the relative safety of Angostura, he devoted himself to the much neglected business of government. If the revolution was stalling, it was because Venezuelans needed to be rallied, allies won, soldiers recruited. Whenever Bolívar's revolution seemed to be going badly, it generally heralded a great leap forward. He worked furiously now to gather more intelligence, produce propaganda, establish diplomacy, outfit his army: a larger plan was forming in his head. As Morillo would write one day, Bolívar *was* the revolution. And he was far more dangerous in defeat than in victory.

~

THE CITY OF ANGOSTURA, WHOSE name means "narrows," sits on a slender strait of the Orinoco River, three hundred nautical miles from the sea. Situated between hills and a rolling current, it is an outpost Humboldt had visited and described as a calm redoubt on a mighty river, flanked by a profusion of natural resources. It had been built fifty years before by the enterprising Spanish crown, which understood the economic importance of moving large shipments of goods from the bountiful interior. Farmlands fanned out along the river; ranchlands flourished immediately behind. Orange, lemon, and fig trees perfumed the balmy air. It had once been a beautiful city. The glistening white houses were ample, low, made of adobe, capped with red tile, handsomely elaborated with wooden windows. Splendid mansions overlooked the river, some with capacious verandas; it was said that Bolívar had given the most splendid of all to his former lover Isabel Soublette as a wedding present. Anyone could see that Angostura had once been a jewel in its riverine setting, but it had fallen to ruin during Piar's long siege and ensuing occupation.

Angostura's houses had been vandalized to such an extent that on Bolívar's return in early June he was moved to write, "It pains me to see that all the houses on the perimeter of town have been ruined or destroyed in order to get at the wood; even those on the main plaza have suffered, particularly the windows and doors." It seemed every city in Venezuela had borne similar depredations. Resources were scant, and whatever was needed was simply ripped from the structures at hand. The armies had come to rely on improvisation: clothes could be made from curtains, carts from doors, spear tips from iron grilles. On the plains, Páez had amassed all the silver his men had captured and melted it down to make money. On the coast, patriot soldiers sold coffee and cocoa in order to buy guns from the Antilles.

Bolívar threw himself into organizing this new capital of the republic. He wanted to establish an effective press, a working congress, diplomatic relations, a foreign legion. By June 27, he had begun publishing a newspaper. He called it *El Correo del Orinoco*, and it was to be the official voice of his future government: an organ in which he could publish laws, decrees, dispatches from the war, news highlights from Europe and North America. Taking an intense personal interest in its publication, he set out a mission from the start: "We are free, we write in a free country, and we seek to deceive no one." It was meant to be a direct counterpoint to the *Gaceta de Caracas*, the mouthpiece of the Spanish crown, which had been publishing pro-royalist propaganda (on Miranda's old printing machine) for almost a decade. Bolívar was passionate about the press, and rightly so. If Spanish kings had been adamant about keeping Americans ignorant, he would be adamant about keeping them informed. "The printing press is the infantry of the Army of Liberation!" his newspaper crowed.

It was on the pages of *El Correo* that readers learned that Bolívar had finally embarked on establishing a congress. Many had wondered why it hadn't happened before. His close friend and confidant Fernando Peñalver—a former president of the old congress of 1812—had finally persuaded him that the question had grown urgent and that it was time for citizens to share the rule. As Bolívar set out to build stores of war matériel—cannon, rifles, gunpowder—he worked to organize an election. And so the last months of 1818 were taken up by a swirl of administrative tasks, forcing Bolívar to be as resourceful behind a desk as he had been on a battlefield.

His letters and papers from this period show a leader engaged in every aspect of creating a republic, a man who, even as he puzzled over the architecture of governments, was working to procure arms and recruits, regularize the currency, stimulate trade along the Orinoco. He fretted about pay for his soldiers; desertions had been dire, and his men could hardly be blamed—they were unclad, penniless, badly nourished. He needed to do something about that. He was also obliged to settle a number of prickly legal disputes. He jailed, then deported the mutinous British mercenary who had tried to drive a wedge between him and Páez; he accepted the resignation of another querulous Englishman, Colonel Gustavus Hippisley, who although he had arrived only weeks before was complaining bitterly about his compensation.

Immediately thereafter, he was presented with two complaints from an American agent, J. Baptis Irvine. This irascible Baltimore newspaperman had been delegated by the United States government to seek

restitution for the seizure of two American ships that had sailed up
the Orinoco with supplies for the Spaniards. His second complaint:
Bolívar's flamboyant Scottish general Gregor McGregor, on furlough,
had turned up on the Florida coast, captured Amelia Island, planted
his own flag, and turned it into a refuge for pirates. McGregor's timing
couldn't have been worse; Secretary of State John Quincy Adams was
trying to pressure Madrid to hand over Florida. The correspondence
shows a courteous but firm supreme chief, standing his ground, trying
to preserve peace with the foreigners. If these conversations weren't
always congenial, they were indicative of a new reality: Bolívar and the
revolution were gradually being recognized in the outside world.

INDEED, THE ORINOCO WAS BUSTLING with outsiders. Admiral Brion,
who was living in one of the lavish mansions on the waterfront, was
overseeing a veritable whirl of activity along the river. Commerce was so
brisk that a French merchant was able to import fine wines to sell to the
residents of Angostura. A Creole matron was draping her bed in European lace. War supplies, too, were suddenly becoming plentiful. In June,
a British ship delivered clothing and supplies for ten thousand men;
days later, Brion himself brought in a valuable cargo of arms. By the
end of July, a large ship had sailed in from London, followed by a brig
from New York, bearing enough muskets, pistols, gunpowder, swords,
and saddles to outfit an entire army. Bolívar purchased any and all such
supplies, paying for them however he could—with mules, fruit, tobacco,
livestock. "Arms have been my constant concern," Bolívar had written
to Luis López Méndez, his agent in London, but now they were flowing
to him in abundance. So much so that at times there was no need for the
equipment. One shipment arrived with fine leather saddles for Páez's
cavalry—saddles his wild horsemen would never use. The remnants of
Wellington's war with Napoleon, nevertheless, were beginning to put
Bolívar's troops at striking advantage. Within a few months, he had
stored away fifty thousand stands of arms.

Wellington's victory had provided something else to the republic:
regiments of seasoned war veterans. As irony would have it, British
soldiers who had fought alongside General Morillo's officers in Spain
were now enlisting to fight against them in Venezuela. The two years

that followed the Battle of Waterloo saw a vast reduction in the size of
the British army. In April of 1817, the London *Times* reported that half
a million ex-soldiers were coming home to Britain's greater population
of 25 million. In good times, this would have been difficult enough; but
these were not good times—England and Ireland had suffered famine,
riots, rampant unemployment—and soldiers were returning to almost
certain poverty. When Bolívar's London agent López Méndez announced he wanted to recruit experienced soldiers to fight in the revolution, he found himself flooded with applicants.

López Méndez had been living in Miranda's house on 27 Grafton
Street since Bolívar had left him there in 1810, acting as a publicist for
the revolution. He had never been able to get official British support for
the Venezuelan republic, but now, with what may have been tacit approval from the Duke of Wellington—who, after all, had once planned
to come to the aid of Miranda—British war veterans rushed to enlist
before their government issued a proclamation that would forbid it.

The offer that López Méndez made to British officers was spelled
out in interviews: pay equal to whatever they had received from the
British army, a promotion to one rank higher, and a salary that would
begin on arrival in Venezuela, with full compensation for travel. A
fierce competition for commissions began, and money began to change
hands to secure places in the regiments. Colonel Gustavus Hippisley had
been one of the first potential commanders to present himself to López
Méndez, offering to raise a corps of cavalrymen. It was called the 1st
Venezuelan Hussars and it consisted of thirty officers and 160 noncom-
missioned officers—including field surgeons, veterinarians, trumpeters,
blacksmiths, a riding master, and a tailor. Scheduled to leave the English
shore in November of 1817, they were to be followed by four more bri-
gades, totaling a detachment of more than eight hundred officers, some
accompanied by their wives.

The preparations to equip these officers in London were detailed,
fastidious, almost laughable, given the primitive conditions for which
they were bound. Colonels took care to outfit their officers with dress
uniforms that featured gold lace and filigreed epaulettes as well as handsome field uniforms with ornamented cuffs and collars, elaborate belts,
leather pouches, sabers, crimson sashes, warm capes, bright caps, and

the current fashion rage among the military—Wellington boots. Gold buttons were cast with the regiments' insignias. Harnesses and saddles were commissioned from London's finest saddleries. Special rifles were ordered. All this was undertaken on the assumption that the commanding colonels and regiments would be reimbursed once they reached Spanish America. It was also undertaken with stunning inattention to the fact that the soldiers would be living in the tropics, serving alongside men who fought barefoot, naked, bareback, with no other weapons but sticks and spears.

Dinners and social events were organized throughout London to celebrate the volunteers and, as the weather grew chillier, members of the regiments could be seen around the city, standing about grandly in their uniforms. A pending proclamation would soon forbid citizens from taking up arms against Spain, but everywhere they went, the Venezuelan regiments garnered breathless, adoring publicity. "The frequency of their mess-dinners, and other parties, in and near the metropolis; the appearance of some of the gentlemen at public places of amusement; and last but not least, the excellence of the regimental band, which attended the officers wherever they dined together, were themes of general conversation" in London.

Of the five ships that sailed from England in November of 1817, only four arrived in Venezuela the following March. One ship, bearing the regiment of lancers, went down in a storm at sea, losing every soul that had signed up to serve in it. By the time the other four were sailing up the Orinoco toward Guayana, the troops were much depleted, having succumbed to malaria or typhus or internecine violence, or the temptation to jump ship along the way. Of the more than eight hundred men who had started out in full uniform and high hopes, only 150 set foot in Angostura. They hadn't been such seasoned veterans, after all. They were adventurers, dreamers, in search of the fabled land of El Dorado. None had actually shown proof of service to López Méndez, and, as it turned out, Gustavus Hippisley, who had reinvented himself as the commanding colonel of the 1st Venezuelan Hussars, had been a mere lieutenant before he applied. Although there were many—the intrepid Irish Colonel James Rooke, for instance, or Daniel O'Leary, Bolívar's aide-de-camp—who were serious and skilled soldiers, there were just as many who had never seen service at all.

They came looking more like a theatrical troupe than rugged soldiers, arrayed in showy uniforms that were utterly useless, except as curiosities to sell. They were, more often than not—and to their superiors' constant consternation—dead drunk. As one historian described it, the Irish, Scots, and English in Venezuela "fought with a rifle in one hand and a bottle in the other." Alcohol saturated every aspect of their lives and they were plied with it generously at all times. "They drank while they were being recruited. They drank while they waited at port for their ship to be ready. They drank while the departure was delayed and they drank while they sailed." Hippisley's correspondence reveals that during the four-month journey, they were often too intoxicated to carry out simple tasks. Men would drink until the inevitable brawl, or they would fail to return from shore, or fall overboard and drown. In a communiqué sent just hours before they pulled into Bolívar's camp in San Fernando, the commanding colonel worried that his men would make a bad impression on Bolívar, who—as it was well known—was not a heavy drinker. "Any man seen drunk, either on or off duty," he warned, "would be punished as severely as the military code would allow."

The British arrived in Angostura in mid-April of 1818. By mid-May, they had made the hard trip upriver to San Fernando on the Apure. They couldn't have arrived at a more difficult time for the republicans: Bolívar had just been defeated spectacularly by Morillo's army at La Puerta; and, only recently, the attempt had been made on his life. When the British officers stepped off their canoes in San Fernando, Bolívar was sick, nursing his suppurating lesions. They laid eyes on an ill-humored little man—impatient, in pain. He welcomed them as cordially as he could, but understandably, he was distracted; he gave confusing orders, was taken aback by the colonel's immediate demands for pay. It wasn't until he had returned to Angostura, his spirit renewed, his energies invigorated, that he saw them for what they were. He quickly identified the priggish buffoon Hippisley as an irritant to be removed. This was a man whose failures of judgment and rampant pretensions might have been comical if they hadn't had such tragic consequences.

Bolívar accepted his resignation, scolding him bitterly for his "ridiculous threats, which I despise." He then jailed Colonel Henry C. Wilson for attempting to undermine his command with Páez. He allowed any of the foreigners appalled by the conditions of his post to leave without reprisals or recriminations. The ones who remained would prove to be an invaluable infusion of grit and dedication. Within a month, he would be sending for more. Within five years, fifty-three ships would bring more than six thousand volunteers from Britain and Ireland to serve in South America; 5,300 actually arrived. The ones who made it up the Orinoco to the plains quickly learned that making war in that faraway terrain was no easy way to earn money. Their contributions made a great difference to the revolution in that precise moment in history. Bolívar was convinced of it. He was known to say that the real Liberator of Spanish America was his recruiting agent in London, Luis López Méndez.

IN AUGUST OF 1818, BOLÍVAR learned that his nephew Leandro Palacios, who was trying to raise guns and men in the Caribbean, had finally located Pepita Machado. His mistress had not returned to Caracas, as gossip had it, but had remained with her mother and sister in the bustling port of St. Thomas, making arrangements for their return. It had been almost two years since Bolívar had laid eyes on her, and he was eager to see her again. But there were questions: Why had she contemplated going back to Caracas? Was she trying to give fuel to his enemies? Had she taken up with another man? "People are saying a million things that strike me as preposterous rumors," he wrote Leandro, "the doubts they arouse in me are making me truly cross." In his next missive, he enclosed a letter for Pepita, entreating her to come. As spring appeared and Bolívar busily planned a major offensive in New Granada, good news arrived from Leandro. Pepita and her family had just boarded a ship for the long journey to Angostura.

Bolívar was delighted. He assumed that Pepita would reach him in time to accompany him on the long march overland, as she had done so often before. But it was not to be. Before she could reach Angostura—before summer had turned the Orinoco into a torrid cauldron—his war plans had called him to move west again.

Imagine, if you will, the drama inherent in this narrative: the clear assumption that his lover would join him on the battlefield; the vision he had of her at his side. Certainly, she had been there for many pivotal moments. She had been present at the end of the Admirable Campaign, glancing back from a cluster of girls as they ushered him to glory. She had been with him during the harrowing evacuation of Caracas, as the two had braved wind and rain to flee Boves. She had joined him on his triumphant campaign from Haiti, forcing an entire expedition to drop anchor while they consummated a happy reunion. And she had been there to witness his flight from Ocumare, when the revolution had seemed irretrievably lost. He hadn't seen her since that disastrous retreat—since the day he had deposited her hastily on the island of St. Thomas.

After Leandro's letter announcing her approach, Pepita's name floats like a wayward wisp into the neverland of legend. History has a poor record of her. But she was less legend than real: a feisty, headstrong, flesh-and-blood woman who was loved by Bolívar and emphatically disliked by his men. It is said that she tried to follow him into battle, but became too ill to travel. Some claim she died along the way. It is argued just as feverishly that she perished of tuberculosis in the town of San Rafael, a mere seventy-five miles into the Orinoco, and never made it to Angostura. Or that she died in Achaguas, which would mean that not only did she reach Angostura successfully, she traveled three hundred miles more, past San Fernando, into the wilderness in his pursuit. We will probably never know what truly happened. What is sure is that Bolívar carried the hope of her pending arrival through the end of that busy year and into the next, as he made sorties, planned a war, organized congress, and solidified the republic.

Come January of 1819, while she was en route, Bolívar was in San Juan de Payara prepared to march toward New Granada, eager to pit his revitalized army against Morillo's troops. But when he heard that a large brigade of British mercenaries was about to arrive, he put Páez in charge, promoted him to major general, and returned to Angostura. There was another reason he needed to be there: the newly elected congressmen from the republican districts had started to gather in Angostura—as they had been instructed to do. Bolívar intended to open their congressional proceedings, unveil his constitution, and air his views on the budding republic.

He made the journey in a long canoe with a small company of men, winding his way down the snake-infested Orinoco, writing the nation's constitution as he went. They skimmed under the majestic palms and giant hardwoods—listening, by night, to the owls, the bats, the bellowing monkeys, the relentless gurgle of frogs. In the swelter of day, he swung in his hammock, batted away mosquitoes, and dictated his thoughts to his secretary. These were theories and ideas he had been formulating since his "Letter from Jamaica," when the revolution's prospects were far more tenuous. In the interim, he had come to know Venezuela more intimately. He had traveled the wide country, ridden from mountain to desolate plain. He had sailed the length of the northern coast, had marched east and west, had seen how topography and peoples could change from island to flatland. He had lived with Páez's cowboys, fought alongside tribesmen, shared rations with former slaves. It was not the kind of company a rich Mantuano ordinarily kept; it was no land easily understood from Madrid, where, as a youth, he had devoured book after book in the Marquis of Ustaríz's library, trying to comprehend his homeland. This was the real Venezuela—no philosopher's mirage, but its crystalline reality—where bandits, horsemen, nomads, sailors, slum dwellers, and jungle Indians now called themselves patriots. This was the America he was trying to liberate.

At noon on February 15, 1819, after a brisk salvo of artillery and three reverberating rounds of cannon, Bolívar took his place in the modest government house in Angostura, ready to mark the inauguration of the Second National Congress. In a clear, stentorian voice, he proceeded to enthrall his listeners with his vision for the republic. The men present represented the greater part of the republic's governing body—twenty-six of the thirty-five—elected into office at the end of the previous year.

Bolívar began by surrendering his power. Nothing was more perilous, he insisted, than allowing one man to stay in control for so long. He went on to explain the colossal scope of the work at hand. He described how the colonies had been robbed, not only of freedom, but also of the right to participate in a true democracy. Spanish Americans had been demoralized, debased, cut off from the world in all matters that related to the rule of nations. The work of building a republic, therefore, would be arduous: they had to reeducate an ignorant nation—a body politic with no notion of justice or fair government, no concept of democracy's high demands. Liberty, as Rousseau had written, was a succulent morsel, but eminently difficult to digest.

As successful as the United States had been at balancing its hard-won liberty, Bolívar argued, its federal system was not a good model for Venezuela. The North American and South American colonies were as different in character as England was from Spain. "Laws need to suit the people for whom they are made," he insisted. And, in every practical respect, according to him, Spanish America at this crucial hour of its molting did not possess the moral fiber to marshal a truly representative government—a system "so sublime that it might be more fitting for a republic of saints."

Venezuela, as Bolívar explained, like the rest of the Spanish American continent, was rent by a great many divisions—geographic, economic, human—and it would not be in congress's interest to enact a government that ignored or exacerbated them. "Unity, unity, unity must be our motto!" he told them. But of all the nation's challenges, the greatest was race:

> Our people are nothing like Europeans or North Americans; indeed, we are more a mixture of Africa and America than we are children of Europe. . . . It is impossible to say with any certainty to which human race we belong. Most of our Indians have been annihilated; Spaniards have mixed with Americans and Africans; their children, in turn, have mixed with Indians and Spaniards. . . . we all differ visibly in the color of our skin: This diversity places upon as an obligation of the highest order. . . . We will require an infinitely firm hand and an infinitely fine tact to manage all the racial divisions in this heterogeneous society, where even the slightest alteration can throw off, divide, or undo its delicate balance.

It wasn't that Spanish Americans were lesser stock; it was that they were a different stock altogether: a new kind of people, forged by three centuries of history, cruelly emasculated by Spain. "When a man loses his freedom," Homer had said, and Bolívar quoted him now, "he loses half his spirit." Codes and statutes were insufficient for a populace laboring under the triple yoke of ignorance, tyranny, and vice; what was needed was wise, considered leadership. It was incumbent on congress to fashion a new kind of government for this new race of man—one capable of governing and nurturing at the same time, for only "virtuous men, patriotic men, learned men can make republics." Toward this end, he proposed a *poder moral* as one of the nation's basic institutions, an educational body that would be responsible for instilling ethics and civic responsibilities.

Indeed, education was of primary concern to Bolívar. He begged the congressmen to establish a strong educational system, guarantee civil liberties, reject any aspect of Spain's old judiciary system, and install a firm central government that united all Venezuela in a single republic, "one and indivisible." He pleaded with them, "as I would plead for my very life," to confirm the absolute freedom of slaves. He favored a powerful president, elected for life. He called for a hereditary senate, similar to the British House of Lords, which would serve as an arbiter between government and the governed. He urged congress to be generous in rewarding the armies, not only with gratitude but also with laurels, since these were soldiers who had fought not "for power, nor fortune, nor even glory, but for liberty alone."

The representatives were brought to tears by the passion and eloquence of Bolívar's address. Not only was it a model of oratory—tautly written, roundly delivered—it was a flood of erudition, containing references to Roman and Greek law, Spartan ingenuity, human history from Genghis Khan to George Washington, bright snatches of wisdom from literature. For many, his frank declarations on race were unprecedented and rattled some deeply held prejudices. But no one could argue with the patriotism, principle, and reason behind the words. At every step along the way, he was interrupted by long, frenzied applause.

As he drew to a conclusion, Bolívar looked out into the crowded room—sweltering in the tropical afternoon, packed with legislators in straw hats and white pantaloons. "I beg you," he said solemnly, "to grant Venezuela a government that is eminently populist, eminently just, eminently moral—one that will put an end to anarchy, tyranny, and recriminations." And then he closed crisply, saying, "Gentlemen, begin your labors. I have finished mine." He had resigned, in effect, all powers as supreme chief, stepped down. But it wasn't long before he would have all those powers back again.

By the next morning, the congress of Angostura had elected Bolívar president and the dignified Granadan professor Francisco Antonio Zea vice president of the republic. Once that was done, they set to work on Bolívar's proposed constitution. Every day for six months, the members—some barefoot and in patches—gathered in the municipal building to make their deliberations. In time, they devised a document that adopted many of Bolívar's ideas but rejected the hereditary senate and the *poder moral*. The republic they had in mind was far from becoming a reality, however. That work would be accomplished not in the halls of government, but on the fields of war.

PÁEZ HAD NOT ALLOWED THE Spaniards to lure him to battle while Bolívar was in Angostura. He had been given a clear command. So loyal was Páez to Bolívar's order that when he heard that Morillo's army was on its way to him in San Fernando, he burned the place to the ground rather than engage the general in combat. Throughout February and March of 1819, Páez had been taunting Morillo's forces in a masterful guerrilla campaign, stinging his flanks enough to fatigue his army, but not enough to provoke him to all-out battle. By the time Bolívar returned, making his way up the Orinoco with a battalion of three hundred English soldiers, Páez's Army of the Apure was itching to fight.

Páez finally was given the go-ahead on the afternoon of April 2. With 150 horsemen, he crossed the River Arauca and approached Morillo's camp on the plains of Queseras del Medio. Ninety of his men waited by the riverbank while three squads of twenty rode at full gallop toward the royalist encampment. Seeing a massive dust cloud rise from the plains, Morillo was persuaded that Bolívar's entire army was on its way. He rallied his corps of a thousand and marched out to meet them. Almost immediately, Páez's horsemen fell into retreat, spurring the enemy to pursue them. Morillo's soldiers opened a resounding fire, and the royalist cavalry raced after. At the most fevered point of the chase, as all horses thundered across the plains toward the river, Páez ordered the squad led by his fiercest horseman, Juan José Rondón, to wheel around and rush the enemy furiously, executing a sudden about-face. The other horsemen followed. The Spanish were momentarily bewildered. They dismounted their horses to better aim their guns at the approaching horde, but Páez and his men, at a full gallop now, were dangling from the far sides of their mounts, invisible. The royalists could hardly see: the failing light, the smoke of their own gunfire, the choking dust, had rendered the battlefield opaque. Páez's men easily overtook them, springing high on their horses to lance royalists left and right, inflicting a swift and terrible punishment. The mayhem of spears, the slash of machetes, and the shrill, barbaric cries of the horsemen were too much for the Spaniards. Their cavalry turned and fled, and their infantry made a frantic run for the forest, abandoning all heavy artillery. Morillo was forced to retreat that night to safer ground, many hours away. It is hard to say whether the Spanish general truly believed what he would later write or whether he simply wanted to blunt his failure, but in his account to Madrid, he reported that Páez had attacked not with 150 men, but seven hundred.

Indeed, Páez's nimble little band of paladins had fought circles around the royalists. Four hundred soldiers of the king died at Queseras del Medio and many staggered away wounded. Páez's men, on the other hand, left the battlefield with trifling losses: two dead, six wounded. It was a glorious victory for the patriots, delivering a powerful psychological blow to the enemy; Bolívar, exultant, generously rewarded the horsemen with citations for their valor. That magnificent clash of so few against so many has lived on in the annals of South American history as the height of revolutionary pluck and mettle—a David and Goliath encounter that marked a turning point in the war. Morillo was never quite the same after that maneuver. Between the wild horsemen of the Apure and Bolívar's newly enlisted British legion, it was clear the patriots had taken on new muscle. Although Morillo commanded a robust army of seven thousand, his communiqués began to reflect a distinct pessimism. He had grown more than a little worried about the fate of his pacification campaign.

And yet the war was far from over. In the ensuing months, patriots and royalists crisscrossed the plains, never quite winning enough

skirmishes to put either side at an advantage. In the east, General Urdaneta's troops had been unable to get closer to Caracas. In the west,
General Santander was building troops, awaiting orders. Bolívar was
eager to carry the war west into New Granada while the weather was
good, but he had hoped to deliver one more deadly blow to Morillo
before undertaking that difficult passage. He grew frustrated, restless.
"Patience," Páez counseled, "for behind every hill, there's a wide open
plain." The aphorism was hardly consoling: plains were precisely what
concerned Bolívar. By May, the rains had begun, and the Orinoco's vast
web of tributaries was threatening to spill onto the land, rot the vegeta-
tion, and drive game to higher ground. As they moved back and forth
in pursuit of Morillo, the patriot soldiers had little food, little rest, and
were forced to traverse the very savannas they had previously reduced to
ash. But they dared not complain. The president himself was enduring
those Spartan conditions.

BOLÍVAR WAS, AT THIS POINT, thirty-five and at the height of his physical
and mental powers. Tirelessly driven, lit by a nervous energy, he slept
little, survived on a soldier's rations, and marched alongside his men,
urging them on, inspiring them to greater sacrifice. His face had lost its
luster of youth and, although his movements were spirited and agile, his
was the countenance of an older man: rawboned, jaundiced. His hair
had grown long and grazed his shoulders in wispy curls; during the day,
he tied it with string. A few errant locks tumbled over his brow, con-
cealing a thinning hairline. His mustache and sideburns were jarringly
blond. His fine, aquiline nose was marred by a small, tumorous growth,
which offended his vanity no end, until it disappeared years later, leaving a scar. An Englishman seeing him for the first time in those plains
remarked at the surprising modesty of his dress—the sandals of jute, the
simple coat, the helmet of a British private. He had, for all the humility
of his appearance, a rare elegance of manner, and it was nowhere more
evident than there, on the fields of war, in the company of rougher men.
If he departed at all from a soldier's rituals, it was in the care he paid to
his bodily hygiene: He bathed at daybreak—sometimes two or three
times a day—and, for all the privations of the battlefield, his teeth were
a radiant white.

Indeed, life in the liberating army was the very essence of privation. Often, a foot soldier made long marches in the scorching heat, obliged to hunt game as he went, and to drink from muddy rivers. His official diet was meat—no salt, no accompaniments—and that, only if he was fortunate enough to be in a company driving cattle. Each soldier received two pounds of beef per day, no more. Páez's horsemen were accustomed to this austere life, and openly disdained the others, especially the British, who called themselves warriors but couldn't break a horse, fight a crocodile, or swim a rushing river. If meat were available, the horsemen were driving it, and they routinely issued the foot soldiers the inferior parts. But even if cattle were close at hand, there were days when no one ate, since vultures or campfire smoke could easily betray their position.

Bolívar took great pains to bring in supplies from Angostura when he could—salt for meat, flour for bread, medicines for the surgeons, tobacco for his officers. Most important, it seemed, were spare shoes for the British, who, unlike the pardos and Indians, were singularly incapable of marching in bare feet. His letters during that time show a commanding general obsessed with details: the precise pattern of horseshoes, the specific soft iron to make them, the way ammunition should be packed for transport, the exact kind of gunpowder. In February, he had left Angostura well stocked with arms and ammunition—even a few uniforms—but food and medicine were rare. The paltry clothes sent by the British were all too easily spotted by the Spaniards, filling them with no little indignation that Bolívar had managed to enlist their former allies. "For the first time," a miffed General Morillo reported to the war ministry in Spain, "we are seeing rebels, suited from head to toe like Englishmen; and even some of the horsemen of the Apure have been seen wearing feathered caps and sitting in British saddles."

IT WAS NO SECRET THAT Bolívar wanted to take his war to the rest of South America. He had said as much in a promise to Granadans, published months before. But time was slipping away, and the skies were issuing a steady drizzle of rain, miring the plains in mud. If the Spaniards had thought Bolívar would try to fulfill his promise of moving the revolution west, they certainly did not think he would do it now. Caracas was still under royalist rule. He had not succeeded in taking it; indeed, he hadn't really tried. Why would he go to New Granada at such a crucial juncture? Only a fool would attempt that journey in the rain, when rivers became seas, valleys disappeared under lakes, and the Andes grew slick with ice, impassable. Bolívar had said nothing to the congress at Angostura about his plan, but now he put it forward to two of his most trusted generals—those he considered essential to the enterprise—Páez and Santander. He swore them to secrecy, insisting that the element of surprise was critical. "This is for your eyes and your eyes only," he wrote Santander. Páez had already said yes.

On May 23, as he and his infantry were making their way west along the Apure, Bolívar called his officers, including Soublette, Pedro Briceño Méndez, James Rooke, José Antonio Anzoátegui, and several others to a council of war. They met in a ramshackle hut in the deserted little village of Setenta. There was no table at which to sit, no chairs. They perched instead on the skulls of cattle—picked over by condors, bleached white by the sun. Although the officers, indeed the entire patriot army, had assumed they would be wintering close by, the Liberator explained that it would be foolish to remain during the rains, when food would be scant, malaria and yellow fever rampant. He confided his plan to take the entire army over the Andes, surprise the enemy on the Granadan side, and astound the world by shifting their campaign from one theater of war to another.

Anzoátegui, Soublette, and a few more important colonels enthusiastically approved the proposal; others took more persuading. But when Páez was presented with unanimous assent, he changed his mind, began to drag his feet. His men wanted to stay on the plains, near what they knew, he insisted; they had no desire to fight in distant lands or imperil their horses in mountainous terrain. He made excuses, hemmed and hawed, then rejected Bolívar's plan altogether. When Bolívar pressed him to provide troops and horses anyway, Páez detached one small corps of horsemen and sent an additional two hundred "scrawny and mangy mares." The Liberator made no effort to hide his fury, but one simple fact remained: he needed Páez. In time, he found a way to make the Lion of the Apure fit his plan. Páez was to ride with his horsemen to Cúcuta, which was easily accessible from the plains, and prevent the Spaniards from moving westward. In the east, Bermúdez and Mariño would keep the pressure on Caracas, with constant forays to Calabozo, where Morillo was quartered. Vice President Zea was to command all other matters, including continuing to seek help overseas.

Bolívar started toward the mountains on May 26, on the very day when the rains began to pelt down in earnest. The soldiers had not been told where they were headed—first, in order to keep the operation fully secret, but just as important, because Bolívar feared they would desert if they knew the perilous direction of their march. As they poured into the town of Guasdualito, the army was finally told, as was the government in Angostura. Bolívar's tight force of 2,100—four infantry battalions and three cavalry squadrons, accompanied by medics, auxiliary forces, women, children, and a herd of cattle—was now poised to undertake one of the most remarkable feats in military history.

On June 4, Bolívar's army crossed the Arauca River and passed into Casanare, where the rains were torrential, savannas flooded, and creatures adrift as far as the eye could see. His soldiers constructed boats of cowhide to transport the ordnance and keep it as dry as possible. They marched with mud sucking at their feet, or wading through waist-high water, or—when floods rose to their highest point—swimming. If they had families, they used their threadbare blankets to shield women from the cold and damp; if they didn't, they used them to protect guns and ammunition. Hungry, weary, drenched through to the skin, they traversed a landscape such as they'd never seen. Men on horseback were no better off than those on the ground. Hooves grew soft in the bog and swamp, rendering animals lame. Feet swelled to such tender misshape that riders could no longer use their stirrups. The army carried on anyway, marching for more than a month, lured by trees that floated like promises of dry earth in those vast inland waterways. The frail were soon sick; the rugged, wounded; the unfortunate, at the mercy of tiny, flesh-eating fish that could strip limbs to bone in seconds. Horses and cattle fell into deep water, never to rise again. Cargo became too heavy to carry; reins too shriveled to use. At night, they camped wherever they could—sleeping in standing water, or on their horses—only to be set upon by mosquitoes, sand flies, and stinging gnats. They finally reached hard land at Tame, where Santander's troops awaited; and there, at long last, the army of liberation gained a measure of relief in dry beds, eating bananas, potatoes, barley, and salt. In the distance, whenever a strong wind cleared the clouds away, they could see the forest of San Camilo, whose tangle of green lined the lower cliffs of the towering Andes.

After a week's rest, on July 1, they were off again, bound for the mighty cordillera—a snowbound, airless barrier of rock and cliff. The patriots, bolstered by Bolívar's enthusiasm, staggered up those slopes, with nothing but dreams of glory. As they rose into thinner air, the icy wind and hyaline numbed some minds, clarified others. Many of Páez's horsemen, who had slogged unhesitatingly twenty miles a day through mud and flood, decided the vertiginous heights and unstable rock were too punishing for their horses. Some gave up on the expedition, deserting the revolution in favor of their afflicted animals. Few beasts would survive the five days' march over the dizzying Páramo de Pisba.

The rain was ceaseless, the cold unrelenting. Within a few days, the remaining livestock were gone: a string of carcasses marked their trail. "The harshness of the peaks we have crossed would be staggering to anyone who hasn't experienced it," Bolívar reported to his vice president. "There's hardly a day or night it doesn't rain . . . our only comfort is the thought that we've seen the worst, and that we are nearing the end of the journey." Often, the streams they crossed were swift and fierce, and travelers had to negotiate them in solid lines, moving hand in hand, until every last person had been dragged through the white water. To traverse ravines, they lassoed trees on either side, then pulled travelers on leather ropes, over the plummeting abyss, suspended in improvised hammocks. Bolívar carried soldiers who were too weak to stand, or the women who had dutifully followed them. "He was," according to one British observer, "invariably humane in his attentions to the sick and wounded." Slipping and sliding over the wet, icy rock, the army kept on the move, ascending to thirteen thousand feet, knowing that to stop and lie down at those bone-chilling heights was to give up and die. By the time they had scaled the Páramo de Pisba, their shoes had no soles, their clothes were in shreds; hundreds had died of hypothermia. Many of the surviving officers, a witness later wrote, "had no trousers, and were glad to cover themselves with pieces of blanket, or whatever they could procure." A full quarter of the British contingent perished in that crossing. Yet there were scenes of extraordinary strength and courage. The patriot women, mistresses or wives, were indispensable medics: tending wounds, giving hope to the ill, evincing an admirable fortitude. Some proved even more sturdy than the men. On the night of July 3, as the army huddled at the very heights of the crossing, Bolívar's aide-de-camp was told that a soldier's wife was there among them, giving birth. The next day he saw her marching along behind her husband's battalion, a strapping newborn in her arms.

On July 6, survivors began to straggle down the other side of the mountain. Weak, famished, in tatters, it was all they could do to pick their way down the steep escarpments. At Socha, jubilant Granadans rushed out to meet them with food and drink, horses and weapons. The village women, filled with sympathy for the half-naked soldiers, set to work, making them shirts, trousers, underwear, and jackets—sewn from their own clothes. Bolívar had chosen the route well, for there was no one to challenge the patriot presence. The Spaniards had dismissed the Páramo de Pisba as too difficult a crossing: there were no guards in the area, no enemy garrisons for miles. The expedition would have precious time to recover.

Over the next few days, while the army rested, the British legion trickled into Socha, lugging the liberating army's trunks and ammunition. Most of it had been badly damaged. Bolívar didn't waste time fretting about the loss. He busied himself organizing supplies, raising troops, making sure the sick were minded and the hungry fed, as well as gathering intelligence on royalist movements. Granadans, who had suffered three years of harsh rule under their tyrannical viceroy, now rushed to enlist in Bolívar's effort, as one village after another welcomed him with open arms. The young Granadan general Santander later wrote of Bolívar's efforts: "Here is where this man distinguishes himself above all the rest, exhibiting extraordinary resolve and energy. In three days, he remounts and arms the cavalry, musters ammunition, reassembles the army; then sends out patrols, energizes the citizens, and plans an all-out attack."

THE LIBERATION OF NEW GRANADA came quickly only days after the last of Bolívar's soldiers descended the snowy heights of Pisba. It was a measure of Bolívar's genius that his army had met with no resistance; the test now would be to spring that army into a winning war. At dawn on July 25, one day after his thirty-sixth birthday, Bolívar's soldiers met the Spaniards in a battle at Pantano de Vargas, a hill-rimmed swampland about 120 miles northeast of Bogotá. Brigadier José María Barreiro and his royalists had all the advantages: higher ground, more troops, better arms and training. But just when all seemed lost for the patriots—a blistering fire on all sides, their forces surrounded—Bolívar shouted to the horseman Rondón, who had been the hero at Queseras del Medio, "Colonel! Save the republic!" The fearless cowboy led his plainsmen in a furious charge up the hill, and, swinging machetes and spears, managed to drive the Spaniards from that promontory. The patriots, elated, now fought with renewed zeal. Rattled by this reversal, the royalists shrank in alarm, then rushed to withdraw, especially as rain began to spill from the darkening heavens. Santander would later say that the battle at Pantano de Vargas was won by the horsemen's intensity and a British calm, and because Bolívar, like some mythic war god, seemed to appear everywhere at once. The patriots had more advantages than that: the core of Bolívar's troops—seasoned, challenged, culled to an able few—were a well-honed fighting force now. The Spaniards, terrified by the Liberator, by his legendary war to the death, by his startling appearance on their side of the Andes, simply lost their nerve. Barreiro's army may have had the numbers, the equipment, the spangled uniforms, the peninsular training, and certainly the optimism of Barreiro himself, but, as Bolívar understood, they had a distinct—and crushing—disadvantage: they were afraid.

The determining Battle of Boyacá was fought a few days later, on August 7. But by now, the balance of power had shifted. It was no longer the Spaniards who were trying to block Bolívar from marching to Bogotá; it was Bolívar trying to block the Spaniards from reuniting with their viceroy and collecting badly needed reinforcements. By mid-morning of that fateful day, the Liberator's army had taken a position near the bridge at Boyacá, on a hill that oversaw the road to the capital, Bogotá. At two in the afternoon, the royalist army appeared. Brigadier Barreiro sent out a vanguard, assuming that the row of patriots he saw on the far bluff was merely a band of observers. He ordered his second in command, Colonel Francisco Jiménez, to scare them off so that the main body of his troops—three thousand strong—could pass. But Bolívar accelerated the patriot march, and before long his entire army coursed over the hill, wave after wave of roaring soldiers. Rondón's horsemen, in galloping charge, plunged like a knife into the royalists' tidy formation, dispersing them like a flock of sheep. General Anzoátegui then fell upon the same soldiers with his hardened veterans; Santander flew after their vanguard and overtook them. By four o'clock, it was done. The Spanish commander, in desperation, tried to retreat to a hillside to regroup his forces, but by then his army had been devastated—two hundred lay dead in the open meadow, the rest were in disarray. When Anzoátegui's cavalry charged up that hill with bloodied lances, the Spaniards laid down their arms. Sixteen hundred royalists were taken prisoner that afternoon. The battle had taken all of two hours.

In the course of that conflagration, many of the British were wounded. O'Leary had taken a gash in the head. Colonel Rooke had sustained a grave wound to his left arm. When the field surgeon amputated that arm in order to save his life, Rooke grasped the hewn limb with his good hand, thrust it high in the air, and shouted, "Viva la patria!" Someone asked, "Which country, England or Ireland?" but the Irishman shook his head. "The one that will bury me," he said. Three days later, his corpse was lowered into Colombian soil.

On the evening of that battle, Pedro Martínez, a twelve-year-old stablehand in Bolívar's retinue, noticed two men crouched in a gully by the river. When he and an armed companion surprised them where they hid, the runaways tried to pay him off with a few gold coins. But the boy refused. By the time the youths had escorted their prisoners back to the patriot camp, they knew that one of them was Brigadier Barreiro. The army had already captured his second in command, Colonel Jiménez.

For all that the Spaniards had agonized about Bolívar's legendary war to the death, not one prisoner taken at the Battle of Boyacá was singled out for execution. Bolívar would be generous to Barreiro and his officers, making it clear that he planned to pursue an exchange of prisoners. But as the battle drew to a close and Bolívar chased stragglers over the rolling hills for many miles and managed to apprehend some, he chanced upon a face he knew. It was Francisco Vinoni, the republican traitor who, in 1812, had thrown open the dungeons of Puerto Cabello and turned over that valuable fortress to the Spaniards—the infamous Vinoni, whose treasonous act had precipitated the most bitter and damaging experience of Bolívar's career. The Liberator had always said that if he ever got his hands on Vinoni, he would extract a cruel revenge. He pulled the prisoner out of the lineup and ordered his men to hang him.

With the road to the capital open now, Bolívar and a small squadron set out for Bogotá. As one of his officers wrote, "A lightning bolt doesn't fall from the sky as swiftly as General Bolívar descended on the capital." He rode, ragged and shirtless, his coat fluttering against bare skin, for all seventy miles of the journey. As he raced through the humid countryside—his wild long hair riding the wind—he hardly looked like a general who had vanquished a king's army. But it was so. His war to the death, discarded so many years before, now worked greatly to his favor: the Spaniards in Bogotá fled the capital with little more than the clothes on their backs, abandoning houses, businesses, the entire viceregal treasury, to the patriot army. Viceroy Juan José de Sámano, author of so many atrocities against New Granadans, had no time to worry about the fate of his people now. The viceroy saved himself, stealing away in the guise of a lowly Indian. By the time Bolívar strode into his palace, he was gone.

In the official report to Spain's Ministry of War, the most important Spaniard in those American colonies, General Morillo, would sum it up this way:

> The rebellious Bolívar has occupied the capital of Bogotá, and the deadly outcome of this battle gives him dominion over the enormous resources of a highly populated, abundantly rich nation, from which he will take whatever he needs to prolong the war. . . . This unfortunate loss delivers into rebel hands—apart from the Kingdom of New Granada—many ports in the South, where he will now deploy his pirates. . . . The interior of the continent, all the way to Peru, is at the mercy of whoever rules in [Bogotá]. . . . In just one day, Bolívar has undone all we have accomplished in five years of this campaign, and in one single battle he has reconquered all the territory that soldiers of the king have won in the course of so many past conflagrations.

~ CHAPTER 10 ~

The Way to Glory

A weak man requires a long fight in order to win. A strong one delivers a single blow and an empire vanishes.

—Simón Bolívar

Bolívar dismounted swiftly and ran up the steps of the viceroy's palace. It was five P.M. and the mountain air was beginning to regain its vigor. It had been unseasonably warm, a stifling day in the capital. Dazed and disbelieving, the republicans of Bogotá had just begun to emerge from the torpid ignorance in which the viceroy had kept them. They had been told the royalists had prevailed at Pantano de Vargas, which was patently untrue; but then came the Spaniards' swift and frenzied departure from the capital, the stores of gunpowder detonating in the distance. As Bolívar rode into the viceregal capital, hurtling along the city streets—windblown and shirtless—citizens ventured out, curious at first, and then in wild, gleeful abandon.

He astonished the throngs, according to one witness, with his memory for names. He greeted Granadans as he went, although it had been more than four years since he had seen them. His movements were quick, economical, with little apparent regard for the grandness of the moment—his energy electric, despite the eight-hour ride. Once he was inside the palace, republican leaders asked if he didn't want to rest a while and he responded, "Absolutely not. I never tire on a horse." He addressed them briskly, courteously, grasping the lapels of his jacket as he spoke. Mainly, he asked questions, and, as they answered, he crossed his arms and listened intently. He asked about his benefactor and supporter Camilo Torres, the former republican president. ("Where Bolívar is," Torres had once said, "*there* is the republic.") The president had been brutally executed and dismembered by Morillo's officers, his head thrust on a spear and displayed a few yards from the very spot where Bolívar now stood. Bolívar asked, too, about President Torices, the young warlord of Cartagena who had welcomed him years before, and whose head had met the same fate as Torres's, on a spear, in front of that palace. As Bolívar glanced about, it was clear that Viceroy Sámano's reign had taken a hard toll on the people. He could see evidence of it etched deeply into their faces.

He wrote to his vice president in Venezuela to report that Bogotá was his now. The viceroy had fled in such a fright that he had left a bag of gold on his desk, a half million pesos in the treasury, and enough arms and munitions to supply an entire army. In the course of a single battle, Bolívar had toppled his iron rule. But not until hours before the Liberator's arrival had Viceroy Sámano realized his reign was over. He had been dining with his courtiers, blithely unaware that his army had been crushed, his commanding officer taken prisoner. Because Brigadier Barreiro had lied to him about the outcome of the battle at Pantano de Vargas, calling himself the victor, the viceroy believed that Bolívar's ragtag soldiers were not a threat and Spain's army was invincible. The viceroy had been bragging about Barreiro to his dinner guests on that evening of August 8 when an official burst into the room with news that the king's army had been vanquished at Boyacá, the commander taken prisoner, and patriot forces were fast approaching the capital. "All is lost!" the official wailed. "Bolívar is upon us!" As a historian of the day recounted it: "The bravura of the viceroy quickly evaporated into terror, and all he could think of was saving his own skin." He fled west to the Magdalena, disguised as a lowly peasant, then embarked incognito for the five-hundred-mile voyage downriver to Cartagena and, eventually,

across the seas to Spain. When Bolívar dispatched a division to apprehend him, he was gone, lost among the crowds—one more traveler on a
busy waterway.

Bolívar went through the viceroy's palace, amazed by the riches that
had been abandoned in the mass evacuation, but he was careful not to
gloat. As far as he was concerned, the war had not ended with the liberation of Bogotá. There was much yet to accomplish: Caracas was not
free; Morillo was still on the loose; and, in spite of all patriot advances,
Spain still controlled a number of vital areas—Coro, Cartagena, Cúcuta,
Pasto, Quito, the viceroyalty of Peru. There was no question that Bolívar
was thrilled by the victory at Boyacá and sure of its consequences, but he
made no public claims. He kept his generals on the move, enlisted prisoners to the patriot side, and worked hard to raise more troops.

Yet even with the seriousness of the work at hand, Bolívar never
failed to enjoy lighthearted pursuits. He played cards with his officers,
bantered with them, rode with them, organized festive celebrations.
Soon after his entry into the capital, he gave a fancy ball for all the leading families of Bogotá. That night, just before dinner, Colonel James
Hamilton, a British officer with whom he had developed a warm
friendship, arrived in such a state of dishabille that Bolívar couldn't help
but express surprise. "My good and brave colonel!" he gasped, when he
saw him, "what a dirty shirt you have on!" There was good reason for
Bolívar's candor: a year before, when he had lost all his shirts in battle,
Hamilton had generously given him six of his own. The Englishman
now apologized for his slovenliness and explained that he was wearing
the only shirt he owned. Bolívar chuckled and ordered his servant, José
Palacios, to fetch the colonel a clean shirt; but Palacios only stared at his
master, until Bolívar was forced to say, "Well, why don't you go?" The
servant stammered, "Your excellency has but two shirts, one is on your
back, the other is in the wash." Bolívar and the colonel laughed heartily at that. Shirts had always been a precious commodity in the revolution: lost in transport, seized in battle, used as tourniquets, robbed from
corpses. Now they had become a source of brief merriment between two
men who, until that war, had never lacked for sartorial finery.

The official celebration of Bolívar's victory was held on September 18, and all Bogotá turned out for the festivities. Church bells pealed,

twenty young beauties in pristine white dresses came forward gamely to bestow crowns of laurels, and Bolívar marched alongside Santander and Anzoátegui in a victory procession that led to the very square where so many of his cohort had died. But even with all the joy and high spirits, few Granadans understood how momentous their victory truly was. In seventy-five days, in a wholly improvised maneuver, Bolívar had freed New Granada and opened the way for the liberation of much of Spanish America. His march over the cordillera had much in common with Hannibal's over the Alps, except that terrain and climate were harsher in the Andes, and Hannibal had taken years to prepare for the challenge. San Martín had crossed the Andes, too, on the far south of the continent, but, like Hannibal, he had trained his soldiers for years in advance. Bolívar's genius was to achieve the feat as an improvisation, fashion his strategy on the fly. As one historian put it: he had fulfilled all of Napoleon's maxims—destroy the army, capture the capital, conquer the country—but he had realized them in one sweeping motion. As Bolívar himself had written prophetically four years before: "A weak man requires a long fight in order to win. A strong one delivers a single blow and an empire vanishes."

For all the grandness of the victory procession, for all the pomp and apotheosis of the ceremony, the Liberator again proved human. He had an eye on one of the beauties in white—a lovely dark-eyed girl of seventeen, Bernardina Ibañez. He had met her six years before, as a guest in her parents' house during his campaign up the Magdalena River. She had been a child then; now she was in the full flower of young womanhood, an irresistible beauty whose charms escaped no one's notice. The British captain Charles Cochrane described her as an ebony-haired Venus with the eyes of a coquette and the lips of an angel. Bolívar was taken with her immediately. He danced with her at the ball and began seriously to court her favor; some historians say she became one of the great infatuations of his life. But she was already in love with one of Bolívar's most able colonels, Ambrosio Plaza, and the young lovers hoped to marry. Although Bolívar considered sending his officer far away so that he could have Bernardina to himself, General Santander interceded. Santander pleaded with Bolívar to allow the young man to stay in Bogotá and remain by Bernardina's side. Eventually, Bolívar agreed, writing to Santander good-naturedly, "No doubt this marriage will please you, for it is sure to increase the population of young Grana-dans. Me, too, for I love this young couple." There was good reason for Santander's interest in the girl's welfare: he had fallen into an ardent affair with her older sister, Nicolasa, a married woman whose royalist husband had fled—all too conveniently—in the evacuation. The Iba-ñez women would be the source of much gossip in New Granada for months, even years, to come.

Triumph, as it turned out, was an aphrodisiac; and balls and parades somehow always managed to sharpen Bolívar's appetite for a woman. But if he couldn't have Bernardina, he could always count on his mis-tress, Pepita. In a letter to Vice President Zea soon after his arrival in Bogotá, he included a personal note: "I hope you will look after the female visitors who await me there." It was a reference to Pepita, her mother, and sister, all of whom, he reasonably assumed, had reached Angostura safely. Months would pass before he learned that Pepita had died trying to reach him. For the moment, however, the very thought of his high-spirited mistress was comfort enough. He was eager to see her again.

Bolívar now threw himself into the business of establishing a government in Bogotá. It was no secret that he wanted to join New Granada to Venezuela and, in so doing, create a larger, more resilient nation. But before he could achieve that more perfect union, he had to return to his fractious land and finish its revolution. He needed to work quickly, keep patriot enthusiasms alive. Within the course of a few weeks, he established the bare bones of government: a supreme court, a system of provincial governors, a police force; he elected a minister of war and a minister of the interior. He appropriated Spain's coveted gold, silver, and emerald mines, putting into practice the recommen-dations made by his old friend Baron von Humboldt. He revoked the king's taxes, confiscated Spanish property, set up a school for orphans, instituted a fund for war widows, and levied fines on priests who con-tinued to support the Spanish cause. He also issued an open letter to Viceroy Sámano, proposing an exchange of prisoners. In trade for the charismatic Barreiro—"the Adonis of Bogotá," as women liked to call him—he hoped to secure the freedom of a number of valuable republicans. But the viceroy, on the run and obsessed with his own safety, never replied to Bolívar, and so the fate of Brigadier Barreiro and his officers was left to chance.

Although Bolívar soon managed to construct a rudimentary government, he had never been a man for the desk. Dealing with the minutiae of paperwork was always sheer torment for him. He needed an amanuensis who could govern the country and attend to details while he moved on to the more pressing business of liberation. In late September, just before he announced his return to Venezuela, Bolívar named General Santander to the post of vice president, entrusting to that methodical, inordinately ambitious, and mercurial man the foundation of a new republic.

No sooner had Bolívar departed Bogotá than Santander began to impose his own stamp on the country. He was a jurist by training—a man of the law, as Bolívar called him—and thus well suited to the business of government. He was also an indefatigable worker, spending long days at his desk, writing memoranda, decrees, statutes. It is no exaggeration to say that Santander constructed the legal foundation for democracy in Colombia. But he was also a complicated man: sullen, calculating, peevish, and far too much in love with money. Along the way, he had acquired a streak of cruelty, and a deep aversion to admitting his own mistakes. The horsemen of Venezuela, with whom he had once served, had never liked him, and said so openly. There was a reason for it: he had always been a mediocre soldier, lacking the physical prowess of a true warrior. But in the halls of government the man shone.

Indeed, Santander had much to offer Bolívar during this crucial period in the history of New Granada. He dove happily into the complex business of administration that Bolívar so deeply abhorred. But on October 11, within days of the Liberator's departure, Bolívar was given a hint of the bad he would have to suffer along with the good in his vice president. Santander summarily ordered Brigadier Barreiro and thirty-eight prisoners of war to be taken from jail and marched to the main square to be executed. They were led four abreast, dragging their noisy chains to the very place on the plaza where so many republican leaders had met bloody ends. Barreiro was ordered to kneel, at which point he realized why he had been brought there; and then he was shot in the back without preliminaries or explanation. After that, all remaining thirty-eight were lined up and gunned down. General Santander watched the killings from atop his horse, peering out from the gate that led to the government palace. He spoke a few words of approval, then led a parade—complete with triumphant song—through the streets of Bogotá. His celebration continued into the night, with a grand ball at the palace.

Republicans were horrified. Barreiro may have been a Spaniard, but the people of Bogotá had had considerable respect—even admiration—for the dashing young officer. They liked his soldierly grit, his personable manner. There was an additional, poignant detail, which surprised no one in those days of jumbled allegiances: the Spanish brigadier was engaged to be married to the sister of a republican soldier. Thrust to his knees, Barreiro came to the swift realization that they meant to kill him, and so asked one thing only: that his executioners remove a tiny portrait of his fiancée from the pocket nearest his heart.

Even in Venezuela, the shootings were seen as cowardly, unnecessary, inhumane. Republican authorities tried to dissociate themselves from the atrocity, refusing to write it into the public acts. If the patriots had learned anything from ten long years of struggle, it was that blood sacrifices—wars to the death—were damaging to their revolution. They wanted no part of them. When Santander tried to explain himself in a private letter to Bolívar, the words rang hollow: "In the end, I had to get rid of Barreiro and his thirty-eight companions. The pressure was making me crazy, the public was up in arms, and nothing good was going to come from keeping them behind bars." He made it seem as if all the prisoners had been Spanish officers—which they were not—and that their very presence on earth had been a threat to New Granada. In closing, he added slyly: "The records have been doctored, but since even you (sadly for America) are not immortal, and since I cannot govern forever, it's essential that your reply cover me for all time." Bolívar's reply did just that; the Liberator's ire barely showed behind the conciliatory phrases:

I have learned with great regret of the deceitful conduct of our prisoners of war, which forced you to shoot them even though we were waiting to negotiate an exchange that might have given honor to the Republic. . . . Our enemies will not believe that our harshness is an act of justice. But be that as it may, I thank Your Excellency for your zeal and dedication in the attempt to save the Republic with such an unpopular measure.

FOR THE NEXT TWO MONTHS, Bolívar moved tirelessly from town to town, gradually making his way to Venezuela. Riding his legendary white horse, Palomo—acquired before the Battle of Boyacá—he traced a circuitous route from Tunja to Bucaramanga to Pamplona. He enlisted troops as he went, raised money for arms, conferred with his officers. In every town he was met by adoring crowds and triumphant processions, and at every point he worked avidly to keep the revolutionary spirit alive. He posted flyers, distributed literature. He was a fervent believer in the power of the written word and, although Spaniards laughed at him for it, he always carried a printing press on military campaigns and into battle. It was a cumbersome contraption, requiring many pack animals for its portage, but—to him—it was as essential a weapon in war as any cannon. There was no maneuver—and certainly no victory tour—that couldn't profit from a well-worded broadside.

There was, too, hardly a stop in that protracted voyage that wasn't accompanied by a jubilant ball celebrating the republic. Bolívar deeply understood the psychological value of a festive ritual: the confidence and loyalty that a high-spirited "bread and circus" could inspire. But there was another reason for hosting a ball at every opportunity. The Liberator loved to dance.

The waltz was his favorite, and he was inclined to dance it for hours at a time if he had a good partner—into the wee hours of morning. He would revel in the music, the physical exertion of it, until, filled with a new energy, he would leave the floor briefly to issue a battery of letters, orders, publications. Like Caesar or Napoleon, he dictated several at once, to two or three different secretaries. He formulated ideas quickly, pacing the room or swinging vigorously in his hammock, and then he would rush back to dance some more. He found that in dancing, concepts became clearer; his writing more eloquent. "There are men," he would say, "who need to be alone and far from the hubbub to be able to think or mull. I deliberated, reflected, and mulled best when I was at the center of the revelry—among the pleasures and clamor of a ball."

But the war was all consuming, even on the dance floor. Revolution was constantly on his mind. As he traveled through New Granada, being toasted for his heroics, he was working to increase his army, which—despite Morillo's fears—was pitifully depleted. In Pamplona, he met his generals Soublette and Anzoátegui, and with them planned an offensive against Morillo, but the Spanish general seemed in no hurry to engage them. He was biding his time in the Venezuelan hills, waiting out the rainy season, putting off hostilities until he received the promised reinforcements from Madrid.

When Bolívar finally crossed into Venezuela, he was given the unexpected news that his vibrant young general Anzoátegui, whose valor had emboldened them all at the Battle of Boyacá, had taken ill and died. Bolívar could hardly believe it. Anzoátegui had seemed, when Bolívar laid eyes on him only days before, the very picture of health—strong, barely thirty, with a wife who anxiously awaited him and an infant he had never seen. Bolívar was devastated, as stricken as he had been to lose Girardot so many years before. But other reports would conspire to vex him.

Surely it was here, as he made his way back to Angostura, that Bolívar learned Pepita was dead, too. He had not been true to her—he had not been true to any one woman since his wife's death—but he had cared for Pepita deeply. She had always been a comfort in difficult times, a vivacious, passionate companion, and he had sorely missed her affections. But as demoralizing as all this news might have been, his personal grief was quickly overshadowed by the intelligence he was receiving about Venezuela itself. He had thought that he was returning to some semblance of the country he had left behind, but as he descended the cordillera, rode across the parched plains, and sailed down the low waters of the Orinoco, he began to hear of the political bedlam that had overtaken Angostura in his absence.

There were rumors of insubordination. The warlords he'd thought he'd tamed had gone back to their old, defiant ways. Páez, he now learned, had ignored his command to march west and check the enemy's movements. Mariño had disregarded orders and refused to join forces with Bermúdez. Worst of all, Arismendi, spinning off into a wild revolution of his own, had had to be apprehended, brought to the capital of Angostura, and thrown into jail.

Vice President Zea may have been an erudite scholar and skilled orator, but he was a weak leader overall and had fallen victim to running gossip that Bolívar had been routed by Morillo's army and was languishing in a dungeon in Bogotá, or that he had simply fled—a deserter and outlaw—into the vast expanse of New Granada. As the reins slipped daily from his hands, Zea found it impossible to control Venezuela's warlords. He was a Granadan, after all—a mousy little foreigner with no military experience—and they had little respect for a chieftain who couldn't swing a sword. Congress, fidgety and nervous, began to worry that in Zea's uncertain hands the republic would surely fail. Before long, members began to conspire with one another and, from captivity, Arismendi shrewdly worked to build a constituency among them. Mariño, whom Zea had unwisely relieved of his command, suddenly appeared in the capital and joined Arismendi in the intrigue. In the face of those two indisputable heroes of the revolution, the bookish Zea didn't stand a chance. Eventually he was forced to step down. In an extraordinary reversal of fortune, the swashbuckling Arismendi went from prison to palace, where he was named vice president of the republic. His first official act was to make Mariño commanding general of the armed forces of the east.

Bolívar arrived in Angostura at three o'clock in the morning on December 11, 1819, well aware by now that the fate of the republic hung in the balance. As always, when things were at their worst, Bolívar was at his calmest. He disembarked in the capital as if all were under control—as if he had hardly left it—although he had been gone for almost a year. Despite the late hour, the citizens rushed to greet him. They were hardly prepared for his arrival, unaware until two hours before that he was alive and on his way. Arismendi was gone, on a tour of inspection; Mariño was in the north, reorganizing his army. Even so, Bolívar was met by resounding cheers and a round of salvos. Surprised, ecstatic, the people of Angostura welcomed their long-gone hero and carried him triumphantly to the palace.

He was careful to treat his minions with great respect and equanimity, even those who had declared the Bolívarian era finished. Exhausted after his arduous sixty-four-day voyage, he rested for two days, took measure of the situation, and received Zea and others privately in his quarters. Arismendi, who had arrived in Angostura only hours after Bolívar, had thought the pealing bells, salvos, and fireworks had been for him, but realized what was happening when he heard the shouts of "Long live Bolívar!" and his own secretary hurrying away, warning him with an ominous, "Farewell, General!" When Arismendi saw him, nevertheless, Bolívar was the essence of collegiality. He congratulated the vice president heartily for reorganizing the military, staging an admirable defense of the capital, and showing just enough muscle to scare off the royalists. "As soon as those two met," an English seaman reported, "Bolívar evinced the same affectionate joy that he would have shown at meeting a brother from whom he had been long separated. He embraced the general, kissed his veteran cheek, encircled him in his arms, and pressed him to his bosom repeatedly, exclaiming as if with the warmest delight '¡Mi querido general!'" Overcome by the Liberator's generosity, Arismendi submitted his resignation. Bolívar returned him to the governorship of Margarita, pretended no knowledge of the intrigues, and reinstated Zea. Allowing everyone to save face, including his petulant warlords, Bolívar was able to restore order. It was as if nothing at all had happened in his absence.

On December 14, Bolívar addressed the members of Congress, calling for the union of Venezuela and New Granada and the creation of a new American nation that straddled the continent from sea to sea. This was the dream for which he had labored on both sides of the Andean cordillera—a goal, he said, he had set almost a decade before, during his earliest fighting days. By the time the legislators voted, that sprawling territory would include the former colony of Quito and embody a remarkably diverse landmass that joined jungle to mountain, valley to desert, and bustling cities to desolate plains. He called it the Republic of Greater Colombia.

The eloquence of Bolívar, the enthusiasm of Zea—the sheer optimism of the moment after what had been such a querulous time—were convincing enough for the beleaguered legislators. On December 17, Congress passed a law joining the former Spanish colonies. In one masterful stroke, Bolívar made Venezuela, a colony that had been struggling fitfully against Morillo, part of the victorious republic that Morillo had just lost. Bolívar and Zea were soon elected president and vice president of that new, larger nation. Santander was confirmed vice president of the state of New Granada; and Roscio, one of the original signers of Venezuelan independence, was named vice president on the Venezuelan side. In their supreme confidence, the congress left the question of Quito's command to be resolved when Bolívar had actually confirmed its liberation. Tired of being traded capriciously between the viceroyalties of Peru and New Granada, Quito had asserted its independence early. But whether the people of Quito or New Granada wanted to be part of Greater Colombia was not even considered. For now, what was important—despite all apparent obstacles—was momentum and revolutionary will.

BOLÍVAR LEFT ANGOSTURA AT THE end of December, eager to press on against the Spaniards while he had them on the defensive. His title of president and Liberator secure, he had the complete loyalty of his officers, and he ordered them now to take strategic positions in the north, along the coast, with all eyes on Caracas. Arismendi would resume control of Margarita; Urdaneta would march toward Caracas; Soublette would escort a fresh infusion of British soldiers down the Orinoco; Bermúdez would command them in the Apure; and Páez would prepare a major offensive to the west. They would squeeze Morillo's army until it had nowhere to go but home.

Bolívar could hardly know it, but he would receive most help from Spain itself, where a major expedition of reinforcements was suddenly halted by a sharp turn in the country's politics. Morillo had asked King Ferdinand for twenty thousand soldiers and a fleet of forty-seven warships to rout Bolívar decisively and drive "all his pirates" from the Caribbean. The Ministry of War had agreed to provide Morillo with at least four thousand of those troops, and had gone so far as to ask Russia for help in the naval transports. But on January 1, 1820, the men who were in Cádiz waiting to be shipped out to America rose up in violent rebellion. Many were veterans of the Napoleonic Wars and, even though they had expelled Napoleon from their shores, they had managed—like much of Europe—to absorb French revolutionary ideas of freedom. They wanted no more of Spain's iron-fisted ways and were deeply angered by King Ferdinand's abolition of the liberal 1812 constitution, whose very goal had been to curb the excesses of a corrupt king. Now they demanded the immediate restoration of the constitution; moreover, they refused to serve in a war effort against the Latin American rebels. A frightened Ferdinand, keen to avoid following his French counterpart to the guillotine, could only comply. On March 9, he reinstated the Cádiz constitution and promised a more equitable political system. The message went out to General Morillo: no reinforcements would be sent; instead, he was to negotiate with the rebels and assure them that, like any other Spanish citizens, they would be granted all freedoms implicit in the constitution. It was proof of how little Spain understood America. By now, Bolívar's rebels were well beyond listening to any king; and they certainly would never accept any constitution they themselves hadn't written. When Morillo received Madrid's instructions, he threw up his hands. "They've gone crazy!" he told his officers. "They have no idea what they're saying."

Morillo could see very clearly that there was no good way out for him. His reports to the Ministry of War grew gloomier by the day. Madrid's decisions, he wrote his minister, "have dashed this army's most fervent hopes and reduced us to total ineptitude and impotence." Being a man of considerable political acumen, Morillo understood that the constitution of 1812 could not fail to have a positive influence on his country, but what was progress in peacetime was not always progress in war. By June, Morillo was forced to publish news of the restoration of the Cádiz constitution. He did this with a heavy heart, knowing full well what it meant for his weary soldiers. How to tell such men, who were far from home and had risked their lives for no pay whatsoever, that they could not aspire to some remuneration? As the constitution spelled out and was reprinted for everyone to see in the *Gaceta de Caracas*, the army was not to touch, much less appropriate private property. The old assumption that soldiers could take whatever booty they could find was now actionable by law. Morillo continued to rule in Caracas and the coastal highlands, but he could see that his war was over. He needed to find a way to cause the least damage to his career.

Morillo may not have known it, but at that moment he had the military advantage. Bolívar was still struggling to fortify the patriot army. Returning to Bogotá, the Liberator knew that he had the support of the Granadan people, but all the adoration and good cheer had not translated into troops. For every republican recruit, there were dozens of soldiers who had deserted out of sheer hunger. The people were tired of bloodshed, dispirited after a long decade of ruin and upheaval. A crippling stupor had invaded the republican soul. Surveying his fellow citizens, Bolívar despaired at their failure to understand what it took to make a democracy. There was bad faith all around, a corrosive lack of will, and the ideals and virtues he spoke of in his speeches seemed to be in scant evidence among his listeners. As he said to Santander: perhaps the poisons of colonialism had gone too deep. "The more I think about it," he confided in a letter, "the more I am convinced that neither liberty, nor law, nor luminous enlightenment will transform us into peace-loving people, much less into republicans and true patriots."

As he worked to consolidate the republic, he made it clear that the black slaves of Greater Colombia were to be free; that he expected them to serve in the liberating army; that it was the height of inequality, not to mention a form of genocide, for whites to be killed in war while blacks were denied the opportunity to show equivalent patriotism. It had been all too evident, as he made his way through the ravaged land, that almost half the white population of Venezuela had been lost to the revolution. But beyond the notion that equal rights demanded equal sacrifices, Bolívar believed in the inherent logic of liberty: "any free government that commits the folly of allowing slavery," he wrote to Santander, "can expect to be punished by revolution." Santander was of a different mind. He saw the freeing of slaves as having grave consequences—both social and economic—for the country. He was careful to avoid argument with the Liberator, but a rift began to grow between them: the president and vice president were learning that they had fundamental disagreements about how America should be free.

There were problems, too, with Páez. The Lion of the Apure continued to be recalcitrant, unreliable. Ignorant of military protocols, he awarded his men titles and privileges far beyond his authority to do so. He was petulant, difficult; he countermanded orders, balked when he was told to follow the rules, complained constantly about money. But Bolívar was all too aware of his value. Loath to provoke Páez to battle, the Spaniards had given the republicans a wide berth. The man was a bulwark in peace, a titan in war. Bolívar decided he was well worth the bluster and insubordination. "A leader needs to learn how to hear even the hardest truths," Bolívar ventured to lecture him, sounding less like a commander than an indulgent teacher. But he let the plainsman do as he pleased.

IF BOLÍVAR WAS AT ODDS with his two most important generals, he was also wrestling with his own heart. In Bogotá, he had many opportunities to see the lovely Bernardina Ibañez and regret that he had ever released her to her young colonel. He began courting her assiduously again. Even when he departed Bogotá less than three weeks later, he couldn't help but ponder her attractions. From the relative quiet of Cúcuta, he wrote pleading letters to the girl, venting the full brunt of his infatuation. She was too shy and frightened to respond, but she was also firmly in love with Colonel Plaza. Frustrated by her reticence, astonished by her neglect, Bolívar became insistent, supplicating, redoubling his efforts to win her. To his delight, the young colonel had done something—strayed, misspoken, the correspondence doesn't make it clear—to break Bernardina's heart. Knowing how close Santander was to all this because of his ongoing affair with Bernardina's sister, Bolívar wrote to the vice president, asking for his intercession. "Tell her whatever she needs to hear, including that I'm tired of writing to her without the courtesy of an answer. Tell her that I, too, am a bachelor, and that clearly she interests me more than she interests Plaza, for I've never been untrue."

In a constant flow of letters about the minutiae of war and the intricacies of managing his officers, a singular portrait emerges, glimpsed only occasionally in the interstices of those idler days: it is the portrait of a lonesome man. Although surrounded by people and difficult demands, he was, as far as love went, as solitary as could be. His mistress of six years was dead. He had heard nothing from the members of his immediate family, who had been scattered mercilessly by war. His oldest sister, María Antonia, a fervent royalist who had stayed on in Havana after her husband died, was at a distance in every sense of the word.

Embittered, staunchly antirevolutionary, she had gone so far as to write to the king, asking to be remunerated for her losses and expressing dismay that her brother had reduced the country to "absolute ruin." Bolívar's other sister, Juana, too, was a widow, whose republican husband had died defending Maturín against Boves's forces. The two sisters had lived together for a while in various ports of the Caribbean until 1817, when Juana had sailed up the Orinoco to Guayana, only to learn that she had lost her son, Guillermo, to a battle outside Angostura. His sisters, in short, were little comfort to him now.

As a result, Bolívar had colleagues, compatriots, and armies that followed and revered him—but precious few intimates. His closest companion in those days of scarce affections was his manservant, the ever constant, much loved José Palacios, to whom he ceded his complete care. It was Palacios who worried over Bolívar's diet, his sleeping habits, his comforts, his day-to-day exigencies; and it was he who spoiled the Liberator with little indulgences, as a thoughtful spouse might do. One can't help but see Bolívar straining toward love in a loveless time, especially in his unrequited infatuation with Bernardina.

Santander dutifully delivered all of Bolívar's sentiments to the vexed girl and reported back to him: "I have yet to see Bernardina, but I will give her your latest message and you shall have her answer. She has told me a thousand times that there is no woman more confused than she. I haven't wanted to get caught up in these affairs, but it's clear that she still hopes that things will work out with Plaza and she mistrusts all the others, including you. Looking at it from afar, the love business doesn't look too promising."

This response may have seemed heartless, but it was true. Bernardina was not inclined to want to commit herself to a difficult, older—and dauntingly famous—man. There were a full twenty years of life separating them, as well as two hundred miles, a world of differing expectations, and a dashing, persistent young colonel. Within the year, Bernardina married Colonel Plaza, and within a year he was dead in battle. In time, she would scandalize Bogotá by bearing a rich man's illegitimate child. Eventually, she married again; this time, her husband, Florentino González, was a pasty-faced newspaper editor who became a powerful Colombian politician. When González learned that Bolívar had once had a strong romantic interest in his fiancée, he began to nurture a bitter hatred against the Liberator. That hostility would play out soon enough in the annals of Greater Colombia.

DESPITE HIS DISAPPOINTMENTS IN LOVE, Bolívar now held the future of the republic in his hands. As he sat in his quiet idyll in Cúcuta, planning his next move on Morillo and Caracas, he began to be inundated by managerial problems, all of them requiring immediate attention, decisions, instructions. The army was in disarray; there was much to do. He soon learned that the newly arrived British troops, who had yet to be paid, were being disruptive, refusing to obey orders. "The Irish are like courtesans," he wrote one of his generals, "they serve you only after the money has crossed hands . . . if you don't pay, they don't kill." Despite the attempt to make light of it, he had no money to give. He had always been able to dig into his own pockets to help pay his soldiers and their widows, but gold and silver were in desperately short supply. It was incumbent on him now to raise it.

There were other worries. In Angostura, Zea was making alarming mistakes. Precious livestock was being sold off to United States slaughterhouses with no thought of feeding the armies of Greater Colombia. Indeed, in a "diabolical mix of ineptitude and confusion," as Bolívar recounted to Santander, the patriot government was buying beef back from the United States. Fully convinced now that Zea was more a scholar than a leader of men, Bolívar made him ambassador from Greater Colombia to Britain, where Zea went on to commit other ineptitudes. But Bolívar had more pressing problems as he looked around in Cúcuta: the recruits, guns, bullets, provisions that he had requested had not appeared, and letters he dictated now in a dizzying flurry to his officers were filled with worry. He worried about the slowness of the mails; about putting soldiers closer to Caracas; about how best to develop his talented young officers. Desperate to bring fresh perspective to the table, he made the youthful colonel Antonio José de Sucre—only twenty-five years old at the time—a general; and then, surprising his ranks further, named him his minister of war.

Bolívar was hardly living the sovereign's life. His routine was Spartan, his meals frugal. In the mornings, he rose at dawn, tended to his horse, Palomo, and read for several hours before breakfast (largely philosophers, especially Voltaire and Montesquieu). He took his first repast of the day with his war minister, his chief of staff, and his secretary, after which he managed the army's affairs, issued edicts, wrote articles for the *Gaceta*, handled diplomatic questions, and fretted over a whirlwind of correspondence. He managed all of this in brisk tempo, dictating to several secretaries, erupting with aggravation if they slowed him in any way or made errors. In the evenings, immediately after dinner, he rode to clear his mind. At night, he conferred with his officers until nine o'clock, when he retired to his hammock and read for another two hours.

Military efficiency was his obsession. He insisted that citizens of New Granada show their patriotism by supporting the army with cold cash—by raising, at the minimum, 30,000 pesos a month to pay salaries and commission uniforms. He instructed Santander to "squeeze" the provinces for the money. Along with his determination to build an invincible fighting force, the possibilities of a favorable armistice were growing daily. The uprising in Spain and the restoration of the constitution of Cádiz had effectively halted Morillo's ability to prosecute the war. In an excited letter to Soublette on June 19, 1820, Bolívar reported having intercepted an official communiqué from Madrid that confirmed King Ferdinand's historic reversal: Spain would send no further expeditions to South America. The soldiers in the port of Cádiz, by their very rebelliousness, had rescued American independence. In yet another letter, Bolívar wrote an English friend exultantly, "Ten thousand enemies were being shipped out against us, and now those ten thousand are our best friends!!!"

Indeed, a little more than two weeks later, on July 6, Bolívar received a message from Morillo's right hand, General Miguel de La Torre, requesting a cessation of hostilities. Morillo had not known where to find Bolívar, La Torre said, and had written to him at numerous addresses. In the process, the captain-general had sent an envoy to Páez and another to the congress of Angostura, proposing that the barbaric war had gone on too long. His earnest efforts to reach Bolívar made an impression on the Liberator: this was either an elaborate trap or the beginning of the end of the revolution. Bolívar responded to La Torre the next day.

"If the object of your mission is anything less than the recognition of the Republic of Colombia, don't expect me to listen." But "if Spain intends to treat Colombia as an independent, free, and sovereign state, we can go forward in peace and friendship."

A period of negotiation followed, in which Bolívar made it readily understood that Greater Colombia—the new amalgamation of northern Latin America—would never again bow to a king. The colonial era was emphatically over. Morillo, seeking nothing so much as a well-defined door and a graceful way to pass through it, was all too accommodating. He had reasons to be. When he had arrived in Venezuela in 1815, Morillo had married a Cádiz woman, with whom he was deeply in love. But she had remained in Spain; the wedding had been by proxy. In all his five years as a married man, he had yet to join her and consummate the marriage. But Morillo had also been seriously injured in the Battle of La Puerta two years before and had never recovered completely from the lance wound that had almost killed him. Certainly, Morillo could see that there was no future for him in the king's pacification campaign, but there were other reasons to go home.

After an exchange of letters between the two leaders in August and September, Bolívar suggested that the most appropriate site for a conference would be in San Fernando de Apure, where he intended to establish headquarters. Morillo wasted no time in giving Bolívar his consent. Cautious about giving away his movements, wary of allowing the enemy to see how weak his army had become, Bolívar delayed the meeting several times. In October, he made a number of quick raids on the border provinces, if only to show Morillo that Greater Colombia needed an armistice less than Spain did, but all the while he maintained a remarkably cordial correspondence with Morillo, in which both generals carefully explained every move. The conference to negotiate an armistice finally came to pass in November in the picturesque mountain town of Trujillo, where Bolívar had decreed war to the death seven years before. General Sucre and two colonels were delegated to meet with the royalist commissioners and work out the details of the armistice. On November 21, the patriots and Spaniards met for the first time.

By November 25, two treaties were ratified. The first called for a six-month armistice; the second recognized Bolívar as president of the republic and set out the terms for an exchange of prisoners. Peace was the ultimate objective. The meetings were cordial, though formal, and Sucre distinguished himself as a coolheaded negotiator. He managed to achieve everything Bolívar wanted. Once the work was complete, Morillo expressed his eagerness to meet the Liberator. A conference was arranged for the morning of November 27 in the scruffy little village of Santa Ana, which lay on a mist-bound limestone ridge between two valleys, some 250 miles southwest of Caracas. Since Santa Ana was well inside Spanish territory, Bolívar took every precaution to put General Urdaneta in command of the army before he, Sucre, and a handful of others set out to see Morillo face-to-face.

So it was that the archenemies of one of the bloodiest episodes of South American history met on a muddy road, far from the medullas of political power. They approached one another from opposite directions, their paths as contrary as their essential natures: Bolívar had come from a long line of aristocrats and wore his pedigree lightly; Morillo, born into a family of peasants, had become Count of Cartagena in the course of an illustrious career. Bolívar was confident, spontaneous, as only the wellborn can be; Morillo was shrewd and deliberate, having scrapped for every honor he had been awarded. Into that historic moment, Bolívar rode a strong mule, was accompanied by a handful of men, and was dressed in the garb of a humble soldier. Morillo, on the other hand, set out on a magnificent horse, was clad in a uniform bespangled with decorations, and accompanied by fifty of his best officers and a full regiment of hussars. As they rode over the bare hills in the damp chill of a November morning, they might have glimpsed the sparkling expanse of Lake Maracaibo in the distance. If they had glanced south, they would have seen the splendid peaks of the cordillera. Weary of war, anxious about their own capacities to execute it, they came to that crossroad with high and not dissimilar hopes.

Morillo was first to arrive, and when he appeared at the appointed place he was soon met by Bolívar's aide Daniel O'Leary, who announced that the Liberator was on his way. As they perched on their horses, peering expectantly down the road, the general asked what kind of escort would accompany the president of the republic. O'Leary replied that Bolívar's retinue amounted to no more than twelve patriot officers and the three Spanish commissioners who had negotiated the armistice in Trujillo. Morillo was taken aback. "Well," he finally managed, "I thought my escort too small for this venture, but I see that my old enemy has outdone me in chivalry. I'll order my hussars to withdraw." He did so immediately. The Liberator's modest party soon appeared on the crest of the hill that overlooked Santa Ana, and Morillo moved forward to meet it. As the two neared one another, General Morillo wanted to know which of the horsemen was Bolívar. When O'Leary pointed him out, the Spaniard exclaimed, "What? That little man in the blue jacket and sergeant's cap; the one riding the mule?" But no sooner had he said it than Bolívar was before him. The generals dismounted and embraced each other heartily. Their words were cordial, warm—filled with the kind of respect and admiration only the most serious rivals can have for one another. They headed to the private house Morillo had commandeered for the occasion, and sat down with their officers for a celebratory lunch.

For all the enmity that had passed between them, the two leaders were instantly companionable, with much to discuss. Morillo had fought in the Battle of Trafalgar only days after Bolívar had trekked to Rome as a young man and made his spirited vow on the heights of Monte Sacro. Morillo had served under the Duke of Wellington, the brother of Richard Wellesley, whose help Bolívar had solicited when the revolution was but an idea, with much blood yet to be shed. There were innumerable toasts made to the end of hostilities and the future of Spanish American understanding. "To the victories of Boyacá!" one Spanish colonel sang out. "To Colombians and Spaniards," General La Torre added, "may they march side by side all the way to hell against the despots and the tyrants!" The men spoke of sacrifices, of heroism, of the past ten years of their lives, which had been steeped in the dark business of war. That very afternoon, Morillo proposed the building of a pyramid to commemorate their meeting, and Bolívar readily agreed to it. Together, they proceeded to the spot of their first embrace and called upon their officers to roll out a first stone. More toasts were had; more libations consumed. "I drink," said Bolívar, "to the heroism of the warriors of both armies . . . to their loyalty, sacrifice, and courage. . . . Eternal hatred upon those who lust for blood and who shed it unjustly!"

The lateness of the hour finally put an end to the exchange, but the generals decided that even nightfall would not separate them. They hung their hammocks in the same room, said their good nights, and slept soundly, compensating perhaps—as one chronicler put it—for the many sleepless nights they had caused one another. The following morning, Morillo accompanied Bolívar to the large rock that marked their peace, whereupon they repeated their promises, embraced once more, and parted, never to see each other again. On December 17, less than a month later, General Morillo boarded a ship in La Guaira and set sail for Spain. General La Torre was left in command of the king's army with a single recommendation from Morillo: "Defend the fortress of Puerto Cabello at all costs!" It turned out to be good advice, as the Spaniards would need that port in the harried evacuation of its expeditionary forces.

Much later, after Bolívar's enemies criticized him severely for being so conciliatory with Morillo, a general whom even Spain had had to censure for his bloodcurdling cruelties, Bolívar had this to say:

> During the entire course of my public life, I have never shown more political acuity or diplomatic cunning than in that crucial hour; and I can say without an ounce of vanity that I think I bested General Morillo then as I bested him in almost every one of my military operations. . . . The armistice of six months fooled Morillo into returning to Spain and handing over his command to General La Torre, who was less skilled, less energetic, and less a consummate soldier than the Count of Cartagena. Let the dolts and my enemies say what they will. . . . Never was a diplomatic game played more successfully than that of the day and night of November 27 in the village of Santa Ana.

AS THE WAR LIMPED INTO its tenth year and rumors of an armistice began to spread throughout the English-speaking world, the eyes of foreign governments turned once again to the struggle for Latin American independence. By now, the English were well acquainted with Bolívar's revolution. Thousands of mercenaries had been recruited to serve the Liberator's cause; some, who had been promised gifts of land in return for their services, had gone so far as to bring their families. Young brigadiers with high hopes had marched through the tropical wilds singing "Ye Gentlemen of England"; few of them would make it home.

Bolívar had been a keen advocate of British recruitment. Three of his aides-de-camp were British. Foreign veterans had become as valuable as gold to republican generals, representing the kind of rigor and training that raw, untested soldiers could emulate. Bolívar's claim that the true Liberator had been Luis López Méndez, his recruiting agent in London, was a blatant exaggeration, to be sure—a generous, diplomatic flourish—but not without a germ of truth.

More accurately, the British mercenary experience in Spanish America, despite its triumphs, was marred with bitter disappointment. As one young English colonel put it succinctly: there had been much to regret. Young men were lured by promises that Venezuela was a richly hung garden, that its partisans of liberty were steadfast and united. What they joined instead was poverty, starvation, and a race war "as black and barbarous as the slave trade." Weakened by typhus, which they had brought with them from Britain, they were especially vulnerable; most died of heat exhaustion, rampant infection, or simply too much rum. Stories began to filter home that the few who had survived were now as barefoot as the locals; that Bolívar was little more than a swindler and bombast; that the only way to survive his revolution had been to sack churches, rob reliquaries. In London's halls of power, however, the view was very different: with Spain in retreat and Bolívar's star rising, a lucrative trade loomed on the horizon. There was money to be made.

In the rapidly expanding United States, a similar awareness was growing. Champions of commerce advocated the recognition of the fledgling South American republics if only because they knew profits were bound to follow. Men of ideals believed that the American nation, itself born of rebellion, should stand behind any impulse to freedom. Some, like Secretary of State John Quincy Adams, however, were slow to see what, if any, advantages diplomatic recognition might bring. Not long before, he had stated with all candor:

Venezuela, though it has emancipated all its slaves, has been constantly alternating between an absolute military government, a capitulation to Spanish authority, and guerrillas black and white, of which every petty chief has acted for purposes of war and rapine as an independent sovereign. There is finally in South America neither unity of cause nor unity of effort, as there was in our Revolution.

He was quite right, of course; even Bolívar had warned the congress of Angostura that the world would never recognize the new republic until it spoke with one voice. "Unity, unity, unity," he had urged. But by 1820, when two large republics—with all their attendant differences—had joined Greater Colombia to stand united behind Bolívar, John Quincy Adams still had not changed his mind. He admitted that he distrusted everything the South Americans said. "There is no community of interests or of principles between North and South America," he stated flatly. And that was where diplomatic relations would remain for three years to come.

Indeed, there were reasons for Adams's reticence. There were the ongoing delicate negotiations between Washington and Madrid about Florida, which Spain owned and the United States wanted. There was the thorny fact that the slave trade was booming in the United States and few legislators in Washington wanted to hear about black revolutionaries or unbridled race mixing. There was also the fact that much of the information Adams was getting about Bolívar was downright negative. In 1818 and 1819, the U.S. government had sent two delegations to Venezuela to meet Bolívar and negotiate the return of American ships that had been seized by privateers in service of Bolívar's revolution. The Baltimore journalist Baptis Irvine had gone in 1818; the naval hero Captain Oliver Hazard Perry followed in 1819. Neither of their experiences had boded well for diplomatic relations. Commodore Perry had made the harsh three-hundred-mile voyage up the Orinoco at the height of the mosquito season only to find that President Bolívar was not in Angostura, but out on a military maneuver. As it happened, Perry had landed on the very day Bolívar had triumphed in Pantano de Vargas in New Granada, following his harrowing march over the Andes. After a fruitless exchange with the long-winded Zea, Perry had had no option but to return, whereupon he began to display sure signs of yellow fever: By mid-voyage to British Trinidad, he was producing a terrifying black vomit. Before he could board his own ship, he was dead.

By then, Baptis Irvine had delivered blistering reports about Bolívar to John Quincy Adams. The South American Liberator, Irvine wrote, was "a charlatan general and mountebank statesman." In numerous discussions with Bolívar, the irascible Irvine had lost his temper, provoking stern responses from the Liberator. It was no surprise that his accounts would be disapproving. "He affects the language of Napoleon," the journalist wrote huffily, which was to say that Bolívar was mimicking a leader any upstanding American should despise. "Without a ray of true political knowledge or a hint of morality, he apes the style and claims the character of Washington. However . . . he can surpass his present competitors by his knack of composition and fluency of speech."

That penchant for oratorical flourish would be on rich display one evening at a dinner given in Irvine's honor. The Liberator, carried away by his own eloquence, reached such heights of exhilaration that he leapt onto the table, and, with no regard to the shivering flowers and crystal, strode up and down the wooden length to make his point. "Thus," he cried, "as I cross this table from one end to the other, I shall march from the Atlantic to the Pacific, from Panama to Cape Horn, until every last Spaniard is expelled!"

There was no question that Irvine's portrait of Bolívar was unrelievedly negative. But there was strong support for Bolívar's revolution from a fervently egalitarian American public at large, as well as from a certain Samuel D. Forsyth, who, hoping to be appointed official agent to South America, had visited with President Monroe and Adams, expressed his high opinion of Greater Colombia, and called the Liberator a great man. Forsyth, who had served as interpreter for Perry in his travels, had not always thought so well of Bolívar, and so his change of heart made for a good impression. Certainly the most ardent supporter of the Spanish American rebels, however, was Henry Clay, the flamboyant congressman from Kentucky, who electrified his fellow members of the House of Representatives by crying out that the revolution's potential beneficiaries were no less than "eighteen million, struggling to be free!" Clay argued passionately for more commercial involvement, claiming that South America—with its rich metal resources and hunger

for North American goods—represented a vast market with endless opportunities. Clay's exhortations were resonant tributes to capitalism and
the democratic spirit, but they were also expressions of pique against
Adams, for, as everyone knew, President Monroe had passed over Clay
to make Adams secretary of state. But no one could deny it: the golden-
tongued orator from Kentucky was a tireless enthusiast for South
American liberty. On February 10, 1821, Clay moved that the House of
Representatives join the American people in their support for the distant revolution. When the Adams-Onís Treaty was proclaimed twelve
days later and the United States purchased Florida for $5 million, the
congressman finally had his way. The delicate negotiations with Spain
were over; official Washington could turn its attention to its southern
neighbors. With a firm foot in Florida, the United States was now only a
small sea away from Bolívar's war.

THE ARMISTICE WITH SPAIN LASTED a scant five months. But it was time
enough for republican forces to strengthen their numbers, discipline
the troops, acquire munitions. Well fed, reasonably well clothed, and
supremely confident in Bolívar, they had a marked advantage over the
Spaniards now. The royalists, in contrast, were exhausted. With no
relief from Spain in sight, they seemed to pass into perpetual limbo.
Soldiers who had been told they would fight for a maximum of three
years had seen three years come and go. Their pay was late; their food
was scarce; many were beset with fevers. Mainly, they wondered why
they were fighting a war that Spain itself had rejected. A corrosive ill-
humor invaded every rank. Even the generals in charge—La Torre and
Morales—were in constant disagreement.

In early 1821, even as Bolívar sent two envoys to Madrid to discuss
terms of peace with the Spaniards, he began to prepare for the next
stage of the revolution. He was haunted by the fear that his negotiators
would lose their nerve and capitulate to Spanish demands. He had given
them permission to trade Quito or even the Isthmus of Panama—lesser
colonies—in return for Colombia's independence, but under no circumstances were they to agree to any constitutional agreements with Spain,
or to subjugation under a prince or potentate from any reigning family

in Europe. "Colombia will be independent, sovereign, and free from all foreign domination, or it will cease to exist," he insisted. Clearly, he had little faith that the dialogue in Madrid would amount to anything, and he was right. Although his correspondence shows that he dearly desired peace, among the first documents he dictated after his friendly meeting with General Morillo was an agenda for renewed war.

It was at about this time that Bolívar learned that the coveted port city of Guayaquil—in what is now Ecuador—had declared independence. The people of Guayaquil, hearing that San Martín's army had landed in Pisco, just south of Lima, expected the Argentine general to sweep north now to liberate them, and they stormed the royalist halls of government in anticipation. Bolívar longed to go to Guayaquil himself to secure the region for Greater Colombia. It was a strategic port, potentially vital to the republic, and he did not want to see it go to San Martín so easily. But Bolívar was also aware that his priority needed to be Caracas, which still languished under Spanish rule. He sent General Sucre to Guayaquil instead.

It was a good decision. By April, the armistice was over. A rebellion had erupted in the Spanish stronghold of Maracaibo, fomented by one of Bolívar's generals, Rafael Urdaneta. It was a clear provocation, and Bolívar had neither sanctioned nor anticipated it. He rushed now to explain to the Spaniards that an unexpected rebellion could hardly count as the willful rupture of a military treaty, but General La Torre was adamant. He demanded the city's return. He informed Bolívar that—failing Maracaibo's restoration to the Spanish crown—the armistice would end on April 28.

Although Bolívar had written to Morillo, to La Torre, even to King Ferdinand himself, in hopes of reaching independence peacefully, he could see that it was no use: he was back at war. Bolívar moved quickly to unite the three armies of the west: his own, Páez's, and Urdaneta's. He knew that his only recourse now was to present the full force of the republic's military power—all at once, and in one great battle. But before he did, he directed General Bermúdez, commander of the army of the east, to prepare to attack Caracas, distract the Spaniards, and force them to split their forces. Bolívar was leaving nothing to chance.

He planned every detail of the engagement with utmost precision. Well aware that General Morales, La Torre's second in command, had been passed over for La Torre's job, he was going to use that resentment to his advantage.

On the morning of April 28, 1821, the mobilization of the three armies began: Páez and his horsemen, accompanied by the British Legion, started the long journey across the rain-whipped Apure to the appointed meeting place in San Carlos, a Venezuelan town on the plains of Carabobo where La Torre's army was garrisoned. Urdaneta undertook the grueling passage along a rough coast and over the mountains from Maracaibo. By early May—as Napoleon lay in St. Helena, surrendering his soul to the hereafter—Bolívar set up camp in the rubble of Barinas, having wended his way down the Magdalena River and recrossed the Andes to Venezuela. One week later, Bermúdez's eastern army invaded and occupied Caracas. Just as Bolívar had hoped, La Torre directed Morales to march on the capital and eject Bermúdez. It was an easy commission. The fierce Morales, commander of Boves's former Legions of Hell, was glad to go off on his own and, with his superior force of two thousand, handily shooed off the patriot soldiers. But all went exactly as Bolívar planned: his diversionary tactic had worked. La Torre, in San Carlos, was left with a weakened defense, and the patriot generals were now able to march overland toward him, unhampered.

On June 11—more than a month later—Páez's horsemen and the British battalion reached the outskirts of San Carlos, where Bolívar awaited them. General Urdaneta and his corps of infantrymen arrived within days, having successfully taken the port city of Coro. The royalist army, aware now of this impressive patriot advance, had withdrawn to the north, as Bolívar had predicted. Five thousand strong, they camped outside the village of Carabobo, fifty miles away. Once informed of their position, Bolívar didn't need to know more: La Torre's forces were clearly in shambles; the Spanish general was doing little more than blocking the road to Caracas and Puerto Cabello, his two strongholds; he was not going to attempt an offensive move. In any case, the patriot army now greatly outnumbered the royalists. By the time Bolívar reviewed his troops on the open fields of Tinaquillo, he had 6,500 soldiers under his command, including some of his most skilled officers. This was the republican army Bolívar had worked so diligently to build—"the largest and most superb ever to bear arms on any battlefield in Colombia," in his own estimation. To have brought them together from such distances, in such an advanced state of readiness, was a true testament to his military acuity.

On the night before the battle, the heavens opened with torrential rains, drenching the open ground and all the warriors who camped on it. The British who had fought in the Napoleonic Wars took it as a good omen; the same had happened before Waterloo. So it was that on June 24, 1821, the morning dawned bright and clear, presenting a cloudless sky. The patriots moved swiftly to carry out Bolívar's orders. Páez's cavalry was dispatched to the west, with instructions to attack the enemy's left flank. Undertaking a forced march for two and a half hours, they rode up and down steep terrain, hacking past tropical undergrowth, fording streams, until they were two miles from the valley where La Torre had taken position. By the time they reached Carabobo, they were laboring under a broiling sun.

The Spanish general had been confident that no cavalry could possibly negotiate the precipitous landscape to his west, and so he expected the republicans to flood into the valley from the south, where a gap in the hills beckoned. But Bolívar's vanguard did not take the bait. Instead, they moved stealthily along a narrow ravine on the western side. Hacking their way up a tangle of green, they scaled the heights and there, past trees and uneven ground, were able to spy the royalists in the valley, preparing for a frontal attack. The patriots spilled over the ridge, assaulting the Spaniards where they least expected it. Initially, La Torre's soldiers shrank back, but rallied with such a murderous volley of gunfire that Páez's men, who had chased them to within a pistol shot, broke and fled in disorder. The British Legion then took up the fight. Wielding their bayonets in their famous "hollow square" formation, they held off the royalists, allowing Páez's forces to regroup. When the horsemen rushed back into the fray, they came at the enemy from the rear, brandishing twelve-foot lances. The Spaniards were helpless in the face of that double onslaught.

Stunned by heavy losses and the abiding fear that they might be taken prisoner, the royalists fled the battlefield even as La Torre was issuing commands. When the smoke of war lifted from that sun-baked sepulcher, the stench of blood was pungent: more than a thousand royalists lay dead; 1,500 more had been taken prisoner; the rest had fled to the hills. The patriots had suffered fewer losses, and yet their dead were never recorded. Eventually, it was reported that six hundred British soldiers lost their lives at Carabobo, along with their commanding colonels, Manuel Cedeño and young Ambrosio Plaza, who had only recently been married to the lovely and highly coveted Bernardina Ibañez. As Bolívar approached to console the dying Plaza, the young man told him, "My general, I die happy here on this battlefield, in a position so far forward that even Páez could not reach it." Indeed, Páez lay in the dirt, not far away. Exhausted, the battle done, he was writhing, foaming at the mouth, being convulsed—as he so often was after a fray—by one of his violent fits of epilepsy. Nearby lay the towering First Negro, who had always protected him in battle—dead now, with a hole in his heart. As soon as Páez regained consciousness, his soldiers erupted in shouts of joy. There was no doubt that Páez's horsemen and the soldiers of the British Legion had won the afternoon, the battle, the war. Bolívar wasted no time in honoring them. There on the field, before the end of day, he promoted Páez to general in chief of the army. Then, as the Irish and English marched off—a bedraggled third of the number that had marched in—Bolívar was overcome with emotion. "Saviors of my country!" he cried after them in gratitude. They returned the praise with a crisp salute.

The victory was complete. The Battle of Carabobo was the last major engagement of the war in Greater Colombia, crucial not only because the patriots had prevailed, but because Bolívar's generals—small-time provincial warlords who heretofore had contributed only sporadically to a nation's welfare—had decided, if only briefly, to commit their allegiance to a greater good. For a brief time they yielded all personal ambition to Bolívar's vision. Some did so blindly; others, because they had become fervent partisans of a national idea whose possibility, until then, was only dimly seen. It didn't matter. Their dedication would be repaid in kind. On July 16, 1821, Bolívar issued a decree with his generals in mind. In it, he assigned the western provinces of Venezuela to Páez and Mariño; the east was placed under the control of Bermúdez. In essence, he was institutionalizing the Latin American warlord. The decree would have deep, subliminal effects on the continent, which would reverberate for centuries to come.

CHAPTER II

The Chosen Son

I am not the governor this republic needs—a soldier by necessity and inclination, I found my destiny in fields of war.

—Simón Bolívar

At times, it seems the hardest road of war is that which leads to peace. For Bolívar, it was ever so. "I am a soldier," he liked to say, even when others begged him to be something more. Despite his well-honed faculties for social justice—despite his gift for imparting democratic ideals—he found the quotidian business of government numbing. He was a man of the sword, not the scepter. But it was the scepter he was handed when he rode triumphantly into Caracas on June 29, 1821, five days after his decisive victory at Carabobo.

Although he reached the city at night and went directly to his house on the cathedral square, delirious crowds engulfed him, eager to embrace their hero. It was morning before he could escape their attentions. The glory of it was seductive, inebriating—but he knew all too well that beyond the fevered joy, there was a deeply demoralized country to govern, and he questioned his patience for carrying out the task. Months before, as he prepared to meet the Spaniards in one last battle, he had written to confess these fears to Antonio Nariño, whom he had just appointed interim vice president of Colombia, which along with

Venezuela and Quito, was a subdivision of Greater Colombia. Nariño was an intellectual as well as a military man and had just returned from prison in Cádiz, where he had been captive more than once in his long, rebellious career. It was he who had translated France's Declaration of the Rights of Man into Spanish, and he who had been credited for instigating the Granadan revolution. Just before marching to battle, Bolívar wrote to ask him to organize the inauguration of a new Colombian congress, and, in the same letter, admitted to strong personal doubts about his own gifts for administration. Colombia was a military camp, not a functioning society, he told Nariño. As one lone man, struggling against the abuses of government, he had seen how venal and corrupt politicians could be, and he had been powerless to control them. It seemed to him that all the good men had disappeared, and that only the bad had multiplied. He wrote on:

> Since I am fully convinced that the command of the army and the control of the Republic must be kept separate, I will tender my resignation. . . . Please, friend, believe me when I say that I have meditated at length on these matters during the eight years I have governed the Republic. I am not versed in the art of government. I cannot and do not wish to govern, for to do it well one must have an inclination or, better yet, an uncontrollable passion for it. For my part, each day I feel a growing repugnance toward the command.

He had never aspired to lead governments. His ambition—as simple as it was ardent—had been to drive out the nation's oppressor. What troubled him now that that task was done was the undeniable evidence that his people were not ready for democracy. On the contrary, they were in urgent need of a strong, authoritative government. Three hundred years of injustice and ten years of hellish war had turned them into a nation of belligerents; they were as feral and rapacious as any horseman of the Apure. "Even I, riding at their head, have no idea what they're capable of," he confessed. He had the ominous feeling that peace would be worse than any war: "We are poised on an abyss; over a volcano, ready to explode." Anyone who thought participatory rule could be handed blithely to the ignorant would be in for a rude shock. Knowing his countrymen as well as he did—having crossed and recrossed the land so many times—Bolívar concluded that Greater Colombia was governable only by a strong hand. That conclusion was far from the teachings of the Enlightenment that had animated his vows—far from Rousseau, Voltaire, and Montesquieu—but it was, he insisted, the hard truth. Any armchair philosopher or graybeard politician who thought otherwise was clouding his head with foolish dreams and imperiling the future of the republic. He said as much to Santander:

> In Colombia the people who count are the army, those who have liberated the country. . . . The rest are old men. . . . This view of reality, which certainly does not derive from Rousseau, will have to be the view we favor in the end, otherwise those old gentlemen will be our ruin. They believe that Colombia is a nation of docile sheep huddled around cozy hearths in Bogotá, Tunja and Pamplona. They haven't bothered to see the Caribs of the Orinoco, the horsemen of the Apure, the boatmen of the Magdalena, the bandits of Patía, the ungovernable people of Pasto, the Guajibos of Casanare, and all the savage hordes from Africa and America who roam like wild deer in the wilderness of Colombia. Don't you think, my dear Santander, that these legislators—ignorant rather than malicious, presumptuous rather than ambitious—are leading us down the road to anarchy, and from there to tyranny, and finally to ruin? I am sure of it. And if the horsemen don't bring us down, the philosophers will.

By "old men" he meant the representatives of congress, who had begun to carp about Bolívar's leadership. In the insular capital of Angostura—uninformed about the nation at large, surrounded by nothing so much as their own gossip—they had begun to question the wisdom of uniting Venezuela and New Granada. They worried about losing their regional authority, fretted about Bolívar's insistence on a centralized government. They had also taken issue with his decision to move the congress to Cúcuta, although it was clear that a governing body could not govern from such a remote location as Angostura. No one could deny that Bolívar was the indisputable leader in the eyes of the people—the victor of a long and dearly won war—but there were many in government who disagreed with him. Even in the face of his ringing achievements, his enemy ranks had grown.

Bolívar did not tarry in Caracas. Within a few days, he went on to visit his estate in San Mateo, which had suffered greatly from the war. It had seen battles, been occupied by royalists as well as patriots, and now the old hacienda was but a phantom of the paradise he'd known as a boy. It was hard to believe that he'd been so rich as all that. By now, his entire fortune had been lost to the war; his finances were in disorder. What little he took in pay, he took in small sums, and that only to purchase life's essentials. For years now, he had refused to collect his government salaries.

While in San Mateo, he freed the few slaves who had stayed behind. Among them was his old wet nurse, Hipólita, who had sustained him as an infant, raised him as a boy, even traveled with him on the battlefield; to him she was "the only father I have ever known." Born in San Mateo almost sixty years before, she had been the product of another time, another order, and had spent her life dedicating herself to the comfort and well-being of the Bolívars. Now, in her sixth decade, she was being released to an unfamiliar world. It doesn't take much to imagine her bewilderment.

After several days, Bolívar traveled on to Valencia, Tocuyo, Trujillo. He was antsy, nervous. He knew he was no longer Venezuelan, but a citizen of something else, the guardian of a larger concept. He felt a strong responsibility to Bogotá. "I belong to the family of Colombia, not of Bolívar," he wrote to his old friend and in-law Fernando de Toro, with whom he had made his vows on the heights of Monte Sacro. But just as urgently, he felt the pull of America at large. He felt a duty to those who still languished under the rule of King Ferdinand—to Quito (the future Ecuador), Quito's ungovernable district of Pasto, and most irresistibly of all, to Lima, the heart of the Spanish viceroyalty. "I need to round out Colombia," he wrote a friend, as he busily planned a campaign in the south. And to another: "I need to give a third sister to the Battles of Boyacá and Carabobo." There were more nations to free, more avenues to greatness. He would not sit and fret about the minutiae of government. "Send me that book about the Incas of Peru," he instructed Santander.

On September 7, he learned that the congress of Cúcuta, in an overwhelming vote, had elected him president of Greater Colombia. Many among the members had argued for a federal system—a union of separate states—and indeed they had borrowed freely from the United States model, but in the end, out of respect for their Liberator, they had put a centralized government in place. It was salve for the moment.

Bolívar accepted the presidency, but only halfheartedly, having joked that if elected, he would always manage to be away from the capital or deathly ill. He was, by then, firmly pointed to the liberation of Quito and Peru. But he also understood that Greater Colombia needed him, if nothing else, for continuity, for stability, for his name. He opted to take the responsibility even as he was moving on, hoping all the while that it was a titular honor, a transitory state. When he went reluctantly to Cúcuta in October to accept the honors, he stood before Congress and spoke his mind:

> I am a son of war, a man whom combat has elevated to the halls of rule. Fortune has brought me to this rank and victory has confirmed it. But mine are not titles that have been consecrated by the scales of justice, by happy circumstance, by the people's will. The sword that has governed Colombia is the whip of misfortune. . . . This sword will be useless in a day of peace and, when that day finally comes, my power will be finished, because I have sworn as much to myself, because I have promised it to Colombia, and because there can be no republic unless people take power into their own hands. A man like me is dangerous to a popular government, a threat to national sovereignty.

He believed that stark evaluation, especially those last words: he was dangerous to anyone who would press full democracy on Colombia too quickly; he was a threat to anyone with narrow, sectarian loyalties; and he was convinced that South America would never know greatness unless it was a seamless, fully integrated whole.

AS BOLÍVAR WARILY ASSUMED THE presidency, eager to march toward Peru, San Martín was already there, establishing a dictatorship in Lima. The Argentine general had been in the viceregal capital for more than a year, blockading the coast and patiently awaiting Lima's capitulation. Eventually, the acting viceroy, General La Serna, was forced to evacuate his formidable army, scattering a force of ten thousand to the sea fortress of Callao or to citadels in Cuzco, Huancayo, and Arequipa. By July 12, 1821, the jittery, intensely Spanish city of Lima was in the hands of San Martín and his liberating army. It had surrendered to him without a drop of bloodshed.

For all the shared ambition between San Martín and Bolívar—for all the history that would forever join them—they were markedly different men. The Argentine was secretive, aloof, impatient with adulators, intolerant of frivolity and excess. He was tall, striking, with lustrous black eyes and hair; his skin was so dark that it was rumored he was the son of an indigenous woman. The aristocrats of Buenos Aires referred to him as "El Indio," "El Cholo," "El Mulato," "El Tapé" (a nickname for Guaraní Indians). Unwilling to speak about his roots, or about the date of his birth—which is disputed—or about anything remotely personal, he did nothing to dispel that gossip. Indeed, he had declared in a gathering of Indian chieftains, "I, too, am Indian, and will finish off all the Spaniards who have robbed you of your ancestral lands." But, according to family record, he was born into a Spanish household in Yapeyú, in the Guaraní territory of Argentina. His father was the governor of Yapeyú and a captain in the Spanish army; his mother was a Creole. At the age of seven, San Martín sailed with his family for Cádiz. By the tender age of eleven, he was a cadet in the Spanish army. Rising steadily through the ranks, the boy was sent to battle in Africa and the Mediterranean; as a young man, he fought with distinction in the Battle of Bailén—alongside Morillo—defending Iberia against Napoleon. By the time the French emperor was driven from Spain, Colonel San Martín had accumulated twenty years of military experience. Along the way, he had befriended the Chilean officer Bernardo O'Higgins and served under two notable British officers: General William Beresford, who once had directed a failed British invasion of Argentina, and the Scotsman Lord MacDuff, who introduced the young soldier to secret lodges of revolutionaries who were conspiring to liberate South America.

They were the very lodges Bolívar had visited. Indeed, in London, Bolívar and San Martín had known many of the same people, walked the same floors in Miranda's house on Grafton Street, spoken with the same British sympathizers. But the paths of the liberators would be as different as their natures. The two had never met. After getting to know the revolutionaries in London—among them Bolívar's old friend and tutor Andrés Bello—San Martín renounced his Spanish citizenship and terminated his service in the king's army. He returned to Argentina—a land he hadn't seen for twenty-eight years—in 1812 on the British frigate *George Canning*. Accompanying him was Carlos Alvear, who had established a secret society in Cádiz, and with whom San Martín would found the Lautaro Lodge, a brotherhood of South American Freemasons dedicated to the ideals of independence. Whereas Bolívar paid only marginal attention to such lodges—availing himself of their connections, yet banning secret societies in the nations he founded—San Martín was resolutely loyal to the Lautaro Lodge, and drew advice and support from its members throughout his revolutionary career.

In Argentina, San Martín proved a brilliant patriot general. He distinguished himself in the decisive Battle of San Lorenzo in February of 1813, defending the port of Buenos Aires against the Spanish navy and gaining such fame that he was granted command of Argentina's Army of the North. As Alvear and others dedicated themselves to the founding of the republic, San Martín ostensibly restricted himself to soldiering. But he was quietly plotting the realization of a secret vision: a plan to press on beyond the borders of independent Argentina and liberate America from Chile to Peru. In the relative seclusion of the Andes, he spent years, as one historian describes it, "conspiring, corresponding, intriguing in his obscure and spidery way, trying to save his great idea of the march on Lima from the dangers that threatened it." He was adamantly uninterested in Argentine politics, refused all promotions, and played no part in the formation of the new nation. With single-minded will, he lobbied to push his way north, getting himself appointed the governor of Cuyo, a ruggedly beautiful region that lay on the Chilean border. With his child bride, a sweet fifteen-year-old girl from a noble family in Buenos Aires, he settled in Mendoza, where he could take closer stock of the situation. It was there that he formed and trained the Army of the Andes, eventually persuading the supreme director of Argentina, Juan de Pueyrredón, to allow him to take his men over the cordillera into Chile. Although Argentina was staggered by poverty, the government hardly able to manage its own affairs, Pueyrredón gave San Martín what he wanted. In November of 1816, the supreme director wrote to his general:

> Here go 40 saddle blankets. By separate post, in a small box, go the only two bugles I've been able to scrounge. By mid December you will receive the 35,000 pounds of jerked beef you've asked for. . . . Here go the 2,000 spare sabers you need. Here go 200 tents, and there are no more. Here goes the World. Here goes the Devil. Here goes the Flesh. I don't know how I shall ever extricate myself from the debts I have incurred for this. . . . God damn it! Don't ask me for anything else, unless you want to hear that I've been found in the fort, hanging from a rafter.

San Martín did not disappoint him. He worked for almost two years to build his war machine, operating a clandestine factory in Mendoza that made bullets from church bells and canteens from bullhorns. "He wants wings for cannon," said the fanatical priest who ran the operation, "and he shall have them." Meanwhile, San Martín disciplined his troops with a rigor hitherto unknown in the republican army. He recruited Indians, freed and enlisted thousands of slaves—half his infantry would be black—and welcomed Chilean patriots who had been forced out of Santiago by Spain's reconquest of the rebel city in 1814. He was stern with his soldiers and brooked no unruliness, but he inspired them to great sacrifice. "If a Spaniard resists," he told them, "split his head open like a pumpkin." If a republican soldier was so incapacitated that he couldn't walk, he was to be left to his fate on the battlefield. By the end of 1816, he had a fierce, disciplined fighting force.

Together with Bernardo O'Higgins, the illegitimate son of a former viceroy, San Martín took an army of four thousand men over the snowy heights of the Americas' tallest peak, Aconcagua, in February of 1817, achieving one of the most astonishing feats in the annals of military history. When 1,200 survivors reached the other side, they surprised the Spanish army and overwhelmed it in the Battle of Chacabuco. The killing field was littered with Spaniards, their forces decimated, their skulls split wide and gaping like smashed pumpkins. With trademark economy, San Martín reported to Buenos Aires, "In twenty-four days, we have completed this campaign, crossed the highest mountains in the world, put an end to the tyrants, and given freedom to Chile."

He was not inclined to stirring dispatches or dazzling oratory. He shunned exaggerated language, preferred to keep a noble silence. Not particularly well read, he wasn't apt at quoting great writers or adding clever flourishes in foreign tongues, as Bolívar was so fond of doing. He was enigmatic, profoundly guarded—and that mysterious nature was not always well received. "There is a timidity of intellect," one English-woman sniffed; another contemporary described him more generously: "It is impossible to know what is happening in that impenetrable soul." Modest to the point of asceticism, San Martín refused salaries and gran-diose ceremonies: admirers who gushed with praise were waved away impatiently. When offered a promotion to brigadier general after lib-erating Chile, he declined it twice; "your approval," he told his govern-ment, "is reward enough." When the jubilant city of Santiago presented him with money to defray the cost of his Andean crossing, he refused it, donating it instead toward the creation of a public library. He was sol-emn, uncomfortable in his skin, easily exasperated.

He was also profoundly ill. As a young soldier in Spain he had suf-fered crippling bouts of rheumatism. After the Battle of San Lorenzo, he began to experience worse: fierce gastric seizures that caused him to hemorrhage and vomit blood. The pain was so excruciating that he was driven to calm it with opium. By 1816, he was deeply addicted to the drug, taking it not only for gastric attacks, but in order to sleep, in order to quiet his nerves, in order to quell disappointment. "An angry hemor-rhage and the consequent debilitating weakness have kept me nineteen days in bed," he wrote a friend, and indeed his cohort began to worry. His speech began to slur, his movements grew unsteady. Friends tried to persuade him to stop abusing the drug; they stole the potent little tubes from his bedside. Somehow, by dint of determination and the close at-tention of medics and aides, he managed the punishing climb over the Andes. On April 5, 1818, with heroic resolve, he triumphed in the decisive Battle of Maipú, driving the Spaniards, once and for all, from Chile. He was so exhausted by battle's close that his report to Buenos Aires was all of three sentences on a soiled scrap of paper. His detractors in the capital accused him of being drunk. "I found the hero of Maipú sick in bed," an Englishman reported soon after, "looking so pale and thin that if it had not been for the brilliance of his eyes I would hardly have recognized him." Within months, the hero would be carried back over the Andes on a stretcher.

All the while, San Martín was carefully preparing for the greatest campaign of his career. By the beginning of 1820, he had risen from his bed, recrossed the Andes, and installed himself near Valparaiso. Several thousand skilled soldiers answered to his command, spurring him to believe he was ready to make a concerted attack on the powerful viceroy in Lima. But at roughly the same time, political disagreements that had plagued Argentina for years erupted in civil war, and chaos overtook the fledgling republic. Suddenly, the viability of San Martín's campaign abroad was called into question. He was ordered to rally his troops, bring his armies home, and defend Buenos Aires. But by then his mission had reached messianic proportions: he believed that the liberation of America superseded internal politics. Gravely sick, his illness compounded by worry, he decided to disobey his government's orders. With a zeal bordering on madness, he insisted on executing his war plan.

The citizens of Argentina rose up in anger against their famous general. San Martín was accused as a traitor, a power seeker—maligned for gross indifference to the Argentine cause. There were rumors that he would be court-martialed if he stepped foot on his native soil. Others claimed that foreign powers had bribed him; that he had made away with a staggering fortune. He protested it all as a grotesque lie. But he refused to change course in favor of the national interest. "I have pledged my honor to the cause of America," he wrote Bernardo O'Higgins, by then the supreme director of Chile. "I have no homeland without it, and I will not sacrifice such a precious gift for anything in the world."

Joining forces with O'Higgins and the veteran British admiral Lord Cochrane, San Martín soon commanded much of the western coast of South America. The infamous Thomas Cochrane—"Wolf of the Seas"—a flamboyant Scotsman convicted of financial fraud in London, had been given full run of the Chilean armada, and, virtually destroying Spanish sea power in the Pacific, had allowed San Martín to launch a successful expedition to Peru.

San Martín and four thousand troops slipped onto Peruvian soil in the fog of August 1820, just as Bolívar was negotiating the peace with Morillo in Venezuela. Spilling onto the white sands of Paracas, not far from the ancient, impenetrable lines of Nazca, his patriot troops quietly moved inland. Soon, the glittering city of Lima—that nexus of power, coveted city of kings—would fall without so much as a sword raised against it. In the course of almost a year, San Martín blockaded it to near starvation. He frightened the rich whites of Lima with his army of blacks and *cholos*, mixed-race natives. He virtually honeycombed Peru with secret agents, winning the sympathies of Spanish Freemasons. He negotiated craftily with Viceroy Pezuela, suggesting that the eminence might appoint his own regency to rule an independent Peru. In January of 1821, an uprising of Spanish army officers deposed the viceroy, and General La Serna was thrust into power. Six months later, after fruitless negotiations with San Martín, the new viceroy and his standing army of thousands evacuated the capital, pinched with hunger. A major earthquake ripped through the coast, as if to mark Spain's historic departure. Terrified, the whites of Lima wailed that the ghosts of the angry Inca were about to wreak their revenge. On July 12, the patriot general entered the capital with no opposition whatsoever. It was a frigid day— one of those dull, dank days of coastal winter—and the place seemed unrelievedly gray, inscrutable.

San Martín was the essence of decorum, taking every precaution to make little of his very large victory. At first, he took lodging at a monastery, accompanied by only one aide, and then he quietly moved to the government palace, where he installed himself with a full delegation of assistants. Two weeks later, with a formidable army of peons behind him, he named himself Protector, waved his flag over the central plaza, and declared the City of Kings a bastion of freedom.

BOLÍVAR WASTED NO TIME IN writing to San Martín to congratulate him. But midway through the flattery, he added, "I hope to heaven that you won't need the Colombian army's services in your liberation of Peru!" It was a barbed remark: Lima may have been liberated; but Peru was not. It was also a prescient observation: Bolívar had no way to know—just yet—of the political bog that would mire his rival in Lima.

General Sucre, too, was soon beset by troubles in Guayaquil. Months before, Bolívar had sent him there with a thousand men to prepare for the liberation of Quito. But Quito remained in Spain's stubborn grip; the people of Guayaquil, who had gleefully declared their independence when San Martín arrived in Peru, were now stalled in fractious argument. Would they join Peru? Or Colombia? Officially, the strategic port city of Guayaquil had been part of the viceroyalty of New Granada, but over the years it had become more closely allied to Peru, with which it did an active trade. Guayaquil was a thriving center of naval commerce; a place where ships were built and where they undertook a busy traffic. Of great importance to Lima, it was also vital to the landlocked colony of Quito.

Bolívar insisted that Santander find five thousand good troops to send ahead to Quito so that he could set out at once and resolve the issue. He was tired of managing, ready to push on. "I'm not going to lose the fruit of eleven years in a standoff," he wrote Santander. "I don't want San Martín to see me as anything but the chosen son." As far as he was concerned, the valuable land poised between the dying viceroyalties would be Greater Colombia's, not Peru's, and certainly not San Martín's.

He arrived in Bogotá on October 21, 1821, and dedicated himself immediately to the business of organizing a decisive southern campaign. He didn't stay long. Before two months had elapsed, he was off, headed for the mountain redoubts of Quito. But he did have time for one personal obligation. On November 27, he bought a magnificent house in the very heart of Bogotá, purchasing it with the salaries due him, which—until now—he had been loath to collect. The mansion was on Santa Clara Street, not far from the cathedral and the old viceregal palace. On the deed of purchase, he designated it as a gift for the mother of Bernardina Ibañez, the young girl whose romantic attentions he had fervently sought and whose valiant young husband had died on the fields of Carabobo. What did that purchase mean? Was it an attempt to compensate for the ultimate sacrifice of Colonel Plaza, whom the Liberator had claimed to love as much as he loved the young officer's fetching wife? Or was it an expression of love for the bereft widow? And why had he paid for the property with his salary—state funds, which he rarely accepted—rather than with personal money? Was it a way to ease his conscience about the gossip to which he and Vice President Santander had subjected the family? Or had the vice president, who went on to keep her sister, Nicolasa, as a mistress for fifteen more years, requested that purchase himself? Historians have conjectured but we may never know the truth.

What we do know is that when Bolívar left Bogotá for Cali on the 13th of December, the Ibañez women had already moved into that comfortable house on Santa Clara Street, and they accepted Bolívar's gift with the fullest gratitude. From Cali, Bolívar would write Bernardina one last letter, professing his ardor and forever leaving open the question whether, in the scant six weeks he had spent in Bogotá, he had been able to win some measure of the widow's love:

> Fussy, beautiful Bernardina, . . . What love can do! I think of nothing but you and your lovely temptations. . . . You are the only one in the world for me. You alone, celestial angel, inspire my most vivid feelings and desires. From you I hope to win whatever happiness and pleasure you deign to give me, for you are what I long for. If I say no more—much more—it is out of modesty and discretion; don't think it is because I don't love you. And stop accusing me of indifference or callousness. You see how time and distance only combine to boost the thrill of memory. It's not right to blame me with empty suspicions. Think only of my passion and my eternal devotion, which you cannot deny.

War would soon conspire to put Bernardina far from Bolívar's mind. The road from Bogotá to Cali was arduous, depleting. Initially, he had thought he would march to the coast and sail to Guayaquil, where he could join Sucre in a coastal attack on the colony of Quito. But word had it that Spanish frigates controlled Ecuadorian shores. It wasn't true. The craft that had caused that fleeting worry was the one depositing the new captain-general. He was Juan Mourgeón, an accomplished soldier who had fought alongside San Martín in the wars against Napoleon and, ironically enough, had once saved the Argentine's life. The Spaniard Mourgeón had sailed from Panama, where he had been governor, and landed on the coast of Ecuador with eight hundred men and orders to fortify Quito.

The faulty intelligence made Bolívar opt for land rather than sea, forcing him to take an army of four thousand across 250 miles of punishing mountain terrain. It was either a fool's or a hero's journey. The Colombians traversed burning plains, perilous rivers, improvising bridges of rope over deadly gorges and cataracts. By the time they reached the other side, the army was a fraction of itself. Those who survived had marched thousands of miles, many of them from as far away as Valencia, some from the battles of Boyacá and Carabobo. Now, as they filed into Cali, they were a shattered force—crushed by exhaustion, hypothermia, disease. Hundreds had deserted. Among those who remained—many of them languishing in litters—few could march, much less muster and fight.

BOLÍVAR STAYED IN CALI LONG enough to learn that Sucre and his troops were trapped in Guayaquil, unable to advance and meet him halfway in Quito. The royalists had blocked the way north, and for all the support Sucre had raised in Guayaquil, he didn't have the manpower to take on the stubbornly defended capital. His vain thrusts to penetrate royalist territory had met with devastating defeat. In desperation, Sucre had called on San Martín in Lima to loan him troops, but he would have to wait months for an answer.

Meanwhile, Bolívar—unable to rely on anyone—forged his way south along the difficult mountain route to Popayán. As he approached that highly fortified town, the Spanish colonel in charge, José María Obando, emerged under a flag of truce and surprised Bolívar by requesting an interview. The Liberator's charisma and passion for the American cause instantly won over the colonel. Not only did Obando surrender, he offered his services—and the services of his entire garrison—to the patriot side. This bit of politicking persuaded Bolívar that he might have similar success with other royalists. If only he could be allowed to talk to them. He wrote to Santander with an idea:

I have been awake all night, thinking about the new challenges. . . . I am certain I will reach the Juanambú River with less than two thousand men. I am equally certain that the enemy will meet me with more than four thousand; if I go on, I will be forced to fight a battle more risky than Boyacá, and I will fight it out of rage and despair. . . . My best hope is to take a political tack and try to win over the enemy leaders and troops, if at all possible. Here then is what I propose . . .

What he proposed was forgery. He instructed Santander to send him letters and documents stating that Spain had yielded the fight and now recognized Greater Colombia's independence. With these false papers and strategically placed "announcements" in the local *Gaceta*, he would fool Quito, force it to let down its guard, and allow him to enter the city. "The object of all this fuss," he wrote Santander, "is to persuade the enemy that there is no other recourse: they must deal with me, and we must prevent more blood sacrifice."

His instructions to Santander were specific. The vice president was to create a trumped-up letter from the Spanish general La Torre, requesting safe passage for a commission that had arrived from Madrid to make peace with the new government of Colombia. Vice President Zea and General Páez were to produce appropriately welcoming responses. Santander obliged without delay and produced the bogus documentation. When all was duly delivered, Bolívar presented these "lies"—for that is what he called them—to Quito's interim president Aymerich as well as the recently arrived Captain-General Mourgeón, and made overtures to Popayán's bishop, requesting his help in ensuring a peaceful transition. But no one was taken in by this deceit, least of all the people of Pasto, diehard royalists who lay between him and the capital, and who preferred all-out war to any talk about reconciliation.

All-out war is what Bolívar finally gave them. On April 7, 1822, Easter Sunday, he led his army to the cliffs of Cariaco, on the side of the volcano where the Spanish army had been seen making an advance. Before he rode off to reconnoiter the area—something he always did alone—he ordered his officers not to have lunch until they had secured the overlooking promontory, which at that hour appeared untaken. When he returned, he saw royalists perched on those heights and his army eating leisurely in the gorge. His second in command had misunderstood his order and was full of remorse. But there was no doubt that the liberating army was now at a distinct disadvantage. Fuming, Bolívar moved to make up for it.

He commanded his men to make a bold, frontal attack. It was a questionable decision, wholly impulsive, built on fury. Wave after wave of patriot lines rushed up the escarpment to sure death. The British battalion—"Rifles"—made a heroic advance with their bayonets drawn, trying to drive the enemy from its fast perch, but to little avail. They couldn't get close enough. It seemed the whole republican force would be obliterated on that maddeningly pitched slope. Bolívar, watching the butchery from below, was convinced the battle was lost. But as the sun slipped over the rocky ridge, creating deep shadows in the ravine, a miracle was at work in the right flank. Soldiers with nothing but bayonets thrust their blades into the steep incline, then, clambering up a ladder of ascending weapons, scaled the cliff. The fighting went well into night, until the moon vanished in a murky haze and darkness engulfed the fray. "Our camp," wrote Obando, the royalist who had defected to the patriots in Popayán, "was a mill of destruction. Our rifles were broken, our equipment burned; all that we might have carried away was destroyed. Dawn came and we were unable to withdraw. A thick fog prevented us from seeing the enemy or the position taken by our own Rifles. The Liberator was in a mood." Bolívar was in more than a mood. For days, he had been fighting a fever. That he had lived through those eight grueling hours was remarkable in itself.

There were those—including Bolívar—who described the Battle of Bomboná as a triumph for the patriot side; others saw it as sheer folly. It was neither. When dusk covered the field and the enemy withdrew like a frightened phantom, no one was sure who had prevailed. The patriots, dazed, remained in the arena, wondering whether hostilities would return with the sun. If nothing else, they could comfort themselves with the knowledge that they had split the royalist camp and distracted it from its defense of Quito. But by morning, it was clear what price they had paid for it. Bodies littered the ground in obscene heaps; a vile stench permeated the air. Every patriot officer save six lay gravely wounded. Bolívar, sick to death, was carried away in a litter.

Though doubts about those bitter losses followed, it soon became clear that the Battle of Bomboná had won something after all. It had been a harbinger of change. The citizens of Pasto and Quito—two stout chambers of the royalist heart—awoke the next morning a little less certain, a little more afraid. General Sucre, now able to push north from Guayaquil, rose masterfully to the occasion.

CHAPTER 12

Under the Volcanoes

I am consumed by the demon of war, determined to finish this struggle.

—Simón Bolívar

"Either I lose my way, or I press on to glory," Bolívar had confessed to Vice President Santander, and indeed he seemed to be fighting battles within as well as without. To those seeing him for the first time, he seemed far older than his age. At thirty-eight, he was grizzled by war, jaundiced by illness and fatigue. Though his movements remained nimble, his voice vibrant, he bore the signs of a soldier too long in the fray. His face was weary, his color wan. His hair was long, thinning, shot through with silver, tied back to curb its wild disorder. He was emaciated, given to fevers and mysterious ailments. He was no longer the brash young man who had fought his way up the Magdalena River and triumphed effortlessly in battle. He was no longer the hero of the Admirable Campaign. Although he paid close attention to his hygiene—maintained a strict regimen of baths, drank little and seldom, and resolutely did not smoke—his health had noticeably deteriorated. He was no longer the infamous, indefatigable Iron Ass. For all the vigor of his will and spirit, he was a prematurely aging soldier, a hard-living, hard-bitten veteran who had fought across thousands of miles of punishing terrain and showed it. Few leaders of nations, apart from Genghis Khan, had spent as many hours—months, years—in a saddle. But twelve years of unremitting effort had taken their toll. He didn't allow his men to see it, but it had become harder for him to tolerate the physical hardship. More than anything, what he needed now was to be assisted by a sprier, younger version of himself: a warrior with all the right instincts, a leader with a common touch, a bright young general who did not question his supremacy and who pledged absolute and undying loyalty to the cause.

That man was Antonio José de Sucre. "If God had given us the right to choose our own families," Bolívar would later say, "I would have chosen General Sucre as my son." The twenty-seven-year-old general of brigade was a vigorous warrior in his prime. Alert, high-spirited, and rigorously disciplined, he was the quintessential officer and gentleman, respected by all who fought under his command. When Bolívar had elevated him, despite his youth, to the most senior of generals, it was because Sucre's talents rivaled his own: Sucre was brave, tireless, uncannily adept at making quick decisions. He insisted on doing everything himself, from maintaining troop records to inspecting his soldiers' rations. He had a sixth sense for battle strategy. In short, Sucre was everything the Liberator admired in the best of soldiers. Together they were the Achilles and Patroclus of the New World.

By May of 1822, the two were laboring toward each other across a volatile terrain—the lava-encrusted avenue of craters that dominated the bitterly contested ground between Colombia and Peru. With the Battle of Bomboná, Bolívar had managed to distract the enemy enough to allow Sucre to move, and the young general proceeded to make his way up the volcano-studded landscape between Guayaquil and Quito, reinforced by a battalion sent to him by San Martín. For a year now, Sucre and three thousand superbly trained soldiers under his command had pointed toward this moment, awaiting word from Bolívar. But the last missive Sucre had received from the Liberator had been sent months before, in December of 1821. By the time he read it, he had been powerless to obey its orders. So much of the war had gone this way: late correspondence, missed opportunities. Seeing now that the enemy was in disorder, he decided to try to take Quito at all costs.

Securing San Martín's support had turned out to be a thorny business for Sucre. The Protector of Peru had announced publicly that he looked forward to traveling north to meet Bolívar, but as time passed, he had grown skeptical about Greater Colombia's ambitions. Within a month of announcing his eagerness to meet his fellow revolutionaries, he began to chafe about Sucre's presence in Guayaquil, convinced that the port's proximity and close commercial ties to Lima made it rightfully Peruvian, and, therefore, under his jurisdiction. In February, after dispatching one of his most talented young colonels, Andrés de Santa Cruz, to help fortify Sucre's army, he worked himself into a state over reports about Bolívar's progress toward Guayaquil. Finally, he had boarded one of Lord Cochrane's ships and hastened north to lay claim on the coveted city. But by the time he got halfway, he saw a copy of a letter Bolívar had sent to Guayaquil's president, José Joaquín de Olmedo. In it, Bolívar claimed peremptorily that the port of Guayaquil belonged to Colombia. A bomb could not have produced a more shattering effect. Seething, San Martín turned around and sailed back to Lima, where he secured authority to go to war.

In his fury, San Martín also recalled Santa Cruz's auxiliary forces, insisting that the colonel return to Peru at once. But the charismatic Sucre soon persuaded Santa Cruz to ignore that order, prepare for greater glory, and join his historic march against Quito. Eventually, San Martín backed down and thought better of prosecuting a suicidal civil war against an equivalent, liberating army. He decided to send one of his generals to take command of the allied forces. Sucre was appalled when he heard of it. But indeed none of those plans came to pass; San Martín was in no position to enforce them. It had all been a tempest in a teacup—a show of martial posturing—but it had revealed everyone's essential character. Bolívar had been high-handed; San Martín, petulant; Sucre, unyielding. And the young Santa Cruz had proved to be divided in his loyalties, as he would continue to be for all time.

By the end of April, Sucre was leading a march to the royalist stronghold of Quito. Bearing west of the Pichincha volcano, he skirted the city and positioned his forces due north of the king's army. He had no way of knowing it, but Mourgeón, the able Spanish captain-general who had arrived only months before, had died suddenly from the complications of a fall, leaving Quito's president, General Aymerich, to fight alone. On May 23, Sucre's forces scaled the icy peak of the volcano and, one day later, descended the other side in an early morning fog. It had rained all night, and negotiating the slippery terrain had been treacherous. Nevertheless, they streamed down on the enemy, meeting them in battle at Riobamba. The hostilities were so close to Quito that the city's inhabitants clambered onto their rooftops to watch the conflict play out on the slope of their looming mountain. The Battle of Pichincha was hardly a surgical strike, and required constantly shifting strategy, but Sucre wasted no effort, giving his every move an object, a rationale. By the end of the day, when it was clear that his army was prevailing, he offered Aymerich a chance to lay down his arms. On May 25, Sucre declared a victory in Quito, taking the capital and securing the capture of more than two thousand prisoners. His treaty was charitable, allowing the royalists to sail to Spain with full military honors; as a result, many of them decided to stay and fight on the patriot side. Hearing that Quito had fallen, the stubborn bastion of Pasto succumbed completely to Bolívar. By a remarkable blend of strategy and bravura, Pasto, Quito, and the valuable port of Guayaquil were now firmly Colombian. Bolívar had only to take his prize.

The Liberator was acutely aware that he owed the victory to his gifted general, and he couldn't help feeling a twinge of jealousy. He fretted that Sucre's battle at Pichincha—not his, at Bomboná—would go down in history as the "third sister" of Boyacá and Carabobo. Indeed, the surrender seemed all askew. Even as Bolívar negotiated the grudging submission of inglorious Pasto, Sucre was accepting the far more glamorous capitulation of Quito from the illustrious Aymerich. Profoundly exhausted, Bolívar wrote to Santander, exhibiting an uncharacteristic smallness of mind: "Sucre had more troops than I did, and fewer enemies," he grumbled. "We, on the other hand, have been in hell, struggling with demons. The victory of Bomboná is far more beautiful than that of Pichincha." He wanted to make sure that Vice President Santander represented it that way.

It didn't take long for Bolívar's spirit to rise, however, as the wider world began to register the triumphs. He entered Quito on June 16, heartened by deafening cheers. He was resplendent in red and gold, mounted on his stately white horse, surrounded by adoring masses. Being a shrewd military man, General Sucre made it a point to leave all glory to the Liberator. The torch of independence was fully ablaze now. The last redoubt of Colombia's royalists had been subdued; the vital Isthmus of Panama had declared itself for Bolívar. Nearly a million square miles of South America—a region far greater than Napoleon's empire—answered to a single man.

ON JUNE 19, THREE DAYS after Bolívar's descent into Quito, and nearly three thousand miles away, an ailing diplomat was admitted to President James Monroe's office. Bent, pained, barely able to propel himself across the brightly polished floors of the White House, he clutched a document in one hand. John Quincy Adams recorded the moment:

> At one o'clock I presented Mr. Manuel Torres as Chargé d'Affaires from the republic of Colombia to the President. This incident was chiefly interesting as being the first formal act of recognition of an independent South American Government. Torres, who has scarcely life in him to walk alone, was deeply affected by it . . . moved even to tears. The President assured him of the great interest taken by the United States in the welfare and success of his country, and of the particular satisfaction with which he received him as its first representative. The audience was, as usual, only a few minutes.

For four long years, Torres had been trying to win diplomatic recognition—not to mention arms, ships, reinforcements—for Bolívar's revolution. But no amount of courtly palaver got the old gentleman very far. In the end, it was Bolívar's successes that changed the American president's mind. As the Battle of Boyacá led to the Battle of Carabobo, and the Liberator set out over the Andes for Quito, there could be no doubt that the tide of revolution was rolling on. Congressman Henry Clay finally persuaded his countrymen of it. After Torres's emotional meeting with Monroe and Adams, the elderly Colombian dragged himself home to Philadelphia full of joy that he could now relay the good news to Bolívar. Less than a month later, Torres was dead. It is unlikely that anyone in the Colombian army knew it, but on the day of their diplomat's funeral, which was attended by representatives of the United States army and navy and accompanied by full military honors, all the ships in Philadelphia's harbor flew their colors at half-staff. Indeed, Bolívar and his army were at such a remove in the depths of the equatorial cordillera that they would not be fully aware of U.S. recognition for another half year.

BOLÍVAR AND HIS ARMY, HARDLY cognizant of the fame they had reaped in the larger world, were living for the moment. Spent by war, reduced by privation, they spilled southward, focused only on the business of staying alive. Few pleasures awaited them. Nevertheless, legend has it that, as Bolívar rode into Quito in his splendid victory parade, he glanced up at the riotously decorated balconies and there saw the woman who would become his greatest love. The truth is probably quite different. The Liberator's first sight of the comely, rapier-witted Manuela Sáenz may have been at a ball given for him that night, or perhaps in an interview that she sought with the new chief of state to resolve questions of her inheritance. But there is no doubt that the meeting—given the exuberance of the moment—was mutually galvanizing. She was as motivated as he, as moody, as curious, as well read. Within days, or even hours, they were lovers, and would remain so until the end of his life.

On the face of things, Manuela Sáenz was a respectable young woman: rich, married, a habitué of liberal aristocratic circles in Quito and Lima. But she was also a woman with a complicated past. Born in Quito twenty-five years before, she was the illegitimate child of a scandalous liaison. Her father had been a wealthy Spaniard about town, an established family man; her mother, a middle-aged spinster from a prominent Creole family. The mother had birthed the child in secret, far away from society's prying eyes, as custom and honor demanded. She had attempted to place her daughter in a good home in Quito, but—failing that—entrusted her to nuns in a convent that was known to take highborn "orphans." Six years later, the mother was dead. For all his social-climbing ambitions, Manuela's father—Simón Sáenz de Vergara—did a surprising thing. He took responsibility for the child. He gave large sums of money to the luxurious convent where she lived, introduced her to his other children, welcomed the pretty little girl into his home. Most important, he gave her the biggest gift a father could offer: the door to a new life. Before her twentieth birthday, he married her off to a wealthy businessman in Lima, an English shipping merchant named James Thorne.

There were many reasons the marriage to Thorne was a welcome union. For Manuela's father, it was undoubtedly advantageous; Thorne probably assisted him in an uncertain economic time. In any case, it was wise for a Spaniard with considerable property to have firm, family connections with a shipping magnate. For Manuela, Mr. Thorne represented the essence of stability. He was twenty years older, sober in nature, generous with his money. Perhaps most important: as a foreigner, he was less inclined to see the circumstances of her birth as an irredeemable flaw.

At the end of 1817, just as Bolívar was preparing to meet Páez on the desolate plains of Venezuela, Manuela traveled to Lima to meet the fiancé to whom she had been promised. He was not a particularly attractive man. Portly, stuffy, a middle-aged fuddy-duddy with no intellectual brio or physical vigor, he could be insufferably dull and adamantly set in his ways. But there was no doubt in her mind that the marriage would give her respectability, a comfortable home, and—in that remote metropolis, far from the gossip of Quito—an enviable social standing. In December, as summer chased off the coastal fog, the couple was married under the vaulting dome of the Parroquia de San Sebastián, the most ancient and elegant of Lima's churches. In time, Manuela's natural grit and intelligence persuaded Thorne that she could manage his affairs, especially during his regular trips abroad.

She was a natural negotiator, a sparkling conversationalist, eager to inject herself into the arteries of intrigue that coursed through the nervous City of Kings. A fervent antiroyalist, she became a regular in patriot circles, and like any woman in the revolutionary effort, she served as spy, courier, and recruiter. There is no question that she celebrated San Martín's arrival in Peru. In time, he favored her with the female version of a distinguished Order of the Sun, an award he had established to honor outstanding patriots. Eventually she became an intimate of Rosa de Campusano, the infamous libertine and fellow Ecuadorian beauty who captivated a long string of Lima suitors as well as the somber San Martín himself.

By late May of 1822, when Manuela Sáenz returned to Quito, she was well known as a revolutionary activist. She had come home because she was worried about her father: a flinty Spaniard with abiding loyalty to the king, a persona non grata among Quito's new patriot masters. Perhaps she knew that he had decided to return to Spain and that this would be her last chance to see him. If so, she was also hoping that, in the new liberal realignment, she could finally claim the inheritance that her fussy maternal family had denied her since she was six, when her mother had died.

It is not difficult to imagine that when this beautiful, irreverent, and irresistibly magnetic woman presented herself at the victory ball on the arm of a patriot officer—her half brother—or when she made pressing claims in the harried halls of his new Colombia, Bolívar was enchanted. She was, as one biographer has described her, a siren with gleaming, ebony hair, bituminous eyes, pearly skin, and a conspicuously pleasing figure. She had an alluring feline grace. She could dance; she could ride. She was also breezily unafraid of scandal. He snatched what pleasure he could with Manuelita—which is what he called her—during those busy weeks, spent a scant few weeks in her thrall, and all the while was able to glimpse an insider's perspective on Lima's rebels, its royalists, San Martín. Before long, he could see that this spunky, brainy woman was unlike any he had ever known. "Madam," he said to her tenderly, "if only my soldiers had your marksmanship, we would have routed Spain long ago."

But San Martín himself came between the lovers. The Argentine general had written to Bolívar, protesting Colombia's designs on Guayaquil. He insisted that the port be allowed to choose its own loyalties in an election. Bolívar fired back without delay: Guayaquil was incontrovertibly Colombian; it had answered to Bogotá since colonial times, and would continue to do so in the future. But he added graciously that he welcomed the opportunity to embrace San Martín and talk about these things man-to-man. He had already offered San Martín the Colombian army's assistance in Peru. Bolívar hastened to Guayaquil, fully aware now that he needed to get there before the Argentine. Tearing himself away from the pleasures of Manuela, he went south to stake his claim.

He didn't get far before she sent him a brash and demanding letter. He wrote an uncharacteristically hesitant response. Perhaps it was because her blatant lack of decorum made him worry for her; perhaps it was because she had triggered something deeper in him, but his letter beseeched her to give him room to think:

> I want to answer, most beautiful Manuela, your demands of love, which are entirely reasonable. But I have to be candid with you, who have given me so much of yourself. . . . It's time you knew that long ago I loved a woman as only the young can love. Out of respect, I never talk about it. I'm pondering these things, and I want to give you time to do the same, because your words lure me; because I know that this may well be my moment to love you and for us to love one another. I need time to get used to this, for a military life is neither easy to endure nor easy to leave behind. I have fooled death so many times now that death dogs my every step. . . . Allow me to be sure of myself—of you. . . . I cannot lie. I never lie! My passion for you is wild, and you know it. Give me time.

HE MADE THE TRIP TO Guayaquil in early July, passing through breath-taking landscapes that thrilled and ignited his imagination. He had always been a lover of nature, and the staggering sight of Ecuador's perpetually snow-covered volcanoes—great white leviathans, rising from carpets of equatorial green—moved him deeply. He had never seen this part of the world before: a fertile terrain that swarmed with earthly life, yet reached boldly for the heavens. The purple skies, the starlit nights, the land's fierce tectonic past—all touched something in his soul.

Had things turned out differently, had he not felt the irresistible pull of war and revolution, he might have been a philosopher in his hacienda, contemplating the miracles of this earth. He thought of this now, as he looked out upon the land. Nowhere in the Republic of Greater Colombia had nature been so prodigal with its gifts as here, outside Quito, where soaring mountains grazed the vaulted skies—taunting ambition with magnificent zeniths.

Chimborazo, believed then to be the tallest peak on earth, spurred him to ponder the heights he himself had mastered. Sometime later, holding the image of that volcano in vivid memory, he wrote about it to his old teacher, Simón Rodríguez. "Come to Chimborazo," he urged:

> Tread if you dare on this stairway of Titans, this crown of earth, this unassailable battlement of the New World. From such heights will you command the unobstructed vista; and here, looking on earth and sky—admiring the brute force of terrestrial creation—you will say: Two eternities gaze upon me: the past and the yet-to-be; but this throne of nature, like its creator, is as enduring, as indestructible, as eternal, as the Universal Father.

He was a writer, after all. And yet historians disagree as to whether Bolívar could be the author of a similarly elegiac document about Chimborazo that appeared three years after his death. "My Delirium on Chimborazo," a prose poem discovered among a Colombian colonel's papers and purported to be written in Bolívar's hand, is a lyrical, phantasmagoric description of his rise to glory. In it, Bolívar is seen astride the very pinnacle of that volcano, high above earth, where Time itself makes him look upon the past as well as an unfurling future. "A febrile ecstasy invades my mind," he writes. "I feel lit by a strange, higher fire."

Bolívar could not possibly have climbed Mount Chimborazo, which measures 20,565 feet and which few mortals have conquered, and yet there are those who read the poem as a literal claim that he did. No, he did not reach the top. The naturalists La Condamine and Humboldt—far more prepared for the feat—attempted it and failed. But it is all too possible that the Liberator climbed some of the way, at least enough to take in the panorama.

Most Latin American scholars of Bolívar do not question that he wrote "My Delirium"; perhaps because it makes perfect sense that he would have, perhaps because it confirms, at least metaphorically, what is known: the Liberator was at the zenith of his glory. He was filled with awe by the transcendence of the moment, by the superhuman vantage it gave him—by the astonishing beauty of his America. He did not feel he was at a loss to describe such emotions. Unlike other warrior heroes who had preceded him in history, he was not afraid to take up the pen.

SAN MARTÍN HAD REACHED SUCH an impasse in Lima that he had no choice but to respond gratefully to Bolívar's magnanimous offer of assistance and the invitation to discuss it in person. "I accept your generous proposal," San Martín wrote back immediately. "Before the 18th, I'll leave from the port of Callao and, as soon as I disembark in Guayaquil, I'll make my way to you in Quito. . . . I have a feeling that America will never forget the day that you and I embrace."

Although San Martín was a proud and headstrong man, there was little he wasn't willing to do for America. But Peru had turned out to be far more complicated than he had anticipated. He was trapped in a political stalemate in Lima—he had produced neither a congress nor a constitution—and, in the process, he had earned many foes. When it was learned that he had sent a delegation to Europe seeking a prince from a royal family to govern the newly independent republic, Lima's republican stalwarts were appalled. High-ranking government officials were soon found guilty of plotting against him. But it wasn't just in government circles that he was drawing fire. His naval blockade had strangled a thriving Peruvian trade, and the powerful merchants hated him for it. He was hated, too, for his tyrannical right-hand man, the Argentine Bernardo Monteagudo, who had assumed the reins as San Martín slipped in and out of an opium haze, and mounted a cruel campaign against Spanish-born citizens. In military matters, too, San Martín's power was crumbling. He was at odds with his admiral, Lord Cochrane, who saw his reticence to attack the king's army as a deficit of courage. He was persona non grata in Argentina for ignoring his president's orders. Perhaps worst of all, his soldiers had been reduced from a bold fighting force to a sluggish army of occupation. Within the course of a short year, the Protector had lost all the momentum he had once had.

Stymied by political minefields, bewildered by the ferocity of his critics, San Martín now found the Peruvian animus against him so crippling that he was unable to carry out strategy or recruit soldiers to his side. There was much he needed from Bolívar. Risking everything, he decided to leave Lima in charge of subalterns to go north and make a desperate alliance with the Liberator. On July 13, he set sail for Guayaquil, intending to march on to Quito.

But Bolívar was no longer in Quito. On the day San Martín received the Liberator's letter, urging him to a meeting, Bolívar was already making a triumphant entrance into Guayaquil. The city's leaders were openly alarmed. President Olmedo, a celebrated poet and orator, had made it clear that he favored joining Guayaquil to Peru, and now, watching the ecstatic crowds rushing to meet Bolívar, the president felt power slip from his hands. Colossal arches glorifying the Liberator's name towered over the magnificent Malecón; women and girls, resplendent in white and blue, flocked down the streets to welcome him. When the municipal council officially welcomed him as Guayaquil's bringer of independence even though independence had been won almost two years before, it was too much for the president and his junta. Offended, they stalked off in protest.

Two days later, Bolívar invited Olmedo and all the members of the junta to a conference in his residence to try to dispel the acrimony. The meeting went rather well. But just as his guests were leaving, a crowd swarmed onto the property, tore down the flag of Guayaquil, and ran up the flag of Colombia. Frightened that this was the start of a violent coup, the junta scurried to safety next door. Bolívar had the flags changed at once. He told his aide O'Leary to make it clear to all present that what they had just seen had been done without his knowledge, and that he highly disapproved of it. But it was just as clear that the demonstrations on behalf of Colombia—and against Olmedo's junta—were growing increasingly more ardent and dangerous. The junta was reconvened to discuss the question, but the debate went on at such length that Bolívar grew impatient and insisted they make an immediate decision. They took the hint. He took command of the city later that day.

LESS THAN TWO WEEKS LATER, San Martín's schooner, the *Macedonia*, and a convoy of Peruvian ships sailed briskly through the dark of an early morning toward the coast of Puna, the lush green island that sits at the mouth of the Guayas estuary. It was July 25, Guayaquil was but hours away, and San Martín was confident that he would now take command of it for Lima. But immediately on dropping anchor, he was told that Bolívar was already in the city, and that the island of Puna—like freed Guayaquil—was Colombian territory now. Stunned, the Protector refused to disembark.

The jolly celebrations for Bolívar's thirty-ninth birthday that had begun the night before were probably still in full throttle in that cool predawn as San Martín deliberated his predicament. Bolívar had not received San Martín's letter; he had no notion the man was on his way. When he arose later that morning, he was astonished to learn that his rival was at such close radius. He sent a delegation of two aides with a letter of welcome and, when he was told that San Martín was unwilling to come ashore, he dispatched another:

No, do not dismiss lightly the eagerness with which I welcome to this Colombian soil the dearest friend of my heart and nation. How is it possible that you have come so far only to deny Guayaquil the corporeal presence of a man we're so anxious to know and, if possible, touch? That cannot be, my admirable friend; I await you, and I will come and meet you wherever you will be so kind as to expect me.

We can imagine San Martín's consternation: the prospect of setting foot on soil that had been snatched so abruptly from his grasp. It was one more indignity in a long string of humiliations, and the proud Argentine was sick at heart. Fleet boats of oarsmen traveled up and down the river, negotiating this delicate exchange between liberators, until, eventually, San Martín responded that he would meet with Bolívar the next day. The *Macedonia* proceeded majestically up the Guayas River through the night and arrived at midday on the 26th. Bolívar went out to meet it. Boarding the Peruvian ship straightaway, he greeted the dour Argentine with all the conviviality and charm he could muster.

San Martín and his official entourage—in all their decorated splendor—were met by a parade formation of Colombian army officers that led all the way from the dock to the imposing Luzárraga mansion, where he would be staying. He walked past throngs of cheering townspeople who had swept down to the docks when they heard that the great San Martín, liberator of Argentina and Lima, had arrived. When he finally entered the house, Bolívar and his officers were there to receive him in the vestibule. Agile, animated, filled with the sudden energy of a man who has been handed every advantage, the Liberator strode forward and vigorously shook his guest's hand. "At last!" he said, for the benefit of the dignitaries who had gathered around, "I am shaking the hand of the famous General San Martín."

Indeed it was an occasion with few precedents in history: two warrior heroes—liberators of a prodigious landmass that stretched half the globe, from north of the equator to Antarctica—had executed one of the most remarkable pincer movements in military history. Moreover, they had succeeded essentially without collaboration until now. Bolívar felt the moment deeply, and showed it. San Martín thanked him and, as was his nature, kept his reserve. Ramrod straight, sober, he replied that it gave him great pleasure to make the Liberator's acquaintance. They walked together to the great salon, where San Martín was given affectionate tributes from the women of Guayaquil. At the close of that ceremony, an exceptionally beautiful girl of seventeen—the youngest of three flirtatious sisters who would correspond with the Liberator for years—approached the venerable Protector and delicately placed a crown of laurel on his brow. Surprised and visibly flummoxed, the general snatched it from his head. Perhaps it was something in the girl's face or in the murmurs around the room that made San Martín see the insult of that gesture. He hurried to say that he didn't deserve her gift, that others merited it far more; that he treasured the hands from which it came, and would always remember the moment as one of the happiest of his life.

The two heroes were left alone to conduct the first of three private conversations. They did so behind closed doors. No secretary, no guard, no third party was present for any of those meetings and the details of their discussions—for almost two centuries now—have remained shrouded in mystery and dispute. With Bolívar likely pacing back and forth, as was his custom, and San Martín sitting stolidly in his chair, they deliberated all that was on their minds, none of it for the record. Nevertheless, looking closely at the considerable correspondence that followed, we can piece together what was said.

The first question that arose was the nationality of Guayaquil. Bolívar assured San Martín that he would hold a vote to determine the democratic will, but added that he was sure the people would choose Colombia. San Martín waved away all further discussion on this, willing to ascribe all problems to the city's fickleness. It was clear he wanted to waste no time. He had told Bolívar in an earlier letter that a few hours between soldiers would suffice, and it was in this spirit that he went directly now to "the last battleground in America," Peru. His strategy for the next campaign, as he described it, was to attack La Serna's army on two fronts, one by land and another by sea, hundreds of miles apart. Bolívar commented, as politely as he could, that he thought it a weak option. It would be far better, he said, to gather the liberating army and drive it into the interior like a hard, steel fist.

His army wasn't large enough for that, San Martín replied. La Serna and Canterac had assembled a mighty legion in the highlands. San Martín had but remnants of his original battalions, and whatever sailors lingered behind after Lord Cochrane angrily abandoned the cause. Recruiting had not been easy. Brought to the last possible question, San Martín went to the heart of the matter: how many Colombians could Bolívar contribute to the task?

Bolívar called for one of his aides to bring some documentation from his office. He wanted to show the Argentine in as concrete form as he could that the Colombian army was neither as vast nor as concentrated a force as he had assumed. The most he could offer, he said, was to return the division led by Santa Cruz, replacing all its losses, and add three battalions of Colombians—a contribution of a little more than a thousand troops. San Martín was flabbergasted. He had counted on the support of Bolívar's entire army, which at that point he calculated to be 9,600 armed men. The only reason he could see for this sudden, alarming parsimony was that Bolívar didn't trust him to lead those troops.

Controlling himself with great difficulty now, the Argentine implored Bolívar to come to Peru himself. He would serve under Bolívar's command, if need be. The Liberator could lead both armies. Bolívar demurred, saying that as president of Colombia, he could not leave the country without congress's consent; and surely, they would never agree to it. There was a nation to secure, a government to build. As to the question of making San Martín his subordinate: such an arrangement was hard to imagine, too delicate to pursue. Here, the Protector sensed Bolívar was being slippery, evasive, and he was hard pressed to understand why. "I couldn't get a clear answer from him," he told a journalist many years later. The only conclusion he could make was that Bolívar wanted all the power and glory to himself.

More likely, Bolívar was caught between desire and common sense. It would have been folly for him to strip a newly independent nation of its army and take on another war. There were problems Colombia had yet to address: Puerto Cabello was still under Spanish rule, Pasto continued to teem with royalist passions, Caracas and Bogotá lacked in defenses, and Guayaquil and Quito had only just been annexed. As for the question of having San Martín report to him, any military man could see that that was a catastrophe waiting to happen—the subordinate would be the hero, the soldier who had made the greater sacrifice, the man with the moral force. But Bolívar didn't say these things to San Martín; he didn't trust him completely. The chemistry between them seemed all wrong.

When they finally spoke about the political system San Martín had in mind for Peru, Bolívar's suspicions were confirmed. The Protector laid out his plan for establishing a monarchy with a European prince in rule. Bolívar had heard rumors about this, but hoped they weren't true. A year before, he had sent one of his aides, Diego Ibarra, to Lima, with a letter of congratulations for San Martín and instructions for Ibarra to learn what he could. Was San Martín considering a monarchical plan and, if so, how deeply was he committed to it? "Sound out the general's spirit," he ordered Ibarra, "and persuade him, if you can, against any project of erecting a throne in Peru, which would be nothing short of scandalous." Now he was hearing about a Peruvian king from the Protector himself. San Martín explained to Bolívar that he had spoken about his plan to both viceroys; that he had sent a delegation of diplomats to England months before to discuss just such a throne and which prince or duke might fill it. If England weren't willing, his delegates would look for qualified candidates in Belgium, France, Russia, Holland, or—even—Spain. It was the reason he had stalled in forming a Peruvian congress or drawing up a Peruvian constitution. As far as

San Martín was concerned, the nation was not ready for democracy—education was in a shambles; ignorance abounded; the pillars upon which democracy could depend did not exist. Bolívar might have agreed on this last point, but he was viscerally opposed to royalty, to kings and queens, to that old, musty European system that had required so much American blood to purge. He would not hear of it.

Bolívar left the meeting as somber and impenetrable as a sphinx. San Martín left it deeply mortified. There had been no question that at every point of discussion, San Martín had been the supplicant, Bolívar the khan. The Liberator had everything the Protector needed: a winning army, the acclaim of his people, the luster of success, the recognition of a major world power. But Bolívar had given nothing; instead he had walked away deeply apprehensive of San Martín's motives.

After the meeting, San Martín made solemn pronouncements from the balcony of that sprawling house, under which throngs of adulators had gathered. He received scores of visitors and heard out their appeals and thanks. But he was cheerless, disconsolate. Later that afternoon, he and Bolívar met for another half hour in the company of their minions. Little was said.

That night, they dined separately, giving them time for ample deliberation. Clearly, they had had plenty of opportunity to take one another's measure, for when they convened again on the next day, they were full of conviction. San Martín had already decided he would leave on the *Macedonia* that same night and had given instructions for his crew to be ready to depart at eleven. He walked from his house to Bolívar's at one in the afternoon and there they proceeded to spend the next four hours in earnest conversation.

Little is known about precisely what was said, but at the end of it Bolívar asked San Martín how the people of Lima would characterize his government. "Satisfactory," San Martín replied. Bolívar nodded. "Well," he said, "the pleasure of our meeting has been marred by news of a revolt there." Bolívar handed him a communiqué he had just received from one of his generals. The report indicated that Bernardo Monteagudo, San Martín's closest advisor, had been driven from power during the Protector's absence. San Martín was visibly stricken by the news. Monteagudo had been ruthless and roundly despised, but he had been his most trusted deputy. Once he recovered from the shock, San Martín confided in Bolívar that it was all finished for him now. He would resign his position, leave Lima. He had already contemplated the possibility. Indeed, he had left his resignation in a sealed envelope before he had boarded the *Macedonia*. But he had hoped Bolívar would save the day.

It was not to be. Whatever was said beyond this, we cannot know. Over the years, there has been much conjecture. Certainly, they went on to speak of Bolívar's vision to create a federation of Latin American nations. San Martín was heartily in favor of it. It was one of the few things upon which they agreed. But by early evening, there was little more to say. When the doors of their meeting room swung open at five o'clock, they walked through them, resolved in very different ways. They appeared shortly thereafter at the banquet Bolívar had planned in San Martín's honor.

Apart from wanting to win Guayaquil for Peru, San Martín had come as an innocent to these proceedings. He was no agent of Argentina, no demagogue in search of a wider power, no seeker of personal glory. As one historian has said: He came to the meeting with not a single trump card up his sleeve. Nevertheless, the moment he decided to leave the deck of the *Macedonia* for the hard earth of Guayaquil, he was on the losing side. Perhaps he knew it. Perhaps he was scrambling to save what he could.

Bolívar, in contrast, had studied his potential collaborator with a hard, cold eye. From Manuela Sáenz and others, he had been given intelligence about San Martín's recurrent illness, his reliance on drugs, his bloodless invasion of Lima, his excess of caution, his willful, angry spats with Lord Cochrane. He knew far more about the Argentine than he let on.

San Martín would leave Guayaquil a defeated man. Bolívar, on the other hand, had been assured the possibility of more triumphs. "Good God, I want no more," he wrote Santander within hours of the banquet. "For the first time I have no further desires." At dinner, he took the head of the table, presiding over a noisy, festive affair. San Martín took the seat of honor at his side. There was lively music, an abundance of good food and wine, and a hearty sense of cordiality. The feast had cost Bolívar 8,000 pesos, by far the largest expenditure he made as Colombia's wars drew to a close. When it came time for toasts, he sprang to his feet: "Gentlemen," he began, "I offer a toast to the two greatest men of South America—to General San Martín, and to me." It was a preposterous thing to say, a diplomatic blunder, but enough wine had been consumed that it hardly mattered. San Martín rose and with exquisite courtesy offered the following: "To the swift termination of this war, to the organization of new nations on this American continent, and to the health of the Liberator." The toasts went on until well into the evening. San Martín repaired to his house to rest awhile before returning for a sprightly ball in his honor, which began at nine.

The celebration was held in the sprawling and sumptuous Municipal Hall, the most imposing structure in the city. Revelers in fancy dress clamored to witness the two most renowned personages in South America demonstrate their friendship, and they were hardly disappointed. When San Martín arrived, they saw a tall, weary, but courtly man greeted with great warmth by Bolívar and his generals. But the elegant Argentine attended the dance without ever participating in it, and it was obvious that his mind was far away, filled with distant preoccupations. Whereas Bolívar danced with gusto, tirelessly, guiding one beauty after another onto the reeling dance floor, San Martín was resolutely unresponsive. The thrumming valses, so beloved of the time, neither interested nor lured him. Dancers swirled by, their euphoria rising with each passing hour, but he seemed to look past the spectacle and bacchanalia, adrift in another world. He stayed as long as patience would allow; but at one o'clock in the morning, he waved to his colonels and told them he could no longer stand the noise.

He left, not through a side door, undetected, as some have claimed, but through the front, with Bolívar at his side. Together they stepped into the night and, as the music and frivolity faded behind them, they walked toward the wide, muddy waters of the Guayas River. A small boat awaited; the *Macedonia* was in the distance; the luggage had already been taken aboard. All was prepared for the Protector's return to Lima. Bolívar sent off his guest with a portrait of himself, "a sincere memento of their friendship." "Sincere" and "friendship" were the last two words San Martín would have used to describe the encounter. As soon as he was securely on board, his schooner set sail for the Pacific. He had spent less than forty hours in Guayaquil.

"General Bolívar beat us to the punch," San Martín told his men. "He is not the man we thought he was." He had left Guayaquil with nothing to show and had been surprised by how little in common he had with his fellow liberator. He had found him superficial, deceitful, childishly vain. The man had seemed—to someone who had worn a uniform since he was twelve—the very antithesis of a soldier. As San Martín sailed down the Guayas River, bound for history and oblivion, his animus grew.

Disembarking in Lima three weeks later, he learned that the information Bolívar had given him about Monteagudo was true. His second in command had been stripped of power, threatened with the death penalty, and driven from Peru. More than ever, San Martín became determined to remove himself from the equation—to allow Bolívar, the fiercer man, reign over the Peruvian quagmire.

Bolívar, for his part, began with more praise than condemnation for his Argentine counterpart. The general had withdrawn gracefully, after all, and he had taken President Olmedo and two hundred disgruntled residents with him. The day after San Martín departed from Guayaquil, Bolívar wrote to Santander: "His character is essentially that of a military man, and he seems quick, no dimwit. His ideas are forthright, interesting, but he doesn't strike me as subtle enough to rise to the sublime." Within two months, Bolívar had changed his tune; he had heard about San Martín's low opinion of him. "San Martín has been taking me apart," he now told Santander. Within six months, Bolívar wouldn't deign to mention him at all.

The first words San Martín uttered before Lima's opening congress on Friday, September 20, announced his resignation. The congress responded by heaping honors on him; but his decision was accepted without debate. Only within his small circle of friends were there any passionate objections. "The scepter has slipped from my hands," he told his followers. There was no arguing about it: the people no longer supported or respected him. In his final address, he assured them that he was leaving the government in excellent order, that independence was all but won, that he would leave it to them to elect a new leader. At nine o'clock on that same winter's night, he stole away on horseback, abandoning the capital for the coast. He was convinced he was helping Peru by clearing the way for Bolívar. But in so doing he left the brand-new republic leaderless, rudderless, and in chaos.

Before he departed, he told his followers and friends that someday they would find documents that explained his sudden and bewildering desertion, but those documents—if indeed they existed—were never found. Pressed by one of his ministers for a better explanation, he gave one that only a bitter heart could muster: "There is no room in all of Peru for General Bolívar and me."

He boarded a ship that very night and skimmed away, unnoticed. He sailed first to Ancón, a port nineteen miles away, where he stayed for a few days, inspiring the rumor that he was waiting to be invited back. No invitation came. With only Pizarro's flag of conquest in hand—a gift that had been given to him months before by the municipality of Lima—he headed for the old glory fields of home.

Wasted by opium, wearied by war, overwhelmed by political labyrinths wherever he turned, he found no comfort in Mendoza. His old cohort was out of power. His twenty-five-year-old wife, hundreds of miles away in Buenos Aires, was dead of tuberculosis before he could reach her. Two years later, he and his eight-year-old daughter moved to a quiet suburb of London. In time, they went on to Belgium and France. Theirs was an impecunious existence—on a meager and irregular pension provided by Peru—but San Martín was hardly as sick as he thought he was. The Protector would be in the world for twenty-seven more years, outliving the Liberator by a full two decades. Eventually, he would transcend the rancor of defeat and find it within himself to write this of Bolívar: "My successes in the war of independence are decidedly trivial compared to those that that general contributed to the American cause." And: "It is reasonable to say that his military achievements have merited his reputation as the most extraordinary man South America has ever produced."

He was too modest. It was because of San Martín that Peru had declared itself a nation without expending a drop of blood. He had arrived with a scant army of four thousand men and scattered the king's far more powerful legions. Whittled by fevers, reduced by an unhealthy climate, his soldiers had held Lima by patience alone. San Martín was not a master of improvisation, but neither was he a reckless or sanguinary man. When he slipped out of Lima, he left no congress or constitution but he left laws by which justice could be dealt, safety might be ensured, and a nation could govern. For all the criticism he endured during his tenure, Peru will always remember him as its most honorable hero. But to win Peru its full liberty, honor would not be enough.

ALTHOUGH BOLÍVAR COULD HAVE LEARNED much from San Martín's swift fall from grace, he had no time to dwell on it. With San Martín gone, Lima spun into a political vortex. A newly formed congress appointed a ruling junta and drafted a constitution, but was soon mired in disarray. Blaming San Martín for its troubles and wanting no further help from outsiders, the junta rejected the Colombian battalions Bolívar sent to Peru, and these now withdrew in bafflement and exasperation. The Spanish general José de Canterac, who lurked close to Lima's gates, found himself poised to take advantage of the vacuum. In January of 1823, he sought out what was left of San Martín's army in Moquegua and routed it completely. By the end of that battle, the Chileans and Argentines who had liberated Lima—1,700 of them—were either dead or in shackles.

In desperation now, the congress in Lima turned to Peru's most respected soldier, Andrés de Santa Cruz, who had just returned from fighting alongside Sucre in Quito. Santa Cruz virtually forced congress to appoint Colonel José de la Riva Agüero to rule over the foundering city-state. Riva Agüero was nothing if not Machiavellian in his quest to wrest all the power and squelch his personal enemies. He proclaimed himself president. But his power began to wane as soon as he assumed the post, and he wrote to San Martín, pleading for him to return and help manage a civil war. Riva Agüero had long been San Martín's supporter, but he had also been pivotal in ousting Bernardo Monteagudo while San Martín had been in Guayaquil, and San Martín had come to despise him. "Impossible!" San Martín lashed back in a scathing letter, "Knave! . . . scoundrel! . . . black soul!" With the Spaniards circling the city and the patriots in angry discord, President Riva Agüero now begged Bolívar for that assistance. No fewer than four delegations of Peruvians traveled from Lima to Guayaquil over the course of the next few months, imploring Bolívar to come to Peru's rescue.

But just as Bolívar had anticipated, Colombia's troubles had begun to flare. The royalists in Pasto had arisen once more—this time under Benito Boves, the nephew of the infamous Boves—and a virulent rebellion threatened to undo all that Bolívar and Sucre had accomplished in that difficult, volcanic terrain. Between the royalists of Peru and the royalists of Pasto, the free districts of Quito and Guayaquil hung in precarious balance. He could hardly leave Colombia now.

There were other worries. Federalists in Caracas, lobbying for more autonomy, had begun to question the Colombian constitution. They proposed reverting to the old constitution established in Venezuela a decade before so that they could establish more independence from Bogotá. Bolívar was furious. To him, the Colombian constitution was sacred, inviolable, and the concept of a strong, centralized government essential. He contemplated going to Bogotá to ensure that Santander stamp out this new threat, but his fulminations alone seemed to persuade the malcontents to back down for the time being. In this brief apogee of glory, Bolívar's moral authority was the strongest it would ever be; there was little the Venezuelan people wouldn't do for him.

The uprising in Pasto, on the other hand, was another story. Young Boves's rebellion had erupted at the end of 1822 in a breathtaking show of violence. Opting for cruelty in the face of cruelty, Bolívar ordered all royalist property in Pasto seized and parceled out to his officers; anyone suspected of supporting the crown was arrested and forced to serve in the patriot army; guns, weapons—all metal objects—were forcibly removed from houses. The populace responded with renewed violence: Bolívar's veteran general Bartolomé Salom reported that Colombia had two choices now: grant absolute pardon for all residents of Pasto or embark on total destruction of the region. "You cannot imagine the obstinacy," Salom wrote to Bolívar. "We have captured prisoner boys who are no more than nine and ten." Finally, with the help of General Sucre, the republican army was able to overtake young Boves in a bloody encounter at Yacuanquer, in which soldiers and civilians, women and children were indiscriminately slaughtered. The carnage did honor to no one; nor was the battle at all decisive. Pasto would need to be tamed again and again. Like an indefatigable Hydra, its royalists would rebound from apparent annihilation to fight again for the king.

Somehow, in this ongoing crucible of history, Bolívar found time for Manuela Sáenz. Their trysts were few and far between, and she complained bitterly about their infrequency. She had stayed on in Quito to be closer to him, refusing to go back to her husband in Lima, but she was learning that life as the Liberator's mistress was one of short, ardent assignations and long, excruciating months of want. As he crisscrossed the Ecuadorean terrain, trying to secure it for Colombia, she was inconsolable. "The victory at Yacuanquer has cost me dearly," she protested. "You'll tell me I'm not a good patriot for what I'm about to say, but I would have preferred my own triumph to ten in Pasto. I can imagine how bored you must be in that little town, but as desperate as you may be, you can't possibly be as desperate as your best of friends—Manuela."

It was probably in the course of his incessant peregrinations to subdue Pasto that Sáenz understood that the only way she was going to be able to see him as much as passion demanded was to travel with him. During the year or more that she stayed on in Quito waiting for him, he had passed through the city only four times. She was lovesick, obsessed. She was also unafraid of danger. A declared patriot before she had ever met him, she was a fanatical partisan of his cause, an excellent horsewoman, comfortable around men, known to savor a good cigar. Moreover, she wanted nothing left to chance. Some have described Manuelita as fierce in her jealousies, capable of mauling his face with her fingernails when she suspected he had been unfaithful. She knew as well as anyone that her lover was a lothario. In any case, sometime during 1823, she likely offered to serve as an informant, secretary, or—as his attentions turned south—a liaison in the republican circles of Lima. He would find Manuelita impossible to resist. "She has a singular configuration," a French physician later said of her, leaving all future historians to contemplate whether the attribute he had in mind was corporeal, psychological, or sexual; whatever it was, it would captivate Bolívar for the rest of his days. He did not object to having her follow.

Her familiarity with Lima was further glue between them. His eye was firmly on Peru's liberation now. He had been coy in committing troops to San Martín, but the moment his rival had fled Callao, Bolívar made it known to Peruvians that he would take up their cause. He now asked the congress in Bogotá for approval to do so. But Santander dawdled, insisting that a man should mind his own house before setting out to salvage another's. By March, with San Martín gone and the original liberation army thoroughly routed, the situation in Lima had deteriorated seriously. Soon, the city began preparing for the worst; people sensed it was only a matter of time before the Spaniards retook Lima. Santander finally took Bolívar's request to congress.

With every return to Guayaquil from the firestorm of Pasto, Bolívar anxiously awaited Bogotá's response. But Colombia's congress, like its vice president, was hesitant to release the president to a foreign war. Bolívar knew Peru could not wait. Lima, the only liberated part of the colony, was about to be overrun by the King's army. He sent it six thousand troops under the command of General Sucre. By the time those reinforcements arrived, however, Lima was already in extremis. On June 18, nine thousand royalist soldiers overwhelmed the capital. Somehow, Sucre was able to whisk congress and his army safely to Callao. But within twenty-four hours, the chaos and intrigue were such that Riva Agüero's government collapsed, he was driven out of Callao unceremoniously, and the Peruvian congress pressed Sucre to accept the presidency of the republic. "The anarchy here is beyond description!" Sucre wrote to Bolívar. "I curse the day I came to Lima. What a task you foisted on me!" He was appalled by the vicious nature of Peruvian politics. Within weeks he had had enough of it, and he handed off the presidency to the Marquis of Torre Tagle, a former mayor of Lima and a republican who had spent most of his life in service to the crown. But Peru hadn't seen the last of Riva Agüero. The former president removed himself to the old, venerable city of Trujillo, where he raised his own army, set up a government, and insisted that he was still in charge.

The fourth and last delegation from Peru to Bolívar arrived in Guayaquil at the end of July. As fate would have it, the mission was led by Olmedo, the erstwhile poet-president of Guayaquil who had gone off in San Martín's ship and become a member of Lima's congress. Now representing the new president, the Marquis of Torre Tagle, Olmedo

showed Bolívar a very different face from the one he had worn in
Guayaquil. He beseeched him to come, make haste: Peru, he said, was
teetering on the verge of a double abyss. If civil war didn't devour it,
the Spanish crown would. "Peru awaits the voice that bonds, the hand
that leads, the genius that opens the way to victory," the official letter
pleaded. "All eyes, all hopes, are naturally on you."

Bolívar composed a careful response to Torre Tagle: "For a long
time now, my heart has drawn me to Peru . . . I have begged permission from [Colombia's] congress to allow me to serve my brothers of the
South; I have yet to receive an answer. This inaction has brought me to
the brink of despair: my troops are already there with you, hovering between hazard and glory; and I linger here, so very far away."

He wrote those words on the evening of August 6. But early the next
day, just as he was about to sign and seal the missive, he received news
that the congress in Bogotá had finally given him permission to go. He
tore up the letter, called for his officers, and—before the hour was out—
boarded a ship for Lima.

CHAPTER 13

In the Empire of the Sun

All the power of the supreme being is not enough to liberate Peru, that accursed country; only Bolívar, backed by true might, can hope to accomplish it.

—José de San Martín

"Peru," Bolívar wrote, "contains two elements that are the bane of every just and free society: gold and slaves. The first corrupts all it touches; the second is corrupt in and of itself." He had written it eight years before, while he languished in Jamaica, his revolution undone. But he was reminded of it now as he stood on the deck of the *Chimborazo*, watching the bare, desolate flank of Peru scroll past on his approach to Lima. It was the 1st of September, and the morning air was still pricked by the raw and damp of a Peruvian winter. By noon, a long, gray spit of land, the port of Callao, came into view, lancing the sea like a mortal wound. Gold. Slaves. Any visitor to the bustling center of Lima could see why Peru was loyal to the crown, why it hadn't been easy to raise an independence army: it was an altogether Spanish city, the richest viceroyalty in the empire. With its palaces, bejeweled aristocrats, and spirited commerce—its streets clattering with six thousand gilded carriages—Lima possessed a magnificence known to few capitals in the

Old World, much less the New. Gold and silver coursed through that harsh landscape; and a vast population of indigenous had been shackled to answer the demands of a brisk world trade.

The schooner dropped anchor at one o'clock. A full-cannon salute announced its arrival and what was left of Lima's patriot army—largely made up of Argentines, Chileans, and Colombians—spilled down the road to Callao, forming a procession for the Liberator's long-awaited entrance into the city. The Spaniards were no longer there: General Canterac had occupied Lima only long enough to wring money, guns, and uniforms from the people, threatening to reduce the capital to ashes if they didn't comply. After a month, Canterac had gone off to rejoin Viceroy La Serna in the highlands, leaving the city to its own chaotic devices. Now Lima was rendering up a cautious welcome for the Colombian Liberator. The streets were festooned with ribbons and flags; church bells pealed; the hum of celebration filled the air. People clamored to get a glimpse of the man who would replace San Martín. Members of Congress, with President Torre Tagle at their head, came down to the port to escort him into the city. He was carried in triumph to the ancient urban heart, where a palatial house had been readied for his stay.

At first, Bolívar refrained from saying much of anything publicly to his Peruvian hosts, aware that the political situation was fragile and that no one was really sure who was in power, nor had anyone said with any specificity what Bolívar's role would be. Sucre had warned him of vicious rivalries: "You could probably get Congress to give you all the power, if that's what you want," he had written Bolívar months before, "but I wouldn't advise it. . . . A son of the soil should govern, and you should dedicate yourself to war." Bolívar followed that advice religiously. The rich Creoles of Lima had worried about the advent of the Colombians. Rumor had it that Bolívar was a mulatto, that his army was a thundering horde of blacks and Indians wanting nothing so much as booty. He was all too conscious of those anxieties. But the expectation that he could save the Peruvian revolution without wielding ultimate power was an illusion. Those who had called for Bolívar's help—first Riva Agüero, then Torre Tagle—thought of him as a brilliant general for hire, a liberator who would serve their interests, not a president of a vast territory with a concrete vision of his own. It was the same error of judgment San Martín had made when he had tried to engage Bolívar's assistance in Guayaquil.

Bolívar understood this. On September 2, when he was offered the supreme military command, he accepted it for what it was. He assured the Peruvian congress that it could count on his service and support. But he warned that he would require radical reforms to be introduced into every branch of the administration—including congress—to address the corruption that plagued it. Those were ominous words. His listeners nodded in agreement, but the demand did not augur well for many of them. President Torre Tagle had raided the public treasury to buy every congressman in the room.

As far as the Peruvian public was concerned, Bolívar seemed the antithesis of the sullen San Martín. He spent those first few days attending the theater, laughing heartily at opera buffa, enjoying a bullfight in the long-neglected ring. He attended parties in his honor, admired the women with their elegant gewgaws and bewitching eyes. He had been at sea for twenty-five long days and the pleasures of a cosmopolitan city were not lost on him. "The men seem to admire me . . . the women are lovely," he wrote Santander, "and that is all very nice." But within days in that city of delights, he was hard at work, addressing the Peruvian juggernaut. There were two presidents to contend with, four patriot armies, a vast and demoralized indigenous population, a seemingly unbridgeable ravine between rich and poor. In private, he called Peru "a chamber of horrors." His closest aide, Daniel O'Leary, called it "a corpse."

He sent Riva Agüero in Trujillo a letter, urging him to give up his misguided efforts to hold on to the presidency; a president and congress were operating perfectly well in the capital. Riva Agüero's act dissolving congress had been a travesty, and Bolívar told him so: the institution was larger than any one man; it had given Riva Agüero the power in the first place—"Stop conducting a war against your nation's offices," he scolded. In an attempt to be conciliatory, Bolívar offered him a way to save face: a role in the military, perhaps, or a diplomatic appointment. But Riva Agüero, in the meantime, had approached the viceroy himself. He had offered La Serna a plan to eject Bolívar and Sucre from Peru altogether—even rid the arena of San Martín, if the Argentine general were to reappear. Riva Agüero had offered the Spaniards an armistice of eighteen months, during which time a permanent peace would be negotiated between Spain and Peru. It was blatant treason. There was no choice now but to forcibly arrest the ex-president. Riva Agüero was apprehended by his own general, sent to prison, and exiled to Chile.

Everywhere Bolívar looked there was evidence of bad faith and duplicity. The Peruvian general Santa Cruz—whose loyalty to Sucre had been so crucial in winning Quito—now marched his army south to devastating losses, spurning all offers of assistance from the Colombian legions. Indeed, since the Colombians' arrival in Peru, Santa Cruz had changed his attitude toward Sucre entirely. He was jealous of his former general, suspicious of his six thousand men, wary of some larger, nefarious design in the Colombian offer. But in that maelstrom of mistrust, even Santa Cruz was accused of questionable ambitions—he had overreached, thought himself a greater general than he had proved to be. His officers worried that he was a puppet of the renegade ex-president Riva Agüero. Some even alleged that Santa Cruz wanted nothing more than to create a personal empire in his native La Paz, in the southern reaches of Peru, where he could control the coveted silver mines of Potosí. No one in this Peruvian enterprise, it seemed, could be trusted. The politics and loyalties seemed utterly alien to Bolívar. Questions of pecking order and jurisdiction were harder to parse. The germ of suspicion that had surfaced between Bolívar and San Martín in Guayaquil seemed to have spread like a contagion in Lima. For the first six months of his tenure in Peru, the Liberator was just as vexed, just as paralyzed as his predecessor had ever been. "I shall always be a foreigner to these people," he wrote gloomily, registering Peru's palpable xenophobia. "I have already regretted that I ever came." But in more sanguine moments, he refused to be cast as another San Martín: "If we lose Peru," he confided privately, "we might as well say adios to Colombia. . . . I'm riding out this storm."

Bolívar noted right away that San Martín's likeness was not on display in the palace in Lima and he commented on it. He was told that Riva Agüero had removed the portrait when San Martín had departed a year before. The Liberator insisted that it be hung again. He made a point to toast San Martín at the first available opportunity, but quickly separated himself from his strategy: America, he insisted, would not tolerate a throne or a king. Nor could Peru afford to be passive in the face of a determined enemy. He made it clear that he would wage an all-out war against the colonizer. It was, as far as he was concerned, a battle for survival: Caracas and Bogotá would not be free until Peru was free; Peru would not be free until La Paz was free; and so on, all the way down the continent. The chain of republics from Venezuela to Argentina had to be defended at all costs, for one weak link might destroy the whole. It was the essence of his revolutionary theory and it could be synthesized in two words: attack and unite. "The soldiers who have come from Argentina, Chile, Colombia, and Venezuela will not return to their fatherlands unless they do so covered with laurels," he told congress. "They will either triumph and leave Peru a free nation or they will die."

It was in this spirit of resolve that Bolívar set out to reconnoiter the very heart of Peru—Cajamarca, Huaraz, and the fertile valley between the two cordilleras of the Andes. He wanted to salvage any damage Riva Agüero might have created, spread word of his liberating mission, and learn something about the potential fields of war. But the links in his chain were already beginning to give way. Argentina pulled out of the Peruvian effort quietly, wanting to expend no more soldiers or funds. A fleet of Chilean ships, which had been making its way up the coast to assist the Liberator, decided to turn around and abandon the operation altogether. Bolívar was now truly alone in Peru. The news from Greater Colombia in recent weeks had been uniformly good—Páez and his plainsmen had finally dislodged the Spaniards from their last bulwark at Puerto Cabello—but here, in this most vital of revolutionary theaters, anarchy reigned. There seemed to be no hope for foreign assistance. His optimism gave way to desperation. He wrote to Santander, expressing grave doubts about the reliability of Peruvians: they lacked mettle, dedication, patriotism. He pleaded with his vice president for a solid battalion of horsemen, a modest contingent of five hundred men from Páez's hordes; within a week he was pleading for an army of twelve thousand. The man called "victory's favorite son" had become a general without any legions.

Sailing back to Lima from Trujillo, he fell ill. On January 1, 1824, his ship found harbor in Pativilca, a tiny village thirty miles north of the capital, and Bolívar was carried ashore, racked with chills and high fevers. In that deserted hamlet, far from hope of medical attention, he slipped in and out of consciousness, struggling for life. He was thought to be suffering from typhus, but it may have been an early manifestation of the tuberculosis that would never leave him. The fever lasted seven days, and he emerged from it a phantom of his former self. Weak, scrawny, he began dictating letters as soon as he could sit up. Officers were brought into his room for conferences, but he insisted they talk to him from the other side of an enormous curtain; it would be weeks before he would allow them to see his face. "You would not recognize me," he wrote to Santander. "I am completely wasted, old. . . . At times I even have episodes of dementia." The envoy from Colombia to Peru, Joaquín Mosquera, stopped in to visit the Liberator a few days later and reported a heartbreaking sight:

> He was so gaunt and skeletal that it almost brought me to tears. He was seated in an old wicker chair, propped up against the wall of a little garden, with his head swaddled in a white kerchief. His trousers were so flimsy that I could see the pointy knees, bony legs; and his voice was hollow and feeble, his face cadaverous. You'll recall that the Peruvian army under Santa Cruz had just fallen to pieces; they'd had to flee the Spaniards. . . . It all seemed a battery of ills designed to finish off the half-dead hero. With a heavy heart, fearing the ruin of our army, I asked him, "And what will you do now?" His cavernous eyes lit up, and he said without hesitation, "Triumph!"

Bolívar stayed in Pativilca for two months, unable to travel, and it was during that time—for all his ordeals—that there were signs that the world, too, was convinced he would triumph. In France, the revered bishop and diplomat Dominique de Pradt urged North Americans to support Bolívar's revolution: South American independence, he insisted, was as important to the United States as its own. Of the Liberator, he had this to say: "When one considers how he began, the obstacles he has overcome and the results of his labors, one has no choice but concede that he has played one of history's most glorious roles. . . . Posterity will exalt his name." If Pradt had worried that President James Monroe wasn't paying attention, he needn't have. Monroe had just issued a warning to the rest of the world that the United States would not tolerate further interference in Spanish America. Any attempt to impose a foreign will on the hemisphere would be considered an act of aggression and would trigger immediate intervention. The Monroe Doctrine had been the brainchild of Secretary of State John Quincy Adams, but it had been prompted by Britain's foreign minister George Canning, who had made it known that his government considered the future of the Spanish empire hopeless. As far as two great world powers were concerned, Spain was on its way out of America. Liberty was on the ascendant. It was all the medicine Bolívar would require.

ON HIS WAY BACK TO Lima before he had fallen ill, Bolívar had eagerly anticipated a reunion with Manuela Sáenz. She had returned from Quito several months before, allowing them to resume their love affair. The Liberator had a roving eye, to be sure, but the love between them was deep and abiding—made all the more ardent by months of separation. Manuela had never been one to shrink from society's censure and she did not hesitate now to raise a collective eyebrow. Her acquaintances were largely artists, liberals, even libertines—she had been seen accompanying a viceroy's courtesan to the theater—and it was whispered that Manuela's closest friend, the actress Rosa de Campusano, had spent nights in San Martín's bed. For propriety's sake, Manuela continued to live in her husband's house, but at night she would hurry to her lover's, where they would spend long, happy hours alone. By then, he had taken up residence in the villa that San Martín had occupied in Magdalena, a quiet suburb far from the hubbub of the city. It was a stucco house with large, comfortable rooms, spacious windows, and a pretty garden that led out to the stables. With a fig tree, a large cherimoya, and clusters of verbena all around, the air seemed perpetually filled with perfume.

By then, Sáenz had persuaded Bolívar to admit her to his entourage. Certainly by December, as he traveled north, she was a permanent member of his staff, maintaining his personal archives. The arrangement was clearly a departure from the ordinary. Women often accompanied their husbands and lovers into battle; they might even take up arms, dress as men, argue for justice in military tribunals; but they rarely were brought into the bureaucracy and paid a salary. Manuela Sáenz had become a full employee of the liberating army—a cavalry soldier, a hussar. That official role would allow her to stay in contact with her lover, communicate with his secretaries and aides, and, most important, keep track of his whereabouts. It was how she came to know that he was ill and convalescing in Pativilca.

When she read of it in a routine report, she had wanted to fly to his side and nurse him back to health, casting her husband's reputation to the winds. But in due course, war itself conspired to bring her north to Bolívar. It had happened in the most unexpected way. Bolívar, struggling with his disease and trying to buy time to rebuild an army, had called on President Torre Tagle to negotiate an armistice with the viceroy. But Torre Tagle had grown thoroughly weary of Bolívar, and, although he agreed to approach the viceroy, he decided to use the conversations as an opportunity to better his own position. He told the Spaniards that he was prepared to change his allegiance altogether, work for them. He had done it before, as had many of his cronies—politicians whose loyalties were so divided between Spain and Peru that they had switched sides again and again, whenever it seemed the other was gaining power. Torre Tagle's strategy began to unfold on February 5, when the demoralized Argentines guarding Callao decided to mutiny and hand over the fortress to Spanish generals. In a panic, the congress declared Bolívar dictator of Peru—a title he found odious, although at the time the word was still hallowed by a republican aura. Passed over entirely by the republican leadership, Torre Tagle now moved to complete his defection. On February 27, he and his top ministers, along with nearly 350 officers of the Peruvian army, declared themselves on the side of the king. The Spaniards issued an ultimatum, announcing that they would retake Lima. Accustomed by now to mercurial transformations, the capital prepared once again to welcome them. In a flight for their lives, the republicans—including Manuela Sáenz—evacuated the city, swarming north along the dunes, toward Pativilca and Trujillo. Two days later, the royalists reentered Lima and the City of Kings swung back under Spanish rule.

When he heard of the Argentine mutiny in Callao, Bolívar had no doubt that royalists would take back the capital. In the darkest of moods, he wrote to his aides in Lima, telling them to send all his possessions to Trujillo. He wrote to his generals in Quito and his vice president in Bogotá, warning them to prepare for a terrible war: Peru was irretrievably lost; the Spanish reinfestation would creep up the coast, work its way overland, and threaten the security of Colombia itself. He wrote to President Torre Tagle—unaware that the president was an embezzler and might well have been party to the mutiny—to warn him that certain Peruvians had stolen government money and others were shamelessly seeking power. It would be weeks before he learned of Torre Tagle's breathtaking betrayal and the defection of so many of Peru's elites to the royalist side.

In defense of Peru, its historians have explained that the four years spent under San Martín and his foreign militias had deeply worried the aristocrats of Lima; they had emerged from the experience persuaded that they had stronger ties to Spain than they did to South America. Certainly they felt they had more in common with their colonial masters than with the mixed-race ruffians of the Chilean and Argentine armies. But in the main, it came down to this: the majority of Lima's Creoles wanted independence handed to them without a fight. They had never wanted to sever their connections to Spain; they had only wanted more economic freedom. And they certainly hadn't expected to forfeit their old privileges in the process. They had learned to be patriots, as one historian has put it, whenever it looked as if Spain was losing, and royalists when the patriots were on the run. But Lima was not Peru, and, convalescing in Pativilca, Bolívar began to realize that the only way he was going to win Peru was to take firm control of the outlying areas and forge his way back into the capital. This was the strategy he had used in Caracas, the one that had worked in Quito. There was something else. Bolívar's battle cry was no longer "Liberate!" It was "Triumph!" A curious thing had happened to his revolution since he had fought his way up from Pasto. The butchery had hardened him. It was less a war of independence now than a crusade; less a call to freedom than a call to win at all costs. He was not unaware of that fundamental sea change. At the nadir of his depression about the loss of Callao he wrote Santander: "I'm through making promises . . . I can't very well tyrannize them into saving their own necks." But within two days, he was telling Santander that he would set up an "itinerant government" in Trujillo. Within three, he was writing out a full battle plan for General Sucre.

By March, the profound depression that had accompanied his disease had lifted. Perhaps it was because of the company of his mistress. Perhaps because world recognition for his struggle had filled him with renewed purpose. Gradually, his health improved, his energy returned. It was summer, and the sun-drenched days and mild sea breezes combined to renew his spirit. He established his headquarters in the main plaza of the city, organized his staff, and made efforts to build a judicial system, lay the groundwork for a university. But rebuilding his army was his major objective and he knew that every day the royalists did not attack was a day he could use toward strengthening military readiness. He instructed Sucre, who had taken his army north of Lima to the mountain city of Huaraz, to hold back from engaging the enemy just yet; he badgered Santander with the endless refrain, "Send troops and we'll win." Almost overnight, he turned Trujillo into a teeming arsenal. Every citizen became a laborer, every metal object a potential weapon. Trujillo's men were assigned to work in improvised forges and factories; women were expected to sew. Highborn señoras along with their servants collected fabric, formed sewing circles, and produced uniforms, flags, tents; no one, no matter how delicate her hands, was exempt. Indians in nearby villages were instructed to produce heavy ponchos and blankets. All available metal was confiscated and melted down for canteens, stirrups, horseshoes. Silver was seized from church altars to melt, mint, and pay for munitions and salaries. Taxes were levied to raise money for food. By force, by persuasion, by whatever means necessary, including outright appropriation, Bolívar made citizens of the north contribute to the war chest. The churches of Piura alone rendered more than 100,000 pesos in silver. Trujillo contributed 300,000 pesos in taxes for the treasury and then went on to give Bolívar 100,000 a month for his liberating army.

Bolívar threw himself into the task, leaving no detail of preparation unattended. He ordered seamstresses to cut patterns in ways that would conserve fabric; he worried about the precise kind of horseshoes needed for mountainous terrain; he oversaw ironworkers forging weapons. Ripping his trousers on a nail as he rose from a chair one day, he was inspired to harvest all nails from Trujillo's furniture for solder. He issued directives about gunpowder, soap, cooking oil, rope—even the number of cattle necessary to feed his troops, the kilos of corn needed to feed the cattle. Lambayeque and Piura produced boots; Huamachuco, belts and saddles. Trujillo milled linen for shirts; Cajamarca, broadcloth for trousers. He sent soldiers off to march thirty miles a day: with Sucre up in the mountains, with General Lara on unforgiving sand. As weeks passed, more and more arrived from Colombia, sent by Santander and Páez. Soon he was expecting them from Panama, greater Guatemala, Mexico. By mid-April he had transformed his war machine. It was, as one aide said, as if Mars had sprung from Jupiter's head, but in place of a single, fully outfitted warrior-god, there was an army of eight thousand. The ranks were overwhelmingly Colombian, heavily reinforced by Peruvian recruits from the countryside; and the army they formed had two distinct advantages: a superb cavalry, made up of horsemen from as far away as Patagonia or Guayana; and a high morale, largely attributable to the fact the men were being paid. Bolívar had insisted on it.

In April, it became evident that they had a third advantage. The Spaniards had been thrown into confusion by the defection of one of their generals, Pedro Olañeta, a diehard conservative who had carved out a principality of his own in the south of Peru. Olañeta accused Viceroy La Serna of being too liberal; he refused to follow orders, marched his divisions south, and proclaimed himself the "only true defender of the crown." La Serna, headquartered in Cuzco, had no choice but to send off a good third of his army to muzzle him. Olañeta's defection had occurred on January 15, just as Bolívar was emerging from the deliriums of his fever, but the news had taken three months to reach him. By then, La Serna's troubles with Olañeta had only multiplied. The viceroy's most talented general, Valdés, was locked in a series of bloody battles with the renegade. The army of the crown, which should have pointed north to Bolívar, was now pointed firmly south, at itself. Here, then, was the reason the royalists hadn't attacked when Bolívar was at his weakest. Olañeta's rebellion turned out to be exactly the diversionary maneuver Bolívar needed. Its chaos became his second chance.

Bolívar eventually wrote to Olañeta to try to persuade him to join the republican side, but speed was of the essence now and he needed to move quickly to win the strategic advantage. He instructed Sucre to meet him in the ancient town of Huamachuco, due east of Trujillo, nestled in the periphery of the Andes. As he left Trujillo, he called for the city to send him more forges, more ironworkers, more nails. The people were to surrender every conceivable military necessity: needles, thread, paper, every last fragment of lead—including whatever could be obtained from the city's statues—every last family jewel. "For God's sake, send me everything, everything, everything!" he implored his secretary-general.

Establishing his quarters in a house of many arches in Huamachuco, he wasted no time. He gathered his war council at the first opportunity, spread out a map of Peru, and posed the strategic question: The enemy was in disorder. Olañeta was on the run; Viceroy La Serna had sent General Jerónimo Valdés and five thousand men against him. Should the patriots strike or should they wait for reinforcements? Bolívar looked around the room at his officers, every one a seasoned general save one, the Irish colonel Francis Burdett O'Connor. He called on O'Connor first. The young officer stood, pointed to the viceroy's position, and then to where a good portion of his army had gone. "As far as I can see," O'Connor said, "our campaign must begin without delay." Bolívar promptly folded up the map. "This youngster has just given us a valuable lesson in the art of war," he said. "There is nothing more to say; nothing more to hear. Tomorrow, we march."

He had already made up his mind. They would follow the Andean cordillera south, tracing the fertile valleys that skirted its base. At Huánuco, they would begin the climb, cross the frigid heights of Cerro de Pasco, and provoke the Spaniards to battle where their garrisons stood thick and fast, protecting their hold on Cuzco. He put his army on the move immediately. At some point in mid-May, Bolívar entered the corridor of green known as the Callejón de Huaylas, which lies at the feet of the towering Cordillera Blanca. All around were the rich fields of sugarcane, corn, wheat, barley carpeting the hills with their abundance. Orchards hung with oranges, guava, and cherimoya surrounded the mud huts that lined the roads. Manuela Sáenz was not at Bolívar's side, but she was only a day's ride away, and by a route that was always kept secret. It was a hellish journey for a woman—through bogs, over rock, in the glacial mountain nights—riding alongside rough men of war and her fearless black female servants, Jonatás and Natán. A superb horsewoman, Sáenz was up to the challenge and, by all accounts, never complained about the hardships. It was a measure of how crucial she felt it was to accompany Bolívar. But she was not with him when he entered the little village of Huaylas to be met by a girl in virginal white.

Manuelita Madroño was ravishingly beautiful, as a writer of the day called her: "an irresistibly fresh doll of eighteen springs." She had been designated by the town council of Huaylas to welcome the Liberator with a crown of flowers. Bolívar was captivated. In high spirits, galvanized by the prospect of war, renewed by his army's remarkable transformation, he pursued the girl with his customary élan. It is said that within forty-eight hours they were inseparable. For a few weeks, she traveled with his troops, brightening his days with her girlish enthusiasms. From Huaylas to Caruaz to Huaraz, as the patriot army advanced through the bosky abundance that bordered the snowcapped Andes, as Bolívar fretted about lances, hooves, flint, and guns, Manuelita was an undisputable tonic. "You will note that though I beg," he wrote Santander, "I am hardly sad." He gamely asked his vice president to give his warm regards to the unattainable Bernardina. On the whole, Bolívar's good cheer was evident in many letters of that time, which are among the wittiest, most profoundly human of his life.

Inevitably, given the garrulousness of men—given the Liberator's roguish fame—news of his sexual infidelity soon reached Manuela Sáenz. She fired off a letter to Bolívar's personal secretary, Juan José Santana, a young soldier she had befriended. "The general has written me only twice in 19 days," she groused. And then, mired in self-pity: "He no longer thinks of me." She asked the secretary for an explanation, accused him of hiding the truth. Was the general indulging in a romantic affair? "You sin by your silence," she huffed, "and it's making me insane." To Bolívar she was more cautious, "My sir. . . . You, who constantly speak of your genial correspondence with friends, fail to write me even one line, and have consigned me to deadly misery. . . . Show me a little love, if only for a fellow patriot."

It isn't clear whether he ever answered that letter. But it's very probable that they reunited at the end of June, when he reached Huánuco, before his army climbed the summit of Cerro de Pasco to meet the Spaniards on the other side. His memory of the Madroño girl, left behind in the valley, was quickly overcome by history—and history would remember her as one more pretty conquest for the Liberator. But she would never forget him, shunning all men until she died of old age, seventy-four years later. "So, how is Bolívar's old lady?" villagers would ask the bright-eyed crone. "As fresh as a little girl," she always answered.

THERE ARE FEW LANDSCAPES AS magnificent or unforgiving as the geologic exuberance that lies between Huaraz and Huánuco. The mighty peaks of Huascarán and Yerupajá pierce the skies and send their melted snows to feed the largest waterway in the world—the Amazon. Like a colossal spine, the Andes run up the very heart of Peru, and there, like a vital organ nestled against bone, lies Cerro de Pasco, the mine that sustained an empire. By 1800, its silver-veined earth had surrendered the equivalent of $12 billion for Spain; a vast indigenous population was enslaved to exhume it. Stalled by revolution and blockade, the town remained the gateway to La Serna's mountain strongholds in Ayacucho and Cuzco. It was through here that Bolívar meant to go.

At more than fourteen thousand feet above sea level, it was neither an obvious nor easy thoroughfare. The approach was a grueling labyrinth of cliffs and gullies; the air was thin, hardly breathable. But Sucre had prepared the way. For more than six months, his troops had combed that treacherous terrain, scouting the best routes, establishing trails, building barrack huts along the way—even stashing cartons of sweets for the officers. There seemed to be little he hadn't thought of in his tireless climbing and reclimbing of that cordillera. He had posted trumpeters at strategic points to help stragglers stay the course; he had stored firewood along the roadside to keep soldiers warm in subzero nights. He had positioned one of his most skilled generals, William Miller—a veteran of the Napoleonic Wars—on the frigid heights of Cerro de Pasco. And he had established depots replete with provisions on the other side.

But as Bolívar's armies advanced over that wasteland there was no avoiding the perils and discomforts. At times, the pathways along precipices were so narrow that they admitted only one person at a time; often, soldiers were overcome by debilitating bouts of altitude sickness, sun poisoning, radiation. A march through a stinging snowstorm could cause temporary blindness; a slippery path could send a soldier into a chasm. Often, in harsher terrain with gorges or waterfalls, night would fall before troops could cross to safety. Some might stray from the march, get lost in the dark; it was not unusual to hear a strange concert of anxious calls, as man and beast wandered adrift in the black and bitter cold.

Following behind them were the Rabonas—hardy Indian women who accompanied the soldiers and provided for their needs, dietary to sexual. They washed, mended, scavenged, minded the pack animals, lit fires, cooked, cut soldiers' hair. Infested with lice, burned by wind and sun, they endured greater misery than most men. What a sight they must have been, with their pots and pans clanging as they hurried over that terrain, far more acclimated to it than any soldier.

For all its idiosyncrasies, it was a brilliantly prepared army, and Bolívar gloried in the sight of its nine thousand disciplined soldiers—fully clad and armed—snaking over that harsh land. Some were from as far away as Caracas or Buenos Aires or Liverpool, and had fought in Boyacá, or Maipú, or the Battle of Moscow. Long columns of Indians trooped behind, shouldering supplies. After them, for as far as the eye could see, an undulating mass of six thousand cattle. It was a solid war machine—trained, equipped, maintained. To Sucre, it seemed the finest patriot force that had ever fought in America. To Bolívar, who delighted in sitting with his officers at mealtimes and freely toasting their exploits, it was an army he loved with all his heart.

On the other side of Cerro de Pasco, wholly unaware of Bolívar's approaching army, was the Spanish general Canterac. His two thousand men—half cavalry, half infantry—were garrisoned in the lush, peaceful valley of Jauja. Exceptionally well regimented, well armed, and well paid, they had had little to fear from the patriots. Most were native Peruvians; indeed, of more than twelve thousand who made up the royal army, only six hundred—a mere five percent—were Spaniards. As Bolívar's liberating army streamed down the promontories of Cerro de Pasco looking for a fight, it had yet to meet the enemy and truly know who they were. The irony was that in Peru the defenders of the king were largely sons of the soil; the freedom fighters were largely foreigners. But General Canterac, too, had yet to meet his enemy; and the one he thought he knew was hardly worth worrying about. Proud, French-born, a brilliant tactician, Canterac had won every battle he had ever fought against the ill-organized seekers of independence. As far as he was concerned, he possessed the superior army: a mighty force that had stymied San Martín, bested Santa Cruz, and taken the city of Lima twice in the past six months. Canterac's fellow general, the fearless Jerónimo Valdés, had persuaded him of their preeminence in a letter assuring him that Bolívar was no threat: The Liberator was a coward, a third-rate military man hated by his troops, a tin-hat general who had won no battles apart from the easy one in Quito. As Sucre's minions swarmed through the nearby villages collecting provisions and securing safe houses for the patriot crossing, Canterac had not lifted a finger to thwart them. It was as if he wasn't concerned in the least, as if he had fallen into a great slumber. Clearly, he was confident that nothing the bumbling patriots could do would put them at an advantage.

On the crisp, clear morning of August 2, Bolívar reviewed 7,700 troops on a towering mesa near Cerro de Pasco. To their west were the snowcapped mountains over which they had just labored; to the east, barren leviathans that ran all the way to Brazil; to the south, the stone forest of Huayllay, its bristling rock reaching up like quills of a mythic porcupine. Directly below, the emerald waters of Lake Chinchaycocha and the marshland of Junín. The view was spectacular, mirroring the high hopes of all who beheld it. As Bolívar inspected the ranks that had followed him far and joined him in many battles, he made the uplifting call:

Soldiers! You are about to complete the greatest task heaven can commend to man—saving a world from slavery.

Soldiers! The enemies you are about to destroy pride themselves in fourteen uninterrupted years of victory. They are worthy of measuring their weapons against yours, which have gleamed in a thousand battles.

Soldiers! Peru and America look to you for Peace. . . . Even liberal Europe contemplates you in awe, for freedom in the New World is the hope of the universe. Will you let it slip away? No, no! You are invincible!

The air was filled with deafening shouts. Viva! Viva! rising into the vault of sky. Two days later, as Bolívar's cavalry made the long descent, riding mules and leading their horses down steep escarpments, they caught a glimpse of one of Canterac's divisions winding through an open valley. Patriot voices filled the air once more, sounding ferocious war whoops. The horsemen of the pampas and llanos were quivering for a fight, eager to pit their legendary skills against the royalist cavalry.

General Canterac finally emerged from slumber on August 6 to ride out on reconnaissance with thirteen hundred troops. He had heard, with the chill of surprise, that the entire patriot army had crossed the Andes under his watch and was headed for the town of Jauja. By then, Bolívar and nine hundred horsemen had already descended to the rim of the lake, looking to provoke the Spanish general to battle. When Canterac spied them on the other side, he decided to circle the lake and attack the patriots in the rear, but the instant he started south, Bolívar hurried to meet him. They finally joined in battle at five o'clock that afternoon on the marshy flats just south of the lake.

The Battle of Junín was fierce and fast, fought entirely with swords and lances. Not one shot was fired; not one cannonball expended. The terrible silence was punctuated only by the sound of steel against steel, wood against wood, the odd bugle call, the pawing of horses, the grunts of men, the thuds and cries of the fallen. At first, when the royalist cavalry loosed a mighty charge across the plain, it seemed they had the advantage. But as combat continued, they drove too far into patriot lines, exposing their own flanks. Bolívar directed the veteran general

Miller to attack those flanks, called for a rush against their rear guard, and ordered his plainsmen to execute their hallmark about-face—a fast retreat, a sudden whirl, a furious charge—and it was here that the royalists began to hesitate, lose ground. Heartened, the patriots ratcheted up the offensive, calling in the Colombian lancers. A horseman's lance was fourteen feet long and, handled nimbly, it could easily outreach any royalist weapon, slamming into a man with such force that it lifted him several feet from his saddle. The stampeding thunder of Bolívar's plainsmen, wrote young Colonel O'Connor, now "made the earth tremble." By dusk—which began to darken the sky an hour later—the patriots had control. Canterac's troops began a swift, disordered retreat, abandoning weapons as they went, marking a path south toward Jauja. Exhausted, suffering the effects of high-altitude combat, the patriots could not have gone on much longer. But just as the sun tipped over the horizon, two colonels rode back from a heated chase shouting, "Victory!" Bolívar took no chances: He sent squadrons of sharpshooters after Canterac, riding two to a mount. Night fell on a plain littered with dead and wounded; riderless horses wandered the battlefield in confusion. The royalists had lost nearly four hundred men, and one hundred more had been taken prisoner. The patriots had lost 145.

That night, Bolívar and his officers made their beds on a grassy knoll by the battlefield. José Palacios, the loyal manservant who had followed Bolívar to every battlefield since Angostura, produced a fortifying meal of cold beef, which he pulled from his saddlebag and handed all around. With that first victory in hand, the men were content to rest on that hard, fiercely won ground, awaking the next morning with frost on their mustaches.

"The brilliant skirmish of Junín," as Bolívar later referred to it, had a powerful psychological effect on both sides, far outweighing the military magnitude of the conflict. Peruvians were suddenly made to realize that the invincible Canterac was not invincible after all: his cavalry had been routed; his infantry had suffered shocking desertions in their mortified retreat—first to Jauja, and then all the way back to the Spanish stronghold in Cuzco. Indeed Canterac confessed to have genuinely been shaken by his experience at Junín, that the rebels under Bolívar were not just a band of beggars after all, but a skilled fighting force. He reported to the governor of Callao that a number of Bolívar's most important officers had been killed in battle, that Bolívar himself had been wounded in the hand—much of his information blatantly wrong—but he did manage to get one thing right: "Our losses may have been few in number," he told the governor, "but they have been overwhelming in spirit." The Spanish governor, terrified to read such words from his fearless general, shut himself up in the fortress of Callao, leaving Lima to the caprices of its patriot population.

THE FORCES OF INDEPENDENCE NOW had the rich, fertile fields of Jauja to themselves. Bolívar took the opportunity to renew the army, strengthen its military prowess, and learn all he could about the territory. As he passed through Jauja, he collected all the equipment the royalists had discarded in their frenzied flight to Cuzco. The royalists had lost more than two thousand men; but they also had abandoned seven hundred guns, a wealth of munitions, livestock, and horses. As Bolívar soon learned, they had burned whole villages during their occupation, executed hundreds—even those convalescing in hospitals— whom they suspected of republican tendencies. "They were Caligula; we were Caesar," as Santander once boasted about the patriots. But as Bolívar headed south, he, too, was not above rough justice. Even as he installed municipal governments and imposed legislation, he threatened to shoot councilors, doctors, and civil servants who didn't do their job. Soldiers who looted and raped peasants were dragged to main squares and executed in public, their bodies drawn and quartered as a lesson to any who would flout the law.

In a further effort to impose order, Bolívar delegated Sucre to join the rear guard, retrace the course of the liberating army, and bring in all the patriots who had been lost or wounded. Sucre balked at the indignity, but complied with the Liberator's orders. At the end, he announced that the experience had been humiliating—that his cohort had laughed at him—and that he was tendering his resignation as a result. Bolívar, who loved Sucre like a son, rushed to make it up to him. "You're out of your mind if you think I meant to offend you. I assigned you a job I myself wanted to do, because I believed you could do it better; it was proof of my esteem, not of your humiliation. . . . If you want to come and put yourself at the head of this army, I'll go to the rear, and then the world can see for itself the destiny I have in mind for you." Before long, he would make good on that promise.

Bolívar traveled tirelessly in the next few months. There was no town in the area he didn't visit. In the course of the next fifty days, while his army rested, he rode through dozens of villages—studied the topography, familiarized himself with the inhabitants—seldom spending more than a day in each stop. Eventually, Manuela Sáenz joined him, having followed him over the freezing cordillera for months. Although there was little time for love, she settled for a while in a comfortable old house in the pretty little town of Jauja. Bolívar was on the move, dictating a steady flow of letters, directing the government in Lima, even trying to manage his navy from that two-hundred-mile remove. But as September became October, the weather began to change. The rain came earlier than usual. By mid-October, the heavens over Jauja and Huancayo had opened and streams that had been easy to cross now became gushing torrents strong enough to fell trees. There was no point in trying to mobilize the army. The land was impassable by man or beast. It wasn't long before Bolívar decided he would return to Lima until the rains abated. There was much to do: establish the capital, win back Callao, receive an influx of foreign troops, govern the newly expanded republic. On October 6, he entrusted the command of the army to Sucre and, along with his aides and secretaries, began the long, rugged ride toward the coast.

When he reached Huancayo on October 24, he was handed yet another reason to descend the cordillera. It was a letter from the Colombian congress in Bogotá, revoking the law that had granted him extraordinary powers. In it, the Liberator was advised that, as of three months before, on July 28, he had been stripped of all his powers. The rationale, described only thinly, was that in accepting the dictatorship of Peru, he had rescinded Colombia's presidency and its military command. Those responsibilities now belonged to Santander. In a subsequent dispatch, Santander was even more stern. He ordered Bolívar to hand over command of all Colombian troops in Peru to Sucre. It was an absurd directive, a rude affront. The men of the military understood—even if their politicians did not—that the liberation of Peru had been undertaken for the greater good and glory of Colombia. That had been the motive in their war on Pasto, the assault on Quito; it had been the understanding in Guayaquil. Santander might have tried to stop congress from taking such harsh actions, but Bolívar could see that his vice president's hand was in them. The trusted "man of laws," as Bolívar called him, had shown his colors. There was no question that long-held jealousies—of Bolívar, of Bolívar's preference for Sucre—had quickened Santander to the task.

When all was said and done, the leadership in Colombia, eager to get on with the business of governing the newly forged and unwieldy republic, had tired of Bolívar's southern campaign. Bolívar's insistence on more and more troops to bolster Peru, more equipment for the army, more horses, had worn thin. Even as Bolívar worked to build military might in Trujillo, Santander had written: "Without a law expressly passed by Congress, I can do nothing, because I have no real power apart from laws, even if the republic ends up going to hell in the process." From the perspective of Bogotá, the ongoing war seemed endless, accruing nothing so much as spiraling expenditures. Some congressmen had even begun to object about soldiers' salaries; others proposed that the government stop issuing uniforms for troops at home and abroad.

Bolívar was outraged. What if he had received these missives relieving him of his position when they had actually been sent—before the triumphant Battle of Junín? What pusillanimous withdrawal would they have caused? Nevertheless, he restrained his anger and communicated the news to Sucre in two memoranda: one was a simple account of Bogotá's decision; the second, a letter for Sucre's eyes only, to be destroyed as soon as it was read. The young general couldn't help but be appalled by the insult delivered to the Liberator. He dutifully informed his officers of congress's decision, although the slight to every warrior in the ranks was clear. The liberating army existed precisely because of Bolívar; to separate the Liberator from it was to separate him from his soul. Sucre and his officers submitted a heated protest to Bogotá, insisting that their leader be allowed to retain his command, but Bolívar refused to send it. He urged Sucre to put the episode behind him, take thorough and aggressive command. His instructions to his general were unequivocal: Sucre was to wait for the propitious moment, engage the enemy in decisive battle, and lead the patriot army to victory once and for all. As for himself, Bolívar stopped sending long candid memos to Santander. His correspondence was clipped, correct, communicating only what was absolutely necessary. On November 10, when the Liberator finally reached the Pacific Ocean at Chancay, a tiny port forty miles north of the capital, he began feverish preparations for a vigorous reentry into Lima.

Bolívar rode into the capital on December 5, 1824, and was met with a jubilant welcome. The people of Lima, more republican now after his victory at Junín, welcomed their dictator with adoration. He wasted no time in focusing on his priorities. Within hours, he imposed a siege to starve the royalists in Callao into submission. He ordered his generals to cut down bridges and destroy any road the Spanish might employ in an assault on Lima. He organized a defensive force of three thousand men, almost all of them fresh arrivals from Colombia, Venezuela, and Panama.

Two days later, he issued an invitation to any and all republics of Spanish America to join a confederation of nations. The institution he had in mind would "serve as a brain trust during major conflicts, a rallying point when facing a common enemy, a faithful interpreter of treaties, a broker of peace when differences between us arise." It was a blunt rejoinder to the Monroe Doctrine. As far as Bolívar was concerned, the newly liberated countries of South America did not need a burly neighbor to protect them. He had fought a fourteen-year revolution without United States help; he had no intention of relying on its muscle now. Banded together as the United States of South America, the former colonies would be self-sufficient, a force for progress, a new world power. It was a dream Bolívar had nursed for more than a decade. "Unity! Unity! Unity!" he had cried five years before at the Congress of Angostura; in the interim, he had changed approach, adjusted strategy, but he had never lost sight of that shining goal. Eventually, his call to union would give birth to a landmark meeting in Panama eighteen months later, the foundations of Pan Americanism for years to come and the modern-day Organization of American States. And for the moment, at least, it allowed the Liberator to rise above the sting of Colombia's ingratitude. His eye was on a higher role.

IN THE RUGGED PERUVIAN LANDSCAPE that lies between the rolling, brown Apurimac River and the mountains of Huanzo, the royalist and patriot armies were stalking each other, moving swiftly, in a constant state of alarm. Sucre's spies had determined that the great mass of the king's army was on the move, with Viceroy La Serna himself at the head, and his two infamously squabbling generals, Canterac and Valdés, close behind. Nine thousand royalists in bright red and gold uniforms— the last bulwark of Spanish rule in America—streamed north of Cuzco, over mountain and vale, in pursuit of the rebel enemy. Valdés had been reined in from battling the ultraconservative Spanish general Olañeta to join La Serna's campaign against the liberating army. After six weeks of a vigorous chase, seven thousand royalists outdistanced Sucre's army and circled around to its flank about thirty miles south of Huamanga.

Sucre, ever unflustered, was not worried by those maneuvers. He had only 5,700 men, but was confident they were superior in every way to the royalists. Mobilizing his troops in a torrential rain, he retreated from a grassy ravine to a more advantageous position. The Spaniards pressed on after them, eager to present battle. Moving with lightning speed, they overtook the patriots again on December 3, nipping them in the rear and annihilating half of the famed British battalion, the "Rifles." Days passed as both armies sought positions for a final conflict. Nearly all the Spanish and patriot forces in Peru would take part in it; there was no doubt it would be the determining battle of Peru's revolution. As December 6 came and went, frantic defections occurred—war prisoners who had been pressed into service on opposing sides ran through the night to rejoin their former cohort.

By December 7—the very day that Bolívar reentered Lima—the two opposing armies had marked their ground. But by then the royalist soldiers had traveled longer, faster, over more precipitous terrain, suffering many privations. They had been marched in strict columns to prevent wholesale desertions; they had not been allowed to enter valleys or villages where provisions (and escape routes) might be found; they had been forced by hunger to eat the flesh of their mules. But on De-

cember 8, they took, at least on the face of it, the stronger position. The
soldiers of the King lined up on the majestic heights of Cundurcunca,
overlooking the broad, flat plain of Ayacucho. Circling the area were
Indian tribes that had pledged to help them; for weeks the local mountain Indians had been raiding patriot encampments and killing men and
cattle; now they vowed to slay any republicans they saw fleeing the field.

Sucre, sighting the royalists as they progressed along the ridges, had
brought his troops to the plain of Ayacucho itself, a dusty mesa surrounded by hulking promontories, more than ten thousand feet above
the sea. His notion was to keep the Spaniards from descending to the
battlefield until the action started, to destroy them as they spilled down
from their perches. The evening before the battle, as dusk cast its long,
dark shadows over the Andes, his troops pressed close to the foot of
Cundurcunca to prevent the enemy from descending in the night. Surrounded on every side by inhospitable nature, the patriots were exactly
where Bolívar would have wanted them to be—in terrain that would
force them to fight with desperate courage.

Dawn on December 9 over the heights of Cundurcunca brought
a resplendent sun. It was one of those cool, crisp Andean mornings in
which the air is a brisk tonic and the land seems suspended in blue. It
was, according to one soldier, the sort of daybreak that lends a warrior
wings. Directly before them was the abrupt rise of Cundurcunca, a
scruffy behemoth of dirt, rock, and shrubbery. To the right, mounting
hills; to the left, a stream; behind, a sheer drop to another plain, and
long vistas as far as the eye could see. There was no place to hide on that
grim plateau. The terrain allowed for no cowards or laggards, no long,
attenuated battle. As the sound of cornets and drums began to resonate
through that theater of war, reechoing against the mountain walls, Sucre's soldiers were well aware that there was no choice for them but to
win. Riding through neatly formed columns of men from every station
of life, every corner of the Americas and beyond, the young general in
chief—then but twenty-nine—was visibly stirred by the significance
of the moment. He stopped and, with a voice brimming with emotion,
shouted words they would never forget: "Soldiers! On your efforts
today rests the fate of South America!" They answered with a resounding roar.

At eight o'clock, as the sun warmed the morning air, one of the Spanish generals, Juan Antonio Monet, a tall, sturdy man with a russet beard, approached the patriot lines and called out to General José María Córdova, whom he knew from former days. Monet told Córdova that in the royalist ranks, as in the patriot, there were soldiers with relatives on the opposite side: would he allow them to greet each other before hostilities began? When General Córdova consulted with Sucre, the general in chief agreed immediately. And so it was that fifty men of opposing sides met on the slopes of Cundurcunca, among them a number of brothers, to embrace and weep—as one chronicler put it—in a heartbreaking display of farewell. Indeed, for Peruvians as for Venezuelans and Colombians before them, revolution meant fratricide, and men who spoke the same language, held the same religion, even shared flesh and blood, would now set upon one another in defense of an idea. Seeing the heart-wrenching scenes, General Monet asked Córdova if there wasn't some way to come to terms and avoid the bloodshed. Córdova answered: Only if you recognize American independence and return peacefully to Spain. Monet was taken aback and said as much: Didn't the young patriot general realize that the Spanish army was vastly superior? Córdova responded that combat would determine whether that was true. Monet walked away shaking his head. There was no turning back.

The battle was fierce, short. The royalists clambered down Cundurcunca in their red, gold, and blue regalia, laboring mightily under the banners, their helmets glinting in the sun. Republicans in dark, somber overcoats lined up to meet them. Cries went up as they watched the enemy troops descend: "Horsemen! Lancers! What you see are hardly warriors! They are not your equals! To freedom!"—and so on, up and down the lines. Before the battle officially began, a young Spanish brigadier was first to attack and first to fall; even so, the royalists took immediate control of the action. General Valdés and his men descended on the republicans like a horde of punishing angels, splitting their formation so wide that it gaped, momentarily helpless. But patriot morale was strong and the setback spurred them to higher resolve. When Córdova cried out, "Soldiers! Man your arms! Move on to victory!" his battalion scrambled to mount a fierce retaliation and soon the course of battle changed. The patriots bayoneted royalists left and right, snatching their silver helmets as trophies. By one in the afternoon, they had taken the heights. By mid-afternoon the field was littered with the fallen. Before sundown, Canterac offered Sucre his unconditional surrender.

Almost three thousand royalists were taken prisoner, surrendering in the face of a daunting republican fervor. Perhaps it was the exhaustion after so many weeks of forced marches; or a terror of Bolívar's famed barbarian hordes; or the dizzying altitude, which, at thirteen thousand feet, can steal the very breath from a man. Or perhaps what prevailed in the end was Sucre's brilliant strategy to make the soldiers of the king work harder, climb higher, march longer; and then strike them with a virulent force. The white-haired viceroy La Serna, fighting bravely to the last, had to be carried off the field with injuries; General Miller, who found him by chance in one of the huts where the wounded were nursed, offered the gallant old soldier tea from his saddlebag and insisted that medics attend to him promptly. The dead amounted to 1,800 for Spain; only 300 for the republicans.

The terms Sucre offered the vanquished were generous, granting every royalist safe passage to Spain, although many chose to transfer to the republican army. But as much as his treaty gave, it extracted. The patriots appropriated Spain's garrisons throughout Peru, confiscated all weapons and supplies, and secured the surrender of Spain's last citadel in the New World, the fort of Callao. When Sucre insisted that General Valdés have lunch with him the next day, the old grizzled Spaniard arrived in full battle dress, in bold contrast to the scarlet and gold of his troops. His heavy wool socks reached high over his knees; his boots were short, his jacket frayed, his vicuña hat pulled low over his skullcap. A long faded white coat reached to his heels, a white poncho was slung over his shoulder. "I drink," said Sucre, "to the man who would have been America's greatest defender, if only he had been born on this side of the sea."

Sucre sent a report to the Liberator immediately, but his messenger was ambushed and killed by Indians. "The battle for Peru is complete," Sucre had written, "its independence and the peace of all America have been signed on this battleground." The news eventually reached Bolívar in Lima more than ten days later, as he was preparing for Spaniards to swarm the capital for a final confrontation—even as he struggled with the Pandora's box that Peru had become. It is said that when he read of his general's victory in Ayacucho, he abandoned all decorum, leapt in the air, and danced through the room, shouting, "Victory! Victory! Victory!" Sucre had won it for him, and Sucre would have his undying gratitude. With Ayacucho, Spain would be evicted from America's shores forever. It was Yorktown, Waterloo. With one single, resounding triumph, all South America would be free.

Anonymous portrait of a young
Bolívar made in Madrid, ca 1799.
Bolívar's wife, María Teresa
Rodríguez del Toro carried
this miniature until her death.
*(Colección Fundación John Boulton,
Caracas)*

The wedding of Simón and María Teresa on May 24, 1802, in Madrid. He was 18;
she was 21. She would die within a year. Tito Salas's painting resides in the *Casa
Natal del Libertador, Caracas.*

Fanny, the countess Dervieu du Villars, with whom Bolívar had an intimate relationship from 1804 to 1806 when he was in Paris to recover from the death of his young wife. *(Ministerio de Educación, Venezuela)*

Bolívar in his full regalia. Painting by Ricardo Acevedo Bernal. *(Palacio Presidencial de San Carlos, Bogotá.)*

Francisco de Miranda, the "Precursor," who boasted friendships with General Lafayette, Thomas Jefferson, Catherine the Great, but whose failed revolution gained him the ire of Bolívar and landed him in the dungeons of Cádiz, where he died. Detail from a painting by Arturo Michelena. *(Galería de Arte Nacional, Caracas)*

The Liberator's "Admirable Campaign" was undertaken in 1813, when Bolívar marched to Caracas and installed the short-lived Second Republic, after liberating New Granada. *(Comisión Para la Conmemoración del Bicentenario de la Independencia, Colombia)*

Manuel Piar, the general Bolívar had executed for trying to start a "race war" during the early days of the Third Republic. *(Anonymous lithograph from Baralt's Resumen, Vol. II, Bethencourt, 1887)*

The Battle of Araure, December 15, 1813, in which Bolívar defeated the superior forces of General Domingo Monteverde. *(Painting by Tito Salas, Casa Natal del Libertador, Caracas)*

The peaks of the Andes in Colombia, over which Bolívar's forces rode many times, most notably before the Battle of Boyacá in 1819. The defining Battle of Ayacucho, which ejected Spain from South America altogether, took place after another of Bolívar's punishing crossings, this time over the Peruvian Andes. *(© Terry Carr/Dreamstime.com)*

The fierce Spanish general Pablo Morillo, Bolívar's nemesis, who negotiated a truce with him in June of 1820, slept in the same room with him after a long night of toasts, and became one of his most admiring correspondents. *(Anonymous painter, courtesy Armada Española)*

General José Antonio Páez, the Lion of the Apure, who helped Bolívar win the Wars of Independence, but ultimately contributed to the Liberator's demise and a rupture with Greater Colombia. Páez rose to the presidency of independent Venezuela three times between 1830 and 1863. *(Library of Congress)*

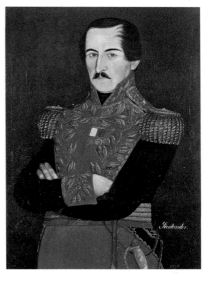

General Francisco Santander, Vice President of Greater Colombia, who went from being Bolívar's right-hand man to being his rival and, perhaps, the mastermind behind the attempt to assassinate him. After the rupture with Venezuela, Santander returned from exile to become president of Colombia. *(Painting by Luis García Hevia, Museo Nacional, Bogotá)*

Bolívar and Santander at the Congress of Cúcuta, 1821, in which Greater Colombia was created from the newly independent regions of Venezuela and New Granada. The congress elected Bolívar and Santander president and vice-president, respectively. *(Painting by Ricardo Acevedo Bernal, La Quinta Museo de Bolívar, Bogotá)*

Antonio José de Sucre, Bolívar's "chosen son," greatest general, and the first president of Bolivia, who was assassinated in the forests of the Andes as he rode home to his wife and baby in Quito in 1830. The assassination had a devastating effect on Bolívar. *(Painting by Arturo Michelena, Colección Gobierno de Bolivia)*

Manuela Sáenz, "The Liberatrix of the Liberator," Bolívar's most enduring lover, who was also an accomplished horsewoman and colonel with the liberating army. Sáenz followed Bolívar from battlefield to palace as he liberated three nations. She saved his life more than once. *(Painting resides in La Quinta Bolívar, Bogotá)*

José de San Martin, the Protector of Lima and liberator of Argentina. After his closed-door meeting with Bolívar in Guayaquil in 1822, he left Lima under the cover of night and relinquished the revolution in Peru to Bolívar. (*Authorship disputed, Museo Historico Nacional, Buenos Aires*)

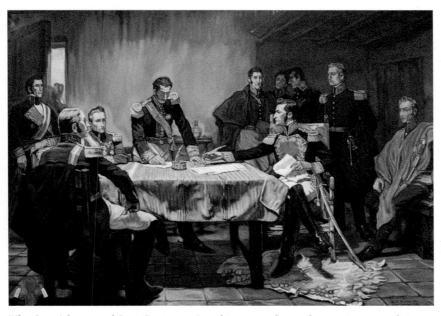

The Spanish general José Canterac signs his surrender to the patriot general Antonio de Sucre after the Battle of Ayacucho, liberating Peru and ending the Wars of Independence in South America. (*Painting by Daniel Hernandez, Lima*)

The presidential palace in Bogotá, the site of the September 25, 1828, assassination attempt on Bolívar's life. At Manuela Sáenz's insistence, he leapt to safety from a window and left her to fend off his assailants. *(Private photo collection)*

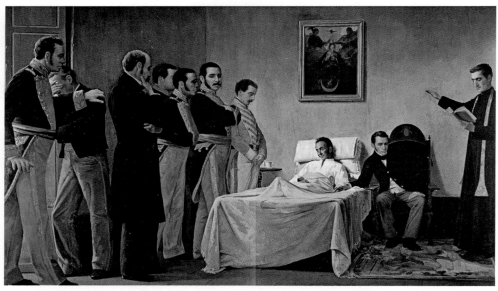

Bolívar died on a sugar plantation in Santa Marta, Colombia, too ill to board a ship and go into exile. *(Painting by Antonio Herrera Toro, Colección Museo Bolivariano, Caracas)*

CHAPTER 14

The Equilibrium of the Universe

*My hope is that our republics—less nations than sisters—will
unite according to the bonds that have always united us, with
the difference that in centuries past we obeyed the same tyrant,
whereas now we will embrace a shared freedom.*

—Simón Bolívar

Bolívar's life had never been short on extremes. But 1824 marked
a new threshold of wild aberrations. He had begun the year in a
sickbed, traveled a veritable wheelwork of triumphs and calamities, and
closed with a victory heard round the world. In London, on the last day
of 1824, Britain announced its recognition of Colombia. In Washington,
on New Year's Day of 1825, Henry Clay stood at a dinner in Lafayette's
honor attended by President Monroe, John Quincy Adams, and Senator
Andrew Jackson, and proposed a toast "to General Simon Bolívar, the
George Washington of South America!" It was just the kind of salute
Bolívar had hoped for from the English-speaking world. The achievements warranted it. Not Alexander, not Hannibal, not even Julius Caesar had fought across such a vast, inhospitable terrain. Charlemagne's
victories would have had to double to match Bolívar's. Napoleon, striving to build an empire, had covered less ground than Bolívar, struggling
to win freedom.

The liberation of South America had created a new world order. The Battle of Ayacucho was not just a military exploit in the faraway dust of Peru, but an action that transformed the hemisphere forever. In banishing Spain from American shores, the revolutionaries had confirmed the fundamental incompatibility between America and Europe; they had drawn a firm line between Europe's conservative worldview and its radical opposite—between ancient monarchies and a fresh democratic ideal. There would be no common ground between Europe's Holy Alliance, now scrambling to preserve its old axis of power, and the Americas North and South, which were committed to turn those hierarchies upside down. As Bolívar pointed out, "European ambition forced the yoke of slavery on the rest of the world, and the rest of the world was obliged to answer with an equivalent force. . . . This is what I call the equilibrium of the Universe." It was the essence of Bolívarianism, a clear admonition to bullies. As far as Bolívar was concerned now that the revolution was won, South America needed no overseer, no higher might, no Monroe Doctrine. In his model, the will to power would come from the people themselves, and—with all the republics united— it would be a prodigious force to be reckoned with.

The next few months were the happiest, most glorious of Bolívar's life. He gave all the credit for his triumph to Sucre—"this splendid victory is due entirely to the skill, valor, and heroism of the general in chief," he announced—and he promoted him to grand marshal. Bolívar received the eminent along with the humble in his capacious house in Lima's suburb of Magdalena; although he reveled in the adulation, he wasted no time reforming Peru according to democratic principle. He reorganized the government, the treasury, the legal system, the schools. He tendered his resignation from the Colombian presidency, telling Santander that he planned to leave Colombia someday and take up residence overseas. When the resignation was read out to congress in Bogotá, the assembly fell into a stunned silence; the man was renowned throughout the world now, adored. Presidents and magnates had toasted the Republic of Greater Colombia because of him. The eminent British diplomat John Potter Hamilton had gone so far as to call Bolívar "the greatest man and most extraordinary character which the New World has ever produced." A few congressmen sounded scattered applause for the Liberator and soon the rest broke into a wild ovation. They moved to reaffirm his presidency of Colombia. In this halcyon moment, even avowed enemies dared not complain.

But Bolívar was hardly ready to leave Peru. There was too much unfinished business. It would take several months to subdue the renegade Spanish general Olañeta, who had turned out to be more monarchist than the viceroy, more authoritarian than the king himself; and it would take another year to flush out the royalists in Callao, who had locked themselves up in the fortress against all reasonable hope of survival. Bolívar announced that he would call the Peruvian congress to session on February 10. That day, he said, "will be the day of my glory, the day on which my most fervent desires will be fulfilled; the day on which, once and for all, I resign my rule." By rule he meant dictatorship; he had every intention of staying on and determining the future of the republic. When February 10 came, an ecstatic Peruvian congress made that possible: he was granted supreme political and military authority for at least another year. The congress also presented him with a gift of one million pesos to compensate him for his victories. He refused to accept it. When the money was offered again—indeed, insisted upon—he asked that it be given not to him but to charitable causes in Venezuela, the republic that had sacrificed most on behalf of Peru.

Those happy days were marred, nevertheless, by the assassination of Bernardo Monteagudo, San Martín's widely despised deputy, who had been expelled from Lima during San Martín's tenure only to return again under Bolívar. Monteagudo, whose agile mind the Liberator respected, had been working on his notion to unite all the republics. The Argentine was found facedown on a street with a kitchen knife plunged deep into his heart and his fingers wrapped tightly around the handle. Dismayed by the crime—and fearing it might be part of a royalist plot to assassinate republican leaders—Bolívar called for an investigation. The inquest soon produced the assassin: a black cook, who worked in the kitchen of one of Monteagudo's associates. When Bolívar questioned the cook himself—in private, in a dimly lit room of the palace—the trembling man confessed that José Sánchez Carrión, Bolívar's highest minister, had paid him 200 pesos in gold to do the deed. The Liberator was flabbergasted; Sánchez Carrión was a brilliant intellectual, a republican stalwart, Bolívar's warmest supporter in Peru. He was also the leader of a powerful secret society. Mysteriously enough, within a few months, Sánchez Carrión, too, tipped over dead. According to a high-ranking official, a Peruvian general had poisoned him. Stranger yet, that general was eventually murdered. It was a murky chain of events and much of it played out after Bolívar had left to tour the country. As far as the people of Lima were concerned, the despised Monteagudo had met a just fate. They had loathed the Argentine when he was San Martín's éminence grise and they loathed him under Bolívar. He was quickly forgotten in the whirl of that triumphant summer. There were festivities to attend—a grand ball in honor of the victory at Ayacucho, a pending assembly of the Peruvian congress. The city was in a celebratory mood.

Bolívar delighted in the public tributes. Seldom had he received such complete adoration. He had lost much in the course of his forty-one years: mother, father, brother, wife, a country to which he would never truly return, countless fellow warriors, and in the course of the past year his best friend, Fernando Toro, who had died after long exile. The Liberator's name was known around the globe, but his intimates were few. He was virtually alone, except for his manservant, José Palacios, and his married mistress.

During those blissful months, Bolívar enjoyed the unbridled attentions of Manuela Sáenz, who basked in the republican glow beside him. Coming and going freely from his house in Magdalena, she scandalized Lima society with her brazen disregard for decorum. She was hardly free of her husband, but she was long past caring about appearances. James Thorne had struck every register of rage—from sputtering indignation to wretched entreaty—to persuade her to end her affair with Bolívar. Thorne was possessive, "more jealous than a Portuguese," according to Manuela, and he was tired of the public humiliation. It may well be that he swallowed his pride and begged Bolívar to release her; he may even have gone so far as to file a legal suit to restrain her. Deeply in love, and adamantly unwilling to give up his pretty young wife, he was prepared to do anything to win her back.

Sáenz was forthright—even brutal—in her rejection of Thorne. She didn't want his money; and she most assuredly did not want him. Even as Bolívar was wending his way back to Lima in late 1823, she had written to her husband in no uncertain terms:

> No, no, no, hombre! . . . A thousand times No! Sir, you are an excellent person, indeed one of a kind—that I will never deny. I only regret that you are not a better man so that my leaving you would honor Bolívar more. I know very well that I can never be joined to him in what you call honor. Do you think I am any less honorable because he is my lover, not my husband? Ah! I do not live by social conventions men construct to torment us. So leave me be, my dear Englishman. We will marry again in heaven but not on this earth. . . . On earth, you are a boring man. Up there in the celestial heights, everything will be so English, because a life of monotony was invented for you people, who make love without pleasure, conversation without grace—who walk slowly, greet solemnly, move heavily, joke without laughing. . . . But enough of my cheekiness. With all the sobriety, truth, and clarity of an Englishwoman, I say now: I will never return to you. You are a protestant and I a pagan—that should be obstacle enough. But I am also in love with another man, and that is the greater, stronger reason. You see how precise my mind can be? Your invariable friend, Manuela

She would later send a copy of this letter to Bolívar, adding coyly that she was hardly a pagan, but had said so for dramatic effect. Certainly to the rest of Lima she seemed diabolically pagan. Even in a city where women smoked cigars, dressed like coquettes, and spoke their minds freely, Manuela was a flagrant eccentric. Jean-Baptiste Boussingault, an overheated young Frenchman whom Humboldt had pressed on Bolívar and who followed the Liberator closely during those years, described her unforgettably in his own memoir:

> At times she behaved like a grand lady, at others like a half-breed; she could dance the minuet or the cancan with equal flair. She was shockingly reckless, promiscuous. The aides told me astonishing tales about her exploits, which Bolívar simply ignored. She was insepa-

rable from her beautiful, young mulatto slave, who often dressed as a soldier. That colored girl was the very shadow of her mistress and, very possibly, her lover—a vice common enough in Peru and one that I myself witnessed. The girl performed lewd, but quite entertaining dances at salon gatherings. And she came and went freely at all hours from Manuelita's room. We can imagine why.

Boussingault had a singular turn of mind in this, to be sure, and it may well be that the twenty-two-year-old was infatuated with Manuela himself. But if it was true that Manuela was erratic, a slave to her senses, it was also true that Bolívar didn't much care. The Liberator's letters to her are filled with tenderness, admiration. He was in love with his mistress's humor, her passion, her courage, her intelligence, and—no doubt, too—her tolerance for his own aberrant ways.

ONCE THE TRIBUTES AND CELEBRATIONS were out of the way, Peru seemed to lose interest in reforming the country. Indeed the entire continent of South America appeared to slide into weary lassitude. The people were exhausted after fourteen years of unremitting violence and chaos. It was as if the very effort of upending the colonial structure had left them without a will to build something new. Far from spurring an era of creativity like the one that now flourished in the United States, newly won liberty gave Spanish Americans a sense that the work was behind them now, that the social challenges were too monumental to tackle—that, having made so many sacrifices, the people had earned the right to sit back and take.

Bolívar wasted no time in trying to inject the country with his spirit of reform. He sent Sucre and his army to La Paz to carry the spirit of liberation into Upper Peru, the region traded back and forth between Lima and Buenos Aires that eventually would be Bolivia. In April, he started out on an overland trip of his own, averaging an astounding twenty-one miles a day, all of it on horseback, and most over rough terrain. The trails along the coast were dry with a choking dust; the gorges stifling, airless. But as he approached the towering volcanoes of Arequipa, he was met with a sight that seldom fails to move a traveler. It was the point that marks the western limit of the desert, where burning sands climb to majestic heights; where a multitude of snowcapped peaks glisten against azure skies. He rode through the desolation and the mountain splendor, visiting every township along the way; he founded schools, laws, municipal governments. But the vigor he brought with him seemed to dissipate the moment he was gone. Appointments, institutions, visions thrived for a while in his wake until they went neglected—then quietly faded away.

In Arequipa, he installed the British Lancaster method of education, putting his old childhood teacher, Simón Rodríguez, in charge. Bolívar had been thrilled to hear that the eccentric, imaginative tutor who had opened his mind to the wider world had returned to South America after decades of exile; he urged Rodríguez to come to Peru. Eventually, he would give Rodríguez the responsibility of revamping the entire school system in Bolivia. But Rodríguez, who had turned up by chance after years of aimless peregrinations around the world, had never been handed so great a responsibility. He was now little more than a bumbling professor, spectacularly unprepared for the task. Like many who were entrusted with vital work at this critical juncture, Rodríguez lacked organizational skills. Building a nation was turning out to be far more thorny than waging an all-out war. San Martín, even from his faraway perch in Brussels, could see the challenge before Bolívar now: "The opus is finished," San Martín wrote to a colleague, "and Americans will begin to see the fruits of their labors and sacrifices; but only if we are wise, and only if twelve years of revolution have taught us to obey—yes, sir, *obey*—for if a man doesn't know how to obey, he will never know how to lead." He had a point. What South America needed now was organization, discipline, a solid foundation of laws. One man couldn't possibly hope to do it all.

On June 25, Cuzco gave Bolívar a welcome unlike any he had ever experienced. Triumphal arches leapt up to greet him along the mountain roads, reminding him of the ones that had welcomed Napoleon to Rome. Cuzco itself was a glorious sight to behold. Gold and silver ornaments were hung from the houses; rich brocades festooned the streets. But as he climbed toward the city, it was the breathtaking panorama and the hardy mountain folk who moved him. Peru here—unlike Lima—it seemed to him, was a fierce original; its Indians a noble breed. The ancient Inca capital had not suffered during the punishing revolution—and yet the Indian civilization had been stalled for three hundred years.

He was presented with a crown studded with pearls and diamonds; golden keys to the city; a horse in a gilded harness, a rich assortment of jewels. In the end, he sent the crown to Sucre, gave the gold and jewels to his aides, and kept only the horse. He stayed for a month, busily issuing laws and decrees. He eliminated all titles of nobility held by descendants of the Inca, just as he had eliminated those that were held by whites; he distributed land to the indigenous peoples; he abolished all race-based taxes. He felt drawn to the plight of the Indians. "I want to do all that is possible for them," he wrote Santander, "first, for the good of humanity; second, because they have a right to it; and, ultimately, because doing the right thing costs so little and is worth so much." Every day brought opportunities to undo Spain's draconian laws: he ordered roads built, demanded that monasteries be converted into schools, built an aqueduct, established the College of Cuzco. But his sympathies for the people of this mountain aerie seemed to confirm that there was something repellent about Peru as a whole—a national character he deeply disliked, forged by a bitter history. He spoke of this aversion only privately, but the prejudice he had brought with him to Lima—the profound conviction that wealth and slavery had ruined the country—ultimately defined his Peruvian experience.

By August, he was traveling the vertiginous route to La Paz, the capital of Upper Peru. The ride was grueling, but conspicuously free of enemies. The last of the Spanish generals, the renegade Olañeta, stubbornly prowling those mountains for two years, had died months before, mortally wounded in battle. Word had it that he had met his end at the hands of his own men; indeed, he had been the only victim in a fleeting skirmish against Sucre's army. Seeing Olañeta fall from his horse, his soldiers—a fraction of his original force—rushed to surrender. It was hardly surprising, as royalist defections after the Battle of Ayacucho had been epidemic; everyone wanted to be on Sucre's side. The grand marshal proceeded to carry out his assignment in Upper Peru admirably.

Sucre met Bolívar on the shores of Lake Titicaca not far from where the old viceroyalty of Peru ended and the old viceroyalty of Buenos Aires began. There, at long last, Bolívar embraced Sucre and thanked him for his many momentous achievements: the victory at Ayacucho, the suppression of Olañeta, the successful occupation of La Paz and Potosí. It had been almost a year since they had seen each other.

Sucre's skirmish with Olañeta represented the last battle against Spain on the American mainland. In the scant year since Bolívar had marched from Trujillo with his hastily improvised troops, an army of eighteen thousand had been brought to ruin. Bolívar's strategies had been masterful, his preparations meticulous, but it had been Sucre who had brought the patriots to their resounding final victory and it was Sucre who soared to fame throughout Peru. He seemed invincible, a colossus among his Latin American contemporaries. Wherever he went, he was cheered, admired, and Bolívar did not grudge him one bit of the adulation. From Pichincha to Potosí, the young general had brought the patriots nothing but glory. Bolívar took every opportunity to say so. When, in La Paz, the Liberator was handed another crown, he passed it—with gallant flourish—to Sucre. "This belongs to the true victor," he said.

But as united as Bolívar and Sucre could be about military matters, they often disagreed about the politics of liberation. It was a measure of how well they worked together: Sucre was unafraid to tell the Liberator things he didn't want to hear, and, from Sucre, Bolívar didn't mind hearing them. Bolívar had not wanted to hear that Upper Peru should be left to determine its own future. The region was something of an anomaly—not a province, not a people. According to founding principles, a new republic was supposed to follow the contours of the viceroyalty that immediately preceded it, and so, by all accounts, Upper Peru should have answered to Buenos Aires. But Bolívar wasn't about to forfeit the mineral-rich region to Argentina, and so his solution had been to make Upper Peru a sovereign republic. Bolívar's thinking seemed to him as just as it was logical: to deliver the region to war-torn Argentina was to deliver it to anarchy; to deliver it to Peru would be to vitiate the founding principles the revolutionaries had long since established. When he had first arrived in La Paz, Sucre had told its citizens that he wasn't there to resolve such questions. He was there to liberate, not govern. Bolívar soon disabused him of that idea. They were there to liberate, to be sure; but they were also there to fashion a new America.

The vastly wealthy Creole aristocrats who guarded the silver-veined hills of Potosí were all too happy to abide by Bolívar's decision to declare themselves an autonomous nation. Most Upper Peruvians had been followers of the ultraconservative, quixotic Olañeta—indeed one of their present political leaders was his nephew—and now they were being assured that they would not have to answer to anyone; that all the riches of Potosí, the treasure of so many kings, would be theirs alone.

A hastily gathered assembly of representatives, "elected" by laws that were clearly arbitrary and racist, met in Chuquisaca on July 10 to formally deliberate the founding. It was hardly a democratic exercise. The Aymara Indians—an overwhelming majority of the population, forty thousand of whom had risen up against their masters forty years before—were given no say, and the pecking order that once had prevailed under Spanish rule was put in place again: the whites would lord over the half-breeds, and the half-breeds would lord over the brown.

On August 6 the members of the assembly officially declared the independence of Upper Peru, changed its name to the Republic of Bolívar, changed it again to Bolivia, and voted to make the Liberator their president. To give him absolute power, they invited the new president to draft their constitution. Bolívar, who was rounding the shimmering, cold waters of Lake Titicaca when he heard of it, was delighted with the news. In the course of one day, his America had acquired a million souls. As maximum leader of three vast republics, Bolívar now ruled over an area that, taken together, exceeded the size of modern Europe. He hurried to accept the honors.

IF BOLÍVAR WAS AT THE zenith of his career, Spanish America, as a whole, appeared to be heading toward its nadir. From the deserts of Mexico to the pampas of Argentina, independence had brought not a bright new world, but a dizzying surfeit of obstacles. Fatigue was soon overtaken by irritability, ushering in an era of discontent. Bolívar seemed to sense it before it happened. He pressed for the conference of new American republics, his Congress of Panama, to take place as soon as possible. He wanted to capture the flush of enthusiasm that accompanied revolution—have his fledgling republics share ideas before they acted on them—and he wanted to be at the vanguard of that process. "If we wait any longer," he told the leaders he had invited, "if each of us waits to see what the other will do, we will deprive ourselves of the advantages." But as 1825 ground on, it was evident that the republics were too mired in their own troubles to think about a wider American ideal. As festivities wound down in Lima at the end of February, Bolívar noted a viral dread creeping into the Creole population, a sense that freedoms would bring social upheaval, and that anarchy would be democracy's next step.

Indeed, anarchy had already begun in Mexico. After the spectacular collapse of Emperor Agustín de Iturbide's reign and his summary execution, the country was in financial ruin: London bankers had stepped in with loans, making the nation a bit player in Britain's vast economic empire. British foreign minister George Canning was euphoric: "We slip in between," he wrote a fellow countryman, "and plant ourselves in Mexico. . . . we link once more America to Europe." He made no secret that in doing so, he felt he had won a victory over Britain's former colony, the swiftly expanding United States.

Greater Colombia, too, had its problems. A corrosive peevishness had set in between Caracas and Bogotá. Páez and Santander, whose hatred for one another was evident, were squabbling, readying for a face-off. Bolívar's proud creation seemed irreparably shot through with fissures. Chile, too, was riven by conflict: its leadership was hesitant, its southern provinces still at war. Argentina was no better. On the verge of declaring war with Brazil over a patch of borderland called the Banda Oriental (Uruguay), the Argentines begged Bolívar to assist them. They courted him throughout his stay in La Paz and Potosí, sending various delegations to convince him to come to their rescue.

Bolívar toyed with the notion of taking his liberating army to the nethermost regions of the American continent, even wrote to Santander to sound out the idea. "The demon of glory will carry us to Tierra del Fuego," he wrote animatedly, "and the truth is: what would we risk?" In many ways, it would have been the apotheosis of Bolívar's American dream, a campaign to fulfill his grand continental ambition. The celebrations in the extravagant heights of Potosí had seemed to persuade

him that there were no limits to possibility—his words so euphoric that
Sucre had cried like a baby and Bolívar's old teacher Rodríguez had
leapt in the air with joy. But when Santander wrote back, exploding in
disbelief at the very notion of a march farther south, Bolívar realized the
folly of it. The conflict between Brazil and Argentina was full of perils;
to enter into it was to declare another war against a colonial empire
and alienate all Europe. Santander reminded Bolívar that there was yet
another reason to say no: Greater Colombia was in shambles. The letter
was unequivocal:

> The miserable state of our financial affairs has forced me to suspend
> all combat. Ten years of peace would set us straight. Today our army
> has estimated costs of 16 to 18 million dollars. Our income is 7 to
> 8. From where will we extract the difference? We need to reduce
> spending unless we want to wither away entirely, and the way to do
> that may be to shrink the army, get rid of the navy.

He was proposing to collapse the very institution that Bolívar had
built so carefully, a military that represented the fusion of all races, the
miraculous engine that had won America's freedom. There was no
doubt: times were dire. Santander was proving true to the appellation
Bolívar had given him. He was the "man of laws," the stern voice of
reason. Sucre, on the other hand, had been Bolívar's "man of war." And
Bolívar, thrashing about to advance an agenda for the hemisphere, had
become—in his own mind, at least—America's "man of difficulties."
The future would bear this out.

BOLÍVAR HAD TOURED THE SOUTH for almost a year when he returned to
Lima on February 10, 1826, and found the capital in a joyous mood. The
royalist forces that had entombed themselves in Callao had just surrendered. Torre Tagle's minions had consumed the last rat in the fortress,
perished by the thousands, and, starved into submission, yielded the last
patch of Spanish soil on America's mainland. The city celebrated for
days. When Bolívar stepped ashore, he, too, was met with elation. But
anyone who thought all was well now would be sorely mistaken.

Almost immediately, Bolívar was handed an agitated letter from

Páez, reporting the miserable state of affairs in Venezuela. "You cannot imagine how ruinous the intrigues have been in this country," Páez told him. "Morillo was right when he said he did you a favor when he killed all the lawyers." But according to Páez, the Spaniards hadn't killed enough of them. It was men of laws, he insisted, who were crippling the republic. He begged Bolívar to return, crown himself king, and wrest a modicum of order from the chaos. Páez didn't tell the whole tale, but he had been accused of brutal methods of recruitment. He claimed that he had only responded to duty, that royalists in Havana were poised to attack the coast and the country was desperate for soldiers. To Páez, and to the many Venezuelans who venerated him, the accusations of violence were only a ruse by lawyers in Bogotá—and, by extension, Santander—to humiliate the army and drive Páez from power. Páez pleaded with Bolívar to return as Napoleon had returned to France: with a crown on his head and a strong arm that brooked no argument.

"Colombia is not France," Bolívar replied to Páez, "and I am not Napoleon." For him, the title of Liberator was far superior to any a monarchy might bestow. But a wider campaign to crown Bolívar was clearly afoot in Venezuela. Bolívar soon received a letter from his sister María Antonia, advising him that if anyone urged him to the throne, he should resist at all costs. "Tell them you will be Liberator or nothing, that is your true title, the one that honors your hard-won glory." Eventually, Sucre told him the same thing. But it was clear that Venezuela was in such turmoil that it was grasping at extreme solutions. Its needs were urgent, and yet his work in Peru was hardly finished. His house in Magdalena had become a hive of Latin American activity. Foreign delegates came and went offering ideas; representatives from new republics constantly appeared with proposals; Peruvians who feared a vacuum of power begged him to stay.

Critics of Bolívar—and Peru is replete with them—say that he should have left Lima there and then. The war was won, the last Spaniard stripped of power, the question of Upper Peru resolved. Why would a lover of liberty with a nation's best interests at heart remain with a vast army of occupation? Bolívar had his reasons. First, he had been beseeched to stay. Second, and more convincing, the political situation in Peru was tenuous, bordering on ruin. During his travels outside

Lima, he had delegated power to José de La Mar, a Peruvian general born near Guayaquil, or to Hipólito Unanúe, the Peruvian doctor who had nursed him to health in Pativilca. But after the serial treacheries of Riva Agüero and Torre Tagle, he harbored an essential distrust of Peruvians; he was reluctant to leave them to themselves. As the days wore on and he concentrated on putting the finishes touches on the Bolivian constitution, he became convinced that the document he was creating was the answer to all of America's ills.

BOLÍVAR'S CONSTITUTION WAS A TESTAMENT to how the social realities of the continent had altered his liberating vision; it was a curious combination of deeply held republican principle and authoritarian rule. He had long feared the lawlessness that a hastily conceived democracy might bring. To hand power too quickly to illiterate masses was to snuff out what little order there was. He had once told a British diplomat in Lima, "If principles of liberty are too rapidly introduced, anarchy and a wholesale purge of whites will be the inevitable consequences." In other words, he had granted all races equality, but he worried that in the process of institutionalizing it, the blacks and Indians would simply kill off the old aristocracy—the very class from which he hailed. It was exactly what had happened in Haiti. Bolívar's new constitution meant to free the people, and yet, for their own good, keep them in a tight harness.

His constitution's proposed division of powers—executive, legislative, judicial—was similar to that of the United States, although he added a fourth branch, a separate electoral college. The legislative branch was to be made up of senators, tribunes, and censors. Senators were to enact and guard the laws; tribunes would deal with money and war; censors would safeguard liberties. The government would offer the people a "moral" education in order to instill principles of civic responsibility. The constitution provided for freedoms of speech, press, work, and passage. It ensured citizens all the benefits of personal security, equality before the law, and a jury-based system of justice. It abolished slavery. It put an end to all social privilege. Up to this point, Bolívar's constitution resembled—even improved on—its British and United States counterparts. Where it differed starkly was in its conditions for the presidency, and it was here that the document ran aground.

Bolívar had stipulated that the president be appointed for life. To him, presidential power was key; upon it would rest the entire Bolívarian concept of order. Although he claimed that he had rendered the position headless and harmless because a president would be powerless to appoint anyone to the legislative government or to the courts, there was no doubt that the presidency would be the most powerful institution in the land. A president's influence would extend into perpetuity by virtue of his ability to choose a vice president, who would be his successor. Thus, Bolívar contended, "we shall avoid elections, which always result in that great scourge of republics, anarchy . . . the most imminent and terrible peril of popular government." He had come a long way from his address to the congress of Angostura seven years before, in which he had roundly averred: "Regular elections are essential to popular government, for nothing is more perilous than to permit one citizen to retain power for an extended period." In the course of taking his wars of liberation south, he had changed his mind entirely.

When the Bolivian constitution was complete, Bolívar sent that "ark of the covenant" off to Sucre in Bolivia, in a special mission led by his personal aide, Colonel Belford Wilson. Eager to promote its adoption in other republics, he had several editions printed and dispatched to Colombia by the very courier who had delivered Páez's message begging him to become king. In Peru, his secretary of state made sure that every member of the electoral college had a copy. Bolívar's constitution, in short, was to be distributed as widely as possible, throughout the Americas as well as strategic points in Europe. As his handiwork circulated, reactions were mixed. The English regarded it as an enlightened charter, generous in its promised liberties, but wise in its mitigation of a "mischievous excess of popular power." In the United States, on the other hand, legislators were outraged by its provision for a president for life; Southern politicians were infuriated by its abolition of slavery. In South America, opinions were divided. In Chile and Argentina, it was received with moderate praise; in Colombia, it was trooped from town to town by a Venezuelan known to have urged Bolívar to the throne, and so it was no surprise that it was seen as a prologue to monarchy. At first, Santander withheld his opinion, knowing that for the vice president to disagree with the president would be impolitic. He wrote to Bolívar that he considered the document "liberal and popular, strong and vigorous." Privately, he complained that it was "absurd, a dangerous novelty." Within months, he was assailing the constitution openly in Bogotá's *Gaceta*.

In Lima, Bolívar's cabal of enemies only grew, fed mightily by this new evidence of his appetite for power. Nevertheless, the secretary of state's firm pressure on the outlying electoral colleges worked. Peru became the first country to adopt the constitution—not one patriot publicly objected—although time and circumstance eventually prevented the charter from ever being put to full use.

The Bolivian congress, on the other hand, didn't approve the constitution right away, and when it did, it did so with great caution. Bolívar had left Bolivia in Sucre's capable hands, urging him to take on the presidency of the republic. Initially, Sucre had demurred: he was a military man, he insisted, not a politician. Furthermore, he ardently hoped to return to Colombia to marry his fiancée, the beautiful Marquesa de Solanda. He was tired of governing and had tendered his resignation repeatedly, but Bolívar had always refused to accept it. "We need to take up the work of founding and fostering nations," Bolívar had said. "We will show Europe that America has men every equal of the heroes of the ancient world." Months later, when the new constitution was adopted in Bolivia along with its provision for a president for life, Sucre was elected to the position, but he agreed to hold office for only two years.

Historians have long pointed to the Bolivian constitution as proof of Bolívar's inordinate love of power. Some have gone so far as to claim that it was the first glimmer of a spiraling madness. There is little doubt that its presidential clause was a blunder of colossal proportions. Just as San Martín had made the error of introducing a monarch into his liberating plan, Bolívar was now introducing a lifelong ruler. But Bolívar did not aspire to wear a crown. He despised hereditary power and had expressly forbidden his family to seek political office. All the same, he adored being called Liberator and longed to be remembered as the founder of his America, the alchemist of its freedom, a living arc of enlightenment. He had made it plain that although he enjoyed a ruler's esteem, he was averse to the quotidian business that attended it.

It is also fair to say that he didn't want the responsibility of ruling over any one nation because he wanted something far larger. He yearned to be the father of a federation of nations and said so very plainly to Santander. You rule Colombia, Bolívar told him, "so that I may be permitted to govern all South America." It was why he would apply himself so vigorously to organizing the Congress of Panama.

He knew this would not be easy. He had always made it clear that the continent could not function as a single, integrated country; the landmass was too sprawling, the population too diverse. To complicate matters, Spain had never encouraged camaraderie among its colonies— travel and commerce had been forbidden and punished by death—and so for three hundred years the colonies had answered to Madrid as spokes to a hub, with no contact whatsoever among them. They did not know one another well enough to be fellow citizens. But Bolívar saw the Spanish-speaking nations of America as potential brothers in a grand fraternity, bound by common laws and protected by a single military. In this, he had some fundamental rules: peace would be kept, the slave trade stopped, international relations encouraged, a coherent system of cooperation established. It was a visionary scheme with vaulting ambition and, soon enough, he saw that it presented overwhelming challenges. Urged on by his advisors, he began to think such a construct might be more appropriate for the countries he himself had liberated. He called this more focused version the Federation of the Andes, and it stretched from Panama to Potosí. Although each nation would remain a separate entity, there would be but one army, one code of racial equality, one face against the world. That face would be embodied in a shared constitution: his own. And to coax it through infancy, the federation would enjoy a special relationship—a protectorate of sorts—with England.

Even as he was conjuring this idea of a tighter Andean federation, Bolívar continued with the Congress of Panama as he had initially conceived it. He had long since instructed Santander, who was managing the details, not to invite Haiti, Brazil, or the United States. They were derived from different nations and cultures, after all. But he also felt they would make awkward partners in the conversation. Haiti was too black, the United States too white, to accept the unconditional equality of races he would require. Moreover, it was evident that with the Monroe Doctrine the United States saw itself as master of the hemisphere; it would fight Bolívar's vision of a robust South American union every step of the way. In this, Bolívar ironically agreed with Count Aranda, an advisor to the Spanish throne, who—long before, in the year of Bolívar's birth—had said of the United States, "There will come a time when she is a giant, a colossus even, much to be feared in those vast regions. Then, she will forget the benefits she received from others and think only of aggrandizing herself." No, Bolívar did not want the United States invited. As for Brazil, it was incompatible with republicanism by virtue of its monarchical tie to Portugal. Santander eventually defied Bolívar's instructions and invited Brazil and the United States anyway, claiming it was in the interest of forging a larger hemispheric union. Bolívar took that insubordination in stride, but it was one more indication that he couldn't trust his vice president.

The conference was to take place on June 22, 1826, on the Isthmus of Panama—an echo, if only symbolic—of ancient Greece's Amphictyonic League, which had met on the Isthmus of Corinth. Bolívar had decided not to attend the proceedings so that it couldn't be said that he had influenced its outcome. But it was precisely to influence the outcome that the Peruvian delegation arrived six months early, hoping to lay the groundwork for its point of view. As deliberations opened, the nations represented were Peru, Greater Colombia (which now consisted of Venezuela, Panama, Ecuador, and New Granada), Mexico, and the Federal Republic of Central America; that is to say, only four of the seven Latin American republics. The Argentines had declined outright, saying that they had "a horror of too early a union," especially one advanced so unilaterally by Colombia. Chile had been too wrenched by internal conflagrations to participate; Bolivia had been willing, but its delegates arrived too late. The kingdom of Brazil, a monarchy with far stronger sympathies for Europe, had also refused, using its war with Argentina as an excuse. The United States, after passionate objection from its slaveholding states, sent two delegates, but one died on the way, the second reached the meeting hall only after the congress was over.

When all was said and done, the congress was a resounding failure. Delegates gathering in the stuffy Franciscan monastery in Panama's sweltering capital had been all too eager to be done with the debate.

Some were ailing, others fearful of the pestilential climate; all were anxious about the motives. The proceedings, which had been meant to go for almost two months, lasted a mere three weeks. Only Colombia ratified the empty initiatives, and nothing was done to advance Bolívar's concept of a league of nations. The only country that made progress worth recording was England, which attended as an observer and walked away with a passel of commercial contracts. Like Mexico, whose failures had become a boon to British financiers, the Congress of Panama became a marketplace for foreign mongers. Bolívar's dream of a larger America had dispersed like a mist in the equatorial sun.

~ CHAPTER 15 ~

Era of Blunders

We have arrived at an era of blunders. In order to fix one, we commit fifty.

—Pedro Briceño Méndez

The Congress of Panama was a bitter disappointment to Bolívar. "The institution was admirable," he wrote Páez, but it ended "like that mythic madman, perched on a rock in the open sea, thinking he could direct the ships' traffic." Just as warlords had plagued the revolution with small-minded ambitions, republics now threatened to undermine one another with toxic distrust.

Little seemed to have gone well since Bolívar's return to Lima. His enemies had grown in number; accusations flowed. Bolívar might have been a hero before he arrived, one Peruvian fumed, "but he is working with a randomness and immorality so thorough that the public has had to reevaluate its opinion." They enumerated the transgressions: the "violent" occupation of Guayaquil; the ouster of its president; his arbitrary appropriation of power in Peru; the forced labor to which he had subjected the people of Trujillo; his summary expulsion of President Riva Agüero. In the end, one writer fretted, Bolívar's resounding victory in Ayacucho had silenced all healthy discourse.

The negative press had a powerful effect. It was as if Peru had forgotten that Bolívar's armies—tattered and colored as they may have been—had won its freedom. As he traveled the countryside and the army of liberation lingered, the people of Lima began to grumble openly. Hadn't the man promised he would throw off the ruler's mantle and leave "without so much as a grain of sand" once the revolution was over? They resented the legions of dark-skinned aliens who remained among them, consuming their sparse supplies like a swarm of locusts. Nor had they forgotten Bolívar's speech after the Battle of Ayacucho, in which he had said that for him to remain would be absurd, monstrous, disgraceful. "I am a foreigner," he had told them, "I came to assist you as a warrior, not to rule over you as a politician. . . . If I were to accept the position your legislators are pressing on me, Peru would become a parasite nation, affixed to Colombia, where I am president and where I was born." But a year and a half had passed since he had uttered those words, and still he was in Lima. Still ruling.

In July of 1826, just as the Congress of Panama collapsed, his staff in Lima discovered a plot to assassinate him. The conspiracy had aimed to expel all Colombians, murder Bolívar, and return power to Peruvian hands. Its organizers, high-level ministers, were summarily deported or executed; Bolívar approved the sentences. But the distrust could not be disposed of so easily. In Lima, the white aristocracy had come to regard Bolívar as a mulatto who was trying to upend their carefully constructed world with ludicrous notions of racial egalitarianism. "Sambo," they called him—Nigger—as if the black blood rumored to course in his veins explained all his harebrained ideals about equality. Yet many of those same aristocrats became genuinely alarmed when they heard Bolívar was finally contemplating a departure. Worried about the government's ability to keep the peace, they streamed to his door to persuade him to stay. The specter of anarchy loomed large in that land of gold and slaves.

But by August Bolívar had made up his mind. Too many troubles threatened his homeland. Páez had broken with Bogotá and, in a brazen coup, tried to assume a separate power in Venezuela. It was, at once, an act of treason and an expression of loyalty to the Liberator. Riding bareback from Valencia to Caracas, raising his rebellion, Páez had shouted for all to hear, "Viva Bolívar! Viva the Republic!" At first the Venezuelan people, frustrated with Bogotá, had responded to Páez's call so enthusiastically that Santander—who had never been adept in the language of truculence—was at a loss as to how to respond. But he knew that he wanted to prevent a full-scale civil war. He begged Bolívar to return and defend the law. Páez, for his own part, begged Bolívar to return and support the military. Both used his name to argue rival positions. As far as they were concerned, only one man could broker the peace. There was no choice for either but to call him home.

Bolívar had other reasons to return. He longed to keep his dream of a unified federation alive; he wanted to ensure that the countries he had liberated adopted his constitution. The Peruvian government, after much debate and, ironically, in order to keep him in Lima a while longer, had finally approved it, as had Bolivia. The Peruvians had gone on to proclaim him president for life. He declined and put the presidency in the hands of General Santa Cruz—a decision he would come to rue. He shipped off the lion's share of the liberating army, leaving three hefty battalions to protect the capital. He then went about giving away every gift Peru had bestowed on him, save one: the jewel-encrusted gold sword given to him by the municipality of Lima. He was determined to leave Peru—as promised—without one grain of its sand, and indeed he left it an impoverished man. In order to liquidate his few debts, he had to borrow from aides. The one million dollars Peru had insisted on paying him after the Battle of Ayacucho—which he hoped would be sent to the poor of Venezuela—had never been produced. Ironically, the liberator to whom Peru would pay a life pension and all the tributes was San Martín, the man who left Lima before completing the task.

Bolívar departed Peru believing all was in reasonably good order. His constitution was in place in Peru and Bolivia, and he was confident that Santa Cruz and Sucre would carry out his vision. He began to think that if he could get those two republics to unite under his constitution— then push through its approval in Colombia—he would have an amalgamated America of sorts. Larger was always better in Bolívar's mind, and that dream seemed large enough for the moment. It wasn't that he was after more power. As he had said many times: he was weary of responsibilities. He was prepared to leave them to Santander. Coalition became his sole purpose and aim.

IN EARLY SEPTEMBER, BOLÍVAR BOARDED a boat for Guayaquil, leaving Manuela Sáenz in Lima. She had long since moved out of Thorne's house and into her own in Magdalena so that she could be closer to her lover. There had been no more pretense, no effort to stand on ceremony. She had broken with her husband and refused all his money. She was known as the Libertadora now. In the company of her loyal black servants, the famously uninhibited Jonatás and Natán, she had come and gone from Bolívar's villa freely.

The romance had not been without its rocky moments. The nine months he had been away in Cuzco and La Paz had tested their love. At first, Bolívar thought it best to end the affair. He was well aware of the scandal Manuela had caused in Lima and the damage such a flagrant affair with a married woman had done to his reputation. It is possible, too, that Thorne persuaded him that it would be in her best interest to let her go. Bolívar wrote soon after his departure: "Dear beautiful and good Manuela, I think of you and your fate constantly. I see no way we can unite in innocence and honor. I see all too well the terrible predicament you're in, having to rejoin someone you do not love (indeed, it makes me tremble); and mine, having to separate myself from someone I adore. . . . My determination to tear myself from your love has done this, and now eternity itself has come between us."

Within a few months, he wrote from Potosí, answering a letter in which she had described "the ill-treatment" to which she was being subjected; we do not know what misery Thorne was inflicting on her, but it was serious enough for Bolívar to suggest she leave Lima and take refuge with friends in Arequipa. The letter was cut-and-dried, hardly the passionate missive she was used to receiving from him. But Manuela proved hard to rebuff. A month later, he was writing again: "What you say about your husband is painful and funny all at once. . . . I don't know how to reconcile our respective happiness with our respective duties; I don't know how to cut a knot that even Alexander's sword would only complicate; it's not a matter of sword or strength, after all, but of pure against guilty love, duty against weakness."

He had had no shortage of affairs in between, and she was well aware of them. Women were always lavishing their attention on the Liberator; he found them impossible to resist. In Lima, before leaving on his travels, he had romanced the doe-eyed American Jeannette Hart, Commodore Isaac Hull's sister-in-law, who had visited Lima with Hull and his wife. It is even said in some Connecticut circles that Bolívar proposed marriage to the brunette beauty, although it is more likely that he only hinted at it, as he was inclined to do when courting a woman.

If legend is to be believed, Bolívar had a string of lovers as he toured Peru and Bolivia. Some were simply the nymphs who welcomed him from town to town; others were more serious entanglements—involving wives of high-placed officials—with lasting complications. One was the formidable and fetching Peruvian heroine Francisca Zubiaga de Gamarra, wife of the prefect of Cuzco, Agustín Gamarra. Little is known about her relationship to Bolívar, apart from two facts. It was she who was chosen to place a crown of laurel on his head when he entered Cuzco; and much later, when her husband was asked why he hated Bolívar even though the Liberator had been so generous to him, Gamarra replied, "He gave me many honors, it's true, but he also took away my wife."

Gamarra's wife, known to all as Doña Pancha or "the Marshalette," was as fierce as she was beautiful. Accompanying her husband in battle, she was fearless, peremptory, taking command when officers grew weak-kneed. She was a consummate horsewoman, knew how to handle a gun, and loved a good cockfight. Like Páez, she was an epileptic and rose to such heights of fury during combat that she would fall to the ground to be trampled by horses and carried off for dead. But in the drawing rooms of Cuzco—and, later, Lima—she was a dazzling presence, as a contemporary recalled: "She had a long, slightly turned-up nose and a large but very expressive mouth; her face was long, with prominent cheekbones; her skin dark but full of vitality." She made no secret of using her beauty and wiles to "exploit situations as the need arose." She had been forged in the fires of revolution and, when Gamarra was elected president, would rise to be first lady of the land. If indeed Doña Pancha had a passing liaison with Bolívar, it was a union on equal terms.

In Potosí, Bolivia, on the other hand, Bolívar had engaged in a dalliance with more lasting consequences. The young woman who placed a wreath on his head this time was María Joaquina Costas, whose Argentine husband was off fighting the war in Chile. She was graceful, elegant, with coal black eyes and a gentle smile. It is said that as Costas was laying her garland on Bolívar's brow, she warned him of a royalist plot brewing against him. At once intrigued and smitten, he invited her to a tête-à-tête. The plot against him never materialized, but he and Costas entered into an ardent affair and, in due course—months after the Liberator was back in Lima—a child was born. That child, José Antonio Costas, would die claiming he was Bolívar's son, but the Liberator never acknowledged him. An enigmatic exchange at a gathering of cronies two years after the child's birth, however, led him to mention that he was hardly sterile, that he had living evidence to the contrary. It was probably wishful thinking.

None of it would have come as a surprise to Manuela. She had long since reconciled herself to Bolívar's philandering ways. He never hid his interest in women; he admired them publicly, kissed their hands, danced with them in her presence. But he always went back to Manuela. When he had returned to Lima from his tour of Cuzco and La Paz, he reunited with her once more. His notes to her en route were as urgent as any young suitor's: "Wait for me at all costs, do you hear? Do you understand? If you don't, you're an ingrate, a traitor, even worse: an enemy."

Their love would not waver again.

Through the years and during the course of her many travels with the army, Manuela had managed to forge lasting friendships with many of Bolívar's men. She was devoted to his campaign, attentive to his soldiers' petitions, and, most important as far as his troops were concerned, brave in extremely perilous circumstances. As a result, she had earned the respect of a number of his generals—Sucre, Heres, and others—and the Liberator's British aides: all the men he loved best. She was, according to a diplomatic report to Secretary of State Henry Clay, a remarkably handsome woman, "generous in the extreme" to officers and soldiers. She was always willing to give them the last dollar in her purse and exhibited "the most zealous humanity" to the sick or wounded. She had become known as the person to whom a desperate soldier could go to win Bolívar's official attention.

Manuela's commitment to her lover's cause was most in evidence when he left Peru and the soldiers of a division he had left behind rose up in a series of mutinies. They claimed that they hadn't been paid full wages, that their rations had been curtailed, that they wanted a share of the fortune Peru had offered to pay Bolívar. As became clear, the insurrection had been concocted in Bogotá by those who, like Santander, wanted to cut short Colombia's military presence in Peru and bring the costly troops home. On January 26, 1827, the 3rd Division expelled Bolívar's generals, seized control of Lima's government palace and the fortress of Callao, and began to make demands. Manuela put on her colonel's uniform, rode out, and tried to win back the mutineers. Doling out money, she implored them to ignore their leader and form a new contingent.

Days later, she was arrested in her home in Magdalena. Peruvian authorities stormed the house at midnight on February 7, detained her, and insisted she leave the country that very night. She pleaded illness. The next morning, she was cast into a cell in a Lima convent, where the abbess received her with open contempt. She tried to object, argue her rights, but all the force of Peruvian vitriol came down on her now. The minister of foreign relations, Manuel Vidaurre—one of Bolívar's most rabid critics—accused her of being wanton, scandalous, "an insult to public honor and morals." On April 11, she was shuffled onto a boat in Callao along with a dozen Colombian officers and 130 sick and wounded men. Without any further ado, they were shipped off to Guayaquil. By the time she arrived, Bolívar would be far away, in a more troubled corner of his new world.

BOLÍVAR SAILED FROM LIMA ON September 3, 1826, promising to return. Indeed he hoped that once his Federation of the Andes was securely in place, he would come back on regular visits, overseeing the country's fortunes. But he would never see Peru again.

By September 13 he was in Guayaquil, where he was received as a hero. He was, in essence, without an army—he had sent the many thousands of Colombian troops in Peru to serve elsewhere—and it must have struck him as peculiar to be back on that hard-won soil without his trusty legions. "I come to you with an olive branch" were the first public words he uttered. That olive branch was his new constitution, but he did not say so right away. He went on to say all the things that Santander and his skittish legislators in Bogotá hoped to hear: He did not aspire to be a dictator; he did not care about political parties; he wanted only to bring harmony to Colombia's troubled shores. "Once more, I offer you my services," he said, "services of a brother. I don't want to know who has been at fault here; I have never forgotten that we are blood brothers, comrades in arms. I come offering an embrace. . . . Here, in the depths of my very being will I carry you, Granadans and Venezuelans alike, the just along with the unjust, the entire liberating army and every last citizen of this great Republic."

But as he moved north, traveling through Quito and Pasto, he exercised every extraordinary faculty he had ever been granted. Technically, he was a returning general—without doubt, a very victorious one—but his presidency had been annulled more than a year before; it was not his place to govern until he reached Bogotá, was formally conferred the presidency, and officially took up the reins. All the same, he was troubled by what he saw. "Everywhere I look," he wrote Santander, "I see only misery and disgust." Citizens felt disconnected from their government; local institutions were in shambles. For all of Santander's laws, the engine of Greater Colombia appeared to have stalled completely. The only way to solve it, as far as Bolívar was concerned, was to return power to the people, renew the social contract, give the outlying electoral colleges more control. To him, a citizen's rights were far more important than any body of statutes.

As he went, he tried to reassure the unhappy public by issuing government appointments, abrogating others. He commuted sentences, gave military promotions to officers who appealed to him, encouraged disgruntled citizens to come forward with protests against Bogotá's laws. He chafed at his aide O'Leary for taking sides with Santander against Páez. And, in the end, he decided that what he needed was more power, not less. He wrote to the vice president, "A dictatorship would solve everything. . . . With constitutional laws you can do nothing about Páez. Authorized by the nation, I can do all." Even as he publicly claimed to abhor the word "dictator," he now privately worked toward being acclaimed one. As he proceeded north, it was precisely what came to pass. The people of Guayaquil and Quito, dismayed by Bogotá's laws and irked by its ignorance about their needs, were only too happy to call Bolívar their dictator.

Santander was furious. According to him, a dictatorship was beside the point, entirely unnecessary in a republic whose laws and institutions—if obeyed—did the work of governing. The established order did not need to change; the disorderly people did. It was true that he had begged Bolívar to come back and restore the peace, but he had meant for the Liberator to come as a figurehead, a symbol. If Bolívar was angling to install his presumptuous Bolivian constitution and upend all the laws put in place in the past five years, Santander wanted no part of it. He had already warned Bolívar to steer clear of governing, as it would only destroy a warrior's glory. He decided to come out and meet the Liberator before Bolívar entered the capital and did any harm.

Bolívar was well into Popayán—350 miles from Bogotá—before he knew how unwelcome he was in Santander's country. It was there that he began to see newspapers out of the capital, filled with hostile editorials against him. It was there, too, that he began to hear that the majority of Granadans thought that the 1821 constitution was best; that they didn't agree with his notions of Pan American unity and constitutional reform; that they were all for Santander's laws and the primacy of Granadans over Venezuelans. They even seemed willing to go to war against Páez to prove it. Bolívar had told Santander months before that laws alone would not bring discipline to the turmoil. An obsession with laws was what had driven Páez to rebel in the first place. What the republic needed now was a strong military hand and every effort to preserve the union. He wrote to Santander again with an even firmer message, reprimanding him for feeding the burgeoning ill will: "I fear that Colombia is lost forever," he lamented. "The old constitution and the laws have reduced the country to a Satan's palace, ablaze in every corner." He threatened to reject the presidency unless congress convened to decide the important questions. But there was no denying he was chastened by the disapproval. Less confident now, he wrote to

Sucre and Santa Cruz, telling them to do what they thought best in Bolivia and Peru, even override him, if that was what the people wanted. But as he made his way through the vast, unfriendly republic, taking the grueling mountain route he had taken years before, suffering the pain of inflamed hemorrhoids, he couldn't help but burn, too, with a consuming fury.

Santander met Bolívar on the outskirts of the capital, before the Liberator began his final ascent to the plains of Bogotá. He was determined to disabuse Bolívar of any duplicity on his part or any bad faith on the part of the government. The meeting was genial, polite, with Santander's every effort directed at personally reassuring his chief. For all intents and purposes, the vice president's strategy worked. They agreed that when they reached Bogotá, Bolívar would resume the presidency under the old constitution—at least for the time being—and that he would take up the extraordinary faculties that the constitution provided in times of peril.

But this rapprochement between Bolívar and his vice president was sorely tested when the Liberator actually made his entrance into the city on November 14. Instead of the wild, exultant acclamations he had received elsewhere for his attendant victories, Bolívar was met with only a few "Vivas!" in his name. The welcome was surprisingly reserved—even grudging—and made largely by supporters of the vice president. The loudest cheers, to the Liberator's dismay, were for the *very* old constitution of 1815—the charter that had formed the original republic of New Granada. There were no triumphal arches, no clamoring masses. The only plaudits were on billboards, and they screamed: *Viva la constitución!* As a chilling rain began to drizzle down, Bolívar found himself riding into the capital virtually alone. At the city limits, he was welcomed with a small ceremony in his honor. But when the presiding official whined on about how the army had violated the republic's laws, Bolívar erupted. He cut off the speaker, ended the harangue, and insisted that patriots should be "celebrating the army's glories, not nattering on about its violation of a few laws." He was livid. When the heavens finally parted to release a drenching rain, all hopes of a triumphal reentry were dampened completely.

The morning sun over Bogotá brought a brighter day. The civic, military, and religious leaders of Colombia greeted Bolívar warmly in the presidential palace and he reciprocated with generous words. Santander made a dazzling, conciliatory speech, in which he congratulated the Liberator, praised the army's astonishing victories, and claimed to be the president's loyal friend. It seemed, too, as conversation continued, that Bolívar's vice president was not completely averse to his Federation of the Andes. Although he didn't say it quite yet, Santander was all for dividing Greater Colombia into separate states, and as long as he ruled New Granada, he was willing to go along with the idea of some form of federal system. The blue sky of possibility seemed to gleam over them now. *Vivas!* for the Liberator rang throughout the capital, and there was talk of a bold, new day. By the end of it, the president and vice president were embracing warmly. It would be their last amicable exchange.

Bolívar did not stay long in Bogotá. A mere ten days after his arrival and two days after being granted dictatorial powers, he was en route again, riding over the same terrain he had crossed when he had descended so spectacularly over the Andes and overpowered the Spaniards at Boyacá. It had been seven long years since that historic moment, and he was all the worse for wear. He was exhausted, unwell, not the warrior he once had been. But he was determined to bring Páez in line and rescue the foundering republic. He wrote to the Lion of the Apure sternly, preparing him for the pending encounter: "General Castillo opposed me and lost," he warned. "General Piar opposed me and lost. General Mariño opposed me and lost. Generals Riva Agüero and Torre Tagle both opposed me and lost. It would seem that Providence curses my personal enemies to hell-fire, Americans and Spaniards alike." But he ended with an outstretched hand: "I believe in you as I believe in my own sword, and I know that it will never be directed against my heart."

When he arrived in Puerto Cabello, Páez was afraid to see him. By then, the truculent plainsman was unwaveringly committed to seceding from Greater Colombia. Santander had stripped Páez of the title of supreme chief of Venezuela and further insulted him by summoning him to Bogotá to be tried for military crimes. Outraged, Páez had ignored the order and made clear that he was poised to go to war to free his country from Bogotá's clutches. He was, after all, the hero of the

Battle of Carabobo, liberator of Puerto Cabello—and Venezuelans were firmly on his side. The great Colombian generals Bermúdez and Urdaneta had declared in no uncertain terms that they would never take up arms against him. This was precisely why Santander had asked Bolívar to intervene.

But hearing of Bolívar's tenure in Bogotá and his evident solidarity with Santander, Páez assumed that the Liberator was now on the opposing side, especially when it became known that Bolívar was advancing on Venezuela with Santander's army. As Bolívar labored over the Andes, fording rivers, covering more than seven hundred miles in the course of twenty-eight days, Páez began to mount a campaign to raise Venezuela against him. He spread the rumor that Bolívar had set out to make himself king—a preposterous fabrication, given the fact that it was Páez himself who had sent emissaries to beg Bolívar to take up the crown. He tried to persuade pardos and blacks, whose opportunities had improved markedly since the revolution, that Bolívar would be like the Mantuanos of old—avaricious, cruel, and adamant about keeping the colored people down.

Bolívar had two choices: negotiate with Páez or see the republic he had toiled to create slide calamitously into civil war. Arriving in Puerto Cabello on December 31, he wasted no time. He issued a unilateral decree granting Páez amnesty for his rebellion, confirmed his title as supreme chief of Venezuela, and invited him to parley. Granadans and Venezuelans were both citizens of Colombia, Bolívar boomed, his voice still electrifying, though the body was frail. He told them they were what they always had been: brothers, comrades in arms, sons of the same destiny. He implored them to see reason and put bitterness behind them. Were they so short of enemies, he scolded, that they would turn on each other in fratricide? To Páez, who in past months had lost much of the support he had ever had among the Venezuelan people, Bolívar wrote, "Enough of the blood and ruin. . . . I came here because you called me. If you want to see me, come. Even Morillo did not mistrust me, and he and I have been friends ever since." Bolívar assured Páez that he had nothing to lose, everything to gain; all he had to do was recognize the Liberator's authority. Páez accepted immediately. On January 4, 1827, he rode out to meet Bolívar in Valencia; but he appeared with armed guards on the chance that the lure was a ruse. Bolívar came alone. When he saw the stout, burly bear of a man without whom he could not have won his America's independence, he strode forward and took him into his arms. Páez later wrote that it was an embrace from which he could hardly release himself: their swords became tangled, locking fast so that the two couldn't break free. "A good omen," Bolívar chuckled, and smiled broadly. But as they struggled to separate their weapons, Páez couldn't help feeling a shudder of dread.

WITH ONE EMBRACE, BOLÍVAR HAD saved the republic. He had always known how to manage his generals. His flexibility in war, his aptitude for employing just the right combination of cordiality and muscle, his natural sympathy for soldiers had served him well among military men. It was dealing with the politicians that would test his patience. He had said so many years before, in 1821, and it would resonate with ever more meaning now:

> When catastrophe forced weapons into my hands and history called me to liberate my country, I put myself at the head of a military venture that has labored for more than eleven years, never dreaming I would be asked to lead governments. With firm resolve, I swore I would never do it. I pledged with all my heart that I was but a soldier, that I would serve only in war; and that, when peace finally came, I would move on to the role of citizen. Ready to sacrifice my fortune, my blood, my very name for the public good, I cannot say I am ready to sacrifice my conscience. I am thoroughly convinced I have no capacities for governing Colombia. I know absolutely nothing about rule. I am not the adjudicator a thriving republic needs. Soldier by necessity and inclination, my destiny has ever been in the battlefield, the barracks.

History had forced his hand. Knowing only one way to manage—the military way, from the top down—he forged on with the enterprise. At every turn, he was given ample encouragement: Every republic he liberated had come to believe, even grudgingly, that Bolívar had an uncanny ability to deal with Gordian knots. If he were present, if he unleashed his spellbinding rhetoric, he could tame a whirlwind, and a whirlwind is what many feared would come without the Liberator at the helm. Caught up in this notion of invincibility, Bolívar began to believe that only he could set things right. "I, too, shall play the game of politics," he had told Santander, and he proceeded to do just that.

On January 12, 1827, he made a glorious entry into Caracas with Páez at his side. It was the first he had been back since the glory days of 1821. They rode through the streets in an open carriage and reveled in the adoration. It was a joyous homecoming, filled with the prospect of seeing family, the childhood haunts, the city of his birth, the nation for which he had sacrified everything. The throngs were so thick and clamorous that the carriage could hardly move. Arches soared over the streets; festive music filled the air. When they reached the square, two pretty women in white came forward to crown him with wreaths: one for besting the Spaniards, another for averting a civil war. He took the laurels in hand and proclaimed, "I value these symbols of victory with all my heart, but allow me to pass them on to the real victors." He put one on Páez's head; the second, he threw to the people.

Bolívar's homecoming was the last leg of an arduous journey—most of it on horseback—that had begun in Lima four months before and had carried him four thousand miles. Awaiting him at the end was family, or what was left of it. There were his sister María Antonia, a royalist throughout the revolution, who had become one of Bolívar's most loyal defenders after the war was over; his favorite uncle, Esteban, who had returned from Europe after an absence of thirty years; his beloved Hipólita, the wet nurse he had freed from bondage. He toured the old houses, visited his properties, and in the comforts of familiar rooms heard news about the others. His patriot sister, Juana, whose daughter had married one of Bolívar's generals, was off in the mountain city of Barinas. His nephew Fernando Bolívar—the seventeen-year-old child of his dead brother—was in Philadelphia, having just graduated from school. Bolívar had paid for Fernando's education. When eminent Americans learned that the Liberator's nephew was among them, they had sought him out. General Lafayette had visited the boy; Thomas Jefferson had corresponded with him; and, on his way to attend Jefferson's new university in Virginia, Fernando had stopped in

Washington and met John Quincy Adams, Henry Clay, and James Monroe.

Bolívar governed Venezuela for the next six months, pledging full faith in Páez, even referring to him as the "savior of the nation." But he was playing politics now. In private, his opinion was very different:

> General Páez is the most ambitious, vain man in the world: he has no desire to obey, only command; it galls him to see me above him in the political hierarchy of Colombia; he doesn't recognize his own incompetence, so blinded is he by pride and ignorance. He will never be more than an instrument of advisors. As far as I am concerned, he is the most dangerous man in Colombia.

He had admitted this to very few. He and Páez took up residence under the same roof and the Liberator soon mollified the disruptive chieftain with assurances that Venezuela would be a separate state in the greater Federation of the Andes. This coddling of Páez would cost Bolívar dearly: his overblown public tributes to a rebel who had broken the republic's laws were an affront to those who had worked diligently to abide by the constitution. But to Bolívar, the rupture between Santander and Páez had become a felicitous opportunity to redefine the republic as he saw fit. First he intended to install his constitution in Venezuela, then nudge Colombia toward adoption. Even as Bolívar confirmed Páez's supremacy, he called for a constitutional convention at which all such matters would be decided. But he was treading on risky ground.

Bolívar tried to do what he could for Venezuela in those months, going about business, trying to boost public morale, but it was evident from the first that Caracas was in heartbreaking disorder. Independence had left it in ruins. All agriculture had halted, the import-export businesses had withered, and a paralyzing torpor had taken their place. He had found similar disrepair in the outlying areas of Greater Colombia. Everywhere he went, he had heard about the wretched state of the national treasury, even though, only two years before, Britain had granted Colombia a loan of $30 million. Where had the money gone? There were many Colombians (and especially Venezuelans) who accused the regime in Bogotá of dissipating it irresponsibly, or even snatching it for themselves. Certainly, the residents of Bogotá lived far more comfortably than their miserable counterparts in Caracas or Quito. The British ambassador complained bitterly that Santander had committed "the most scandalous abuses," siphoning off money for his friends under the guise of assigning commercial contracts. Bolívar had not been shy to ask about such allegations. He recalled all too well that, in correspondence with Santander not long before, he had had to point out that heads of nations could not afford to involve themselves in money schemes. His vice president had seemed to have a poor understanding of this principle.

Learning that the Liberator had openly impugned his honor, Santander took offense. "Let's ignore for the moment what you've been saying in public," he wrote Bolívar sharply. "Páez is called the savior of his nation, whereas I, as ruler of this country as well as of Congress, am considered criminal, delinquent, forced to defend myself against these charges." He felt cheated, betrayed. He had called on Bolívar to rein in Páez, not glorify him; he had furnished the Liberator with troops in order to intimidate the Lion of the Apure, not parade through Caracas exalting the man's crimes.

Santander had tried to temper his messages, not being entirely candid about the extent of hostility he and his circle felt about Bolívar's constitution, his call for a life presidency, his dictatorial powers, his evident disregard for a system Santander had worked so carefully to create. To be blamed for the disastrous financial state of Colombia was simply infuriating. He wrote out a long report in his own defense. But by then Bolívar had had enough of him. He informed Santander bluntly that he would write to him no longer—between them there was nothing more to say.

The intricacies of the British loan turned out to be far more complicated than anyone understood at the time. The problems had begun in 1822, when the former vice president of Colombia, Francisco Zea—as flamboyant with money as he was with words—had been sent to London to raise funds for the revolution. It had taken two years for Britain to respond, but by 1824 when a loan of $30 million was approved, Zea had already frittered away a good third of it through reckless spending, questionable negotiations, and rampant debt. The other $20 million had been swallowed immediately by the military's yawning deficit. For five years running, Colombia essentially had underwritten the liberation of six countries. Taxes had brought the government $5 or $6 million a year, but the army and navy were spending double that—$13 or $14 million—and much of it on foreign ground. The ever expanding wars of independence had become a vast maw that needed to be fed. Santander was all too aware of it; it was why he had constantly carped about military costs. There was no doubt that government corruption was endemic: tax collectors, commercial middlemen, official bursars were flagrantly dishonest, promoting rank fraud and embezzlement; the vice president had had to impose the death penalty on the most brazen of these. But the facts were incontrovertible: the loan was gone, the republic had been forced to beg Britain for another one, and the republic's economy was in ruin.

Even as he stewed about the financial state of affairs, Bolívar proceeded to address the crippling discontent in Venezuela. He had put a stop to civil war, but insurrections now flared like wildfires around the country. He deployed General Páez and his stalwart in eastern Venezuela, General Mariño, to quell them. He felt personally responsible for ameliorating his country's problems, having ignored Venezuela for so long. But by April, as he sorted through the financial and military muddle, he was given evidence of Santander's duplicity on a very different matter: the insurrection by Colombian troops Bolívar had left behind in Lima. It had taken three months for news of that January coup to reach him. Whether or not Santander personally inspired the 3rd Division's uprising has never been proven—General Sucre believed he did, so did Bolívar—but there is no question that Santander and his minions in Bogotá saw it as a godsend, since they had been weary of paying for Lima's defense. When they heard that Colombian soldiers in Lima's garrisons had overthrown their generals and rejected Bolívar's constitution, the people of Bogotá spilled into the streets to celebrate. The coup, in itself, did not implicate Santander. But his reaction did. He strolled out into the night to listen to the music and join in the revelry, an act hardly befitting the dignity of his station. A few days later he wrote to José Bustamante, the leader of the revolt, and congratulated him. Bustamante's actions, the vice president announced, were to be highly commended; the republic deeply appreciated the patriotic instincts that had prompted them. A few days later Santander signed the order promoting Bustamante to colonel.

Enraged, Bolívar had his secretary of state fire off a stinging rebuke to Santander's minister of war. Bustamante's rebellion, the missive claimed, was a clear contravention of the military's most sacred laws. Soldiers had risen up against commanders, and yet Colombia had had the gall to congratulate them! "The Liberator is astonished by this evidence of moral decay in the government. . . . He doesn't know which is worse: the crime committed by Bustamante or the act undertaken with all deliberation to give the man a prize." Santander shot back, arguing that to absolve Bustamante for his rebellion in Peru was equivalent to absolving Páez for his rebellion in Venezuela. But Bolívar remained adamant. He wrote in candor to one of his generals: "Santander is a snake . . . I can no longer abide him. I trust neither his principles nor his heart."

The revolt of the 3rd Division had a resounding impact on Peru. The government Bolívar had cobbled together in Lima was finished, his constitution abrogated. General Santa Cruz, to whom Bolívar had virtually handed the presidency, had done nothing to curb the fall. Santa Cruz now attempted Bolívar's old, trusted gesture of relinquishing all power, so sure was he that it would be given back. But the Peruvian congress astounded him by accepting his resignation, and then began organizing a new election.

Colonel Bustamante and his rebel division went on to create more trouble. They departed secretly from Lima, swept north, invaded Guayaquil, and replaced the city's staunchly pro-Bolívarian head with a Peruvian general. Five years after the infamous Guayaquil standoff between Bolívar and San Martín, it looked as if Peru finally was taking hold of that disputed port. To what extent the invasion was instigated by Peru has never been clearly established, but Peruvians were widely blamed for it. The bizarre enterprise of a Colombian division running amok, invading the Colombian republic, was enough to set even Santander's teeth on edge. He did not condemn Bustamante's division outright, but he ordered it to desist.

Little seemed to be going well in the querulous Republic of Greater Colombia. As Bolívar's confidant Pedro Briceño Méndez put it, "We

have arrived at an era of blunders. In order to fix one, we commit fifty."
Bolívar could see that the only way for him to retake control and address those errors was to return to Bogotá, perhaps even mount a new
military campaign and show the republic that he meant business. He
had been working at the periphery for too long; he needed to attend
to the center. But the center had long since become exasperated with
Bolívar. On June 20, Santander decided to abolish Bolívar's dictatorial
powers and reinstate the law of the land; and so, with one stroke of the
pen, all of Bolívar's improvised mandates were annulled. It would take
more than a Hercules to win back Bogotá now.

Have no doubt, Bolívar told Páez, "I'm ready to do whatever it takes
to liberate my people. I would even declare war to the death all over
again." He gathered up the mighty army that Bogotá had provided him
and readied it to double back against the capital. A notice went out to
all Colombians: "The Liberator has resolved to march against the traitors who have stained the Republic's glory and are working even now
to dismember it." As Manuela Sáenz was sailing north from Peru to
Guayaquil, still stinging from the mortification of her eviction, Bolívar
sailed in the opposite direction, from Caracas to Cartagena, in what he
remembered as the most pleasant voyage he had ever made. From there,
he mobilized his generals: Urdaneta in Maracaibo, Páez in central Venezuela, all the troops he could muster in Cartagena, and told them to
prepare to move on Bogotá. He continued on toward the capital, upriver
on the Magdalena, with a force powerful enough to quell all the rebels
of Guayaquil and Peru put together.

When the politicians and pundits who had heaped every possible
abuse on Bolívar learned of his march on Bogotá, they trembled with
alarm. The most vociferous among them feigned illness and left the
capital. Santander tried to dissuade Bolívar from advancing any farther,
arguing weakly that to bring too many troops into Bogotá would put an
untenable burden on the city: soldiers would die of hunger; there was
not enough food to go around; their presence would be a scandal. But
the Liberator pressed on. Grasping at straws now, Santander reminded
Bolívar that he had no power, that he had never actually taken the oath
of the presidency, that his "extraordinary faculties" had all been rendered null; but this, too, had no effect. The vice president even went so

far as to plan a preposterous scheme in which he would mount a new revolutionary force to repel Bolívar. The minister of war, Carlos Soublette, rejected the proposal out of hand. Suddenly, it seemed all tables had turned. The very heart of the republic was awaiting Bolívar's wrath. If anyone noted the irony, few had the nerve to say it: the revolution had twisted so far upon itself that the people of Bogotá were afraid of their own liberator.

CHAPTER 16

Man of Difficulties

Nobody loves me in New Granada . . . they think of me as a necessary evil. Why should I sacrifice myself for them? With weapons. I defended their rights, and now, with weapons, I must force them to do what they should?

—Simón Bolívar

Before his arrival in Bogotá on September 10, 1827, Bolívar let it be known that he expected nothing less than absolute power. "Let me say this as clearly as I can," he announced in advance, "The republic will be lost unless it gives me the fullest authority." He was no longer willing to delegate the presidency in order to pursue a larger vision. That vision had been utterly shattered: there would be no federation now. "Can you believe it!" he fumed, "They ask me to dismember the army even as they report the latest calamities!" Peru had declared itself an enemy; the territory of Ecuador had been invaded; Sucre was reporting trouble in Bolivia. As far as Bolívar was concerned, Vice President Santander and a diabolical congress had been the ruin of his ambition for Latin America. They had undermined the army, frittered away the money, imposed a political system that worked only in Bogotá. It would take a colossal military effort to travel the distances and subdue the mess. He communicated to the president of the senate that he expected to take the oath of the presidency immediately upon entering the capital. His demands were clear: a congressional assembly was to receive him on his arrival, his old mansion of La Quinta was to be made available, and—although he didn't have a peso to his name—he would scrounge money from friends until he could pay it back. Not one government cent was to be spent on his behalf.

Trying to make the best of an exceedingly nervous situation, the government of Bogotá sent a welcoming party to greet him a hundred miles from the city. Among that number was the secretary of war, Carlos Soublette, an associate of his for years, who over time, Bolívar suspected, had lost some of his love for him. But a gaggle of good friends, too, insisted on riding out to welcome the prodigal warrior. It was a civil but solemn rendezvous, made somewhat lighter by the Liberator, who burst out laughing when he heard that he had sent his most raucous critics running for the hills.

On they went into the crowded streets of Bogotá, which had been abundantly decorated for the occasion. Grateful that he was entering in peace, the city had rushed to erect triumphal arches along the Calle Real; colorful bunting hung from the stately houses. For as far as the eye could see, balconies were filled with elegantly turned out ladies. But, overall, it was a muted reception. Citizens didn't know how to respond. Santander, who had spewed every imaginable accusation against Bolívar—comparing him to the cruel Spanish general Morillo—now found himself powerless in the face of congress's decision to receive Bolívar according to the Liberator's wishes. He sat in the presidential palace and anticipated the worst.

The senators had all gathered at the nave of the ancient convent of Santo Domingo and seated themselves in a double circle of chairs. Before them was a table with a thick Bible on it. As Bolívar made his way through the capital, a noisy congregation crowded into every possible cranny of the church. Gossiping, buzzing, the people glanced over their shoulders in anticipation, placing bets on when the Liberator would appear and whether he would actually take the oath. He had, after all, tried to renounce the presidency numerous times. From time to time, a false rumor that he had arrived would electrify the crowd, and the more audacious would stand on their seats, craning to see the door.

He entered the church at three in the afternoon and, though bells pealed and bands played when he passed through the doors, the crowd instantly quieted to see the gaunt, weary figure before them. As he walked slowly down the aisle, he seemed in acute discomfort. His stride was steady, yet awkward: the gait of a man too long in the saddle. No longer was he the nimble warrior who—only eight years before—had leapt from his horse to dart up the steps of the viceroy's palace. At forty-four, he was the very picture of old age.

The applause was reserved, but he didn't pay it much mind. He seemed dazed, his health badly shaken by the journey. When he reached the senators, he bowed low, motioned them to sit, and placed his cocked hat on the table. The oath was administered promptly, as he had re-quested: The president of the senate, Vicente Barrero, fixed his small, fierce eyes on the Liberator, laid his hand on the Bible, and asked him to repeat the words. Bolívar did so firmly. A few cheers rippled through the crowd and the music started up again, but the newly confirmed president called for silence. In a weak, hoarse voice, he began to speak. He seemed agitated, confused; more than once he wiped his brow, said things twice. Mary English, the widow of a British colonel, described it this way:

> My heart bled for him. . . . He spoke of his distress and mortification at the late political disturbances. He said that intrigue and calumny was a monster with a hundred thousand heads, but if his further devotion, his sword and self-sacrifice, could restore tranquility to his bleeding country, he offered all, all to its service.

It was, despite the frailty of its orator, a moving speech, and he ended it with a flourish by announcing that a constitutional convention to decide the controversial issues would take place in Ocaña within six months. The announcement itself was a breach of sorts: because the congress of Cúcuta had ruled in 1821 that the constitution would be in-violable for ten years. To consider changing the country's charter before 1831 was to shuffle all the rules. But Bolívar believed that dire times required dire measures. He had hinted about such a convention when he had arrived in Venezuela, and now he decided to hold one and throw rules to the wind.

Bolívar had long abandoned a number of constitutional rulings. On the day he stepped foot in Colombia from Peru, he had taken power unilaterally into his hands, not bothering to confer with Bogotá about any of his actions. He had flouted the law when he had absolved Páez for his insurrection and made him supreme chief of Venezuela. More serious still, Greater Colombia had been operating for months without a legal executive. Bolívar was, in truth, no longer president. Santander had been acting illegally as vice president. Congress had decreed that Bolívar could hold extraordinary powers until January 1, 1827—the end of his appointed term—after which both men's authority would lapse. The popular election of December 1826 had reinstated both of them, but the official oath had never been administered. On January 2, when that ceremony was supposed to have taken place, Bolívar was on a march to Caracas, resolved to fix the troubles with Páez. Short of a necessary quorum, congress was unable to convene to decide the question of rule. By law, all power at that moment should have commuted instantly to the president of the senate, the very official who now stood in church with the flashing eyes, swearing in the Liberator. But when Bolívar was informed of the situation, he had cavalierly instructed Santander to appropriate his command; and the vice president, for all his obsession with laws, had gone along with it. Eager to preserve his clout, Santander had written to the president of the senate, claiming Bolívar had granted him all authority. He then issued a decree to confirm it. In other words, Santander himself had acted in full contravention of the constitution. No one could call him "the man of laws" now.

Once the presidential oath was taken, Bolívar repaired to the government palace, where Santander awaited. As he made his way down the old cobblestone streets, the Liberator was showered with roses, thronged by a swarming multitude. The people were eager to witness his meeting with his vice president, and they followed with fevered curiosity, supporters and critics alike. When Bolívar arrived at the foot of the palace stairs—the steps he had taken so readily after his victory at Boyacá—Santander descended apprehensively to greet him. Their encounter was ceremonious, chilly, but not without cordiality. Bolívar could rise to the occasion when necessary and he rose to it now, summoning every bit of charm to put Santander at ease. Santander reciprocated graciously by inviting him to a late lunch at his table. Over polite conversation at that meal, Bolívar told his vice president that those who had evacuated Bogotá fearing persecution should come back at once; they would not be punished for their opinions. For a fleeting moment, peace reigned between rivals.

Early the next morning when Bolívar was still in bed, Santander appeared in full uniform at the palace; the Liberator received him with no little surprise. Santander apologized for his handling of the rebel leader of the 3rd Division; Bolívar listened, then deftly turned the conversation to reminiscences of their friendship, their long and intimate correspondence, the glories they had seen together. They went from bedroom to dining room and lunched together again. It was as it had always been and always would be: in Bolívar's presence, maintaining high wrath was impossible. "His force of personality is such," Santander soon confessed, "that on countless occasions when I have been filled with hatred and revenge, the mere sight of him, the instant he speaks, I am disarmed, and I come away filled with nothing so much as admiration."

But by that afternoon, suspicions came hurtling back. Goaded by followers, the two lost any hope of true reconciliation. Partisan rancor ran deep in Bogotá. The revolution, in which Bolívar had led bickering diehards toward a single goal, had been replaced by a peace in which harmony seemed impossible. Had laws been held sacrosanct, had petty rivalries not taken center stage—had Bolívar himself been firmer about holding his generals to a single standard—perhaps a strong, unified republic might have emerged to forge a different future. As it was, animosities were too extreme, political parties too blinded by narrow aims to compromise. Even as Britain, France, Holland, Germany, Brazil, and the Holy See recognized the republic and sent their congratulations to "the illustrious Liberator"—as Colombia began to find some small measure of glory abroad—a hellfire of belligerence consumed the capital. On the pages of newspapers, in the halls of debate, and at social *tertulias* throughout Bogotá, Bolívarians and Santanderistas unleashed their fury at one another; and in turn, political reputations teetered. Within a year, as one historian put it, Greater Colombia would be the laughingstock of the world.

~

IT WAS NO SECRET THAT the journey from Caracas had drained him of all vigor. Bolívar was spent. The widow of Colonel English had observed it, and although she noted several days later at a palace ball that he seemed somewhat refreshed, it was evident he needed the quiet refuge of La Quinta. He didn't mingle much at that party, apart from chatting with Mrs. English. He didn't dance. "He is exhausted," a flyer announced months before his arrival. "He is weary of serving during the most painful times the Republic has ever known . . . and he is thinking that perhaps the best contribution he can make toward peace is simply to forfeit his destiny and return to a private life." For the six months between the oath of presidency and the grand constitutional convention that was to take place in Ocaña, he aspired only to be with his mistress and renew his fragile health.

"The frost of my years melts at the very thought of your beauty and grace," he wrote to Manuela Sáenz soon after reaching Bogotá. "Your love gives hope to this dwindling existence. I cannot live without you, cannot will away my Manuela. . . . Even at this distance, I see you. Come, come, come!" She could not do otherwise. "I am going because you call me," she responded, but she hadn't heard from him in almost a year and so couldn't help but add a warning: "Don't tell me to go back to Quito once I arrive."

Nature soon gave them a warning of its own. On November 16, a few weeks before her departure from Quito, a major earthquake struck Bogotá, heaving whole buildings from their foundations. The government palace and the sturdy church of Santo Domingo where Bolívar had taken the oath of the presidency surrendered to the undulating earth, their walls collapsing to rubble. Clouds of white dust hung over the city, thinning into an ominous veil that shrouded the valley for days. The convulsion occurred at a quarter past six on a Friday evening, when Bolívar was in his house at La Quinta, at a remove from the city, but he had no doubt that its magnitude was as great as that of the earthquake he had survived in Caracas fifteen years before. As the chill night fell and stars glimmered overhead, it was impossible for him to see the extent of the destruction through the milky haze below, or witness how the desperate were streaming to safety on the open plain. The lurching ground deeply unsettled him, and a terrible sickness clawed at his stomach. He could not summon the strength to leave his house.

Come morning, it was clear that the city's infrastructure—more squat and square than that of Caracas—had spared lives. Few were lost, although many were injured; and the city suffered its losses with great equanimity. But the rumbling went on into the night and tremors continued for a full week. Eighty miles away, the ancient volcano of Tolima sighed a long column of smoke, sending a trail of ash over the ruins. "The city is rendered helpless," Bolívar reported, "and deeply sad." The rabid politics of Bogotá was suspended—but not for long.

When Manuela arrived a few months later, the lover she saw was hardly his former self. As he paced the brick floors of La Quinta in his blue uniform, he seemed thinner than she remembered him. His hairline had receded; his curly mane had grown sparse. His eyes appeared clouded with worry until rare, galvanizing moments when they flashed with fury. But for all the toll that thousands of miles of travel had taken on the man, she was still deeply in love with him and made no secret of it.

She moved into a house within yards of the presidential palace, but whenever he retreated to La Quinta, she lived with him openly, scandalizing the citizens of Bogotá, who felt a mistress should keep her distance and a president should show more decorum. It was bad enough that she was a foreigner, but that she was married, outspoken, and a brazen exhibitionist, who showed no respect for the nation's capital, was intolerable. She was ridiculed mercilessly by his enemies. Even so, anyone could see she was made of strong stuff: She had traveled hundreds of miles through unfriendly territory with the Liberator's precious personal archives and a modest entourage of five. She had crossed the formidable Andes, canoed hundreds of miles down crocodile-infested waters. This was no routine voluptuary. She cared for Bolívar like a tigress. She burst in on parties to which she hadn't been invited, shocking the guests and annoying her lover no end. She was politically astute, aggressive—labeling politicians as either trustworthy or "vile." Adored by some officers, despised by many more, she was unafraid to stand up to his generals. But to him she was the soul of tenderness. Slowly she nursed him to health; and, ignoring the censure of an outraged public, bustled about La Quinta and made it a sanctuary of repose.

La Quinta, which had been Bolívar's home over the years whenever he was in Bogotá, was hardly an opulent mansion. A charming cottage nestled in the hills above the city, it stood in the shadow of two towering peaks that pierced the sky behind it. Ringed by high walls, set back by a driveway of stately cypresses, the house was a one-story, one-bedroom abode in the old colonial style, its rooms furnished in handsome mahogany. Under its red-tiled roof were three fine salons, a dining room, and a game room; outside, a scenic overlook, an orchard and vegetable garden, and a covered pool fed by a rushing stream where the Liberator took his daily bath. During cold mountain nights, fireplaces and braziers afforded warmth; during the day, balconied windows opened to fragrant gardens of honeysuckle, violets, wild roses, and ancient cedars. In the back was a spare room for Bolívar's manservant, José Palacios. Bustling with servants, gleaming with crystal and silver, La Quinta was the getaway that Bolívar and Sáenz sorely needed after their hard journeys, and it was there that they found a brief interval of joy.

BOGOTÁ WAS CERTAINLY NO LIMA, as Manuela was swift to observe. It was not as wealthy, not as grand, not as easy to get lost in as the City of Kings. The Colombian capital was a mere 25,000 souls; Lima's population was nearly its triple. But Bogotá was trying to manage an unwieldy amalgamation of territories—the departments of Venezuela, New Granada, Quito, and Panama—and that fact alone made it a thrilling experiment. For the time being, Venezuela had simmered down under Páez and the region Bolívar called Ecuador had calmed under General Flores, but at any time, it seemed, this lumbering republic might come whirling apart at the seams.

As Bolívar worked to gain Greater Colombia a place in the world and diplomats began to arrive to confirm it, time worked against him. There was a mounting sense—especially in the United States—that South Americans were no better off for their revolution. Hoping to maintain relations with his northern neighbors, Bolívar sent off a letter to Henry Clay, thanking him for his brilliant advocacy on behalf of South America. As we have seen, the congressman from Kentucky had been an ardent ally of Bolívar's, summoning his name in government and banquet halls, exhorting fellow Americans to support the Liberator's call for freedom. As Abraham Lincoln later recounted, Clay's name was well known and well loved in the southern hemisphere: "When South America threw off the thralldom of Spain," as Lincoln put it, "Clay's speeches were read at the head of her armies by Bolívar." For the soldiers of the liberating forces, Clay was a kindred spirit, an American brother, his very name a rallying call.

Imagine, then, Bolívar's surprise when he read Clay's response to his heartfelt letter of gratitude. The chilly missive echoed every accusation Santander had ever made:

> Sir. . . . The interest which was inspired in this country by the arduous struggles of South America, arose principally from the hope that along with its independence would be established free institutions, insuring all the blessings of civil liberty. To the accomplishing of that object we still anxiously look. We are aware that great difficulties oppose it, among which not the least is that which arises out of the existence of a large military force, raised for the purpose of resisting the power of Spain. Standing armies, organized with the most patriotic intentions, are dangerous instruments. They devour the substance, debauch the morals, and too often destroy the liberties of a people. Nothing can be more perilous or unwise, than to retain them after the necessity has ceased which led to their formation, especially if their numbers are disproportioned to the revenues of the state.
>
> But notwithstanding all these difficulties, we had fondly cherished and still indulge the hope that South America would add a new triumph to the cause of human liberty, and that Providence would bless her as he had her northern sister, with the genius of some great and virtuous man, to conduct her securely through all her trials. We had even flattered ourselves that we beheld that genius in your excellency. . . .
>
> I cannot allow myself to believe that your excellency will abandon the bright and glorious path which lies plainly before you, for the

bloody road passing over the liberties of the human race, on which the vulgar crowd of tyrants and military despots have so often trodden. I will not doubt that your excellency will in due time render a satisfactory explanation to Colombia, and to the world, of the parts of your public conduct which have excited any distrust. . . . H. CLAY.

Clay had been disappointed—perhaps even humiliated—by the dismal results of Bolívar's Congress of Panama. After all, it was Clay who had argued volubly that the United States should send delegates to that table. But the tone of Clay's letter suggests something more, and it is equally probable that, having been newly appointed as secretary of state, Clay had begun to read blistering reports from United States diplomats, who were being courted assiduously by Bolívar's enemies. In Lima, where Bolívar by now was roundly resented, the American consul, William Tudor, had gone from ardent admirer to almost pathological detractor, describing Bolívar in dispatches to Washington as a hypocritical usurper and "madman." In Bogotá, on the other hand, the American chargé, Beaufort Watts, believed Bolívar to be a strong moral force, and had implored him—quite improperly—to hurry back from Caracas, resume the presidency, and "save the country." William Henry Harrison, a future president of the United States, soon replaced Watts as resident diplomat in Bogotá and made no secret that he was consorting with Bolívar's enemies. Harrison had heard that Bolívar favored the British style of government and he misguidedly took this to mean that the Liberator was a monarchist. His judgment of the Liberator was harsh, based entirely on hearsay: "Whether Bolívar is himself the author of these measures," he wrote back to the secretary of state, "and whether, under the mask of patriotism . . . he has really been preparing the means of investing himself with arbitrary power . . . I have not the least doubt." Eventually, Harrison even had the effrontery to write Bolívar a long and insulting letter, scolding him for flaws his enemies had ascribed to him:

The mere hero of the field and successful leader of armies may for the moment attract attention. But . . . to be esteemed eminently great, it is necessary to be eminently good. . . . Are you willing that your name should descend to posterity amongst the mass of those, whose fame has been derived from shedding human blood, without a single advantage to the human race? Or shall it be united to that of Washington, as the founder and father of a great and happy nation. The choice lies before you. The friends of liberty throughout the world, and the people of the United States in particular, are awaiting your decision with intense anxiety.

Andrew Jackson, another future president, was of a different mind about Bolívar. How could "he who has made such liberal sacrifices and exerted such great powers, physical and moral . . . ever consent to exchange the imperishable renown . . . for the fleeting and sordid gratification of personal aggrandizement"? he later asked his secretary of state, Martin Van Buren. Jackson was correct. Bolívar didn't want a crown; he had made it clear from the beginning that the notion of according a liberated republic to a monarch was abhorrent to him. But John Quincy Adams, who was then president of the United States, was not so sure:

> The conduct of Bolívar has for many years been equivocal. As a military leader, his course has been despotic and sanguinary. His principles of government have been always monarchical, but for himself he has repeatedly played off the farce of renouncing his power and going into retirement. He still holds out this pretense, while at the same time he cannot disguise his hankering after a crown.

What Bolívar couldn't disguise—what he had no intention of disguising—was that he vastly preferred the British system of government with its built-in controls to the American model. As he had said repeatedly since the early days of the revolution, Spain had kept Latin America in benighted ignorance for so long that the ordinary citizen was manifestly unprepared for the full, blazing light of democracy. A leader had to take undisputed power, hold on to it, and employ it to enlightened ends. The objective he had in mind—the complete social and educational transformation of a continent—was impossible to achieve in the short term; it needed lifelong, applied dedication. In this, as far as he was concerned, the British parliamentary system, with its presumed noblesse oblige and educated legislators, was superior to the American model. Moreover, he felt that the North American concept of federalism—meant to unite what had once been divided—was inappropriate for Spanish America, where federalism would only divide what had previously been united. But for leaders in Washington, any preference for British ways was anathema. The allergy was understandable enough, but something had been lost in the translation.

To be sure, Bolívar understood that the differences between America north and south were deep. Hadn't Montesquieu's *Spirit of Laws*, the precursor to the United States constitution, insisted that laws be tailored to those for whom they are meant; that it would be an astonishing fluke if one nation's laws were applicable in another? South America had an obligation to construct a constitution appropriate to its needs, "not one that was written for Washington!" Later, in an unbridled fit of anger, he complained to Santander that "liberals" like Santander—his anti-militarist, anticentralist circle of Bogotá lawyers—were blindly aping the United States without considering the radical differences. Beware of "American hucksters," he wrote his vice president. "I detest that lot to such a degree that I would not want it said that a Colombian did anything the same way they do." As time and political necessity had worn on, Santander had used that intemperance against Bolívar, and now it was coming a cropper in the official Washington response.

When Bolívar read Harrison's insult, he wrote to the British chargé d'affaires in a fury, "The United States seems destined by Providence to plague America with torments in the name of freedom."

Indeed, Bolívar's relations with the British were far friendlier, and the Americans in Washington couldn't help wondering why. Not only had Bolívar written to King George IV, thanking him for the heroics of so many British soldiers in the liberating army, but he had developed a close camaraderie with the British chargé in Colombia, Colonel Patrick Campbell. The sunny diplomat was thoroughly enchanted by the Liberator and said so at every opportunity. In Bolívar, he saw the only leader who could purge the nation of the rank political corruption, armed insurgencies, and rampant ignorance that plagued it; to Campbell, Bolívar was indefatigable, admirably disinterested, patriotic, awe-inspiring, capable of commanding the cooperation of all good men. Soon, Campbell began hoping out loud that Bolívar would be given absolute power—the presidency for life, perhaps—with the right to choose a successor from among the princes of Europe. Bruiting about this notion of a "monarchical project," the Englishman persuaded himself that Bolívar himself aspired to such a model. Campbell breezily reported to London's Foreign Office that certainly every thinking person in Colombia favored a monarchy. "I cannot suppose," he wrote in a confidential memo, "that Bolívar would be an obstacle in the erection of Colombia into a constitutional monarchy—but I do not think that he would, himself . . . accept the crown."

Bolívar's enemies leapt on the "monarchical project" as proof of the Liberator's burgeoning megalomania. Unearthing letters from loyalists—Páez, Briceño Méndez, Urdaneta—who had lobbied openly to persuade their hero to mount a throne, those enemies decided they had incontrovertible evidence.

The Liberator may well have been bullheaded, militaristic, deluded by blue-sky ideas of Pan Americanism. He may even have seen himself as a benevolent overseer, a sage of sages, capable of supervising a broader American union. But he had never wanted to be king.

IN SUCH A STATE OF high blame and vitriol did Bolívar now face the Great Constitutional Convention. He had often said that the convention was Colombia's last hope—an opportunity to forge a stable nation. But unlike Santander, who busied himself campaigning to pack the hall with delegates, Bolívar did little to ensure that Bolívarians would be there to argue his side. He had stressed the convention's importance for months as he traveled the countryside; fretted openly about Santander's bookish young "liberals" and their separatist fantasies; made every effort to court conservative institutions—the generals, the merchants, the priests—as a foil against the lawyer-bureaucrats. But ultimately, aside from insisting that delegates be chosen from among the nation's best and brightest, he made no preparations. He had decided to let fate take its course.

Santander, on the other hand, left nothing to chance. The general who had never led a battlefield victory now conducted a formidable paper war, deploying journalists to write incendiary assaults against Bolívar. "In my line of work," he wrote to Vicente Azuero, the most rabid of Bolívar's critics, "one avoids frontal combat against a powerful enemy, especially if it is possible to destroy him with forays, surprise ambushes, and all manner of lesser hostilities." Santander was tireless in those maneuvers. He traveled to outlying villages to rub elbows with small-town politicians; he visited the taverns and drank chicha with the people. He invited potential candidates to dine at his table, made flamboyant promises, offered them all the comforts of his house. Throughout, he spoke constantly of the Liberator's alleged plot to hijack the constitution and mount a throne.

Bolívar knew very well that the convention would decide between him and Santander; between a national and a federalist state; between a new and an old constitution. But he kept out of the elections, full of conviction that, as the highest executive of the republic, he could hardly stoop to those tactics; a president did not use his power for personal ends. In his mind, at least, there was a difference between assuming a dictatorship for the good of the republic and trying to sway an election. When it was suggested that he attend the convention in order to keep a firm hold on its decisions, he rejected the notion out of hand. He sent the delegates a written message instead. All this was good news to Santander, who quickly realized his opportunity.

Santander's vigorous efforts to pack the convention paid off. The "liberal" party won a majority of the delegates and Santander was elected as the representative of six provinces, including Bogotá. Bolívar was astonished. At first, he accused his vice president of fraud, but realizing how petty and foolish that sounded, backed off and accepted the humiliation. In resignation, he wrote, "All New Granada has conspired against me. . . . Santander is the idol of this place."

Although the convention was uppermost in his mind, Bolívar had much to occupy his days. He was still president of Greater Colombia, after all, from Panama City to Guayaquil. With prophetic foresight, he commissioned a British engineer to survey the Panamanian isthmus for the possible construction of a canal between the seas. Envisioning Colombia as the gatekeeper of a mighty commerce, he studied the trade routes that had developed in the region. But Latin American conflagrations kept getting in the way of progress. In the north, Venezuelans were arming themselves against a possible Spanish invasion from Cuba. In the south, President Sucre had been wounded in a skirmish when two separatist Peruvian generals, Gamarra and Santa Cruz, had tried to topple Sucre's "foreign" presidency and win Bolivia for themselves.

There were other, more immediate dangers. In Cartagena, two sworn enemies—a white aristocrat and a mulatto sailor—were vying for power. General Mariano Montilla and his nemesis, the black admiral José Padilla, had been wrangling over supremacy in Cartagena for years. Padilla was a giant of a man and, as one contemporary put it, as strong and scarred by life as a Cyclops; sometimes he was so full of hatred for the white race that he was helpless to contain it. The feisty, adventurous son of a ship's carpenter, Padilla had survived the Battle of Trafalgar, transformed himself into a hero of the revolution, and now boasted a popular following. Montilla, on the other hand, was the army's local commander in chief, a refined, erudite man from one of the leading families in Caracas. Padilla suspected Montilla of being on the verge of staging a coup, and so decided to storm Cartagena. With a band of colored followers, Padilla invaded the port city and declared himself its intendant. But the struggle between Padilla and Montilla had deeper political ramifications: Padilla was a New Granadan and loyal to Santander; Montilla, a Venezuelan, was an agent of Bolívar. It was an extension of the larger feud.

Bolívar could hardly be in three places at once. He decided to set out for Cartagena immediately. He hadn't gone far before word came that Montilla had quelled the coup and sent Padilla running to Santander's side just as the convention was getting under way in Ocaña. Bolívar decided to take fuller measure of the situation. He stopped in Bucaramanga, a picturesque little town in the verdant, wooded hills, ninety miles from Ocaña, and there he stayed—close enough to monitor the convention's proceedings, far enough to appear as if he were doing nothing of the kind. But Bolívar's enemies suspected that he had always intended to come to Ocaña and keep an eye on Santander. When Bolívar sent his aides to sit in on all the debates, they were certain of it. The truth was simpler: Bolívar had stated very clearly to his staff that the stakes at Ocaña were too high to ignore, that what was decided there would frame the future of the republic. It would affect all he had ever struggled for. With the volatile Padilla taking refuge there under Santander's wing, the convention had taken on a possibly explosive dynamic. Bolívar wanted to know precisely what was being said.

As days passed and the deliberations in Ocaña dragged on, Bolívar surrendered himself to a quiet life in the green vales of Bucaramanga. He took over a cluster of elegant country houses where he and his officers could dine together, discuss the news of the day, and govern the republic. They set up a system of mail deliveries to keep him informed of developing events in Ocaña, Bogotá, and Caracas. As he waited to hear the fate of the nation, he visited the local church, played cards with his aides, wrote letters, went on brisk runs, rode out into the wilds at full gallop. At meals, he presided over long, ruminative conversations, in which he discussed his long-ago marriage, his generals, the various attempts on his life over the years, his alternating respect and contempt for Napoleon. The Liberator adapted easily to life in that rustic sanctuary. He ate modestly, prepared his own salads, drank little, bathed often, and allowed no one to smoke in his presence. He even undertook to teach his more uncultivated companions a little table manners.

He had shaved his beard and mustache, and he wore his hair short, affecting a look of Spartan practicality. He had little time or taste anymore for an elaborate toilette. No longer did he dress to impress the ladies nor, for that matter, did he attend Bucaramanga's dances. He wore comfortable linen clothing and a wide straw hat. His face was an atlas of wrinkles, his skin cured to a deep, leathery tan; he seemed far older than his forty-four years. Thin to cadaverous, he had grown ever more delicate, his thighs and legs emaciated. He suffered from fevers, night sweats, deliriums—sure signs of his advancing tuberculosis. In response, his doctor tried to treat him with emetics, but these only exacerbated the condition. All the same, his spirit was strong. When he laughed, his eyes fairly twinkled; they had, as was often said, an expression of soul and energy impossible to capture. When he brooded, they grew pinched, his lower lip large: he could also be, according to even his most devoted admirers, decidedly ugly.

He was generally up at five in the morning, tending his horses. When he wasn't out on a jaunt through the wilds, he was swinging vigorously in his hammock, dictating letters or reading from a store of books that traveled with him—works by Homer, Virgil, Montesquieu, Locke, or the eloquent Bishop de Pradt. By early evening, exhausted by the sheer stress of waiting, he was ready for bed. Mostly, during those days of forced idleness, he vacillated between determination and pessimism. He was as moody as a tiger in a cage. What he was hearing from Ocaña was not good: José María del Castillo, a loyal partisan to his cause, had been elected president of the convention, but the man couldn't get Bolívarians to agree and vote as a unified bloc. The Venezuelans, particularly, had turned out to be unreliable advocates, inclined to pursue personal agendas in lieu of the greater good. The Santanderistas, on the other hand, ate together, moved together, consulted on every point, and worked as a uniform offensive.

On the first order of business, both sides were in unanimous agreement: the old constitution needed to be overhauled. But beyond that, as delegates began to pull tedious drafts of a new charter from their pockets, debates quickly degenerated into long windy harangues or shouting matches, freighted with personal animus. Bolívar's followers were accused of being tyrants; Santander's, cunning conspirators. In time, a rumor began to spread that Santander had ordered one of his men to steal out to Bucaramanga and assassinate the president. Immediately, Bolívar's retinue tightened the security around him. But nothing came of it; and the Liberator, apprised of these machinations, dismissed them as entirely ridiculous.

By the end of May, Santander's front had made real headway in the deliberations. Azuero, the journalist who had issued the most scathing condemnations of Bolívar, put forward the group's recommendations for a new constitution: They would abolish the law that allowed Bolívar emergency dictatorial powers. They would curb the president's power in general, dismember the republic, federalize the nation into twenty provinces, and give congress broad powers over the executive. It was Bolívar's nightmare. Fully aware of this, his followers demanded that the Liberator be allowed to go to Ocaña and present his side. But Santander took the floor and argued vehemently against it. No, the vice president insisted, he cannot come. "For if he does, there will be no will, no ideas other than his own!" The assembly roundly agreed.

Castillo sensed the reins slipping out of his control. He considered boycotting the proceedings—walking out with just enough members to prevent a legitimate vote. When Bolívar heard of it, he was appalled. Had it come to this? Had one bully so stalled the democratic process that men of principle would be forced to walk away? Had the convention, his great hope for the republic, been so futile? But Azuero's proposals for the nation were worse. "Do what you must," Bolívar told his delegates, "and I will do my duty."

The more he thought about it, the more determined he became. In idler days, he had fantasized going home to join his retired, war-battered cohort in Venezuela. Now, he was incapable of abandoning the fight. "My doctor often has told me," he wrote Briceño Méndez, "that for my flesh to be strong, my spirit needs to feed on danger. This is so true that when God brought me into this world, he brought a storm of revolutions for me to feed on. . . . I am a genius of the storm."

On the 10th of June, nineteen conventioneers walked out of the proceedings at Ocaña, leaving fifty-four delegates in the room—one person short of a quorum. The Great Constitutional Convention was over. By then, Bolívar was on his way to the capital. "The bull is in the arena," he wrote his minister of foreign affairs, "and now we'll see who's got guts." As he rode on, he got word that Bogotá's ministers were demanding that he take supreme dictatorial powers. He didn't know it yet, but one of his generals, Pedro Herrán, had summoned the people of Bogotá to the main square. The constitution, Herrán had told them, was in tatters; the convention, a failure; the country, verging on chaos. Bolívar was riding back to renounce his presidency, Herrán said, and a bloody civil war would surely follow. Was that what they wanted? With eight hundred of Herrán's armed soldiers just beyond the square, there was considerable weight to the question. The council of ministers did not hesitate. They voted to disregard all decisions at Ocaña, suspend elected officials, and confer unlimited power on Bolívar. When the Liberator entered the city on June 24, he was welcomed euphorically as the savior of the republic.

It was a genuine torrent of gratitude. The citizens of Bogotá sensed they had peered into a maw of anarchy and pulled back, just in time. Bolívar may have had enemies in the halls of government—Santander had elevated them, made them appear mightier than they truly were—but on the streets, among ordinary people, there was no doubt who was the nation's leader. For many, Bolívar represented freedom itself: the polestar of a new identity. As he rode into view on that warm summer's day, they roared with wild approval.

Two months later, in a ceremony that formalized Colombia's "Organic Decree," Bolívar was pronounced president-liberator. His acceptance address was puzzling, odd, filled with a rare ambivalence: "Colombians," he said in closing, "I won't even utter the word 'liberty,' for, if I am good on my promises, you will be more than liberated, you will be *obeyed*. Moreover, under a dictatorship, how can we speak of liberty? On this then let us agree: Pity the nation that obeys one man as we should pity the man who holds all power."

He was that man; he held absolute power; and his uneasy romance with authority would come to define a continent. A few days later, José Padilla was put behind bars. Francisco de Paula Santander was stripped of all command. The office of vice president was abolished. In a pale show of national appreciation, Bolívar offered Santander an ambassadorship in Washington. But it was clear that if the failed general didn't accept, he would be setting sail all the same. "Santander will leave the country," Bolívar announced, "one way or another."

In the end, Santander would go for an entirely different reason.

WHILE BOLÍVAR WAS IN BUCARAMANGA awaiting news of the convention, Manuela Sáenz was coming and going freely from La Quinta, his house overlooking Bogotá. She was ever bolder in her eccentricities, her predilection for dressing like a man, her lavish parties with naughty skits and dances. Among her guests at those ribald affairs were some of Bolívar's closest friends—including an emerald magnate named Pepe París and a jolly Englishman named Colonel John Illingworth. They were captivated by Manuela's warmth, her raffish wit and humor, but they were drawn, too, by her closeness to the Liberator. She was La Presidenta, La Libertadora: a door to his intimate circle. That she adored him was patently obvious; that she despised anyone who didn't was amusing.

"Paula, Padilla, Páez!" she had complained to Bolívar, "all those P's! . . . God, let them all die! It will be a great day for Colombia when they do." She had—as South Americans like to say—no hair on her tongue. "We adored her," one of his friends confessed. "She would receive visitors in the morning, dressed in a fetching robe. She tried covering her arms, but essentially they were bare; and, embroidering away, with possibly the prettiest fingers in the world, she spoke little, smoked fetchingly . . . and shared the most interesting news of the day. Later on, she would ride out in an officer's uniform."

A month after his return, on Monday, July 28, Manuela held an extravagant party in La Quinta to celebrate Bolívar's forty-fifth birthday. The festivities were open to the public and held on the sloping meadows that surrounded the house. La Quinta itself was hung in patriotic bunting. Outside, a military band did the honors, soldiers performed drill formations, revelers danced or splashed in the river, and an abundance of food and drink was offered: grilled meats, fresh bread, countless barrels of chicha. Inside the house, where the Liberator's personal friends were received, the fare was more elegant. Bolívar, as chance would have it, was in town, busy, and could not attend, but his generals and old cronies filled the rooms, toasting his name with champagne. As the evening wore on, tributes grew uninhibited and vinous, until—in the wee hours of morning—someone mentioned the name of Santander. It was like holding a match to gunpowder: Someone else proposed that they hold a mock trial and hang the irksome ex–vice president in effigy. Off they went, clapping and hooting, to fashion Santander from a sack of grain, a three-cornered hat, long black stockings, and a sign that read: "F.P.S. dies, Traitor." An officer improvised a firing squad, a priest gave last rites, and—to the apparent delight of all—the puppet was pounded with gunshot.

It was a disgrace, a scandal—and all of it in public. Some claimed that Manuela Sáenz was to blame. That, at least, was the opinion of General José María Córdova, a young officer in Bolívar's service, who had despised her since the ship's voyage he had taken with Manuela after the harried evacuation of Peru. We don't know whether the cause for that animus was a heated argument or, as some popular historians claim, a failed flirtation. But to Córdova, the Libertadora was obstreper-

ous, spiteful, a meddler in government affairs; she was corrosive to the
very fiber of the country. In high dudgeon, he told the Liberator that he
would do well to be rid of her.

"I know you're angry with me," Sáenz wrote her lover just after the
scandal broke, "but I'm not at fault." According to her, others had been
responsible. She hadn't seen it; she'd been fast asleep—all of which may
or may not have been true. She offered to lie low in her own house for a
while. "The best thing now, sir, may be for me to stay away, unless you
want to see me."

Bolívar was furious, knowing that even though he hadn't been present, he would be blamed for the whole affair. He tried to dismiss it as
a prank, an instance of too much mirth and drink—unfortunate, but
ultimately harmless. But he knew he had to respond. "I'll suspend the
commanding officer," he told Córdova. "As for the lovable madwoman,
what can I say? I've tried my best to be rid of her, but she's impossible to
resist. . . . Even so, once we're past this, I think I'll send her back to her
country, or wherever she wants to go."

He would do nothing of the kind. She was indispensable to him.
Other than his manservant, José Palacios, who had served him for years
and kept a close catalog of every penny he spent and every well-worn,
earthly scrap in his possession, Manuela was the most intimate companion Bolívar had ever known. She was the only other human being who
worried over him, tended to his every need, kept a keen eye on his entourage, and said what no one else had the courage to say.

What few had the courage to say was that whispers of an impending coup were beginning to be heard in the capital. Manuela, who had
her ear well to the ground, became suspicious of just such a plot in early
August, as the council of ministers readied itself to grant absolute power
to Bolívar. A cabal of young intellectuals loyal to Santander began to
speak openly of "tyrannicide" as the only way to save the republic.
Although the people and the army were firmly on Bolívar's side, these
youths were adamantly not. They were a motley alliance with one thing
in common: they had spent their short lives in the shadow of revolution and, as far as they were concerned, the country needed to move on.
Bolívar was of their parents' generation: a throwback, a warmonger, a
diehard of the old guard. As far as they were concerned, in suspending

the law and usurping power, Bolívar had committed high treason. He was little more than a common criminal. "Off with the Tyrant's head!" became the rallying cry. To any casual observer, the young liberals were only quoting literature. But the tight cabal was plotting the president's assassination.

Among the conspirators was Florentino González, a young editor who had taken over Azuero's newspaper and married Bernardina Ibañez, the stubborn young beauty with whom Bolívar had been so infatuated a decade before. González was pale, volcanic, gifted with words; and, like Azuero, he despised Bolívar with a passion. His conspirators were Pedro Carujo, a young artillery officer with literary pretensions, who had always harbored royalist sympathies; Agustín Horment, a French liberal, suspected of being a Spanish spy; Luis Vargas Tejada, whom Santander had chosen to be his secretary in his pending ambassadorship to the United States; and, finally, Colonel Ramón Guerra, chief officer of the city's garrison, whom no one would have suspected of being involved in the skullduggery.

The first plan was to kill Bolívar at a masked ball to be held at the Coliseum Theater on August 10, the tenth anniversary of the historic Battle of Boyacá. The mayor had approved the festivities with one proviso: guests had to wear costumes that corresponded to their gender. To enforce it, he stood near the door as guests filed into the ball. One by one, he peered behind their masks. Among the early arrivals was a partygoer dressed as a hussar. When the mayor asked him to lift his mask, he refused. Barred admission, the hussar whispered she was Manuela Sáenz, but the mayor was firm: not even the Liberator's mistress would be admitted dressed as a man. Manuela, who feared precisely what the conspirators had planned—a swarm of assassins, dispatching their Caesar with a battery of well-aimed daggers—did what she had come to do. She raised an earsplitting ruckus. She shouted, screamed, argued frantically, until there could be no doubt who was at the door, trying to gain entry. Bolívar, already inside and in sure danger, was so thoroughly embarrassed that he excused himself and left. Manuela had been disgraceful yet again, but she had made sure Bolívar would leave alive.

The second plan to murder him came on September 21, three weeks after the "Organic Decree" granted him absolute power. It was

Sunday—a crisp, cool day—and Bolívar had decided to take a long walk to Soacha, a pretty little suburb five miles from the city's center. His companions, as the conspirators had learned, were to be few—one friend, one aide—and the stroll would be on a country road: the ideal scenario for a murder. Carujo prepared six assassins for the task, but the conspirators were called off at the last minute by Santander, who told them emphatically that the public wasn't ready to be rid of Bolívar. It was best to wait, to use legal arguments where possible; and in any case he wanted to be as far away as possible when the moment came "so that no one will say I had anything to do with the intrigue." The new date was set for late October, when Santander, as the newly appointed ambassador to the United States, would be on a ship and long gone from the capital.

By now the scheme to kill Bolívar involved more than 150 collaborators, the great majority of whom were soldiers in Colonel Guerra's barracks, a short walk from the presidential palace. The leaders worked actively to coordinate the assault, aware that with so many in their ranks they ran a high risk of exposure. Their plan was to storm the palace in full force and dispatch Bolívar along with two of his most loyal generals—Urdaneta and Castillo. Florentino González had been elected to sound out Santander: was Santander ready and willing to assume the presidency? He responded vaguely that, if the "criminals" were out of the way, he would serve his country. All was set, then. It was a matter of time.

Time ran out, however, on the 25th of September, when the head of the garrison, Colonel Guerra, alerted his fellow conspirators that they were in danger of being discovered. An army captain had just reported to him that a revolution was afoot, that Bolívar's life was in peril, and that a number of soldiers in Guerra's garrison were involved. The informant had not imagined that such a high-ranking officer as Guerra would be part of the nefarious plan. It was late in the afternoon when González, Carujo, and Horment received Guerra's message, but they understood immediately that there was no choice but to act that night, before any details leaked to Bolívar. Indeed, rumors of a pending coup were so widespread by then in Bogotá that a woman had been emboldened to go directly to the palace and report what she had heard to

Manuela Sáenz. When Manuela fretted about it to Bolívar, he consulted his entourage, but nothing came of it. The men had a good laugh and concluded that it was like women to imagine things.

Wasting no time now, the chief conspirators gathered at seven that night in the house of Santander's deputy, Luis Vargas Tejada. Methodically, they began to send word to all 150 collaborators that they were about to execute the plan. Call it cowardice, call it change of heart: the majority failed to respond. Even Colonel Guerra decided to play it safe by visiting one of Bolívar's ministers that night to play a friendly game of cards. Nevertheless, by half past ten, the group in Vargas Tejada's house had formed a tight fist of committed assassins. They left for the palace at about half past eleven: ten armed citizens under the command of Horment; sixteen seasoned soldiers under Carujo. It was a typical September night in Bogotá—a brisk rain had drenched the city and left streets slick with mud—but the moon was bright and full.

THAT NIGHT, EVERYONE IN BOLÍVAR'S circle was ailing. The palace had been reduced to a clinic. Bolívar was sick with fever. José Palacios was confined to bed, severely ill. Two aides were suffering from bad colds, Colonel Ferguson so much so that he had gone off with a burning throat to be treated at the army hospital, and Colonel Andrés Ibarra was suffering his infirmities in his room. Even Fernando Bolívar, the Liberator's nephew, freshly arrived from school in Virginia, was unwell and indisposed. Seldom had Bolívar been more unattended.

At six o'clock, he sent a message to Manuela's house and asked her to come and accompany him, but Manuela demurred. She, too, had a terrible head cold and didn't want to venture out in the inclement weather. But Bolívar insisted that she was far better off than he. He was achy, feverish, in need of her tender ministrations. Yielding to his entreaties, she put on her galoshes and hurried to him through the damp night.

When she arrived, he was in the tub, giving himself a cooling bath to ease the fever. He seemed melancholy—understandably so. He was a sick man in a sick house, with much to trouble him: the Peruvian navy had just attacked Colombia in Guayaquil; the president of Peru, General La Mar, had marched north to take command of the offensive; and the wounded General Sucre, who had lost Bolivia to Peruvian generals, was about to disembark in Guayaquil and face the hostilities. All in all, he said to Manuela—with a heavy dose of gallows humor—it's time for a palace coup. She scoffed. "Ten coups could be in the offing right now, for all the attention you pay!"

"Don't worry," he comforted her, "nothing will happen." Despite the few guards stationed around the palace that night—a fact she had seen for herself as she wended her way there—Bolívar was unpreoccupied. Colonel Guerra had assured him that an entire garrison was standing by should the slightest trouble emerge. The Liberator's only protection at that moment was the sword and the pistol that rested in the next room, sheathed and holstered, on the bureau.

He asked Manuela to read to him while he soaked in the tub, thinking that words might soothe his misery. When he climbed into bed shortly thereafter, he fell into a heavy, torpid sleep, as did his exhausted mistress. But at some point near midnight, she was brought wide awake by the raucous barking of dogs. Bolívar's mastiffs were yawping wildly in the courtyard. She heard a few dull thuds, as if something were being struck, cut down, and then the sound of men's voices, ringing through the dark.

Alert to the possibility of danger, she roused Bolívar from deep sleep. His first instinct was to grab his weapons and go, in his nightshirt, to the door. She stopped him and pleaded with him to get dressed, which he did calmly and quickly. But when he looked around for shoes, there were none. His only pair of boots had been taken away to be polished. In desperation, Manuela pressed her galoshes on him and, somehow, he was able to squeeze into them. "Now what?" he said, taking up his pistol and sword. "Shall we brave the storm?"

Thinking fast—for the clamor was only growing as the intruders burst through the hallways—she pointed to the window. She reminded him that only days before he had told Pepe París it would make a perfect getaway. Bolívar had said it in jest, but now with marauders at the door, pounding their fists and shouting, he saw how right he had been. The window opened onto the street—it was an easy jump to the cobblestones. Manuela peered out to see if the way was clear, and made him wait a few seconds until it was. Just as he leapt through the casement into the night, his assailants began to force an entry.

Manuela took up her sword and unbolted the latch with as much calm as she could muster. She could hear the yelling on the other side: "Long live liberty!" "Death to the tyrant!" And then she flung wide the door.

"There appeared in the doorway," González later recounted, "a strikingly beautiful woman, sword in hand, who, with admirable presence of mind and very courteously, asked us what we wanted."

"Bolívar!"

"He's not here," Manuela answered. "See for yourselves." Horment and the others pushed past her, looking for Bolívar. Until then, they had had little trouble moving toward their target, and they wanted none now. Carujo and his sharpshooters had shot a guard and slit the throats of a number of sentries on their way through the palace gates, and then they had sped away to take on the Vargas battalion, Bolívar's most faithful unit, while the armed civilians rushed inside. Horment, González, and the others had raced up the few steps toward the Liberator's quarters on the mezzanine. They had wounded Ibarra, who, hearing the din, had run from his bed, disheveled and febrile but carrying a sword.

The conspirators had daggers in hand, pistols in holsters strapped to their chests. Manuela could see that they meant business. Carrying lanterns aloft, they pushed past her and inspected the rooms, feeling the bed to see if it was still warm. But Bolívar was nowhere to be found. Frustrated, they seized Manuela by the arm and questioned her gruffly, demanding to know where he had gone. She responded that he was in the council rooms, down the hall. It was the only plausible excuse that sprang to mind. When one of the men shouted that a window was gaping, Manuela insisted that she had just opened it herself. They believed her; they couldn't imagine that Carujo's soldiers would leave that side of the street unattended. She led them this way and that down the circuitous hallways, trying to throw them off track and hoping to buy Bolívar precious time. When at last they had been led to every floor of the palace and back again, they suspected that she was toying with them. She crossed her arms, standing her ground against the lot of them. "He's safe!" she admitted finally. "I helped him flee! So kill me!" They flung her to the floor, kicked her head, and began beating her with their swords, but González pulled them off. "I didn't come here to fight women," he said. They vanished down the hall as quickly as they had come, just as cannon fire exploded outside: Carujo's gunners were attacking the Vargas regiment. As Manuela staggered back to the room, she heard the sharp clatter of boots outside. Glancing out into the moonlight, she made out Bolívar's aide Ferguson, sprinting back from the barrack hospital. She tried to warn him, but he refused to halt. "What's going on?" Ferguson cried when he saw his fellow colonel Carujo, wielding a gun, shouting orders. Carujo killed him with a single shot before he could reach the door.

As Bolívar lit on the cobblestone street beyond the bedroom window, he saw his pastry cook scurrying from the palace. Together, they ran as far as they could, along the river, taking refuge under a dank bridge as Bogotá came to life with shouts, bustle, and gunfire. For three hours, they shivered in the dark, listening to the clatter of horse hooves overhead, the staccato of steel-studded boots on stone, the cries of frightened citizens as they flung open and slammed shut their windows. The conspirators had freed Padilla from the barrack prison—killing his jailer in the process—and the black general staggered into the moonlit night with no idea that a coup was afoot. Street by street, Bolívar's faithful Vargas battalion, led by Córdova and Urdaneta, worked at beating back the conspirators, taking some prisoner, chasing others until they scattered, never to be found. Sometime after the bell tower struck two, the uproar finally began to die down. Bolívar's fever had mounted in the humid mountain chill, but he couldn't risk coming out just yet. He sent the cook out to learn what he could from the barracks. The man came back with good news: the army had remained loyal to Bolívar; the citizens were outraged; the conspirators had vanished into the night. When General Herrán came riding down the street to cries of "Viva, Bolívar!" the Liberator knew, at last, that he might venture out and take measure of the situation.

Soaked to the bone, slathered in mud, hardly able to speak, he was taken to the main plaza, where he was received with boundless elation. Urdaneta, Castillo, París, Córdova, and every last soldier on the square rushed to embrace him, their eyes glistening with tears. He was near delirious, on the verge of fainting, but told them, "Here I am, dying of grief, and you're trying to kill me with joy."

The grief was indeed palpable. He was humiliated, shaken. Until then, he had blithely dismissed all rumors of danger as the gibberish of a harmless fringe. He had never imagined that soldiers in his own army—his "patriots"—would raise swords against him. It was a shattering revelation, especially when he learned that his house had become a killing field, his mistress so battered she could hardly walk. Indeed, something in Bolívar died during that predawn vigil under the bridge—it was as if his heart were broken, his spirit mortally wounded. He had survived two assassination attempts before, but this one would torment him for the rest of his life.

By four in the morning, he was back in the palace, thanking Manuela for her nimbleness of mind and courage. "You are the Liberatrix of the Liberator," he told her tenderly. Again and again, he asked her to recount the details as they unfolded, responding gloomily every time, "I don't want to hear any more." But then he would toss and turn until he sat up and asked her to tell it all over again.

Bolívar's first impulse when he met with his ministers later that morning was to resign the presidency and pardon the conspirators. He didn't even want to hear who his attackers were. "My heart is in pieces," he told his confidants. He admitted to Castillo that he was profoundly saddened and wanted nothing so much as to leave the country. He added that he preferred to die rather than live; he was simply carrying on for the glory of the republic. With that, Castillo could see that the man before him was gravely ill. He advised him to think closely about the ramifications. If he did as he said, Bolívar would signal to the world that the anger of a very few was more important than the welfare of many; that Colombia's Liberator would rather resign than fight for his republic's glory.

Castillo's counsel was persuasive. By the next day, Bolívar's officers had put Santander, Guerra, Padilla, Horment, and Carujo under arrest.

They rounded up suspects, began a full investigation of the conspirators. One by one, the people of Bogotá turned them in. Colonel Guerra, who had spent the evening playing cards with Castillo, appeared at the palace as if it were just another day; as if he had never been part of the plot. He was seized and taken off to prison. General Urdaneta—Bolívar's loyal combatant since the Admirable Campaign and Santander's most bitter enemy—was given charge of dispensing justice. Within a month, Bolívar wrote to tell Sucre that he was certain his former vice president was the brain behind the assassins' scheme. "I am crushing the aborted conspiracy," he said. "Every accomplice will be punished, one way or another. Santander is the highest-ranking among them, but he is also the most fortunate. My generosity protects him."

In the end, of the fifty-nine men identified as principal actors, eight were acquitted for one reason or another, largely because they were willing to testify against the rest. Fourteen were condemned to death and executed outright, among them Guerra, Horment, and Padilla. Facing the firing squad, General Padilla—who was certainly a rebel, but by no means an assassin—refused to wear a blindfold and, like Piar, who had been executed so controversially a decade before, was unapologetic to the finish, shouting "Cowards!" before he succumbed to gunshot. Other conspirators either escaped or were imprisoned for only a short while. Carujo and González, the true ringleaders, saved their necks via one machination or another; González (married to the coveted Bernardina) swore to tell Urdaneta and the judges everything he knew. Santander, who was dragged through the courts and from prison to dungeon, was issued a death sentence, but Bolívar munificently commuted it to banishment.

In spite of his decision to let the courts punish the aggressors, the Liberator didn't have the stomach for all-out revenge. "I've got conspiracy up to the eyeballs," he said, in exasperation. Manuela later insisted that he was the soul of clemency: he had forbidden the courts to force her to testify and be part of the bloodletting; he had asked Manuela to visit Padilla in his prison cell and console him; he had looked the other way when she harbored fugitives in her house. She had never forgotten that, in the heat of the moment—when she was defenseless, her head to the floor—Florentino González had prevented his goons from killing her. If culprits were inexplicably freed and pardoned, it was because human circumstances such as these prompted Bolívar's mercy.

If Bolívar had not leapt from his bedroom window on that moonstruck night, he might have been a dead man and the country in bloody ruin. A mistress and a pastry cook had turned the tide of history. A pair of galoshes had saved the day. And yet it is fair to say that the assassins accomplished what they wanted. The Liberator was never the same again. His body and spirit slipped into a fatal spiral. A death knell began to sound.

~ CHAPTER 17 ~

Plowing the Sea

No one achieves greatness with impunity: No one escapes the fangs of envy along the way.

—Simón Bolívar

In the days that followed, Bolívar's health plunged to a dangerously fragile state. Apart from the heartbreak of the attempted assassination, there was the physical strain: squatting under a bridge for three hours in the cold damp of night would have taxed a healthier man, and he had been racked by fever to begin with. The ordeal profoundly affected his lungs, which were teeming with undiagnosed tuberculosis; he withdrew to La Quinta to convalesce. Even as Manuela's bruises faded and she began to bustle about the house, managing affairs, Bolívar remained weak, and the frailty showed.

He decided to stay on at La Quinta, for he felt more secure in that hillside redoubt, and it was there that visitors were obliged to call. The newly appointed ambassador from Paris, Auguste Le Moyne, who arrived three months after the foiled conspiracy, made his way up the hill to present his credentials to the president. Le Moyne had endured a rough, two-month voyage up the Magdalena in a canoe propelled by twelve near-naked men—the ambassador had seen his share of crocodiles, drunken locals, riotously colored parrots—but he was never so struck by those sights as he was by the figure before him now:

> We arrived at la Quinta and were received by Manuela Sáenz. . . . Moments later there appeared a man in a miserable state, with a long, jaundiced face, a cotton cap on his head, wrapped in a robe, and his legs all but lost in a pair of wide flannel trousers. At first mention of his health: "Ay!" he said, pointing to his emaciated arms, "it isn't nature that has reduced me to this, but the pain gnawing at my heart. My fellow citizens couldn't kill me with daggers, so they are trying to kill me with ingratitude. When I cease to exist, those hotheads will devour each other like a pack of wolves, and what I erected with superhuman effort will drown in the muck of rebellion.

As he dogged ahead, trying to recover some semblance of stability, he was painted by a soldier from the glory days of Boyacá. Although the artist strove to give him a distinguished bearing, he couldn't help but record the specter: the thin hair, sunken cheeks, the eyes that lacked all radiance. No longer was the Liberator the spirited warrior of the triumphalist canvases of La Paz and Lima. His muscles had withered. His skin was slack; his face, dug with furrows. The jaw—once fine and strong—had grown weak with a thousand doubts. The bold stance had become tentative.

Bolívar agonized over the punishment to be meted out to the conspirators, changing his mind constantly as to whether sentences should be harsh or merciful. He was all too willing to be led in this, listening in turns to Sucre, Manuela, and Santander's mistress, Nicolasa Ibañez, who pleaded for mercy on Santander's behalf. Urdaneta's jury had found the vice president indisputably guilty. According to them, Santander had known about the plot, given the conspirators advice, and never once made an attempt to notify the authorities. But as much as the courts looked for evidence that linked him to the crime, they found none. Bolívar was persuaded Santander was at the bottom of it, but he also worried about the ramifications of executing so popular and eminent a man. In the end, he listened to his council of ministers, who recommended leniency. Bolívar commuted the sentence to banishment and Santander was shipped off to await it in a fetid cell in the dungeons of Cartagena. Bolívar couldn't help worrying about that, too. Was it right to grant clemency to a white man who had dealt with traitors when a black man—Padilla—had been executed for the same crime? Would Colombia ever forgive its Liberator for putting to death its greatest black heroes: Padilla and Piar? He confided to a friend that the blood of so many had come to haunt him.

Bolívar's intense preoccupation with justice now colored all his decisions. He hesitated, wavered. He was tormented by the fact that his enemies called themselves "liberals" and arrogated to themselves such concepts as "freedom" and "justice" when he had invoked precisely those words at every step of the revolution. Hadn't he promised equality, freedom, the rights of man? Hadn't he delivered independence? But in peace it all seemed a carousel of empty rhetoric. The meaning of "liberal" had been twisted, used to hostile ends, and then sent around to plague him. He grew more and more irritated with people who urged him to be his old self, renew his energies; couldn't they see he was mortally tired, that his energies were spent? As one historian put it: it was during those days of unrelieved anguish—realizing his failures as a politician—that he reached a peak of personal greatness. He understood now with rare lucidity what it meant to hold unlimited power; he knew, too, that a ruler should be loath to use it. "Beware the nation in which one man rules," he had told his fellow patriots, "for it is a nation of slaves." He hadn't meant to find himself in that position. He had assumed dictatorial power because the country was in shambles and he needed to get things done; he had set the date of the constituent congress—January 2, 1830—as the day he would surrender it. But the night of September 25 had shown him just how unrealistic his goals had been, how bitter the animus against him. So it was that the most radical and impetuous of world revolutionaries became filled with a mortal hesitancy. Bolívar had become a man of qualms; he could hardly budge; and he saw the tragedy of it clearly.

As usual, it was his generals and friends who pressed him on. They knew that wherever Bolívar went, some semblance of order would follow; and wherever the man was not was bound to fall into disrepair. It now became crucial to prop him up, keep him in power, for he seemed the only certainty in an increasingly uncertain republic. Every political advance, every institution, every step in world recognition had been achieved by virtue of the Liberator's stature. Santander himself had said it: "You are the anchor of all our hopes; the essence of our vitality. . . . Only you can save us in these perilous times." As O'Leary so aptly put it: people believed that Bolívar could calm troubles by his very presence, by "the magic of his prestige."

No one knew more than Bolívar how imperfect the work had been. Independence had been achieved—enlightened forms of government considered—and yet the victors had emerged with no singleness of purpose, no spirit of collegiality. Warlords still wanted to rule their little fiefdoms, their undersized dreams a match for undersized abilities. It was as true in Bolivia as it was in Venezuela: Notions of a larger union seemed pompous, foreign, vaguely threatening. The colonies were dead, but the colonial mentality was very much alive. The new republics were as insular and xenophobic as Spain had encouraged its American satellites to be. Venezuelans saw Peruvians as arrogant royalists. Coastal dwellers saw mountain dwellers as benighted Indians. Southerners saw northerners as outlandish Negroes. "Goodbye, sambo!" someone yelled as General Sucre pulled out of La Paz. No one seemed to want the dream of an amalgamated America.

The cost of liberty, as Bolívar well knew, had been staggering—far more so than in the United States. Vast, populated regions of Latin America had been devastated. A revolution begun by polite society on the assumption that its wins would be painless had become mired in two decades of catastrophic losses, rivaling in carnage the twentieth century's more heavily armed conflicts. Populations had been cut in half. Regional economies had come to a rumbling halt. Indeed, the republics Bolívar had liberated were far worse off economically than they had been under the Spaniards; whole provinces had been laid waste. Silver mines had been abandoned; farmlands burned to ash, textile production stopped cold. The chance for a new America to create a robust, interregional market had been lost to squabbling border struggles. Although indigenous and black generals appeared in the army for the first time—a phenomenon that would transform the face of South America—the

great masses of Indians and blacks were no better off after the revolution. For a long while, they would be far worse off than they had been
under Spain's oppressive laws. Slavery, which Bolívar had worked hard
to eradicate, had been supplanted by other forms of subjugation; Creoles
had appropriated the Spanish rule. The Americas that were emerging
under Bolívar's horrified eyes were feudalistic, divisive, militaristic, racist, ruled by warlords who strove to keep the ignorant masses blinkered
and under bigoted control. Eventually this would change. There is a
vast difference, after all, between slavery and freedom; between opportunity and a shut door; between a ballot and totalitarian rule. But those
fundamental transformations would take a century and a half to work
through the continent. Latin America lay in financial and social ruin, its
cities on the verge of anarchy. It was hardly the enlightened world the
Liberator had envisioned.

Bolívar needed time to mull these questions and vent his sorrows.
He decided to leave the stifling ambit of Bogotá altogether for a long rest
in the country. But before he departed, he moved to divest himself of at
least part of the crushing burden of leadership. He wrote to the general
he loved best, Antonio Sucre, who had just arrived in Guayaquil. "You
will see in the attached documents," Bolívar told Sucre, "that I am nam-
ing you absolute ruler of southern Colombia. All my powers—the good
along with the bad—I now cede to you. Make war, make peace, save or
lose the South; you are master of your fate, and I invest all my hopes in
you. . . . Ask Flores and O'Leary to read this, too, so that they can know
that I have willed you the very essence of Simón Bolívar."

THERE WAS A REASON BOLÍVAR had wanted Flores and O'Leary to read
the letter in which he invested his "favorite son" with so much power.
Flores was the general in charge of the region Bolívar called "Ecuador,"
the southern portion of Greater Colombia he had just handed to Sucre;
Bolívar knew the news would surprise Flores. He expected O'Leary to
explain.

At age twenty-seven, General Juan José Flores had already spent
sixteen years in the liberating army. Abandoned by his father, orphaned
by his mother's death, he had joined the Venezuelan revolution at the
age of twelve, when child recruits were being swept into service by des-

perate generals. His life had been spared when Boves's hordes stormed through Valencia in 1813, reducing the city to flames and slitting the throats of all revolutionaries; they had taken pity on the soldier boy. Flores had gone on to serve under Páez, from whom he had learned gall, grit, and the art of disciplining a fighting force. By fifteen, he was a lieutenant; by seventeen, captain. Bright, curious, he had taught himself to read and write. He went on to fight with Bolívar in Carabobo, Bomboná, Pichincha. Eventually, Bolívar had put him in charge of Pasto, the most stubborn and difficult region in the republic. Ruling Pasto with a deft hand, Flores had managed to quell its ardently royalist population without resorting to the rampant butchery it had endured during the "liberation." He had made up his mind that he would govern the entire region, including Quito, someday. Even so, he was no Sucre—no victor of the defining Battle of Ayacucho, no shaper of nations—no "shining, unblemished" exemplar of all Bolívar imagined a great American could be. Now Flores was being told in no uncertain terms that Sucre was to be the Liberator's successor.

Sucre did not want the job. After five years in Peru and Bolivia, the great warrior of Ayacucho had looked forward to returning to his elegant bride in Quito, whom he had married by proxy. He had already served the revolution in capacities he had never sought or wanted—in faraway governments, overseeing populations that regarded him by turns as savior and occupier. The disintegration of Bolivia had been a soul-killing experience. Generals Santa Cruz and Gamarra—skilled soldiers of the revolution—had invaded Bolivia from Peru and overthrown his presidency. He had had to speed away with a bullet in his arm, and the nation had gone on to replace him with three presidents in five harrowing days, two of whom were assassinated. All Sucre aspired to now was a quiet life, away from all that. The last thing he wanted was to encroach on anyone's command and he said so—emphatically— to Flores and O'Leary.

Time and circumstance would force his hand. On November 12, 1828, as Bolívar recuperated in the tiny village of Chia, hoping to rid himself of the black mood that had descended on him since the attempted assassination, a disgruntled colonel led a rebellion in the very region that fell under Flores's and Sucre's command. José María

Obando, the offending colonel, had begun his career as an officer in the Spanish army. But in 1822, when Bolívar undertook his historic march from Bogotá to Guayaquil, Obando had switched sides and fought as a revolutionary. In the intervening years, Obando had grown disenchanted with Greater Colombia. He considered himself first and foremost a Granadan. At first, he showed his displeasure by simply resigning from the army. But months later, in a breathtaking about-face, he wrote to General La Mar and offered Peru his services in the impending Peruvian invasion of Colombia. To show that he meant business, Obando attacked Popayán, seized control of the city, ejected its Bolívarian governor, and declared himself at war with the Liberator.

Bolívar had known for a long time that a confrontation with Peru was inevitable. It was why he had put Sucre in charge. For months, Bolívar had been sparring with Peru's ambassador—an adversary appointed, quite obviously, to goad him. He refused to see the man. Bolívar announced that he was raising a robust army of forty thousand to settle the border squabbles; he communicated to Peru that its refusal to repay a $3.5 million debt to Colombia was, in itself, a casus belli. Bolívar had been planning a wartime strategy even as he had sat in his bath on that fateful night when the conspirators had sped through the palace intending to slay him in bed. War with Peru had always been certain. And a war couldn't be won without Colombian solidarity. He instructed Flores and O'Leary to go to Guayaquil on the pretense of ne-gotiating peace with Peruvians who—by then—had blockaded the city, but in reality, he was trying to buy time so that he could consolidate his forces after Obando's defection. The last thing Bolívar needed now was a rebel colonel fanning enemy fires in that nervous region. The ailing liberator had not fully recovered—he was only ten days into a convales-cence that should have lasted two months—but he cut short his cure and rushed back to Bogotá. He was working on instinct now.

By early December, fueled by little more than Herculean will, Bolívar undertook the arduous six-hundred-mile trip over the Andes to the menaced border. Seized by violent fits of coughing, he could barely ride two hours at a time. The rains were incessant, the heat and pestilence intolerable. But speed was imperative and he directed one of his most skilled and audacious officers, General Córdova, to put down

Obando's rebellion. Not yet thirty, Córdova had been one of the heroes of Ayacucho and Boyacá; he was loyal, quick-thinking, fierce—a charismatic leader of men. As Bolívar moved overland, Córdova made a quick course for Obando. By January of 1829, the young general had scattered Obando's forces in a relentless guerrilla campaign.

In February, Sucre, Flores, and O'Leary finally mobilized against Peru. General José de La Mar had been made the Peruvian president, and his army had swarmed into Guayaquil and occupied it a month before, eager to separate it from Colombia. But La Mar's army hadn't stopped there; it had overtaken the city of Cuenca and was preparing another incursion north. President La Mar had been born in that disputed land, and he, like General San Martín before him—indeed like many Peruvians—resented its appropriation by Bolívar. He was determined to free it from Colombia's clutches and annul Peru's war debt to Bogotá.

That outright provocation gave Sucre no choice. Resigned to take up his sword one last time, he led fifteen hundred men against La Mar's army of five thousand. They met in the high buttes south of Guayaquil, in the rarefied air of Tarqui. Like most battles Sucre waged, the odds at the Battle of Tarqui were out of kilter, against the grain, with far fewer men under his command than troops charging toward him. Nevertheless, despite the rain and treacherous mountain passes—despite Obando's rebels, who seemed to materialize out of nowhere to block the way—Sucre prevailed. The Colombians were poorly armed, poorly fed, but by now they thought themselves invincible; they gave Peru no quarter. Fifteen hundred Peruvian soldiers were killed, a thousand more wounded or taken prisoner. Sucre offered La Mar an honorable surrender and, for the time being at least, the Peruvians retreated to their stronghold in the south. Weary unto death, Sucre wrote to Bolívar and reported the victory. It had seemed inconceivable that he had had to raise weapons against the very people for whose liberty he had fought so ardently in Ayacucho. But it was done. The war with Peru was over. He told Bolívar that he had assumed command only because the circumstances were urgent; that he would take no such responsibilities in the future. He submitted his resignation. His young wife was expecting their first child in July, and all he wanted now was to be by her side.

As Sucre was winding his way home through the volcanoes, Bolívar arrived in Pasto. Using the tactic he had employed two years before with Páez, Bolívar now offered the rebels complete amnesty and urged them to rejoin the republic. Obando had little choice. The rescue he had sought from Peru had become impossible. He seized on Bolívar's bait. A peace treaty was signed, and then to seal it Bolívar promoted Obando to full general. Córdova, who had labored mightily against the insurrectionist, was outraged. How could the Liberator be so peremptory? He railed against the injustice of it—the arbitrariness. Impulsive, frenzied, the young general rode off to vent his indignation. He complained to Bolívar's friends; he complained to his enemies. He even sought out Obando to gauge the man's intentions. But by then, General Córdova would have yet another reason to be furious.

MANUELA SÁENZ WAS NEVER SO celebrated in Bogotá society as she had been during the months that followed her bold rescue of Bolívar. His name for her, "the Liberatrix of the Liberator," had passed into legend, as had the image of her standing squarely at his bedroom door, brandishing a sword against his assailants. All the invective General Córdova had summoned against her scandalous conduct—the male dress, the pasted mustache, the naughty servants, the high-spirited execution of Santander's effigy—seemed to wane against the evidence of her cool aplomb. She was admirable; she was heroic. The glow would not last long. But for the moment foreign diplomats clamored to meet her; she made the rounds of a brisk social life; she was even made part of a closed circle that brainstormed the future of the republic.

The foiled assassination attempt had deeply shocked Bolívar's council of ministers. What if the colluders had succeeded? What if Bolívar had died? Surely, Colombia would have spun into unspeakable violence, another monstrous civil war. Bolívar's strongest partisans—his stalwart minister of war General Urdaneta, acting president José María Castillo, foreign minister Estanislao Vergara, and minister of the interior José Manuel Restrepo—now took it upon themselves to avert potential chaos. Taking a cue from Bolívar's long-held belief that Colombia would not succeed until it had the backing of a world power, they began to look abroad for salvation. They threw themselves into a frenzied plan to recruit a foreign monarch. They knew they were working against time; anyone could see that Bolívar's health was failing. They also knew that he would resolutely oppose them. He had made his views against crowns and thrones very clear. They decided to keep the plan secret from him for the time being.

Their notion was simple, and their hope was that it would eradicate the schisms that plagued the young republic. As they saw it, Bolívar would be at the helm until he died, at which point all power would go to a European prince who had been carefully readied for succession. A constitutional monarchy such as England's promised to be the ideal solution to Colombia's lurching instability: it would vest power in an indisputable leader, ensure the populace's hard-won freedoms, yet give government a strong hand over a racially diverse and disorderly nation. Urdaneta, Vergara, and Restrepo had approached French and British diplomats to assist them in the search. As talks continued throughout April and May, they began to favor a prince of the French royal family on the assumption that a nobleman with Catholic roots would have more in common with South American subjects. But for all the ministers' studiously contrived secrecy, by June Bolívar was well apprised of the scheme. O'Leary had reported much of it; and the British chargé d'affaires—in all his calculating enthusiasm for a monarchical plan—had written the Liberator to ask his opinion.

Whether Manuela informed Bolívar of the plan, we do not know; but as a close friend of Urdaneta's she was surely aware of it. In any case, she had every reason to support the idea. She believed her lover to be a great man and she wanted to perpetuate his vision and ensure his place in history. With all her customary worldliness and gusto, she hosted a glittering party for King Charles X's official French delegation, which arrived to discuss the monarchical project in early May. Virtually every member of the capital's diplomatic community swirled through Manuela's rooms that evening—all, that is, except for the U.S. representative, William Henry Harrison, and a few others who were viscerally opposed to a monarchist state. It isn't hard to imagine the French delegates' eagerness as they quaffed champagne in Manuela's house and toasted the Liberator: Napoleon had always had an eye on the Americas;

now, with a Bourbon king back on the throne and much of the French navy plying American waters, an irresistible opportunity had presented itself. The charming soiree in the home of Bolívar's mistress augured well for the empire of Charles X. Within little more than a year, however, all of it would be a pipe dream: Parisians would revolt, hurling stones into the king's gardens, and Charles X would evacuate the Palais-Royal in the black of night.

But in the mists of Bogotá, Bolívar's ministers could not imagine such an outcome. A monarchy promised order, permanence, and a foreign link—all the rudiments thought necessary for the survival of the republic. When they finally presented the idea to Bolívar, he waved them off with an exasperated hand. There were a thousand reasons why it wouldn't work, he said: What European prince would want to rule in that utter chaos? How would Colombia support the staggering expense of a monarchy? Most important, Colombia's humbler classes, accustomed by now to freedom, wouldn't stand for inequalities of empire. Nor was it likely that a monarchy would be tolerated by Colombia's new generals, who stood to be stripped of all power and command.

No, he had no stomach for kings. Since his days in Madrid—days of Miranda, days of San Martín—Bolívar had adamantly rejected all argument that favored a monarchical system. He rejected it now. The monarchy question was like a summer swarm of gnats: constant, annoying, yet so insignificant in his mind as to be swatted away. Some historians claim he ignored it because he had already declared a wish to abandon power; the decision was no longer his. But there were other reasons for Bolívar's dismissal: his distance from the capital, the delicate question of Córdova's disaffection, his inability to see the maneuvering at first hand. But his wan response, twisted artfully, was used by his enemies to suggest that he had always hankered after a throne. Indeed, those who prayed for Bolívar's ruin—including Páez and the supporters of Santander—feigned support for a monarchy at first, knowing that the only means to destroy Bolívar was to make Colombians believe that he, too, wanted it for himself. And didn't he, after all? Hadn't his ministers put it forward? Surely Bolívar himself had instigated it—indeed, been angling for it—all along. When the young, impetuous General Córdova heard about Bogotá's machinations, his response was immediate and unequivocal. He decided Colombia needed to be rid of Bolívar. For all his past loyalty to the Liberator, he decided to break all ties and dedicate himself to one burning cause.

By August, when Bolívar had reentered Guayaquil and La Mar had receded into the margins of history, Córdova was on the loose in the rich, green valleys of northwest Colombia, his native home. With little more than three hundred followers, he began a campaign to overthrow Bolívar. He approached Bolívar's steadfast supporter General Mosquera in the deluded belief that he could recruit Mosquera to his way of thinking; he tried to persuade the rebel Obando to reclaim his seditious stand. He wrote to Páez, congratulating him for his separatist spirit and inviting his support. Córdova had been incomparably brave in the past; indeed Bolívar had honored him with one of the jeweled crowns Peru had given him after the victory at Ayacucho. But Córdova was also rash and egotistical. Thinking he would divvy out the republic piece by piece—Venezuela for Páez, Ecuador for Flores, New Granada for himself—thinking, too, that an army was all he needed to govern a country, Córdova was the essence of a military mirage that would persist into the twenty-first century. For him, it was enough to rule by brute force, not as a government of the people. It was a foolish, atavistic, colonial frame of mind, and it was bound for failure.

But Bolívar hardly had a chance to respond to the insolence. He was unwell when Córdova had seen him in Pasto six months before, and Córdova had noted the striking deterioration. Bolívar had been sick again upon arrival in Quito: so weak, and so emotionally overcome by the sight of Sucre that he could hardly speak; he cried like a baby. Bolívar continued the backbreaking schedule, nevertheless: dictating scores of letters at a time, managing the republic, negotiating with Peru, moving restively from one trouble spot to another. He was determined to broker a sturdy peace. He knew that Peruvians expected him to invade and be the warmonger they made him out to be; he wanted to prove them wrong. Shortly after his arrival in Guayaquil at the end of July, however, the Liberator fell into an illness far graver than any he had experienced. He was delirious, bird-thin, incapacitated, spitting black. He reported that it was a passing incidence of black bile—gastric in nature—but anyone could see that it was a desperate battle for survival, and all too clearly in his lungs.

We know now that the slightest frailty can admit dormant tuberculosis in its fiercest form; once the sparks of disease ignite, it can rage through a body like consuming wildfire. As soon as Bolívar's illness began to devour him, even he couldn't refute that something was deeply wrong. But he didn't allow himself to rest until peace with Peru had been established. Forced to spend twelve feverish days in bed, he continued to dictate letters and give orders, even as he floated in and out of delirium. The equatorial heat was relentless, the humid, pestilential climate ruinous to his delicate condition, and yet he could claim considerable progress: Guayaquil had been retaken easily; the Peruvians had simply slipped away, too distracted by their own reversals to oppose him. In Lima, the government had crumbled in a surgical coup; President La Mar had been deported to Guatemala at bayonet point, in shackles. The new chief of state, Antonio de La Fuente, had always been well disposed toward Bolívar—and was willing to talk peace. La Fuente would last only months at Peru's helm, giving way to the Machiavellian hand of General Agustín Gamarra and his power-hungry, bellicose wife, but for the time being, in the beastly heat of the Guayas River, it seemed as if Bolívar's peace would last.

All the same, by September, when Bolívar had recovered enough to take in the situation around him, he understood the extent of betrayal that had been mounted against him by the brave and beloved General Córdova. It had been one thing to be attacked by Santander's lawyers and city "liberals"; it was something else entirely to be despised by a trusted general. The wound this betrayal inflicted on the Liberator was lasting and deep, and, although he tried to dismiss it, he rose from his sickbed to a dark night of the spirit. His correspondence in the next months exhibits a level of torment—an almost pathological frustration—that was completely unlike the vigorous, determined Liberator who had marched into Bogotá only a year before. Bolívar wrote to O'Leary: "My strength is almost entirely gone. You wouldn't believe the state I'm in. . . . My spirit and body have suffered so much that I have no energy for the slightest task, and I feel powerless to rekindle it."

A mere five years earlier, after the fateful victory at Ayacucho, he had called America the hope of the universe, the long desired promised land. Now, the revolution seemed little more than a chimera; its heritors, madmen. As far as Bolívar was concerned, all the colonies had been duped by their illusions, like a flock of foolish children. "We have tried everything under the sun," he wrote to Urdaneta, "and nothing has worked. Mexico has fallen. Guatemala is in ruins. There are new troubles in Chile. In Buenos Aires they have killed a president. In Bolivia, three presidents took power in the course of two days, and two of them have been murdered." His America, like his body, was riddled with maladies.

It was during this time that he learned just how far his star had fallen: in France, the renowned thinker Benjamin Constant denounced Bolívar as an outright despot. In England, George Flinter, a British officer in Venezuela, published a blistering letter to King George IV, warning against issuing support for Simón Bolívar, "who has murdered thousands in cold blood and swindled the British nation out of millions." In New York, Luis Ducoudray, the French mercenary who had served Bolívar in Angostura, released a lacerating memoir, prompting a British reviewer to conclude that Bolívar was less a lion of liberty than a snake. In Washington, William Henry Harrison's condemnations were being heard by Congress and disseminated by the press. In Chile, the outcast Riva Agüero—who still called himself president of Peru—was claiming that the Liberator was a despicable Negro and that his long-dead wife, María Teresa del Toro, had been the illegitimate daughter of a cook.

"I'm being accused of an inferno of abominations," Bolívar confessed. At the end of his tether, he wrote to General O'Leary insisting that someone else be president and that O'Leary should promote that idea in Bogotá. At best, Bolívar told his old aide, a liberator might be a gadfly to goad the machinery of government—not run it. He was too weary to go on as head of state.

Was he being calculating, as some historians have claimed? Spaniards, Argentines, Peruvians—all with good reasons for their antipathy to Bolívar—have argued that he was an unabashed autocrat, a crypto-monarchist whose goals became more and more twisted with each victory. He refused laurels, those critics say, because he knew they would be offered again. He rejected power only to accept it anew in an hour of crisis, at which point he could apply it with abandon. To some extent, these accusations were true: he had turned down the presidency numerous times, resigned outright, before being persuaded to take it again. He was suspect in this. He had said that he wanted to please, serve, unify. But, since the liberation of Peru, he had come to believe that he could do none of these without wielding absolute control. In order to preserve liberties, in other words, he had assumed a dictatorship, under which—as he himself had said—all talk of liberty was impossible. Now, in this strange echo chamber of will and intent, his loyalists (as well as his enemies) wondered whether he was insisting that he wanted to leave precisely because he wanted to stay.

He continued to work. He drew up a treaty with Peru, although it wasn't clear that it would last. He oversaw an ingenious plan to finance Colombia's crippling deficit with vigorous exports of Venezuelan tobacco. He signed off on improvements in universities, schools, courts. He sent military reinforcements to Panama to protect it against the Spanish presence in Cuba. He congratulated the army on its efforts to put down Córdova's rebellion. And always—always—he found the strength to dictate a multitude of letters to his officers, relying on the power of the word. But the correspondence in which he was engaged was largely bureaucratic. He no longer had an aide whom he could trust enough to dictate his most private thoughts. "I have no one to write for me," he lamented in one of his missives; and he certainly didn't have the energy to do it himself. Worse, few of his correspondents were informing him about sensitive matters—as Santander had done so masterfully in happier days. He felt out of reach, out of touch.

Hoping for a bit of clarity, Bolívar published a circular that asked Colombians to state exactly what they wanted from government, but his enemies recalled that Napoleon, too, had ordered a plebiscite just before making himself emperor. Bolívar, they insisted, was no patriot sounding the public will, but a manipulator plotting his coronation. Bolívar threw up his hands. "There is no such thing as good faith in America," he concluded. "Treaties are worth little more than the paper they're printed on; constitutions are pamphlets; elections, an excuse for war; liberty has dissolved into anarchy; and for me life has become a torment." Forces against him were too strong now. Years of serial abandonment by officers who had once been loyal—Santander, Páez, Padilla, Obando, Córdova—had had their cumulative effect. "I hope you haven't forgotten what I told you," he wrote O'Leary. He was less coy with Mosquera, who visited him on an emerald isle just south of Guayaquil where he had gone to recuperate. He wanted to leave, he told his old friend bluntly, travel to Europe, live out his days in peace, taking nothing more from America than his memories. He was determined to step down at last.

IN JULY OF 1829, SANTANDER, whom Bolívar could neither abide nor safely destroy, was released from Bocachica dungeon and set on a journey that would ultimately take him to Hamburg. His first stop would be Venezuela, where he would be held until he was allowed to board a foreign vessel in Puerto Cabello. It must have been sobering for Bolívar when he heard of it. Santander had been friend and foe; collaborator and saboteur. Bolívar had always known that having a Granadan in the vice presidency was good cement for the republic—the only way Bogotá would accept a Venezuelan in the presidency. Santander was hardworking, ambitious, detail-oriented, and he had served Bolívar loyally for many years. But the fundamental distrust between Granadans and Venezuelans had been there from the start, and, for all their effort to overcome it, they couldn't rid themselves of a sick germ of suspicion.

The germ had been planted long before, when they had faced off as young men on the border between New Granada and Venezuela, at the start of the Admirable Campaign. Bolívar, head of the consolidated army, had ordered Santander to continue his march into Venezuela, and Santander had refused, unwilling to fight someone else's war. "March at once!" Bolívar had barked at him. "You have no choice in the matter! March! Either you shoot me or, by God, I will certainly shoot you." Eventually, Santander obeyed him; indeed, as the revolution unfolded, he obeyed the Liberator with utter dedication. Bolívar had every reason to make him his trusted colleague. In time, their correspondence revealed an alliance unparalleled in South American history. Now, after years of mounting bitterness, Santander was being ejected from the fatherland he had served all his life, and it spoke volumes about the inherent fissures in Greater Colombia. A deep, fratricidal impulse had crept into Spain's disgruntled children. Nowhere was this more apparent—and more polarizing—than in the relationship of these two men.

Although Bolívar had saved Santander from the firing squad and commuted his sentence to exile, the former vice president had been made to suffer a seven-month internment in the dank, grimy dungeons of Bocachica. This was not without its logic: Bolívar's council of ministers had feared Santander might seek revenge, join Peru, and march against the Liberator. Manuela Sáenz, too, had a deep, unshakable distrust of the man; so much so that she engaged a spy to ferret out whatever information he could about Santander's intentions. But Santander, desperate to free himself from the miseries of internment, denied he had any such reprisals in mind. He wrote an impassioned plea to Bolívar, promising he would not go to Peru or anywhere else in Latin America for that matter. He swore that he had opposed the would-be assassins with tears in his eyes, beseeched Carujo not to carry out his nefarious plot against the Liberator. Santander even went so far as to beg protection from Andrew Jackson, a fellow Freemason who had just been elected president of the United States; he told Jackson that he, too, had once been a head of state, reduced now to wretched prisoner of fortune. He needed a powerful champion to plead his case.

President Jackson never responded to Santander's plea. But the former vice president turned out to have plenty of champions in Colombia itself. Sucre and Mosquera, Bolívar's most loyal henchmen, had long respected Santander and had both corresponded with him in jail. They now began to entreat Bolívar to grant him his freedom. Even Páez, Santander's archenemy, seemed to take pity on the man. When the captive of Bocachica—reduced to illness and terror—was finally taken from his dungeon cell, shipped to Puerto Cabello, and forced to look out at the very bay from which Miranda had started his voyage to ignominious death, he made a heartfelt appeal for Páez's mercy. The Lion of the Apure assured Santander that he would be given safe passage. He was as good as his word and had reason to be: no one agreed with Páez more than Francisco Santander. For all the acrimony that had passed between them, for all their conspicuous attempts to foil one another,

Páez and Santander concurred single-mindedly on one thing: secession. They both sought to disband the republic; they both yearned to reduce their nations to manageable regions they could command freely. As one historian put it, they wanted fiefdoms equivalent to their aspirations—Cundinamarca for Santander, the Apure for Páez—provincial patches with little influence in a larger world. It was not magnanimity but unbridled ambition that led Páez to allow Santander to sail off into the Caribbean.

As Santander floated out to sea, Bolívar proceeded north toward Bogotá, racked not only by disease but by the small-mindedness of his generals, who prepared to carve up the republic just as Alexander the Great's generals had done when Alexander lay dying. Stopping in Quito to catch his breath, Bolívar published his deeply pessimistic "Panoramic View of Spanish America," in which he described the rampant lawlessness that prevailed from Mexico to Argentina. But his own land was most on his mind, and his despair about it was evident; he claimed he had been as good as assassinated: "Colombians," he grieved,

> The second man to head the Republic has assassinated the first; the Third Division invaded the south; Pasto rebelled against the Republic; Peru laid waste to her liberator's homeland; and there is hardly a province that has not exceeded its powers and prerogatives. Throughout this ill-fated time there has been nothing but blood, chaos, and destruction. There is nothing left for you to do but muster your spiritual strength and establish a government vigorous enough to curb ambition and safeguard freedom. Otherwise, you will become the laughingstock of the world and the victims of your own undoing.

The constitutional congress scheduled for January was only two months away and, as far as Bolívar was concerned, it couldn't come soon enough. He called on Colombians to rise to their better natures and prepare for it.

Páez knew well that he needed to make a move before congress convened and, seeing an advantage now that Santander was out of the way, dispatched a letter to Bolívar via personal messenger. It reached him in Popayán in the early days of November. Páez's missive was respectful, querying Bolívar about the monarchical plan, the health of the republic, the succession. But anyone could read his meaning between the lines: he would preserve the union only if he could rule it. He had suffered indignities visited on him by Santander; he had stood by for almost a decade while his nemesis had run Greater Colombia. It was his turn now.

Bolívar rallied all the diplomacy he could muster and answered Páez in the clearest terms: a monarchy was out of the question; he had always fought against it, and he was fighting against it now. Moreover, he was leaving the presidency for good. "I give you my word of honor," he told his old comrade, "I will happily put myself at your orders if you are elected our chief of state, and I'd like you to make me the same promise if someone else is chosen to lead us."

From Popayán, he also wrote an unequivocal response to his council of ministers, scolding them for going too far with the monarchical nonsense. Everything he had heard to date had been mere rumor and insinuation, but in Popayán hard evidence of efforts to make him king awaited in the form of official documents.

"You will now suspend completely all negotiations with the governments of France and England," he wrote back in high dudgeon. To Urdaneta, he was gentler: "Just leave congress to do its duty," he urged Urdaneta; "it will be easier for them to appoint a president than a prince." This dressing-down was not taken lightly in Bogotá. Ministers proffered their resignations, claiming they had only followed orders. His orders had not been vague: he had directed his diplomats to seek European protection, which he saw as essential to the fledgling status of the republic; by no stretch of the imagination had he meant them to seek a European prince. He had been too much on the move, too plagued by illness, too busy battling the Hydra of chaos to see the damage a monarchical smear might inflict on him. Both Páez and Santander, though ardent enemies, had tarred Bolívar with an imperial brush. If he had been more decisive on the question—clipped back suspicion at the very start—history might have played out differently. But history, as we know, is impossible to foresee.

Being South America's roving defender of liberty, he now admitted, had exacted a punishing price. For all the laurels and dictatorial authority he had garnered, he had no power to speak of. He had left it behind at every turn, relinquished control to deputies who simply didn't understand or endorse his vision. Ruling from a remove had proved impossible in a republic whose cities were separated by jungles, savannas, a towering cordillera. Information about statecraft had been scant, slow; by the time it arrived, the political landscape had changed, the national mind-set shifted. Improvisation, so crucial in war, was proving to be deadly when it came to government.

BY THE TIME BOLÍVAR REACHED Popayán, there was more to engage him than a stack of pressing dispatches. An uprising had come and gone in Colombia, rattling through like a row of collapsing cards. Córdova's rebellion had reached a fever pitch, growing more in renown, perhaps, than in strength of numbers. But it tumbled as quickly as it rose, and then it shocked everyone with its terrible, final resolution.

As Córdova galloped through the lush valleys of Medellín, Páez realized that this could well be the opening he had waited for. Circumstances couldn't have been more ideal. Santander was at sea, well removed from the competition, and Córdova's pugnacity seemed to serve Páez's purpose. Like Páez, the feisty young general was unwilling to bow to a European prince; and, also like Páez, he wanted to separate Venezuela from New Granada. But it was Bolívar himself who gave Páez the most felicitous opportunity of all, the plebiscite in which he had asked citizens to stand forth and say what they truly wanted from government. The wily plainsman seized that opportunity with two fists. Even before he received Bolívar's reply to the letter he had sent by messenger, he began rallying politicians to respond to Bolívar's call. He sent his agents out into the provinces, insisting on signatures for three demands: total rejection of any union with New Granada, Páez's elevation to president of the independent nation, "and down with Don Simón. Everybody must ask for this or be treated as an enemy." Soon Páez had the support of some of Bolívar's most loyal generals, fervid Venezuelans all: Arismendi, who had joined the revolution in its earliest days; Bermúdez, the intrepid hero of Cumaná; Soublette, who had fought alongside the Liberator since the Admirable Campaign; Mariño, who after years of sparring with Bolívar for control of the east, had become his trusty defender. On November 25, in the convent of San Francisco, the old, venerable church where Bolívar had been named Liberator sixteen years before, Páez announced what it was that the citizens of Venezuela truly wanted. Total independence. From Bolívar, from Colombia, and from the impossible gossamer dream of Latin American unity.

By the time Páez announced secession, Bogotá had dealt with Córdova's rebellion. Urdaneta had sent O'Leary and a thousand seasoned veterans to hunt down Córdova in the hills outside Medellín. They found him in Santuario with a motley band of three hundred—a hasty coalition of craftsmen, students, and peasants. The rebel Córdova could see that his cobbled-together little militia would be no match for Colombia's legions. As the army troops drew near, he called out to O'Leary, appealing to their old friendship, hoping to convince former comrades to join his side. Seeing the provocation for what it was, O'Leary ordered a full-fledged attack. Córdova fought fiercely, but there was no hope against a hardened war machine. His rebels dispersed in alarm. Badly wounded, Córdova managed to drag himself to safety in a nearby hut. O'Leary was quick to act when he learned of it; he directed one of his most fearless mercenaries, a notorious drunk named Rupert Hand, to storm the hideaway and rout the rebel. The Irishman burst into the little shack, found Córdova sprawled on the floor dying, and dispatched him handily with two thrusts of the sword.

The short-lived rebellion clarified things. Brash, independent-minded warriors like Córdova, who had once been the life's blood of the revolution, had become the blight of Bolívar's republic. Scarred by two decades of war, they seemed singularly unprepared for peace—battlegrounds had become their ultimate courts of justice. And so it had come to this. A beloved general was dead and, as far as the world could see, Colombia was devouring its heroes, just as Saturn had swallowed his children: one by one, even as they emerged, threatening to overthrow their father. For Bolívar, it was a hard truth to suffer. His patriots were cannibalizing their ranks, dying at one another's hands. The country's politicians were radicalized against one another. In the end, he would be blamed for all of it. O'Leary's corrective against Córdova had saved the union, but it had poisoned the nation's soul. The torment of that reality weighed on Bolívar until it crystallized in the form of a stark conclusion: Colombia was no longer worth the sacrifice. Bolívar wrote to his minister of interior, recommending that the republic be divided into three separate states: Venezuela, Colombia, and Ecuador. He added that after the constitutional congress in January of 1830 he would depart for foreign shores.

Few balked. In Bogotá, the gears of politics were whirring freely now; there seemed to be less and less patience for Bolívar. In Caracas, the rage against him was flagrant, led by his old friend Páez. Graffiti filled the walls, accusing the Liberator of being a hypocrite, a tyrant, a traitor to his countrymen. The lie that he would mount a throne—a phantom concocted by his enemies and embraced bizarrely by his followers—had brought passions to a white-hot fever. As Páez declared that he would go to war against Bolívar if he had to, city councils began to bar Bolívar from ever stepping foot in Venezuela again.

Everything happened quickly after that. The American diplomat William Henry Harrison was booted unceremoniously from Colombia for his scandalous attempts to meddle with internal affairs. The French delegation left in a huff, as did its English counterpart. When the Liberator entered the capital for the last time on January 15, 1830, hardly a voice was raised in welcome. The streets were hung in festive bunting and four thousand soldiers lined the way, but the people were eerily silent, as if something calamitous was afoot. There were rounds of cannon, choruses of music, and yet the air rang with anything but merriment. When Bolívar finally came into view, he was tiny, skeletal—a wasted specter with lackluster eyes whose voice was barely audible. It was apparent to everyone that the Liberator was not long for this earth. His grief was palpable. Lost in thought, reduced by fatigue, he made one last ride to the presidential palace.

~ CHAPTER 18 ~

The General in His Labyrinth

If my death can heal and fortify the union, I go to my tomb in peace.

—Simón Bolívar

On January 20, 1830, five days after Bolívar's arrival in the capital, congress gathered to define a new government. It was the fourth time in the twenty-year history of the republic that a constitutional convention was called to the task. The representatives elected to serve were so esteemed—such indisputable heroes of the revolution—that the body became known as "the admirable congress." As they arrived from every corner of the republic, hopes ran high that they would heal the discord that plagued the land.

The day began with a twenty-one-gun salute and a solemn Mass in the Cathedral. That venerable structure, with its soaring arches and towers, had just been restored after the ravages of the 1827 earthquake, and it loomed over the proceedings now like an ancient witness to history. Almost three hundred years had passed since Fray Domingo de Las Casas had celebrated the first Mass on those grounds. It was a typical January day in Bogotá. The crisp mountain breezes had surrendered to the morning sun, and an air of anticipation hung over the crowd as it watched its fragile president proceed from palace to altar. Only days before, he had been despondent, inconsolable; one of his letters suggests he was even contemplating suicide: "I am seeking," he had written his stalwart Castillo, "that desperate moment when I can end this humiliating existence." But he had a startling ability to overcome his dark moods when occasion demanded it. After receiving Communion from the archbishop, he led a procession across the square to the assembly hall, where, with all the pomp and formality the ceremony required, he was sworn in and offered his presidential seat.

There was no doubt Bolívar was still master among those men. Here, with so many of his esteemed generals and advocates in attendance, his prestige and charisma were hardly questioned. For all their distinction he seemed head and shoulders above the rest, a colossus in a gallery of mediocrities. It was he, after all, who had had the foresight to convoke this gathering more than a year before, pledging to surrender his dictatorial control. Congress welcomed him, lauded him, and for a fleeting moment it seemed the Liberator's power might live forever. It appeared especially so when Sucre—the man he had handpicked to succeed him—was elected to take charge of the proceedings. "I withdraw in utmost confidence," Bolívar declared, "for Sucre is my worthiest of generals." He meant it with all his heart, but it was a rash, impolitic thing to say. General Urdaneta, who had ruled Colombia for almost a year, laboring to preserve Bolívar's place in it, was visibly wounded. A British emissary reported that he clutched his head in dismay. It wasn't the first time Bolívar had passed over someone for Sucre. "I, too, had my desperate hour," General Flores commiserated with the pained Urdaneta. "I'll never forget when Bolívar dismissed me, sent me home, and then handed my whole army to Sucre."

It was an awkward moment among anxious souls. Perhaps noting so many strivers under one roof—and perhaps eager to reduce the tension—Bolívar stood, handed Sucre his speech, and left him to deliver it in his absence. If anyone harbored the fear that the Liberator would make one last lunge for power, the words Sucre read aloud made it clear that he had no such ambition. Although congress had paid him polite tribute—although the public seemed to be in his favor—few politicians gave him unequivocal support, and he knew it. His words bristled with customary candor. He wanted no part of the presidency. He had no desire to extend his power one more day:

> Spare me, I beg you, the disgrace that awaits me if I continue to fill a role that can never be free of the charge of ambition. Believe me, a new leader is absolutely vital to the republic. The people wonder if I will ever cease to rule. Our American neighbors regard me with a weary eye, contemplating what ills I will now inflict on them. In Europe, there are those who fret that I have besmirched the radiant name of liberty. Ah! How many conspiracies and assaults have been aimed at my life and authority! . . . Fellow citizens, prove yourselves worthy of the free nation you represent by banishing the idea that I am necessary to the republic. If any one man were indispensable to a state's survival, that state should not and will not exist. . . .
>
> Do as you will with this presidency; I respectfully return it to your hands. . . . I am ashamed to admit it, but independence is the only thing we have won, at the cost of everything else.

It was a bitter admission. Never before, except in letters to close confidants, had he confessed failure or despaired so openly about the future. Never had he felt so powerless to guide his country from the abyss. Now, more than ever, he warned, Colombia needed strong institutions, better citizens, a more efficient treasury, a radically reorganized military, a judiciary that protected the rights of man. He appealed to the senators to preserve and protect the Catholic religion, for in the absence of unity the Church represented the only cohesion South Americans had.

"Today, I cease to rule," began the public proclamation he issued that afternoon, and a broadside with that headline was posted immediately throughout the capital. In the course of twenty years, he told his countrymen, he had served as their soldier and chief. Now all he wanted was to rescue his tattered glory:

> Colombians! I have been the victim of reprehensible slander, deprived of a chance to defend my honor and principles. The seekers of

power have gone to great lengths to rip me from your hearts, smearing me with their own ambitions, making me out to be the author of schemes they themselves concocted; ascribing to me aspirations to a crown, which they offered me more than once and which I rejected with staunch republican indignation. Never, never, I swear to you, have my thoughts been tainted by lust for a kingdom. . . . In the name of Colombia, remain united; do not allow it to be said that you were a nation's assassins and your own executioners.

Defending his reputation had become his paramount goal. In the next days, with what little strength he had, he dedicated himself to it. He met with foreign diplomats, wrote to his ambassador in London, José Fernández Madrid, exhorting him to dispel the negative press against Bolívar in Europe. There was so much to defend: the hard-won liberation, the human costs, the iron discipline, the need for unity, the Pan American vision, the Bolivian constitution, the executions. Ambassador Madrid was to insist that Bolívar had never forced the Bolivian constitution on Colombia, nor had he been the one to install it in Peru. It had been put in place by Peruvian ministers, and only after he was gone. This was technically true, although it was well known that Bolívar had mounted a vigorous campaign in Peru's outlying provinces. Bolívar also instructed his ambassador to refute all charges of duplicity; everything he had ever said or done, he insisted, had been honest, straightforward, with no intent to dissimulate. He rejected all charges that he had been unnecessarily cruel to dissidents and Spaniards; if harsh measures had been taken, he argued, it was in the spirit of wartime reprisal. He maintained all he had ever done was free of self-interest, a fact no one could question. He was a virtual pauper; he had rejected salaries, given away everything he owned. Finally, he denied that any of his actions had ever been governed by cowardice; every attack, every calculated retreat had required grit and daring. In short, Bolívar's campaign to salvage his name was among the most ardent he ever undertook—and it quickly became a losing proposition. Even at home, he was hardly referred to as "Liberator" anymore; his closest allies had begun calling him simply "the General." There is no record that he objected to this, but he can't have helped but notice it. By then, he had convinced himself that he could let go of all worldly assets—power, possessions, even his homeland—except the one thing he prized most. His glory.

He retired to his house at La Quinta, where Manuela awaited him. Loving him as she did, she must have been shocked to see him so physically reduced, so emotionally ravaged. In seven short years, he had gone from being a commanding presence, a vibrant lover, to the remnant that appeared before her now. She received him with customary cheer, but it had to have been disorienting. She was a woman in the prime of life—a spirited, vivacious, thirty-two-year-old—and he an old man in rapid ruin.

Despite his determination to leave the presidency, it became impossible to let go of the reins entirely. Congress rejected his resignation as it had done on three earlier occasions, but this time it was for practical reasons. The country needed to project some semblance of stability as it went about electing a new leader. Even those who despised him feared that without him at the helm, the country would spiral into chaos. He was pressed, as he had always been, into staying just a little while longer.

There were moments when glimmers of the dream returned, a vestigial impulse he couldn't quite control. On January 27, even as congress busily hammered out a new constitution, he volunteered to lead an expedition to try to talk Páez out of secession. Colombia's ministers, recalling his earlier blunders with Páez, insisted a president could not travel at such a crucial time. Hamstrung and frustrated, he wrote to one of his closest friends in Caracas, José Angel Alamo: "I've asked Colombia to speak up about how it wants to be governed. Let it speak up, then! The whole South has gone and done whatever it felt like doing. Some want a populist government, democratically elected officials, regular change; others, a monarchy; and yet others . . . *sheer idiocies*! Let Venezuela be what it will be. Let it separate, federate, do whatever its heart desires. I don't care at all, at all, AT ALL! The only thing I want is what any soldier or slave wants—my discharge, my freedom."

He was feeling petulant, peevish. Seized by another attack of what he called black bile, he appointed General Domingo Caicedo acting president and announced he was setting out to convalesce in a country retreat a few miles southwest of La Quinta. The government could hardly refuse. It was clear to all except perhaps Bolívar that he was on the verge of physical collapse. With a small retinue of intimates, including José Palacios and his nephew Fernando, Bolívar went off to a house by a pretty little brook, away from the ferment of the capital. He had released all executive power for good. He would never rule Colombia again.

EVER SINCE HE HAD CONFIDED to General O'Leary that he intended to relinquish the presidency and leave the country, Bolívar had worried about his means to make that possible. He had no money. He had turned down every compensatory award every government had offered him. He had pressed his salaries on others, or neglected to collect them. By the end of March, he realized the urgency of his situation: he was destitute. He sold his silverware in hopes that it would cover his expenses, but it fetched little more than $2,000—hardly enough for a transatlantic passage and the cost it would take to sail up the Magdalena to Cartagena. He had nothing to live on come the day he arrived at wherever he was going: whether it was Europe or a stopover in Curaçao or Jamaica.

His one last financial hope lay in his copper mines in Aroa, a property worth more than the equivalent of $10 million. But work there had ground to a stop and the mines were frozen in legal limbo. He had instructed his sister María Antonia to sell them to pay her bills; and, indeed, a buyer in London had surfaced. But niggling questions of title and liens had interfered, and the lucrative mines, owned outright by the Bolívars since 1773, had ended up in Venezuelan courts, their ownership disputed. The owner, it was claimed, was nowhere to be found. It was clear to anyone who cared to look that this was out-and-out harassment.

In short, the man who had freed Americans from Panama to Potosí, who had commandeered the gold and silver of the Indies—who had been awarded jewel-encrusted crowns and scabbards and million-dollar bonuses, and given it all away—had little to show for the sacrifice. He had claimed he didn't care about money, that he needed no more than what was given any soldier. But he had ended up with less: he had no income and no pension. Eventually, when Venezuela outlawed the sale of the Aroa mines completely, all hope that he would ever recover his rightful inheritance was lost.

He was not surprised. Bogotá had tried to assassinate him, and now in Caracas, where Páez had whipped up a mighty belligerence, they were killing his very name. Bolívar's old comrades began turning against him with signal relish. His old pal Bermúdez accused him of being "a despot with criminal designs." Arismendi, at whose side he had fought many years before, called him a tyrant with an evil brain. He was persona non grata—a man who had forced his country to kowtow to another capital. Now he would be shown no mercy. He was stripped of his citizenship, his property, his right to ever go home again. At first, when he heard of the court's ruling, he was outraged, but as weeks turned into months, rage turned into resignation. He wrote to a friend who was trying to assist María Antonia in her legal battles, "Give up trying to defend me. Let the judge and his cronies take my property. I know them. Scoundrels! Don't do one more thing on my behalf. I'll die the way I was born: naked. . . . I can't take any more humiliation."

María Antonia, too, had had her share of chagrin. In her attempt to manage her brother's affairs, she had encountered nothing but opprobrium. As Bolívar languished in limbo, unable to eat or sleep—his health dwindling alongside his prospects—her door was hung with threats:

> María Antonia, don't be a fool,
> But since you are, just mind this rule:
> Should you ever want to see Bolívar,
> Go on, you'll find him in the graveyard.

She was barely able to fend for herself. She could hardly be expected to fend for his financial affairs, too.

This is not to say that Bolívar was living like an impoverished man. He was a head of state, slept in palaces, ate well. But the presidency would soon go to someone else, and he was facing penury in a foreign land. He had anticipated neither of these eventualities. He had made no contingent plans. The worst of it was that his fellow Venezuelans had pushed him to the brink of poverty, although few knew how desperate his situation was. He had been celebrated, glorified wherever he went; it would have been natural for them to assume he had become ever more prosperous along the way. Even his old mistress in Paris, Fanny du Villars, had written to him and pleaded for money, imagining the Liberator a vastly rich man. But Bolívar had always been profligate with what little he had. War widows in distress, soldiers who had been incapacitated, officers struggling under debt—legions had benefited from his largesse. He had spent twenty years emptying his pockets for liberty.

While Bolívar considered the meager options left to him, Colombia continued to swirl in discord. Congress labored to write a constitution for the greater republic even as its constituent states sped off on separate tracks. Ecuador readied to declare itself a country. Páez announced that Venezuela's sovereignty was nonnegotiable: laws would be regarded as null and void if they were concocted in Bogotá. If that wasn't clear enough, Páez added that he would not deal with Bogotá until Bolívar was ejected permanently from the country.

A flurry of vacillations followed as Bolívar considered taking up the reins one last time—a whim that arose as mercurially as one of his fevers. He worked himself into a temper, accused General Urdaneta of making a mess of the republic; Urdaneta barked back that Bolívar had killed the republic long ago by pardoning Páez and giving him license. Wanting to fix things once and for all, Bolívar put in a bid for reelection. When Bogotá's ministers—all of them his friends—came to tell him that this was madness, that for him to stay was a threat to domestic peace, Bolívar erupted in a fury. What was he now then? What had his hard work come to? In what capacity would he be leaving the presidency? They answered as evenly as they could: he would leave as First Citizen. When he calmed, he saw that there was no other way.

BOLÍVAR RESIGNED THE PRESIDENCY ON April 27, 1830. Although Venezuela and New Granada were eager to be rid of him, Ecuador offered him safe haven. In a warm letter to the Liberator, General Flores expressed outrage at Colombia's ingratitude. "Come live in our hearts," he wrote, "and receive the homage and respect that the genius of America deserves." They were pretty words, but Flores was hardly interested in pursuing Bolívar's vision of unity. He was seeking a nationhood of his own.

Having returned to Bogotá in March to campaign for reelection,

Bolívar was soon given plenty of reasons to leave. Not one vote had been cast in his favor. Sucre, the man he hoped would succeed him, had been barred from running at all. The new constitution stipulated that a president had to be at least forty; everyone knew that Sucre was only thirty-five. Even so, with all the barriers Bolívar's enemies had raised against him, a Bolívarian went on to win the majority of votes. But as that winner's name was being read out, the announcer was shouted down; the people of Bogotá balked. Citizens ran out into the streets, roaring that Bolívar had tampered with the election. Panicked, the congressmen who had voted for Bolívar's party now rushed to change their ballots. When these were recounted, Colombia had a new president, a leader both parties could live with, Joaquín Mosquera. None of this augured well for the democratic process. And what it said about Bolívar was clear.

On May 7, three days after congress unveiled its stillborn constitution, rioting hordes surged through the city, cursing the Liberator's name. Fearing for Bolívar's life, friends urged him to evacuate the palace and move into the house of one of his generals, but even there he could hear young men milling about the streets, shouting taunts. Terrified that another assassination attempt was in the offing, the newly elected vice president, Domingo Caicedo, insisted on spending the night under the same roof with Bolívar, so that his very presence might be a shield.

Reviled, mortally ill, Bolívar departed Bogotá the next day. Manuela had come to see him off, and they said their hurried goodbyes in a dim corridor of that humble house. With typical resolve, she had decided to stay until the Liberator returned in glory or sent for her from some foreign shore. Their parting was sad and sweet, and shortly after he was striding into the chill of morning.

A throng of loyalists had gathered out front, but as Bolívar emerged he could see that Bogotá's most powerful were not among them. The archbishop made only a brief, perfunctory appearance. President Joaquín Mosquera was still making his way to the capital from Popayán. Vice President Caicedo, attempting some measure of courtesy, handed him a letter expressing Colombia's gratitude. Reading it, Bolívar was momentarily overcome. His hands trembled; his face reddened; he mounted his horse with brimming eyes. He rode off, escorted by a phalanx of congressmen, diplomats, soldiers, friends, citizens, foreigners, who were resolved to accompany the Liberator until he was well outside the turbulent city. But they couldn't protect him completely. As he rode through Bogotá's main plaza, a knot of rabble ran alongside, pointing, laughing, and barking insults. "Hey, Sausage!" they called out, using the nickname of a well-known madman who staggered around the city decked out in military gear.

We can only imagine Bolívar's cavalcade as it snaked out of Bogotá, making its grim way through the fog-hung morning. There couldn't have been much to say—only a hard, dour silence. When at last the escort stopped and watched its former president recede until he was no more than a speck in the rising mist, the English ambassador turned away with a sigh and said, "He is gone, the gentleman of Colombia."

In Bogotá, few seemed to mourn his departure. By noon, an angry mayhem reigned. Bolívar's enemies had circulated a rumor that he wasn't going to Cartagena, after all. Word had it that he was headed for Ocaña, where two thousand soldiers were billeted and waiting for him in the garrisons; two thousand more were said to be waiting for him farther north. Bolívar's plan, according to his foes, was to march on Caracas, win it from Páez, then double back with renewed muscle and overrun Bogotá. By afternoon, the capital was teeming with rioters and looters. Vice President Caicedo had been powerless to stop them.

General Sucre had set out late to join Bolívar's escort, but mobs had already begun to flood the streets, blocking his way. Protesters yelled anti-Bolívarian slogans, burned images of Bolívar. In the palace of justice, a throng of hooligans pulled down the Liberator's portrait and ripped the canvas to shreds. When Sucre finally made it to the house where Bolívar was staying, intent on warning him of danger, Bolívar was gone. Heartsick, Sucre wrote him a final valediction.

When I came to your house to accompany you from the city, you had already departed. Perhaps it was just as well, since I was spared the pain of an impossible farewell. Now, with my heart breaking, I don't know what to say. Words cannot express my feelings for you. You have known me for some time now so you are well aware that it is not your power but your friendship that inspires my most tender affection for you. . . . Goodbye, my general. Take, as a measure of my fondness, these flowing tears.

Bolívar was in the northern town of Turbaco, more than six hundred miles away, when he read Sucre's letter, and it must have deepened his sense of loss to leave such a friend behind. The trip had not been easy on his health or spirit. After an arduous ride to Honda, he had had to wait for a craft sturdy enough to make the six-hundred-mile journey down the Magdalena. All along, there had been too much time to fear the worst. A few miles outside Bogotá he wrote to Manuela Sáenz, full of worry. The more distance he had put between them, the more he fretted about leaving her behind. Envisioning all the perils—not least her reckless nature—Bolívar dashed off an anxious note:

My love, I am glad to report that I am fine, but I am filled with your grief—and mine—over our separation. I love you, my darling, but I will love you more if you show great prudence, now more than ever. Be careful in all you do, for if you don't you are bound to bring ruin on yourself, and so destroy us both. Your ever-faithful lover, Bolívar.

By the time he reached Turbaco at the end of May, his condition had worsened. The voyage down the Magdalena, that brown, airless, mosquito-infested river he had navigated so easily in the past, had broken what little vigor he had. He was riding those waters at the peak of the rainy season, and the river spilled onto the banks, sending snakes, crocodiles, and eels swirling out of the depths. The journey had to have been hard; the rapids, bone-rattling. But the relentless, fetid heat of the coast was worse, aggravating his pulmonary infirmities. Even so, there was a bit of good news at the end. He received word that the new government in Bogotá had granted him an annual pension equivalent to $15,000. It was enough, at least, to live on. But when would it begin? How long would he have to wait in that suffocating heat to be able to afford his passage? The scant money he had raised by pawning his household knickknacks in Bogotá was all but gone. To make matters worse, his passport was slow in coming, and finding a ship to carry him away had turned out to be a complicated ordeal.

He reached Cartagena at the end of June and set about querying the port about passing ships that might take him. Before long, he learned that a British packet boat was on its way, but the authorities told him it was relatively small, uncomfortable, hardly fit for a debilitated passenger. When he learned that it would be full of women, he consented to let it go. A second boat arrived, and the authorities counseled him against that, too, but this time Bolívar wouldn't hear of it. He instructed José Palacios to take his luggage down to the beach, wait for the boat's arrival, and carry it all on board. As he and his servant stood at the water's edge, awaiting their fate with a crowd of well-wishers, they watched the boat speed toward them. It must have been heartening to see that fleet craft with a full wind in its sails. But the gusts were so strong that the boat soon careened out of control. As they watched, it ran aground, shattering its hull. Undaunted, Bolívar declared he would sail as soon as repairs were made, but the captain of the damaged ship had a better idea. A British man-o'-war bound for Jamaica and England was due within the week. It promised a steadier voyage, larger accommodations, a doctor on board. When the *Shannon* arrived, its English captain was the soul of munificence. He offered Bolívar his own room and every amenity he could afford, but he added that the ship's first stop would be the Venezuelan port of La Guaira, where Bolívar could not legally go. The captain suggested that he wait a month until the *Shannon* returned to Cartagena, at which point he would gladly ferry Bolívar to Jamaica and beyond. Bolívar agreed, and took advantage of the ship's route to Caracas to send a letter to his executor, requesting some desperately needed cash. Relieved that he had been spared the grueling months-long voyage, his friends spirited him off to convalesce in a modest cottage at the foot of Mount La Popa.

The cash from Caracas never came. What did come as Bolívar awaited his fate was a slew of letters and a bit of remarkable news. Whole provinces of Venezuela had rebelled in his favor. They were calling Bolívar back into the fray. His spirits lifted. He knew perfectly well that for him to return to Venezuela was to risk war with Páez, and yet . . . it was tempting to think that he might live out his days in the land of his fathers—the land for which he had sacrificed all. As he mulled this unexpected turn of events, June slipped into July, ships came and went, and more bulletins arrived. But nothing would affect him as deeply as the tragic news he received on the morning of July 1.

Sucre had been assassinated. Unable to find the Liberator in the churning chaos of the capital, the general had decided to undertake the long ride home to his wife and infant in Quito. But days into the trip, he had been ambushed in the thickest part of a forest, deep in the heart of that most fractious and willful of regions: Pasto. He had set out in the dim light of dawn and was traversing a rocky mount when he heard someone call his name. He whirled around in his saddle to meet a quick battery of gunshot. When his three traveling companions caught up with him, they found him sprawled on the ground with a bullet in his heart, two more in his brain. His dazed mule was standing by.

Days later, a band of suspects was arrested, dragged to Bogotá, and put on trial. In the course of conflicting testimony, none of which was ever substantiated, the leader of the group confessed that he had been dispatched by General Obando. There was logic to this: Obando was the notorious rebel who had sought Peru's help against Sucre; in a desperate effort to unify the region, Bolívar had forgiven Obando, even promoted him to a position of prominence. The directive Obando had given to Sucre's killers, according to one of them, was as urgent as it was explicit. The men were to stop Sucre from returning to Quito—at all costs. It was essential, urgent, a matter of state security: Bolívar's "favorite son" was in the process of mounting a colossal crime against the Ecuadorian people. He was galloping home, Obando told them, to prepare the country for Bolívar's coronation.

Whether Obando was complicit was never established. Whether the crime originated in Pasto or Bogotá would remain a mystery as well. But everyone seemed to recall that three days before the murder, *El Demócrata,* a "liberal" newspaper in Bogotá, had published this in one of its editorials: "Maybe Obando will go ahead and finally do to Sucre what we failed to do to Bolívar." It was obvious that a contract of some sort had been carried out on Bolívar's chosen successor. General Flores, whom Bolívar had shunted aside for Sucre, was also accused of having ordered the assassination, as was anyone who had any reason to want Sucre gone.

No one was ever made to answer those accusations. By the time Bogotá moved to deliberate the question of Obando's complicity, Ecuador had proclaimed its independence from Colombia. It was—for all intents and purposes—a perfect hit.

THE NEWS OF SUCRE'S MURDER couldn't have been more devastating to a sick man on the brink of exile. Bolívar had been prepared to lose all he had—homeland, family, fortune. But to lose a brave man who had served his dream so loyally was more than he had bargained for. Sucre had been Bolívar's ideal: a skilled leader who was also a devoted acolyte, a brilliant warrior on whose honesty and principles he could rely. He had won some of Bolívar's most resounding victories—Ayacucho, Pichincha, Tarqui. He had presided over Bolivia, the nation that bore the Liberator's name. He had shared in the most intimate aspects of Bolívar's life, sealing a warm friendship with Manuela. He had warned Bolívar of impending dangers, told him truths no one else dared say. He was the best friend and defender the Liberator had ever had. How could Sucre, a blameless hero—a man who served liberty so selflessly—have been struck dead by a compatriot's hand? It was barbaric, inconceivable. "Holy God!" Bolívar roared when he heard of it, "If there is justice in heaven, hurl down your vengeance now!" That night, Bolívar's condition worsened; he was overcome by an insuperable sense of dread. He had agonized over his mistress's welfare, worried about his sisters—he had thought them the most vulnerable—but it was his fearless warrior who had been hunted and killed. If it could happen to Sucre, it could happen to anyone. Shaken to his very soul, he issued a warning to his second most favorite general, Flores, "Be careful," he wrote him. "Mind your safety as if you were a pretty little girl."

Manuela, on the other hand, was flaunting her safety, comporting herself like anything but a little girl. She was dressing like a Mameluke soldier, galloping through Bogotá with her ostentatious servants, inviting trouble. The city's demonstrations had provoked her to out-and-out war. On the very day Bolívar departed, she began a calculated campaign against the new president, Joaquín Mosquera, who had yet to step foot in Bogotá. As far as she could see, his first order of business had been to vilify the Liberator: the riots seemed thoroughly provoked; the editorials full of vitriol; and public smears had targeted her, too.

By now, Manuela was well accustomed to insults. Making fun of the Liberator's mistress had been elevated to public sport. In newspapers she was referred to as "the Foreigner"; in drinking establishments the names for her were more lewd and piquant. On June 9, the eve of the religious festival of Corpus Christi, Manuela learned that gigantic caricatures of her and Bolívar had been erected on the capital's main square. For as long as anyone could remember, it had been customary on the eve of Corpus Christi for Bogotá's citizens to poke fun at government authorities—all in the name of public merriment. But the effigies that appeared on the plaza that afternoon were particularly vicious. They were colossal grotesques, obvious enough in their likenesses, and they loomed over a platform that had been fashioned as an elaborate castle. Bolívar was wearing a crown and labeled "Despot!" Manuela was in regal dress, branded "Tyranny!" They were deliberate provocations, and they did what they were meant to do: they aroused an infuriated response.

Manuela rode to the plaza, dressed in her colonel's uniform and accompanied by her black servants, the smart-mouthed Jonatás and Natán, toting all manner of knives and pistols. At Manuela's command, the women rushed at the soldiers guarding the display. The men, astounded by the sudden hostility, pulled their bayonets to the ready. That only spurred Jonatás and Natán to a higher fury. They came at the guards now with such raw truculence that they had to be forcibly disarmed, arrested, and sent to prison. Manuela went home in a huff. All the same, she had made her point. So had her critics. The offending caricatures were dismantled and carried away. A few days later, the liberal tabloid *Aurora* reported:

An unhinged woman, a devotee of General Bolívar who always shows up in clothes that do not correspond to her sex, and who— truth be told, insists that her servants show up the same way—burst onto the scene, offending the decorum, disrupting the order, and breaking the law of the land. . . . She proceeded to the plaza with two soldiers (who were, indeed, her black, female servants), flaunted a pistol, declaimed against the government, liberty, and the people. . . . When the black women were arrested, we thought the regime might take the opportunity to punish their crimes with serious penalties. Instead, the authorities freed them, and the vice president in charge ended up by going to the house of "the Foreigner" and paying her a friendly visit.

Days later, when President Mosquera was finally expected to enter Bogotá, Manuela decided to watch from her perch on her second-floor balcony. It was a comfortable enough place to pass the time, and she had often gone there to sit and sew. As she settled into her chair, she could see that a great many people had streamed into the public spaces. A good crowd of revelers had gathered under her balcony. They were young, loud, obstreperous—eager to welcome the new head of state. But before long, they were shouting expressions that hardly corresponded to the occasion: "Down with despots! Down with tyranny!"—aimed clearly at Manuela's house. The slogans, well known by now, were code for Bolívar, meant to offend. A mounting fury rose in Manuela. But the parade had begun in earnest now, and just as President Mosquera came into view, a string of fireworks pealed down the street to announce him. Music, cheering, and a resounding din rocked the air. Whether or not it was intentional, a few sputtering flares veered dangerously close to her balcony. They seemed aimed straight at her, and they caused her no shortage of alarm. She shot out of her chair. "You think that man is president?" she yelled at them fiercely. "Wrong! He is no president! The real one is Bolívar, liberator of nations!"

Soon, she was in an angry exchange. Fists punched the air, fingers jabbed in opposing directions; within moments her servants appeared on the balcony, lit firecrackers in hand, ready to defend their mistress. They lobbed their ammunition into the throng, scattering people in terror. Outraged, the men below started hurling rocks. Then one of her male servants ran into the street, waving a gun. Someone managed to wrench it away, but not before Manuela and Jonatás had dashed downstairs, grabbed their rifles, and burst through the doors to join him. Flailing the air with weapons, they tried to push the angry crowd from the house. A tragedy might have followed had it not been for General Mariano París, a close friend of Bolívar's, who rode back from the president's parade and put a quick end to it all.

The government understood that it had a formidable foe in the Liberator's mistress. It fought back with steely resolve, describing her as ravenously promiscuous, a voluptuary who took on lovers even as Bolívar was making his way to exile. She was no longer the valiant Liberatrix, who stood fast against assassins. They mocked her eccentricities, her manly poses, her Quito accent. Before the brawl, the government had harassed her for little more than shouting "Viva Bolívar!" Now they called her impertinence treason and made it a matter of state. They did so flagrantly, without any interference from President Mosquera or Vice President Caicedo, the very men Bolívar had counted on to protect her. Both president and vice president, however, had fallen under the thrall of Santander's liberals. Days after Mosquera arrived in Bogotá, he appointed Bolívar's most ardent critics—the sharp-tongued journalist Vicente Azuero and the convicted conspirator Pedro Carujo—to top positions in his government. There was a reason: he owed his election to their party. Mosquera and Caicedo were decent men, trusted by both factions, but they soon proved to be weak executives. When pressed to put Santander's liberals in high positions, they acquiesced. When those liberals gave orders to punish Manuela, they looked the other way. Mosquera had become the very antithesis of the leader Bolívar had expected him to be: soft, spineless—scared of his own shadow, doing everyone else's bidding. "My hero has turned into a pumpkin," Bolívar would later say.

In time, the pressures on Manuela grew intolerable. The regime tried to seize Bolívar's archives, but she fought it fiercely. "In answer to your demands, let me just say that I have absolutely nothing in my possession that belongs to the government," she wrote back. "What I do have is the personal property of His Excellency, the Liberator. . . . I will not surrender one sheet of paper, one book, unless you can produce a ruling that proves he is in breach of the law."

Little by little, she meant to break the back of the liberals and stage a comeback for Bolívar. It was why she had stayed in the capital in the first place. She courted the regiments with beer and cigars; she plastered the capital's walls with propaganda; she wrote letters to editors, insisting that she was the victim of a small, pernicious cabal. She firmly believed that the Colombian people were overwhelmingly for Bolívar, that they weren't being allowed to have their say. But before she could make much headway, the government moved to destroy her. Azuero, now the minister of the interior, initiated a formal investigation into her wanton and "scandalous comportment." The mayor of Bogotá let it be known that he would seek her imprisonment. She received so many death threats that her friends finally persuaded her to leave the capital. What had happened to Sucre, they argued, could happen to her. In mid-August, wearily Sáenz packed up her possessions, mounted her horse, and left Bogotá, riding west toward the Magdalena River.

But the winds of change were such that within two weeks, the entire political climate of Colombia had reversed. The rich conservatives of Bogotá, aghast at their flagrantly inept government, began making demands: They wanted General Urdaneta reinstated as minister of war, the journalist Azuero removed as minister of the interior; they wanted all who had been implicated in the attempt on Bolívar's life ousted from office; they insisted on fewer liberal appointments, more balance, more conservatives in high command. The Church was firmly on their side, as was the military. It was evident to all that Mosquera had made a great error in handing so much power to Bolívar's enemies. The government was unbalanced, and the people felt marginalized, ignored. By the time a band of angry Bolívarian rebels overcame government forces in a skirmish outside the capital, the tide had begun to turn. Days later, Mosquera left Bogotá, claiming he was unwell; on September 5, he and Caicedo were deposed. General Urdaneta, who had been behind the coup all along, wasted no time. He seized power, warily proclaiming victory for Bolívar, although he had opposed the Liberator only months before. Like so many others, Urdaneta was using Bolívar's glory for his own purposes. Cagily, with little to lose, he promised to rule for the time being, only until the Liberator returned.

Bolívar was long past returning. Broken by Sucre's assassination, stung by ingratitude, he had slipped into the mortal grip of his affliction. Manuela did not know this. She believed the rumors of his decline had been lies, advanced by enemies. "The Liberator is immortal," she crowed, and, as far as she was concerned, it was so. She sent one of her friends to Cartagena to confirm it. Her lover had been ill before—in Peru, in Guayaquil—and he had always sprung back to win wars, liberate nations, dance. She was convinced he would flourish once more when he reached England, or wherever he decided to go. But by September 25, the second anniversary of the assassination attempt, Bolívar had become a spectral shadow. From time to time, vestiges of the old Liberator would emerge, quixotic, abiding, flickering in the gloom, but they quickly receded with the bleak march of his disease.

In October, buoyed momentarily by a surge of popular support, he claimed he would march south with three thousand troops—"If they offer me an army, I'll accept. If they send me to Venezuela, I'll go." But he admitted later that he had said so only to boost his supporters. When General Urdaneta sent a delegation to request that he come to Bogotá and take command, Bolívar responded with an unequivocal no. The delegation could see why: he was deathly sick; his only goal seemed to be to get well enough to travel. He told friends that he was largely in the dark—too exhausted, too weak to think.

It was only partially so. His body may have been wasted, but his mind was in perfect order. He knew he didn't want any part of this new, makeshift Colombia. In Urdaneta's wild caprices, in Páez's "crazy fandango," Bolívar recognized the chaos he had always feared for Latin America. "I cannot live between rebels and assassins," he confided. "I refuse to be honored by swine, cannot take comfort in empty victories." For him Urdaneta's rebellion was illegitimate—as illegal as any act by Córdova, Piar, or Páez—even if it promised Bolívar a return to glory. Where was the legal process? Where was the orderly democratic vote? He could not accept power on the basis of rank mutiny. He felt he had been diminished enough already in the public eye—by Santander's intrigues, by Páez's vicissitudes, by his own party's ill-advised project to crown him king—"and now here they are, wanting to strip me of my personal honor, reduce me to an enemy of the state." They were asking Bolívar to take power at any cost. It was too much.

"Mosquera is the legitimate president," he wrote to Urdaneta. "That is the law. . . . I have no right to his title. Nor has he ceded it." To a confidant, he spoke with emphatic pessimism: "I no longer have a fatherland for which to sacrifice my life." He believed with all his heart that the dogs of anarchy were running loose now. He had always been animated by adversity, willing to try extreme measures of constitutional law if they could save the country. But why would he want to impose his will on an effort that was already lost? "Believe me," he wrote, in a feverish spurt of epistolary energy, "I've never looked on insurrections kindly; I've even come, at this late stage, to deplore the one we mounted against Spain. . . . I don't see much good coming for our country."

It was during this time that he received a letter from General Lafayette, the revolutionary hero now living on a magnificent estate outside Paris. Bolívar had treasured his correspondence with Lafayette, just as he had treasured warm letters from Bishop de Pradt, or the one from George Washington's family that acknowledged Bolívar as "the Washington of the South." Lafayette was deeply respectful, almost adoring in his praise. As far as he was concerned, Bolívar had accomplished more than Washington; he had freed his people in far more difficult circumstances. North America's revolutionaries had been uniformly white, after all; and their values had been shared ideals, their faith overwhelmingly Protestant. In South America, on the other hand, Bolívar had cobbled liberty from a gallimaufry of peoples and races; and he had done so by "sheer dint of talent, tenacity, and valor." The tribute to the Liberator was crisp, cordial, and bighearted, but Lafayette dealt him two lasting wounds in its delivery: he made it clear that the lifetime presidency Bolívar had proposed in the Bolivian constitution did not square with democratic principle; and he urged Bolívar to forgive, bring home, and join forces with Santander. The message was tidy, straightforward. And it was more than a dying man could bear.

"I am old, sick, tired, disillusioned, besieged, maligned, and badly paid," he protested to a friend. "And I ask for nothing more than a good rest and the preservation of my honor. Alas, I don't think I will ever find either."

IN FORTY-SEVEN YEARS OF LIFE—traversing more than 75,000 miles of hard terrain—Bolívar had been the essence of vigor. He had rarely experienced physical weakness, much less the spiritual anguish that so often accompanies it. He had truly been "Iron Ass": hale, able to outrun and outride far younger soldiers, blessed with a seemingly inexhaustible stamina. Certainly, he had experienced bouts of exhaustion in his time, but drastic circumstances had helped explain them: feats in high altitudes, freezing promontories, waist-high floods, jungle swelter. It seemed there was no adversity he could not surmount. Fussy about hygiene, abstemious, he was free of debilitating vices, neither a smoker nor a drinker. He was able to function with a minimum of rest. As the years wore on and he went from battlefield to battlefield, he was crimped by a touch of this and that: malaria, dysentery, punishing hemorrhoids that followed long campaigns on a horse. But these were rare setbacks in an otherwise vigorous constitution. He had always been war-ready, prepared for hardship, remarkably fit, even if he couldn't always explain why.

To find himself so suddenly helpless—unable to overcome simple fatigue, unable to ride or walk for even a short distance—was disorienting. By October, it was clear that he was too incapacitated to do more than dictate letters from bed. He had shooting pains in his abdomen, an angry cough, and his appetite had dwindled emphatically. He asked for a little dry sherry to spur it, a fresh vegetable perhaps, but when presented with food, he lost all interest. The heat of Cartagena was debilitating, its effect on his ills so pronounced that his entourage decided to move him inland to Barranquilla, where the air seemed slightly more salubrious. But any relief he gained from the move was soon dwarfed by a passel of different discomforts. In Barranquilla, he was swaddled in wool from head to toe, fighting off chills. Soon, he was longing for a quick voyage at sea, convinced that the Caribbean air would do him good, that a little nausea from a rocking ship might serve as a welcome purgative. But all the while, he adamantly refused medicines, took no palliatives; even the most acute pain could not persuade him to do otherwise. There was no doctor whose opinion he trusted. "I've deteriorated to such a degree," he wrote Urdaneta, "that I've come to believe I'm dying. . . . You would find me absolutely unrecognizable."

Indeed he was dangerously emaciated, a living skeleton, so wisplike that he could hardly stand. "Today, I had a bad fall," he wrote in early November. "I toppled half-dead from my feet for no reason. Fortunately, it turned out to be no more than a passing vertigo, although it left me quite confused. All of which proves how feeble I am." Climbing a few steps had become an arduous undertaking. Crossing a large room had become an impossible task. His symptoms so shocked and horrified him that he fretted over each, an anxious hypochondriac, charting the evidence of his own decline. He had barely enough strength to sit and play cards; he was ill-humored, slept badly. When he ate, he took no more than a few bites—a little tapioca, a spoonful of lentils—and so he was growing weaker by the day. "I'm very, very alarmed by his physical state," his close aide, Belford Wilson, reported. "There is no way this man can participate in public office; he is physically and psychologically impaired."

But for all the afflictions that gripped his body and spirit, his mind was sharp. He received visitors from Venezuela, where Páez's bid for power had spun into open bedlam; he heard out Granadans who wanted him back in Bogotá. He pleaded with Colombians to make peace with their enemies. He warned rebels that they could bring ruin on America. He told Justo Briceño, the rebel governor of an outlying province, that if he didn't reconcile with Urdaneta, the republic would tumble like a house of cards. "Believe me," he said in no uncertain terms, "you two will end up like Páez and Santander, whose rift caused my downfall and wreaked havoc on us all." To Urdaneta, he spoke as plainly: "Building one good accord is better than winning a thousand arguments. I have no doubt that my inability to make peace with Santander has been our undoing." It was as if—in that rapidly waning body—he was reaching a higher plane. He seemed to see his failures all too clearly: "Many generals," he counseled, "know how to win wars, but too few know what to do with their victories." He worried openly about the legitimacy of his successor and told Urdaneta that until he held an election he was no more than a tin-pot usurper. "I wouldn't be surprised if they kill you," he said, "and then plunge into total anarchy. If they do, it will be because you didn't obey the laws." He instructed Urdaneta to burn those letters as soon as he read them; they were too candid, too disapproving; he didn't want his words twisted against Urdaneta after he was dead and gone. No one in that roiling stew of ambition could count on holding power for long.

To General Flores, the new president of Ecuador, his message was just as dire: "Avenge Sucre's murder," he advised Flores, for it was the vilest crime America had ever known, "then get out while you can." In a passage that has become a classic in the Bolívarian canon, he went on to list what two decades of rule had taught him:

1. America is ungovernable; 2. he who serves a revolution ploughs the sea; 3. all one can do in America is leave it; 4. the country is bound to fall into unimaginable chaos, after which it will pass into the hands of an undistinguishable string of tyrants of every color; 5. once we are devoured by all manner of crime and reduced to a frenzy of violence, no one—not even the Europeans—will want to subjugate us; 6. and, finally, if mankind could revert to its primitive state, it would be here in America, in her final hour.

He was never so lucid, and yet he was not entirely sane. Like a Shakespearean king wandering through the wreckage, he couldn't help but issue commands to his faraway generals, warn them of the collapse to come. For all his pessimism about Colombia, however, he believed, beyond all evidence to the contrary, that his sickness was curable, that it was only a matter of time before he would walk away from it all. When he did, he would sail for the blue mountains of Jamaica. Then on to London, with Manuela.

One of his most loyal supporters, General Mariano Montilla, who was then in command of the northwestern coast of Colombia, soon took interest in his condition. When Bolívar wrote to him asking for help in procuring a few supplies, Montilla responded by doing far more. He hired a brig to ferry Bolívar to Santa Marta, a quiet enclave in a Caribbean cove just fifty miles east of Barranquilla. The voyage would be swift, easy, precisely the cathartic Bolívar had in mind. But Montilla did not stop there. He found Bolívar a doctor of sorts, a Frenchman who had served as a medic in Napoleon's army; and he persuaded the brig's owner, a rich Spaniard named Joaquín de Mier, to give the Liberator refuge in his sprawling hacienda on the lip of the sea.

Bolívar arrived in Santa Marta on the 1st of December, accompanied by his nephew Fernando; his servant, José; and a retinue of loyal friends, among them Perú de Lacroix, whom Manuela had sent from Bogotá. It had taken a mere two days to skirt the coast in those calm December waters. As they rounded the last jut of land and sailed into an embrace of bay, they saw the glistening white beaches of Santa Marta. Behind were the verdant hills, alive with a riot of birds and orchids. And behind that, like a hoary old giant stretching his legs in the sea, stood the snowcapped Sierra Nevada. Alexander von Humboldt, who had recounted such sights to a far younger Bolívar, had traveled this shore in wonder, recording its snakes, fruits, and shimmering insects—hacking his way past palm trees to chance upon a row of tiny volcanoes, barely taller than a man.

When the ship pulled into harbor, Joaquín de Mier was there to greet it, his face a mask of alarm. The dread author of the war to the death had been reduced to a human cinder; the only sign of life, as far as the Spaniard could see, was the fevered eyes—black as onyx—still smoldering in the meager frame. The officers lowered Bolívar from the ship's deck in a cradle of locked hands. With infinite care, they laid him on a pallet, then carried him off to the stately old mansion that housed the Spanish consulate. There, on that tiny patch of Spain—as ironic a destination as an American hero might imagine—he was received with the utmost courtesy and consideration.

Alejandro Révérend, the doctor whom Montilla had engaged to care for the ailing Liberator, took careful notes of the occasion:

> His excellency arrived in Santa Marta at seven thirty in the evening and, unable to walk at all, came to shore in a chair of human arms. I found him in the following state: extremely thin, exhausted, pained expression, high-strung. Hoarse voice; profound cough, producing a thick, green sputum. Even, but rapid pulse. Labored digestion. The patient exhibited considerable suffering. In sum, His Excellency's illness struck me as most grave, and my immediate impression was that his lungs were sadly damaged. In Barranquilla, he had been given little more than a few tablespoons of cough syrup.

For the next few days, Révérend cared for him, securing a second opinion from a United States naval surgeon, whose ship, by chance, had dropped anchor in Santa Marta. The American surgeon corroborated Révérend's diagnosis: the Liberator's illness was largely in his lungs, most probably tuberculosis.

With every day, Bolívar's condition grew more dire. He was jaundiced, hardly able to sleep more than two hours at a time; at night, he was feverish, delirious; come morning, he was seized by nausea. His bones ached. His scrawny frame, reduced to less than eighty pounds, shook with coughs or occasional fits of hiccups. He was, as victims of tuberculosis can be, grizzled, balding, shriveled: ancient before his time. Five days later, Révérend decided to transport him in a comfortable sedan to Mier's sugar plantation, where, at the very least, Bolívar would be in more pleasant surroundings, surrounded by an attentive staff.

At first, Mier's splendid estate at San Pedro Alejandrino seemed to be just the cure that Bolívar needed. The house was bright, open, with large windows that welcomed fresh breezes from the sea. Palm trees and tamarinds swayed gently in the adjacent gardens. Under a warm sun and a vaulting blue sky, the patient's spirits rose. The sweet fragrance of sugar invaded his senses. It was an aroma he knew well, having grown up on a sugarcane plantation in San Mateo. As he lay in a hammock strung between two tamarind trees, he may well have remembered the hewn cane, the mashed pulp, the black pits of sorghum that perfumed his childhood. He gained a little energy, wrote a few remarkably eloquent letters. Sometime before, he had sent word to Manuela, beseeching her to come. Where was she?

More visitors arrived: couriers bursting with news, a solemn bishop, a crisply efficient notary public, generals and colonels eager to see their hero. The officers made themselves comfortable. They played cards, drank rum, hired musicians to raise the fading Liberator's spirits. Rolling cigars, puffing on pipes, they smoked until the corridors were hung with gray. When the stench of one general was so noxious that Bolívar asked him to move back his chair, the man was taken aback. "Excuse me, Your Excellency, I don't think I've soiled myself!" "Not at all," Bolívar said, "it's just that you smell like hell." The general laughed and replied that Bolívar would have never said such a thing to Mistress Manuela, whose love of tobacco was well known. Bolívar's face was suddenly filled with infinite sadness. His eyes welled with tears. "Ah, Manuela," he said. "Very well."

Sometime later, when Dr. Révérend was at his side, Bolívar took it upon himself to ask, "Doctor, what brought you to these parts?" "Liberty," the doctor answered. "And have you found it?" Bolívar queried. "Yes, my General." "Well, then," Bolívar sighed, "you are more fortunate than I. Go back to your beautiful France . . . eventually you'll find that life is impossible here, with so many sons of bitches."

By the night of December 9, he was feverish again, raving. The last, fatal seizures of consumption took grip of his bony frame. When he came to his senses the next morning, the bishop pressed him to take his last sacraments; General Montilla, beside himself with grief, pleaded with him to put his house in order, make a will. Bolívar balked at first. Accustomed to fight, he was not prepared for surrender. "How will I ever get out of this labyrinth?" he cried out in dismay. But as the day wore on, he saw the sense in it. With friends at his side as witnesses, he commended his soul to God, declared the long-dead Teresa del Toro his lawfully wedded wife, and avowed that he had no descendants. For all the dozens of mistresses he had romanced in the past, for all the love he had professed to Manuela and Pepita, his bid to posterity confirmed what he had sworn as a young man: no woman would ever take Teresa's place. He had buried his baptismal garments with her body and fulfilled his vows to the church. The rest was a matter of earthly cargo. He bequeathed 8,000 pesos (from the pension he had yet to receive) to his life-long servant José Palacios, his disputed property in Venezuela to his two sisters, his most valuable books to the University of Caracas, his sword to Sucre's wife. That night, he received last rites from a humble Indian priest who had been called from a neighboring village. Those rituals done, he turned his remaining strength to address his countrymen one last time. The notary took down his final words:

Colombians! You have witnessed my efforts to launch liberty where tyranny once reigned. I have labored selflessly, sacrificing my fortune and my peace of mind. When it became clear that you doubted my motives, I resigned my command. My enemies have toyed with your confidence, destroyed what I hold sacred—my reputation, my love of liberty. They have made me their victim and hounded me to my grave. I forgive them.

As I depart your midst, my love for you impels me to make known my last wishes. I aspire to no other glory than the consolidation of Colombia. . . . My last vote is for the happiness of our native land. If my death can heal and fortify the union, I go to my tomb in peace.

As Bolívar's companions gathered around his bed, the notary read out those last lines. The Liberator was a living ghost—he could hardly keep his eyes open, hardly talk, hardly breathe—but his mind was clear enough to grasp that his words had made an impression: in that circle of hard-bitten soldiers, there was scarcely a dry eye.

A man could do little more but die. And so it came to be. Within hours, he was weaving in and out of delirium. His urine burned, doubling him over with pain; his hands and feet were as cold as the Andean snow. His pulse galloped; he passed blood, and then he started to babble incoherently. "José!" he called out, "Let's go! Let's go! They don't want us! Take my luggage on board!" In time, he lost the ability to form words at all. When asked whether he was in pain, he seemed to be signaling no. Six days passed in this harrowing limbo.

At noon on December 17, the strange wheeze that was coming from his chest gave way to desperate gasps. Life would not depart Bolívar's body easily. But there was no mistaking it: he was taking his last, deep gulps of mortality. Something about that urgent rattle startled Dr. Révérend. He called the men from the room next door. "Gentlemen, if you want to be present for the Liberator's last breath and his final hour," he said, "come now." They filed in quickly, somberly. At one o'clock in the afternoon, exactly eleven years to the minute after his famed declaration of independence in Angostura, Bolívar's soul passed from his shattered body. His lips went white, his brow softened in beatific repose.

Bolívar was dead, Greater Colombia was gone, and the dream he had held so dear slipped imperceptibly into the vast hereafter. But there was no question about the triumph: Six new nations—Venezuela, Colombia, Ecuador, Panama, Bolivia, and Peru—would emerge one by one to confirm it.

~ Epilogue ~

O nly after Bolívar was dead and gone did his legend take root and grow. Few heroes have been so exalted by history, so venerated around the world, so memorialized in marble. In time, the rancor that dogged his last days became rampant adulation.

But that reversal—perhaps unique in the annals of history—was slow to come. As life ebbed and the corpse grew cold, only the loyal were there to mourn him. Bolívar died reviled, misunderstood, slandered in every republic he had liberated. For all the wealth into which he had been born, he died a pauper. For all the treasuries he had commanded, he had eschewed financial reward. He departed this life penniless, powerless, dispossessed. Driven from Bogotá, loathed by Peru, yearning to return to his beloved Caracas, he soon found that even his native land had barred his homecoming. He died mourned by only a few: his manservant, his stalwart lieutenants, his sisters, his brother's son, a scattering of friends. There was scant sympathy otherwise. "Goodbye to the spirit of evil!" the governor of Maracaibo crowed—"the author of all misfortune, the tyrant of the fatherland!" Twelve years passed before Bolívar's bones were carried home to Caracas in triumph.

As three rounds of cannon fire sounded from a nearby fort, marking the Liberator's passing, his doctor, the town pharmacist Révérend, undertook to perform an autopsy. From the cadaver's discoloration, the choked lungs, pronounced tubercles, advanced atrophy, he could draw but one conclusion: Bolívar had died of acute pulmonary failure, most likely tuberculosis. After working all night to embalm him, the doctor met light of day with one more responsibility. There was no one else to dress the dead man; no garment available but the shabby tunic in which he had died. A clean shirt had to be borrowed from a kind neighbor, after which some semblance of a funeral was arranged and paid for by a volunteer.

On December 20, 1830, the Liberator's corpse was transported from public view at the customhouse to the cathedral, some blocks away. A modest procession wended its way through the sleepy streets of Santa Marta. Bells tolled, a requiem was sung, but no important officials were there to hear them. The bishop of Santa Marta, who had fallen ill days before, did not preside over the Mass. Bolívar's remains were deposited in a tomb within the cathedral walls, and there they lay as Greater Colombia fell to pieces, the continent spun into petty wars, and Bolívar's generals scrambled to advance self-important visions. Within months, Bolívar's nemesis José Antonio Páez was elected president in Venezuela. General Urdaneta, who had lobbied to make Bolívar king, was toppled ignominiously in Bogotá. General Santander, in exile for the attempted assassination, was brought back to rule independent Colombia. General Flores, wanting more elbow room for Ecuador, prepared a flank attack on the parent republic. Panama, trying to declare itself a republic, looked around anxiously for a leader. Bolivia, under Andrés Santa Cruz, struggled to surmount the chaos. And Peru—the anxious heart of a lapsed empire—proceeded to have twenty presidents in the next twenty years. But, for all that, the Liberator's paramount achievement was irreversible: the Spaniards never returned.

The news of Bolívar's death—like all news in those distant days—was slow to spread through the Americas. Manuela had been making her way upriver toward him, confident that rumors of his decline were exaggerations, when she was stopped cold by a letter from Perú de Lacroix: "Allow me, esteemed madam, to weep with you over the immense loss you have suffered along with the rest of the nation. Prepare yourself for a final death notice." She was taken aback, momentarily unhinged. Somehow, she got hold of a venomous snake and put it to her throat, but it sank its fangs into her arm instead. When she recovered, she regained her rock-hard determination. "I loved the Liberator when he was alive," she wrote General Flores. "Now that he is dead, I *worship* him." Less than two years later, Santander—back in power—packed her off to foreign shores.

She sailed to Jamaica, then Guayaquil, but her passport was revoked along the way and so she landed in Paita, a tiny fishing village on the coast of Peru, where the only wayfarers were Yankee whalers. Undaunted, striving to make the best of a bad situation, she took over an abandoned house not far from the wharf and hung a sign over her door: "Tobacco. English Spoken. Manuela Sáenz." For a modest fee, she offered to write letters on behalf of illiterate sailors. She prepared and sold sweets, embroidered linens, and, one way or another, managed to eke out a meager living. But she lived in virtual poverty for the rest of her days, visited from time to time by such eminences as the Italian military hero Giuseppe Garibaldi, or the celebrated Peruvian writer Ricardo Palma. As years went by, she learned that her husband, James Thorne, had been murdered along with his mistress as they strolled through the sugar fields, not far from Lima. There were perhaps many reasons why. Thorne had had numerous mistresses and illegitimate children since Manuela had left him. At the very end of her life, Sáenz was joined by Simón Rodríguez, Bolívar's teacher, who arrived in Paita when he was eighty, destitute, and more than a little touched by madness. He limped off a boat in 1853 and died the following year. Manuela died two years later. We can only imagine the conversations between those feisty old revolutionaries who loved Bolívar above all men.

Dead, Bolívar became less man than symbol. As the years went by—as chaos continued to plague the region—South Americans recalled the extraordinary feat of freeing so many nations in so dire a time. His failures as a politician receded. His successes as a liberator took center stage. Indeed, the accomplishments were irrefutable. It was he who had disseminated the spirit of the Enlightenment, brought the promise of democracy to the hinterlands, opened the minds and hearts of Latin Americans to what they might become. It was he who, with a higher moral instinct than even Washington or Jefferson, saw the absurdity of embarking on a war for liberty without first emancipating his own slaves. It was he who had led the armies, slept on the ground with his soldiers, fretted about their horses, their bullets, their maps, their blankets—inspired men to unimaginable heroism. Revolutionaries called for him in Mexico, Chile, Cuba, Argentina. He rode, "fighting all the way," as Thomas Carlyle put it, "more miles than Ulysses ever sailed. Let the coming Homers take note of it!" Never before in the history of the Americas had one man's will transformed so much territory, united so many races. Never had Latin America dreamed so large.

But in the course of forging a new world, compromises had been made. More than once, Bolívar found himself tossing ideals by the wayside. As he rode through the roiling hell of a brutal war, through the abattoirs of improvised military justice, he didn't always have the luxury of employing the principles he so eloquently espoused. From time to time he made questionable decisions. Bolívar's critics are quick to cite them: The decree of a war to the death, for instance, with which he meant to shock and awe the colonizer. The execution of General Piar, a young, ambitious patriot who, Bolívar suspected, was trying to incite a race war under his very nose. The massacre of eight hundred Spanish prisoners at Puerto Cabello, which seemed expeditious at the time, as a prison uprising was feared and there were insufficient guards to contain them. The betrayal of his aging fellow liberator, Francisco Miranda, who, according to Bolívar, had lacked courage, capitulated too easily, and sold out the revolution to Spain. Last, and certainly not least, was Bolívar's exercise of dictatorial powers.

He had good arguments for all of it. There was, to begin, a continent's staggering ignorance, the result of conditions under which it had labored for hundreds of years. In his darkest hours, Bolívar wondered whether his America was truly ready for democracy. There was, too, the swift, draconian response Spain let loose on revolutionaries. After the Napoleonic Wars, the *madre patria* emerged fiercer, more terrible— more sharpened by combat—than the patriots could have anticipated. Violence was met by ever more violence, and soon escalation became the only rule of war. The result was a bloody conflict that wiped whole cities from the map, reduced civilian populations by a third, and virtually obliterated Spain's expeditionary forces.

Bolívar was a master of improvisation, a military commander who could outwit, outride, and outfight a vastly more powerful enemy. But that very talent, that genius for moving swiftly from strategy to strategy—for rebounding quickly, for making decisions on the fly—had its liabilities in times of peace. It is difficult to build a democracy on a wartime model. It was why he made hasty decisions, last-ditch promises, political blunders. It was why he pardoned Páez. It was why he mishandled Santander. It was why he tried to patch his way through the labyrinths of political process, saying different things to different men.

But, for all his flaws, there was never any doubt about his power to convince, his splendid rhetoric, his impulse to generosity, his deeply held principles of liberty and justice. As the years went by and South Americans remembered that greatness, they understood that their Liberator had been ahead of his time. Leaders who followed seemed wanting in comparison, dwarfed by the shadow of a colossus. Venezuelans were appalled that they had allowed their most distinguished citizen to die in penury, in another country, forbidden even to come home. Colombians recalled that it was on their soil that he had begun his march to freedom. Ecuadorians, Bolivians, Panamanians, Peruvians began to revive the legend. Cities and provinces took his name. Public plazas raised monuments to his victories. In marble or bronze, Bolívar's flesh took on a serenity it never had in life. The restless, fevered Liberator was now the benevolent father, devoted teacher, good shepherd striving to build a better flock. Astride a horse, galloping into an eternal void, the enduring image was complete: here was a vigorous life, lived in a single trajectory, aiming to forge a people, a continent. America.

No one knew more than Páez the power of that Bolívarian image. Struggling to maintain his grip on the Venezuelan presidency, Páez reached once again for Bolívar to help him shore up an unstable nation. Never mind that Bolívar was dead. Never mind that Páez's vision for Venezuela was in stark counterpoint to that of Bolívar. In November of 1842, almost twelve years after the Liberator's death, Páez had the hero's remains exhumed from their serene resting place in the Cathedral of Santa Marta and brought by a naval fleet to the port of La Guaira. To pacify Colombia, Páez granted it permission to keep the Liberator's heart, and so that part of him remained behind, preserved in a small urn interred at Santa Marta. When Bolívar's eviscerated corpse arrived in La Guaira, it was welcomed home by an enormous delegation of military men, diplomats, clerics, and government dignitaries. As the

funeral procession made its way over the mountain to Caracas, an adoring public poured into the streets to greet it. So began the posthumous
glorification of a hero, the birth of the cult of Bolívar.

As years passed—not only in nations he had liberated, but throughout the world—Bolívar became the personification of Latin American
greatness: a man with a resolute love of liberty and an unwavering sense
of justice; a hero willing to risk everything for a dream. But as the legend grew, each version building on the last, the man took on a protean
quality. Politicians, whether they were left or right, used him to defend
their positions. Priests quoted him in righteous sermons. Poets lauded
him in ecstatic verse. History texts swooned over his exploits. Teachers
pointed to his brilliance. Fathers urged sons to emulate him. Schoolchil-
dren memorized his speeches: "Soldiers!" they all learned to roar, just as
Bolívar had done after the Battle of Ayacucho, "You have given South
America its freedom and now a quarter of this world is a living monument to your glory!"

In time, historians, too, took up the task of glorification. Whole
institutions and scholarly apparatuses were put in place to defend him.
And defend him they would, for doubts about him were beginning to
creep back. Peruvians, who had always resented the Venezuelan liberator, complained that Bolívar had cheated Peru of land in the course of
building nations, that he had robbed the Inca of their nobility. Indeed,
by 1825, Lima's wealth and influence had shrunk; the viceregal city that
had once overseen a large swath of South America had far less presence,
far less power. All the same, it was an exaggeration to say that Bolívar
had ruined Peru. Peru hadn't existed before the revolution. Peru hadn't
lost land; it hadn't owned land to begin with. As for the descendants of
the Inca, Bolívar hadn't singled them out especially. He had abolished
all rank, outlawed Freemasons, secret societies, any semblance of legis-
lated superiority. To him, indigenous nobility was just another form of
oppression. In other words, Bolívar had changed all the rules in Peru.
And Peru, once the most powerful nexus of the Spanish Metropolis—
the most loyal of Spain's colonies—never forgot it.

The debunkers would be many—Argentines who preferred to glorify San Martín, Spaniards who felt obliged to defend the *madre patria*,
Andeans who felt crimped by their borders, mercenaries who never got

paid, even the vociferous Karl Marx, who called Bolívar "the dastardly, most miserable and meanest of blackguards." But all that came later, By the time of the one-hundredth anniversary of Bolívar's birth, the myth was in place, augmented with surprising flourishes. The intervening century had made Bolívar a good Catholic, a moral exemplar, an unwavering democrat—none of which he had been during his life. The story had less to do with the man than with a romantic ideal. He was our better angel, our prince valiant. Even the imperfections (the dozens of mistresses, the take-no-prisoners bravado, the penchant for dictatorship) were seen as natural parts of the persona, what every young man should aspire to be. As the writer José Martí so famously wrote of Bolívar in those centennial years: "Nothing is more beautiful than that craggy forehead, those cavernous eyes, that cape flapping against him on the back of a winged horse. . . . From son to son, for as long as America shall live, the echo of his name will resound in our manly hearts."

The echo certainly resounded in the manly heart of President Antonio Guzmán Blanco, who, like Páez half a century before, was trying to keep a firm grip on the Venezuelan nation. Guzmán had come to power in 1870, ruled flamboyantly for eighteen years, and presided over great growth as well as rampant corruption. He was far from anything like Bolívar. But he, too, knew the power of the image. Taking his cue from Páez, he had Bolívar's remains exhumed and transported from the cathedral to the newly completed National Pantheon. He purchased Bolívar's family home in Caracas, announced the publication of a thirty-two-volume history of the Liberator's career, then presided bombastically over the centenary of Bolívar's birth, memorializing no one so much as himself in the process. Bolívar, we can only imagine, would have been horrified at the spectacle of being preyed on so publicly by a man who embodied all that he despised: sycophancy, corruption, pomposity, Freemasonry, and a full-bore attack on the Church. But the scheme worked: Guzmán stayed in power for a staggering eighteen years, driving out one political opponent after another, until his antiCatholic campaign backfired and he was cast out by an angry nation.

One hundred years later, in 1982, following those predecessors' examples, Hugo Chávez, an ambitious young captain in the Venezuelan army, established a leftist party he called the Bolívarian Revolutionary Movement. After a decade of secret machinations, he attempted a coup on the sitting government, was arrested and sentenced to prison. Nevertheless, he emerged to ride Bolívar's legacy to the presidency in 1998. The following year, Chávez rewrote the constitution and renamed the country the Bolívarian Republic of Venezuela. He made televised speeches with Bolívar's image behind him, had his followers chant, "Bolívar! Bolívar!" in the streets. Think of the irony in this: there is no George Washington party in the United States of America, no registered adherents of a founder, no declared enemies. There are no people who shout Napoleon's name in the streets of Paris today. But in Latin America, Bolívar lives on as a galvanizing force, a lightning rod for political action.

Bolívar had been aped by many pretenders in his mercurial afterlife, but never so bizarrely as by Chávez, a radical socialist, whose goals were a far cry from Bolívar's. Once again, in a period of national instability—in 2010, the bicentenary year of the start of the revolution—Bolívar's bones were exhumed. This time, President Chávez had them taken from his sarcophagus in the National Pantheon in what can only be described as a macabre freak show. Throughout, Chávez narrated, prayed, rhapsodized in what looked to anyone witnessing it like a highly stylized performance by astronauts in moon gear. Behind, above, everywhere on display was the flag of Venezuela. The purpose of this outlandish ballet was the same as it had been for two hundred years: to become one with the spirit of the Liberator, to bask in "the magic of his prestige." But this time Chávez hoped to prove something more than brotherhood. He had Bolívar's DNA tested in order to show that the Liberator had been poisoned by Colombian autocrats, landed gentry who couldn't tolerate his "socialist" impulses—but the tests gave inconclusive results. In bolstering his own faded reputation, in lobbing a stiff accusation across the border, Chávez had played a very old hand. But he had also brought Bolívar full circle. Harassed to the end of his days by those who accused him of being too fond of dictatorial powers, Bolívar was now being touted by a military despot as the apotheosis of liberal thought.

Certainly, it was not the first time the legend was twisted to preposterous ends; nor were Chávez, Guzmán, and Páez the only strongmen to try it. Countless dictators who came after independence tried to manipulate Bolívar's image in some way in the process of burnishing their own. Bolívar purported to hate dictatorships—he claimed he had taken them on only for limited periods and as necessary expedients—but there is little doubt that he created the mythic creature that the Latin American dictator became.

In centuries to come, dictators came in a multitude of varieties. But the trajectory was always the same. Indeed, many of the most tyrannical and barbaric started out as liberals. South American history is replete with such men. As the Argentine writer Ernesto Sábato once said: "The most stubborn conservatism is that which is born of a triumphant revolution." Bolívar had feared it would be so. He died convinced that a bloody-minded era would follow, and follow him it did. In Bolivia, a famously debauched dictator, fleeing retribution, was tracked down and killed by his mistress's brother; in Ecuador, a deeply religious despot who had installed himself for a third term was butchered on the Cathedral steps in the full light of morning; in Quito, a liberal caudillo who tried to seize power too many times was thrown in prison, murdered, and dragged through the cobbled streets. There is a reason why blood trickles down roads and heads roll out from under bushes in Latin American literature: this is not magical realism. It is history. It is true.

In many ways, the revolution is still afoot in Latin America. Although Bolívar's name has been conjured by every -ism that succeeded him, his burning ideals seemed lost in the bedlam that ensued. Principles of the Enlightenment were cast aside as rich whites scrambled to appropriate the wealth and power the Spanish overlords had left behind. Equality, which Bolívar had insisted was the linchpin of justice, was quickly replaced by a virulent racism. The rule of law—indispensable to a free people—was abandoned as one dictator after another rewrote laws according to his caprices. Democracy, equality, fraternity: these were slow to come to South America. Unity, which might have made the continent a mighty force, was never realized. And yet Bolívar's dream never would die.

Perhaps that is because his life has always spoken so clearly to the Latin American people. Here is an all too imperfect man who, with sheer will, a keen mind, an ardent heart, and admirable disinterest carried a revolution to far corners of his continent. Here is a leader whom fate presented with one opportunity and a glut of insuperable hurdles. A general betrayed by his officers; a strategist who had no equals on whom he could rely; a head of state who oversaw nothing that resembled a vigorous, unified team of rivals. With a stamina that is arguably unmatched in history, he prosecuted a seemingly unwinnable war over the harshest of terrains to shuck the formidable banner of Pizarro. From Haiti to Potosí, there was little that stopped him. On he rode, into the void, fighting against unimaginable odds. Until he remade a world.

~ Acknowledgments ~

Before I acknowledge the living, I must pay tribute to the dead: my ancestors, whose very frowns drove me to write this book.

When I was an unruly child in Lima, Peru, I was made to atone for my misbehavior by sitting alone on a hard stool in my grandparents' living room. It was an airless chamber, shuttered against the coast's alternating sun and fog. There were musty books in shaky bookcases, an ornately carved piano, marble-topped tables, bronze busts of illustrious Romans, and five immense ancestral portraits that seemed to regard me with pointed reproach. Two of the likenesses were of my beloved grandparents peering down with what I never saw on their real faces—sharp looks of haughty surprise. But the other three were of earlier vintage, painted 125 years before I was born.

One was of an imposing general named Joaquín Rubín de Celis, my great-great-great-grandfather, the first Spaniard to charge and the first to fall at the Battle of Ayacucho. His defeat won Peru its freedom. The wistful beauty who stared at him from the other wall was the daughter he never knew: Trinidad. She was born a few weeks after a rebel sword pierced his heart. At sixteen, Trinidad married a rebel general, my great-great-grandfather Pedro Cisneros Torres, who had rushed down the Andes with Bolívar's forces on that crisp December day to fight against her father.

After three hundred years of Spanish rule, with two of my ancestors battling each other in the dust of the cordillera, the yoke of colonialism was broken, the war of independence won. And so, although I had been instructed to sit in that room and ponder my wanton badness, I could only wonder at the glories of rebellion. A lifetime later, those faces are still with me. They hang in my study today. I only hope that I have done their history credit in this book about the man at the crucible of American possibility, Simón Bolívar.

There is no shortage of books about Bolívar. In the Library of Congress alone there are 2,683 volumes. Most are in Spanish, many are in Bolívar's words or written by his contemporaries; many more, unfortunately, tend to be filled with hagiography or vitriol. He was a controversial man. But I owe a large debt of gratitude to a number of writers and historians whose portraits animated me: Daniel Florencio O'Leary, José Manuel Restrepo, Vicente Lecuna, Gerhard Masur, Indalecio Liévano Aguirre, David Bushnell, John Lynch, and Gabriel García Márquez. I have benefited from the friendship of others who have written about Latin American history in general: among them, Mario Vargas Llosa, John Hemming, Larrie Ferreiro, the late Germán Arciniegas, Natalia Sobrevilla, Pamela Murray, Lawrence Clayton, and Lester Langley.

In the course of researching Bolívar's life, I visited many libraries and museums throughout the hemisphere, but I could not have written this book without the help of two great American institutions: the Library of Congress and Brown University. At the Library of Congress, I was fortunate to be made a Distinguished Scholar at the John W. Kluge Center, where I took up residence in 2009 and proceeded to immerse myself in the library's extensive Latin American collection. I thank the eminent James H. Billington, Librarian of Congress, who generously granted me that privilege. I am indebted to the Director of the Kluge Center, Carolyn Brown, and her staff members, Mary Lou Reker and Patricia Villamil, as well as Georgette Dorn, Chief of the Library's Hispanic Division and her deeply knowledgeable colleagues; and the Map Division's specialist Anthony Mullan, who turned out to be—of all things!—the great-great-grandson of the Lion of the Apure, José Antonio Páez. There is such wit in history.

I am grateful beyond words to Ted Widmer, former director of the John Carter Brown Library, who invited me to be a Fellow at his remarkable institution—so rich in Latin American holdings—at the very start of my research. It was a thrill to read and write in a room alive with Bolívariana, dedicated entirely to the Liberator's achievements. Ted's support was invaluable, as was the help I received from his staff: Valerie Andrews, Michael Hamerly, Ken Ward, Leslie Tobias Olsen; and a string of venerable JCBL veterans, including Norman Fiering and José Amor y Vásquez.

Years ago, when I was in the thick of research, I received a note from Thor Halvorssen, who is one of the few living direct descendants of the Bolívar family. His lineage is matrilineal, and derives directly from Bolívar's sister Juana. Thor, who is founder and president of the Human Rights Foundation, was generous with his gifts: his master's thesis on Bolívar's views of the Enlightenment, some precious family books, even a DNA swab of his grandfather's cheek, which did not corroborate what some of Bolívar's enemies believed—that the Liberator was largely black-blooded and therefore unsuitable (to them) as a leader. To Bolívar those allegations were meaningless. He spent no time arguing them, instead recruiting blacks to his ranks. But more than likely he would have been amazed that a biographer would be able to trace his haplogroup in cells harvested from a very elderly great-great-grandnephew.

I count myself fortunate indeed to be represented by my agent, Amanda "Binky" Urban, whose fortitude and friendship over the years have been my rock. Binky has seen me through many a genre and caprice, and proved her mettle when I told her I intended to leap from fiction to history. She didn't flinch. I am grateful, too, to Binky's colleagues in London, Gordon Wise and Helen Manders, for their ongoing faith in my work.

A biographer couldn't have better luck than to be edited by Bob Bender, the Simon & Schuster vice president and senior editor whose astute eye and unfailing instincts have made this book better in every way. Thanks also to my publisher, Jonathan Karp, who immediately understood that Simón Bolívar deserved to have his life's story told again, in an English-language version, and differently. I am grateful to many good people at Simon & Schuster who helped bring this book to life: Johanna Li, Tracey Guest, Maureen Cole, Michael Accordino, Gypsy da Silva, Joy O'Meara, and my phenomenally eagle-eyed copyeditor, Fred Chase.

Thanks to all my friends at *The Washington Post*, who have been a fount of support over the years. Thanks, too, to my brilliant siblings, Vicky and George, to whom this volume is dedicated. But, in truth, I could not have written any of it—or any of my books, for that matter— without the love and daily sacrifices of my husband, Jonathan Yardley, who read the manuscript of *Bolívar* at every stage, made dinners when I was oblivious, did all the shopping, walked the dog, fed the cat, and kept the cabinet stocked with good wine.

In the last days of my parents' lives, each gave me a distinct piece of her or his mind, so characteristic of the differences between them. My father, being a traditionally minded Peruvian, insisted that I take my time. The book had better be good, he said; he didn't want any daughter of his embarrassing the family. My mother, on the other hand, being a forward-thinking American, would sing her impatience: Hurry! When are you going to finish that thing? Don't you know I'm on tenterhooks, waiting?

Papi, Mother, bless you for that. I couldn't have done it without you.

∼ Notes ∼

Abbreviations

BANH Biblioteca de la Academia Nacional de la Historia, Caracas
BOLANH Boletín de la Academia Nacional de la Historia, Caracas
DOC *Documentos para la historia de la vida pública del Libertador de Colombia*, José Félix Blanco and Ramón Azpurúa, eds.
FJB Fundación John Boulton, Archives, Caracas
HAHR Hispanic American Historical Review
JCBL John Carter Brown Library, Brown University, Providence, Rhode Island
LOC Library of Congress
O'L *Memorias del General O'Leary*, Daniel Florencio O'Leary, 32 vols.
O'LB *Bolívar and the War of Independence*, Daniel Florencio O'Leary
O'LN *Memorias: Narración*, Daniel Florencio O'Leary, 3 vols.
PRO/FO Public Records Office, Foreign Office, Great Britain
SB Simón Bolívar
SBC *Cartas del Libertador corregidas conforme a los originales*, Vicente Lecuna, ed., 10 vols.
SBO *Obras (Cartas, Proclamas, y Discursos)*, Vicente Lecuna, ed., 3 vols.
SBSW *Selected Writings of Bolívar*, Vicente Lecuna and Harold A. Bierck, Jr., eds., 2 vols.

EPIGRAPH

PAGE
ix *"You can't speak with calm"*: José Martí, *Amistad funesta* (Middlesex: Echo, 2006), 39–40.

CHAPTER 1: THE ROAD TO BOGOTÁ

PAGE
1 Epigraph: *We, who are as good as you:* Oath at the coronation of the monarch, Aragón, Spain, as reported by Antonio Pérez, secretary to Philip II of Spain. Viscardo y Guzmán, *Letter*, 74.
1 *magnificent horse:* Espinosa, *Memorias*, 260. Espinosa was a soldier in the Granadan rebel forces who became a painter. His portraits are among the most famous of SB. He painted SB from life, so spoke with him often. Hermógenes Maza, the fellow soldier present at this scene, may well have relayed the dialogue that Espinosa quotes.

1   *small, thin:* Ibid.

1   *"Here comes one of those losing bastards":* Ibid.

1   *He had been captured and tortured:* Delgado, *Hermógenes Maza*, 28.

1   *"Halt! Who goes there?":* Espinosa, 260.

2   *"¡Soy yo!":* Ibid., 261. Also Delgado, 73.

2   *sweltering afternoon:* Groot, *Historia*, IV, 20.

2   *barely alive, scarcely clothed:* O'LB, 158.

2   *He had lost a third:* Lecuna. *Crónica*, II, 307–17.

2   *abandoned their houses:* Groot, IV, 20; also O'L, I, 578–80.

2   *deafening detonations:* Groot, IV, 20.

2   *cold-blooded execution:* Gaceta de Caracas, 1815, no. 14, 120–21.

2   *he, too, had been ruthless:* SB to Zea, Tasco, July 13, 1819, SBO, I, 393.

3   *raced ahead, virtually alone:* Groot, IV, 21.

3   *He was gaunt, shirtless:* Peñuela, *Album de Boyacá*, 319–20.

3   *"God bless you, phantom!":* José Peña, *Homenaje de Colombia al Libertador Simón Bolívar* (Bogotá: Imprenta Nacional, 1883), 304.

3   *dismounted in one agile movement:* Juan Pablo Carrasquilla, quoted in Blanco-Fombona, *Ensayos Históricos*, 303 fn.

3   *five foot six inches, etc.:* O'LB, 139.

4   *population one and a half times:* Bethell, *Cambridge History*, III, 26. Humboldt estimated the population of Spanish America in 1800 to be 16.9 million. U.S. census figures (www.census.gov) show that of the U.S. in 1820 to be 9,638,453. The total population of Canada in 1822 was 427,465. Joseph Bouchette, *The British Dominions in North America* (1832), II, 235.

4   *Washington of South America:* Langley, *Simón Bolívar*, ix.

6   *neglected to take the bag:* O'L, XVI, 431 (*Boletín del Ejército Libertador*, Aug, 11, 1819).

6   *hoard of pesos:* SB to Zea, Bogotá, Aug. 14, 1819, SBO, I, 395. Bolívar's letter claims it was one million pesos, but the amount in the treasury was actually 500,000 pesos in coins and 100,000 pesos in gold bars (O'LB, 164).

6   *the serene trickle:* Carlos Borges, in Restrepo de Martínez, *Así era Bolívar*, 24.

7   *predatory sexual escapades:* Madariaga, *Bolívar* (English edition), 23.

7   *gather in the house's parlor:* Blanco-Fombona, *Mocedades*, 45.

7   *ponderous carved mahogany, etc.:* Ibid.; Restrepo de Martínez, 13–32.

7   *chamber next to the living room:* Blanco-Fombona, *Mocedades*, 45.

7   *aware that she was ailing:* Gómez Botero, *Infancia*, 13.

8   *one of their prized female slaves:* Ibid., 12.

8   *Inés Mancebo, the Cuban:* SB to Pulido, Gobernador de Barinas, Aug. 18, 1813, SBO, II, 222.

8   *Juan Vicente's lively blue eyes:* Camacho Clemente, "Juan Vicente," in *La Revista de Buenos Aires*, I (Buenos Aires: Imprenta Mayo, 1863), 278.

8   *looked far older than his years:* Gómez Botero, 12.

8   *replied with youthful energy:* Blanco-Fombona, *Mocedades*, 46.

8   *portrait in the elaborate gold frame:* Restrepo de Martínez, 16.

8   *descendant of the powerful Xedlers:* Madariaga (English edition), 12.

9   *He arrived in Santo Domingo, etc.:* Humbert, *Les origines*, 62.

9   *He introduced large-scale agricultural, etc.*: de la Cruz Herrera, *Don Simón de Bolívar*, 35.

9   *conceived and built the port*: Arístides Rojas, *Estudios*, 191.

10   *Queen Isabel and the Church*: Pope Alexander VI, the bull *Inter Caetera*, 1493. Especially: "We command you . . . to appoint to the aforesaid mainlands and islands worthy, God-fearing, learned, skilled, and experienced men, in order to instruct the aforesaid inhabitants and residents in the Catholic faith and train them in good morals." *New Iberian World*, I, 273; also, Ferdinand I and Isabella I, *Instructions to Christopher Columbus*, March 14, 1502, especially: "You are not to take slaves, but if a native should ask to come, for the purpose of learning Our language and returning, you are to give him passage." *New Iberian World*, II, 107.

10   *instructing them in the Christian faith*: Las Casas, *Devastation*, 41.

10   *"Forasmuch as my Lord"*: Isabel I, *Decree on Indian Labor*, 1503, *New Iberian World*, II, 263.

11   *"Slaves are the primary source"*: Las Casas, quoted in Sullivan, *Indian Freedom*, 60.

11   *"Spaniards are still acting like ravening beasts"*: Ibid., 127.

11   *to "a population of barely two hundred"*: Ibid., 29.

11   *stolen more than a million*: Ibid., 50.

11   *"Deep, Bloody American Tragedy," etc.*: Las Casas, *A Brief Account of the Destruction of the Indies*, penultimate paragraph (www.gutenberg.org/files/23466/23466-h/23466-h.html).

11   *"humble, patient, and peaceable"*: Las Casas, *Devastation*, 28.

11   *ten thousand African slaves*: Salcedo-Bastardo, *Bolívar*, 4.

12   *Chained, herded in gangs*: At the port of Buenos Aires in 1630, Governor Pedro de Avila declared that he had witnessed the open sale of 600,000 Indians over the course of two years—a striking number, since the population of the entire city at that time was only 20,000. Miller, *Memoirs of General Miller*, I, 5.

12   *Indian men who had no facial hair, etc.*: Ibid., 12.

13   *a cosmic race*: This term was coined by the Mexican philosopher-politician José Vasconcelos in his famous 1925 essay, "La raza cósmica."

13   *population counted 5,000 Spaniards, etc.*: Salcedo-Bastardo, *Bolívar*, 5.

13   *Venezuela had 800,000 inhabitants*: Ibid.

13   *Today, more than two thirds*: Francisco Lizcano Fernández, "Composición étnica de las tres áreas culturales del continente americano," *Revista Argentina de Sociología*, 38 (May–Aug. 2005), 218.

13   *Nowhere else on earth*: Salcedo-Bastardo, *Bolívar*, 16.

13   *he bought the title outright*: Lecuna, *Adolescencia y juventud*, BANH, no. 52, 484–533.

14   *Josefa's mother was an Indian from Aroa*: Rafael Diégo Mérida, SB's declared enemy and virulent detractor (whom SB called "El Malo"), claimed this. See Mijares, *The Liberator*, 14.

14   *a black slave from Caracas*: Claimed by SB's Peruvian nemesis, José de la Riva Aguero, who was deposed by SB but eventually returned to the presidency of Peru. Ibid.

15   *age of sixteen, served the Spanish king, etc.*: Masur, *Simón Bolívar*, 30.

15   *a sexual profligate, etc.*: Madariaga (English edition), 23–24, 659.

15   *He began to molest, etc.*: Madariaga, *Bolívar* (Mexico: Editorial Hermes, 1951) I, 67–72. From the Spanish edition of this biography, which is more complete in these details

than the English translation. Madariaga quotes from a "reserved file" in the Archives of the Archbishopric of Caracas, titled *San Matheo. Año de 1765. Autos y sumarios contra Don Juan Vicente Volíbar sobre su mala amistad con varias mujeres.*

15 *When the bishop of Caracas, etc.:* This was Diego Antonio Diez Madroñero.

16 *"fearing his power and violent temper":* Madariaga (Spanish edition), 67–72.

16 *"this infernal wolf," etc.:* Ibid.

16 *"loose ways with women":* Ibid.

17 *"by force of law":* Madariaga, *Bolívar* (English edition, and hereafter), 24.

17 *sent to the convent at four:* Ducoudray, *Memoirs,* I, 40.

17 *on the corner of Traposos:* Mijares, 8.

17 *elite were close acquaintances:* Ferry, *The Colonial Elite,* 218.

17 *a baby had just been born:* www.euskalnet.net/laviana/palacios.

18 *decorated the heavy sideboards, etc.:* Carlos Borges, in Restrepo de Martínez, 24.

19 *"incapable of filling":* Viscardo y Guzmán, 69.

19 *a sentiment held for years:* Norman Fiering, ibid., vii.

20 *A Bourbon minister mused:* Manuel de Godoy, as quoted in Lynch, *Simón Bolívar,* 7.

20 *"The Indies and Spain are two powers":* Charles de S. Montesquieu, *The Spirit of Laws,* II (Cincinnati: Clarke, 1873), 51.

20 *letter proposing revolution, etc.:* Juan Vicente de Bolívar, Martín de Tobar, and Marqués de Mixares to Miranda, Caracas, Feb. 24, 1782, *Colombeia,* II (Caracas, 1979). The editor of this collection remarks that the letter may be inauthentic. Miranda's biographer Karen Racine (*Francisco de Miranda,* 27–28) claims it is probably a forgery; she suggests it was written by Miranda himself. Even so, it is a reflection of the sentiments of Venezuelans of his time and class.

21 *Don Juan Vicente's nephew:* Fundación del Mayorazgo de la Concepción, por el presbítero Dr. Don Juan Félix Xerez de Aristiguieta. Caracas, Dec. 8, 1784. Archivo del Registro Principal de Caracas. Quoted in Juan Morales Alvarez, "Los bienes del mayorazgo de la concepción," Instituto de Altos Estudios de America Latina, Universidad Simón Bolívar, Feb. 2011, www.iaeal.usb.ve/documentos/nro_91/morales.

21 *died in 1785 with no direct heirs, etc.:* Camilo Calderón, *Revista Credencial Historia,* no. 144 (Bogotá, Dec. 2001).

21 *Juan Vicente's will and testament, etc.:* Madariaga, 22.

22 *"whose milk sustained my life"* and *"the only father I have ever known":* SB to María Antonia, July 10, 1825, SB, *Cartas: 1823–1824–1825,* 339.

22 *Willful, irascible:* de la Cruz Herrera, 138.

22 *No one scolded him:* Arístides Rojas, *Historia patria,* II, 252.

23 *brought him to live:* There is some dispute about this. José Gil Fortoul, for instance, recorded it in his initial history of Venezuela, but edited the material out in a new edition. Francisco Encina, in his *Bosquejo psicológico de Bolívar,* calls it total "invention." The historian Arístides Rojas, on the other hand, fully describes Bolívar's stay in Sanz's house, and quotes Sanz's daughter as the source for many stories about the stern lawyer and naughty boy.

23 *"You're a walking powder keg," etc.:* Arístides Rojas, *Historia patria,* II, 254.

23 *locked Simón in a room, etc.:* Ibid., 254–55.

23 *hired a learned Capuchin, etc.:* Ibid., 255.

24 *returned to Caracas and died, etc.*: Pereyra, *La juventud*, 67.

24 *"Concepción decided to lay her illness"*: Encina, *La primera república*, 314.

24 *she had bled for seven days, etc.*: Ibid. Don Feliciano's letter, quoted above, specifies that she began to bleed on Saint Peter's day, which was a week before her death.

24 *Within two months, he married, etc.*: Ibid., 338.

24 *her uncle Dionisio Palacios*: Pedro Mendoza Goiticoa, *Los Mendoza Goiticoa* (Caracas: Cromotip, 1988), 39. (Quotes records, Catedral de Caracas, Libro IX de Matrimonio, folio 58.)

24 *a connecting passageway*: Encina.

25 *net worth equivalent today*: Polanco Alcántara, *Simón Bolívar*, 11. Polanco gives the wealth in terms of 1976 dollars ($8 million), which are translated here according to the current (2010) U.S. Consumer Price Index.

25 *Juan Vicente was put in the custody, etc.*: Lecuna, *Catálogo*, I, 64.

25 *time in the company of street boys*: Cited in court records: *Litigio ventilado ante la real audiencia de Caracas sobre domicilio tutelar y educación del menor Simón Bolívar: Año de 1795*, p. 32.

26 *no attempt to develop factories*: Bethell, III, 3.

26 *Five thousand clerics*: Robertson, *Rise of the Spanish-American Republics*, 22.

26 *King Carlos IV made it very clear*: Sherwell, *Simón Bolívar*, www.fullbooks.com, chapter I.

26 *Contraband was punishable by death, etc.*: Restrepo, *Historia de la revolución*, I, 105–24.

27 *Caracas was awash in smuggled goods*: Robertson, *Rise*, 15.

27 *Books or newspapers*: Restrepo, I, 105–24.

27 *Only the Spanish-born were allowed*: Sherwell.

27 *It earned $60 million a year*: DOC, II, 5. The peso was roughly equivalent to the dollar.

27 *Factories were forbidden*: Bethell, 13.

27 *profit of $46 million a year*: DOC, II, 390.

27 *"Nature has separated us from Spain"*: Vizcardo y Guzmán, 81.

28 *overwhelmingly populated by pardos*: Lombardi, *People and Places*, 132.

28 *slave ships had just sold 26,000 Africans*: Blanchard, *Under the Flags of Freedom*, 7.

28 *reduced to a third*: Salcedo-Bastardo, *Bolívar*, 3.

28 *Cédulas de Gracias al Sacar, etc.*: Bethell, 30.

29 *Túpac Amaru II*: His birth name was José Gabriel Condorcanqui.

29 *first written to the crown's envoy*: DOC, I, 151.

29 *"I have decided to shake off"*: Ibid., I, 147.

29 *costing the Indians some 100,000 lives*: Bethell, 36.

29 *"I only know of two"*: Viscardo y Guzmán, from introduction by David Brading, 20.

30 *signaled the end of Spanish dominion*: Winsor, *Narrative and Critical History*, 317.

30 *Chirino . . . had traveled from Venezuela*: Pedro Arcaya, *Insurrección de los negros de la serranía de Coro* (Caracas: Instituto Panamericano de Geografía y Historia, 1949), 36.

CHAPTER 2: RITES OF PASSAGE

PAGE

32 Epigraph: *"A child learns more in one split second,"* Simón Rodríguez, *Sociedades americanas en 1828* (Lima: Comercio, 1842), 60.

32 *sent Simón to an elementary school: Expediente de la real audiencia de Caracas sobre el "domicilio tutelar del menor don Simón Bolívar, en el mes de junio de 1795,"* BANH, no. 149; also Polanco Alcántara, 12.

32 *as the black revolutionary Chirino fled, etc.:* Ramón Aizpurúa, *La insurrección de los negros, 1795,* BANH, no. 283, 705–23.

32 *Simón, too, decided to run: Litigio ventilado,* 17.

32 *where his old wet nurse, Hipólita:* Gómez Botero, 114.

33 *On July 31, he filed a lawsuit: Litigio ventilado,* 30.

33 *"We've already warned his guardian," etc.:* Ibid., 31.

33 *"Slaves have more rights":* Ibid., 23.

33 *"a highly respected and capable":* Ibid., 33.

33 *punching the boy's chest:* Ibid., 28.

34 *A court-ordered inspection: Expediente de la real audiencia,* Ibid.

34 *Three days later, Rodríguez reported, etc.:* Encina, 342.

34 *return him to "the harbor": Expediente de la real audiencia,* Ibid.

34 *"hire a respectable teacher": Litigio ventilado,* 58.

34 *praised by no less than the great naturalist:* SB to Santander, Arequipa, May 20, 1825, SBC, IV, 333.

34 *other esteemed Caracans of the day:* These were Fernando Vides, José Antonio Negrete, and Guillermo Pelgrón. SB to Santander, ibid.

35 *born in Caracas in 1771, birthed in secret, etc.:* Jesús Andrés Lasheras, from the Introduction, Rodríguez, *Cartas,* 17.

36 *what their revolution had in mind, etc.:* Gil Fortoul, *Historia contitucional,* III, 94.

37 *barbers, priests, doctors, etc.:* Salcedo-Bastardo, *Historia fundamental,* 238–39.

37 *attended Rodríguez's trial:* Masur, *Simón Bolívar,* 38.

37 *Sanz, argued the teacher's defense:* Rourke, *Bolívar,* 26.

37 *Rodríguez escaped conviction:* Masur, *Simón Bolívar,* 38.

37 *without so much as a goodbye:* Alfonso Rumazo González, "Simón Rodríguez," in *Manuel Gual y José María España* (Caracas: Latina, 1997), 635.

37 *In order to satisfy the conditions:* Esteban Palacios to Carlos Palacios, Madrid, Sept. 24, 1794, in Lecuna, *Adolescencia,* 526.

37 *"I keep worrying about the boys":* Esteban Palacios to Carlos Palacios, June 28, 1797, ibid., 538.

37 *"Keep a good eye on him":* Carlos to Esteban, Oct. 1799, ibid., 562.

38 *back to Venezuela in a canoe, etc.:* Esposición arrancada á José María de España estando en cadenas, Caracas, May 4, 1799, DOC, I, 345.

38 *A vial of poison:* Larrazábal, *Correspondencia,* I, 26.

39 *ship's commander was generous, etc.:* Lecuna, *Catálogo,* I, 93.

39 *After loading seven million silver coins:* Polanco Alcántara, 45.

40 *borrow 400 pesos:* SB to Pedro Palacios y Sojo, Vera Cruz, March 20, 1799, SB, *Cartas: 1799–1822,* 37.

40 *"The city of Mexico reminds one of Berlin":* Humboldt, *Oeuvres,* 186.

41 *snatch a few private moments, etc.:* Ramón Urdaneta, *Los amores de Simón Bolívar,* 30.

41 *already had quite a reputation, etc.:* Saurat, *Bolívar,* 36.

41 *the most beautiful woman:* Mme. Calderón de la Barca, *La vida en Mexico*, Colección "Sepan cuentos" (Mexico City: Porrúa, 1967), 64.

41 *making its wary way past the Bahamas, etc.:* Clarence Haring, *Trade and Navigation Between Spain and the Indies in the Time of the Hapsburgs* (Gloucester: P. Smith, 1964), 220.

42 *As the king whiled away the hours, etc.:* Hans Madol, *Godoy* (Madrid: Occidente, 1933), 91.

42 *The new object of her concupiscence, etc.:* Lecuna, *Catálogo*, I, 89.

42 *a rich young aristocrat from the Indies:* Madariaga discusses songs of the time, which referred to young rich Americans and the demand for them among marriageable Spaniards. Madariaga, 53.

42 *"He has absolutely no education":* Esteban to Carlos Palacios, Madrid, June 29, 1799, Lecuna, *Adolescencia*, 552.

43 *minister of the auditing tribunal:* Esteban to Carlos Palacios, Madrid, Oct. 23, 1798, ibid., 544.

43 *Simón arrived in Madrid, etc.:* Lecuna, *Catálogo*, I, 104.

43 *his ship had been seized:* Ibid., 101.

43 *"We do enjoy some favor":* Pedro to Carlos Palacios, Madrid, Aug. 1, 1799, Lecuna, *Adolescencia*, 553–54.

44 *He hired a tailor to outfit the boy, etc.:* Ibid., 477.

44 *He arranged special tutors:* Pedro to Carlos Palacios, Madrid, Aug. 22, 1799, ibid., 556.

44 *the marquis's resplendent mansion:* Lecuna, *Catálogo*, I, 115.

44 *The only surviving letter:* SB to Pedro Palacios, March 20, 1799, SB, *Cartas 1799–1822*, 37; SBO, I, 15.

45 *Disguised in a monk's cape, etc.:* Rourke, 20.

45 *"There is no woman," etc.:* French minister Charles J. M. Alquier, in Pereyra, 166.

45 *"The Queen's favorite in the year 1800":* Henry Adams, *History of the United States, 1801–09* (New York: Albert & Charles Boni, 1930), 347.

46 *"How could Ferdinand VII":* SB, in Larrazábal, *Vida*, I, 4–5. Also Mosquera, *Memorias*, 9.

46 *Esteban and Pedro moved out:* Lecuna, *Catálogo*, I, 104.

47 *As the marquis and her father, etc.:* Liévano Aguirre, *Bolívar*, 62.

47 *"sweet hex of my soul":* Dalmiro Valgoma, *Simón Bolívar y María Teresa del Toro* (Madrid: Cultura, 1970); also in Polanco Alcántara, p. 69.

48 *granted a passport:* Lecuna, *Catálogo*, I, 105.

48 *applied for a marriage license:* Lecuna, *Adolescencia*, 568.

48 *One of the main stipulations, etc.:* SB to Pedro Palacios, Sept. 30, 1800, SBSW, I, 38.

48 *Madrid's Parish Church of San José:* Lecuna, *Adolescencia*, 568. According to Lecuna, this church no longer exists. Originally, it was on the corner of Calle de la Libertad and Calle Gravina. Bernardo Rodríguez del Toro's house was at No. 2 Calle de Fuencarral, a few blocks away.

48 *festooned with flowers:* Polanco Alcántara, 66.

48 *a few carefree months, etc.:* Lecuna, *Catálogo*, I, 125.

48 *house his uncle Carlos had coveted, etc.:* Esteban to Carlos Palacios, June 28, 1797, Lecuna, *Adolescencia*, 538.

49 *Bolívar had hoped to take her, etc.:* Lecuna, *Catálogo*, I, 125.

49 *But he never accomplished this, etc.:* Ibid. Lecuna makes the point that she did not die in San Mateo, as other historians have assumed. Bolívar would not have taken his wife to live at a property that rightfully belonged to his brother; and Bolívar's haciendas, though important properties, did not have lavish enough houses.

CHAPTER 3: THE INNOCENT ABROAD

PAGE

50 Epigraph: *"I was suddenly made to understand":* SB to Fanny du Villars, Paris, 1804, SBO, I, 22–24.

50 *laid to rest in an open coffin:* Lecuna, *Catálogo*, I, 126.

50 *richly decorated gown, etc.:* Mijares, *The Liberator*, 87.

50 *Simón's grief was so extreme:* O'L, I, 18.

50 *"I had thought of my wife":* Mosquera, 11.

50 *"May God grant me a son":* SB to Pedro Palacios, Sept. 30, 1800, SBC, I, 38.

51 *"Had I not become a widower":* Perú de Lacroix, *Diario*, 98–100.

51 *in a legal dispute:* SB to the Captain-General, Caracas, Jan. 31, 1803, SB, *Escritos*, II, 13, 111.

51 *letter scolding his uncle Carlos Palacios:* SB to Carlos Palacios, Oct. 13, 1803, SBO, I, 20. Also SB to Pedro Palacios, Aug. 28, 1803, SBO, I, 20.

51 *bored beyond imagining:* SB to Déhollain, March 10, 1803, in Polanco Alcántara, 82–83.

51 *books by Plutarch, Montesquieu:* Mancini, *Bolívar y la emancipación*, 81.

52 *detailed instructions to his agent:* SB to Jaén, Cádiz, Jan. 29, 1804, SBO, I, 21.

52 *still in mourning clothes:* Larrazábal, *Vida*, I, 11.

52 *weeping with Don Bernardo:* Mosquera, 7.

52 *the crown issued a decree:* Bando (official order), Madrid, March 25, 1804, JCBL.

52 *the violet fields:* J. S. M., "Spring Flowers of the South of Europe," *Phytologist*, IV (Oct. 1860), 289–96.

52 *They arrived in Paris:* Lecuna, *Catálogo*, I, 144.

52 *Napoleon . . . review:* Boussingault, *Memorias*, III, 11. Perú de Lacroix relates the same story, except that in his version it occurs in 1805 in Montechiaro, after Napoleon is crowned in Italy.

53 *"I worshiped him as the hero":* O'Leary, *Bolívar y la emancipación*, 80–83.

53 *Duvernoy's virtuosic horn, etc.:* Aexandre Dratwicki, "La réorganisation de l'orchestre de l'Opéra de Paris en 1799," *Revue de Musicologie*, 88 (Paris, 2002), 297–326.

53 *one of Bolívar's favorite haunts:* Trend, *Bolívar and the Independence*, 40.

53 *With Simón Rodríguez:* O'LB, 16.

53 *lit by newfangled gas lamps, etc.:* Paris in 1804, as described by Madame de Rémusat, *Mémoires*, II (Paris: Calmann Lévy, 1880), 83ff.

54 *"He was another man entirely":* Flora Tristan, "Cartas de Bolívar," in Marcos Falcón Briceño, *Teresa: La confidante de Bolívar* (Caracas: Imprenta Nacional, 1955) 44.

54 *Legend has it:* From material on the descendancy of Jean Elie, the first Denis, Lord of Trobriand-en-Plougasnou: rootsweb.ancestry.com.

54 *Fanny was frankly promiscuous:* Liévano Aguirre, 38.

54 *She was golden-haired, vivacious:* Luis A. Sucre, "Bolívar y Fanny du Villars," *BOLANH*, XVII, no. 68 (Oct.–Dec. 1934), 345–48.

55 *"His spirit, his heart, his tastes":* Tristan, Ibid.

55 *Dancing with Fanny:* Liévano Aguirre, 71.

55 *call one another "cousin":* Sucre, "Bolívar y Fanny du Villais."

55 *The old count, believing, etc.:* Ibid., 348.

55 *soon became lovers:* Lecuna, *Catálogo*, I, 146.

55 *She was Thérèse Laisney, etc.:* SB and Thérèse (Teresa) Laisney's affair is recorded in three letters preserved by Flora Tristan and published eight years after SB's death. Tristan's account is riddled with errors of detail, compounded by the fact that she wrote in French and mistakes obviously were made in translation or orthography. Clearly, she was also relying on her mother's memory. One of SB's most respected biographers, the Venezuelan historian Vicente Lecuna, assumed that those three letters, which were published in an unsigned article in Peru's *El Faro Militar* in 1845, actually were written by SB to Fanny du Villars, and that SB, out of grief, called Fanny by his dead wife's name, Teresa. That assumption has no basis in fact, but, because its author was a great Bolívarian scholar, the fantasy was repeated in many works and created an endless string of misinformation. In 1955, a year after Lecuna's death, Marcos Falcón Briceño identified an earlier publication of Tristan's article in the French newspaper *Le Voleur* (July 31, 1838) that clearly identified her as the author and included references to her father, Mariano Tristan, and her uncle, Pío Tristan. The Peruvian publication *El Faro Militar* had suppressed these details. Falcón Briceño, 26, 53.

55 *"Eight months after my father left Bilbao":* Tristan, "Cartas de Bolívar," 43.

56 *"Turning onto the Rue Richelieu":* Ibid., 44.

56 *"All in all":* Gil Fortoul, *Historia constitucional*, III, 332.

56 *"I loved my wife very much":* Mosquera, 10.

56 *"With his keen appreciation for pleasure":* Quoted in Liévano Aguirre, 70, taken from Serviez's memoirs, issued anonymously as *L'aide de camp ou l'auteur inconnu. Souvenirs de deux mondes*, published in Paris in 1832.

57 *in Fanny du Villars's house:* du Villars to SB, April 6, 1826, BANH, no. 52, 581–82.

57 *met him through Carlos Montúfar:* Humboldt to Zaccheus Collins, May 20, 1804, Archives, 129; Academy of Natural Sciences, Philadelphia.

57 *from Jefferson's White House:* Margaret B. Smith, *The First Forty Years of Washington Society*, ed. Gaillard Hunt (New York: Scribner's, 1906), 395–96.

57 *He had advised the president:* Ulrike Moheit, *Alexander von Humboldt: 1799–1804* (Berlin: Akademie Verlag, 1993), 296.

57 *"We have lately had a great treat":* Letter from Mrs. James (Dolley) Madison, June 5, 1804, quoted in Hermann R. Friis, "Baron Alexander von Humboldt's Visit to Washington," *Records of the Columbia Historical Society*, 44 (1963), 23–24.

57 *he had met Bolívar's sisters:* Lecuna, *Catálogo*, I, 160.

57 *lodged with his in-laws:* R. A. Palacio, *Documentos para los anales de Venezuela*, IV (Caracas: Imprenta del Gobierno Nacional, 1890), 336.

58 *a frequent guest at Humboldt's:* Larrazábal, *Vida*, I, 13.

58 *collection of sixty thousand botanical specimens:* Humboldt to Hermann Karsten, Paris, March 10, 1805, in Karl Bruhns, ed., *Alexander von Humboldt*, I (Leipzig: Brockhaus, 1872), 408.

58 *part Spanish, part English, part French:* Charles Willson Peale, in Lillian Miller, *The*

Selected Papers of Charles Willson Peale and His Family (New Haven: Yale University Press, 1983), 683.

58 *Although Humboldt and Bonpland cannot:* du Villars to SB, April 6, 1826, BANH, no. 52, 581–82.

58 *became friends:* SB to Humboldt, Bogotá, Nov. 10, 1821, SBC, I, 541–604. Also du Villars to SB, Ibid.

58 *Bolívar made a passionate case:* O'LB, 17.

58 *"On that day, so notable":* Fabio Puyo Vasco, *Muy cerca de Bolívar* (Bogotá: FMC, 1988), 18.

58 *Hiram Paulding confirms this story:* Paulding, *Un rasgo de Bolívar*, 201.

59 *"He made himself emperor":* O'L, I, 15.

59 *"a sad reverse for all mankind":* Wordsworth, quoted in *The Cambridge History of English and American Literature* (Cambridge: Putnam's, 1907–21), XI, v, 7.

59 *"I regarded the crown":* Perú de Lacroix, 64.

59 *his temper erupted at a banquet:* Tristan, "Cartas de Bolívar," 49.

60 *"Colonel, I have known you":* SB to Mariano Tristan, Paris, 1804, SB, *Escritos*, Doc. 25, 141, 153.

60 *He was not well:* O'LB, 17.

60 *He had lost a fortune:* O'L, I, 19.

60 *Having fled during the Gual-España:* Rodríguez admitted he was "president of a secret society of conspirators," Manuel Uribe Angel, "El Libertador, su ayo y su capellán," *Homenaje de Colombia al Libertador Simón Bolívar en su primer centenario* (Bogotá: Medardo Rivas, 1884). But he is not listed in the official litany of suspects and convicted conspirators.

61 *"I don't want to be like trees":* Simón Rodríguez, quoted in Cazaldilla Arreaza, J.A., *El libro de Robinson* (Caracas: Siembraviva Ediciones, 2005), 7.

61 *a noted Austrian chemist:* Waldo Frank, *Birth of a World* (Boston, Houghton Mifflin, 1951), 32.

61 *where Rousseau purportedly:* Maurice Cranston, *Jean-Jacques* (Chicago: University of Chicago Press, 1982), 119.

62 *an inveterate gambler:* Madariaga, 57.

62 *Boccaccio, Petrarch, and Dante, etc.:* O'L, I, 18.

62 *Fanny was there:* du Villars to SB, June 18, 1820, and Feb. 5, 1821, in Aníbal Noguera, *Bolívar: Epistolarios, Bolívar y las damas, las damas y Bolívar* (Caracas: Ediciones de la Presidencia de la República, 1983), 124–27. In the second letter, Fanny states that she was pregnant when she saw him in Italy, although her child (Eugène, whose official godfather was Prince Eugène de Beauharnais) was conceived in late July, long after the coronation festivities.

62 *Napoleon stared back:* Perú de Lacroix, 45.

62 *"Perhaps he will think":* Ibid.

62 *Eugène de Beauharnais, viceroy:* Larrazábal, *Vida*, I, 12.

63 *Florence is said to have delighted, etc.:* O'L, 18–19.

63 *on the Piazza di Spagna:* Lecuna, *Catálogo*, I, 152.

63 *"I found Rome brick":* Suetonius, *Augustus*, 28.

63 *filled Bolívar with purpose:* O'L, I, 19.

63 *saw Alexander von Humboldt again, etc.:* O'L, XII, 234; SBC, III, 264; V, 212.

63   *his brother, Wilhelm, etc.:* Gabriele von Bülow, *Gabriele von Bülow, Daughter of Wilhelm von Humboldt* (London: Smith, Elder & Co., 1897), 19.

63   *a gathering place:* Ibid., 30.

63   *a number of European intellectuals:* These included the German poet August Wilhelm von Schlegel, the Swiss historian Jean Charles de Sismondi, and the Danish sculptor Bertel Thorvaldsen, whose eloquent stone tribute to Pope Pius VII resides in St. Peter's Basilica.

64   *Humboldt maintained a strict objectivity:* A. P. Whitaker, "Alexander von Humboldt and Spanish America," in *Proceedings of the American Philosophical Society*, 104, no. 3 (June 15, 1960), 317.

64   *"How could a minority":* Humboldt, *Personal Narrative*, II, 472–76.

64   *complacent, indolent, etc.:* *Humboldt-Lettres*, Aug. 12, 1804, quoted in Madariaga, 62.

64   *"During my time in America":* Humboldt to O'Leary, Berlin, 1853, in Charles Minguet, *Las relaciones entre Alexander von Humboldt y Simón Bolívar* (Caracas: A. Filippi, 1986–92), 746.

65   *Vargas Laguna, Spain's ambassador, etc.:* O'LN, I, 68.

65   *On August 15—a hot, etc.:* Manuel Uribe, "El Libertador, su ayo y su capellán," in *Homenaje de Colombia al Libertador* (Bogotá: M. Rivas, 1884), 72–74; also Simón Rodríguez, *El Libertador al mediodía de América* (Arequipa, 1830); also SB, *Escritos*, IV, 16.

66   *"I will not rest until":* Uribe. Also de la Cruz Herrera, 325.

66   *"Do you remember when":* SB to Rodríguez, Pativilca, Jan. 19, 1824, Simón Rodríguez, *Cartas*, 109.

66   *"From boyhood I thought of little else":* Paulding, 71.

67   *Paris lodge of the Freemasons:* Perú de Lacroix, 73. The author recounts that SB mentioned having joined the Freemasons in Paris out of curiosity, but that his fleeting association with it was enough to judge it as a "ridiculous institution" of "large children." This aligns with SB's later prohibition of all secret societies in 1827.

67   *lists him as being inducted:* Miriam Blanco-Fombona de Hood, "La masonería en nuestra independencia," *Reportorio Americano*, I (1979), 59–70, quoted in Polanco Alcántara, 145. Also Américo Carnicelli, *La masonería en la independencia de América*, I (Bogotá: Lozano & Cía., 1970), 123. Some sources give the precise induction date in Paris as Nov. 11, 1805.

67   *she was pregnant with her son Eugène:* Lecuna, *Catalogo*, I, 152. The birth notice is recorded in www.guebwiller.net/fr/index, listed under Dervieu du Villars, No. 26362.

67   *listed on the child's birth certificate:* www.guebwiller.net.

67   *might have been his:* du Villars to SB, Lyon, Feb. 5, 1821, and Paris, April, 28, 1823, SB, *Epistolarios*, 126, 129.

67   *an engraved ring:* du Villars to SB, Paris, April 6, 1826, ibid., 135.

67   *she would try to borrow money, etc.:* du Villars to SB, ibid.

67   *scores of pleading letters:* du Villars to SB, Paris, May 14, 1826, ibid., 140.

67   *Take this copy of my likeness:* SB to Leandro Palacios, Cartagena, Aug. 14, 1830 (the portrait was delivered by Señor Lesca), Palacios to SB, Paris, Nov. 20, 1830, O'L, IX, 396. Also Boulton, *El rostro de Bolívar*, p. 70.

68   *under the name of Mr. George Martin:* Racine, 155.

68   *a textile factory and a bakery:* Ibid., 2.

68 *including Juan Vicente de Bolívar:* As mentioned, there is some doubt about this letter. It is part of Miranda's archives and is signed by Juan Vicente Bolívar, Martín Tovar Blanco, and Juan Nicolás de Ponte, but Racine suspects Miranda himself may have forged it. Ibid., 28.

68 *"a mulatto, a government henchman":* Ibid., 6.

68 *a position his father bought:* Ibid., 11.

69 *visiting whorehouses:* José Amor y Vázquez, "Palabras preliminares al XXVIII Congreso del Instituto Internacional de Literatura Iberoamericana," in Julio Ortega, *Conquista y Contraconquista* (Mexico City: El Colegio de México, 1994), 19.

69 *documents describing Spain's fortifications:* Racine, 106.

69 *sharing their wardrobes and:* Ibid., 75.

69 *a brigadier general:* André-Jean Libourel y Edgardo Mondolfi, eds., "Brevet de Maréchal de Camp," in *Francisco de Miranda en Francia* (Caracas: Monte Avila, 1997), 42.

69 *"traveled to great advantage":* Racine, 91.

69 *one of the Revolution's heroes:* Ibid., 116–30.

69 *"What a country!":* Ibid., 129.

70 *"We have before our eyes":* Miranda to Gual, London, Dec. 31, 1799, *Archivo del General Miranda,* XV, 404.

70 *left New York harbor:* Lloyd, *The Trials of William S. Smith and Samuel G. Ogden,* 2.

70 *Among them was William Steuben Smith:* Ibid., 22.

70 *ill-prepared and badly equipped:* Racine, 160–70.

70 *as many as four thousand:* Ibid., 163.

70 *total of eleven days:* Ibid., 164.

71 *"On August 10th, this officer":* Madariaga, 95.

71 *the talk of New York:* Lloyd, 215.

71 *"He'll only do harm":* SB to Alexandre Déhollain, Paris, June 23, 1806, SBO, I, 28.

71 *2,400 francs:* Madariaga, 97.

71 *had arrived in Paris sometime before:* Mijares, on the other hand, claims that Anacleto traveled with SB in 1803, but gives no source for this. There are no letters, nor is there a mention by du Villars, Rodríguez, or Tristan to confirm it. Lecuna says SB may have brought Anacleto to Paris in 1803, but definitely left Hamburg with him in 1806. SB to Anacleto Clemente, Lima, May 29, 1826, SBC, V, 319; Lecuna, *Catálogo,* I, 167.

71 *Napoleon's hussars:* J. T. Headley, *The Imperial Guard of Napoleon* (New York: Scribner, 1852), 57.

71 *Germany through Holland:* Lecuna, *Catálogo,* I, 165.

71 *Charleston in January of 1807:* Déhollain to SB, London, Aug. 20, 1820, Polanco Alcántara, p. 92.

72 *Mr. M. Cormic of Charleston:* Manning, *Independence,* II, 1322.

72 *by June he was home:* Proceso de Briceño contra Bolívar, BANH, no. 52, 605.

72 *slavery was the most profitable:* Wood, *Empire of Liberty,* 3.

72 *one of the most highly commercialized nations:* Ibid., 2.

72 *business and profit more glorified:* Ibid.

73 *the most evangelically Christian nation:* Ibid., 3.

73 *"During my short visit":* Pérez Vila, *La formación intelectual del Libertador,* 81.

73 *the rancorous trial:* The charges against Smith were filed on April 1, 1806, and the case was closed with a not guilty verdict on July 26, 1806. See Lloyd, 215.

73 *On the stand, Smith recounted:* Ibid., 118ff.

73 *in clear violation of the Neutrality Act:* Ibid., 91.

74 *"My fear":* Jefferson to Archibald Stuart, Paris, Jan. 25, 1786, Paul Ford, ed., *The Works of Thomas Jefferson*, IV, 188.

74 *"agreeable to the United States":* John Adams to John Jay, London, May 28, 1786, E. Taylor Parks, *Colombia and the United States: 1765–1934* (Durham: Duke University Press, 1935), 36.

74 *"You might as well talk about":* Whitaker, *The United States and the Independence*, 37.

74 *"corrupt and effeminate":* Ibid.

74 *"It accords with our principles":* Jefferson to Gouverneur Morris, 1792, in Ford, VI, 131.

74 *Jefferson moved to make that clear:* Jefferson, "Proclamation on Spanish Territory," Washington, Nov. 27, 1806, Multimedia Archive, Miller Center, University of Virginia.

CHAPTER 4: BUILDING A REVOLUTION

PAGE

76 Epigraph *"They say grand projects need to be built with calm!":* SB, Speech to the Patriotic Society, July 3–4, 1811, SB, *Doctrina*, 7.

76 *alongside his slaves:* Lynch, *Simón Bolívar*, 41.

77 *battled his neighbor:* Proceso de Briceño contra Bolívar, 7.

77 *in sparkling salons:* Larrazábal, *Vida*, I, 48; Lecuna, *Catálogo*, I, 180–81.

77 *recited his translations of Voltaire:* Larrazábal, *Vida*, I, 31.

77 *chanced upon some papers:* M. Lafuente, *Historia General de España*, IV (Barcelona: Montaner y Simón, 1879), 428.

77 *the king wrote to Napoleon, etc.:* Ibid.

78 *permission to march 25,000 troops:* Ibid., 389.

78 *sent quadruple that number:* Ibid.

78 *a secret plan to escape:* Restrepo, II, 98.

78 *annual salary of 1.5 million pesos:* Ibid., 100.

78 *Talleyrand would write:* Charles M. de Talleyrand-Périgord, *The Memoirs of Prince Talleyrand* (London: Griffith, Farran, Okeden, and Welsh, 1891), II, 24.

79 *two old, dog-eared issues:* Amunátegui, *Vida de Don Andrés Bello*, 37–51.

79 *The facts were confirmed:* Capt. Beaver to Sir Alexander Cochrane, HMS *Acasta*, La Guayra, July 19, 1808, in Larrazábal, *Vida*, I, 39–41.

80 *Within days of arrival in Caracas:* Ibid.

80 *a letter from Francisco Miranda:* Miranda to Marqués del Toro, Londres, Oct. 6, 1808, in Miranda, *América espera*, 382.

80 *little patience for those who would take up:* Conjuración de 1808 en Caracas, Instituto Panamericano de Geografía y Historia, Comisión de Historia, Comité de Orígenes de la Emancipación, 148–50.

80 *dwarfed the sea that separated him:* Unamuno, *Simón Bolívar*, ix.

80 *refused to compromise:* Conjuración de 1808, 112.

80 *On August 3, etc.:* Polanco Alcántara, 185.

81 *"But I'm totally innocent!":* BANH, no. 52, 616.

81 *"For the first time":* Díaz, *Recuerdos sobre la rebelión*, 73.

81 *Tovar drew up a formal letter, etc.:* Recorded on Dec. 1, 1808, Lecuna, *Catalogo*, I, 175–79.

82 *Napoleon had recommended him:* Napoleon Bonaparte, *Correspondance de Napoléon Ier* (New York: AMS Press, 1974), 212–13.

82 *blessed by Napoleon's bitterest enemy:* Polanco Alcántara, 199.

83 *the escapes from servant quarters:* Gaceta de Caracas, Oct. 24, 1808, and ff., quoted in Polanco Alcántara, 201.

83 *Emparan had Bolívar taken aside:* Heredia, *Memorias*, 163.

84 *Bolívar hurried down to La Guaira:* Díaz, 64.

84 *at three in the morning on Maundy Thursday:* Ibid., 64–72, for this whole account, including testimony about the possible presence of the Bolívar brothers.

84 *Whether Bolívar was there:* A number of biographers contend that SB may have been confined to his hacienda in Yare (e.g., Polanco Alcántara) or that he took off for San Mateo (e.g., Lynch, Parra-Pérez), but there appears to be no documentary evidence for this. His aide-de-camp, Daniel O'Leary, claims that SB was too much a friend of Emparan to be present at his ouster, although he dearly desired it; and that he was too much of an enemy of the crown to take part in a coup that was essentially monarchist. Larrazábal and Díaz, two of SB's contemporaries, however, place him on the scene. SB himself never claimed to be present at city hall on April 19, 1810.

85 *large crowd of activists in long capes:* Díaz, 67.

85 *"To city hall, Governor!":* Parra-Pérez, *Historia*, I, 383.

85 *Cortés, swept grandly into the room:* Ibid.

86 *"No! No! We don't want it!" etc.:* Ibid., 384; also Gil Fortoul, *Historia*, I, 168.

86 *recorded into the meeting's minutes:* Masur, *Simón Bolívar*, 98.

86 *Within two days, Emparan:* Mancini, II, 30.

87 *junta was organizing diplomatic missions:* Parra-Pérez, *Historia*, I, 380

87 *offered to pay all costs for the diplomatic mission:* O'LB, 21.

88 *expressly by Lord Admiral Cochrane:* Cochrane to the Junta de Caracas, May 17, 1810, published in *Gaceta de Caracas*, II, no. 102 (June 8, 1810), 4.

88 *twelve times the size of Venezuela:* Wayne Rasmussen, "Agricultural Colonization and Immigration in Venezuela, 1810–1860," *Agricultural History*, 21, no. 3 (July 1947), 155.

88 *Lord Wellesley had expressed:* Rich Wellesley's letter to his brother Henry, ambassador to Cádiz, July 13, 1810, Foreign Office, Spain, 93, confidential dispatches, nos. 2 and 22, quoted in Mancini, 59.

88 *a calculated scheme to force:* Ibid.

89 *immense and resplendent lobby:* Apsley House (London: English Heritage, 2005), 42–49.

89 *His French was superb:* Polanco Alcántara, 229, fn. 11.

89 *He gave Wellesley a spirited account, etc.:* Amunátegui, 49.

89 *"eager to shake off":* Minuta de la sesión, July 16, 1810, *Revista Bolívariana*, II, Nos. 20–21, Bogotá, 1830, 531.

90 *When he was done, the minister looked up:* Mancini, 61.

90 *Bolívar was speechless:* Ibid. Also Amunátegui, 89.

90   *tempestuous French wife:* Richard Holmes, *Wellington: The Iron Duke* (London: Harper, 2003), 24. Hyacinthe Gabrielle Rolland was a French courtesan who lived with Wellesley and bore him several children before they were married. She had left him during this period because of his rampant womanizing.

91   *an incorrigible voluptuary:* Ibid., 157.

91   *"The events in Caracas":* Lord Harrowby, minister without portfolio, in a report dated June 1810, *Bolívar y Europa*, Ediciones de la Presidencia de la República (Caracas, 1986), I, Doc. 86, 388. From a Spanish translation.

91   *"Despite his age":* Amunátegui, 93.

91   *his house at 27 Grafton Street:* Today the house is 58 Grafton. A plaque on the front wall identifies it as Miranda's house from 1803 to 1810, although his wife and son occupied it until the 1840s. *Survey of London*, vol. 21 (1949), 50–51, http://www.british history.ac.uk/report.aspx?compid=65170.

92   *"The only person with whom we consulted":* López Méndez to Venezuelan secretary of state, London, Oct. 3, 1810, quoted in Lynch, *Simón Bolívar*, 49.

92   *the Foreign Office had been on the verge:* Mijares, *The Liberator*, 183.

93   *the three preeminent figures:* Carnicelli, *La masonería en la independencia de América*, 76. Despite numerous South American histories that insist that Miranda's lodge was, at one point or another, visited by San Martín, O'Higgins, and Bolívar, it's worth mentioning here that William Spence Robertson says this is "hardly more than a legend" (Robertson, *Rise*, 53).

93   *agents intercepted a letter:* The letter was dated Oct. 28, 1811, and was one of several from the Argentine Carlos Alvear to Rafael Mérida in Caracas. The letters— intercepted by Antonio Ignacio Cortavarría and reported to the viceroy of New Granada, Don Francisco de Montalvo—were on an English ship, sailing from London to Caracas. Archivo Histórico de Colombia en Bogotá, Sección Histórica, XIII, folios 00581–2, quoted in Carnicelli, 123.

93   *Given his later criticisms:* Gould, *Library of Freemasonry*, IV, 180.

93   *made a point to study its public services:* Racine, 54–64.

93   *He spoke of irrigation, mines, schools:* Mijares, 186.

94   *the portraitist Charles Gill:* Mancini, 315.

94   *"singular adventure":* Perú de Lacroix, *Diario (version sin mutilaciones)*, 57.

94   *police had raided the White Swan:* "Police. Bow Street," London *Times*, July 10, 1810, Issue 8029. Also "Police. Diabolical Club in Vere-Street," *The Morning Chronicle*, July 16, 1810.

95   *Bolívar was dismayed:* O'L, XXVII, 35.

95   *"a deadly animosity exists":* Robert Semple, *Sketch of the Present State of Caracas* (London: Robert Baldwin, 1812), 57.

96   *only member of the junta:* Juan Germán Roscio to Andrés Bello, June 8, 1811, *Epistolario de la primera república*, II, 200.

96   *Expecting to be greeted as the leader:* Miranda to Francisco Febles, London, Aug. 3, 1810, *Archivo*, XXIII, 490.

96   *The coat was sky blue:* Angell, *Simón Bolívar*, 11.

96   *"I saw Miranda enter in triumph":* Díaz, 88.

97   *had bombastically opposed his return:* Roscio to Bello, *Epistolario*, 200.

97   *where he would lodge:* Miranda, *América espera*, 650.

97   *a title of lieutenant general: Toma de Razón, libro de registro de nombramientos y actos oficiales,* 1810–1812 (Caracas: Ministerio de Relaciones Interiores, Imprenta Nacional, 1955), 177–78.

97   *demoted him from lieutenant colonel:* Ibid., 285–86.

97   *took control of the* Gazeta de Caracas: Lynch, *Simón Bolívar,* 55. The spelling of *Gazeta de Caracas* changed to Gaceta, depending on which side was publishing the newspaper. Under the editorship of José Domingo Díaz, it was spelled *Gaceta.* This accounts for the different spellings that occur throughout this book. The *Gaceta de Colombia,* however, was always spelled the same. Pacheco, Carlos, et al, *Nación y Literatura* (Caracas: Bigott, 2006), 178.

98   *Miranda's Patriotic Society was well in the lead:* Madariaga, 154–55.

CHAPTER 5: THE RISE AND FALL OF MIRANDA

PAGE

99   Epigraph: *"Liberty is a succulent food":* From Jean-Jacques Rousseau, Letter to the Polish People, *Oeuvres Complétes,* V (Paris: Dupont, 1825), 280.

99   *"He listened to toasts":* Germán Roscio to Bello, June 8, 1811, *Epistolario de la primera república.*

99   *the marquis received more than one letter:* Oct. 6, 1808, Miranda, *América espera,* 650.

100   *he refused to be disloyal:* Cristóbal de Mendoza, Prefacio, *Documentos relativos a la vida pública del Libertador de Colombia y del Perú Simón Bolívar* (Caracas, 1826), I, ix.

100   *too raw a soldier, . . . too impulsive:* A. Rojas, *Obras escojidas* (Paris: 1907), 573.

100   *absconded with the War Department's plans:* Díaz, 32. Also Parra-Pérez, *Historia,* II, 50.

100   *the moment had come to discuss:* Parra-Pérez, *Historia,* II, 51.

100   *"Let us valiantly lay the cornerstone":* SB, *Discursos* (Caracas: Lingkua, 2007), 17.

101   *"Among all the rest":* Richard Colburn, *Travels in South America* (London, 1813), cited in Gabriel E. Muñoz, *Monteverde, cuatro años de historia patria,* BANH, I, no. 42, 143–44, translated from the Spanish.

101   *All night long, young revolutionaries, etc.:* Díaz, 33.

101   *Miranda took the floor, etc.:* Angell, 26. Also Díaz, 33.

102   *duped Juan Vicente into believing:* Parra-Pérez, *Historia,* I, 446–48.

102   *Blacks taunted the wellborn, etc.:* Flinter, *History of the Revolution,* 22.

102   *"carried insolence so far":* Ibid., 23.

102   *cutlasses, muskets, and improvised tin shields, etc.:* Díaz, 34.

102   *"Unless we spill blood":* Germán Roscio to Bello, June 8, ibid.

103   *Only citizens who owned property, etc.: Constitución Federal de 1811 (21 de Diciembre, 1811),* http://www.dircost.unito.it/cs/docs/Venezuela%201811.htm. Also Parra-Pérez, *Historia,* I, 370–86.

103   *"enjoy the benefits": Constitución Federal.*

104   *the old nobleman . . . had proceeded to correspond:* Angell, 21.

104   *"Because he is a dangerous young man":* Austria, *Bosquejo,* I, 128.

104   *"How can you refuse me":* Larrazábal, *Correspondencia,* I, 97.

105   *he singled out Bolívar for his valor:* Yanes, *Relación documentada,* I, 5.

105   *But privately, he was more critical:* Mancini, 127.

105 *"Where are the armies":* O'L, XXVII, 46.

105 *debilitating number of dead:* There were 4,000 troops total under Miranda's command during the Valencia campaign. Eight hundred died, 1,500 were wounded (among them, Fernando del Toro, SB's friend and cousin who traveled with him to Rome): Admiral Fraser to Rowley, July 21, 1811, in W. S. Robertson, *Francisco de Miranda and the Revolutionizing of Spanish America* (American Historical Association, 1909), I, 450. Also, Eduardo Blanco, *Venezuela heroica,* xv; and Pedro Rivas, *Efemérides americanas* (Barcelona: Ramírez, 1884), 255.

106 *hemming and hawing about the rights of man:* Lynch, 58; also Eduardo Blanco, *Venezuela heroica,* XV.

106 *named the new nation Colombia: Constitución Federal.*

107 *made himself head of his own army:* Sherwell, 33.

107 *the sun was oppressively hot, etc.:* Díaz, 98–102, for all subsequent details.

107 *heaving and rippling:* Humboldt, *Personal Narrative,* 451.

107 *A cacophony of bells, etc.:* Díaz, 98–102.

107 *Trinity collapsed to its foundations:* Heredia, 46.

108 *severed limbs, crushed corpses:* Flinter, *History of the Revolution,* 35.

108 *"I will never forget that moment":* Díaz, 98–102.

108 *More than ten thousand, etc.:* Heredia, 46.

108 *Survivors, caked with dust and blood:* Mancini, 127.

108 *The looting began almost instantly, etc.:* Flinter, *History of the Revolution,* 34.

108 *Bolívar's house had been seriously damaged, etc.:* Mancini, 118.

108 *dug with their bare hands:* Humboldt, *Personal Narrative,* p. 452.

109 *"On your knees, sinners", etc.:* Mancini, 118. For all subsequent details.

109 *He combed the ruins, etc.:* O'L, XXVII, 50–51.

109 *men of means married slaves:* Flinter, *History of the Revolution,* 34. Also O'L, XXVII.

109 *colossal wooden crosses:* Flinter, *History of the Revolution,* 34.

109 *proceeding in devastating opposition:* Humboldt, *Personal Narrative,* 451.

109 *Strange natural phenomena occurred:* Ibid., 454.

109 *the loss of life at 30,000:* Flinter, *History of the Revolution,* 34.

109 *as high as 120,000:* O'L, XXVII, 49.

109 *the only house that remained standing:* Mancini, 118.

109 *crushed in their barracks:* Humboldt, *Personal Narrative,* 451.

109 *there was hardly a brick out of place:* Ibid., 454.

110 *the gallows to which dissident Spaniards, etc.:* Díaz, 98–102.

110 *he had no trouble recruiting troops:* Heredia, 47.

110 *blazing comet:* J. Zeilenga de Boer, *Earthquakes in Human History* (Princeton: Princeton University Press, 2005), 129.

110 *its epicenter between Memphis and St. Louis, etc.:* Ibid., 126–29.

110 *news of the Caracas disaster:* When the U.S. Congress learned of the extent of damage in Venezuela, it approved a gift of $50,000 in aid. Many North Americans complained that the country had not provided the same to its own citizens. Ibid., 129.

110 *"The period is portentous and alarming":* Ibid.

110 *hang a ball from a string:* E. S. Holden, *Catalogue of Earthquakes on the Pacific Coast, 1769–1897* (Washington, DC, Smithsonian, 1898), 33.

110 *a volcano on the Caribbean island:* W. A. Garesché, *Complete Story of the Martinique and Saint Vincent Horrors* (Chicago: Monarch, 1902), 155.

110 *rumblings went on for months, etc.:* Holden, 32–33.

111 *forty percent of all U.S. exports:* J. H. Coatsworth, "American Trade with European Colonies, 1790–1812," *William & Mary Quarterly*, Series 3, 24 (April 1967), 243.

111 *a virtual monopoly in Latin America:* T. O'Brien, "Making the Americas," *The History Compass*, 2 (2004), 1–29.

111 *In the address, etc.:* President Madison's message to Congress, Nov. 5, 1811, in J. Richardson, *A Compilation of the Messages and Papers of Presidents*, www.gutenberg.org. Also W. S. Robertson, "The Recognition of the Hispanic American Nations by the United States," *HAHR*, 1, no. 3 (Aug. 1918), 239–69.

111 *Congress issued a dry statement:* Dec. 10, 1811, ibid., 242.

111 *when John Adams had first heard:* Adams to James Lloyd, Quincy, March 26, 1815, *The Works of John Adams* (Boston: Little, Brown, 1856), X, 140.

112 *Monroe met with Ambassador Orea:* Robertson, "Recognition," 239–69.

112 *republican population decimated:* The population of Venezuela in 1810 was estimated at 800,000. The republican population was a small fraction of that. The Caracas population in 1810 was 40,000. Citations for the numbers of dead in the earthquake (throughout Venezuela) range from 20,000 to 50,000. See Bethell, 150.

112 *"not without misgivings":* Austria, 299.

112 *powerful enemies of the revolution, etc.:* Parra-Pérez, *Historia*, 440.

112 *the day after Monteverde readily took:* O'L, XXVII, 56.

112 *Many were farm boys, etc.:* Becerra, *Ensayo histórico*, II, 219–20.

113 *Miranda had six thousand, etc.:* Heredia, 49. Some sources (e.g., Sherwell, 35) cite up to 12,000 soldiers for Miranda.

113 *defected to the Spanish side:* O'L, XXVII, 56.

113 *Even the Marquis del Toro:* Archivo General de Indias (Sevilla), Caracas, 385, in McKinley, *Pre-Revolutionary Caracas*, 211.

113 *massive slave insurrection:* Paz del Castillo to Miranda, Caracas, July 5, 1812, *Archivo del General Miranda*, XXIV, 288. Also G. R. Andrews, *Afro-Latin America, 1800–2000* (New York: Oxford, 2003), 59.

113 *something turned in Miranda:* "Acta de la decisión," La Victoria, July 12, 1812, Miranda, *América espera*, 461.

113 *an act that freed slaves:* The Conscription Act, Robertson, *Francisco de Miranda*, 466.

113 *he had instructed a diplomat:* Miranda to L. M. Martín, La Victoria, July 2, 1812, Miranda, *América espera*, 460.

113 *half the province of Caracas:* M. Lucena, "La sociedad de la provincia de Caracas a comienzos del siglo XIX," in *Anuario de Estudios Americanos*, XXXVII, 8–11.

113 *"As much as I desire liberty":* Miranda to John Turnbull, Dover, Dec. 6, 1798, in *Archivo del General Miranda*, XXIV, 207.

114 *fragrant gardens, well-kept houses, etc.:* Flinter, *History of the Revolution*, 50, for all subsequent details.

114 *"The graveyard of Spaniards":* Ibid.

114 *to attend his own wedding:* Madariaga, 170.

114 *Taking advantage of his absence, etc.:* Lecuna, *Crónica*, I, xxi.

115   *urging the renegades to reconsider:* Ibid.

115   *most of the republican munitions, etc.:* SB's report to Miranda, Puerto Cabello, quoted in full in O'L, XXX, 517.

115   *the captain in charge of defending:* Parra-Pérez, *Historia*, p. 489.

115   *five hundred of Monteverde's troops:* Ibid., 490.

115   *chatting breezily of Jefferson:* Pedro Gual, *Testimonio y declaración*, Quinta de la Paz, Bogotá, Feb. 15, 1843, published in Robertson, *Francisco de Miranda*, 470.

115   *"Generalísimo, At one o'clock":* SB, *Escritos*, IV, 85, in Puyo Vasco and Gutiérrez Cely, *Bolívar día a día*, I, 126. Also Yanes, 46.

116   *"You see, gentlemen":* Miranda to his men (Sata y Bussy, Roscio, Espejo, Gual), as recorded by Gual, *Testimonio*, in Robertson, *Francisco de Miranda*, 471.

116   *retinue of five ragged officers, etc.:* Lecuna, *Crónica*, I, xxii.

116   *They stole along the coast:* SB, in his report to Miranda, O'L, XXX, 517.

116   *a swarm of Spanish ships, etc.:* Communication of Luis Delpech, Feb. 27, 1813, as given to the British by Tomás Molini, PRO/FO: Spain, 151.

116   *"my spirits are so low":* SB to Miranda, Caracas, July 12, 1812, SBO, I, 35.

117   *crushed under the ruins:* O'L, XXX, 528.

117   *"Venezuela is wounded in the heart":* Miranda to his men, in French, as recorded by Gual, *Testimonio*, in Robertson, *Francisco de Miranda*, 471.

117   *next morning, before dawn:* Ibid., 472.

117   *"They've probably stormed the plaza by now":* Ibid.

117   *did not dare raise the possibility, etc.:* Heredia, 52.

117   *suggested that the generalísimo convene, etc.:* Mancini, 137.

117   *He wanted nothing more:* Heredia, 52.

117   *The republic was in extremis, etc.:* Mancini, 136.

118   *Casa León happily volunteered:* Heredia, 53.

118   *republicans launched a modest attack:* Yanes, 47.

118   *charter a ship for his evacuation, etc.:* Austria, 316–22; Mancini, 139.

118   *22,000 pesos:* M. M. Las Casas, Defensa Documentada del Comandante de La Guaira 33, in Lecuna, *Catálogo*, I, 239; and Austria, 150.

118   *proof incontrovertible:* Masur, *Simón Bolívar*, 145.

118   *The pact did seem to ensure:* O'LB, 37.

118   *made to give up their arms:* Heredia, 54.

119   *banner of independence was lowered:* Rafter, *Memoirs of Gregor M'Gregor*, 47.

119   *had not confided his plans:* Fermín Paúl, as quoted in Pereyra, 500.

119   *no provision in the capitulation for their safe passage:* Rafter, 47.

119   *why hadn't he passed the scepter:* Lecuna, *Crónica*, I, xxiv.

119   *less than three hundred of Monteverde's:* Lynch, *Simón Bolívar*, 62.

119   *a city of fourteen thousand:* J. Kinsbruner, "The Pulperos of Caracas and San Juan During the First Half of the 19th Century," *Latin American Research Review*, 13, no. 1 (1978), 65–85.

119   *in hopes of reconstituting the army, etc.:* Lecuna, *Crónica*, I, xxv.

120   *no vessel could leave:* O'L, XXVII, 74. Also P. Briceño Méndez, *Relación histórica* (Caracas: Tipografía Americana, 1933), 10, quoted in Lecuna, *Catálogo*, I, 254.

120   *suffocating heat, etc.:* Mancini, 136, for subsequent details.

120   *The sea, ruffled:* Mancini. Also Lecuna, *Catálogo*, I, 252.

120   *Miranda's baggage had been sent:* Robertson, *Francisco de Miranda*, 473.

120   *22,000 pesos:* Las Casas, Defensa Documentada.

120   *Gual stubbornly doubting, etc.:* Gual, *Testimonio*, in Robertson, *Francisco de Miranda*, 472–73. Pedro Gual was the nephew of Manuel Gual, the rebel in the Gual-España conspiracy.

121   *had already communicated with Monteverde:* M. Picón Salas, *Miranda* (Caracas: Aguilar, 1955), 247. Also Parra-Pérez, *Historia*, II, 443; Baralt and Díaz, *Resumen*, I, 102–3; and Gual, *Testimonio*, in Robertson, *Francisco de Miranda*, 472–73.

121   *sought out Las Casas and Peña:* O'LB, XXVII, 38.

121   *contempt for his countrymen:* "He preferred his real countrymen, the English and French, saying that [Venezuelans] were brutes, incapable of following commands, and that they had better learn how to handle a gun before donning epaulettes, &c." Conversation in Edificio Guipuzcoana, Austria, 159–60.

121   *charge him with treason, etc.:* Lecuna, *Crónica*, I, xxv–vi.

121   *He put his troops on alert, etc.:* Austria, 160.

121   *"Too soon!" Miranda growled:* Carlos Soublette, SBC, I, 246. Also see letters between Soublette and Restrepo, BANH, nos. 77, 23, and for all subsequent details.

122   *encountered a party of couriers, etc.:* Austria, 160–61.

122   *"It's no small surprise to me":* Parra-Pérez, *Historia*, 441.

122   *The USS Matilda:* Slatta and Lucas de Grummond, *Simón Bolívar's Quest for Glory*, 66.

122   *succeeded in evading capture:* Lecuna, *Crónica*, I, xxvi.

122   *hastily improvised a disguise:* Larrazábal, *Correspondencia*, I, 132.

123   *thrust into the dank crypts:* Becerra, 294.

123   *hustled onto a shabby little boat:* Letter from Miranda to the president of the Spanish courts, June 30, 1813, in Becerra, 300–7.

123   *"Miranda by a shameful":* Scott to James Monroe, Nov. 26, 1812, State Department MSS, Bureau of Indexes and Archives, Consular Letters, La Guayra, I; in Robertson, *Francisco de Miranda*, 468.

123   *labeling him an outright coward:* Baralt and Díaz, 124.

124   *the reward of money:* Miranda to Nicholas Vansittart, La Carraca, May 21, 1814, and April 13, 1815.

124   *"Proto-leader":* From Rumazo González, "Francisco de Miranda: Protolíder de la independencia americana."

124   *skilled at plotting grand schemes, etc.:* Robertson, *Francisco de Miranda*, 488.

124   *hatching of revolutions:* Ibid.

124   *opportunity to clear his honor:* SB to Miranda, Caracas, July 12, 1812, SBO, I, 34.

124   *"a loathsome leader, despot":* SB, *Manifiesto*, Valencia, Sept. 20, 1813, O'L, XIII, 366.

124   *"To the last hour of his life":* Wilson to O'Leary, London, March 4, 1832, O'L, I, 75.

124   *"General Bolívar invariably added":* Wilson to O'Leary, London, July 14, 1832, O'L, I, 76.

125   *kind man with a large heart:* Larrazábal, *Correspondencia*, I, 137.

125   *flung alkali against the walls:* Sherwell, 37.

125   *pulled from a fleeing boat:* Larrazábal, *Correspondencia*, I, 133.

125   *Six of the most respected:* E.g., Montilla Mirés, Paz Castillo, who were SB's cronies, ibid.

125   *"eight monsters":* Gil Fortoul, *Historia constitucional*, I, 196.

125 *One thousand five hundred:* Ibid., 197.

125 *offering himself as a guarantee, etc.:* Larrazábal, *Correspondencia*, I, 137–38.

126 *"Here is the commander":* Gil Fortoul, *Historia constitucional*, I, 193.

126 *August 27, Bolívar sailed:* Zerberiz to Monteverde, Guayra, Aug. 28, 1812, ibid., 138.

126 *face turned a deathly white:* Masur, *Simón Bolívar*, 150.

CHAPTER 6: GLIMPSES OF GLORY

PAGE

127 Epigraph: *The art of victory is learned in failures:* SB, in Larrazábal, *Vida*, I, 580.

127 *Storms bedeviled his journey, etc.:* SB to Iturbe, Sept. 10, 1812, Curaçao, O'L, XXIX, 13.

127 *they confiscated his baggage, etc.:* Ibid.

127 *beginning to see his straitened circumstances:* Ibid., 14.

128 *he had secured a loan:* O'L, XXVII, 83.

128 *he seemed more deliberate, judicious, mature:* Mancini, 187.

128 *words were as valuable as weapons:* SB arrived in Cartagena in mid-November (O'L, I, 85) and decamped to his first military assignment on Dec. 1 (Mancini, 187). It is very possible that he actually wrote the Cartagena Manifesto in Curaçao or even on board the ship.

128 *Bolívar lodged in a modest house, etc.:* German Arciniegas, *Bolívar, de Cartagena a Santa María,* 10.

128 *illusions of grandeur:* J. de la Vega, *La federación en Colombia* (Bogotá, 1952), 106–10.

129 *Manuel Rodríguez Torices:* Although Rodríguez was his surname, it was a common enough name that he was referred to by his matronymic, Torices. This is also true for the del Toros, who were also surnamed Rodríguez.

129 *hotbed of pirates and opportunists:* Isidro Beluche Mora, "Privateers of Cartagena," *Louisiana Historical Quarterly,* 39 (January 1956), 74–5, 79.

129 *wealth and abounding whiteness:* According to Restrepo (in Liévano Aguirre, 93), New Granada had 887,000 whites; Venezuela had 200,000. New Granada had 140,000 free blacks and pardos; Venezuela had 431,000. New Granada had 313,000 indigenous and mestizos; Venezuela had 207,000. New Granada was thus overwhelmingly white in comparison with neighboring Venezuela. As Liévano says, in New Granada: "the classes had more in common . . . more sympathy than hatred."

129 *He and his fellow Venezuelan revolutionaries:* O'L, XXVII, 86.

129 *assumed that their military experience:* Masur, *Simón Bolívar,* 156.

129 *General Labatut knew these men too well:* Ibid., 98.

129 *on the deck of the USS* Matilda: "Généalogie et Histoire de la Caraïbe," 87 (Nov. 1996), 1786, http://www.ghcaraibe.org/bul/ghco87/p1786.html.

129 *eluding enemy cannons:* Yanes, 55.

129 *presumptuous letters to President Antonio Nariño:* O'L, XXVII, 96–97.

129 *On December 1, 1812:* Mancini, 187.

130 *published General Monteverde's official proclamations:* R. Domínguez, *Don Vicente Texera* (Caracas: Lit. Vargas, 1926), 83, LOC. Also Parra-Pérez, *Historia,* 469.

130 *"I am . . . a son of unhappy Caracas," etc.:* SB, "Memoria dirigida a los ciudadanos de la Nueva Granada" (Cartagena Manifesto), Dec. 15, 1812, SBO, I, 43–50.

131 *Andrés Bello later compared him:* Bello, "Alocución a la Poesía," SB, *Obras Completas,* III (Santiago: Ramírez, 1883), 38.

131 *met with landowners from the Valle:* M. A. Suárez, "Movimiento independentista," in *Becas culturales* (Bogotá: Observatorio del Caribe Colombiano, 2006), 77.

131 *She wrote a letter on his behalf:* Lenoit to Loperena, Salamina, Nov. 3, 1812, ibid., 78. Also P Castro, *Culturas aborigenes cesarences e independencia* (Bogotá: Casa de la Cultura, 1979), 203–6.

132 *the scant seventy men under his command:* O'L, XXVII, 99.

132 *came from the dregs of society, etc.:* Mancini, 442.

132 *They took off on ten* champanes, *etc:* All details about the Magdalena River campaign are taken from O'L, XXVII, 99–101; and Lecuna, *Crónica*, I, 6–9.

132 *He summoned the townspeople:* SB's speech to the people of Tenerife, Dec. 24, 1812, SB, *Escritos*, IV, 127–30.

132 *"Wherever the Spanish empire rules":* Ibid.

133 *by hand and ax:* D'Espagnat, *Souvenirs de la Nouvelle Grenade*, in Mancini, 440.

133 *the widow Loperena and other wealthy:* Suárez, *Movimiento independentista*, 78–79. Also Castro, 212–15.

133 *"every defensive action," etc.:* SB, "Memoria dirigida," SBO, I, 43–50.

133 *five hundred punishing kilometers:* O'L, XXVII, 102.

133 *the entire length of the river:* SB, Oficio al Congreso, Jan. 8, 1813, O'L, XIII, 133.

133 *The operation had taken him fifteen days:* Ibid.

133 *Bolívar's name was known and admired:* Lecuna, *Crónica*, I, 9.

133 *"I was born in Caracas":* Revista de la Sociedad Bolívariana de Caracas, 38, nos. 129–32, (1981), 21.

133 *sacking, plundering, and sending its governor:* Marcucci, *Bolívar*, 85.

133 *accused Bolívar of insubordination:* Lecuna, *Crónica*, I, 9.

133 *even making a trip to the capital:* Larrazábal, *Correspondencia*, I, 155.

134 *As the mill of souls ground on:* Lecuna, *Crónica*, I, 31.

134 *confiscated the Creoles' land:* Ibid., 1–25.

134 *An official who arrived from Madrid:* Refers to Pedro Urquinaona. From W. S. Robertson, "Bibliografía General," *The American Historical Review*, 22, no. 4 (July 1917), 893.

134 *appalled by Monteverde's reign of terror:* P. Urquinaona, *Relación documentada del origen y progreso del trastorno* (Madrid: Impresa Nueva, 1820), 2nd Part, 119.

134 *"Happiness. Prosperity. Liberty," etc.:* Gaceta de Caracas, III, Dec. 6, 1812.

134 *"pompous and extravagant promises":* Ibid., Oct. 4, 1812.

134 *they had insulted the king by seeking help:* Ibid.

135 *a wanton truculence, etc.:* Mijares, 220–21; Heredia, 154; Baralt and Díaz, II, 114–15.

135 *lop off their ears, etc.:* Gazeta de Caracas, IV, Sept. 16, 1813.

135 *"If it were possible":* Mijares, 250.

135 *Even Franciscan priests:* Heredia, 135.

135 *"spare no one over the age of seven!":* Ibid.

136 *a well-born Granadan with a large ego, etc.:* Ducoudray, I, 39.

136 *in charge of his uncle, José Félix Ribas:* SB's second in command; O'L, XXVII, 103.

137 *President Torices instructed him to join:* Ducoudray, I, 40.

137 *made their way through February rain:* O'L, XXVII, 104.

137 *Spanish general Ramón Correa:* Son-in-law of failed Captain-General Miyares: Heredia, 127.

137   *Bolívar was joined by Castillo, etc.:* Restrepo, I, 199.

137   *Correa's troops were double the force:* Ibid., 200.

137   *Correa fell to the ground:* SB to Torices, Feb. 28, 1813, O'L, XIII, 150.

138   *a vast supply of food and ammunition, etc.:* Ibid.

138   *only two dead and fourteen wounded:* Ibid.

138   *Bolívar was lauded:* Groot, III, 232.

138   *including a raging fever:* Mancini, 200.

138   *"Loyal republicans!," etc.:* SB, Proclamation to his soldiers, March 1, 1813, Cuartel general de San Antonio de Venezuela, DOC, IV, 770.

138   *"If one country wears chains":* SB to Camilo Torres, March 4, 1813, in Austria, 191–92.

139   *"mad undertaking":* Masur, *Simón Bolívar,* 167.

139   *anathema to his principles:* Ibid.

139   *a friendly letter as a palliative:* SB, SBSW, I, 27.

139   *"March at once!," etc.:* O'L, XXVII, Part I, 123.

139   *"General, if two men are enough":* Rafael Urdaneta, *Memorias,* 14.

140   *tell him about the true condition of his troops:* SB to the president of the union (Antonio Nariño), May 3, 1813, SB, *Cartas: Santander–Bolívar,* 2–4; also Santander to SB, April 30, 1813, SB, *Cartas: Santander–Bolívar,* 3.

140   *The march to Trujillo promised to tax:* SB to Nariño, May 8, 1813, in Austria, 195–96.

140   *"I will await the result":* Ibid.

140   *leading one Spanish commandant:* Heredia, 128–29.

140   *murdered some of his own relatives, etc.:* Díaz, 39; also Baralt and Díaz, II, 198, 218.

140   *posted a Royal Order:* "Real Orden de 11 de enero de 1813," published in Caracas as a broadside on March 13, 1813, and by Cmdt. Gen. Antonio Tizcar in Barinas on May 3, 1813; Lecuna, *Catálogo,* I, 271; also Austria, 199.

141   *took off on a bloody campaign:* O'L, XXVII, Part I, 124–5.

141   *his 143 soldiers:* Díaz, 93.

141   *one of the heads—along with a letter:* Larrazábal, *Vida,* I, 170.

141   *"the work of Satan":* Ibid.

141   *saw himself as the anointed liberator:* Urdaneta, *Memorias,* 21.

141   *twenty Spanish heads, etc.:* V. Dávila, *Investigaciones Históricas,* in Mijares, 246.

141   *The news came as a great blow, etc.:* O'L, XXVII, Part I, 125.

142   *"We've run out of goodness":* SB, Cuartel general, Mérida, June 8, 1813, in Larrazábal, *Vida,* I, 170.

142   *All night he pondered it:* Larrazábal, *Vida,* I, 171–72.

142   *"SPANIARDS AND CANARY ISLANDERS":* Austria, 197.

143   *an outright abomination:* See Blanco-Fombona, "La proclama de guerra a muerte"; also Larrazábal, *Vida,* I, 172–73.

143   *the deadly Royal Order:* "Real Orden de 11 de enero de 1813."

143   *"Either Americans allow themselves":* SB to the British governor of Curaçao, J. Hodgson, Valencia, Oct. 2, 1813, SB, *Escritos,* V, 173–80.

143   *hundreds of royalist troops defected:* Sir Walter Scott, ed., *The Edinburgh Annual Register for 1816,* Vol. IX, Ballantyne, Edinburgh, 1820, 136–37.

143   *if they defected and fought for Spain:* Trend, 96.

144   *"I worry that our illustrious":* Larrazábal, *Vida,* I, 185.

144 *took more than four hundred prisoners:* Rafael Urdaneta, *Memorias*, 7.

144 *a rapid preemptive strike on the city of Barinas:* O'L, XXVII, Part I, 136.

144 *fourteen-year-old soldier:* Blanco-Fombona's note, SBC, *1799–1822*, 70.

144 *"The glorious hero":* SB to Antonio Rodríguez Picón, Cuartel general de Araure, July 25, 1813, SBC, ibid., 70–71.

145 *"Pause now your weeping to remember":* Cecilio Robelio, *El Despertador: Periodico semanario*, No. 5 (Jan. 29), Cuernavaca, 1896, 7.

145 *Monteverde had found himself doing too little:* Lecuna, *Crónica*, I, 66.

145 *two or more men to an animal, etc.:* Ibid.

145 *offered the Spaniards amnesty, etc.:* Larrazábal, *Vida*, I, 192.

145 *"to show the world":* Ibid.

145 *"Here, your Excellency":* SB to Torres, O'L, XIII, 327.

146 *He rushed to La Guaira in a panic, etc.:* Heredia, 145.

146 *horde of six thousand royalists:* Larrazábal, *Vida*, I, 193; Flinter, *History of the Revolution*, 49.

146 *set sail for Curaçao:* Ducoudray, I, 44–45.

146 *elbowed their way onto canoes:* Heredia, 152.

146 *cast off the clothes:* SB to the Nations of the World, Valencia, Sept. 20, 1813, DOC, IV, 732.

146 *entered Caracas on August 6:* O'L, XXVII, Part I, 145.

146 *He arranged to be met, etc.:* Ducoudray, I, 44–45; also, *Gazeta de Caracas*, IV, Aug. 26, 1813.

146 *There were rounds of artillery, etc.:* Larrazábal, *Vida*, I, 196; also *Gazeta de Caracas*, IV, Aug. 26, 1813.

146 *stepping off his cart to embrace:* Larrazábal, *Vida*, I, 196.

146 *Colorful silks hung, etc.:* Flinter, *History of the Revolution*, 50.

147 *could not restrain tears of joy:* Larrazábal, *Vida*, I, 196.

147 *the faithful mastiff Nevado:* Carlos Chalbaud Zerpa, *Historia de Mérida* (Mérida: Universidad de los Andes, 1983), 365. Also Lynch, *Simón Bolívar*, 78.

147 *daughter of a prosperous bourgeois family, etc.:* Liévano Aguirre, 149.

147 *as dungeons emptied of rebel prisoners:* Ducoudray, I, 49.

147 *She had full lips, a hearty, infectious laugh, etc.:* Liévano Aguirre, 150.

148 *"The most important business":* Ducoudray, 49.

CHAPTER 7: THE LEGIONS OF HELL

PAGE

149 Epigraph: *"All murderers shall be punished":* Voltaire, *Oeuvres complètes de Voltaire, Droit*, www.voltaire-integral.com/Html/18/droit.htm.

149 *When the governor of Barinas, etc.:* Gil Fortoul, *Historia*, I, 221.

150 *Even as Santiago Mariño:* Lecuna, *Crónica*, I, 142–43.

150 *"will look ridiculous":* SB to Mariño, Dec. 16, 1813, SBC, I, 88.

150 *"Spain does not treat with insurgents":* General Monteverde, quoted in A. Walker, *Colombia*, II (London: Baldwin, Cradock, and Joy, 1822), 346.

150 *imprisoned the priest:* Palacio Fajardo, *Bosquejo*, 91.

150 *he decided to stage a funeral:* Larrazábal, *Vida*, I, 230–31.

151 *A British traveler in the employ of Spain, etc.:* Flinter, *History of the Revolution*, 60.

152 *"Kill him!":* Ibid.

152 *an enormous head, etc.:* H.N.M., Escuelas Cristianas, *Historia de Venezuela* (1927), 127, quoted in Cunninghame Graham, *José Antonio Páez*, 65.

152 *"Of all the monsters":* O'L, XXVII, Part I, 172.

152 *needed few worldly goods, etc.:* Cunninghame Graham, 107–25.

152 *nearly eradicated them, along with their horses:* Mitre, *Emancipation of South America*, 338.

152 *slaughtered them all:* O'L, XXVII, Part I, 175.

153 *former haberdasher and a former butcher:* Austria, 265; and T. Peréz Tenreiro, *Para acercarnos a don Francisco Tomás Morales* (Caracas: Academia Nacional de la Historia, 1994), 12.

153 *killing every last inhabitant:* G. Crichfield, *American Supremacy* (Cambridge: Cambridge University Press, 1908), 21.

154 *"Citizens!":* SB, *Escritos*, VI, 4–9.

154 *"There are more illustrious citizens," etc.:* Larrazábal, *Vida*, I, 267.

155 *in order to forge bullets, etc.:* Lecuna, *La guerra a muerte*, XVIII, 150, in Masur, *Simón Bolívar*, 209.

155 *categorically refused to sell arms:* Whitaker, 95, 113–14.

155 *some historians claim:* Lecuna, *La guerra a muerte*, XVII, 365, in Masur, *Simón Bolívar*, 210.

155 *letter to Lord Wellesley:* SB to Wellesley, Maracay, Jan. 14, 1814, SBO, I, 85.

155 *haughty, ambitious—the privileged son:* J. M. Gómez, *Libertadores de Venezuela* (Caracas: Meneven, 1983), 266–71.

155 *a brig and five schooners:* Slatta and Lucas de Grummond, 91.

155 *he had ordered Piar to withdraw:* Baralt and Díaz, 178.

156 *but the Liberator of the East never showed up:* Larrazábal, *Vida*, I, 278.

156 *hanging in little pieces:* Austria, 265.

156 *Skeletons dangled from trees:* Larrazábal, *Vida*, I, 287.

156 *Some soldiers deserted:* Archer, *Wars of Independence*, 36.

156 *children as young as twelve:* Larrazábal, *Vida*, I, 183.

156 *army of a thousand slaves:* Mitre, *Emancipation of South America*, 366.

157 *the blood of old men:* Baralt and Díaz, 191.

157 *found a lone priest:* M. Briceño, *Historia de la isla Margarita, Biografías del General Juan B. Arismendi* (Caracas: El Monitor, 1885), 40.

157 *But a sack flung on the roadside:* Larrazábal, *Vida*, I, 282.

157 *Leandro Palacios:* Ibid., 284.

157 *What sprang to mind:* SB confesses this in a letter to Archbishop Narciso Coll y Pratt, in which he tries to justify the killings (Feb. 8, 1814, SBO, I, 91). It's worth mentioning here that the dates of the executions given in various accounts don't align. SB's letter to the archbishop is cited as Feb. 8, for instance, the evidence being the handwritten note in the margin; but documentation by Palacios in La Guaira indicates that the executions took place between Feb. 13 and 16.

157 *"Without delay":* Larrazábal, *Vida*, I, 284.

157 *to the letter, and with relish:* Baralt and Díaz, 195.

157 *more than one thousand:* This number ranges from 800 to 1,200, depending on the

source: Lecuna, *Crónica*, I, 215 (1,200); *Gaceta de Caracas*, no. 14, 1815 (1,200); Heredia (close to 900); Larrazábal, *Vida*, I, 284 (866); Díaz (866); Baralt and Díaz (more than 800); O'Leary (800).

157 *over the course of four days:* Palacios to SB, quoted in Gil Fortoul, *Historia*, I, 225.

157 *mark him as a brutal man:* The killing of bound prisoners was certainly not unique in 1813–14; the Legions of Hell had already done a fair amount of it. Archer (29, 36) comments that there was simply more of an official record on SB's order in La Guaira and, therefore, more of an opportunity to point an accusing finger.

158 *visible as far as thirty miles away:* Wood, 691.

158 *pocketed a few knickknacks:* William Seale, *The President's House* (Washington, DC, White House Historical Association, 1986), 133.

158 *supped on the president's wine:* Wood, 691.

158 *sporting squirming babies:* Flinter, *History of the Revolution*, 140.

158 *asking him to cease unnecessary cruelty:* Ibid., 141.

158 *Boves's response to Cajigal:* Ibid., 142.

158 *Gunfire set the tall grasses:* Ibid., 153.

158 *four thousand of the enemy's horses:* Larrazábal, *Vida*, I, 312.

159 *at the head of his roaring horde:* Restrepo, *Historia*, I, 758.

159 *Boves signed a treaty:* Austria, 311–13.

159 *stunned and deeply grateful:* Flinter, *History of the Revolution*, 169.

159 *A Spanish general later recounted:* Heredia, 203; also Larrazábal, *Vida*, I, 319.

159 *he beheaded them all:* Flinter, *History of the Revolution*, 171.

159 *sweep of all the precious silver and gold:* Larrazábal, *Vida*, I, 325–28.

159 *as an unrelieved rain fell:* Lecuna, *Crónica*, I, 295.

159 *almost the entire population:* Lila Mago de Chópite, "La población de Caracas (1754–1820), *Anuario de estudios americanos*, LIV-2, July–Dec., Sevilla, 1997, 516. Between 1809 and 1815, Caracas lost one third of its inhabitants to the earthquake or the wars, reducing the population from about 30,000 to 20,000. Mago de Chópite cites parochial church figures, and says they are far more accurate than Humboldt's or Depons's.

159 *dwindled to a force of twelve hundred:* Lecuna, *Crónica*, I, 295.

159 *trudge through swamps, etc.:* A. Guinassi Morán, *Estudios históricos* (Caracas: Ministerio de la Defensa, 1954), 36.

159 *Soldiers took the incapacitated, etc.:* Lecuna, *Crónica*, I, 295, 302.

160 *For twenty-three days, etc.:* Ibid.

160 *drowned in floods, etc.:* Guinassi, 36.

160 *cholera and yellow fever:* O'LB, 68. Also Guinassi, 36.

160 *Bolívar told of a starving mother:* O'LB, 68.

160 *His hair was long, etc.:* This portrait is informed by the famous painting of the evacuation, *Emigración a Oriente*, by Tito Salas. It was painted in 1913 and benefited from Salas's consultations with Lecuna, who commissioned the artist to paint pivotal scenes of SB's life.

160 *plagued by hemorrhoids:* Lynch, *Simón Bolívar*, 229. Also Slatta and Grummond, 268; and a paper presented by Paul G. Auwaerter, M.D., M.B.A., associate professor and clinical director in the Division of Infectious Diseases at the Johns Hopkins University School of Medicine, www.physorg.com/news191680201.html.

160 *Bolívar never let on:* Larrazábal, *Vida*, I, 214.

160 *He would not allow his sisters:* Lecuna, *Crónica*, I, 294–95.

160 *like the Marquis de Casa León:* Madariaga, 231.

160 *the pyramids of skulls:* Lecuna, *La guerra a muerte*, XVIII, 161, 379, in Masur.

160 *María Antonia, Juana, etc.:* Guinassi, 36.

161 *following Bolívar from battle to battle:* Ramón Urdaneta, *Los amores de Simón Bolívar*, 16.

161 *to the island of St. Thomas:* Lynch, *Simón Bolívar*, 86.

161 *sent on to Curaçao:* Polanco Alcántara, 407.

161 *a force of eight thousand, etc.:* Baralt and Díaz, I, 261.

161 *only hope for equipping a renewed republican offense:* Ibid., 282.

161 *Mariño had placed the treasure:* Lecuna, *Crónica*, I, 488.

161 *Bolívar sent Colonel Mariano Montilla, etc.:* Parra-Pérez, *Mariño y la independencia*, I, 440.

162 *the command to open fire:* Ibid., 441.

162 *cowardice, desertion, and conspiring to steal, etc.:* Lecuna, *Crónica*, I, 494.

162 *began to have misgivings, too:* Parra-Pérez, *Mariño y la independencia*, 454.

162 *forced to turn over the trunks:* Larrazábal, *Vida*, I, 329.

163 *He set sail from the turbulent coast:* Ibid.

163 *intending to shoot them both:* Parra-Pérez, *Mariño y la independencia*, 456.

163 *white flags and a nervous archbishop:* Larrazábal, *Vida*, I, 318.

163 *On the road, he had made it clear:* Austria, 316.

163 *red-faced and speechless:* Ibid., 317.

163 *sulked and sent off bitter complaints:* Gil Fortoul, *Historia*, I, 229.

163 *Boves issued a proclamation:* Austria, 311–13.

163 *archbishop of Venezuela:* Arístides Rojas, *Obras escojidas*, 692.

163 *beggars were sent off, etc.:* Langley, 52.

163 *Pardos rose to high positions, etc.:* McKinley, 172; also Heredia, 160.

164 *whites were treated as dangerous foes:* Gil Fortoul, I, 232.

164 *more than ten thousand:* Ibid.

164 *General Piar ignored Field Marshal Ribas's:* DOC, VI, 103.

165 *Boves had killed eighty thousand:* SB to the editor of *The Royal Gazette*, Kingston, Aug. 15, 1815, SBC, 1799–1822, 29; Blanco-Fombona, Introduction, SBC, I, 95. The Spaniard Díaz additionally writes in his *Recuerdos* that the Creole population was virtually wiped out (193).

165 *war to the death, too, had executed thousands:* McKinley points out that there were only 7,000–8,000 European-born Spaniards in the province of Caracas (171). SB's "war to the death" policies were strictly in place during the period from June 15 to August 6, 1813, as he marched to the capital, but there is no number for Spanish and royalist deaths directly attributable to the edict.

165 *"all Europeans" he encountered:* McKinley, 171; also Madariaga, 210.

165 *calculated result of strategies:* McKinley, 171.

165 *killing in cold blood sickened him:* Heredia, 157.

165 *unborn child struggling for life:* Larrazábal, *Vida*, I, 222.

165 *took pleasure in watching a boy:* Miller, I, 42–43.

165 *hospitals were overrun with invalids:* Baralt and Díaz, II, 268–69.

165 *"There are no more provinces left":* Trend, 109.

166 *certainly like no revolution since:* Lecuna, *Crónica*, I, 107.

166 *no uniform group of like-minded whites:* D. Armitage, "The Americas on the Eve of Independence Movements," paper presented at the LOC, Friday, Nov. 19, 2010 (Conference on Creating Freedom in the Americas).

166 *"They must be for, or against us," etc.:* Andrew Jackson, in Robert Remini, *Andrew Jackson* (New York: Palgrave Macmillan, 2008), 93.

166 *"Destiny elected me to break your chains":* SB, Manifiesto de Carúpano, Sept. 7, 1814, *Derecho constitucional colombiano* (Universidad de Medellín, 2007), 431–32.

167 *in the palace of the Spanish bishop:* Ducoudray, I, 77.

167 *sharing that grand manse with a family:* Ibid. The sisters were Soledad and Isabel. Soledad, who was a little girl at the time, would grow up to marry SB's most loyal aide-de-camp, Daniel F. O'Leary. Eventually, Isabel married Juan Bautista, an Italian immigrant. The world of these revolutionaries was so small that Isabel later married Miranda's son, Leandro, and she and her child, Teresa, lived with Leandro in Miranda's house on Grafton Street, in London. Ramón Urdaneta, *Los amores*, 61.

167 *irresistibly flirtatious, etc.:* Ducoudray, I, 77; also Lynch, *Simón Bolívar*, 97; Angell, 97; C. Hispano, *Historia secreta de Bolívar* (Medellín: Bedout, 1977), 134.

167 *insinuated herself into his political affairs:* Ducoudray, I, 49.

167 *the gift of a house:* Jesús Rosas Marcano, column in *El Nacional*, Caracas, July 24, 1983; quoted in Ramón Urdaneta, *Los amores*, 61.

168 *nest of intrigue:* Ducoudray, I, 77–88.

168 *"General, as long as your sword lives on":* Código militar de los Estados Unidos de Colombia (Bogotá: Zapata, 1883), 315.

168 *"I give you my word of honor," etc.:* SB to Juan Jurado, Campo de Techo, Dec. 8, 1814, SBC, I, 99–102.

168 *a glorious Mass in his honor:* F. Rivas Vicuña, *Las guerras de Bolívar*, Vol. 51 (Bogotá: Imprenta Nacional, 1934), 147.

169 *set out to blacken Bolívar's reputation:* SB to Torres, Cuartel general de Santafé [Bogotá], Jan. 22, 1815, SBO, I, 119–20; also O'L, XIV, 43–44.

169 *a mad course toward civil war, etc.:* Larrazábal, *Vida*, I, 356.

169 *as smallpox and cholera tore:* Ibid., 357.

169 *poisoned its water supply:* O'LN, I, 259.

170 *began to sweep down the Magdalena:* Ibid., 362.

170 *raising arms against a fellow republican:* Ibid., 360.

170 *"I have offered to withdraw":* Mosquera, 161.

170 *On April 24, he sent Bolívar:* Larrazábal, *Vida*, 361; also Mosquera, 162.

170 *sixty ships, etc.:* Parra-Pérez, *Historia*, 30; also Mosquera, 162.

170 *mortal impatience with the tenets of democracy, etc.:* Mijares, *Liberator*, 231.

170 *"Death to the Constitution!":* Quoted ibid.

170 *resign his commission and separate himself:* SB to Torres, Cuartel general de la Popa, May 8, 1815, SBO, I, 132–33.

171 *his cousin Florencio Palacios:* Ducoudray, I, 100.

171 *"I treated them all with respect," etc.:* Pablo Morillo, *Mémoires du général Morillo* (Paris: Dufart, 1826); also DOC, VII, 356.

172   *as Bolívar's ship lost sight:* Larrazábal, *Vida*, I, 367.

172   *"Some day . . . God will punish":* Morillo, broadside, Pampatar, April 15, 1815, JCBL.

172   *"The army of King Ferdinand VII has entered":* Ibid.

172   *five thousand of Boves's finest:* Flinter, *History of the Revolution*, 186.

173   *once beautiful, prosperous city, etc.:* G. J. Rodríguez y Carrillo, "Carta Pastoral," sermon by the bishop-elect, Madrid, July 14, 1816, JCBL.

173   *Every donkey, etc.:* Pablo Morillo, quoted in *Gaceta de Caracas*, Dec. 6, 1815. Also Jesús María Henao and Genardo Urrubula, *History of Colombia* (Chapel Hill: University of North Carolina Press, 1938), 272.

173   *Every day, three hundred corpses:* Ducoudray, I, 117.

173   *pale light of a new moon:* NASA, Phases of the Moon: 1801–1900, http://eclipse.gsfc.nasa.gov/phase/phases1801.html.

173   *two thousand patriots, etc.:* Gil Fortoul, *Historia*, I, 242.

173   *honored with a lavish Mass, etc.:* Larrazábal, *Vida*, I, 322.

174   *sat in its iron cage for a thousand days:* Eduardo Blanco, *Las noches del panteon: Homenaje a Antonio José de Sucre* (Caracas: El Cojo, 1895), 22.

174   *His widow, Josefa Palacios:* Blanco-Fombona, *Mocedades*, 36; also Larrazábal, *Vida*, II, 63.

174   *the oil had consumed the flame:* Larrazábal, *Vida*, I, 389.

174   *"I have seen the ravening fire" etc.:* SB to Wellesley, Kingston, May 27, 1815, SBO, I, 138–40.

175   *"What could I think of revolutions":* Adams to James Lloyd, Quincy, March 30, 1815, *The Works of John Adams*, X (Boston: Little, Brown, 1856), 150.

175   *proclamation that prohibited United States citizens:* Madison, Proclamation No. 17, Sept. 1, 1815, Respecting an Apprehended Invasion of the Spanish Dominions; also Robertson, *Hispanic-American Relations*, 28.

175   *He offered Bolívar the battleship:* SB to Brion, Kingston, July 16, 1815, SBO, I, 152–53.

175   *Bolívar wrote editorials:* Jocelyn Almeida, "Sullen Fires Across the Atlantic," Long Island University, Praxis Series, http://www.rc.umd.edu/praxis/sullenfires/almeida/almeida_essay.html.

175   *an astonishingly prescient letter:* "Letter from Jamaica," SB to "un caballero de esta isla," Kingston, Sept. 6, 1815, SBO, I, 161. The first known manuscript of this letter, as Pedro Grases explains in his essay on bibliographic conundrums of Bolívarian history, was published in Jamaica in English, translated by Gen. John Robertson. It appeared in 1818 and once more, in 1825, in *The Jamaica Quarterly and Literary Gazette*. The version in Spanish was not published until 1833, three years after SB's death. Grases y Uslar Pietri, "Temas de Simón Bolívar," in P. Grases, *Escritos selectos* (Caracas: Biblioteca Ayacucho, 1989), 188–89.

175   *an Englishman in Jamaica:* This was Henry Cullen. Lynch, *Simón Bolívar*, 92; also Grases, 187.

176   *"wicked stepmother":* SB, "Letter from Jamaica," SBO, 161–77.

177   *afforded him two tiny rooms:* Larrazábal, *Vida*, I, 407.

177   *"I am . . . living in uncertainty and misery":* SB to Brion, Kingston, July 16, 1815, SBO, I, 152–53.

177   *Bolívar was no longer there:* SB to Hyslop, Kingston, Dec. 4, 1815, SBO, I, 188.

177 *attacked the man in the hammock, etc.:* Royal Gazette of Jamaica, Dec. 16, 1815, and Dec. 23, 1815, quoted in Annette Insanally, "L'enjeu Caraibéen," in Alain Yacou, ed., *Bolívar et les peuples de nuestra America* (Paris: Centre d'Études et Recherches Cara-ibéenes, 1990), 117–18.

177 *"A Negro is killing me!":* Ibid., 117.

177 *2,000 pesos, etc.:* Ibid. Also, O'L, XV, 28–30; Larrazábal, *Vida*, I, 407.

177 *lolled abed with Julia Cobier:* Insanally, 118; also Liévano Aguirre, 143.

177 *dinner at Hyslop's:* Insanally, 117.

177 *Polish Jew in Kingston:* O'L, XV, 28–30.

178 *sailed with food and supplies, etc.:* O'LN, I, 313.

178 *Hyslop's wealthy colleague Robert Sutherland:* W. F. Lewis, "Simón Bolívar and Xavier Mina," *Journal of Inter-American Studies*, 11, no. 3 (July 1969), 459.

178 *Haiti's de facto minister of trade and finance:* M. E. Rodríguez, *Freedom's Mercenaries* (Ann Arbor: Hamilton, 2006), 92.

178 *and an active gunrunner:* B. Ardouin, *Études sur L'histoire d'Haïti*, 2nd edition (Port-au-Prince, 1958), VI, 21–69. The Sutherland connection is also noted in Lewis, 458–65.

178 *Sutherland received him, etc.:* SBC, I, 254.

179 *"I was immediately drawn to him":* Pétion to José Gaspar Rodríguez de Francia; quoted in "A Few Great Leaders," *The Freeman*, Indianapolis, July 5, 1890, 7.

179 *"No, don't mention my name":* Azpurúa, *Biografías de hombres notables de Hispano-América*, III 214–17.

179 *one thousand guns, etc.:* Lewis, 458–65. With Pétion's blessing, Sutherland provided the supplies. Among the ships were the *Bolívar, Mariño, Píar, Brion, Constitución*, and *Consejo*.

179 *married one of Bolívar's cousins:* McGregor's biographer, David Sinclair, called it "a shotgun wedding" in *The Land That Never Was* (Cambridge: Da Capo, 2003), 151.

179 *challenge Bolívar to a duel:* Lecuna, *Crónica*, I, 430.

179 *Bermúdez continued his insubordination:* Ibid.

180 *affair with the irresistible young Isabel Soublette:* Ducoudray, I, 308; also Lynch, *Simón Bolívar*, 97.

CHAPTER 8: A REVOLUTION STRUGGLES TO LIFE

PAGE

181 Epigraph: *"Our people are nothing like Europeans":* SB, "Discurso al Congreso de Angostura," Feb. 15, 1819, DOC, VI, 589.

181 *year without a summer, etc.:* Mount Tambora erupted in April of 1815. It took many months for the ash particles to travel around the planet, but by spring of 1816 the volcano's effects were in full force in the northern hemisphere. A. Gates and D. Ritchie, *Encyclopedia of Earthquakes and Volcanoes* (New York: Facts on File, 2007), 252.

181 *"darkling in the eternal space":* From "Darkness," by Lord Byron, 1816. First lines: "I had a dream, which was not all a dream./The bright sun was extinguish'd, and the stars/Did wander darkling in the eternal space."

181 *freak imbalance:* M. Z. Jacobson, *Atmospheric Pollution* (New York: Cambridge University Press, 2002), 336–37.

181 *causing a crippling famine, etc.:* J. D. Post, *The Last Great Subsistence Crisis in the Western World* (Baltimore: Johns Hopkins University Press, 1977), 122–25.

181 *Food riots gripped England:* C. Knight, *Popular History of England*, VIII (London: Bradbury & Evans, 1869), 55.

181 *Luddites torched textile factories:* Ibid., 61.

182 *castle in rain-pelted Switzerland:* M. Shelley, *Frankenstein* (London: Penguin, 1992), Introduction.

182 *stunned by the fiery skies:* Jacobson, 336–37.

182 *new age of medical discovery:* Post, 122–25.

182 *arrived a month sooner:* L. Dupigny-Giroux and C. J. Mock, *Historical Climate Variability and Impacts in North America* (London: Springer, 2009), 116–19.

182 *the revolution's cruelest year:* S. K. Stoan, *Pablo Morillo and Venezuela* (Columbus: Ohio State University Press, 1974), 83–84.

182 *installed draconian laws, etc.:* Archer, 35, for all subsequent details.

182 *Committee of Confiscation, etc.:* "Junta de Secuestros," described in Lynch, *Simón Bolívar*, 92. Also O'LN, I, 297–98; Stoan, 83–84, 163.

182 *largest and most retaliatory confiscation:* Lynch, *Simón Bolívar*, 92.

182 *"traitors to the king":* Morillo's term, quoted in Prago, *Revolutions*, 191.

182 *condemned to heavy labor, etc.:* Ibid.

183 *shot in the back:* Larrazábal, *Vida*, I, 382; also Petre, *Simón Bolívar*, 164.

183 *Morillo had created a strategic problem:* Adelman, *Sovereignty and Revolution in the Iberian Atlantic*, 273–74.

183 *Venezuelan rebels with nothing to lose:* O'L, XXVII, 345.

183 *A ship holding a million pesos, etc.:* Adelman, 273–74, for Morillo's problems.

183 *Frustrated, ill-humored:* Ducoudray, I, 200.

183 *began to imagine the worst:* L. Ullrick, "Morillo's Attempt to Pacify Venezuela," *HAHR*, 3, no. 4 (1920), 535–65; also Stoan, 134–46; R. Earle, *Spain and the Independence of Colombia* (Exeter: University of Exeter, 2000), 70–73.

183 *disputatious officers, querulous wives:* Ducoudray, 142.

183 *a paucity of wind:* Restrepo, II, 337; also Mosquera, 180.

183 *corresponding anxiously for months:* Ducoudray, I, 141.

184 *were probably in danger without him:* Polanco Alcántara, 410–11.

184 *more than two days, etc.:* Ducoudray, I, 143, for subsequent details.

184 *Just as Marc Antony:* Soublette to O'Leary: "Here is where love came in. You know very well that Anthony [*sic*], despite all the perils through which he sailed, lost precious moments with Cleopatra." Quoted in O'L, XXVII, 351.

184 *cousin Florencio Palacios:* Ducoudray, 142.

184 *the dawn of the third republic:* Blanco Fombona, *Bolívar, pintado por sí mismo*, 72–73.

184 *liberation of Spanish America:* SB, *Escritos*, IX, 132.

184 *end to his war to the death:* Blanco-Fombona, *Bolívar, pintado por sí mismo*, 179–80.

185 *tall, athletic, muscular, etc.:* *Recollections of a Service of Three Years* (Anonymous), 32–33.

185 *"exhibits a peculiar ferocity":* Ibid.

185 *Caribbean pirate Beluche:* Renato Beluche was a pirate-soldier from New Orleans, where his father ran a wig shop as a front for smuggling. Before joining SB, Beluche

had business dealings with the pirate Lafitte and fought in the Battle of New Orleans alongside General Andrew Jackson. A good portrait of Beluche can be found in J. Lucas de Grummond, *Renato Beluche* (Baton Rouge: Louisiana State University Press, 1983).

185 *"enough arms and munitions," etc.*: SB to Leandro Palacios, March 21, 1816, SBC, I, 227.

185 *bringing a black revolution*: Madariaga, 536.

185 *as hurricanes blew record winds*: Dupigny-Giroux and Mock, 116–18.

186 *largely made up of officers*: Lecuna, *Crónica*, I, 445.

186 *more than triple that number*: SB was only able to raise 800. *New American Encyclopedia*.

186 *"I have come to decree, as law"*: SB, *Escritos*, IX, 185–86.

186 *risked alienating fellow Creoles*: O'L, XXVII, 346.

186 *had written to his superiors in Spain, etc.*: Cevallos to the Secretary of State and the Council of the Indies, Letter no. 42, Caracas, July 22, 1815, Archivo General de las Indias, *HAHR*, 33, no. 4 (November, 1953), 530, for all subsequent quotes. Also in Archer, 180.

187 *Soublette sent his aide-de-camp*: Lecuna claims that Soublette himself may have been the source of the miscommunications. Soublette, he argues, was miffed with SB for dallying with Pepita. She was constantly at SB's side through this expedition and some claimed she was a distraction. We should remember here, too, that SB had had a dalliance with Soublette's sister, Isabel. All this can be found in Lecuna, *Crónica*, I, 474–76.

187 *no more than three miles away*: Ibid., 468.

187 *but Villaret stalled, arguing*: Ibid., 467.

187 *Making matters worse, Francisco Bermúdez*: SB to Bermúdez, Ocumare, July 8, 1816, SBC, XI, 71. SB asked him to leave because his presence was causing disorder in his ranks.

187 *"Events were clouded by love"*: O'L, XXVII, 351.

187 *deal with Pepita and her family*: Brion to Arismendi, Bonayre [*sic*], July 1816, DOC, V, 456. Brion says he saw the warship *Indio-Libre* still in harbor when he arrived, and heard the news that SB had escaped three nights before with a few of his officers and the women.

188 *"The gang of criminals"*: Rodríguez Villa, *El teniente general Don Pablo Morillo*, IV, 82–83.

188 *Few events in Bolívar's life*: Masur, *Simón Bolívar*, 283.

188 *admitting much later*: SB to Madrid, Fucha, March 6, 1830, SBSW, II, 757. Also SBC, IX, 241.

188 *tried to deliver a few arms*: Lecuna, *Crónica*, I, 472.

188 *He sent Admiral Brion*: Brion took three of the warships (*Bolívar, Constitución*, and *Arismendi*). The *Bolívar*, which held officers Brion, Villaret, and Beluche, wrecked at Isla Pino, off Panama, but the men survived. The mission to the U.S. did not. Yanes, I, 311.

188 *deposit Pepita and her family*: They were deposited on the island of Tortola, very close to St. Thomas. SB contracted a ship's captain to take them the short distance. Lecuna, *Crónica*, I, 480.

188 *He did not reach the eastern port*: Madariaga, 284.

188 *a man with a ready sword, etc.*: Ibid.

189 *"Down with Bolívar!"*: Larrazábal, *Vida*, I, 436.

189 *10,000 pesos for his head:* Sherwell, 97.

189 *drawing his sword into the air:* Larrazábal, *Vida*, I, 437.

189 *"Never," asserted a witness, had "Bermúdez's arm moved":* Ibid.

189 *forbidden from assuming the title:* Mosquera, 186.

190 *"Bolívar's cowardice has emerged":* Ducoudray, II, 22.

190 *Bolívar had never been inclined:* Lynch, "Bolívar and the Caudillos," *HAHR*, 63, no. 1 (Feb. 1983), 9.

190 *Pétion was generous in his praise:* Larrazábal, *Vida*, I, 441.

190 *a letter from a Spanish insurrectionist:* Ibid., 442.

190 *charming his way through Boston:* Ibid., 443.

190 *Mina had actually managed to raise men:* Ibid., 442.

191 *One was from Arismendi, etc.:* Ibid., 444–45.

191 *"and try to forget those lamentable scenes":* Ibid.

191 *the patriots had made heartening advances:* Lecuna, *Crónica*, I, 484–94.

191 *Arismendi openly hated Mariño, etc.:* Larrazábal, *Vida*, I, 444–45, for all details on these hatreds.

191 *eventually met Javier Mina:* O'LN, I, 356.

191 *who had limped into Haiti:* Yanes, 311; also Larrazábal, *Vida*, I, 444–45.

191 *he issued a proclamation:* Lecuna, *Crónica*, I, 497; also SB, *Proclamas y Discursos*, 151.

192 *"Our arms will have destroyed":* SB to Cortés Madariaga and Roscio, Port-au-Prince, 1816, SBC, 1799–1822, 256.

192 *"General, I am the best friend":* SB to Mariño, Villa del Norte, Dec. 29, 1816, Archivo General de Indias, BANH, No. 62, 185.

192 *impossible without their cooperation:* Lynch, *Simón Bolívar*, 13–14.

192 *he set about recruiting Indians:* O'Leary, 370.

192 *an army ten times the size:* Larrazábal, *Vida*, I, 456.

192 *Urdaneta, who had fought with Páez:* Rafael Urdaneta, *Memorias*, 101–7.

192 *"I hardly know you!" etc.:* Larrazábal, *Vida*, I, 456.

192 *On the afternoon of February 9:* Lecuna, *Crónica*, I, 527.

193 *"I've come to embrace the liberator," etc.:* Larrazábal, *Vida*, I, 458.

193 *"Small divisions cannot":* SB to Piar, Barcelona, Jan. 10, 1817, in Azpurúa, III, 378.

193 *Páez had left the royalist camp:* Páez, *Autobiografía*, 56–57.

194 *consistently overestimated their numbers:* Vásconez, *Cartas de Bolívar*, 8.

194 *outnumbered three times by Morillo's:* Páez, *Autobiografía*, 118.

194 *"We had hardly advanced":* Vásconez, *Cartas*, 8.

194 *they abandoned horses, swords, guns:* Páez, *Autobiografía*, 126.

194 *fully outfitted in Madrid finery:* Ibid., 130.

194 *"Fourteen consecutive attacks":* Ibid.

194 *Bolívar was thrilled:* Vásconez, 9.

194 *He understood:* SB to Piar, Azpurúa, III, 378.

194 *"We've just had the best news":* SB to Leandro Palacios, Barcelona, Jan. 2, 1817, SBO, I, 226.

195 *"Destiny is calling us":* SB to Briceño Méndez, Jan. 1, 1817, in O'L, XXVII, 365.

195 *On March 25, when Bolívar set out:* Lecuna, *Crónica*, I, 537.

195 *arrived there in early May:* Lecuna, *Crónica*, II, 18.

196   *handsome, blue-eyed, ruddy-skinned:* Guzmán Blanco, "El Capitán Juan José Conde, subalterno del General Piar y testigo presencial de su ejecución, hace una relación minuciosa," DOC, VI, 105.

197   *in poor health:* SB, "Manifiesto del Jefe Supremo a los pueblos de Venezuela," Cuartel general de Guayana, Aug. 5, 1817, SB, *Doctrina*, 68–73.

197   *"The nation needs you":* SB to Piar, San Félix, June 19, 1817, SBO, I, 244.

197   *"I rose to General in Chief":* The witness, J. F. Sánchez, is quoted in Liévano Aguirre, 187.

197   *the black governor, Andrés Rojas, scoffed:* Ibid.

197   *"If I have been the essence of moderation":* SB to Briceño Méndez, June 19, 1817, O'L, XXIX, 113–14.

198   *accountable for the death:* Piar and Bernardo Bermúdez were bitter rivals. Lecuna implies that Piar led Bernardo into the trap that ended in his execution in 1813. Lecuna, *Crónica*, II, 37.

198   *"I want to denounce openly":* SB, "Manifiesto," SB, *Doctrina*, 68–73.

198   *"The accused is the same General Piar":* O'L, "Proceso de Piar," XV, 351–424.

199   *it is said he wept:* Testimony of Briceño Mendez, in O'L, XXVII, 427.

199   *At five o'clock on the following afternoon, etc.:* J. J. Conde, in Guzmán Blanco, "El Capitán," DOC, VI, 106–9.

199   *the citizens of Angostura, etc.:* Rourke, 167.

199   *Tears welled in his eyes:* O'L, XXVII, 427.

199   *"The death of General Piar":* Perú de Lacroix, 116–7.

200   *But, as Bolívar told them now:* O'L, XXVII, 428–9.

200   *The power of the warlord, etc.:* Trend, 122.

200   *almost thirteen thousand now:* Díaz, 214.

200   *confirmed as the supreme chief:* Gil Fortoul, *Historia*, I, 247.

200   *a pay structure written into law:* SB, "La ley de Repartición de Bienes Nacionales entre los Militares del Ejército Republicano," Oct. 10, 1817, SB, *Doctrina*, p. 73.

200   *when Bolívar had set out for Guayana, etc.:* Gil Fortoul, I, 246.

200   *four hundred soldiers garrisoned in the convent:* Casa Fuerte was in the convent of San Francisco, which SB left under the leadership of Gen. P. M. Freites, Larrazábal, *Vida*, I, 460.

200   *English captain named Chamberlain, etc.:* Ibid., 463; also Azpurúa, 225.

201   *possibly avoidable moment:* Larrazábal, *Vida*, I, 463–64.

201   *began spreading the rumor:* Gil Fortoul, I, 246; Larrazábal, *Vida*, I, 464.

201   *a regional warlord could not hope:* Lynch, *Simón Bolívar*, 104.

202   *as easy to dissolve as cassava:* SB to Tovar, Guayana, Aug. 6, 1817, SBO, I, 256.

202   *"I've resisted writing a single word," etc.:* Ibid.

202   *"if he submits voluntarily":* SB to Sucre, Angostura, Nov. 11, 1817, SBO, I, 277–78.

203   *two of the most capable generals:* SB to Mariño, Maturín, Nov. 5, 1818, SBO, I, 368–69.

CHAPTER 9: THE HARD WAY WEST
PAGE

204   Epigraph: *"A lightning bolt doesn't fall from the sky,"* etc.: Santander, "El General Simón Bolívar en la campaña de la Nueva Granada de 1819. Relación escrito por un Granadino," *Gazeta de Santa Fé*, Oct. 4, 1819, JCBL.

204 *Bolívar had dreamed of so often:* SB to Leandro Palacios, Barcelona, Jan. 2, 1817, SBO, I, 228.

205 *a seamless, unified America:* SB to Pueyrredón, June 12, 1818, SBO, I, 295–97. This letter was in answer to a letter from Pueyrredón to SB dated Nov. 19, 1816, which was full of congratulations for SB, although by then he had had to flee Ocumare and return to Haiti.

205 *Páez could neither read nor write:* Cunninghame Graham, 108.

205 *eat with a knife and fork, etc.:* Páez, *Autobiografía*, 144.

205 *child of indigent Canary Islanders:* Ibid., 1.

205 *a paltry few cents a week, etc.:* Ibid., 5–11, for subsequent details about this job.

206 *one officer commanded him to give up his horse, etc.:* Ibid., 57–58.

206 *regiment of more than a thousand men, etc.:* Ibid., for subsequent details about this army.

206 *They sat on skulls of bulls:* Ibid., 6.

206 *making lightning incursions into his camp, etc.:* Recollections of a Service, 179.

207 *as Morillo later admitted:* Morillo, "Cuenta al Rey," Ministerio de Guerra, Madrid, Oct. 26, 1818, JCBL.

207 *When Bolívar sent two colonels:* Páez, *Autobiografía*, 136.

207 *He explained to his army:* Ibid., 153. As for the size of Páez's army, it's difficult to put numbers on his troops. He counts, at one point, no fewer than 40,000 horses. Ibid., 136.

207 *a company of Cunaviche Indians:* Ibid., 138 fn.

207 *stormed the Spanish encampment fearlessly:* My great-great-great grandfather, Joaquín Rubín de Celis, was a young soldier for Morillo, one of the thousands brought from the peninsula to fight in the wars of pacification. He was present at this battle in San Fernando, fighting against Páez and the Cunaviche Indians. He would go on to become a brigadier and die in the decisive battle of Ayacucho, fighting against another of my ancestors, the man who would marry his daughter, Gen. Pedro Cisneros Torres of the republican forces.

207 *Páez finally met the supreme chief, etc.:* Páez, *Autobiografía*, 172–73.

208 *He was given to epileptic fits, etc.:* Recollections of a Service, 185–86; also Cunninghame Graham, 92–93; Slatta and Lucas de Grummond, 147.

209 *Start the march, he said animatedly, etc.:* The exchange between SB and Páez that follows is taken from accounts in Páez's *Autobiografía* (141) and O'L (XXVII, 444). Lecuna's account (*Crónica*, II, 135) is quite different. In it, Bolívar shouts, "Is there a guy among us who would dare take one of those boats himself?" and Páez shouts back, "Yes, there is!" Apparently, Lecuna's account was taken from General A. Wavell, *Campagnes et croisières* (sic for Vowell, *Campaigns and Cruises*) (Paris, 1837), 70. The action in all versions, however, is the same.

209 *the men slid their saddles, etc.:* Páez, *Autobiografía*, 142.

209 *thought they would be blown to bits:* Mosquera, 252.

209 *they had captured fourteen boats:* Páez, *Autobiografía*, 142; also Mosquera. O'Leary says it was seven all together, O'L, XXVII, 444.

209 *"It may appear inconceivable":* From Recollections of a Service, 178.

209 *one can easily imagine their initial suspicions:* Liévano Aguirre, 185.

210 *On a dare, he had leapt into a lake, etc.:* Perú de Lacroix, 39, 169.

210 *"I confess it was crazy of me":* Ibid., 169.

210 *left Páez and his horsemen behind to lay siege:* Morillo, report to King Ferdinand VII, Ministerio de Guerra, Madrid, Oct. 26, 1818, JCBL. As Morillo reported, during Páez's siege of San Fernando, a company of 650 men was forced to subsist on a small daily ration of toasted corn, which soon ran out. The soldiers continued to be in virtual imprisonment from Feb. 6 to March 7, subsisting "on horses, donkeys, cats, dogs, and leather."

210 *descending on his post:* O'L, XXVII, 445.

210 *"Fly, fly, join me now!":* SB to Páez, Calabozo, Feb. 24, 28, 1818; O'L, XV, 600–601.

211 *a string of loud arguments:* Páez, *Autobiografía,* 154.

211 *losses on the patriot island of Margarita:* Yanes, II, 22.

211 *had been reduced to seven hundred:* Ibid., 298–99.

211 *asked to be relieved:* Polanco Alcántara, 469.

211 *Páez wanted to continue to pressure:* Páez, *Autobiografía,* 154.

211 *keep pushing toward the capital:* Soublette, *Boletín del Ejercito Libertador,* Feb. 17, 1818, O'L, XXVII, 580.

212 *"In a few hours":* Feliciano Palacios, quoted in Madariaga, 307.

212 *more than a thousand infantrymen, etc.:* Morillo to J. Barreiro, Valencia, May 5, 1818, in O'L, XI, 478; also O'Leary, *Detached Recollections,* 39–40.

212 *a band of eight royalists came upon, etc.:* Larrazábal, *Vida,* I, 344–46.

212 *by the light of a waxing moon:* NASA, Moon Phases, 1801–1900, Sec. 1816–1820.

213 *a painful case of anthrax pustules:* SB to Gen. M. Cedeño, San Fernando, May 5, 1818, SBO, I, 286. Bolívar refers to his *"carbuncos,"* which are lesions from anthrax, a painful condition of the flesh that is transmitted from diseased or dead horses and other animals.

213 *"My lesions are getting better":* Ibid.

213 *an unruly English colonel:* Wilson, who together with Col. G. Hippisley was among the first British recruits to join SB's wars of independence. See Páez, *Autobiografía,* 170.

213 *he had been cleverly planted:* Hippisley, *Narrative of the Expedition,* 515.

213 *"They say the Machados":* SB to L. Palacios, Angostura, July 11, 1818, SBO, I, 308.

213 *Bolívar was the revolution:* Morillo to King Ferdinand VII, quoted in Aristide Rojas, *El elemento Vasco en la historia de Venezuela* (Caracas: Imprenta Federal, 1874), 33.

214 *outpost Humboldt had visited:* Humboldt, 6.

214 *Orange, lemon, and fig trees:* Hippisley, 334–35, for much of this description.

214 *ample, low, made of adobe, etc.:* The chaplain of the *John Adams* (Commodore Perry's ship), described Angostura in the *National Intelligencer,* Oct. 2, 1819, quoted in Polanco Alcántara, 474.

214 *Splendid mansions overlooked the river, etc.:* Hippisley, 332–35, for subsequent descriptions.

214 *"It pains me to see":* SB to the Municipality, June 20, 1818, quoted in C. J. Reyes, *El mundo según Simón Bolívar* (Bogotá: Icono, 2006), 34.

214 *amassed all the silver:* Páez, *Autobiografía,* 130.

214 *sold coffee and cocoa:* Polanco Alcántara, 469.

215 *"We are free, we write in a free country":* El Correo del Orinoco, Oct. 1, 1818, JCBL.

215 *keeping Americans ignorant:* King Carlos IV in 1785 pronounced, "It's always best not

to enlighten Americans." See V. Bulmer-Thomas et al., eds., *The Cambridge Economic History of Latin America* (New York: Cambridge University Press, 2006), 432.

215   *"The printing press is the infantry"*: El Correo del Orinoco, Facsimile ed. (Bogotá: Gerardo Rivas Moreno, 1998), ix.

215   *on the pages of* El Correo: *El Correo del Orinoco,* Oct. 1, 1818, JCBL.

215   *establishing a congress:* SB, Discurso, Angostura, Oct. 1, 1818, SB, *Escritos,* XIV, 310–16.

215   *regularize the currency:* Páez's silver money was suddenly recalled in an effort to impose some controls, but it was issued again later, in seeming frustration. Hippisley, 458.

215   *his men could hardly be blamed:* O'L, XI, 455.

216   *correspondence shows a courteous but firm:* Madariaga, p. 317.

216   *recognized in the outside world:* O'L, XI, p. 473.

216   *import fine wines, etc.:* Hippisley, 336–37.

216   *clothing and supplies for ten thousand:* Madariaga, 315.

216   *valuable cargo of arms:* SB to Palacios, Angostura, Aug. 7, 1818, SBO, I, 324; also Madariaga, 316.

216   *large ship had sailed in from London, etc.:* Ducoudray, 233; Polanco Alcántara, 468–85.

216   *"Arms have been my constant concern":* SB to López Méndez, Angostura, June 12, 1818, SBSW, 156.

216   *fine leather saddles for Páez's cavalry:* Ibid.

216   *he had stored away fifty thousand stands:* Ducoudray, 234.

217   *tacit approval from the Duke of Wellington:* Col. Hippisley, who had fought in Spain under Wellington, intimates this when he describes his first visit to López Méndez in London: Hippisley, 3. Madariaga makes the connection more explicit: Madariaga, 310.

217   *before their government issued:* In Nov. 1817, the Duke of San Carlos, Spanish ambassador to the Court of St. James's, persuaded the British to issue an order forbidding citizens from joining the Spanish American revolution. Alfred Hasbrouck, *Foreign Legionaries* (London: Octagon, 1969), 56, 111.

217   *The offer that López Méndez made, etc.:* The descriptions of the British mercenaries on the following pages are all from Hippisley, 12–25, 532, 632ff.

218   *"The frequency of their mess-dinners":* Ibid., 25.

218   *the fabled land of El Dorado:* Madariaga, 311.

218   *None had actually shown proof:* López Méndez, letter to the *Morning Chronicle,* London, dated Jan. 15, published Jan, 18, 1819, quoted in Hippisley, 648–50.

218   *had been a mere lieutenant:* Britain War Office, *A List of the Officers of the Army and of the Corps of Royal Marines,* London, 1827, http://books.google.com, 533.

219   *"a rifle in one hand and a bottle in the other," etc.:* K. Racine, "Rum, Recruitment and Revolution," *Irish Migration Studies in Latin America,* 4, no. 2 (March 2006), 47–48.

219   *Hippisley's correspondence:* Hippisley, 548.

219   *the commanding colonel worried:* Ibid., p. 585.

219   *"Any man seen drunk":* Ibid.

220   *"ridiculous threats":* SB to Hippisley, Angostura, June 19, 1818, ibid., 628.

220   *more than six thousand volunteers, etc.:* E. Lambert, "Los legionarios británicos," in *Bello y Londres,* Bicentenario, 2 vols. (Caracas, 1980–81), I, 355–76, quoted in Lynch, *Simón Bolívar,* 122.

220   *faraway terrain:* Hamilton, *Travels Through the Interior,* I, 31.

220 *He was known to say:* C. Pi Sunyer, *Patriotas americanos en Londres* (Caracas: Monte Avila, 1978), 242.

220 *finally located Pepita Machado, etc.:* SB to Palacios, Angostura, Aug. 8, 1818, SBO, I, 325; also Polanco Alcántara, 412–14.

220 *"People are saying":* SB to Palacios, Angostura, July 11, 1818, SBO, I, 308.

220 *major offensive in New Granada:* SB, "Proclamation," Angostura, Aug. 15, 1818, SBSW, I, 165.

220 *had just boarded:* Palacios to SB, San Tomás, Oct. 14 1818, Archivos de Gran Colombia (Caracas: Fundación Boulton), C.XXIV, 230232.

220 *accompany him on the long march:* Polanco Alcántara, 468–85.

221 *tried to follow him into battle:* O. R. Jiménez, "Los recuerdos, Josefina Machado," *El Universal*, May 5, 1983, Caracas.

221 *died along the way, etc.:* Ibid.; also Julián Rivas, Bicentenario, enfoques365.net, Venezuela, April 30, 2010.

221 *reach Angostura successfully:* Polanco Alcántara claims this, 414.

221 *a large brigade of British mercenaries, etc.:* O'L, XI, 492.

222 *This was the real Venezuela:* Polanco Alcántara, 529.

222 *the Second National Congress:* SB, Congressional Inauguration Address, Feb. 15, 1818, O'L, XI, 493ff. English translation, SBSW, I, 173–97.

222 *twenty-six of the thirty-five, etc.:* Larrazábal, *Vida*, I, 548.

223 *"Laws need to suit the people," etc.:* O'L, XI; SBSW, I, 173–97. All quotes and summaries in the next pages are from the address.

224 *long, frenzied applause:* Larrazábal, *Vida*, I, 549.

224 *straw hats and white pantaloons:* See *Recollections of a Service*, 46.

225 *Every day for six months:* O'L, XI, 522.

225 *some barefoot and in patches:* *Recollections of a Service*, 46.

225 *rejected the hereditary senate:* Larrazábal, *Vida*, I, 569, O'L, XI, 522.

225 *With 150 horsemen, etc.:* The full account is in "Campañas de Apure," BOLANH, no. 21, 1192–94; also Páez, *Autobiografía*, 181–4; and Lecuna, *Crónica*, II, 279–81.

226 *his account to Madrid:* Morillo to the Ministerio de Guerra, Madrid, May 12, 1819, in Rodríguez Villa, 20–25; also Lecuna, *Crónica*, II, 285.

226 *Four hundred soldiers of the king, etc.:* Ibid, 281.

226 *a robust army of seven thousand:* O'L, XI, 483.

226 *more than a little worried:* Morillo to L X. Uzelay, in Lecuna, *Documentos inéditos para la historia de Bolívar*, XVIII.

227 *"Patience, . . . for behind every hill":* Páez, *Autobiografía*, 183.

227 *By May, the rains had begun:* Ibid., 203.

227 *soldiers had little food, etc.:* O'LB, 150.

227 *height of his physical and mental, etc.:* Ibid.; also O'L, I, 486–87, 539.

227 *His face had lost its luster, etc.:* Boulton, *El rostro de Bolívar*, 26.

227 *His mustache and sideburns, etc.:* O'LB, 139.

227 *An Englishman seeing him:* Vowell, *Campaigns and Cruises*, 66–67.

227 *sometimes two or three times a day:* O'L, I, 487.

228 *essence of privation:* Lecuna, *Crónica*, II, 285; also Santander, in Restrepo, II, 368.

228 *two pounds of beef per day:* Lecuna, *Crónica*, II, 285.

228 *openly disdained the others:* Restrepo, 367.

228 *vultures or campfire smoke:* Cunninghame Graham, 94.

228 *Bolívar took great pains, etc.:* Lecuna, *Crónica*, II, 286, 300; also Oficio, April 11, O'L, XVI, 301.

228 *a commanding general obsessed, etc.:* SB to López Méndez, Angostura, June 12, 1818; also SB to Páez, Angostura, Sept. 29, 1818, SBO, I, 293, 351.

228 *"For the first time":* Morillo, Oficio al Ministerio de Guerra, Atamaica, Feb. 28, 1819, in Rodríguez Villa, 10, quoted in Lecuna, *Crónica*, II, 286.

228 *a promise to Granadans:* SB, "Proclamation to the People of New Granada," Angostura, Aug. 15, 1818, published in *El Correo del Orinoco*, Aug. 22, 1818.

228 *issuing a steady drizzle of rain:* Páez, *Autobiografía*, 181–4.

229 *"This is for your eyes":* SB to Santander, Cañafistola, May 20, 1819, SB, *Cartas: Santander–Bolívar*, I, 92.

229 *Páez had already said yes, etc.:* O'LB, 152.

229 *assumed they would be wintering close by:* Vowell, 153.

229 *"scrawny and mangy mares,":* SB to Páez, Arauca, June 5, 1819, O'L, XVI, 395–96.

230 *rains began to pelt down in earnest, etc.:* Vowell, 66–67.

230 *feared they would desert:* By June 3, they had already deserted. SB sent Páez a letter on June 5, reporting that 50 hussars had fled their ranks, and warning him to take severe measures with them. O'L, XVI, 395.

230 *force of 2,100, etc.:* O'LB, 153.

230 *On June 4, Bolívar's army, etc.:* O'LB, 154–57.

230 *savannas flooded:* Anzoátegui to his wife, Bogotá, Aug. 28, 1819, quoted in Slatta and Lucas de Grummond, 194–95.

230 *Hooves grew soft, etc.:* Cunninghame Graham, 167–68.

230 *marching for more than a month:* SB to Zea, June 30, 1819, SBO, I, 291–92.

230 *flesh-eating fish:* Vowell, 157.

230 *Horses and cattle fell into deep water, etc.:* Cunninghame Graham, 167–68.

230 *sleeping in standing water:* Anzoátegui to his wife, in Slatta and Lucas de Grummond, 194–95.

231 *potatoes, barley:* Vowell, 203–4.

231 *the forest of San Camilo:* Liévano Aguirre, 217.

231 *bolstered by Bolívar's enthusiasm:* Lecuna, *Crónica*, II, 313.

231 *Some gave up on the expedition:* O'LB, 158.

231 *"The harshness of the peaks," etc.:* SB to Zea, Paya, June 30, 1819, SBO, I, 392.

231 *Often, the streams they crossed, etc.:* Vowell, 159–62.

231 *"He was . . . invariably humane":* Ibid.

231 *"had no trousers":* Ibid., 163.

231 *A full quarter of the British contingent:* Lynch, *Simón Bolívar*, 128.

232 *The next day he saw her marching:* Ibid.

232 *set to work, making them shirts:* Anzoátegui to his wife.

232 *dismissed the Páramo de Pisba:* Sámano to Barreiro, Santa Fé [Bogotá], June 29, 1819, *Los ejércitos del rey*, II (Bogotá: Fundación para la Conmemoración, 1989), 185.

232 *"Here is where this man distinguishes himself":* Santander, "El General Simón Bolívar en la campaña. Relación escrito por un Granadino," *Gazeta de Santa Fé*, Oct. 4, 1819, JCBL.

233 *"Colonel! Save the republic!" etc.*: Lecuna, *Crónica*, II, 339.

233 *as rain began to spill*: Barreiro to Viceroy Samáno, Campo de Pantano de Vargas, July 25–26, 1819, *Los ejércitos del rey*, 354–55, 594–95.

233 *Santander would later say, etc.*: Santander, *Archivo*, II, 46, quoted in Lecuna, *Crónica*, II, 339.

233 *a well-honed fighting force*: Lecuna, *Crónica*, II, 339.

233 *by his legendary war to the death*: Liévano Aguirre, 224.

233 *the optimism of Barreiro himself*: Polanco Alcántara, 551–53.

233 *they were afraid*: Liévano. Also O'LB, 160.

233 *balance of power had shifted, etc.*: Liévano, 222.

233 *Barreiro sent out a vanguard, etc.*: Lecuna, *Crónica*, II, 346–48.

234 *Sixteen hundred royalists, etc.*: O'LB, 163.

234 *Rooke grasped the hewn limb, etc.*: O'LN, I, 559; Hasbrouck, 202–3; Mijares, 362; and Masur, *Simón Bolívar*, 380.

234 *"Viva la patria!"*: Masur, ibid.

234 *a twelve-year-old stablehand, etc.*: José Segundo Peña (Senator), Address to the Congress of Colombia, April 12, 1880, *Boletín de historia y antigüedades*, Academia de Historia Nacional, I (Bogotá, 1903), 652–55.

234 *Bolívar chased stragglers*: O'LB, 163.

234 *Vinoni, the republican traitor, etc.*: Lecuna, *Crónica*, II, 346–48.

235 *"A lightning bolt doesn't fall"*: Santander, "El General Simón Bolívar en la campaña."

235 *He rode, ragged and shirtless, etc.*: For details about Bolívar's ride into Bogotá, see notes for Chapter 1, where the ride is described in full.

235 *"The rebellious Bolívar has occupied"*: Morillo to Ministerio de Guerra, Valencia, Sept. 12, 1819, quoted in Rodríguez Villa, 49–55.

CHAPTER 10: THE WAY TO GLORY
PAGE

236 Epigraph: *"A weak man requires a long fight in order to win," etc.*: Bolívar to the editor of the *Royal Gazette*, Kingston, Sept. 28, 1815, SBO, I, 179.

236 *Bolívar dismounted swiftly, etc.*: J. P. Carrasquilla, quoted in Blanco-Fombona, *Ensayos históricos*, 303 fn.

236 *It was five P.M.*: O'LN, 578.

236 *a stifling day in the capital*: Groot, IV, 29.

236 *greeted Granadans as he went*: Carrasquilla, in Blanco-Fombona, *Ensayos históricos*, 303 fn. for subsequent details.

236 *despite the eight-hour ride*: O'LN, 578.

237 *"Absolutely not," etc.*: Carrasquilla, in Blanco-Fombona, *Esayos históricos*, 303 fn.

237 *"Where Bolívar is"*: O'Leary, *Detached Recollections*, 38.

237 *it was clear that Viceroy Sámano's*: SB to Zea, Bogotá, Aug. 14, 1819, SBO, I, 394–96.

237 *fled in such a fright*: Lecuna, *Crónica*, II, 350.

237 *left a bag of gold*: O'L, XVI, 431 (*Boletín del Ejército Libertador*, Aug. 11, 1819).

237 *a half million pesos*: O'LB, 164.

237 *dining with his courtiers, etc.*: Larrazábal, *Vida*, I, 596.

237 *"All is lost!"*: Mariano Torrente, quoted ibid., 596–97.

237 *"The bravura of the viceroy"*: Larrazábal, *Vida*, I, 596–97.

238 *he gave a fancy ball:* Hamilton, 232.

238 *"My good and brave colonel":* Ibid.

238 *lost all his shirts in battle:* Hippisley, 443.

238 *"Well, why don't you go?":* Hamilton, 232.

239 *many of his cohort had died:* Manuel B. Alvarez, the uncle of Nariño, and, for a time, his successor in Cundinamarca, was also drawn and quartered on that square.

239 *As one historian put it:* Masur, *Simón Bolívar,* 384.

239 *"A weak man requires a long fight," etc.:* SB to the editor of *Royal Gazette.*

239 *an ebony-haired Venus, etc.:* Charles Stuart Lord Cochrane, quoted in Mario Javier Pacheco García, *El fin del imperio latinoamericano* (Bogotá: Gobernación de Norte de Santander, 2008), 238.

239 *one of the great infatuations:* Bushnell, *Simón Bolívar,* 110.

240 *"No doubt this marriage":* SB to Santander, Pamplona, Nov. 8, 1819, SBO, I, 401–2.

240 *the source of much gossip:* Lynch, *Simón Bolívar,* 130.

240 *"I hope you will look after":* SB to Zea, Bogotá, Aug. 13, 1819, SB, *Escritos,* XVI, 213.

240 *Within the course of a few weeks, etc.:* SB, Oficio, Sept. 14, 1819, ibid., 267; Decreto, Sept. 15, 1819, ibid., 270; Resoluciones, Sept. 15–16, 1819, ibid., 274. Also Lecuna, *Crónica,* II, 352–55.

240 *instituted a fund for war widows:* This was with his own salary, DOC, XIV, 514.

240 *an exchange of prisoners:* Lecuna, *Crónica,* II, 354.

240 *"the Adonis of Bogotá":* J. M. Henao, *Historia de Colombia* (Bogotá: Bernardus, 1910), 358 fn.

241 *sheer torment for him:* Masur, *Simón Bolívar,* 392.

241 *a man of the law:* SB to Santander, Lima, Feb. 9, 1825, SBO, II, 1044–46.

241 *in love with money:* Santander's will, *Boletín de la Historia y Antiguedades,* IV, 1907, 161.

241 *always been a mediocre soldier:* Rafael Urdaneta, *Memorias,* 103.

241 *But on October 11, etc.:* O'LB, 166, for all subsequent details of this event.

242 *engaged to be married, etc.:* Slatta and Lucas de Grummond, 196.

242 *Republican authorities tried to dissociate:* O'LB, 166.

242 *"In the end, I had to get rid":* Santander, in *El reportorio colombiano,* VI (Bogotá: Librería Americana y Española), 229.

242 *"The records have been doctored":* Ibid.

242 *"I have learned with great regret":* O'L, XVI, 515.

243 *always carried a printing press, etc.:* Larrazábal, *Vida,* I, 432.

243 *accompanied by a jubilant ball, etc.:* Perú de Lacroix, I, 19.

243 *"There are men":* Ibid.

244 *Bolívar was devastated:* O'LB, 169; also Lecuna, *Crónica,* II, 360.

244 *sorely missed her affections:* SB to Zea, Bogotá, Aug. 13, 1819.

244 *the intelligence he was receiving:* Lecuna, *Crónica,* II, 366–69.

244 *the political bedlam:* SB to Santander, Soatá, Nov. 14, 1819, SBO, I, 403–5.

244 *Mariño had disregarded orders:* Arismendi to SB, Angostura, Sept. 16, 1819, O'L, XI, 390–91.

245 *Worst of all, Arismendi:* O'LB, 170.

245 *fallen victim to running gossip:* Larrazábal, *Vida,* I, 600.

245 *he was forced to step down:* O'LB, 170.

245 *His first official act:* Larrazábal, *Vida,* I, 602.

245 *Arismendi was gone, on a tour, etc.:* O'LB, 171.

246　*declared the Bolívarian era finished:* A congressman: "Whether or not Bolívar was de-feated, as has been reported, we should prepare to move on without him and without his tutelage." Larrazábal, *Vida*, I, 601.

246　*arduous sixty-four-day voyage:* Azpurúa, I, 223–27.

246　*thought the pealing bells, salvos, etc.:* O'LB, 171.

246　*"Long live Bolívar!," etc.:* Ibid.

246　*congratulated the vice president heartily:* Vowell, 121.

246　*"As soon as those two met," etc.: Recollections of a Service,* 4, 38, 41, 43.

246　*a goal, he said, he had set almost a decade before:* SB, *Proclamas y discursos,* 244–45.

247　*elected president and vice president, etc.:* Lecuna, *Crónica,* II, 372–73.

247　*asked King Ferdinand for twenty thousand soldiers, etc.:* Liévano Aguirre, 229.

247　*drive "all his pirates":* Morillo to the Ministerio de Guerra, Valencia, Sept. 12, 1819, Rodríguez-Villa, III, 50.

248　*"They've gone crazy!":* Morillo to his officers, in Liévano Aguirre, 230.

248　*"have dashed this army's":* Morillo to the Ministerio de Guerra, Valencia, April, 29, 1820, Rodríguez Villa, IV, 170.

248　*Morillo was forced to publish:* Constitution of Cádiz, proclaimed in Caracas on June 6 and 7, 1820, *Gaceta de Caracas,* Ediciones 308, 309, JCBL.

248　*not to touch, much less appropriate:* Ibid.

249　*Bolívar despaired at their failure, etc.:* SB to Santander, June 1, 1820, Carrera Damas, *Simón Bolívar Fundamental,* I (Caracas: Monte Avila, 1993), 170.

249　*"The more I think about it":* Ibid.

249　*made it clear that the black slaves:* SB to Santander, San Cristóbal, April 20, SBO, I, 426.

249　*almost half the white population:* Morillo reported to Spain's Ministry of War, "The whites have disappeared from Venezuela": Blanco-Fombona, *Bolívar y la guerra a muerte,* 199. Also J. F. King, *HAHR,* 23 (Nov. 4, 1953), 535. Also "Memorial presentado al rey en Ma-drid por el Pbro. Doctor don José Ambrosio Llamozas," *BOLANH,* 18 (1935), 168.

249　*"any free government that commits":* SB to Santander, San Cristóbal, April 20, SBO, I, 42.

250　*"A leader needs to learn":* SB to Páez, San Cristóbal, April 19, 1820, SB, *Escritos,* XVII, 223.

250　*From the relative quiet of Cúcuta:* O'LB, 176.

250　*pleading letters, etc.:* Arciniegas, *Las mujeres y las horas,* 87.

250　*To his delight:* SB to Santander, Cúcuta, June 10, 1820, SBO, I, 453.

250　*"Tell her whatever she needs to hear":* SB to Santander, Cúcuta, Aug. 1, 1820, ibid., 490.

250　*He had heard nothing:* SB to Domingo Ascanio, San Cristóbal, May 25, 1820, ibid., 442.

251　*to write to the king:* Archivo Nacional, Habana, *Asuntos políticos,* nos. 17, 5 and 18, 2, quoted in Madariaga, 400. Also M. Garrito, *Historia Crítica,* no. 31 (Jan.–June 2006), 205–6.

251　*"absolute ruin":* María Antonia to Ferdinand VII, Habana, Feb. 14, 1819, in Madar-iaga, 400.

251　*when Juana had sailed:* Ibid.

251　*much loved José Palacios, etc.:* M. L. Scarpetta, "José María Palacios Antunes," in S. Vergara, ed., *Diccionario biográfico de los campeones de la libertad* (Bogotá, 1870), 431.

251　*"I have yet to see Bernardina":* Santander to SB, Bogotá, Aug. 12, 1820, SB, *Cartas: Santander–Bolívar,* II, 322: 271.

251 *a rich man's illegitimate child:* Bernardina had a daughter by Miguel Saturnino Uribe, an influential millionaire, who, it was said, fathered many. "Las Ibañez somos así," *Revista semana*, Bogotá, May 22, 1989. Two more sources on the Ibañez sisters: López Michelsen, Alfonso, *Esbozas y Atisbos* (appendix) (Buenos Aires: Avellaneda, 1980), and Jaime Duarte French's *Las Ibañez* (Bogotá: El Ancora, 1987).

252 *bitter hatred against the Liberator:* Madariaga, 357; also Polanco Alcántara, 982–83, 988–89.

252 *newly arrived British troops:* SB to Santander, Cúcuta, June 22, 1820, SBO, I, 460.

252 *"The Irish are like courtesans":* SB to Montilla, Cúcuta, July 21, 1820, ibid. 479.

252 *Precious livestock:* SB to Santander, ibid., 461.

252 *"diabolical mix of ineptitude":* Ibid.

252 *the recruits, guns, bullets, etc.:* SB to Santander, Cúcuta, June 25, 1820, ibid., 462–63.

252 *the slowness of the mails:* SB to Soublette, Cúcuta, June 19, 1820, ibid., 455–57.

252 *putting soldiers closer to Caracas:* SB to Santander, Cúcuta, May 19, 1820, ibid., 437–38.

252 *his talented young officers:* SB to Santander, June 25, 1820, ibid.

252 *Antonio José de Sucre:* O'LB, 188. O'Leary writes: "On seeing him, I, who did not know him, asked the Liberator who the poor horseman approaching us was. 'He is one of the best officers in the army,' he replied. 'I am determined to bring him out of obscurity, for I am convinced that some day he will rival me.' "

252 *routine was Spartan, etc.:* O'LB, 176–77, for subsequent details about the order of his days.

253 *30,000 pesos a month:* SB to Santander, San Cristóbal, April 14, 1820, SBO, I, 424.

253 *"squeeze" the provinces:* Ibid.

253 *an excited letter to Soublette:* SB to Soublette, Cúcuta, June 19, 1820, ibid., 455–57.

253 *"Ten thousand enemies":* SB to W. White, San Cristóbal, May 1, 1820, ibid., 430.

253 *written to him at numerous addresses:* SB to M. de La Torre, San Cristóbal, July 7, 1820, ibid., 468; also SB to Morrillo, Carache, Nov. 3, 1820, ibid., 506.

254 *"If the object of your mission":* Ibid.

254 *Morillo had married:* Rodríguez Villa, 45.

254 *had never recovered:* A. Révesz, *Milicia de España. Teniente general don Pablo Morillo* (Madrid: Editorial Gran Capitán, 1947).

254 *a remarkably cordial correspondence:* SB to Morillo: Trujillo, Oct. 26; Carache, Nov. 3 (two); Trujillo, Nov. 13; Mocoy, Nov. 16; Trujillo, Nov. 17; Trujillo, Nov. 20, 1820; SBO, I, 503–12.

255 *A conference was arranged:* O'Leary, *Bolívar y la emancipación*, XVIII, 38–43.

255 *Bolívar rode a strong mule, etc.:* Ibid.

256 *"I thought my escort too small":* Ibid.

256 *"What? That little man":* Ibid.

256 *"To the victories of Boyacá!" etc.:* All subsequent toasts can be found ibid.

257 *"Defend the fortress of Puerto Cabello":* Quoted in Líevano Aguirre, 238.

257 *even Spain had had to censure:* Adelman, 276–77.

257 *"During the entire course":* Perú de Lacroix, 121–23.

257 *Thousands of mercenaries, etc.:* See especially Celia Wu's fascinating *Generals and Diplomats: Great Britain and Peru*. Wu claims that 3,000 British, Irish, and German soldiers volunteered for SB's army. Others put that figure as high as 7,000–8,000 (Rourke, 213–14).

258 *singing "Ye Gentlemen of England":* Trend, 127.

258 *the true Liberator had been:* Pi Sunyer, Carlos, *Patriotas americanos en Londres* (Caracas: Monte Avila, 1978), 242.

258 *one young English colonel:* Chesterton, *Narrative of Proceedings in Venezuela.*

258 *"as black and barbarous," etc.:* Ibid., vi, 7–8, 20–22.

258 *"Venezuela, though it has emancipated":* Adams to A. H. Everett, Dec. 29, 1817, *The Writings of John Quincy Adams,* VI (New York: Macmillan, 1916), 282.

259 *"Unity, unity, unity":* SB, "The Jamaica Letter," Kingston, Sept. 6, 1815, *El Libertador: Writings of Simón Bolívar,* 48.

259 *He admitted that he distrusted:* "I feel distrust of everything proposed and desired by these South American gentlemen": John Quincy Adams, *Writings,* VI, 51.

259 *"There is no community of interests":* Adams, *Memoirs of John Quincy Adams,* notes for Sept. 19, 1820, V (Philadelphia: J. B. Lippincott, 1875), 176.

259 *the slave trade was booming:* Wood, 3.

259 *Perry had made the harsh, etc.:* D. F. Long, *Gold Braid and Foreign Relations: Diplomatic Activities of U.S. Naval Officers* (Annapolis: U.S. Naval Institute, 1988), 59.

259 *Perry had landed on the very day:* J. N. Hambleton, *Journal of the Voyage of the USS "Nonsuch" up the Orinoco, July 11–August 23, 1819,* in J. F. Vivian, "The Orinoco River and Angostura, Venezuela, in the Summer of 1819," *Americas,* 24, no. 2 (Oct. 1967), 160–83.

259 *sure signs of yellow fever:* Ibid.

260 *"a charlatan general":* Hanke, "Baptis Irvine's Reports on Simón Bolívar," 360–73.

260 *"He affects the language":* Ibid.

260 *"Without a ray of true":* Ibid.

260 *a dinner given in Irvine's honor:* Rourke, 234–35.

260 *"Thus, . . . as I cross this table":* Ibid.

260 *Samuel D. Forsyth, etc.:* Hambleton, p. 182 fn.; also John Quincy Adams, *Memoirs,* 49–50.

260 *"eighteen million, struggling to be free!":* Clay, May 24, 1818, quoted in Randolph Adams, *History of the Foreign Policy of the United States,* 171.

260 *Clay argued passionately:* Annals of Congress, 15th Congress, 1st Session, II, no. 1485, quoted ibid.

261 *Clay moved that the House of Representatives:* Motion "that the House of Representatives participates with the people of the United States in the deep interest which they feel for the success of the Spanish provinces of South America, which are struggling for their liberty and independence": report by the Committee of Foreign Affairs, in E. McPherson, *The Political History of the United States During the Great Rebellion* (Washington, DC: Chapman, 1882), 351.

261 *fight for a maximum of three years, etc.:* L. Duarte-Level, in Unamuno, 132.

261 *He was haunted by the fear:* SB to Guillermo White, Barinas, May 6, 1821, SBO, II, 560.

262 *"Colombia will be independent":* SB to José Revenga and José Echeverría, quoted in Robertson, *Rise of the Spanish-American Republics,* 244.

262 *an agenda for renewed war:* SB to Santander, Trujillo, Dec. 1, 1820, SBO, I, 520–22.

262 *written to Morillo, to La Torre, even to King Ferdinand:* SB to Morillo, Barinas, Dec. 11, 1820, and Bogotá, Jan. 26, 1821; SB to La Torre, Bogotá, Jan. 25, 1821; SB to Fernando VII, Bogotá, Jan. 24, 1821, SBO, I, 510–32.

263 *planned every detail:* Duarte-Level, in Unamuno, 146.

263 *Morales . . . had been passed over:* From an unnamed British officer's account of the Battle of Carabobo, quoted in Charles Dickens's magazine, *All the Year Round*, XIX, March 28, 1868 (London: Chapman, 1868), 368. The account also appears in Mulhall, *Explorers in the New World*, 232ff.

263 *The royalist army, aware now:* Lecuna, *Crónica*, III, 35.

263 *La Torre's forces were clearly in shambles:* Ibid., 34.

264 *"the largest and most superb":* SB to Santander, Valencia, June 25, 1821, SBO, II, 571.

264 *the heavens opened with torrential rains, etc.:* Dickens, 369.

264 *Páez's cavalry was dispatched:* For a good overall description of the battle, see Duarte-Level's essay in Unamuno's *Simón Bolívar*.

264 *laboring under a broiling sun:* Prago, 204.

264 *they scaled the heights, etc.:* Lecuna, *Crónica*, III, 47–48.

264 *"hollow square" formation:* Prago, 205. A tight square or rectangular formation of 500 men in two to four rows, armed with muskets, rifles, or fixed bayonets: essentially a defensive tactic used against a charging enemy. Soldiers in the "hollow square" would withhold fire until chargers were 100 feet away, at which point they would mow down their attackers, creating piles of bodies that served as obstructions to further attacks.

265 *more than a thousand royalists lay dead, etc.:* Lecuna, *Crónica*, III, 52.

265 *six hundred British soldiers lost their lives:* Mulhall, 232.

265 *"My general, I die happy":* Mosquera, 420; also Lecuna, *Crónica*, III, 51.

265 *one of his violent fits of epilepsy:* Lecuna, *Crónica*, III, 50.

265 *Nearby lay the towering First Negro:* Mijares, 396.

265 *"Saviors of my country!," etc.:* Mulhall, 232.

266 *he was institutionalizing the Latin American warlord:* Lynch, *Simón Bolívar*, 142.

CHAPTER 11: THE CHOSEN SON

PAGE

267 Epigraph: *"I am not the governor this republic needs," etc.:* SB to the secretary of state, Cúcuta, April 8, 1813, SBO, I, 53–55.

267 *"I am a soldier":* Ibid.

267 *he reached the city at night:* Masur, *Simón Bolívar*, 434.

267 *he questioned his patience:* O'LN, I, 578.

267 *written to confess these fears:* SB to Nariño, Barinas, April 21, 1821, SBSW, I, 64–65.

268 *Colombia was a military camp:* Ibid.

268 *all the good men had disappeared:* SB to F. Peñalver, Valencia, July 10, 1821, SBO, II, 577–78.

268 *"Since I am fully convinced":* SB to Nariño.

268 *not ready for democracy, etc.:* SB to Santander, San Carlos, June 13, 1821, SBSW, I, 267–68.

268 *as feral and rapacious:* SB to P. Gual, Guanare, May 24, 1821, SBO, II, 563–64.

268 *"Even I, riding at their head":* Ibid.

268 *"We are poised on an abyss":* Ibid.

269 *governable only by a strong hand:* SB to Santander.

269 *"In Colombia the people":* Ibid.

269 *begun to question the wisdom, etc.:* Polanco Alcántara, 610–25.

270 *his finances were in disorder, etc.*: Lynch, *Simón Bolívar*, 141.

270 *he freed the few slaves:* O'LB, 196.

270 *Among them was his old wet nurse, Hipólita:* "Hipólita Bolívar," in *Diccionario de historia de Venezuela*, I (Caracas: Editorial Ex Libris, 1992).

270 *"the only father I have ever known":* SB to María Antonia, July 10, 1825, SBC, *1823–1824–1825*, 339.

270 *He was antsy, nervous:* O'LB, 197; also SB to Santander, Valencia, July 10, 1821, SBO, II, 576–77. O'Leary describes him as "suffering indescribable torment" from political enemies. In SB's July 10 letter to Santander, he admits that he is sick and tired, and that his life is far too frenetic. Polanco Alcántara (610) mentions that a long exhaustion had taken SB sometime before. SB mentions this in a May 7, 1820, letter to Santander, in which he says, "I was very sick in San Cristóbal and so came here [to Cúcuta] to recover. I still don't know what I had but I know very well that I'm still a wreck, with a strong propensity to sleep all the time or to want to rest, which for me represents a serious illness." SBO, I, 432–34.

270 *"I need to round out Colombia":* SB to Castillo Rada, Trujillo, Aug. 24, 1821, SBO, II, 588.

270 *"I need to give a third sister":* SB to Santander, Tocuyo, Aug. 16, 1821, SBO, II, 582.

270 *"Send me that book":* SB to Santander, Cúcuta, June 1, 1820, SBO, I, 451. SB asks him to have his friend Pepe París send him a copy of "Los Incas del Peru," by which he very well could have meant Inca Garcilaso de la Vega's magisterial book, *Comentarios Reales de los Incas*. Inca Garcilaso was the son of a conquistador and an Inca princess; his record of Inca customs and traditions was the first work ever written by an American. The Spanish king forbade its publication or circulation in 1780, after Túpac Amaru II's rebellion in Peru. San Martín had also read the book (and carried it with him) before his liberating army entered Lima in 1821.

271 *having joked that if elected:* SB to L. E. Azuola, Trujillo, March 9, 1821, SBO, II, 547–48.

271 *I am a son of war:* Address to the president of the General Congress of Colombia, Cúcuta, October 1, 1821, DOC, VII, 122, quoted in SBSW, I, 285.

272 *scattering a force of ten thousand:* Paz Soldán, *Historia del Perú*, II, 435. The exact number quoted in the army document is 9,530.

272 *his skin was so dark, etc.:* María Joaquina de Alvear, granddaughter of the Spanish brigadier Diego de Alvear, left a journal (Jan. 23, 1877) in which she claimed that San Martín was the illegitimate son of her grandfather and an indigenous woman—San Martín's wet nurse, Rosa Guarú. The journal says, furthermore, that the Alvear family offered the child to be adopted into the San Martín family. Indeed, throughout his childhood and youth, San Martín was close to the Alvear family and founded the Lautaro Lodge with Carlos Alvear, who, according to María Joaquina, was his half brother. Complicating the proof of his origins, his birth date is inconsistent in military records, a record of baptism was never found, and his father, Juan de San Martín, is said to have been away from home for the entire year that preceded San Martín's presumed February birth. None of this has been proven beyond Joaquina de Alvear's words and subsequent arguments made by Argentine historian Hugo Chumbita, who has written copiously on the matter. See Chumbita, *El manuscrito de Joaquina: San*

Martín y el secreto de la familia Alvear (Buenos Aires: Catálogos, 2007); also Chumbita, *El secreto de Yapeyú* (Buenos Aires: Emecé, 2001). Mary Graham, the widow of a British naval captain, also wrote about San Martín's presumed "mixed breed" background in an 1823 fragment published in *De Don José de San Martín* (Santiago: Editorial Barros Browne, 2000). Madariaga claims San Martín's mother was a half-caste, and that as a result he bore a "*mestizo* resentment" (Madariaga, 425). Mitre says his birth predisposed him to be "an enemy of the race" of Spaniards (Mitre, *Historia de San Martín*, III, 193, 218, 225). The inherent prejudice in both cases speaks for itself.

272 *"El Indio," "El Cholo," etc.:* A. J. Lapolla, "El origen mestizo del General San Martín," *La Fogata Digital*, www.lafogata.org/07arg/arg1/arg-9-2.htm.

272 *"I, too, am Indian":* Galasso, *Seamos libres*, 200.

272 *served under two notable British officers:* R. Rojas, *San Martín* (New York: Cooper Square, 1967), 22–23.

273 *Accompanying him was Carlos Alvear:* This, including the information about the Masonic lodges and Lautaro, can be found ibid., 21–24.

273 *banning secret societies:* Gould, 180.

273 *"conspiring, corresponding, intriguing":* Madariaga, 405.

274 *"Here go 40 saddle blankets":* Pueyrredón to San Martín, Nov. 2, 1816, Buenos Aires, Documentos Archivo General San Martín (DAGSM), IV (Buenos Aires: Coni), 526.

274 *"He wants wings for cannon," etc.:* Padre Luis Beltrán, quoted in R. Rojas, *San Martín*, 99.

274 *half his infantry would be black:* Bethell, 128.

274 *"If a Spaniard resists":* R. Rojas, *San Martín*, 112.

274 *illegitimate son of a former viceroy:* O'Higgins was the "hijo natural" of Ambrosio O'Higgins, an Irishman who fought for the Spanish crown and became governor of Chile as well as viceroy of Peru. His mother was from an aristocratic family. Despite the illegitimacy, his father took a great interest in his education and his fortunes, although the two never met. See Benjamin Vicuña Mackenna, *Vida del capitán jeneral de Chile Don Bernardo O'Higgins* (Santiago: Jover, 1882).

275 *"In twenty-four days":* San Martín to Pueyrredón, *Anales de la Universidad de Chile*, IX (Santiago, 1852), 140; Mitre, *Historia*, II, 19.

275 *Not particularly well-read:* Mary Graham, *De Don José de San Martín*.

275 *"There is a timidity of intellect":* Ibid.

275 *"It is impossible to know":* Georg Gottfried Gervinus, quoted in R. Rojas, *San Martín*, 76.

275 *refused salaries, etc.:* Ibid., 120–21.

275 *"your approval . . . is reward enough":* Ibid., 119.

275 *crippling bouts of rheumatism:* Ibid., 66.

275 *deeply addicted to the drug:* The most persuasive evidence in this regard is a letter from President Pueyrredón: "I've tried to persuade San Martín to quit using opium; but unsuccessfully, for he tells me that he will surely die without it." Pueyreddón to T. Guido, Buenos Aires, June 16, 1818, Guido y Spano, *Vindicación histórica* (Buenos Aires: Librería de Mayo, 1882), 117; also R. Rojas, *San Martín*, 67, 80, 127–28; Galasso, 125.

275 *"An angry hemorrhage":* San Martín to Godoy Cruz, Jan. 19, 1816, DAGSM, V, 529–30.

275 *stole the potent little tubes:* Guido, who admits to doing this, is quoted in R. Rojas, *San Martín*, 127.

276   *all of three sentences:* "We have just obtained a complete victory. Our cavalry pursues them to finish them. The country is free." San Martín to General Headquarters, April 5, 1818, in R. Rojas, *San Martín*, 144.

276   *accused him of being drunk:* Ibid.

276   *"I found the hero of Maipú":* Samuel Haigh, quoted in R. Rojas, *San Martín*, 159.

276   *Several thousand skilled soldiers:* Ibid., 157.

276   *accused as a traitor, etc.:* Ibid., 160.

276   *"I have pledged my honor":* Ibid., 158.

276   *"I have no homeland":* Ibid.

277   *San Martín and four thousand troops:* He had counted on 6,000 but only had 4,000. Wu, 13–15.

277   *He virtually honeycombed Peru:* Madariaga, 406–7.

277   *suggesting that the eminence might appoint his own regency:* Galasso, 375. Also Barros Arana, *Compendio elemental*, 479. Capt. W. Bowles, the British naval station head at the mouth of the Río Plata, reported in early 1817 that San Martín had confided long before "his desire to establish monarchies under British protection in Spanish America" and that the information was sent at once to the British Foreign Office: Rippy, *Rivalry of the United States and Great Britain*, 12.

277   *A major earthquake:* Occurred on July 10, 1821, in Camaná, south of Lima, and was measured at 8.2 magnitude. Known casualties: 162. U.S. Geological Survey, Dept. of the Interior, earthquake.usgs.gov/earthquakes/world/historical_country.php.

277   *ghosts of the angry Inca:* Attributed to the historian Mariano Torrente, in R. Rojas, *San Martín*, 181.

277   *At first, he took lodging at a monastery:* Ibid., 182.

277   *named himself Protector, etc.:* San Martín proclaimed independence on July 28, 1821. On August 3, he issued a proclamation announcing that the supreme powers of the military and government were vested in himself, under the title of Protector. San Martín, *Decreto*, Lima, Aug. 3, 1821, *Collección de documentos literarios del Peru*, IV (Lima: Imprenta del Estado, 1877), 318; also Robertson, *History of the Latin-American Nations* (New York: Appleton, 1922), 184.

277   *waved his flag:* R. Rojas, *San Martín*, 183.

277   *wasted no time in writing to San Martín:* SB states in his letter that he is sending Diego Ibarra to facilitate communication. Col. Ibarra was SB's first aide-de-camp. He was also related to SB through SB's dead wife and the extended family of del Toros. It was rumored in Lima that Ibarra was a spy.

277   *"I hope to heaven":* SB to San Martín, Trujillo, Aug. 23, 1821, SBO, III, 586.

278   *stalled in fractious argument:* Barros Arana, 467.

278   *He was tired of managing:* SB to Soublette, Cúcuta, Oct. 5, 1821, SBO, III, 599.

278   *"I'm not going to lose":* SB to Santander, Tocuyo, Aug. 16, 1821, *Cartas: Santander–Bolívar*, III, 132.

278   *On November 27, he bought, etc.:* The deed of sale, finalized in the presence of the ministers of the treasury, is transcribed in Duarte French, *Las Ibañez*, 76–77. See also Polanco Alcántara, 641–42.

278   *the Liberator had claimed to love:* SB to Santander, Pamplona, Nov. 8, 1819, SBO, I, 401–2.

279 *as a mistress for fifteen more years:* Polanco Alcántara, 641–42; Duarte French, 76–77.

279 *moved into that comfortable house:* Polanco Alcántara, 641.

279 *"Fussy, beautiful Bernardina":* SB to "The Fussy and more than fussy, beautiful Bernardina," Cali, Jan. 5, 1822, SBO, II, 619. In a footnote, Lecuna comments that the letter, which belonged to E. Naranjo Martínez, the Colombian consul in Boston, was written in Bolívar's hand, and purchased from the collector Francis Russell Hart (1868–1938) in Boston.

279 *Spanish frigates controlled:* Lecuna, *Crónica*, III, 85–86.

280 *had once saved the Argentine's life:* Parte de la batalla de Arjonilla, June 23, 1808; original document available at http://abc.gov.ar/.

280 *landed on the coast of Ecuador:* Lecuna, *Crónica*, III, 85–86.

280 *an army of four thousand:* Lecuna, *Crónica*, III, 83.

280 *the army was a fraction of itself:* A third had been lost: Ibid., 88–89.

280 *had met with devastating defeat:* For an account of Sucre's frustrations, ibid., 119–34, 148–51.

280 *Sucre had called on San Martín:* Ibid., 147–48. Sucre had called for San Martín to lend him the Numancia Battalion, a force of native Colombians who had fought for Spain, then defected to the rebels. San Martín refused to send the Colombians, but sent another force led by Colonel Andrés de Santa Cruz.

280 *Obando, emerged under a flag of truce, etc.:* J. M. Vergara y Vergara, *Almanaque de Bogotá* (Bogotá: Gaitan, 1866), 158.

281 *"I have been awake all night":* SB to Santander, Popayán, Jan. 29, 1822, SBO, II, 623–27.

281 *What he proposed was forgery, etc.:* Ibid.

281 *"The object of all this fuss":* Ibid.

281 *His instructions to Santander, etc.:* Ibid.

281 *Quito's interim president Aymerich:* SB to Aymerich, Popayán, Feb. 18, 1822, SBO, II, 635–36.

281 *recently arrived Captain-General:* SB to Mourgeón, Popayán, Jan. 31, 1822, ibid., 627–28.

281 *overtures to Popayán's bishop:* SB to Salvador Jiménez, Obispo, Jan. 31, 1822, ibid., 628–29.

281 *ordered his officers not to have lunch:* SB had ordered his second in command, Gen. Torres, to take the heights of Cariaco. Torres was not to direct mess officers to dispense the midday meal until they did. Mosquera, 441; also Lecuna, *Crónica*, III, 97–98.

282 *Wave after wave of patriot lines, etc.:* Lecuna, *Crónica*, III, 97–101; also López, *Recuerdos históricos*, 63–68; Obando, *Apuntamientos*, I, 38–40.

282 *clambering up a ladder:* Bartolomé Salom, *Boletín del Ejercito Libertador*, April 8, 1822, O'L, XIX, 236–40; also Guzmán Blanco, *Bolívar y San Martín* (Caracas: La Opinion Nacional, 1885), 40. Andrés Bello would later describe it in his "Fragmentos de un poema titulado 'América,' " *Obras Completas*, III (Santiago: Ramírez, 1883), 59.

282 *"Our camp . . . was a mill":* Obando, 38–40.

282 *including Bolívar:* SB to Col. J. Lara, Cariaco, April 15, 1822, O'L, XIX, 251–52.

282 *split the royalist camp:* Salom, *Boletín del Ejercito Libertador* (Buenos Aires: Instituto Samatiniano, 1971), O'L, XIX.

282 *Every patriot officer:* Lecuna, *Crónica*, III, 98.

282 *carried away in a litter:* Lynch, *Simón Bolívar*, 169.

CHAPTER 12: UNDER THE VOLCANOES

PAGE

284   Epigraph: *"I am consumed by the demon of war"*: SB to Sucre, Huaraz, June 9, 1824, O'L, XXIX, 503.

284   *"Either I lose my way"*: SB to Santander, Tocuyo, Aug. 16, 1821, SBO, II, 582.

284   *he seemed far older*: From *Notes on Colombia, Taken in the Years 1822–3, Reviewed in The United States Literary Gazette* (New York, 1827), I, 418–32.

284   *grizzled by war, etc.*: Physical descriptions of him at this point in his life abound, but perhaps the most persuasive are in Boulton, *El rostro de Bolívar*; these show the changes in progressive portraits of SB.

285   *harder for him to tolerate the physical hardship*: This was evident in his weakness at the Battle of Bomb022, but he mentions his exhaustion in SB to Marqués del Toro and Fernando del Toro, Quito, June 21, 1822, SBO, II, 648–49; and SB to Santander, Guayaquil, Aug. 29, 1822, ibid, 680–82.

285   *"If God had given us the right"*: SB to his loyal friend Gen. Mosquera, quoted in Antonio José de Sucre, *Documentos selectos* (Caracas: Bib. Ayacucho, 1993), vii.

285   *last missive Sucre had received*: SB to Sucre, Cuartel general de la Plata, Dec. 22, 1821, SBO, I, 115–16.

286   *The Protector of Peru had announced*: Vicente Lecuna, "Bolívar and San Martín at Guayaquil," *HAHR*, 31, no. 3, 372–73.

286   *worked himself into a state*: Madariaga, 428.

286   *a copy of a letter Bolívar had sent*: SB to J. J. de Olmedo, Cali, Jan. 2, 1822, SBO, II, 616–17.

286   *A bomb could not have produced*: The exact words of Lecuna in "Bolívar and San Martín at Guayaquil," 372–73.

286   *authority to go to war*: Espejo, *Recuerdos históricos*, 110.

286   *persuaded Santa Cruz to ignore*: Masur, "The Conference of Guayaquil," 195.

286   *He decided to send one of his generals*: José de la Mar, a Peruvian Creole who had started out as a royalist, but defected to the patriots after San Martín entered Lima. La Mar turned out to be the wrong person to send to the thoroughly patriot enclave of Guayaquil. Lecuna, *Crónica*, III, 189. Also SB to La Mar, Guaranda, July 3, 1822, SBO, II, 654–55.

286   *skirted the city, etc.*: Lecuna, *Crónica*, III, 173–77; and O'Leary, *Bolívar y la emancipación*, 165–69.

286   *Mourgeón . . . had died suddenly*: P. F. Cevallos, *Resúmen de la historia del Ecuador*, III (Lima: Imprenta del Estado, 1870), 381.

287   *It had rained all night*: Sobrevilla, *Caudillo of the Andes*, 62.

287   *clambered onto their rooftops*: Prago, 206.

287   *with full military honors*: Sobrevilla, 62.

287   *"Sucre had more troops"*: SB to Santander, Pasto, June 9, 1822, SBO, II, 642–44.

288   *greater than Napoleon's empire*: The landmass of Bolívar's liberated nations at this point in mid-June of 1822 amounted to roughly 935,000 square miles. Napoleon's empire, at its peak, measured 810,815 square miles.

288   *"At one o'clock I presented"*: John Quincy Adams, *Memoirs*, VI, 23.

288 *arms, ships, reinforcements:* Torres had been responsible for the shipload of arms that Juan Vicente Bolívar, Simon's brother, was trying to bring back to Venezuela in 1811, when his ship went down in the Caribbean. Whitaker, 68.

288 *dragged himself home to Philadelphia:* Ibid., 69.

288 *day of their diplomat's funeral, etc.:* Ibid. Torres was the grand-nephew of the famous archbishop-viceroy of New Granada, Antonio Caballero y Góngora. He had come from Spain with the viceroy and was radicalized after spending several years in Cartagena. He lived in Philadelphia from 1796 until his death in 1822, and came to be highly esteemed by Henry Clay and many other distinguished Americans of his time. Arciniegas, *Bolívar y la revolución*, 124–26.

289 *not be fully aware of:* O'Leary, *Bolívar y la emancipación*, 240; *Gaceta de Lima*, Jan. 18, 1823, I, JCBL.

289 *legend has it:* The legend of Manuela Sáenz on a Quito balcony comes from "Diarios de Quito," a diary that was purported to be hers. But it has come into question, as have many unverified letters attributed to her. Indeed there is a veritable minefield of uncorroborated accounts about Sáenz. These "Diarios" are published in C. Alvarez Saá's *Manuela: Sus diarios perdidos y otros papeles* (Ecuador: Imprenta Mariscal, 1995).

289 *at a ball given for him, etc.:* Murray, *For Glory and Bolívar*, 30.

289 *the illegitimate child, etc.:* Ibid., 9–15.

290 *Thorne probably assisted him, etc.:* Ibid., 15–16.

290 *fuddy-duddy with no intellectual brio:* Sáenz to Thorne, Oct. 1823, Vicente Lecuna, "Papeles de Manuela Sáenz," *BOLANH*, 28, no. 112 (1945), 501–2. Murray claims that it is more likely that this letter was written in 1829. It is undated in the Archivo del Libertador in Caracas.

290 *a regular in patriot circles:* Murray, *For Glory and Bolívar*, 22–23.

290 *distinguished Order of the Sun:* "Al patriotismo de las más sensibles," Decreto de San Martín y B. Monteagudo, Jan. 11, 1822, *Gaceta del gobierno del Peru independiente*, Jan. 12, 1822.

291 *Rosa de Campusano:* R. P. Pimentel, *Diccionario biográfico del Ecuador*, www.diccionario biograficoecuador.com/tomos/tomo6/c3.htm.

291 *By late May of 1822, etc.:* Murray, *For Glory and Bolívar*, 28, and for subsequent details.

291 *gleaming, ebony hair, etc.:* Ibid., 33.

291 *"Madam, . . . if only my soldiers":* Bolívar to Sáenz, quoted in Ospina, *En busca de Bolívar*, 116.

291 *protesting Colombia's designs:* San Martín to SB, Lima, March 3, 1822, *San Martín, su correspondencia* (paginated by date).

291 *Bolívar fired back:* SB to San Martín, Quito, June 22, 1822, SBO, II, 653–54.

292 *blatant lack of decorum:* SB to Sáenz, Ica, April 20, 1825, *La más hermosas cartas de amor entre Manuela y Simón* (Caracas: Ed. de la Presidencia de la República, 2010), 47.

292 *"I want to answer":* SB to Sáenz, Cuartel general en Guaranda, July 3, 1822, 17.

292 *thrilled and ignited his imagination:* O'Leary, *Bolívar y la emancipación*, 169.

292 *a lover of nature, etc.:* Ibid.

292 *He thought of this now, etc.:* Ibid., 169–70.

293 *the tallest peak on earth:* Until the early 1800s, it was believed Chimborazo was the world's tallest peak. This is not so.

293   *"Come to Chimborazo":* SB to Rodríguez, Pativilca, Jan. 19, 1824, SBO, II, 885–86.

293   *And yet historians disagree:* Lecuna includes it in his collection, Madariaga doesn't mention it at all, and Masur calls it "forgery, and poor forgery at that" (see Lecuna in the citation below about Col. Vicente Aguirre; Masur, *Simón Bolívar*, 463). Polanco Alcántara believes it to be in SB's hand, as does Pedro Grases (*Escritos Selectos* [Caracas: Bib. Ayacucho, 1989], 191). Bushnell includes it in *El Libertador: Writings*. Lynch prefers to remain "agnostic" (Lynch, *Simón Bolívar*, 171).

293   *similarly elegiac document:* I owe this comparison to the Colombian writer Frank D. Bedoya Muñoz, who wrote about it in the magazine *Gotas de Tinta*, no. 1, Feb. 2010.

293   *discovered among a Colombian colonel's papers:* The original was never found. But Lecuna, the chief editor of SB's papers, mentions the copy found in Quito, among the family papers of Col. Vicente Aguirre, an officer in the Colombian army. "My Delirium" was published for the first time in 1833, three years after SB's death, in F. J. Yanes and Cristóbal Mendoza, eds., *Colección de documentos relativos a la vida pública del Libertador* (Caracas, 1826–33). See Lecuna, "Mi delirio," *BANH*, vols. 27–28, 138.

293   *Most Latin American scholars:* Lynch, for one, says this, although he is not entirely convinced. Lynch, *Simón Bolívar*, 171.

294   *offer of assistance and the invitation:* SB to San Martín, Quito, June 17, 1822, SBO, II, 647, and June 22, 1822, SBO, II, 653–54.

294   *"I accept your generous proposal":* San Martín to SB, July 13, 1822, Lima, O'L, XIX, 335.

294   *seeking a prince from a royal family:* San Martín had sent his doctor, the Englishman James Paroissien, and J. García del Río in Dec. 1821, Paz Soldán, I, 271; see also San Martín to Gen. Miller, Brussels, April 9, 1827, *Documentos, Archivo de San Martín*, VII, 411. Nevertheless, San Martín's emissaries apparently never had the chance to present his monarchical plan to a single chancellery in Europe. Robertson, *Rise of the Spanish American Republics*, 215.

294   *found guilty of plotting:* L. Ornstein, "La guerra terrestre y la acción continental de la revolución argentina," in *Historia de la nación argentina*, VI, 510–11.

294   *powerful merchants hated him for it:* Masur, "The Conference of Guayaquil," 197.

294   *mounted a cruel campaign:* Bethell, 136.

294   *He was at odds with his admiral:* Lord Cochrane to San Martín, Valparayso, Nov. 19, 1822, *Noticias del Perú*, vol. 13, *Lima justificada* (1822), 57–58.

295   *On July 13, he set sail:* San Martín to SB, Lima, July 13, 1822, O'L, XIX, 335–36.

295   *Colossal arches:* Espejo, 61.

295   *resplendent in white and blue:* Ibid., 31.

295   *stalked off in protest:* O'Leary, *Bolívar y la emancipación*, 177.

295   *Bolívar invited Olmedo:* Ibid., 180; and O'Leary, *Detached Recollections*, 32.

295   *tore down the flag of Guayaquil, etc.:* O'Leary, *Bolívar y la emancipación*, 180–81.

295   *that he highly disapproved of it:* O'Leary, *Detached Recollections*, 32. At first, the people of Guayaquil believed SB was coming because he was sailing from their port back to Colombia (Espejo, 60), but it became evident that his was an occupying force. He went through the motions of holding a popular vote. In fact, an electoral college vote was discussed at the July 13 conference with SB; in compliance with his later promise

to San Martín, the vote was taken on July 31. The vote favored Colombia. But at that point, of course, the city was well under SB's control, and San Martín was long gone. C. Destruge, *Historia de la revolución de octubre y campaña libertadora de 1820–1822* (Guayaquil: Elzeviriana, 1920), 342. Also R. Andrade, *Historia del Ecuador*, III (Guayaquil: Reed & Reed, 1934), 1353.

295 *The junta was reconvened, etc.:* O'Leary, *Detached Recollections*, 33.

295 *He took command of the city:* O'Leary, *Bolívar y la emancipación*, 180–81.

296 *take command of it for Lima:* San Martín's aide-de-camp Rufino Guido later confirmed that the Protector's secret purpose was to take possession of Guayaquil before making his way overland to meet with the Liberator in Quito. R. Guido, *San Martín en la historia y en el bronce*, "Año del Libertador General San Martín" (Buenos Aires: República Argentina, 1950), 171, quoted in Lecuna, *La entrevista de Guayaquil*, 321.

296 *in that cool predawn:* "Average Temperature and Rainfall in Guayaquil," http://www.hacienda-ecuador.com/Ecuador/Ecuador_4.html.

296 *"No, do not dismiss lightly":* SB to San Martín, Guayaquil, July 25, 1822, SBO, II, 658–59.

296 *Fleet boats of oarsmen:* "Relación de Rufino Guido," quoted in Espejo, 95.

296 *eventually, San Martín responded:* Mosquera, in *El Colombiano*, Bogotá, Oct. 28, 1861, cited in Villanueva, *Bolívar y el general San Martín*, 233.

296 *met by a parade formation:* Espejo, 96.

297 *"At last!":* Ibid., 97.

297 *Bolívar felt the moment deeply:* Lecuna, *La entrevista de Guayaquil*, 382.

297 *tributes from the women:* Espejo, 97–98.

297 *youngest of three flirtatious sisters:* The young women of the Garaycoa family, with whom SB came to be quite friendly. Joaquina made an impression on him when she first met him; she called him "El Glorioso." He called her "La Gloriosa" after that, or *loca gloriosa*, or *amable loca*. His long correspondence with Joaquina and Manuela Garaycoa makes for lively reading. Some historians have concluded that a romance flared briefly between SB and Joaquina, although it may have been a merely well-documented flirtation.

297 *snatched it from his head, etc.:* Espejo, 97–98.

298 *The first question that arose:* Masur, "The Conference of Guayaquil," 212.

298 *a vote to determine the democratic will:* Ibid. Also SBC, III, 61.

298 *ascribe all problems to the city's fickleness:* Masur, "The Conference of Guayaquil," 212.

298 *a few hours between soldiers:* SBC, III, 57.

298 *"the last battleground in America":* San Martín to SB, July 13, 1822, O'L, XIX, 335–36.

298 *commented, as politely as he could:* O'LN, II, 173.

298 *army wasn't large enough for that:* San Martín to Miller, *San Martín, su correspondencia, 1823–1850*, 66.

298 *called for one of his aides:* Mitre, *Historia*, VI, 81.

298 *a little more than a thousand:* San Martín to SB, Lima, Aug. 29, 1822, quoted in Masur, "The Conference of Guayaquil," 203–5. This letter has been disputed by Lecuna, but Masur defends it persuasively. It was never disputed by Larrazábal, Mitre, or Paz Soldán, who refer to it with confidence. The strongest defense of its authenticity is that it was published by San Martín's acquaintance Gabriel Lafond de Lurcy, *Voyages autour du monde* (Paris, 1843), during San Martín's lifetime. San Martín, who died in France

in 1850, never disputed it, although he was known to dispute other documents after his withdrawal from Peru.

298 *he calculated to be 9,600:* San Martín to SB, July 13, 1822, O'L, XIX, 335–36.

298 *Controlling himself with great difficulty:* Masur, "The Conference of Guayaquil," 215.

298 *implored Bolívar to come to Peru, etc.:* San Martín to SB, July 13, 1822, O'L, XIX, 335–36.

299 *too delicate to pursue:* Ibid.

299 *"I couldn't get a clear answer":* D. F. Sarmiento, *Vida de San Martín* (Buenos Aires: Claridad, 1950), 186. The interview with Sarmiento was on July 15, 1846.

299 *The only conclusion:* Gen. T. Guido, *San Martín y la gran epopeya* (Buenos Aires: El Ateneo, 1928), 242.

299 *he didn't trust him completely:* Masur, "The Conference of Guayaquil," 220.

299 *his plan for establishing a monarchy:* SB to Sucre, Guayaquil, July 29, 1822, SBO, II, 663–65; SB to Santander, July 29, 1822, ibid., 667.

299 *"Sound out the general's spirit":* Briceño Mendez to Ibarra, Maracaibo, Sept. 7, 1821, O'L, XVIII, 497–98. This is a memo with SB's instructions, signed by his secretary (and nephew-in-law) Pedro Briceño Méndez.

299 *sent a delegation of diplomats:* San Martín to Gen. Miller, Brussels, April 9, 1827, *Documentos del Archivo de San Martín*, VII, 411.

300 *as somber and impenetrable:* Mitre, *Historia*, 75.

300 *deeply mortified:* Masur, "The Conference of Guayaquil," 218.

300 *pronouncements from the balcony, etc.:* "Relación de Rufino Guido," in Espejo, 80.

300 *Little was said:* Ibid.

300 *Little is known:* Masur writes that they spoke about San Martín's political quandaries, but this can be said for the whole visit. Masur, "The Conference of Guayaquil," 216.

300 *how the people of Lima would characterize:* Larrazábal, *Vida*, II, 160.

301 *resign his position, etc.:* SB to Sucre, ibid.

301 *resignation in a sealed envelope:* Ibid.

301 *not a single trump card:* Masur, "The Conference of Guayaquil," 202.

301 *From Manuela Sáenz and others, etc.:* Langley, 81.

301 *"Good God, I want no more," etc.:* SB to Santander, ibid.

302 *cost Bolívar 8,000 pesos:* SB to Santander, Guayaquil, Aug. 27, 1822, SBO, II, 676. "I haven't had any extraordinary expenses, except for the dinner in San Martín's honor, on which I spent eight thousand pesos."

302 *"Gentlemen, . . . I offer a toast":* Espejo, 100. Also E. Colombres Marmol, *San Martín y Bolívar* (Buenos Aires: Coni, 1940), 67–68.

302 *"To the swift termination of this war":* Espejo, ibid.

302 *greeted with great warmth:* Ibid.

302 *San Martín was resolutely unresponsive:* Colombres Marmol, 68.

302 *not through a side door, undetected:* Villanueva, 253.

302 *"a sincere memento":* San Martín to Gen. Miller, Brussels, April 19, 1827, *Documentos del Archivo de San Martín*, VII, 411.

303 *the last two words San Martín would have used:* Villanueva, ibid.

303   *less than forty hours in Guayaquil:* He arrived midday on July 26 and left on July 28, at 2 A.M. Espejo, 94–96, 102.

303   *"beat us to the punch":* "El Libertador nos ha ganado de mano," in Mitre, *Historia*, VI, 81.

303   *"He is not the man":* San Martín to O'Higgins, Callao, ibid.

303   *He had found him superficial, etc.:* San Martín to Guido, Brussels, Dec. 18, 1826, June 21, 1827, *Documentos del Archivo de San Martín*, VI, 504, 529. Also Mitre, *Historia*, VI, 81; Masur, "The Conference of Guayaquil," 218.

303   *bound for history and oblivion:* San Martín received little attention from Latin America in his last years. His fame was largely posthumous. He lived in impecunious circumstances in Europe during his last years and grew blind. When governor of Buenos Aires Juan Manuel Rosas visited him in France in 1849, one year before his death, the Protector could no longer see. R. Rojas, *San Martín*, pp. 338–39.

303   *his animus grew:* Col. Heres, San Martín's aide-de-camp, is quoted to this effect in O'LN, II, 195.

303   *second in command had been stripped:* O'Leary, *Bolívar y la emancipación*, 186.

303   *"His character is essentially":* SB to Santander, Guayaquil, July 29, 1822, SBO, II, 666.

303   *"San Martín has been taking me apart":* SB to Santander, Cuenca, Oct. 27, 1822, ibid., 699.

303   *"The scepter has slipped," etc.:* Guido, 232–43.

303   *In his final address, he assured them:* San Martín, address to congress, in Mitre, *Historia*, VI, 108.

304   *that someday they would find documents:* Guido, quoted in Mitre, *Historia*, VI, 110.

304   *"There is no room":* R. Vargas Ugarte, *Historia general del Perú*, 6 vols. (Barcelona: Milla Batres, 1966), 240.

304   *He boarded a ship:* The ship was *El Belgrano*, which belonged to San Martín. Mitre, *Historia*, VI, 101; also Col. Heres in O'Leary, *Bolívar y la emancipación*, 186.

304   *Pizarro's flag of conquest:* The flag was presented to him by the municipality of Lima on April 2, 1822. This was purportedly the standard Francisco Pizarro had flown when he entered Peru in 1532. San Martín's last will and testament returned the flag to Lima upon his death in 1850, but it was later lost in a riot (R. Rojas, *San Martín*, 349–50). The box in which the flag was presented to him (complete with an engraved dedicatory plaque) turned up empty in Boulogne-sur-Mer, San Martín's last place of residence. Many years later, the box was presented to the cellist Pablo Casals as a gift from French admirers. In 2008, by chance, it was given to me by Casals's widow, Marta Casals Istomin, and her second husband, the pianist Eugene Istomin, close friends of mine.

304   *"My successes in the war":* San Martín to Guido, Dec. 18, 1826. *Documentos del Archivo de San Martín*, VI, 504.

304   *"It is reasonable to say:* San Martín, quoted in Sarmiento, *Obras de D. F. Sarmiento* (Buenos Aires: Mariano Moreno, 1899), 31.

304   *It was because of San Martín, etc.:* Paz Soldán, I, 348.

305   *1,700 of them:* Ibid., II, 56.

305   *pleading for him to return:* R. Rojas, *San Martín*, 300.

305   *"Impossible!," etc.:* San Martín to Riva Agüero, Oct. 23, 1823, San Martín, *San Martín, su Correspondencia*, 338.

306   *No fewer than four delegations:* O'LB, 220–39.

306   *To him, the Colombian constitution was sacred, inviolable:* Ibid., 230.

306   *guns, weapons—all metal:* SB to Santander, Jan. 8, 1823, SBO, II, 715–17.

306   *responded with renewed violence:* O'LB, ibid.

306   *"You cannot imagine," etc.:* Salom to SB, Pasto, Sept. 25, 1823, quoted in Madariaga, 458.

307   *women and children were indiscriminately slaughtered:* O'LB, 227–28.

307   *"The victory at Yacuanquer," etc.:* Sáenz to SB, Dec. 30, 1822, in Lecuna, "Cartas de mujeres," 332.

307   *only four times:* Bernal Medina, *Ruta de Bolívar*, VII, map and graphic.

307   *She was lovesick, etc.:* Murray, *For Glory and Bolívar*, 36.

307   *a fanatical partisan, etc.:* All these traits are amply described in Murray's excellent biography. See also Rumazo González, *Manuela Sáenz.*

307   *capable of mauling his face:* Boussingault, III, 209.

307   *she likely offered to serve as an informant:* Murray, *For Glory and Bolívar*, 36.

307   *"She has a singular configuration":* Boussingault, 206.

308   *Bolívar made it known to Peruvians:* SB to José de la Mar, Loja, Oct. 14, 1822, SBO, II, 696–97; Cuenca, Oct. 28, ibid., 700–2; SB to Riva Agüero, Guayaquil, April 13, 1823, ibid., 735–37.

308   *a man should mind his own house:* SB quotes Santander in SB to Santander, Cuenca, Sept. 29, 1822, ibid., 693.

308   *Santander finally took Bolívar's request:* Santander al Presidente del Senado, Bogotá, May 10, 1823, *Actas y correspondencia* (Bogotá: Biblioteca de la Presidencia de la República de Colombia, 1989), I, Doc. 46, 286.

308   *He sent it six thousand troops:* SB to Riva Agüero, ibid.; SB to Manuel Valdés (commandant of Colombian troops in Peru), Guayaquil, April 14, SBO, II, 737–38.

308   *"The anarchy here is beyond description!":* Sucre to SB, Callao, June 19, 1823, O'L, I, 47.

308   *insisted that he was still in charge:* A good account of this and of Riva Agüero's subsequent treason is in A. Gutiérrez de La Fuente, *Manifiesto que di en Trujillo en 1824* (Lima: Impreso Masias, 1829), 2–5.

309   *"Peru awaits the voice that bonds":* Olmedo to SB, O'Leary, *Bolívar y la emancipación*, 237.

309   *"For a long time now":* Ibid., 238.

309   *before the hour was out:* Ibid.

CHAPTER 13: IN THE EMPIRE OF THE SUN

PAGE

310   Epigraph: *All the power of the supreme being:* San Martín, quoted in Bulnes, *Ultimas campañas*, 282.

310   *"Peru . . . contains two elements":* SB, Contestación de un americano meridional a un caballero de esta isla ("Letter from Jamaica"), Kingston, Sept. 6, 1815, SBO, I, 161–77.

310   *he was reminded of it now:* O'Leary, *Bolívar y la emancipación*, 252.

310   *It was the 1st of September:* Ibid.

310   *the morning air:* The *Chimborazo* sailed along the foggy coast in the morning, approached Callao at noon, dropped anchor at 1 P.M., and at 3 P.M. the procession began. See *Gaceta de Gobierno*, Sept. 3, 1823, *BANH*, no. 104, 321.

310   *Any visitor to the bustling center, etc.:* Liévano Aguirre, 302.

310   *six thousand gilded carriages:* Ibid.

311   *dropped anchor at one o'clock:* O'Leary, *Bolívar y la emancipación*, 252.

311   *procession for the Liberator's long-awaited entrance, etc.:* Proctor, *Narrative of a Journey*, 245; also O'Leary, *Bolívar y la emancipación*, 252.

311   *refrained from saying much of anything:* Proctor, 245.

311   *"You could probably get Congress":* Sucre to SB, Lima, May 15, 1823, in O'L, I, 35–36.

311   *Rumor had it that Bolívar was a mulatto:* Martha Hildebrandt, a Peruvian linguist, notes that SB was called "una pasa" (a raisin), which was a term used by whites of Spanish extraction to refer to blacks. Hildebrandt, *La lengua de Bolívar*, 234. Ricardo Palma also recorded this Peruvian attitude toward Bolívar's swarthiness and curly hair in *Tradiciones peruanas.* To this day, many Peruvians assume Bolívar was part black.

311   *his army was a thundering horde:* Liévano Aguirre, 312.

312   *to address the corruption:* S. Lorente, *Historia del Perú desde la proclamación de la independencia* (Lima: Callé de Camaná, 1867), 188.

312   *Torre Tagle had raided the public treasury:* O'Leary, *Bolívar y la emancipación*, 253; also Paz Soldán, I, 253–57, quoted in Madariaga, 461–62.

312   *He spent those first few days:* Proctor, 246–51.

312   *"The men seem to admire me," etc.:* SB to Santander, Lima, Sept. 11, 1823, SBO, II, 805–8.

312   *"a chamber of horrors":* Lynch, *Simón Bolívar*, 187; "Un campo de Agramante," O'L, XXVIII, 240.

312   *called it "a corpse":* O'Leary, *Bolívar y la emancipación*, 206.

312   *sent Riva Agüero in Trujillo a letter, etc.:* SB to Riva Agüero, Lima, Sept. 4, 1823, SBO, II, 799–801.

312   *"Stop conducting a war":* Ibid.

312   *approached the viceroy himself:* Lecuna, *Crónica*, III, 326–28.

313   *now marched his army south:* SB to Santa Cruz, Lima, Sept. 8, 1823, SBO, II, 801.

313   *He was jealous, etc.:* Lecuna, *Crónica*, III, 309–15.

313   *"I shall always be a foreigner," etc.:* SB to Santander, Lima, Sept. 11, 1823, SBO, II, 805–8.

313   *"If we lose Peru," etc.:* SB to Santander, Lima, Oct. 13, 1823, SBO, II, 821–22.

313   *San Martín's likeness was not on display:* Villanueva, 249.

313   *a point to toast San Martín:* Bulnes, 283; also Larrazábal, *Vida*, II, 212.

314   *two words: attack and unite:* Belaunde, *Bolívar and the Political Thought*, 136.

314   *"The soldiers who have come," etc.:* Paz Soldán, II, 168.

314   *anarchy reigned:* Rivadeneira to San Martín, Lima, July 26, 1823, San Martín, *San Martín, su correspondencia*, 286.

314   *expressing grave doubts:* SB to Santander, Pallasca, Dec. 8, 1823, SBO, II, 845.

314   *a solid battalion of horsemen:* Ibid.

314   *army of twelve thousand:* SB to Santander, Trujillo, Dec. 21, 1823, ibid.

314   *"victory's favorite son":* Larrazábal, *Vida*, II, 212.

315   *thought to be suffering from typhus:* J. Herrera Torres, *Simón Bolívar, vigencia histórica y política* (Caracas: Editiones Bolívar, 1983), II, 558.

315   *from the other side of an enormous curtain:* O'Connor, *Recuerdos*, 54.

315 *"You would not recognize me":* SB to Santander, Pativilca, Jan. 7, 1824, SBO, II, 868–70.

315 *"He was so gaunt and skeletal":* Mosquera, quoted in Bulnes, 461–63.

315 *In France, the revered bishop, etc.:* Bishop de Pradt and SB had already been in correspondence for some time; see SB to Revenga, San Cristóbal, May 20, 1820, *Doctrina*, 126. SB had also mentioned de Pradt's views of America in his "Letter from Jamaica," Sept. 6, 1815. This particular citation refers to de Pradt's publication of *L'Europe et L'Amerique en 1821,* 2 vols. (Paris: Béchet Ainé, 1822).

315 *"When one considers how he began":* de Pradt, II, 329–30. These sentiments were repeated in de Pradt's later volumes, published in 1824.

316 *George Canning, who had made it known:* The Polignac memorandum (a report on Canning's conversation with the French ambassador to Britain, Prince Polignac), Oct. 1823. See Bethell, III, 212. Also Sir Adolphus W. Ward, *The Cambridge History of British Foreign Policy: 1815–1866* (London: Octagon, 1970), 67.

316 *a viceroy's courtesan:* The infamous Peruvian diva, La Perricholi (Micaela Villegas, 1748–1819), who maintained a fourteen-year romance with Viceroy Manuel Amat y Juniet—even had a child by him—and loved to scandalize Lima by appearing at his side. According to Von Hagen, Sáenz was often a guest in La Perricholi's box at the Coliseo de Comedias. Von Hagen, *The Four Seasons of Manuela*, p. 21.

316 *It was a stucco house, etc.:* Details from a personal visit and research by the docent staff, Museo Casa de Bolívar, Plaza Bolívar, Pueblo Libre, Lima, Peru, March 2011.

317 *might even take up arms, etc.:* Inés Quintero, paper presented at the symposium "Creating Freedom in the Americas, 1776–1826," LOC, Nov. 19, 2010.

317 *rarely . . . paid a salary:* Murray, *For Glory and Bolívar*, 37. Murray explains that Sáenz's salary was paid out from SB's account. Since he had refused a salary from Peru, this may well have been from his expense allotment.

317 *a cavalry soldier, a hussar:* SB to O'Leary, Lima, Sept. 28, 1823, Alvarez Saá, *Manuela*, 76.

317 *When she read of it in a routine report:* Sáenz to SB, Lima, Feb. 27, 1824, ibid., 77.

317 *called on President Torre Tagle to negotiate:* SB to Col. Heres, Pativilca, Jan. 9, 1824, SBO, II, 872–76.

317 *a title he found odious:* SB to the Peruvian Congress, in Larrazábal, *Vida*, II, 235. "I would have preferred never to have seen Peru again—preferred even our defeat—to the frightening title of Dictator."

317 *still hallowed by a republican aura:* Wu, 14.

317 *On February 27, he and his top ministers, etc.:* Sáenz to SB, Lima, Feb. 27, 1824, Alvarez Saá, 77. Also O'Leary, *Bolívar y la emancipación*, 289. Joining Torre Tagle were the famous Diego Aliaga (whose ancestor had come to Peru with Pizarro) and Minister of War Berindoaga.

317 *including Manuela Sáenz:* Heres to SB, Chanquillo, Feb. 13, 1824, O'L, V, 67.

318 *He wrote to his generals, etc.:* SB to Gen. Salom, Pativilca, Feb. 10, 1824, SBO, II, 916–18; SB to Santander, Feb. 10, 1824, ibid., 918–21; SB to Sucre, Feb. 13, 1824, ibid., 921–26; SB to Gen. La Mar, Feb. 14, 1824, ibid., 926–27.

318 *stronger ties to Spain:* S. O'Phelan, "Sucre en el Perú," *La independencia en el Perú: De los Borbones a Bolívar* (Lima: Pont. Univ. Católica del Perú, 2001), 379–406.

318   *mixed-race ruffians:* Ibid.

318   *They had learned to be patriots:* The historian is Morote, *Bolívar: Libertador y enemigo no. 1 del Perú*, 48.

319   *"I'm through making promises":* SB to Santander, Pativilca, Jan. 23, 1824, SBO, II, 887–89.

319   *"itinerant government":* SB to Santander, Pativilca, Jan. 25, 1824, SBSW, II, 433–35.

319   *full battle plan for General Sucre:* SB to Sucre, Pativilca, Jan. 26, 1824, SBO, II, 896–901.

319   *"Send troops and we'll win":* SB to Santander, Pativilca, Feb. 10, 1824, ibid., and Trujillo, March 16, 1824, ibid.

319   *turned Trujillo into a teeming arsenal, etc.:* O'Leary *Bolívar y la emancipación*, 296.

319   *Silver was seized from church:* SB to Sucre, Trujillo, March 21, 1824, SBO, II, 939–42.

319   *more than 100,000 pesos, etc.:* Morote, 57.

320   *ordered seamstresses, etc.:* O'Leary, *Bolívar y la emancipación*, 296. Also Lecuna, *Crónica*, III, 396.

320   *cattle necessary to feed his troops:* SB to La Mar, Huaraz, June 14, 1824, SBO, II, 984–85.

320   *Lambayeque and Piura, etc.:* Ibid., 58.

320   *Panama, greater Guatemala, Mexico:* SB to Sucre, Trujillo, April 9, 1824, SBSW, II, 444–47; also SB to Heres, Huamachuco, April 23, 1824, SBO, II, 958–59.

320   *as if Mars had sprung:* O'Leary, *Bolívar y la emancipación*, 297.

320   *an army of eight thousand:* Lynch, *Simón Bolívar*, 191.

320   *In April, it became evident, etc.:* SB to Heres, Otuzco, April 15, 1824, SBO, II, 953–54.

321   *Bolívar eventually wrote to Olañeta:* SB to Olañeta, Huaraz, May 21, 1824, ibid., 975–77.

321   *"For God's sake, send me":* SB to Pérez, Huamachuco, May 6, 1824, ibid., 963–65.

321   *spread out a map of Peru, etc.:* O'Connor, 67.

321   *Valdés and five thousand men:* Lecuna, *Crónica*, III, 402, 404. The royalists had 20,000 troops in Peru. Sixteen thousand were active soldiers; the rest were guarding garrisons around the area.

321   *"As far as I can see":* O'Connor, 68.

321   *"This youngster has just given us":* Ibid.

321   *rich fields of sugarcane, etc.:* Paulding, 48.

322   *only a day's ride away:* Murray, *For Glory and Bolívar*, 38.

322   *"an irresistibly fresh doll," etc.:* From the great nineteenth-century Peruvian essayist-historian Ricardo Palma, *Mis últimas tradiciones peruanas* (Barcelona: Editorial Maucci, 1908), 146.

322   *"You will note that though I beg":* SB to Santander, Huamachuco, May 6, 1824, SBO, II, 966–68.

322   *regards to the unattainable Bernardina:* Ibid.

322   *the wittiest, most profoundly human:* Madariaga, 479.

322   *"The general has written me only twice," etc.:* Sáenz to Santana, Huamachuco, May 28, 1824, Lecuna, "Cartas de mujeres," 332.

323   *"My sir," etc.:* Sáenz to SB, Huamachuco, May 26, 1824, *Las más hermosas cartas* (Caracas: Editorial El Perro y La Rana, 2006), 35.

323   *they reunited at the end of June:* Murray, *For Glory and Bolívar*, 38.

323   *seventy-four years later:* Palma, *Tradiciones*, 162 fn.

323   *"So, how is Bolívar's old lady?":* Ibid.

323 *the equivalent of $12 billion:* Cerro de Pasco had produced £170 million by 1803. According to http://www.parliament.uk/documents/commons/lib/research/rp2002/rp02-044.pdf the value today would be over $12 billion. Report of the Commissioner of General Land Office, for the year 1867 (Washington: GPO, 1867); *The Colliery Engineer*, 27 (1907), 134; Dan De Quille, *History of the Big Bonanza* (San Francisco: Bancroft, 1876), 463.

323 *But Sucre had prepared the way, etc.:* Miller, II, 122–28; O'Connor, 66–68.

324 *strange concert of anxious calls:* Miller, II, 122–28.

324 *Following behind them, were the Rabonas, etc.:* Flora Tristan wrote about the Rabonas in her *Peregrinations of a Pariah*, 179–81. Also see A. García Camba, *Memorias del General Camba*, Rufino Blanco-Fombona (Bib. Ayacucho, 1916), VII, 205; R. Gil Montero, "Las guerras de independencia en los andes meridionales," *Memoria Americana*, no. 14 (Ciudad Autónoma de Buenos Aires, 2006), online version ISSN 1851–3751.

324 *a brilliantly prepared army:* Miller, II, 122–28; O'Connor, 64–67; O'Leary, *Bolívar y la emancipación*, 305.

324 *Bolívar gloried in the sight, etc.:* Masur, *Simón Bolívar*, 530.

324 *nine thousand disciplined soldiers:* Miller, II, 122–28; O'Leary, *Bolívar y la emancipación*, 297.

324 *from as far away as Caracas, etc.:* Miller, II, 122–28. O'Connor, 64–67.

324 *six thousand cattle:* Miller, II, 125.

324 *the finest patriot force, etc.:* Masur, *Simón Bolívar*, 530.

324 *delighted in sitting with his officers:* Paulding, 53–60.

324 *His two thousand men, etc.:* Lecuna, *Crónica*, III, 410.

325 *well regimented, well armed, etc.:* Miller, II, 125.

325 *only six hundred, etc.:* Wu, 14; O'Connor, 85.

325 *assuring him that Bolívar was no threat:* Valdés to Canterac, Cochabamba, May 3–4, 1824, *Documentos para la historia separatista del Perú por el conde de Torata, nieto del General Valdés*, IV (Madrid: Minuesa, 1898), 291–94.

325 *Sucre's minions swarmed through:* Miller, II, 128.

325 *fallen into a great slumber:* Ibid., 128–29.

325 *Clearly, he was confident:* Lecuna, *Crónica*, III, 405.

325 *On the crisp, clear morning:* Miller, II, 128–29.

325 *reviewed 7,700 troops:* O'Leary, *Bolívar y la emancipación*, 305. General Miller (II, 128) cites 9,000, but he is probably including the 1,500 guerrillas, whom O'Leary mentions, and who may not have arrived until later.

325 *on a towering mesa, etc.:* Miller, II, 128–29.

326 *"Soldiers! You are about to complete":* O'Leary, *Bolívar y la emancipación*, 306.

326 *The air was filled, etc.:* Miller, II, 129.

326 *a glimpse of one of Canterac's divisions, etc.:* López, 115; Miller, II, 130.

326 *quivering for a fight:* Miller, II, 130–1.

326 *reconnaissance with thirteen hundred troops, etc.:* Lecuna, *Crónica*, III, 414.

326 *with the chill of surprise:* A. García Camba, *Memorias*, II (Madrid: Hortelano, 1846), 254–55.

326 *Bolívar and nine hundred horsemen:* Lecuna, *Crónica*, III, 415.

326 *looking to provoke the Spanish general to battle:* Ibid., 412.

326 *he decided to circle the lake:* Canterac to Viceroy La Serna, quoted in O'Leary, *Bolívar*

y la emancipación, 312. This was revealed in a letter intercepted by the patriots. There is no reason to doubt Canterac's word that he was after the patriot rear guard, but O'Leary adds that the Spanish general was rushing south to block SB from marching on Jauja, since they appeared to be going in that direction.

326 *battle at five o'clock:* Santa Cruz, Parte oficial de la batalla de Junín, in O'L, XLIV, 422.

326 *fought entirely with swords and lances, etc.:* O'Leary, *Bolívar y la emancipación*, 308.

326 *directed the veteran general Miller, etc.:* Lecuna, *Crónica*, III, 415–19.

327 *lance was fourteen feet long:* Miller, II, 133.

327 *"made the earth tremble":* O'Connor, 76.

327 *darken the sky an hour later:* Miller, II, 133. Miller claims the action lasted three quarters of an hour. Larrazábal (*Vida*, III, 253) says it took an hour. Masur (*Simón Bolívar*, 532) cites one and a half hours.

327 *the effects of high-altitude combat:* The plains of Junín are 13,232 feet above sea level. *Encyclopaedia Britannica*, 21 (1911), 267.

327 *could not have gone on much longer, etc.:* O'Connor, 76–77, for subsequent details.

327 *"Victory!":* Madariaga, 482.

327 *sent squadrons of sharpshooters:* Ibid.

327 *José Palacios, the loyal manservant:* Ibid.

327 *"The brilliant skirmish of Junín":* Larrazábal, *Vida*, II, 253.

328 *"Our losses may have been few in number," etc.:* Canterac to Rodil, O'Leary, *Bolívar y la emancipación*, 312–13.

328 *shut himself up in the fortress of Callao, etc.:* Baralt and Díaz, II, 134.

328 *collected all the equipment, etc.:* Larrazábal, *Vida*, II, 254.

328 *had burned whole villages:* Gen. Miller to Sucre, O'L, XXII, 417; Lecuna, *Crónica*, III, 409–11.

328 *executed hundreds, etc.:* Larrazábal, *Vida*, II, 255.

328 *"They were Caligula; we were Caesar":* Santander, "El General Simón Bolívar en campaña," *Gazeta de Santa Fé*, Oct. 4, 1819, JCBL.

328 *installed municipal governments, etc.:* Bulnes, 547–48.

328 *he threatened to shoot councilors:* Ibid. Also Madariaga, 484.

328 *Soldiers who looted, etc.:* Madariaga, 484.

328 *"You're out of your mind if you think":* Villanueva, 151.

329 *There was no town in the area:* Bulnes, 549.

329 *while his army rested:* Larrazábal, *Vida*, II, also SB to Sucre, Huancarama, Sept. 28, 1824, SBO, II, 993–94.

329 *dozens of villages:* See the list of these in SBO, II, 991–93.

329 *she settled for a while:* Murray, *For Glory and Bolívar*, 39. A number of historians—Rumazo González, Alvarez Saá, Claire Brewster—have claimed that Sáenz marched with SB over Cerro de Pasca and fought in the Battle of Junín. But there appears to be no basis for that claim. Murray and many serious Latin American scholars hold that the legend (and material that supports it) is apocryphal.

329 *The rain came earlier than usual, etc.:* Bulnes, 551.

329 *he had been stripped of all his powers, etc.:* Lecuna, *Crónica*, III, 436–37.

330 *"man of laws":* SB to Santander, Lima, Feb. 9, 1825, SBO, II, 1044–46. "You are the man of laws and Sucre is the man of war." Also Monsalve, *El ideal político del Libertador*, 56.

330 *"Without a law expressly passed":* Santander to SB, Bogotá, Feb. 6, 1824, O'L, III, 137.

330 *Some congressmen had even begun to object, etc.:* This growing resentment was eventually described in the letter from Santander to SB, Bogotá, May 6, 1825, O'L, ibid., 168–76.

330 *news to Sucre in two memoranda:* Heres to Sucre, Oct. 24, 1824 (two letters with this date), O'L, XXII, 525–26. Heres was Bolívar's secretary general.

330 *to be destroyed:* Lecuna, *Crónica*, III, 436–37.

330 *to separate the Liberator from it:* Heres to Sucre, ibid. (the first, personal letter).

330 *submitted a heated protest:* Sucre to Heres, O'L, XXII, 542. Also Lecuna, *Crónica*, III, 437–38.

331 *correspondence was clipped:* See SB to Santander, Chancay, Nov. 13, 1824, SBO, II, 1008–9.

331 *more republican now:* This sentiment was surely aided by Lima's despotic royalist commandant Ramírez, "the Robespierre of Peru," who sat in the Convent of La Merced and entertained himself by shaving the head of every young male passerby he suspected of being a republican. Liévano Aguirre, 342.

331 *imposed a siege, etc.:* Lecuna, *Crónica*, III, 440.

331 *"serve as a brain trust":* SB to the governments of Colombia, Mexico, Argentina, Chile, and Guatemala, Lima, Dec. 7, 1824, SBO, II, 1016–18.

331 *South America did not need a burly, etc.:* Arciniegas, *Bolívar y la revolución*, 133–36; A. Lleras Camargo, *El primer gobierno del Frente Nacional*, II (Bogotá: Imprenta Nacional, 1960), 21.

331 *he had no intention of relying:* Arcieniegas, *Bolívar y la revolución*, 133–36; Lleras Camargo, 21.

332 *Nine thousand royalists:* López, 141; Larrazábal, *Vida*, II, 268.

332 *not worried by those maneuvers, etc.:* Sucre's report to the Minister of War, Dec. 11, 1824, quoted in O'Leary, *Bolívar y la emancipación*, 354.

332 *in a torrential rain, etc.:* Miller, II, 158–59, and for subsequent details.

332 *frantic defections occurred:* Ibid., 10, 174.

333 *His notion was to keep the Spaniards, etc.:* O'Connor, 100.

333 *pressed close to the foot of Cundurcunca, etc.:* López, 134.

333 *exactly where Bolívar would have wanted:* SB to Sucre, quoted in Masur, *Simón Bolívar*, 536.

333 *brought a resplendent sun, etc.:* López, 137; Miller, II, 167.

333 *according to one soldier:* López, 137.

333 *a scruffy behemoth of dirt, etc.:* Ibid., 138.

333 *the sound of cornets and drums, etc.:* Ibid., 143.

333 *no choice for them but to win:* Ibid., 141; O'Connor, 99.

333 *"Soldiers! On your efforts":* O'Connor, 99.

334 *At eight o'clock, as the sun, etc.:* López, 143–44.

334 *as one chronicler put it:* Ibid.

334 *General Monet asked Córdova, etc.:* López, 145–50, and for subsequent details.

334 *helmets glinting in the sun:* Miller, II, 174.

334 *dark, somber overcoats:* Madariaga, 488.

334 *"Horsemen! Lancers! What you see," etc.:* López, 151.

334   *a young Spanish brigadier was first to attack:* This was Col. Joaquín Rubín de Celis, my great-great-grandfather. My great-grandfather Pedro Cisneros was fighting him on the patriot side. (See Acknowledgments.)

334   *splitting their formation, etc.:* López, 154.

334   *"Soldiers! Man your arms!":* Miller, II, 168.

334   *snatching their silver helmets:* Ibid., 174.

335   *By mid-afternoon, etc.:* Ibid., 172.

335   *three thousand royalists were taken:* Lecuna, *Crónica*, III, 463.

335   *found him by chance in one of the huts, etc.:* Miller, II, 176. Apart from his gallantry to La Serna, Miller invited Canterac to bed down in his hut, along with other officers. Canterac talked into the night, saying: "General Miller—General Miller—all this appears to be a dream! How strange is the fortune of war! Who would have said twenty-four hours ago, that I should have been your guest? but it cannot be helped: the harassing war is now over, and, to tell you the truth, we were all heartily tired of it." Ibid., 178.

335   *The dead amounted to, etc.:* Lecuna, *Crónica*, III, 463.

335   *The terms Sucre offered, etc.:* Ibid.; Sucre to SB, Dec. 10, 1824, quoted in O'Leary, *Bolívar y la emancipación*, 364–67.

335   *His heavy wool socks, etc.:* Bulnes, 614.

335   *"I drink . . . to the man":* Ibid.

335   *ambushed and killed by Indians:* Miller, II, 170 fn. By Indians of the Huando tribe.

335   *"The battle for Peru is complete":* Sucre to the Minister of War, Dec. 11, 1824, O'Leary, *Bolívar y la emancipación*, 364–67.

336   *the Pandora's box that Peru had become:* O'Leary, *Junín y Ayacucho*, 211.

336   *"Victory! Victory! Victory!":* Blanco-Fombona in a footnote to the 1915 edition of O'Leary's *Bolívar y la Emancipación*, 368.

CHAPTER 14: THE EQUILIBRIUM OF THE UNIVERSE

PAGE

337   Epigraph: *"My hope is that our republics":* SB to Hipólito Unanue, Plata, Nov. 25, 1825, O'L, XXX, 154–56.

337   *"to General Simon Bolívar," etc.: National Intelligencer,* Jan. 3, 1825; quoted in R. V. Remini, *Henry Clay* (New York: Norton, 1991), 257.

337   *Not Alexander, not Hannibal, etc.:* Pérez Silva, *Bolívar, de Cartagena a Santa Marta,* 18 (Introduction). And for subsequent comparisons.

338   *"European ambition forced the yoke": Gaceta de Caracas,* No. 30, Dec. 31, 1813, quoted in Larrazábal, *Vida,* I, 251.

338   *"this splendid victory is due entirely":* SB, Decreto, Dec. 27, 1824, O'L, XXII, 605–6.

338   *He tendered his resignation:* Dec. 22, 1824, cited in Lecuna, *Catálogo,* III, 368.

338   *planned to leave Colombia someday:* SB to Santander, Lima, Dec. 20, 1824, SBO, II, 1022–26; also SB to Santander, Lima, Jan. 23, 1825, ibid., 1040–41.

338   *assembly fell into a stunned silence, etc.:* Lynch, *Simón Bolívar,* 194.

338   *"the greatest man and most extraordinary":* Hamilton, I, 230.

339   *"will be the day of my glory":* DOC, IX, 480.

339   *presented him with a gift of one million pesos, etc.:* O'L, XXVIII, 340–43.

339   *Monteagudo, whose agile mind:* Monteagudo, *Ensayo sobre la necesidad de una federación general entre los estados hispano-americanos y plan de su organización* (Lima: J. González, 1825; uncompleted and posthumously published.)

339   *found facedown on a street, etc.:* A. Íñiguez Vicuña, *Vida de Don Bernardo Monteagudo* (Santiago: Imprenta Chilena, 1867), 171.

339   *might be part of a royalist plot:* SB to Santander, Lima, Feb. 9, 1825, SBO, II, 1044–46.

339   *a black cook, who worked in the kitchen:* Íñiguez Vicuña, 173–74.

339   *in private, in a dimly lit room:* Mosquera, Popayán, Sept. 20, 1878, quoted in Ricardo Palma, *Cachivaches* (Lima: Torres Aguirre, 1900), 233. Mosquera would later become president of Colombia.

339   *had paid him 200 pesos:* Ibid.

339   *The Liberator was flabbergasted:* Ibid.

340   *a Peruvian general had poisoned him, etc.:* Mosquera, 233–34.

340   *It was a murky chain of events:* SB himself thought it might be a plot undertaken by the Holy Alliance: SB to Santander, Feb. 9, SBO, II, 1044–46. Others have posited that it was a Masonic intrigue, since Sánchez Carrión was leader of the secret society that had pledged to exile Monteagudo from Peru and kill him if he ever returned. Indeed, Sánchez Carrión had written an article for *El Tribuno*, saying that every Peruvian had a right to exterminate Monteagudo: Ricardo Palma, *Mis últimas tradiciones peruanas* (Barcelona: Editorial Maucci, 1908), 541–70.

340   *she scandalized Lima society:* Murray, *For Glory and Bolívar*, 40.

340   *"more jealous than a Portuguese":* Ibid., 33–34; Sáenz to Thorne, Lecuna [n.p., n.d.] Archivo del Libertador, Caracas, 1961, roll 34; also Lecuna, "Papeles de Manuela Sáenz," 501.

340   *he swallowed his pride and begged, etc.:* Boussingault, 208; Murray, *For Glory and Bolívar*, 33–34.

341   *"No, no, no, hombre!":* Sáenz to Thorne, Lecuna, 501.

341   *Even in a city where women:* Murray, *For Glory and Bolívar*, 21.

341   *"At times she behaved like a grand lady":* Boussingault, 205–11.

342   *was infatuated with Manuela:* Lecuna claims that Boussingault was "madly in love" with her. Lecuna, *Catálogo*, III, 219.

342   *Bolívar didn't much care:* Boussingault, 208.

342   *filled with tenderness:* These are too many to cite, but see especially SB to Sáenz, La Plata, Nov. 26, 1824, O'LN, II, 376–77.

342   *Far from spurring an era of creativity:* I owe this insight to Colombian historian and diplomat (president of the United Nations General Assembly) Indalecio Liévano Aguirre, *Bolívar*, 351–52. See also O'Leary, *Bolívar y la emancipación*, 416.

342   *Upper Peru:* A counterintuitive geographic term. Although it suggests north, it is the opposite: it lay south of Peru as we know it, and north of Chile.

342   *an astounding twenty-one miles a day:* O'Leary, *Bolívar y la emancipación*, 410.

342   *a sight that seldom fails to move:* Tristan, *Peregrinations of a Pariah*, 85. Tristan, mother of Paul Gauguin, whose parents were acquaintances of Bolívar's, made a similar trip eight years later.

343   *dissipate the moment he was gone:* Madariaga, 508–9.

343   *returned to South America after decades of exile:* Simón Rodríguez arrived in Guayaquil in 1824, Rodríguez to SB, Guayaquil, O'L, IX, 511.

343 *"The opus is finished"*: San Martín to D. Vicente Chilavert, Brussels, Jan. 1, 1825, San Martín, *San Martín, su correspondencia*, 172.

343 *gave Bolívar a welcome, etc.*: O'Leary, *Bolívar y la emancipación*, 415–17.

343 *Gold and silver ornaments, etc.*: Ibid., 417.

343 *a fierce original, etc.*: SB to Olmedo, Cuzco, June 27, 1825, SBO, III, 1121–23.

344 *He was presented with a crown, etc.*: O'Leary, *Bolívar y la emancipación*, 418

344 *he sent the crown to Sucre, etc.*: Lecuna, *Catálogo*, III, 370–71. Sucre eventually gave the crown to the national museum of Colombia: *Cuerpo de leyes de la República de Colombia*, Jan. 30, 1826 (Caracas: Imprenta Espinal, 1840), 421.

344 *eliminated all titles of nobility, etc.*: O'Leary, *Bolívar y la emancipación*, 418–22.

344 *"I want to do all that is possible"*: AV to Santander, Cuzco, June 28, 1825, SBO, III, 1125–27.

344 *he ordered roads built, etc.*: O'Leary, *Bolívar y la emancipación*, 418–22.

344 *something repellent about Peru*: "The Venezuelans are saints in comparison. The people of Quito and Peru have this in common: They are vicious unto infamy and low to the extreme." To be fair, this was written while he was still emerging from illness in Pativilca, but his antipathy to Peru is evident throughout his correspondence. SB to Santander, Pativilca, Jan. 9, 1824, O'L, XXIX, 376. See also the account in Paulding, *Un rasgo*, 58–59: "He condemned Peruvians in general: he called them cowards, claimed that as a people they had no manly virtues. In sum, he made no effort to mask his bitter disdain."

344 *at the hands of his own men, etc.*: L. Lumbreras, *Historia de América andina* (Quito: Libresa, 1999), IV, 124 fn; also Morote, 164.

344 *a fraction of his original force*: Lecuna, *Crónica*, III, 497; see also O'Leary, *Bolívar y la emancipación*, 430.

345 *and the old viceroyalty of Buenos Aires began*: This was actually the viceroyalty of Río de la Plata, ruled out of Buenos Aires.

345 *From Pichincha to Potosí*: Larrazábal, *Vida*, II, 273.

345 *Liberator was handed another crown*: O'Leary, *Bolívar y la emancipación*, 455.

345 *"This belongs to the true victor"*: Ibid.

345 *to deliver the region to war-torn Argentina, etc.*: SB to Santander, Feb. 18, 1825, SBO, II, 1047–49.

346 *Bolívar soon disabused him*: O'Leary, *Bolívar y la emancipación*, 435–42.

346 *laws that were clearly arbitrary and racist*: Lynch, *Simón Bolívar*, 199.

346 *delighted with the news*: SB to Santander, La Paz, Aug. 19, 1825, SBO, III, 1169–70.

347 *"If we wait any longer"*: SB to the Governments of the Republic of Colombia, Mexico, the River Plate, Chile, and Guatemala, Lima, Dec. 7, 1824, SBO, II, 1016–18.

347 *Bolívar noted a viral dread*: SB to Santander, Lima, Feb. 18, 1825, SBO, II, 1047–49.

347 *"We slip in between," etc.*: H. Temperley, "The Later American Policy of George Canning," *American History Review*, XI, 781, quoted in Whitaker, 584.

347 *toyed with the notion of taking his liberating army*: SB to Santander, Potosí, Oct. 10, 1825, SBO, III, 1193–98.

347 *"The demon of glory will carry us"*: SB to Santander, La Paz, Sept. 8, 1825, SBO, III, 1179–80.

348 *Sucre had cried like a baby*: L. Diez de Medina, *El Libertador en Bolivia* (La Paz: Ministerio de Defensa Nacional, 1954), XXXIII, 49.

348 *leapt in the air with joy:* Ibid.

348 *But when Santander wrote back:* Santander to SB, Bogotá, Jan. 21, 1826, O'L, III, 235.

348 *"The miserable state of our financial affairs":* Ibid.

348 *"man of laws":* SB to Santander, Lima, Feb. 9, 1825, SBO, II, 1044–46.

348 *an agitated letter from Páez:* Páez to SB, Caracas, Oct. 1, 1825, SBO, III, 1292–94.

349 *"You cannot imagine how ruinous":* Ibid.

349 *brutal methods of recruitment:* Gaceta de Colombia, Aug. 27, 1826, no. 254, "Parte no oficial," 3 (1826–28), 358. Also Páez, *Autobiografía*, 288–92.

349 *royalists in Havana were poised to attack:* Ibid., 284.

349 *as Napoleon had returned to France:* Ibid.

349 *"Colombia is not France":* SB to Páez, Magdalena, March 6, 1826, SBO, III, 1290–91.

349 *"Tell them you will be Liberator":* María Antonia to SB, Caracas, Oct. 30, 1825, SB, *Obras completas*, II, 311–13.

349 *Sucre told him the same thing:* Sucre to SB, Chuquisaca, April 27, 1826, O'L, I, 314–17.

350 *"If principles of liberty," etc.:* Reported in Rickets to Canning, Lima, April, 25, 1826, British National Archives, PRO/FO, 61–67, quoted in Lynch, *Simón Bolívar*, 202.

351 *rendered the position headless and harmless:* SB, Message to the Congress of Bolivia, Lima, May 25, 1826, SB, *Selected Writings*, II, 596–602.

351 *"we shall avoid elections":* Ibid.

351 *"Regular elections are essential":* SB, Address, Inauguration of the Congress of Angostura, Feb. 15, 1819, DOC, VII, 141ff.

351 *"ark of the covenant":* SB to Sucre, Magdalena, May 12, 1826, SBO, III, 1328–32.

351 *courier who had delivered Páez's message:* This was Antonio Leocadio Guzmán, a member of the Caracas Club, which together with Páez was campaigning to have SB crowned king. Bushnell, *Simón Bolívar*, 170–71.

351 *"mischievous excess of popular power":* Rickets to Canning, Lima, May 30, 1826, British National Archives.

351 *In South America, opinions were divided:* O'LB, 315–16. (In O'Leary, *Bolívar y la emancipación*, 604–5.)

352 *"liberal and popular, strong":* O'LB, 316.

352 *"absurd, a dangerous novelty":* Monsalve, *El ideal político*, 54. For Santander's duplicity in saying one thing to SB and another to his cohort in Bogotá, see Masur, *Simón Bolívar*, 616; and Rourke, 314.

352 *he was assailing the constitution openly:* La Gaceta de Colombia, Oct. 22, 1826; G. Hernández de Alba and F. Lozano y Lozano, *Documentos sobre el Doctor Vicente Azuero* (Bogotá, 1944), VI, 183. The piece was written by Azuero, but the printing was paid out of Santander's pocket and it was considered to be essentially his views. Bushnell, *The Santander Regime in Gran Colombia*, 336.

352 *not one patriot publicly objected:* O'LB, 319.

352 *it did so with great caution:* Ibid.

352 *"We need to take up the work of founding":* O'L, XXXI, 35.

352 *"We will show Europe":* Ibid.

352 *Some have gone so far as to claim:* Fabio Lozano, *El maestro del Libertador* (Paris: Ollendorff, 1914), 96; Gil Fortoul, 349; Jorge Vejarano, *Simón Bolívar* (Bogotá: Iqueima,

1951), 516; Victor Andrés Belaunde, "La constitución boliviana," BANH, XI, no. 44, 377; Masur, *Simón Bolívar*, 561.

352   *expressly forbidden his family:* SB to María Antonia, Magdalena, July 10, 1826, SBO, I, 13.

352   *averse to the quotidian business:* SB to Santander, Magdalena, June 23, 1826, SBO, III, 1383–85.

353   *yearned to be the father of a federation:* SB to Santander, Chuquisaca, Nov. 11, 1825, SBO, III, 1236–39; and Plata, Nov. 26, 1825, ibid., 1246–47.

353   *You rule Colombia, etc.:* SB to Santander, Chuquisaca, ibid.

353   *could not function as a single, integrated country:* SB, "Letter from Jamaica," Kingston, Sept. 6, 1815, SBSW, I, 103–22.

353   *Spain had never encouraged camaraderie:* The notion that the lack of relations between colonies was eventually lethal to the unity of South America is elaborated in Belaunde, *Bolívar and the Political Thought*, 163; and Basadre, *Historia de la república del Perú*, Introduction.

353   *a grand fraternity, bound by common laws, etc.:* SB, *Un pensamiento sobre el congreso de Panama*, Archivo del Libertador, Caracas, published by Lecuna in Jan. 1916 for the Second Pan-American Congress in Washington.

353   *the Federation of the Andes:* O'Leary, *Bolívar y la emancipación*, 583–87.

353   *Although each nation would remain a separate entity, etc.:* SB to Sucre, Magdalena, May 12, 1826, SBO, III, 1328–32; also Bolívar to La Fuente, Magdalena, May 12, 1826, ibid., 1332–34.

353   *That face would be embodied in a shared constitution, etc.:* SB to La Fuente, Lima, June 17, 1826, O'L, XXXI, 228–30.

353   *not to invite Haiti, Brazil, etc.:* SB to Santander, Arequipa, June 6, 1825, SB, *Cartas: Santander-Bolívar*, IV, 388.

354   *"There will come a time," etc.:* Count of Aranda to King Carlos III, quoted in *Historia general de España y de sus Indias*, VI (Habana: Librería de la Enciclopédia, 1863), 308. Aranda's next sentence was almost prophetic: "First, she will grab the Floridas."

354   *Bolívar had decided not to attend:* SB to Santander, Lima, June 28, 1825, SB, *Obras*, SBO, II, 1125–27.

354   *"a horror of too early a union":* Official letter from the government of Argentina to Santander, quoted in Liévano, 408.

355   *Some were ailing, others fearful, etc.:* Briceño Méndez, Report on the Congress of Panama, Bogotá, Aug. 15, 1826, O'L, XXVIII, 572.

CHAPTER 15: ERA OF BLUNDERS

PAGE

356   Epigraph: *"We have arrived at an era of blunders":* Briceño Méndez to SB, on board the *Macedonia*, July 26, 1826, O'L, VIII, 208–13.

356   *"The institution was admirable":* SB to Páez, Lima, Aug. 8, 1826, O'L, XXVIII, 665.

356   *accusations flowed:* One notable critic was a former officer of San Martín, Federico Brandsen, whose "To the Peruvian Nation" was printed in Lima (1825, JCBL) and distributed widely.

356 *"but he is working with a randomness":* Anonymous, "Ensayo sobre la conducta de General Bolívar," reprint of nos. 11, 13, and 14 of *Duende de Buenos Aires* (Santiago: Imprenta de la Independencia, 1826), published in *Noticias del Perú*, vol. 9, JCBL.

356 *one writer fretted:* Brandsen, "To the Peruvian Nation."

357 *people of Lima began to grumble openly:* Restrepo, III, quoted in Madariaga, 521.

357 *throw off the ruler's mantle:* In a broadside to all Peruvians, SB called it the "odious" mantle. Cuartel de Trujillo, March 11, 1824, SB, *Discursos*, 264.

357 *"without so much as a grain of sand":* Ibid.

357 *"I am a foreigner":* SB, speech before congress, Lima, Feb. 10, 1825, ibid., 112.

357 *Bolívar approved the sentences:* SB to Unanúe, Plata, Nov. 25, 1825, SBO, III, 1244–45.

357 *"Sambo," they called him:* I know this from my own Peruvian grandparents, who heard it from older generations; but it is also mentioned in Madariaga, 16; also Hildebrandt, 234; and Gott, *Húgo Chávez and the Bolivarian Revolution* (London: Verso, 2005), 91.

358 *"Viva Bolívar! Viva the Republic!":* *Revista de Madrid*, Segunda Serie, IV (Madrid: Imprenta de Vicente de Lalama, 1840), 12.

358 *He begged Bolívar to return:* Santander to SB, Bogotá, March 30, 1825, SB, *Cartas de Bolívar: 1825–1827*, 226.

358 *He then went about giving away every gift:* O'Leary, *Bolívar y la emancipación*, 610.

358 *the jewel-encrusted gold sword:* SB's sword ("Espada del Perú"), which was eventually inherited by his sisters (Last Will and Testament, SBSW, II, 766–68), was appropriated by Hugo Chávez, taken from its display case in Caracas's Banco Central, and removed to the government palace in Feb. 2010. *El Comercio*, Peru, June 5, 2010.

358 *The one million dollars:* Colección de leyes, decretos y ordenes publicadas en el Perú, 1820–1840, VII (Lima: Masías, 1845), Art. 8, Feb. 12, 1825, 486.

358 *had never been produced:* Solicitudes de los herederos del Libertador, DOC, X, 231.

358 *the liberator to whom Peru would pay a life pension:* San Martín's regular pension (15,000 pesos) appears in Peruvian government documents, some of which were regularly published in the *Gaceta del Gobierno*: *Gaceta*, II, nos. 7–6 (Jan. 24, 1825), 29. The pension was passed into law by the Peruvian congress on Feb. 12, 1825 (the same day one million pesos was offered to SB and rejected), and is clearly referred to in Juan Oviedo, ed., *Colección de leyes, decretos y ordenes*, 16 (Lima: Ministerio de Hacienda y Comercio, 1872), 352. Ironically, Peru and Chile paid San Martín pensions; Argentina, his homeland, did not.

358 *if he could get those two republics to unite:* SB to Santander, Lima, Aug. 17, 1826, SB, *Cartas: Santander–Bolívar*, VI, 19.

358 *As he had said many times:* SB to Santander, Lima, Feb. 9, 1825; Ocaña, May 8, 1825; Cuzco, July 10, 1825; La Paz, Sept. 8, 1825; Potosí, Oct. 27, 1825; all in SB, *Cartas: Santander–Bolívar*, IV, V.

359 *He was prepared to leave them to Santander:* SB to Santander, Potosí, Oct. 27, 1825, ibid.

359 *She had long since moved out:* William Tudor to U.S. Secretary of State Henry Clay, Lima, March 23, 1827, Dispatches from U.S. consuls in Lima, 1823–54; referred to in Murray, *For Glory and Bolívar*, 41, 173.

359 *famously uninhibited Jonatás:* Boussingault, 215–16.

359 *Bolívar thought it best to end the affair:* SB to Sáenz, Ica, April 20, 1825, SBO, III, 1089–90.

359 *It is possible, too, that Thorne persuaded him:* Murray, *For Glory and Bolívar*, 40.

359 *"Dear beautiful and good Manuela":* SB to Sáenz, April 20, 1825, SBO, III, 1089–90.

359 *"the ill-treatment":* SB to Sáenz, Potosí, Oct. 13, 1825, ibid., 1204.

359 *"What you say about your husband":* SB to Sáenz, Plata, Nov. 26 [1825], ibid., 1246.

359 *"how to cut a knot":* The reference is obviously to the Gordian knot, which was said to be too intricate to untie. Alexander the Great cut it with his sword.

360 *doe-eyed American Jeannette Hart:* From *Family Histories* (a genealogy of several Connecticut families, including the MacCurdys and Harts), 3 vols. (privately published by E. E. Salisbury, 1892), 13. Housed at Cornell University Library.

360 *who had visited Lima with Hull:* Long, *Gold Braid and Foreign Relations*, 83–84.

360 *Bolívar proposed marriage to the brunette beauty:* M. C. Holman, "The Romance of a Saybrook Mansion," *Connecticut Magazine*, 10 (Hartford, 1906), 50–51; also *Family Histories*.

360 *chosen to place a crown of laurel:* C. Matto de Turner, *Bocetos al lápiz de americanos celebres*, I (Lima: Bacigalupi, 1890), 146.

360 *"He gave me many honors":* Sucre, quoting Gamarra, to SB, Guayaquil, Sept. 18, 1828, quoted in Liévano Aguirre, 380; also C. Hispano, *Historia secreta de Bolívar* (Medellín: Bedout, 1977), 185; and Ramón Urdaneta, *Los amores de Simón Bolívar*, 137.

360 *Doña Pancha or "the Marshalette," etc.:* La Mariscala. According to Flora Tristan, she had accompanied Gamarra in battle since 1823: Tristan, *Peregrinations*, 290–96; also Matto de Turner, *Bocetos al lápiz*, 143–47. Matto de Turner cites her participation in combat especially in Bolivia in 1828, after Sucre's departure.

360 *she was an epileptic, etc.:* Tristan, *Peregrinations*, 300.

360 *"She had a long, slightly turned-up nose":* Ibid., 293–94.

360 *"exploit situations as the need arose":* Francisca Gamarra, quoted ibid., 295.

361 *María Joaquina Costas:* Her face was preserved for all time in a portrait by José Gil de Castro, an Afro-Peruvian artist of great renown who painted Bolívar, San Martín, Bernardo O'Higgins, and many other figures of the day. The painting of Costas (1817) hangs in the Museo Nacional de Bolivia, in La Paz.

361 *warned him of a royalist plot, etc.:* Diez de Medina, 47.

361 *entered into an ardent affair:* Cacua Prada, *Los hijos secretos de Bolívar*, 251–53; also Ramón Urdaneta, *Los amores de Simón Bolívar*, 137.

361 *José Antonio Costas, would die claiming:* H. Muñoz, "Los hijos del Libertador," *El Espectador*, Bogotá, May 31, 2008. According to this and other sources, Costas died in Caiza at the age of sixty-nine in 1895.

361 *he was hardly sterile:* Perú de Lacroix, 96. See also A. Costa de la Torre, *Descendencia de los libertadores Bolívar y Sucre en Bolivia* (La Paz: Tamayo, 1982), 35, 67, 249. José Antonio is mentioned, too, in Lynch, *Simón Bolívar*, 201.

361 *danced with them in her presence:* A. Maya, *Jeannette Hart: La novia norteamericana de Simón Bolívar* (Caracas, 1974), 28–35; also in *La mujer en la vida del libertador* (Ed. conmemorativa del sesquicentenario, Cooperativa Nacional, 1980), 191.

361 *"Wait for me at all costs":* SB to Sáenz, Lima, [April 6] 1826, SBO, III, 1313.

361   *she had earned the respect of, etc.*: Palma, *Tradiciones peruanas completas*, 1133.

361   *"generous in the extreme," etc.*: Tudor to Clay, Lima, March 23, 1827, Dispatches from U.S. consuls in Lima, microfilm roll 1, quoted in Murray, *For Glory and Bolívar*, p. 49.

361   *"the most zealous humanity," etc.*: Ibid.

362   *the insurrection had been concocted in Bogotá*: Sucre to O'Connor, Feb. 22, 1827, quoted in O'Connor, 166; also Sucre to SB, La Paz, March 11, 1827, O'L, I, 422–25; Lecuna, *Catálogo*, III, 206–16; Ricketts to Canning, Lima, Feb. 8, 1827, PRO/FO 61/11 ff 65–85, quoted in Murray, *For Glory and Bolívar*, 45.

362   *the 3rd Division*: Its leader was Colonel José Bustamante, a New Granadan, who ousted General Lara and a number of other Venezuelan officers and took over the position of commandant of the Colombian forces in Peru.

362   *Days later, she was arrested, etc.*: Sáenz to Armero, Lima [n.d.], in Lecuna, "Papeles de Manuela Sáenz," 507; Murray, *For Glory and Bolívar*, 46.

362   *"an insult to public honor and morals"*: Vidaurre letter, Pilar Moreno de Angel, *Santander, su iconografía* (Bogotá: Litografía Arco, 1984), 351, quoted in Murray, *For Glory and Bolívar*, 47.

362   *shuffled onto a boat, etc.*: Moreno de Angel; Murray, *For Glory and Bolívar*, 49.

363   *"I come to you with an olive branch"*: SB, *Proclama a los colombianos en Guayaquil*, Sept. 13, 1826, in Groot, V, 147.

363   *That olive branch was his new constitution*: Guerra, *La convención de Ocaña*, p. 81.

363   *"Once more, I offer you my services"*: Ibid.

363   *it was not his place to govern*: SB's contemporary and minister, Restrepo, who later became a historian of record in Colombia, says this. Restrepo, III, 549.

363   *"Everywhere I look"*: SB to Santander, Ibarra, Oct. 8, 1826, SB, *Cartas: Santander–Bolívar*, VI, 43.

363   *The only way to solve it*: SB to Santander, Pasto, Oct. 14, 1826, ibid., 59.

363   *issuing government appointments, etc.*: Restrepo, 549, quoted in Guerra, 88.

363   *He chafed at his aide O'Leary*: SB to Páez, Bogotá, Nov. 15, 1826, SBO, III, 1458–60.

363   *"A dictatorship would solve everything"*: SB to Santander, Sept. 19, 1826, ibid., 1441–42.

364   *abhor the word "dictator"*: SB to the governor of Popayán, quoted in Guerra, 90.

364   *it was precisely what came to pass*: Before leaving Lima, SB had sent Leocadio Guzmán, who traveled throughout Colombia, including Panama, to spread the word about SB's constitution; Guzmán had urged leaders to press SB to assume dictatorial powers. Ibid., 75, 82–84.

364   *Santander was furious, etc.*: Santander to SB, Bogotá, Oct. 8, 1826, ibid., 85–7.

364   *Santander wanted no part of it*: O'Leary, *Bolívar y la emancipación*, 775.

364   *had already warned Bolívar*: Santander to SB, Bogotá, July 19, 1826, ibid., 738.

364   *began to see newspapers, etc.*: Guerra, 89.

364   *had told Santander months before*: SB to Santander, Magdalena, July 8, 1826, SBO, III, 1395–97.

364   *"I fear that Colombia," etc.*: SB to Santander, Neiva, Nov. 5, 1826, SBO, III, 1456–58.

364   *he wrote to Sucre and Santa Cruz*: SB to Santa Cruz, Pasto, Oct. 14, 1826, and Popayán, Oct. 26, 1826, SBO, III, 1449–50, 1453–56. In these, SB asks Santa Cruz to relay the contents to Sucre.

365   *suffering the pain of inflamed hemorrhoids*: Slatta and Lucas de Grummond, 268.

365 *He was determined to disabuse, etc.*: Bushnell, *Simón Bolívar*, 172.

365 *met with only a few "Vivas!" etc.*: Guerra, 91.

365 Viva la constitución!: Ibid.

365 *As a chilling rain began to drizzle, etc.*: Ibid, 90–91, and for all subsequent details.

365 *"celebrating the army's glories"*: Ibid.

366 *a dazzling, conciliatory speech, etc.*: Santander's final words: "I will be a slave to the Constitution and to the laws, but a constant and loyal friend of Bolívar." Ibid.

366 *vice president was not completely averse*: Bushnell, *Simón Bolívar*, 173.

366 *talk of a bold, new day, etc.*: Guerra, 91.

366 *"General Castillo opposed me and lost," etc.*: SB to Páez, Cúcuta, Dec. 11, 1826, SBO, III, 1472–74.

367 *Bermúdez and Urdaneta had declared*: Liévano Aguirre, 436.

367 *Bolívar was advancing on Venezuela*: SB to Páez, Puerto Cabello, Dec. 31, 1826, SBO, III, 1486–87.

367 *He issued a unilateral decree, etc.*: SB, Proclama a los colombianos, Puerto Cabello, Jan. 3, 1827, *Discursos*, 280–81.

367 *Were they so short of enemies*: SB said some version of this on several occasions, most notably on his arrival in Guayaquil, stepping ashore in Colombia after many years in Peru: "What!? Colombia now finds itself short on enemies? Are there no more Spaniards in the world?" Proclama en Guayaquil, Sept. 13, 1826, *Discursos*, 274; also Proclama en Maracaibo, Dec. 17, 1826, ibid., 278.

367 *Páez . . . had lost much of the support*: O'Leary, *Ultimos años*, 109–14; DOC, XI, 74–77; O'L, II, 318–19, and VI, 20–21.

367 *"Enough of the blood and ruin"*: SB to Páez, Puerto Cabello, Dec. 31, 1826, SBO, III, 1486–87.

367 *but he appeared with armed guards, etc.*: Bushnell, *Simón Bolívar*, 175.

368 *Páez later wrote, etc.*: Páez, *Autobiografía*, 370 fn.

368 *"A good omen," etc.*: SB, quoted ibid., 370.

368 *a shudder of dread*: Ibid., 371.

368 *"When catastrophe forced weapons into my hands"*: SB to the president of the Congress of Colombia, Cúcuta, Oct. 1, 1821, in O'L, XVIII, 541.

369 *"I, too, shall play the game"*: SB to Santander, Potosí, October 27, 1825, SBSW, II, 547–49.

369 *in an open carriage, etc.*: Páez, 372, and for subsequent details.

369 *"I value these symbols of victory"*: Ibid., 373.

369 *had carried him four thousand miles*: Liévano Aguirre, 454.

369 *Esteban, who had returned from Europe*: SB to Esteban Palacios, Cuzco, July 10, 1825, SBSW, II, 514–15.

369 *an absence of thirty years*: SB says twenty-five to thirty. SB to Santander, Cuzco, July 10, 1825, ibid., 515–19.

369 *His patriot sister, Juana*: She was not in Caracas, as some others have claimed. She was in Barinas with her daughter, Benigna, who had a child that year. That she was not in Caracas is confirmed in SB to Briceño Méndez, Caracas, Jan. 13, 1827, and Jan. 25, 1827, SBO, III, 1494–1504. Benigna had a child in Barinas, Juana Clara Briceño y Palacios, born 1827: V. Dávila, *Próceres trujillanos* (Caracas: Imprenta Nacional, 1971),

328. Benigna had married Briceño Méndez, one of SB's generals, who had since been appointed secretary of state in Bogotá. Not only was Briceño Méndez Bolívar's nephew-in-law, he was also Santander's brother-in-law. SB to Briceño Mendez, Caracas, Jan. 12, 1827, and Jan. 13, 1827, SBO, III, 1493–95.

369 *just graduated from school, etc.:* This was Germantown Academy, which was founded in 1759 and still exists today. The father of Louisa May Alcott (A. Bronson Alcott) was its headmaster at the time. Rivolba, *Recuerdos y reminiscencias,* 20–26. (Rivolba is the pseudonym of Fernando Bolívar, and an anagram for the name Bolívar.)

369 *General Lafayette had visited, etc.:* Ibid., 36–40.

370 *"savior of the nation":* Páez, *Autobiografía,* 369.

370 *"General Páez is the most ambitious":* Perú de Lacroix, 71–72.

370 *He had admitted this to very few:* Ibid.

370 *an affront to those who had worked:* Guerra, 125.

370 *a felicitous opportunity to redefine the republic:* Bushnell, *Santander Regime,* 331.

370 *trying to boost public morale:* Páez, *Autobiografía,* 369.

370 *Everywhere he went, he had heard:* SB to Briceño Méndez, Valencia, Jan. 6, 1827, SBO, III, 1492–93.

370 *dissipating it irresponsibly:* The most complete analysis of the financial situation in 1823–27 and the accusations of corruption against the Santander regime can be found throughout Bushnell's excellent *The Santander Regime in Gran Colombia.*

371 *"the most scandalous abuses," etc.:* Patrick Campbell to Lord Aberdeen, June 4, 1829, PRO/FO, Colombia, LIV., LXV., LXXIII., quoted in Petre, 372.

371 *He recalled all too well, etc.:* When SB was in Potosí, Santander had proposed that the Liberator take personal ownership of an enterprise to build a canal between the Pacific and Atlantic. "Your name would facilitate the business venture," he wrote (Santander to SB, Bogotá, Sept. 22, 1825, SB, *Cartas: Santander–Bolívar,* V, 54). SB had responded with alarm: "No one would be pleased to see either you or me, who sit at the head of our government, mixing in purely speculative projects. . . . I refuse to involve myself in this or any business of a commercial nature" (SB to Santander, Magdalena, Feb. 22, 1826, ibid., 151).

371 *"Let's ignore for the moment":* Santander to SB, Bogotá, March 9, 1827, O'L, III, 373–74.

371 *extent of hostility he and his circle felt:* Bushnell, *Santander Regime,* 346–8.

371 *To be blamed for the disastrous financial state:* Santander to SB, *Exposición,* Bogotá, Aug. 17, 1827, DOC, X, 203–8.

371 *He informed Santander bluntly:* SB to Santander, Caracas, March 19, 1827, in O'Leary, *Ultimos años,* 149; and in Santander to SB, Bogotá, April 29, 1827, O'L, III, 390–92.

371 *reckless spending, questionable negotiations, etc.:* Bushnell, *Santander Regime,* 113. SB called Zea "Colombia's greatest calamity": SB to Santander, Jan. 14, 1823, SBO, II, 718–20.

372 *Colombia essentially had underwritten the liberation of six, etc.:* Bushnell, *Santander Regime,* 95ff.

372 *the vice president had had to impose the death penalty:* Ibid., 87.

372 *General Sucre believed he did:* Sucre to SB, La Paz, March 19, 1827, Sucre, *De mi propia mano,* 323–24. But Posada argues that Santander did not know Bustamante, and had to look up his name and rank in order to congratulate him for the uprising. Posada Gutiérrez, *Memorias,* I, 60.

372 *so did Bolívar:* SB to José Félix Blanco, Caracas, June 6, 1827, Bolívar, *Obras Completas*, IV, 1597.

372 *He strolled out into the night:* Baralt and Diaz, 202. Santander himself denies this in his own report to SB, but that report reflects a very different tone (and different information) from his letter to Bustamante. Santander to SB, Bogotá, n.d., O'L, III, 370–73.

372 *wrote to José Bustamante:* Santander to Bustamante, Bogotá, March 14, 1827, O'L, III, 434–36.

373 *signed the order promoting Bustamante:* Minister of War to Bustamante, in Baralt and Diaz, 204–7.

373 *"The Liberator is astonished," etc.:* Revenga to Ministry of War, April 18, 1827, O'L, XXV, 260–62.

373 *equivalent to absolving Páez:* Santander to SB, quoted in Liévano, 458.

373 *"Santander is a snake," etc.:* SB to Urdaneta, Caracas, April 18, 1827, O'L, III, 383–84.

373 *the city's staunchly pro-Bolívarian head:* Col. Tomás Mosquera, who would go on to become president of Colombia numerous times.

373 *the invasion was instigated by Peru:* Bushnell, *Santander Regime*, 348–50.

373 *"We have arrived at an era of blunders":* Briceño Méndez to SB, on board the *Macedonia*, July 26, 1826, O'L, VIII, 208–13.

374 *On June 20, Santander decided to abolish:* Guerra, 179.

374 *"I'm ready to do whatever it takes":* SB to Páez, Caracas, March 20, 1827, O'L, XXXI, 367–69.

374 *"The Liberator has resolved to march against":* Revenga to Santander, Caracas, June 19, 1827, O'L, XXV, 392–93.

374 *As Manuela Sáenz was sailing, etc.:* Murray, *For Glory and Bolívar*, 51.

374 *the most pleasant voyage:* SB to the Marqués del Toro, Cartagena, July 12, 1827, O'L, XXXI, 433–34. SB was traveling on the English frigate *Druid*, which had been made available to him by Sir Alexander Cockburn, the British envoy to Colombia. Cockburn himself accompanied SB on the voyage. Posada Gutiérrez, I, 61.

374 *he mobilized his generals, etc.:* Ibid., I, 60.

374 *a force powerful enough to quell:* SB, Proclama, Caracas, June 19, 1827, O'L, XXV, 394–95.

374 *they trembled with alarm, etc.:* Santander, *Escritos autobiográficos*, 69; Guerra, 179.

374 *feigned illness and left the capital:* Among these were were Dr. Soto and Vicente Azuero. Petre, 380.

374 *soldiers would die of hunger, etc.:* Santander to SB, Bogotá, DOC, XI, 515; also Masur, *Simón Bolívar*, 620.

374 *Santander reminded Bolívar that he had no power, etc.:* Guerra, 180.

375 *plan a preposterous scheme, etc.:* Ibid.; Posada Gutiérrez, I, 72.

CHAPTER 16: MAN OF DIFFICULTIES

PAGE

376 Epigraph: *"Nobody loves me in New Granada":* SB to José María de Castillo, Ríobamba, June 1, 1829, DOC, IV, 61–63.

376 *"Let me say this as clearly as I can," etc.:* SB to José Rafael Arboleda, La Carrera, Aug. 24, 1827, O'L, XXX, 463–64.

376   *"Can you believe it!":* Ibid.

376   *a diabolical congress:* SB's words were "The devil is in congress." Ibid.

376   *communicated to the president of the senate:* He asked his friend Mosquera to deliver the message. Posada Gutiérrez, I, 73.

377   *a congressional assembly was to receive him:* He sent the minister of the interior, Restrepo, ahead to Bogotá with these instructions. Slatta and Lucas de Grummond, 273.

377   *his old mansion of La Quinta, etc.:* SB to Pepe París, Mahates, Aug. 10, 1827, O'L, XXX, 456.

377   *Not one government cent:* "I don't want the government or anyone, for that matter, to spend one cent on me," he told París. "If I am to be fed when I arrive, borrow the money; I'll pay it back." Ibid.

377   *had lost some of his love for him:* Madariaga, 550. Others (e.g. Posada Gutiérrez, I, 7) claim that Soublette was always faithful to Bolívar. Among his friends who were present: Pepe París, Col. Herrán, Gen. Mosquera.

377   *burst out laughing when he heard:* Larrazábal, *Vida*, II, 409.

377   *triumphal arches along the Calle Real, etc.:* Mary English to William Greenup, Bogotá, Sept. 10, 1827, Papers of Mary English and the British Legion, Private Collection, Bonhams, New Bond Street, London. Mary English was the wife of James Towers English, who was one of the first Englishmen to enlist to participate in the South American revolution. As described earlier, he died on the island of Margarita in 1819. His widow, who stayed in Colombia, later married Greenup.

377   *elegantly turned out ladies, etc.:* Ibid.

377   *Santander, who had spewed every imaginable accusation, etc.:* Posada Gutiérrez, I, 73.

377   *sat in the presidential palace:* English to Greenup. Also Larrazábal, *Vida*, II, 409.

377   *the ancient convent of Santo Domingo:* It had been founded in 1550. The nave of the original was destroyed in the earthquake of 1785, but the church was rebuilt on the same plan. The *Virgin of the Conquistadors*, the image that looked down on the congregation, had been painted in Seville in the sixteenth century.

377   *double circle of chairs, etc.:* English to Greenup, Papers of Mary English and the British Legion.

377   *Gossiping, buzzing, the people, etc.:* Ibid.

377   *placing bets on when the Liberator:* Posada Gutiérrez, I, 73. Also Masur, *Simón Bolívar*, 621.

377   *stand on their seats, craning, etc.:* English to Greenup, Papers.

378   *He entered the church at three:* Posada Gutiérrez, I, 73. Larrazábal, *Vida*, II, 409.

378   *he seemed in acute discomfort, etc.:* "My health, badly shaken by the journey." Bolívar wrote these precise words to Páez, confirming the troubling impression he made. SB to Páez, Bogotá, Sept. 29, 1827, SBSW, II, 663.

378   *fixed his small, fierce eyes, etc.:* English to Greenup, Papers.

378   *A few cheers rippled through, etc.:* Ibid, and for subsequent details.

378   *"My heart bled for him":* Ibid.

378   *a moving speech:* Larrazábal, *Vida*, II, 408.

378   *constitution would be inviolable for ten years:* Constitución adoptado en Colombia, Seccion 3, Título 10, Revisión de la constitución, Article 1, *Constitutional Documents of Colombia and Panama, 1793–1853* (Leipzig: Grueter, 2010). Also Gil Fortoul, I, 317.

379 *He had flouted the law, etc.:* All gubernatorial changes (his delegation of power to Santander) should have been cleared with congress, according to the constitution of 1821: Gil Fortoul, I, 314. SB's show of support for Páez was a legal affront to congress. Ibid., 421.

379 *Bolívar was, in truth, no longer president, etc.:* Guerra, 133–37.

379 *By law, all power:* Ley de 2 de mayo, fijando el término de la duración del presidente y vicepresidente de la república, May 1, 1825, Bogotá, *Cuerpo de leyes de la República de Colombia, 1821–1827* (Caracas: Espinal, 1820), 361–63.

379 *the president of the senate, the very official:* To be precise, the senate president who swore in SB was Vicente Barrero. His predecessor, Luis Andrés Baralt, was the man who should have been handed the rule on Jan. 2; it was to Baralt that Santander wrote to say that SB had assigned him (Santander) the power. Confirmation of the Barrero/Baralt tenures: *Gaceta de Colombia*, No. 311, Sept. 30, 1827, and No. 312, Oct. 7, 1827.

379 *he had cavalierly instructed Santander:* SB to Santander, Cúcuta, Dec. 12, 1826, O'L, XXIV, 568; Santander to SB, Bogotá, Dec. 21, 1826, O'L, ibid., 485–86. Also Posada Gutiérrez, I, 61.

379 *Santander had written to the president of the senate:* Restrepo, III, 577; also Santander to Baralt, Dec. 22, 1826, quoted in Guerra, 137.

379 *He then issued a decree:* Parte Oficial, June 9, 1827, Bogotá, *Gaceta de Colombia*, Sept. 2, 1827, No. 307.

379 *Santander himself had acted in full contravention:* Posada Gutiérrez, I, 64.

379 *No one could call him "the man of laws" now:* Ibid., 63.

379 *the Liberator was showered with roses, etc.:* English to Greenup, Papers.

379 *When Bolívar arrived at the foot, etc.:* Ibid. Also ("apprehensively") Larrazábal, *Vida*, II, 409.

380 *inviting him to a late lunch, etc.:* Madariaga, 550.

380 *Early the next morning, etc.:* Ibid.

380 *deftly turned the conversation:* Mosquera, who was present, reported this, in ibid.

380 *"His force of personality is such":* Larrazábal, *Vida*, II, 427.

380 *But by that afternoon, suspicions, etc.:* Mosquera, in Madariaga, 550.

380 *"the illustrious Liberator":* Posada Gutiérrez, I, 99. For countries that sent diplomatic representation, see Gil Fortoul, I, 380.

380 *a hellfire of belligerence:* Posada Gutiérrez, I, 98.

380 *at social tertulias:* These are social gatherings typical throughout the history of Latin America, in which educated people met in one another's homes to discuss literature and politics, and perhaps listen to music and poetry. They were also known as *salones.*

380 *political reputations teetered:* Posada Gutiérrez, I, 98.

380 *the laughingstock of the world:* Ibid., I, 99. Note: Posada was Colombian.

381 *she noted several days later:* English to Greenup, Bogotá, Sept. 11, 1827, Sept. 24, 1827, Papers.

381 *"He is exhausted":* The opinion of a citizen of Colombia in Bogotá, 1827, DOC, XI, 314.

381 *he aspired only to be with his mistress:* Liévano Aguirre, 464.

381 *"The frost of my years":* SB to Sáenz, Bogotá, 1827, SBC, 1825–27, 438, quoted (in a different translation) in Masur, *Simón Bolívar*, 625.

381 *"I am going because you call me," etc.:* Sáenz to SB, Nov. 27 [1827], Lecuna, "Cartas de mujeres," 334. Quoted also in Murray, *For Glory and Bolívar*, 51.

381 *a major earthquake struck, etc.*: Nicholas Mill to the *Quarterly Journal of Science*, Bogotá, Nov. 23, 1827, Royal Institution of Great Britain, XXV (London: Henry Colburn, 1828), 379–82.

381 *The government palace and the sturdy church, etc.*: *Gaceta de Colombia*, no. 919, DOC, XI, 640–41.

381 *Clouds of white dust, etc.*: Mill, for subsequent details about the earthquake and climate.

381 *when Bolívar was in his house*: *Gaceta de Colombia*, 640–41.

381 *he had no doubt that its magnitude*: Mill, 382.

382 *a terrible sickness clawed at his stomach*: Ibid., 382. Dr. Mill claims he felt this as well, as did many residents of Bogotá.

382 *Few were lost, although many were injured, etc.*: *Gaceta de Colombia*, 640–41.

382 *Tolima sighed a long column of smoke*: Ibid.

382 *"The city is rendered helpless"*: SB to Briceño Méndez, Bogotá, Nov. 23, 1827, O'L, XXX, 506–7.

382 *As he paced the brick floors of La Quinta, etc.*: From Rumazo González, quoted in Masur, *Simón Bolívar*, 625–26.

382 *eyes appeared clouded with worry*: The painter Roulin, who produced an important sketch of Bolívar in Feb. 1828, made these observations. Busaniche, *Bolívar visto por sus contemporáneos*, quoted in Polanco Alcántara, 876–78.

382 *within yards of the presidential palace, etc.*: Murray, *For Glory and Bolívar*, 53–58, for many of these details.

382 *married, outspoken, and a brazen exhibitionist*: Rumazo González, quoted in Masur, *Simón Bolívar*, 625–26; Murray, *For Glory and Bolívar*, 53–58.

382 *through unfriendly territory, etc.*: Sáenz to Mosquera, Pasto, Jan. 5, 1828, Archivo Central del Cauca.

382 *burst in on parties to which she hadn't been invited*: BOLANH, 16 (Caracas), 334.

382 *labeling politicians as, etc.*: Sáenz to SB, Bogotá, March 28, 1828, Lecuna, "Cartas de mujeres," 335; also Murray, *For Glory and Bolívar*, 59.

382 *unafraid to stand up to his generals*: Murray relays an incident in which Sáenz confronted SB's minister of war, Col. Heres, refusing to give him a letter he requested. Ibid., 42–43.

383 *A charming cottage nestled in the hills, etc.*: La Quinta has been preserved as a museum and is open to tourists. The description here is taken from numerous public sources. See also www.quintadebolivar.gov.co.

383 *a mere 25,000 souls, etc.*: *The Literary Chronicle for the Year 1825* (London: Davidson, 1825), 171. Bogotá's population was about one third that of Lima, which was 70,000 in 1820.

383 *Bolívar sent off a letter, etc.*: SB to Clay, Bogotá, Nov. 27, 1827, Lecuna, *Cartas*, VI, quoted in Mallory, Daniel, *The Life and Speeches of the Honorable Henry Clay*, I (New York: Bixby, 1843), 99.

384 *"When South America threw off the thralldom of Spain," etc.*: A. Lincoln, Eulogy on Henry Clay, Springfield, Ill., July 6, 1852, in *The Language of Liberty: The Political Speeches and Writings of Abraham Lincoln* (Washington, DC: Regnery, 2009), 130.

384 *"Sir . . . The interest which was inspired"*: Clay to SB, Washington, Oct. 27, 1828, in Mallory, 99. Also Calvin Colton, *Life and Times of Henry Clay* (New York: Barnes, 1846), I, 244–45.

385 *Clay had been disappointed:* Speech, Lewisburg, Va., Aug. 30, 1826, quoted in *Niles' Register*, XXXI, 60–62.

385 *it was Clay who had argued volubly:* Mallory, 145–46.

385 *usurper and "madman":* Iñaki Erraskin, *Hasta la coronilla* (Bizkaia: Txalaparta, 2009), 72; also Eduardo Galeano, *Faces and Masks* (New York: Perseus, 2010), 139.

385 *had implored him—quite improperly:* Clay to J. Q. Adams, Lexington, July 2, 1827, *The Papers of Henry Clay*, VI, Secretary of State, 1827 (Lexington: University Press of Kentucky, 1981), 727.

385 *"Whether Bolívar is himself the author":* Harrison to the U.S. State Department, Manning, *Diplomatic Correspondence*, II, 1333–34.

385 *"The mere hero of the field":* W. H. Harrison, U.S. State Department Archives, Dispatches, Colombia, VI, quoted in Rippy, "Bolívar as Viewed by Contemporary Diplomats of the United States," *HAHR*, 15, no. 3 (Aug. 1935), 290.

386 *"he who has made such liberal sacrifices":* Martin Van Buren to Thomas P. Moore, referring to a comment from Andrew Jackson: *A Digest of International Law*, IV (Washington, DC: Government Printing Office, 1906), 789.

386 *Bolívar didn't want a crown:* Repeated often in speeches and letters, and stated strongly to San Martín, but two sturdy references: Bolívar to Páez, Magdalena, March 6, 1826, SBSW, II, 577–78; and Bolívar declaration, Government Palace, Bogotá, Nov. 23, 1826, O'L, XXIV, 512–13.

386 *"The conduct of Bolívar":* Adams, *Memoirs*, VIII, 190, quoted also in Rippy, 287–97.

386 *vastly preferred the British system:* Bushnell, *The Santander Regime*, 348–50.

387 *superior to the American model:* Bushnell, "Simón Bolívar and the United States: A Study in Ambivalence," Air University Review, USAF (July–August 1986), www.air power.au.af.mil/airchronicles/aureview/1986/jul-aug/bushne ll.html.

387 *federalism would only divide:* Belaunde, 174.

387 *Hadn't Montesquieu's* Spirit of Laws, *etc.:* SB, Address, Inauguration of the Congress of Angostura, Feb. 15, 1819, DOC, VII, 141ff. Also SB, *Discursos y Proclamas*, 75.

387 *"not one that was written for Washington!":* SB, Address.

387 *"American hucksters," etc.:* SB to Santander, Potosí, Oct. 21, 1825, SBSW, II, 539–46.

387 *"The United States seems destined by Providence":* SB to Col. Campbell, British chargé d'affaires, Bogotá, Guayaquil, Aug., 1829, SBSW, II, 731–32.

387 *had Bolívar written to King George IV:* SB to George IV, King of the United Kingdom, Bogotá, Dec. 20, 1827, O'L, XXX, 529–30.

387 *a close camaraderie, etc.:* Rippy, 183.

387 *the only leader who could purge, etc.:* Ibid., quoting Campbell to Dudley, Oct. 14, 1827, PRO/FO, Colombia, XVIII, 42.

388 *Campbell began hoping out loud, etc.:* Ibid., 184–87.

388 *"I cannot suppose" etc.:* Ibid., 185, quoting Campbell to Secretary Aberdeen, Confidential, May 14, 1829, PRO/FO, Colombia, XVIII, 64.

388 *leaped on the "monarchical project" as proof, etc.:* "Probabilidades sobre el establecimiento de la federación," in DOC, XIV, 167.

388 *incontrovertible evidence:* According to Bushnell, when SB asked his ministers to explore the possibility of obtaining a British protectorate for Greater Colombia, they assumed he meant a return to monarchy, because they assumed Britain would expect

Colombia to conform to the "European model." Bushnell, "Simón Bolívar and the United States." See also Restrepo, VII, 220–50.

388 *nation's best and brightest:* SB to Fernández Madrid, Bogotá, Feb. 7, 1828, Lecuna, *Cartas*, II, 256.

389 *"In my line of work," etc.:* Santander to Azuero, quoted in Líevano, 466.

389 *He traveled to outlying villages, etc.:* SB to Carabaño, April 12, 1828, SBO, IV.

389 *full of conviction that, as the highest executive, etc.:* Perú de Lacroix, 17.

389 *"All New Granada":* SB to Arboleda, Bogotá, Jan. 22, 1828, O'L, XXXI, 16.

389 *he commissioned a British engineer:* J. A. Lloyd, "Account of Levellings Carried Across the Isthmus of Panamá," Nov. 26, 1829, *Philosophical Transactions, Royal Society of London*, CXX (London: Taylor, 1830), 59.

390 *wrangling over supremacy in Cartagena for years:* See Díaz, 267–69.

390 *Padilla was a giant of a man, etc.:* P. D. Martin-Maillefer, *Los novios de Caracas* (Caracas: República de Venezuela, 1954), 91; also G. R. Peñalosa, "José Prudencio Padilla," in *Gran enciclopedia de Colombia*, IX (Bogotá: Circulo de Lectores, 1994).

390 *When Bolívar sent his aides to sit in:* SB to Wilson, Bucaramanga, March 31, 1828, Lecuna, *Cartas*, II, 293.

390 *Bolívar had stated very clearly:* Perú de Lacroix, 17. Also Restrepo, IV, 98.

391 *convention had taken on a possibly explosive dynamic:* Rafael Urdaneta, 418.

391 *They set up a system of mail, etc.:* Perú de Lacroix, 18, 52ff. Information about Bolívar's habits at Bucaramanga is recorded amply in Lacroix's account.

391 *he visited the local church, etc.:* Ibid., 94, 67.

391 *played cards with his aides, etc.:* Ibid., 127–40, for subsequent details.

391 *an expression of soul and energy:* English to Greenup, Bogotá, Sept.–Oct. 1827, Boulton *El arquetipo iconografico de Bolívar* (letter accompanying Rollin sketch).

392 *He was generally up at five in the morning, etc.:* Perú de Lacroix, 201.

392 *Castillo, a loyal partisan to his cause:* Guerra, 276. Castillo was the cousin of Manuel Castillo, SB's rival in 1813. After refusing to join SB's Admirable Campaign, Manuel Castillo took hold of Cartagena and defended it against SB and the Spaniards. When Morillo conquered Cartagena, Manuel Castillo was taken into custody and shot. Nevertheless, his cousin proved faithful to SB.

392 *The Venezuelans, particularly:* SB to Ibarra, Bucaramanga, May 22, 1828, O'L, XXXI, 121.

392 *On the first order of business, etc.:* Larrazábal, *Vida*, II, 425.

392 *Bolívar's followers were accused of being tyrants:* Ibid., 428.

392 *In time, a rumor began to spread, etc.:* Perú de Lacroix, 31–32.

392 *demanded that the Liberator be allowed to go:* SB to Urdaneta, Bucaramanga, May 8, 1828, O'L, 96.

393 *"For if he does," etc.:* Larrazábal, *Vida*, II, 427.

393 *When Bolívar heard of it, he was appalled, etc.:* SB to Arboleda, Bucaramanga, June 1, 1828, Lecuna, *Cartas del Libertador*, II, 365. Briceño Méndez to SB, Ocaña, April 9, 1828, O'L, VIII, 239.

393 *Had it come to this?:* SB to Wilson, Bogotá, Aug. 21, 1828, O'L, XXXI, 182–85.

393 *"Do what you must," etc.:* SB to Briceño Méndez, Bucaramanga, June 8, 1828, O'L, XXXI, 139–41.

393 *"My doctor often has told me," etc.:* Ibid.

393 *nineteen conventioneers walked out, etc.:* Restrepo, IV, 100.

393 *"The bull is in the arena":* SB to Vergara, Bucaramanga, June 3, 1828, O'L, XXXI, 137–38.

393 *As he rode on, he got word:* SB to Restrepo, Cipaquirá, June 21, 1828, O'L, XXXI, 145.

393 *The constitution . . . was in tatters, etc.:* Herrán, Proclama, June 13, 1828, quoted in Posada Gutiérrez, I, 105–6.

393 *welcomed euphorically:* "All these towns are receiving me with incomparable happiness," SB reported as he rode to Bogotá. "It is greater than the reception in 1819." SB to Soublette, June 20, 1828, O'L, XXXI, 144. Also SB to Mendoza, June 28, 1828 O'L, XXXI, 148.

394 *Bolívar may have had enemies, etc.:* These, according to SB after the fact, were a mere dozen, but they had been given great power by Santander. SB to Carabaño, Aug. 9, 1828, O'L, XXXI, 178–79.

394 *"Colombians, . . . I won't even utter the word 'liberty' ":* SB to the Republic of Colombia, Bogotá, Aug. 27, 1828, SB, *Proclamas y Discursos*, 305–6.

394 *"Santander will leave the country":* SB to Briceño Méndez, Bogotá, Sept. 5, 1828, O'L, XXXI, 199–201.

394 *Among her guests at those ribald affairs, etc.:* Murray, *For Glory and Bolívar*, 72.

395 *"Paula, Padilla, Páez!" etc.:* Paula is Francisco de Paula Santander. Sáenz to SB, Bogotá, March 28, 1828, Lecuna, "Cartas de mujeres," 335.

395 *"We adored her," etc.:* Boussingault, 213.

395 *The festivities were open to the public, etc.:* The entire account of this event is in Cordovez Moure, *Reminiscencias* (Bogotá: Epigrafe, 2006), 569–71. Also in Herrán to Restrepo, Bogotá, Aug. 5, 1828, Archivo General de la Nación, Bogotá, Sección República, Historia, IV, 170–75; and Murray, *For Glory and Bolívar*, 62.

395 *An officer improvised a firing squad:* This was the Irish colonel Richard Crofton, head of the Granaderos, who, according to Posada, was a coarse and vulgar man. Posada Gutierrez, I, 121.

395 *the opinion of General José María Córdova:* Córdova to SB, Bogotá, Aug. 1, 1828, PRO/FO, Colombia, XVIII, 56.

395 *despised her since the ship's voyage:* Córdova was a ladies' man, and some have conjectured that he and Manuela had a brief, ultimately bitter romantic brush on that voyage. About the voyage: Córdova to SB, Quito, May 19, 1827, O'L, VII, 369–73; also Murray, *For Glory and Bolívar*, 49. About the possible flirtation: L. F. Molina, "José María Córdova," *Gran enciclopedia de Colombia*, Sección militar.

396 *"I know you're angry with me," etc.:* Sáenz to SB, [n.p., n.d.], Lecuna, "Cartas de mujeres," 334.

396 *"I'll suspend the commanding officer," etc.:* SB to Córdova, Bogotá, July, 1828, Lecuna, *Cartas*, II, 419.

396 *kept a close catalog of every penny:* He was well known for the trunks of secondhand clothes he took along in his travels with SB. He stashed SB's old caps, torn epaulettes, threadbare shirts, faded jackets; and SB would dispense them to soldiers or officers who needed them. Aristides Rojas, *Obras escojidas*, 606; S. Vergara, *Diccionario biográfico de los campeones de la libertad* (Bogotá: Zaragosa, 1870), 431.

396 *began to speak openly of "tyrannicide"*: Mijares, *The Liberator*, 535. Boussingault, III, 224–25.

396 *the country needed to move on, etc.*: González, *Memorias*, 117.

397 *"Off with the Tyrant's head!"*: The full verse, written by L. Vargas Tejada, Santander's intended deputy: "Take the first and last letter from Bolívar, and we're left with 'Oliva' [olive branch]. In other words, cut off the Tyrant's head and feet in order to enjoy a lasting peace." Mijares, 535.

397 *Florentino González*: Bernardina Ibañez was the younger sister of Santander's long-time mistress, Nicolasa. That Florentino González was about to marry Bernardina can be found in Lecuna, *Catálogo*, III, 283. Having such intimate relations with sisters, we can assume that González and Santander knew one another before González called on him specifically to discuss the conspiracy. See Santander's testimony, Dec. 13, 1828, O'L, XXVI, 545.

397 *González was pale*: V. Pérez Silva, in the Introduction to González, 3.

397 *volcanic, gifted with words*: Larrazábal, *Vida*, II, 447.

397 *Pedro Carujo, a young, etc.*: Posada Gutiérrez, I, 113.

397 *Horment, a French liberal*: Cordovez Moure, *Reminiscencias*, 1129–30.

397 *to kill Bolívar at a masked ball, etc.*: Ibid., 744–45; Larrazábal, *Vida*, II.

397 *The second plan to murder him, etc.*: Posada Gutiérrez, I, 114; also Bolívar to Montilla, Sept. 21, 1828, O'Leary, *Ultimos años*, 215–17; also "Testament of an eyewitness, 1828," O'Leary, *Bolívar y la emancipación*, 409–15 (cited hereafter as "Testament").

398 *one friend, one aide, etc.*: Mijares, 536.

398 *Carujo prepared six assassins, etc.*: "Testament"; also Mijares, 536.

398 *called off at the last minute by Santander*: "Testament." González paid a visit to Santander on Sept. 17 or 18, just days before the planned assault, and evidently it was then that Santander responded generally to the plot. That Santander knew about the general plot and that he responded specifically to the Sept. 21 plan: González, 117, 123.

398 *"so that no one will say"*: "Testament"; also Posada Gutiérrez, I, 113; González, 119.

398 *set for late October*: For Oct. 28, the birthday of Saint Simón. On that day, Santander would have been well on his way to his diplomatic posting in Washington. González, however, claims that the coup was set for Sept. 28, which makes little sense, since Santander told him that he wanted to be long gone when it happened. Santander was still in Bogotá, hardly ready to leave and somewhat unwell, on Sept. 25.

398 *Their plan was to storm the palace in full force, etc.*: Some conspirators were told (and they believed) that they were only going to apprehend Bolívar. It became evident during the trial that this was why some had been persuaded to join. See also Sept. 26–Nov. 13, 1828, O'L, XXVI, 460–503.

398 *An army captain had just reported, etc.*: González, 125.

398 *a woman had been emboldened to go directly, etc.*: Sáenz to O'Leary, Paita, Aug. 10, 1850, O'Leary, *Bolívar y la emancipación*, 416–23.

399 *in the house of Santander's deputy, etc.*: "Testament." One of the ministers was Castillo, one of three original targets, along with Bolívar and Urdaneta. González, 127.

399 *rain had drenched the city*: Sáenz to O'Leary, O'Leary, *Bolívar y la emancipación*.

399 *slick with mud*: Posada Gutiérrez, I, 121.

399 *the moon was bright and full*: NASA, Moon Phases, http://eclipse.gsfc.nasa.gov/phase/

phases1801.html; also Posada Gutiérrez, I, 115; also Sáenz to O'Leary, O'Leary, *Bolívar y la emancipación.*

399 *That night, everyone in Bolívar's circle was ailing, etc.:* This and all following details and quotations from Sáenz to O'Leary, O'Leary, *Bolívar y la emancipación.*

400 *Peruvian generals:* These were generals Gamarra and Santa Cruz.

400 *it's time for a palace coup:* The ensuing account and all quotations: Sáenz to O'Leary, O'Leary, *Bolívar y la emancipación.*

400 *Despite the few guards:* "Testament." There were only thirty to thirty-five for the entire palace that night.

400 *Colonel Guerra had assured him, etc.:* Sáenz to O'Leary, O'Leary, *Bolívar y la emancipación.*

400 *He asked Manuela to read to him, etc.:* Ibid.

400 *in his nightshirt:* Boussingault, III, 232. Boussingault claims this information is from Manuela's lips. Sáenz, in her testimony to O'Leary, says only that he was undressed.

400 *His only pair of boots, etc.:* Sáenz to O'Leary, O'Leary, *Bolívar y la emancipación,* and subsequent details.

401 *"There appeared in the doorway," etc.:* González, 127.

401 *"He's not here," etc.:* Boussingault, III, 226.

401 *Carujo and his sharpshooters, etc.:* González, 130–31; also Boussingault, III, 232.

401 *The conspirators had daggers in hand, etc.:* Sáenz to O'Leary, O'Leary, *Bolívar y la emancipación.*

402 *She crossed her arms, standing her ground, etc.:* Boussingault, III, 227.

402 *"He's safe!," etc.:* Ibid.

402 *"I didn't come here to fight women":* Sáenz to O'Leary, O'Leary, *Bolívar y la emancipación;* also González, 131.

402 *as cannon fire exploded outside, etc.:* González, 131.

402 *the sharp clatter of boots, etc.:* Sáenz to O'Leary, O'Leary, *Bolívar y la emancipación.*

402 *"What's going on?":* Posada Gutiérrez, I, 120.

402 *he saw his pastry cook, etc.:* Sáenz to O'Leary, O'Leary, *Bolívar y la emancipación.*

402 *no idea that a coup was afoot:* Posada Gutiérrez, I, 119.

402 *Sometime after the bell tower struck two:* Larrazábal, *Vida,* II, 452.

402 *the conspirators had vanished, etc.:* Posada Gutiérrez, I, 119.

402 *Soaked to the bone, slathered in mud, etc.:* Ibid., 121.

403 *eyes glistening with tears, etc.:* Posada Gutiérrez, I; also Larrazábal, *Vida,* II, 453.

403 *"Here I am, dying of grief," etc.:* Posada Gutiérrez, I, 121.

403 *his "patriots":* SB to Carabaño, quoted in Larrazábal, *Vida,* II, 454.

403 *so battered she could hardly walk:* Boussingault, III, 228; also Larrazábal, *Vida,* II, 454; Murray, *For Glory and Bolívar,* 66; Sáenz to O'Leary, O'Leary, *Bolívar y la emancipación;* Posada Gutiérrez, I, 116.

403 *By four in the morning:* Posada Gutiérrez, I, 121.

403 *"You are the Liberatrix of the Liberator," etc.:* Sáenz to O'Leary, O'Leary, *Bolívar y la emancipación.*

403 *Bolívar's first impulse, etc.:* Posada Gutiérrez, I, 121–22.

403 *"My heart is in pieces," etc.:* Larrazábal, *Vida,* II, 454. For his general demoralization: Restrepo, IV, 119.

403 *he preferred to die, etc.:* Posada Gutiérrez, I, 121–22.

404 Colonel Guerra, who had spent the evening: Larrazábal, Vida, II, 454.

404 "I am crushing the aborted conspiracy" etc.: Bolívar to Sucre, Oct. 28, 1828, O'L, XXXI, 230–33.

404 In the end, of the fifty-nine men identified, etc.: These verdicts are expressed in an official memorandum from Castillo, Vergara, and Córdova to the Secretary of State, Nov. 10, 1828, Bogotá, O'L, XXVI, 493–98.

404 Santander . . . was issued a death sentence: O'L, XXVI, 493–98.

404 "I've got conspiracy up to the eyeballs": Lynch, Simón Bolívar, 242.

404 that he was the soul of clemency, etc.: Sáenz to O'Leary, O'Leary, Bolívar y la emancipación; Manuela was not the only one to note Bolívar's forgiveness. Among others, Carujo, who deserved death more than most, gave him the same tribute: Carujo to the Sons and Inhabitants of Bogotá, Nov. 13, 1828, O'L, XXVI, 502–3.

404 González had prevented his goons from killing her: Sáenz to O'Leary, O'Leary, Bolívar y la emancipación. Looking back on this, one has to wonder whether González was spared because he was affianced to Bernardina Ibañez, for whom the Liberator had once cared, and who was, after all, the widow of one of Bolívar's beloved officers.

405 inexplicably freed and pardoned: In Nov. of 1828, Carujo eluded a death sentence and was sent to prison in Bocachica (where Santander, too, spent time). Thereafter, he lived an eventful life in and out of favor. González was sentenced to solitary confinement in Bocachica, but after eighteen months was set free. He returned to Colombia in 1831 to serve in Santander's administration and marry Bernardina Ibañez. Years later, he ran unsuccessfully for president of the republic. In time, he emigrated to Argentina.

405 slipped into a fatal spiral: Restrepo, IV, 119.

CHAPTER 17: PLOWING THE SEA

PAGE

406 Epigraph: No one achieves greatness with impunity: SB to Restrepo, Bucaramanga, June 3, 1828, O'L, XXXI, 136.

406 he withdrew to La Quinta to convalesce: Liévano Aguirre, 486.

406 Le Moyne, who arrived three months after, etc.: J. O. Melo, Introduction, "El ojo de los franceses," in Augusto Le Moyne, Viaje y estancia en la Nueva Granada (Bogotá: Ed. Incunables, 1985).

406 voyage up the Magdalena in a canoe, etc.: Ibid.

407 "We arrived at la Quinta," etc.: A. Le Moyne, Voyages et séjour (Paris, 1880), in Liévano Aguirre, 486.

407 painted by a soldier: This was José M. Espinosa, who created some of the most renowned likenesses of Bolívar. His initial sketches—done from life—were transformed into numerous portraits, the majority of which reside in Caracas. Espinosa wrote about the revolution in his memoir, Memorias de un abanderado, from which the opening scene of this biography is taken.

407 the thin hair, sunken cheeks, etc.: Boulton, Los retratos de Bolívar, 110–11.

407 listening in turns to Sucre, Manuela, etc.: Sucre to SB, cited in Polanco Alcántara, 992; Nicolasa Ibañez to SB, Bogotá, Duarte French, Las Ibañez, 100.

408 Was it right to grant clemency to a white, etc.: SB to Briceño Méndez, Bogotá, Nov. 16, 1828, O'L, XXXI, 239–40.

408   *the blood of so many:* SB to Briceño Méndez, Bogotá, Nov. 28, 1828, ibid.

408   *his enemies called themselves "liberals":* SB to Briceño Méndez, Bucaramanga, April 23,
      1828, O'L, XXXI, 73–75; also SB to Urdaneta, Purificación, Jan. 1, 1829, ibid.,
      281–85.

408   *As one historian put it, etc.:* Mijares, 538.

408   *"Beware the nation," etc.:* SB, Discurso, Caracas, Jan. 1, 1814, SB, *Doctrina*, 28.

408   *most radical and impetuous of world revolutionaries:* Arciniegas, *Bolívar y la revolución*, 345.

408   *filled with a mortal hesitancy:* SB to Briceño Méndez, Bogotá, Nov. 16, 1828, O'L,
      XXXI, 239–40.

408   *They knew that wherever Bolívar went:* Lynch, *Simón Bolívar*, 252–53.

409   *"You are the anchor of all our hopes," etc.:* Santander to SB, Bogotá, June 8, 1826, O'L,
      III, 265–66.

409   *"the magic of his prestige":* O'L, II, 639.

409   *"Goodbye, sambo!":* Madariaga, 380.

409   *Populations had been cut in half:* B. Hammett, "Popular Insurrection and Royalist
      Reaction," in Archer, 50. Also see Jay Kinsbruner, *Independence in Spanish America*,
      (Santa Fe: University of New Mexico Press, 1994), 153–57.

409   *Regional economies had come to a rumbling halt, etc.:* Kinsbruner, 130–31.

410   *The Americas that were emerging, etc.:* Liévano Aguirre, 512–13.

410   *Eventually this would change, etc.:* Kinsbruner, xvii.

410   *vent his sorrows:* SB to Briceño Méndez, O'L, XXXI, 239–40; SB to Alamo, Nov. 19,
      1828, ibid., 242.

410   *"You will see in the attached documents," etc.:* SB to Sucre, Bogotá, Oct. 28, 1828, ibid.,
      230–33.

410   *"favorite son":* "If God had given us the right to choose our own families," SB had once
      said, "I would have chosen General Sucre as my son." Sucre, *Documentos selectos* (Ca-
      racas: Biblioteca Ayacucho, 1993), vii.

410   *He expected O'Leary to explain:* SB to Flores, Bogotá, Oct. 8, 1828, O'L, XXXI,
      223–24.

410   *Flores had already spent sixteen years, etc.:* Vásconez Hurtado, *Cartas de Bolívar al Gen-
      eral Juan José Flores*, Introducción.

411   *He had made up his mind that he would govern:* Madariaga, 582.

411   *"shining, unblemished" exemplar:* SB's description of Sucre in SB to Sucre, O'L, XXXI,
      230–33.

411   *Now Flores was being told in no uncertain terms:* SB to Flores, ibid.

411   *his elegant bride in Quito:* Mariana Carcelén Larréa, the marquesa of Solanda, whom
      Sucre had met in Quito. He had given power of attorney to General José María Pérez
      de Urdininea to effect the marriage in 1823. Sucre, *De mi propia mano*, 470.

411   *He had had to speed away with a bullet, etc.:* Sucre also left behind a mistress: Ro-
      salía Cortés, a Bolivian, with whom he had had a relationship in La Paz. Their ille-
      gitimate son, born on Jan. 13, 1826, was José María. Ibid., 464.

411   *hoping to rid himself of the black mood:* SB to Alamo, Chia, Nov. 19, 1828, O'L, XXXI,
      241–2.

412   *he wrote to General La Mar:* Obando to La Mar, Pasto, Dec. 14, 1828, O'L, III, 481; also
      from Guáitara, Dec. 29, 1828, ibid., 483.

412   *impending Peruvian invasion of Colombia:* La Mar, "El Ciudadano General La Mar, Presidente de la República, a los Peruanos," in O'Leary, *Bolívar y la emancipación,* 496–98.

412   *Obando attacked Popayán:* Obando's close colleague in this pro-Granadan rebellion was José Hilario López, a native of Popayán, who was a fervent loyalist of Santander. In time, Santander, López, and Obando all became presidents of the Republic of New Granada.

412   *a confrontation with Peru was inevitable:* SB to Ibarra, Bogotá, July 16, 1828, O'L, XXXI, 166.

412   *sparring with Peru's ambassador:* This was José de Villa, the former private secretary and close friend of Gen. Berindoaga, who had abandoned the patriots to join the Spaniards alongside Torre Tagle. Bolívar had had Berindoaga executed for treason. Madariaga, 580.

412   *a robust army of forty thousand:* SB to O'Leary, Bogotá, Aug. 15, 1828, O'L, *Ultimos años,* 475.

412   *a convalescence that should have lasted two months:* SB to Alamo, ibid.

412   *He was working on instinct now:* SB to Flores, Oct. 8, 1828, O'L, XXXI, 223–24.

412   *barely ride two hours at a time, etc.:* Posada Gutiérrez, I, 140.

412   *rains were incessant, etc.:* SB to Urdaneta, Paniquitá, Jan. 22, 1829, O'L, XXXI, 304–6.

413   *it had overtaken the city of Cuenca:* Peruvian president La Mar's birthplace. Although he had fought with SB and Sucre in the effort to liberate Peru from Spain, the fact that Cuenca and Guayaquil had been appropriated by Bogotá had always rankled him.

413   *he led fifteen hundred men, etc.:* The actual number of troops (not all represented in the battle): 4,000 Colombians; 8,000 Peruvians. Posada Gutiérrez, I, 146.

413   *who seemed to materialize out of nowhere, etc.:* Monsalve, *El ideal político,* 196.

413   *The Colombians were poorly armed, poorly fed, etc.:* Ibid.

413   *Sucre wrote to Bolívar, etc.:* Sucre to SB, Cuenca, March 3, 1829, O'L, I, 521–22.

413   *the very people for whose liberty he had fought:* After the battle, Sucre had a monument erected on the battlefield. It was engraved as follows: "On February 27, 1829, eight thousand men of the Peruvian army invaded the land of their liberators and were vanquished here by four thousand stouthearted Colombians." The discrepancy in numbers is due to the fact that Sucre was using the size of total armies, not numbers of troops on the battlefield. Posada Gutiérrez, I, 146.

413   *He told Bolívar that he had assumed command, etc.:* Sucre to SB, ibid.

413   *As Sucre was winding his way home:* SB to Vergara, Hato Viejo, Feb. 28, 1829, O'L, XXXI, 328–29; and SB to Urdaneta, Pasto, March 9, 1829, ibid., 330–31.

414   *Bolívar now offered the rebels complete amnesty, etc.:* SB to Vergara, Popayán, Jan. 28, 1829, O'L, XXXI, 307–10; also Monsalve, *El ideal politico,* 192.

414   *Bolívar promoted Obando to full general:* Posada Gutiérrez, I, 150.

414   *Córdova, who had labored mightily, etc.:* Ibid., 136–40.

414   *Manuela Sáenz was never so celebrated, etc.:* O'Leary to Bolívar, Bogotá, May 9, 1829, and Aug. 18, 1829, FJB, Archivo Libertador, Nos. 633, 641.

414   *foreign diplomats clamored to meet her, etc.:* O'Leary to SB, ibid.

414 *a frenzied plan to recruit a foreign monarch, etc.:* O'Leary, *Detached Recollections*, 12–15.

415 *O'Leary had reported much of it:* Ibid.

415 *British chargé d'affaires—in all his calculating enthusiasm:* Campbell to SB, Bogotá, May 31, 1829, in Liévano Aguirre, 491–92.

416 *much of the French navy plying American waters:* A. Sheldon-Duplaix, "France and Its Navy During the Wars of Latin American Independence," presentation, 2011 McMullen Naval History Symposium, Sept. 16, 2011, Annapolis.

416 *a thousand reasons why it wouldn't work, etc.:* Bolívar to Vergara, Campo de Buijó, July 13, 1829, O'L, XXXI, 422–27.

416 *Bolívar had adamantly rejected, etc.:* His views on monarchy have been discussed amply elsewhere in this book. He refers to his enemies' persistent attempts to tar him with a monarchical brush in SB to Urdaneta, Bojacá, Dec. 16, 1828, O'L, XXXI, 268; tells Urdaneta that a monarchy is untenable: SB to Urdaneta, Guayaquil, July 13, 1829, *Documentos para los anales*, 54–56. Also Larrazábal, *Vida*, II, 493–517.

416 *Some historians claim he ignored it because, etc.:* Liévano Aguirre, 482–83.

416 *other reasons for Bolívar's dismissal, etc.:* Ibid.

416 *But his wan response, twisted artfully:* Not only SB's enemies but some of his biographers have misguidedly claimed he had monarchical aspirations. The Spaniard Salvador Madariaga, whose book on SB is relentlessly negative, claims he wanted to be king, as does a highly tendentious biography by former Argentine president Bartolomé Mitre.

416 *Indeed, those who prayed for Bolívar's ruin, etc.:* Páez had written to Urdaneta to say that he supported any form of government SB wanted, even a monarchy. Among those who trumpeted the notion that SB wanted a crown (especially in Antioquia, Córdova's region) were the Montoyas and Arrublas, lawyers who were friends of Santander's. O'Leary, *Detached Recollections*, 15.

417 *With little more than three hundred followers:* Masur, *Simón Bolívar*, 659.

417 *recruit Mosquera to his way of thinking:* Mosquera's testimony, *Causa contra el presidente*, I, Anales del Congreso, Imprenta de la Nación, Bogotá, 1867, 589; also Posada Gutiérrez, I, 142–43.

417 *He wrote to Páez:* Córdova to Páez, Medellín, Sept. 18, 1829, in Páez, 544–47.

417 *honored him with one of the jeweled crowns:* Cordovez Moure, 1067.

417 *an army was all he needed to govern a country, etc.:* Mosquera, quoted in *Causa contra el presidente*.

417 *he could hardly speak; he cried like a baby:* Larrazábal, *Vida*, II, 474.

417 *He was determined to broker, etc.:* J. M. del Castillo, in "Report of the President of the Council of Ministers," Bogotá, Jan. 25, 1830 (translation), in British and Foreign State Papers, XVII, 1829–30, 1273–81.

417 *his arrival in Guayaquil at the end of July:* July 21 to be exact. SB to Restrepo, Guayaquil, July 23, 1829, O'L, XXXI, 439–41.

417 *spitting black, etc.:* SB to Restrepo, Guayaquil, Aug. 20, 1829, O'L, XXXI, 482; SB to Briceño Méndez, Guayaquil, Aug. 21, 1829, ibid., 488; SB to Páez, Guayaquil, Sept. 5, 1829, ibid., 513.

418 *all too clearly in his lungs:* "When we arrived with the army at the Mayo River [where

Obando and the rebels were], the Liberator suffered a grave pulmonary attack."
Mosquera, quoted in Posada Gutiérrez, I, 142; also Mosquera's testimony about his
general state, *Causa contra el presidente*, 588–89.

418 *Forced to spend twelve feverish days:* SB to Briceño Méndez, O'L, XXXI, 488; also SB to
Restrepo, ibid., 482.

418 *The equatorial heat was relentless, etc.:* SB to Urdaneta, Guayaquil, Aug. 20, 1829, O'L,
XXXI, 480; SB to Restrepo, ibid., 483.

418 *La Mar had been deported, etc.:* SB to Col. Wilson, Guayaquil, Aug. 3, 1829, O'L, XXX,
462–66.

418 *The new chief of state, Antonio de La Fuente:* La Mar's immediate successor was La
Fuente, who held the position of supreme chief for three months, before Gamarra
took over. Bolívar was well disposed to La Fuente probably because La Fuente had
done him the service of removing Riva Agüero. La Fuente immediately wrote a conciliatory letter to the Liberator. SB to Briceño Méndez, Guayaquil, July 22, 1829, O'L,
XXXI, 435–36.

418 *The wound this betrayal inflicted on the Liberator, etc.:* Posada Gutiérrez, I, 143; also SB,
Proclamas y discursos, 34–35. Masur claims Córdova didn't worry Bolívar in the least,
but it is difficult to find a South American historian who would agree.

418 *although he tried to dismiss it:* SB to Urdaneta, Guayaquil, Aug. 3, 1829, O'L, XXXI,
458–60.

418 *"My strength is almost entirely gone":* SB to O'Leary, Guayaquil, Sept. 8, 1829, O'L,
XXXI, 516–19.

419 *called America the hope of the universe:* SB, Proclama, Aug. 2, 1824, DOC, IX, 343.

419 *little more than a chimera, etc.:* SB to Leandro Palacios, Guayaquil, July 27, 1829, O'L,
XXXI, 451–52.

419 *"We have tried everything under the sun":* SB to Urdaneta, Buíjo, July 5, 1829, ibid.,
416–18.

419 *denounced Bolívar as an outright despot:* Constant is referred to in SB's letters from
Guayaquil: Urdaneta, July 22; M. Montilla, July 27; R. Wilson, July 28; and Palacios,
July 27, 1829; ibid., 442–50.

419 *"who has murdered thousands," etc.:* G. D. Flinter, letter to King George IV, Island of
Margarita, Jan. 28, 1829 (Gazette, Hollman & Co., 1829), JCBL.

419 *less a lion of liberty than a snake:* "Review: Memoirs of Simón Bolívar," by Gen. H. S. V.
Ducoudray-Holstein, *The Gentlemen's Magazine* [a compendium of 1829 publications],
C-147, I (London: Nichols, 1830), 48–51.

419 *disseminated by the press:* The prevalence of negative press against SB was reported in
the American Masonick Record, *Albany Saturday Magazine*, II, no. 52 (Jan. 24, 1829),
415.

419 *In Chile, the outcast Riva Agüero, etc.:* Lecuna, *Catálago*, III, 87ff. and 101; also A. Rey
de Castro Arena, *Republicanismo* (Lima: Universidad de San Marcos, 2010), 238.

419 *still called himself president of Peru:* Riva Agüero had been ejected from Peru in 1823
for siding with the Spaniards, along with Torre Tagle. Basadre, I, 32–36, 87.

419 *"I'm being accused of an inferno":* SB to O'Leary, Guayaquil, Aug. 17, 1829, O'L,
XXXI, 478–79.

419   *he wrote to General O'Leary insisting, etc.*: SB to O'Leary, Guayaquil, Aug. 21, 1829, ibid., 483–86.

419   *calculating, as some historians have claimed*: See Madariaga's last chapters for a thoroughly negative and distorted portrait of SB, in which SB only pretends to reject the crown because he so ravenously hungers for it. Mitre, an Argentine who far preferred his countryman San Martín to SB, portrayed SB as pathologically duplicitous and dangerously authoritarian. Most recently, the Peruvian historian Morote attributes to SB a diabolical plan to crush Peru.

420   *under which—as he himself had said*: SB, Proclama, Aug. 27, 1828, Bogotá, quoted, with special piquancy, in Santander, *Apuntamientos*, 116.

420   *wondered whether he was insisting, etc.*: This is most apparent in the correspondence from James Henderson, the British consul general, to the Foreign Office, accusing SB of the lowest motives. PRO/FO, 18/68, Doc. 24, 25, and Henderson's letters. The emissary was heavily influenced by Santander and Córdova. Also: Henderson's thirteen-year-old daughter, Fanny, had been maintaining a romantic correspondence with Córdova, which Henderson had read. Madariaga, 592–612.

420   *drew up a treaty with Peru, etc.*: SB to Vergara, Guayaquil, Sept. 20, 1829, O'L, XXXI, 520.

420   *ingenious plan to finance Colombia's crippling deficit*: Mijares, 539.

420   *improvements in universities, etc.*: Restrepo, Order 654, Bogotá, in O'L, XXVI, 414–16.

420   *sent military reinforcements to Panama*: SB to Vergara, O'L, XXXI, 520.

420   *He congratulated the army*: SB to Urdaneta, Quito, Oct. 26, 1829, *Documentos para los anales*, 56–57.

420   *"I have no one to write for me"*: SB to Vergara, O'L, XXXI, 520.

420   *published a circular, etc.*: An open referendum. Posada Gutiérrez, I, 171–72. On his genuine disinterest: C. Cantú, *Historia de cien años: 1750–1850*, II (Madrid: Rivera, 1852), 523–24; also Restrepo, IV, 256–59.

420   *"There is no such thing as good faith," etc.*: SB, "Una mirada hácia la america española," in Pérez Vila, *Doctrina*, 286–87.

421   *"I hope you haven't forgotten"*: SB to O'Leary, Babahoyo, Sept. 28, 1829, O'L, XXXI, 526.

421   *He wanted to leave, etc.*: Mosquera testimony, *Causa contra el presidente*, 590.

421   *In July of 1829, etc.*: Restrepo, IV, 186. He was in Puerto Cabello in August; Páez, 548.

421   *But the fundamental distrust between Granadans, etc.*: Santander, *Apuntamientos*, 21–22.

421   *"March at once!," etc.*: O'L, XXVII, Part I, 123.

422   *a seven-month internment*: Santander, *Apuntamientos*, 55.

422   *Bolívar's council of ministers had feared*: Restrepo, IV, 185.

422   *she engaged a spy to ferret out*: Montebrune to Sáenz, Guaduas, Nov. 19, 1828, quoted in Cordovez Moure, 748; also in Murray, *Simón Bolívar*, 69.

422   *He swore that he had opposed, etc.*: Santander to SB, Bocachica, Dec. 18, 1828, quoted in *Proceso Seguido al General Santander* (Bogotá: Biblioteca de la Presidencia de la República, 1988), Prólogo.

422   *protection from Andrew Jackson*: Santander to Jackson, Bocachica, May 19, 1829, quoted ibid.

422   *corresponded with him in jail*: Santander, *Apuntamientos*, 55; also Cordovez Moure, 1206.

422 *Even Páez, Santander's archenemy:* Blanco-Fombona, in O'Leary, *Bolívar y la emancipación*, 683 fn.

422 *The lion of the Apure assured Santander:* Páez to Santander, Puerto Cabello, Aug. 20, 1829, in Páez, *Autobiografía*, I, 550.

423 *they wanted fiefdoms equivalent to their aspirations:* Liévano Aguirre, 501.

423 *"The second man to head the Republic," etc.:* SB, "A Panoramic View of Spanish America," DOC, XIII, 493; also in SBSW, II, 741–48.

423 *Páez's missive was respectful, etc.:* Páez to SB, Caracas, July 22, 1829, *Documentos para los anales*, II, 132–34; also in Páez, *Autobiografía*, I, 509. As for reading the meaning, see Liévano Aguirre, 498–99.

424 *"I give you my word of honor," etc.:* SB to Páez, Popayán, Dec. 15, 1829, *Documentos para los anales*, 134–37.

424 *"You will now suspend completely," etc.:* SB to Vergara, Popayán, Nov. 22, 1829, SB, *Obras completas*, III, 365.

424 *"Just leave congress to do its duty":* SB to Urdaneta, Popayán, Nov. 22, 1829, ibid., 367, 370.

424 *Ministers proffered their resignations, etc.:* Restrepo, IV, 244; also O'Leary's notes in Sept. 1829, *Detached Recollections*, 16–17.

424 *Both Páez and Santander, though ardent enemies:* Larrazábal, *Vida*, II, 513 fn.

424 *If he had been more decisive on the question, etc.:* Restrepo, SB's minister of the interior and a loyalist, was critical of SB on this score. Perhaps rightfully, he blames SB for not making a stronger attempt to clarify his position and kill the monarchical campaign from the outset (José Manuel Restrepo, quoted in Guerra, *La convención de Ocaña*, 82; also in Restrepo, *Historia de la revolución*, III, 534; also quoted in Larrazábal, *Vida*, II, 511). President Belaunde of Peru, who wrote amply on Bolívar, feels that his last years reflect an essential weakness: He vacillated when he should have been firm. But for Belaunde, SB's weakness is only human (Belaunde, xiii).

424 *had exacted a punishing price:* SB, "A Panoramic View," DOC, XIII, 493.

425 *An uprising had come and gone, etc.:* Before O'Leary's campaign to quell the rebellion, SB had tried a number of strategies to pacify Córdova. He had offered to promote him to minister of the navy, but the general had only scoffed, as there was no navy to speak of in Colombia. SB had then offered him a diplomatic post in Holland. Córdova ignored that, too.

425 *gave Páez the most felicitous opportunity, etc.:* Posada Gutiérrez, I, 226–30; also Larrazábal, *Vida*, II, 525.

425 *He sent his agents out into the provinces:* DOC, XIII, 706.

425 *"and down with Don Simón":* Ibid.

426 *O'Leary and a thousand seasoned veterans, etc.:* Posada Gutiérrez, I, 208.

426 *O'Leary was quick to act, etc.:* Ibid., 208–9.

426 *a notorious drunk named Rupert Hand:* Ibid.

426 *two thrusts of the sword:* FJB, *Archivo O'Leary*, Marinilla, Oct. 17, 1829, quoted in Polanco Alcántara, 1014; also Posada Gutiérrez, I, 209.

426 *just as Saturn had swallowed his children:* I owe this image to Masur, *Simón Bolívar*, 659.

426 *In the end he would be blamed for all of it:* Posada Gutiérrez, I, 209–10.

426 *The torment of that reality, etc.:* Larrazábal, *Vida*, II, 521–24.

426   *Bolívar wrote to his minister of interior:* Restrepo, IV, 260; also *Documentos para los anales*, I, 481.

427   *Graffiti filled the walls, etc.:* DOC, XIII, 714 ff.

427   *Páez declared that he would go to war, etc.:* Páez to SB, Caracas, Dec. 1, 1829, Páez, *Autobiografía*, 557–59.

427   *When the Liberator entered the capital, etc.:* Posada Gutiérrez, I, 230.

427   *four thousand soldiers lined the way, etc.:* Ibid., 230–31.

427   *a wasted specter with lackluster eyes, etc.:* Ibid.; also Masur, *Simón Bolívar*, 669–70.

427   *It was apparent to everyone, etc.:* Posada Gutiérrez, I, 231.

CHAPTER 18: THE GENERAL IN HIS LABYRINTH

PAGE

428   Epigraph: *"If my death can heal and fortify the union":* SB's last words, Restrepo, IV, 412.

428   *"the admirable congress":* Ibid., 319; also Larrazábal, *Vida*, II, 519.

428   *a twenty-one-gun salute, etc.:* Posada Gutiérrez, I, 233.

428   *Fray Domingo de Las Casas:* Cousin of the great humanist Bartolomé de Las Casas. Groot, I, 48.

428   *an air of anticipation hung over the crowd, etc.:* Posada Gutiérrez, I, 233; also Larrazábal, *Vida*, II, 521.

429   *"I am seeking":* SB to Castillo Rada, Jan. 4, 1830, SBC, IX, 227, quoted in Mijares, 553.

429   *After receiving Communion, etc.:* Posada Gutiérrez, I, 233.

429   *gallery of mediocrities:* I owe this image to Lynch, *Simón Bolívar*, 271.

429   *the foresight to convoke this gathering, etc.:* SB, "Manifesto Justifying the Dictatorship," Bogotá, Aug. 27, 1928, SB, *El Libertador: Writings*, 141–42.

429   *Congress welcomed him, lauded him:* Posada Gutiérrez, I, 233–4.

429   *"I withdraw in utmost confidence":* Ibid.

429   *was visibly wounded:* W. Turner, report to the British Foreign Minister, PRO/FO 18/68, no. 75, quoted in Madariaga, 617.

429   *he clutched his head in dismay:* Ibid.

429   *"I, too, had my desperate hour," etc.:* Flores to Urdaneta, Quito, March 27, 1830, O'L, IV, 288–89.

430   *"Spare me, I beg you, the disgrace":* SB, "Mensaje del Libertador," Bogotá, Jan. 20, 1830, SBO, III, *Discursos*, 145–53.

430   *Now, more than ever, he warned:* Ibid.

430   *"Today, I cease to rule":* Larrazábal, *Vida*, II, 521.

430   *"Colombians! I have been the victim":* Ibid., 521–22.

431   *He met with foreign diplomats:* Ibid., 529; also Posada Gutiérrez, I, 231.

431   *wrote to his ambassador in London, etc.:* SB to J. Fernández Madrid, Bogotá, Feb. 13, March 6, 1830, SB, *Fundamental*, I, 609–13.

432   *retired to his house at La Quinta:* Liévano Aquirre, 502.

432   *She received him with customary cheer:* Ibid.

432   *Congress rejected his resignation, etc.:* DOC, XIV, 123–24.

432   *recalling his earlier blunders with Páez:* Masur, *Simón Bolívar*, 671.

432 *"I've asked Colombia to speak up"*: SB to Alamo, quoted in Larrazábal, *Vida*, II, 512.

432 *attack of what he called black bile*: Ibid., 532; Posada Gutiérrez, I, 250; Madariaga, 621.

432 *a country retreat a few miles southwest*: This was the Villa Fucha, mentioned in Posada Gutiérrez, I, 251; Madariaga, 621; Mitre, *Emancipation of South America*, 468.

432 *It was clear to all except perhaps Bolívar*: Mijares, 555.

433 *Ever since he had confided, etc.*: SB to O'Leary, Guayaquil, Aug. 21, 1829, O'L, XXXI, 483–86.

433 *By the end of March, he realized, etc.*: Larrazábal, *Vida*, II, 541.

433 *fetched little more than $2,000*: Larrazábal reports that when SB sold his personal silverware to the government mint, it produced $2,535, which represented all the money SB had. Larrazábal, *Vida*, II, 541.

433 *Europe or a stopover in Curaçao or Jamaica*: SB to Gabriel Camacho, Guaduas, May 11, 1830, quoted ibid., 542–43.

433 *lay in his copper mines in Aroa, etc.*: SB refers in many letters to his attempts to sell these. See especially SB to Alamo, Soatá, March 26, 1828, O'L, XXXI, 54–55; SB to Ibarra, Bogotá, Aug. 28, 1828, ibid., 192–93; SB to Briceño Méndez, Popayán, Feb. 5, 1829, ibid., 316–17. SB aspired to private life as early as 1825, even as he was making a victory tour of Upper Peru, and counted on the sale of Aroa to support him: SB to Peñalver, Potosí, Oct. 17, 1825, and Magdalena, March 4, 1826, O'L, XXX, 182.

433 *the equivalent of $10 million*: SB had asked Lord Cochrane to go and see the mines himself, in order to confirm their estimated worth of $500,000 (SB to Cochrane, Oct. 18, 1825, *Escritos*, 188). The dollar in 1830 would be worth $20 today ("Comparative Value of the U.S. Dollar," http://mykindred.com/cloud/TX/Documents/dollar/). The mines represented an annual income of the equivalent of $250,000. "Bolívar Empresario," a monograph by the Venezuelan historian Antonio Herrera-Vaillant, www.hacer.org/pdf/Bolívar.pdf, 17, 21.

433 *owned outright by the Bolívars since 1773*: This was when Juan Vicente Bolívar, SB's father, confirmed ownership. The mines were inherited by SB's grandmother, Josefa Marín de Narváez, whose family had owned them since the 1600s. P. Verna, *Las minas del Libertador* (Caracas: Ed. de la Presidencia de la República, Imprenta Nacional, 1976).

433 *He had claimed he didn't care about money*: There is much on the record to support this, e.g., SB to Santander, Lima, Oct. 30, 1823, SBO II, 829: "I have always thought that he who labors for liberty and glory should have no other compensation than liberty and glory." For an interesting analysis of SB's disposition to money, see Herrera-Vaillant, 8–12.

433 *when Venezuela outlawed the sale*: Ibid., 47–49.

434 *"a despot with criminal designs"*: Bermúdez, Proclama, Feb. 16, 1830, in Larrazábal, *Vida*, II, 540.

434 *a tyrant with an evil brain*: Arismendi, Bando, Feb. 25, 1830, in Larrazábal, *Vida*, II, 540.

434 *"Give up trying to defend me," etc.*: SB to Alamo, Popayán, Dec. 6, 1829, DOC, XIV, 26–27.

434 *unable to eat or sleep*: Posada Gutiérrez, I, 250.

434 *"María Antonia, don't be a fool," etc.*: Liévano Aguirre, 503.

435   *Even his old mistress in Paris:* Fanny du Villars to SB, Paris, April 6, May 14, 1826, O'L, XII, 293–300.

435   *But Bolívar had always been profligate, etc.:* Mijares, 556–57; Ducoudray Holstein, 94; Petre, 428.

435   *Páez announced that Venezuela's sovereignty, etc.:* Restrepo, IV, 267–71.

435   *He worked himself into a temper, etc.:* Masur, *Simón Bolívar*, 672–73.

435   *came to tell him that this was madness:* Restrepo, IV, 309.

435   *What was he now then?, etc.:* Ibid.

435   *"Come live in our hearts," etc.:* Flores (and forty-two other signatories) to SB, Quito, March 27, 1830, in Larrazábal, *Vida*, II, 537.

435   *Having returned to Bogotá in March, etc.:* Restrepo, IV, 299.

436   *Not one vote had been cast:* Ibid., 312; also Larrazábal, *Vida*, II, 538.

436   *a Bolívarian went on to win, etc.:* This was Eusebio Canabal. Restrepo, IV, 299; also Posada Gutiérrez, I, 307.

436   *the announcer was shouted down, etc.:* Restrepo, IV, 299.

436   *had tampered with the election:* Posada Gutiérrez, I, 307–8.

436   *On May 7, three days after congress unveiled, etc.:* Ibid., 317–18.

436   *move into the house of one of his generals, etc.:* General Herran's house. Larrazábal, *Vida*, II, 539.

436   *milling about the streets, shouting taunts:* Restrepo, IV, 312–33.

436   *Caicedo, insisted on spending the night:* Ibid., 317.

436   *hurried goodbyes in a dim corridor, etc.:* Rumazo González, 263.

436   *Their parting was sad and sweet, etc.:* Murray, *Simón Bolívar*, 74; Lynch, *Simón Bolívar*, 274.

436   *striding into the chill of morning:* Rumazo González, 263.

436   *His hands trembled, etc.:* Posada Gutiérrez, I, 322.

436   *He rode off, escorted by a phalanx, etc.:* Larrazábal, *Vida*, II, 540.

437   *"Hey, Sausage!":* Groot, III, 460.

437   *the fog-hung morning, etc.:* Rumazo González, 263.

437   *"He is gone, the gentleman of Colombia":* Col. Campbell, quoted in Larrazábal, *Vida*, II, 540.

437   *enemies had circulated a rumor, etc.:* Posada Gutiérrez, I, 321; also Restrepo, IV, 318–19.

437   *Vice President Caicedo had been powerless:* Caicedo was in charge in the absence of Mosquera, the president-elect, who was still making his way to the capital from Popayán.

437   *Protesters yelled anti-Bolívarian slogans, etc.:* Slatta and Lucas de Grummond, 291.

437   *"When I came to your house," etc.:* Sucre to SB, Bogotá, May 8, 1830, O'L, I, 571.

438   *Bolívar was in the northern town of Turbaco, etc.:* SB to Sucre, Turbaco, May 26, 1830, in *Itinerario documental*, Homenaje al Dr. Vicente Lecuna, Caracas, 1970, 349.

438   *he had had to wait for a craft, etc.:* Ibid.

438   *"My love, I am glad to report":* SB to Sáenz, Guaduas, May 11, 1830, SBC, IX, 265.

438   *at the peak of the rainy season, etc.:* H. Chisholm, "Colombia: Fauna and Flora," in *Encyclopedia Britannica*, VI, 704.

438   *the relentless, fetid heat of the coast, etc.:* Posada Gutiérrez, I, 392, 397.

438   *an annual pension equivalent to $15,000, etc.:* According to Restrepo, $30,000; Restrepo, IV, 317–18. Peso to dollar value: *Consular Reports*, vol. LX, GPO, Washington, DC, 1899, 663.

438 *The scant money he had raised:* Posada Gutiérrez, 393.

438 *his passport was slow in coming:* SB to Caicedo, Turbaco, June 1, 1830, SBC, IX, 272.

439 *a British packet boat was on its way, etc.:* Posada Gutiérrez, I, 397.

439 *learned that it would be full of women:* SB to Mosquera, Cartagena, June 24, 1830, SBC, IX, 275.

439 *Bolívar wouldn't hear of it, etc.:* Posada Gutiérrez, I, 397, and for all subsequent details about this incident. Also see SB to "mi General," Cartagena, June 29, 1830, SBC, IX, 277.

439 *took advantage of the ship's route to Caracas:* SB to Leandro Palacios, Cartagena, Aug. 14, 1830, SBC, IX, 285.

439 *a slew of letters and a bit of remarkable news:* Rivolba, 64.

440 *the tragic news he received on the morning of July 1:* Larrazábal, *Vida*, II, 547.

440 *he had been ambushed, etc.:* "Sucre," República del Ecuador, Diario Oficial, Quito, May 24, 1889, no. 61, 1–3, and for all subsequent details in this paragraph.

440 *Days later, a band of suspects, etc.:* L. Villanueva, *Vida del gran mariscal de Ayacucho* (Caracas: Tip Moderna, 1895), 567–72.

440 *The directive Obando had given:* The head assassin, Apolinar Morillo, when questioned, quoted Obando as saying in the presence of Com. Antonio María Alvarez: "The country is in great peril of being taken over by tyrants, and the only way to save it is to get rid of General Sucre, who is coming from Bogotá to force Ecuador to crown the Liberator. To this end, it is necessary that you march this very day to join José Erazo [the second assassin] in Salto de Mayo." L. Villanueva, *Vida del gran mariscal* (Caracas: Moderna, 1895), 570; see also Restrepo, IV, 611–12. (Restrepo's version of the testimony is stronger, quoting Morillo as saying: "The only way to save Ecuador is to go to Salto de Mayo, find Sucre, and kill him.")

440 *"Maybe Obando will go ahead" etc.:* Editorial, *El Democrata*, June 1, 1830, quoted in *Documentos para los anales*, IV, 544.

440 *General Flores . . . was also accused, etc.:* L. Urdaneta, "*Relación desnuda*, July 24, 1830," *BOLANH*, 28, no. 111 (July–Sept. 1945), 347–48. SB later said, "Some claim that [Sucre's assassination] was carried out on Flores's orders, but this is false." SB to Madrid, Cartagena, July 24, 1830, SBC, IX, 284.

441 *"Holy God! . . . If there is justice, etc.":* SB, upon hearing about Sucre's assassination. Rumazo González, 266.

441 *That night, Bolívar's condition worsened:* He experienced a severe pulmonary attack within hours of hearing the news about Sucre. Larrazábal, *Vida*, II, 560.

441 *an insuperable sense of dread:* Bolívar to Flores, Cartagena, July 1, 1830, SBC, IX, 279.

441 *He had agonized over his mistress's welfare, etc.:* Ibid.; also Larrazábal, *Vida*, II, 549.

441 *but it was his fearless warrior:* Bolívar to Flores, July 1, 1830, SBC, IX, 279.

441 *"Be careful. . . . Mind your safety," etc.:* Ibid., 280.

441 *She was dressing like a Mameluke, etc.:* Cordovez Moure, 752.

441 *she began a calculated campaign:* L. A. Cuervo, *Apuntos historiales* (Bogotá: Editorial Minerva, 1925), 201.

442 *referred to as "the Foreigner":* Editorial, *Aurora*, June 10, 1830, in Rumazo González, 269–70.

442 *But the effigies that appeared on the plaza, etc.:* The scene is described in the government hearing about Sáenz's alleged misbehavior. "Documentos inéditos," *Boletín de Historia*

y Antiguedades, Bogotá, no. 47, May–June, 1960, 373–402; also Rumazo González, 267–96; and Murray, *For Glory and Bolívar*, 75–76.

442 *Manuela rode to the plaza, etc.:* Rumazo González, 269–70; Murray, *For Glory and Bolívar*, 76, and for subsequent details.

442 *"An unhinged woman, a devotee," etc.:* Editorial, *Aurora*, quoted in Rumazo González, 269–70.

443 *Manuela decided to watch from her perch, etc.:* "Documentos inéditos."

443 *"Down with despots!":* Ibid.; also Rumazo González, 269–70; Murray, *For Glory and Bolívar*, 76.

443 *A mounting fury rose in Manuela, etc.:* "Documentos inéditos," 390–93.

443 *a resounding din rocked the air, etc.:* Ibid.; Rumazo González, 270; Murray, *For Glory and Bolívar*, 76, and for subsequent details.

443 *"You think that man is president?" etc.:* "Documentos inéditos."

444 *a voluptuary who took on lovers, etc.:* There were rumors (persisting through history) that Manuela had love affairs with other men, most notably Nimian R. Cheyne. None of these rumors was substantiated, and indeed she never was known to have another lover after her exile from Colombia. Lecuna, "Papeles de Manuela Sáenz," 497.

444 *her Quito accent:* Rumazo González, 270.

444 *harassed her for little more than shouting, etc.:* Lecuna, "Papeles de Manuela Sáenz," 517–18.

444 *made it a matter of state, etc.:* Cordovez Moure, 751.

444 *the sharp-tongued journalist Vicente Azuero:* Azuero, who had been exiled along with Santander and others after the attempt on SB's life, was made minister of the interior. F. Cevallos, *Resumen de la historia del Ecuador*, IV (Guayaquil: La Nación, 1886), 423.

444 *they soon proved to be weak executives, etc.:* SB to Briceño Méndez, Cartagena, Sept. 20, 1830, SBC, IX, 320.

444 *Mosquera had become the very antithesis:* Ibid.; also SB to Soledad, Oct. 25, 1830, SBC, IX, 342.

444 *"My hero has turned into a pumpkin":* SB to Briceño Méndez.

444 *The regime tried to seize, etc.:* Rumazo González, 265; also Murray, *For Glory and Bolívar*, 78.

444 *"In answer to your demands," etc.:* Murray, *For Glory and Bolívar*, 78.

444 *she meant to break the back, etc.:* Ibid., 78–80.

444 *She courted the regiments with beer, etc.:* Azuero, in particular, complained bitterly about this. Rumazo González, 266; "Documentos inéditos," 380–85.

445 *initiated a formal investigation, etc.:* "Documentos inéditos," 375, for all these details.

445 *The mayor of Bogotá let it be known:* Lecuna, "Papeles de Manuela Sáenz," 519–20.

445 *She received so many death threats, etc.:* Turner to Aberdeen, Bogotá, Aug. 12, 1830, PRO/FO, 18:77, 14–18; also José Manuel Restrepo, *Diario político y militar*, II (Bogotá: Imprenta Nacional, 1954), 102; also Murray, *For Glory and Bolívar*, 80–81.

445 *Sáenz packed up her possessions, mounted her horse, and left:* Restrepo, *Diario*, II, 102.

445 *entire political climate of Colombia had reversed, etc.:* All the particulars in this paragraph are described in SB to Briceño Méndez, Cartagena, Sept. 1, 1830, SBC, IX, 287. See also Posada Gutiérrez, I, 482–83.

445 *skirmish outside the capital:* Battle of Santuario, Aug. 27, 1830. Restrepo, *Historia*, IV, 366–67.

445 *on September 5, he and Caicedo were deposed:* Ibid., 372. Also DOC, IV, 480–85.

445 *General Urdaneta, who had been behind the coup, etc.:* Restrepo, *Historia*, IV, 372.

445 *using Bolívar's glory for his own purposes, etc.:* SB knew it. Writing to General Montilla six months before, he said, "A few swine who were behind the monarchical project have imagined they could sell my soul in order to save themselves; but I am resolved to maintain my dignity, my honor and glory, in spite of their perfidious projects." SB to Montilla, March 21, 1830, SBC, IX, 230.

445 *"The Liberator is immortal," etc.:* Sáenz to D. Logan, Guaduas, Nov. 24, 1830, *BANH*, 29, no. 74 (July–Dec., 1949), 277–80.

445 *She sent one of her friends:* This was Perú de Lacroix, who was at his side until the end. Villalba, *Epistolario*, 32–33.

445 *flourish once more when he reached England:* Arciniegas, *Las mujeres y las horas*, 288.

446 *march south with three thousand troops:* SB to Justo Briceño, Cartagena, Sept. 15, 1830; SB to Castelli, Sept. 18, 1830; SB to Urdaneta, Sept. 18, 1830; all in SBC, IX, 306–13.

446 *"If they offer me an army," etc.:* SB to Briceño Méndez, Cartagena, Sept. 20, 1830, ibid., 320–22.

446 *he had said so only to boost his supporters:* "I offered these things vaguely, in order to dissimulate, but I was not going to Bogotá, not going to rule." SB to Vergara, Sept. 25, 1830, ibid., 323–28.

446 *he was deathly sick, etc.:* Villalba, *Epistolario*, 32–33.

446 *Páez's "crazy fandango":* "un fandango de locos," SB to Briceño Méndez, Cartagena, Sept. 1, 1830, *Documentos para los anales*, 266–67.

446 *"I cannot live between rebels," etc.:* SB to Briceño Méndez, Sept. 20, 1830, ibid.

446 *Where was the legal process? etc.:* SB to Briceño Méndez, Cartagena, Sept. 10, 1830, SBC, IX, 304.

446 *He felt he had been diminished, etc.:* Ibid.

446 *"and now here they are, wanting to strip me":* Ibid.

446 *"Mosquera is the legitimate president," etc.:* SB to Urdaneta, Cartagena, Sept. 25, 1830, SBC, IX, 320–23; also in Larrazábal, *Vida*, II, 556.

446 *"I no longer have a fatherland":* SB to Vergara, Sept. 25, 1830, SBC, IX, 323–28.

447 *"Believe me, . . . I've never looked on insurrections":* SB to Vergara, Sept. 25, 1830, SBC, IX, 323–28.

447 *a feverish spurt of epistolary energy:* Bolívar dictated fifty-two letters in the course of a month, from mid-Oct. to mid-Nov. 1830. Polanco Alcántara, 1024.

447 *a letter from General Lafayette:* Lafayette to SB, Lagrange, June 1, 1830, DOC, XIV, 236.

447 *from George Washington's family:* SB to Lafayette, Lima, March 20, 1826, SB, *El Libertador*, 171.

447 *"the Washington of the South":* The letter included a commemorative medal and a lock of George Washington's hair. G. W. Custis to SB, Aug. 26, 1825, *The United States of Venezuela* (New York: Government of Venezuela, 1893), 144. (Published for the World's Columbian Exposition in Chicago.)

447 *"I am old, sick, tired, disillusioned," etc.:* SB to Briceño Méndez, Cartagena, Sept. 20, 1830, *Documentos para los anales*, 266–67.

447   *more than 75,000 miles:* 120,000 kilometers. This figure is cited in many works on SB, including Alvaro Vargas Llosa's review of John Lynch's *Simón Bolívar* in *The New Republic*, June 19, 2006; or monographs such as R. D. Favale's "Las casas más importantes de Simón Bolívar," http://www.scribd.com/doc/19325625/Las-casas-mas-importantes-de-Bolívar. Also see Bernal Medina, Introducción.

447   *He had rarely experienced physical weakness, etc.:* O. Beaujon, *El Libertador enfermo,* Sociedad Venezolana de Historia de la Medicina, conference, June 27, 1963 (Caracas: Grafos, 1969), 105ff.

448   *too incapacitated to do more than dictate, etc.:* SB to Urdaneta, Soledad, Oct. 25, 1830, SBC, IX, 345–49.

448   *shooting pains in his abdomen, etc.:* SB to Montilla, Soledad, Oct. 27, 1830, ibid., 349–51.

448   *He asked for a little dry sherry, etc.:* SB to Montilla, Barranquilla, Nov. 8, 1830, ibid., 374–75; also SB to Mier, Barranquilla, Nov. 19, 1830, ibid., 393.

448   *The heat of Cartagena was debilitating:* SB to Briceño Méndez, Dec. 4, 1830, ibid., 405.

448   *swaddled in wool from head to toe:* Arciniegas, *Los hombres y los meses,* 290.

448   *longing for a quick voyage at sea, etc.:* SB to Montilla, Barranquilla, Nov. 11, 1830, SBC, IX, 384–85; also SB to Urdaneta, Barranquilla, Nov. 8, 1830, *Documentos para los anales,* 253–54.

448   *adamantly refused medicines, etc.:* SB to Urdaneta, Soledad, Nov. 6, 1830, SBC, IX, 369.

448   *There was no doctor, etc.:* SB to Montilla, Soledad, Oct. 27, 1830, ibid.

448   *"I've deteriorated to such a degree," etc.:* SB to Urdaneta, Soledad, Oct. 31, 1830, ibid., 355.

448   *a living skeleton, etc.:* SB to Urdaneta, Soledad, Oct. 16, 1830, ibid., 333–38.

448   *"Today, I had a bad fall," etc.:* Ibid.

448   *Climbing a few steps, etc.:* SB to Justo Briceño, Barranquilla, Nov. 24, 1830, ibid., 395–96; also Wilson to O'Leary, Santa Marta, Oct. 31, 1830, O'L, XII, 131.

449   *He had barely enough strength to sit, etc.:* José Vallarino to Panama, Nov. 10, 1830, *BO-LANH,* no. 104, 258ff., quoted also in Madariaga, 643–44.

449   *a little tapioca, etc.:* Vallarino to Panama, Nov. 10, 1830, BOLANH, no. 104, 258 ff.

449   *"I'm very, very alarmed," etc.:* Wilson to O'Leary, Oct. 31, 1830, O'L, XII, 131.

449   *his mind was sharp, etc.:* Polanco Alcántara, 1024–25.

449   *"Believe me, . . . you two will end up like Páez":* SB to Justo Briceño, Soledad, Oct. 31, 1830, SBC, IX, 356.

449   *"Building one good accord is better":* SB to Urdaneta, Nov. 16, 1830, ibid., 390.

449   *"Many generals . . . know how to win":* SB to Urdaneta, Turbaco, Oct. 2, 1830, ibid., 329.

449   *"I wouldn't be surprised if they kill you":* SB to Urdaneta, Soledad, Nov. 4, 1830, ibid., 362–65.

449   *instructed Urdaneta to burn those letters:* Ibid.

449   *could count on holding power:* SB to Urdaneta, Soledad, Oct. 16, 1830, ibid.

449   *"Avenge Sucre's murder," etc.:* SB to Flores, Barranquilla, Nov. 9, 1830, ibid., 370.

450   *he believed, beyond all evidence to the contrary:* SB to Urdaneta, Barranquilla, Nov. 26, 1830, ibid., 399–400.

450   *he would sail for the blue mountains of Jamaica, etc.:* SB to Urdaneta, ibid. Also Ar-

ciniegas, *Los hombres y los meses*, 313; and Belford Wilson to O'Leary, Barranquilla, Nov. 27, 1830, O'L, XII, 140.

450   *loyal supporters, General Mariano Montilla:* SB and Montilla had not always been friends. Montilla served under Brigadier Manuel Castillo, who was SB's bitter enemy, from the Admirable Campaign through the siege of Cartagena. But after 1815, Montilla was an indefatigable supporter. Parra-Pérez, *Historia*, I, 21.

450   *When Bolívar wrote to him asking for help, etc.:* SB to Montilla, Barranquilla, Nov. 8, 1830, SBC, IX, 374–75.

450   *He found Bolívar a doctor of sorts, etc.:* M. L. Scarpetta and S. Vergara, "Révérend, Alejandro Prospero" in *Diccionario biográfico de los campeones de la libertad en Nueva Granada* (Bogotá: Zalamea, 1879), 507.

450   *Bolívar arrived in Santa Marta on the 1st of December, etc.:* Journals of Dr. A. P. Révérend, *Gaceta de Colombia*, Bogotá, Jan. 1, 1831 (Facs. nos. 494–566, Banco de la República), xxix. Also Révérend, "Relación del Dr. Révérend," in DOC, XIV, 464–74.

450   *a retinue of loyal friends:* Belford Wilson, Laurencio Silva, Mariano Portocarerro, and Diego Ibarra, among numerous others. Perú de Lacroix to Sáenz, Cartagena, Dec. 18, 1830, in Villalba, *Epistolario*, 185.

450   *among them Perú de Lacroix, etc.:* Ibid.

450   *those calm December waters:* M. Maza, "Subtidal Inner Shelf Currents off Cartagena de Indias," *Geophysical Research Letters*, 33 (Nov. 9, 2006), L21606, 5.

451   *Alexander von Humboldt, etc.:* Alexander von Humboldt and W. MacGillivray, *The Travels and Researches of Alexander von Humboldt, Being a Condensed Narrative of His Journeys in the Equinoctial Regions of America* (New York: Harper, 1835), 272.

451   *his face a mask of alarm, etc.:* Liévano Aguirre, 509.

451   *reduced to a human cinder:* Arciniegas, *Los hombres y los meses*, 313.

451   *a cradle of locked hands:* Révérend, "Relación," DOC, XIV, 464–74.

451   *they laid him on a pallet, etc.:* Ibid.

451   *"His excellency arrived in Santa Marta":* Ibid.

451   *"his lungs were sadly damaged":* Révérend brought an American surgeon, Dr. George W. McKnight, from the United States warship *Grampus* to confirm this diagnosis. Dr. McKnight called it a chronic lung catarrh. There was also some question as to whether it was malaria, and he was given quinine. Ibid.

451   *a United States naval surgeon:* This was Dr. McKnight. In many references he is inaccurately referred to as Dr. Night. Department of State, *A Register of All Officers, Civil, Military, and Naval, in the Service of the United States*, W. A. Davis, City of Washington, 1830, 125.

451   *most probably tuberculosis:* Gil Fortoul, I, 493.

451   *jaundiced, hardly able to sleep, etc.:* Révérend, "Relación," DOC, XIV, 464–74.

452   *reduced to less than eighty pounds:* Langley, 105.

452   *an aroma he knew well, etc.:* SB's sugar plantation in San Mateo, Díaz, 154.

452   *a hammock strung between two tamarind trees:* http://www.museobolivariano.org.co.

452   *Sometime before, he had sent word to Manuela:* Posada to Sáenz [place undetermined], Oct. 14, 1830, cited in Lecuna, "Papeles de Manuela Sáenz," 494–525. Gen. Posada had written to her to say that although SB knew she was planning to come in December, he hoped she would come sooner.

452   *couriers bursting with news, etc.:* Arciniegas, *Los hombres y los meses*, 314.

452   *They played cards, drank rum, etc.:* Ibid.

452   *When the stench of one general was so noxious, etc.:* Révérend, "Relación del Dr. Révérend," in DOC, XIV, 470.

452   *"Excuse me, Your Excellency":* Ibid., 471.

452   *"Ah, Manuela," etc.:* Ibid; also in Masur, *Simón Bolívar*, 591.

452   *"Doctor, what brought you to these parts?" etc.:* From Révérend, "Relación," 471; also in Gil Fortoul, I, 494.

453   *he was feverish again, raving, etc.:* Révérend, "Relación," DOC, XIV, 469.

453   *Montilla, beside himself with grief:* Gil Fortoul, I, 494.

453   *Bolívar balked at first, etc.:* Rivolba; also Révérend, "Relación," DOC, XIV, 472.

453   *"How will I ever get out of this labyrinth?":* Révérend, "Relación," DOC, XIV, 472.

453   *he commended his soul to God, etc.:* "Testament of Simón Bolívar," DOC, XIV, 463; SBSW, II, 766–68.

453   *8,000 pesos, etc.:* "Testament of Simón Bolívar."

453   *last rites from a humble Indian priest:* A cleric from the village of Mamatoco, Révérend, "Relación," DOC, XIV, 456.

453   *Colombians! You have witnessed":* SB, Proclama, *Documentos para los anales*, 280.

454   *but his mind was clear enough:* Révérend, "Relación," DOC, XIV, 472.

454   *weaving in and out of delirium:* Ibid., 473.

454   *His urine burned, etc.:* Ibid.

454   *"José! . . . Let's go!":* Ibid., 471. More editions: *La última enfermedad, los últimos momentos y los funerales de Simón Bolívar, por su médico de cabecera* (Paris: Imprenta de H. A. Cosson, 1866), 20–30; quoted in B. B. Celli, "La enfermedad y muerte del Libertador," *Revista de la Sociedad Venezolana de Historia de la Medicina*, 58 (Caracas, 2009), 63–70.

454   *When asked whether he was in pain:* Révérend, "Relación," DOC, XIV, 471; Celli, 66.

454   *the strange wheeze, etc.:* Révérend, "Relación," 473.

454   *"Gentlemen, if you want to be present":* Ibid., 474.

454   *At one o'clock in the afternoon, etc.:* Ibid.

454   *exactly eleven years to the minute:* Larrazábal, *Vida*, II, 565.

454   *his brow softened in beatific repose:* Révérend, "Relación," 473.

EPILOGUE

PAGE

455   *"Goodbye to the spirit of evil!", etc.:* I. S. Alderson, *Los funerales de Bolívar, BANH*, Caracas, XI, no. 41, 49.

455   *As three rounds of cannon fire, etc.:* DOC, XIV, 475.

456   *On December 20, 1830, the Liberator's corpse, etc.:* Ibid.

456   *looked around anxiously for a leader:* General José Domingo Espinar, the military commander of the Isthmus of Panama, offered Bolívar the presidency of the Panamanian republic after he declared its independence on Sept. 26, 1830. Bolívar declined, urging him to return Panama to Greater Colombia.

456   *"Allow me, esteemed madam," etc.:* Perú de Lacroix to Sáenz, Cartagena, Dec. 18, 1830, *Trofeos*, III, no. 14, Feb. 20, 1908, 384; also Unamuno, 273.

456   *Somehow, she got hold of a venomous snake, etc.:* Boussingault, III, 217. Boussingault comments that she may have been trying to die like Cleopatra.

456   *"I loved the Liberator when he was alive," etc.:* Rumazo González, 255.

457   *she landed in Paita:* Murray, *For Glory and Bolívar*, 105–29.

458   *He rode, "fighting all the way," etc.:* Thomas Carlyle, "Dr. Francia: Funeral Discourse Delivered on Occasion of Celebrating the Obsequies of His Late Excellency," *Foreign Quarterly Review*, no. 62 (1843).

458   *Never had Latin America dreamed so large:* I owe this to the Colombian poet and novelist William Ospina, in Ospina, 9.

458   *reduced civilian populations by a third:* Archer, esp. 35–37 and 283–92.

459   *In marble or bronze, Bolívar's flesh, etc.:* Ospina, 9.

459   *preserved in a small urn:* Historians were unable to find that urn or duly document its existence. See José Ignacio Méndez, *El ocaso de Bolívar*, Santa Marta, 1927, 212–13, in Masur, *Simón Bolívar*, 693.

461   *"the dastardly, most miserable":* Karl Marx to Fredrich Engels, Feb. 14, 1858, quoted in Enrique Krauze, *Redeemers* (New York: HarperCollins, 2011), 464.

461   *"Nothing is more beautiful," etc.:* José Martí, "Discurso pronunciado en la velada de la Sociedad Literaria Hispanoamericana," speech in New York, Oct. 28, 1893, in Unamuno, *Simón Bolívar*, 196.

461   *publication of a thirty-two-volume history:* This was O'Leary's *Memorias*, which contain Bolívar's letters, proclamations, and a narrative history. It is the mainstay of all research on Bolívar's life and work.

462   *in 2010, the bicentenary year of the start of the revolution:* To be precise, the exhumation was on July 16, 2010. The revolution began on April 19, 1810.

462   *had them taken from his sarcophagus, etc.:* G. Pereira, "Dead Commodities," in *Forensic Architecture*, http://www.forensic-architecture.org/docs/cabinet_43_dead_commodities _0.pdf.

462   *narrated, prayed, rhapsodized:* "My God, my God . . . my Christ, our Christ, while I was praying in silence watching those bones, I thought of you! . . . How much I wanted and would have liked for you to arrive and order, as you did to Lazarus: rise Simón, this is not the time to die!" Two entries on Hugo Chávez's Twitter account (7:41 A.M. and 7:48 A.M., July 16, 2010). See <twitter.com/chavezcandanga>, quoted in Pereira.

462   *astronauts in moon gear:* The bizarre ceremony can be seen in many videos, including one accompanied by a voice-over of President Chávez's comments, but this was one of the first videos released: http://www.youtube.com/watch?v=vqRT4q7zOg8&feature= related.

462   *"the magic of his prestige":* The phrase used by Gen. Daniel O'Leary, as referred to earlier in this book.

463   *many of the most tyrannical and barbaric:* G. García Márquez, "Una naturaleza distinta en un mundo distinto al nuestro," April 12, 1996, *La Jornada*, Bogotá, Oct. 28, 2010, 4.

463   *"The most stubborn conservatism," etc.:* E. Sábato, "Inercia mental," in *Uno y el universo* (Buenos Aires: Editorial Seix Barral, 2003), 90.

463   *In Bolivia, a famously debauched dictator, etc.:* This is Mariano Melgarejo, who was killed in exile, in Lima, in 1871. See Clayton, *The Bolivarian Nations*, 22.

463   *in Ecuador, a deeply religious despot, etc.:* This is Gabriel García Moreno, an intensely Catholic president, who was a bitter rival of President José Eloy Alfaro. Ibid., 23.

463   *in Quito, a liberal caudillo, etc.:* President José Eloy Alfaro, a liberal Freemason, who tried to dismantle the Church's power in Ecuador. Ibid., 36.

463   *Equality, which Bolívar had insisted was the linchpin of justice:* Bolívar to Vergara, Dec. 16, 1828, in Larrazábal, *Vida*, II, 511.

464   *Until he remade a world:* Vicuña MacKenna, quoted in Blanco-Fombona, "Bolívar escritor," Unamuno, 295.

~ Bibliography ~

PRIMARY SOURCES

Austria, José de. *Bosquejo de la historia militar de Venezuela.* 2 vols. Caracas: Academia Nacional de la Historia, 1960.

Baralt, Rafael María, and Ramón Díaz. *Resumen de la historia de Venezuela desde el año de 1797 hasta el de 1830.* 2 vols. Paris: Fournier, 1841.

Blanco, José Félix, and Ramón Azpurúa, eds. *Documentos para la historia de la vida pública del Libertador de Colombia, Perú y Bolivia.* 15 vols. Caracas: Ediciones de la Presidencia, 1977.

Blanco-Fombona, Rufino, ed. *Bolívar, pintado por sí mismo.* Caracas: Ministerio de Educación, 1959.

Bolívar, Simón. *Cartas de Bolívar: 1799–1822.* Ed. Rufino Blanco-Fombona. Paris: Louis-Michaud, 1912.

———. *Cartas de Bolívar: 1823–1824–1825.* Ed. Rufino Blanco-Fombona. Madrid: Editorial-América. 1921.

———. *Cartas de Bolívar: 1825–1827.* Ed. Rufino Blanco-Fombona. Madrid: Editorial-América. 1922.

———. *Cartas del Libertador corregidas conforme a los originales.* 10 vols. Ed. Vicente Lecuna. Caracas, 1917.

———. *Doctrina del Libertador.* Ed. Manuel Pérez Vila. Caracas: Fundación Biblioteca Ayacucho, 1992.

———. *El Libertador: Writings of Simón Bolívar.* Ed. David Bushnell. New York: Oxford, 2003.

———. *Epistolarios: Bolívar y las damas, las damas y Bolívar.* Caracas: Ediciones de la Presidencia de la República, 1983.

———. *Escritos del Libertador.* Caracas: Sociedad Bolívariana, 1964.

———. *Fundamental.* 2 vols. Ed. Germán Carrera Damas. Caracas: Monte Avila, 1993.

———. Letters, executive decrees, proclamations, broadsides. Maury Bromsen Collection, John Carter Brown Library, Brown University, Providence, Rhode Island.

———. *Obras (Cartas, Proclamas, y Discursos).* 3 vols. Ed. Vicente Lecuna, 1929–30. Caracas: Ediciones de la CANTV, 1983.

———. *Obras completas.* 6 vols. Madrid: Maveco de Ediciones, S.A. 1984.

———. *Proclamas y discursos.* Caracas: Gobierno de Venezuela, 1939.

———. *Proyecto de constitución para la república de Bolivia y discurso del Libertador.* Buenos Aires: Hallet y Cía., 1826.

———. *Selected Writings of Bolívar.* 2 vols. Comp. Vicente Lecuna. Ed. Harold A. Bierck, Jr. Trans. Lewis Bertrand. New York: Colonial Press, 1951.

Bolívar, Simón, y Luis Brión. *Correspondencia entre el Libertador y el Almirante Luis Brión.* Caracas: Ediciones de la Presidencia de la República, 1984.

Bolívar, Simón, y José Antonio Páez. *Bolívar: Epistolarios, Bolívar–José Antonio Páez, José Antonio Páez–Bolívar.* Caracas: Ediciones de la Presidencia de la República, 1983.

Bolívar, Simón, y Coronel Andrés Santa Cruz. *Bolívar y Santa Cruz: Epistolario.* Ed. Armando Rojas. Caracas: Gobierno de Venezuela, 1975.

Bolívar, Simón, y Francisco de Paula Santander. *Bolívar y Santander: Correspondencia, 1819–1820.* Bogotá: Imprenta del Estado Mayor General, 1940.

———. *Cartas: Santander–Bolívar, 1813–1830.* 5 vols. Bogotá: Biblioteca de la Presidencia de la República, 1988.

Bolívar, Simón, y Antonio José de Sucre. *Bolívar y Sucre: Dialogo epistolar de la grandeza.* Ed. J. L. Salcedo-Bastardo. Caracas: Ministerio de Educación, 1974.

Bolívar, Simón, y Rafael Urdaneta. *Bolívar: Epistolarios, Bolívar–Rafael Urdaneta, Rafael Urdaneta–Bolívar.* Caracas: Ediciones de la Presidencia de la República, 1983.

Boussingault, Jean-Baptiste. *Memorias.* 5 vols. Trans. Alexander Koppel de León. Bogotá: Banco de la República, 1985.

Breckenridge, H. M. *Voyage to South America, Performed by Order of the American Government, in the Years 1817 and 1818, in the Frigate* Congress. Published by the Author. Baltimore, 1819.

Campbell, John. *The Spanish Empire in America.* London: M. Cooper, 1747.

Chesterton, George Laval. *A Narrative of Proceedings in Venezuela, in South America, in the Years 1819 and 1820.* London: John and Arthur Arch, 1820.

Díaz, José Domingo. *Recuerdos sobre la rebelión de Caracas: 1829.* Caracas: Academia Nacional de la Historia, 1961.

Documentos para los anales de Venezuela. 8 vols. Academia Nacional de la Historia. Ed. R. Andueza Palacio. Caracas: 1830–1890.

Duane, Col. William. *A Visit to Colombia in the Years 1822 & 1823, by Laguayra and Caracas, over the Cordillera to Bogota, and Thence by the Magdalena to Cartagena.* Philadelphia: Thomas H. Palmer, 1826.

Ducoudray Holstein, Gen. H. L. V. *Memoirs of Simón Bolívar, President Liberator of the Republic of Colombia.* 2 vols. Boston: S. G. Goodrich & Co, 1829.

Espejo, G. *Recuerdos históricos: San Martín y Bolívar, entrevista en Guayaquil.* Buenos Aires: Goodby, 1873.

Espinosa, José María. *Memorias de un abanderado: Recuerdos de la patria boba, 1810–1819.* Bogotá: El Tradicionista, 1876.

Flinter, George Dawson, Esq. *A Letter to His Most Gracious Majesty, George the Fourth, King of Great Britain and Ireland, etc.* Port of Spain: John Hollman & Co., 1829.

Flinter, Major (George Dawson). *A History of the Revolution of Caracas.* London: T. and J. Allman, 1819.

Gaceta del Gobierno del Perú. Periodo de gobierno de Simón Bolívar. 4 vols. Caracas: Fundación Eugenio Mendoza, 1967.

García y García, José Antonio, ed. *Relaciones de los virreyes del Nuevo Reino de Granada, ahora*

Estados Unidos de Venezuela, Estados Unidos de Colombia y Ecuador. New York: Hallet & Breen, 1869.

Gazeta de Caracas, Gaceta de Caracas, Gaceta de Colombia, facsimile editions, JCBL.

González, José Florentino. *Memorias de Florentino González, 1853.* Medellín: Bedout, 1971.

Graham, María. *Journal of a Residence in Chile During the Year 1822, and a Voyage from Chile to Brazil in 1823.* Ed. Jennifer Hayward. Charlottesville: University of Virginia Press, 2003.

Guzmán Blanco, General José Félix. *Documentos para la historia de la vida pública del Libertador de Colombia, Perú y Bolivia.* 4 vols. Caracas: La Opinión Nacional, 1875.

Hamilton, John Potter. *Travels Through the Interior Provinces of Columbia* [sic], 2 vols. London: John Murray, 1827.

Heredia, José Francisco. *Memorias sobre las revoluciones de Venezuela.* Paris: Garnier Hermanos, 1895.

Heres, Tomás de. *Historia de la independencia americana: La emancipación del Perú, según la correspondencia del General Heres con el Libertador (1821–1830).* Ed. Rufino Blanco-Fombona. Madrid: Editorial-América, 1919.

Hippisley, Gustavus M. *Narrative of the Expedition to the Rivers Orinoco and Apure in South America.* London: John Murray, Albemarle-Street, 1819.

Humboldt, Alexander von. *Oeuvres d'Alexandre de Humboldt. Correspondance inédite scientifique et littéraire receuillie et publiée par M. de la Roquette.* Paris: E. Ducrocq, 1865.

———. *Personal Narrative of Travels to the Equinoctial Regions of America.* 3 vols. London: George Bell, 1900.

Lafond, Gabriel. *Voyages autour du monde et naufrages célebres: Voyages dans les Amériques.* Paris: Administration de Librairie, 1843.

Las Casas, Bartolomé de. *The Devastation of the Indies.* Trans. Herma Briffault. Baltimore: Crossroad, 1974.

Larrazábal, Felipe. *Vida y correspondencia general del Libertador Simón Bolívar.* 2 vols. New York: Eduardo O. Jenkins, 1866.

———. *Vida del Libertador Simón Bolívar.* 2 vols. New York: D. Appleton, 1887. (English: *Life of Bolívar.* 2 vols. New York: Edward O. Jenkins, 1866.)

Lecuna, Vicente, ed. "Cartas de mujeres." *Boletín de la Academia Nacional de la Historia*, 16 (April–July 1933): 332–98.

———. "Papeles de Manuela Sáenz." *Boletín de la Academia Nacional de la Historia*, 28, no. 112 (1945).

Litigio ventilado ante la real audiencia de Caracas sobre domicilio tutelar y educación del menor Simón Bolívar: Año de 1795. Caracas: Imprenta Nacional, 1955.

Lloyd, Thomas, stenographer. *The Trials of William S. Smith and Samuel G. Ogden for Misdemeanors Had in the Circuit Court of the United States for the New-York District, in July, 1806.* New York: I. Riley & Co., 1807.

López, Manuel Antonio. *Recuerdos históricos del Coronel Manuel Antonio López, ayudante del Estado Mayor General Libertador.* Bogotá: J. B. Gaitán, 1878.

Manning, William R. *Diplomatic Correspondence of the United States Concerning the Independence of the Latin-American Nations.* 3 vols. New York: Oxford University Press, 1925.

Martí, Obispo Mariano. *Documentos relativos a su visita pastoral a la Diócesis de Caracas, 1781–1784.* Caracas: Fuentes para la Historia, 1969.

Mejía Pavony, Germán, ed. *Proceso seguido al General Santander: Por consecuencia del acontecimiento de la noche del 25 de septiembre de 1828 en Bogotá.* Bogotá: Biblioteca de la Presidencia de la República, 1988.

Mérida, Rafael Diego. *Vindicación y repulsa a las inicuas acusaciones de la maledicencia, que publicó en 1819, Rafael Diego Mérida, secretario de Gracia y Justicia, que fue en esa época, del jeneral Bolívar.* Lima: Imprenta Juan Ross, 1827.

Miller, John. *Memoirs of General Miller in the Service of the Republic of Peru.* 2 vols. London: Longman, Rees, Orme, Brown, and Green, 1829.

"Minuta de la sesión tenida, el 16 julio, 1810, a las ocho de la tarde, entre el marqués Wellesley y los comisionados de la junta suprema de Caracas, en Apsley House, Londres." *Revista Bolivariana*, 2 nos. 20–21 (Bogotá, 1930).

Miranda, Francisco de. *América espera.* Selección y prólogo por J. L. Salcedo-Bastardo. Caracas: Biblioteca Ayacucho, 1982.

———. *Archivo del General Miranda.* 25 vols. Caracas: La Nación, 1929–33.

Mosquera, Tomás Cipriano de. *Memoria sobre la vida del General Simón Bolívar: Libertador de Colombia, Perú y Bolivia.* New York: Imprenta Nacional, 1853.

Niles, John M. *A View of South-America and México, by a Citizen of the United States.* New York: H. Huntington, Jr., 1825.

Notes on Colombia, Taken in the Years 1822–3. With an Itinerary of the Route from Caracas to Bogotá; and an Appendix. By an Officer of the United States' Army. Published anonymously, but credited later to Richard Bache. Philadelphia: Carey & Lea, 1827.

Noticias del Peru. 13 vols. Collection gathered by Henri Ternaux-Compans, including letters, broadsides, and other publications in Peru from 1807 to 1864. John Carter Brown Library, Brown University, Providence, Rhode Island.

Obando, José María. *Apuntamientos para la historia.* 2 vols. Lima: Imprenta del Comercio, 1842.

O'Connor, Francisco Burdett. *Independencia americana: Recuerdos de Francisco Burdett O'Connor.* Madrid: Sociedad Española de Librería, 1915.

O'Higgins, D. Bernardo. *Epistolario de D. Bernardo O'Higgins.* 2 vols. Ed. Ernesto de la Cruz. Madrid: Editorial-América, 1920.

O'Leary, Daniel Florencio. *Bolívar and the War of Independence.* Trans. and ed. Robert F. McNerney, Jr. Austin: University of Texas Press. 1970.

———. *Bolívar y la emancipación de Sur-América.* Trans. and ed. Simón B. O'Leary. This is a useful republication of vols. 27–28 of O'Leary's *Memorias*, with a change of title, and a biographical and critical preface by Rufino Blanco-Fombona. Madrid: Sociedad Española de Librería, 1915.

———. *The Detached Recollections of General D. F. O'Leary.* London: Institute of Latin American Studies, 1969.

———. *Junín y Ayacucho.* Madrid: Editorial América, 1919.

———. *Memorias: Narración.* 3 vols. Caracas: Imprenta Nacional, 1952.

———. *Memorias del General O'Leary.* 32 vols. Caracas, 1879–88.

———. *Ultimos años de la vida publica de Bolívar (Memorias del General O'Leary: Tomo apéndice).* Madrid: Editorial-América, 1916.

Páez, J. A.: *Archivo, 1818–1820.* Bogotá, 1939.

Páez, General José Antonio. *Autobiografía del General José Antonio Páez.* New York: Hallet & Breen, 1867.

Palacio Fajardo, Manuel. *Bosquejo de la revolución en la América Española* (first published as *Outline of the Revolution in South America: By a South American*). London: Longman, Hurst, Rees, Orme and Brown, 1817.

Paulding, Hiram. *Un rasgo de Bolívar en campaña.* New York: Don Juan de la Granja, 1835.

Perú de Lacroix, Louis. *Diario de Bucaramanga, vida pública y privada del Libertador, versión sin mutilaciones.* Caracas: Edicion: Centauro, 1976.

Posada Gutiérrez, Joaquín. *Memorias histórico-politicas: Últimos días de la Gran Colombia y del Libertador.* 3 vols. Bogotá: Foción Mantilla, 1865.

Proceso del 25 de septiembre: Documentos sobre el proceso de la conspiración del 25 de Septiembre de 1828. (Originales del Fondo Pineda y del Archivo Histórico.) Bogotá: Prensas de la Biblioteca Nacional, 1942.

Proctor, Robert. *Narrative of a Journey Across the Cordillera of the Andes, and of a Residence in Lima and Other Parts of Peru in the Years 1823 and 1824.* London: Archibald Constable & Co, 1825.

Rafter, M. *Memoirs of Gregor M'Gregor: Comprising a Sketch of the Revolution in New Grenada [sic].* London: J. J. Stockdale, 1820.

Recollections of a Service of Three Years During the War-of-Extermination in the Republics of Venezuela and Colombia, by an Officer of the Colombian Navy [Anonymous]. 2 vols. London: Hunt and Clarke, 1828.

Restrepo, José Manuel. *Historia de la revolución de la República de Colombia.* 10 vols. Paris: Librería Americana, 1827.

Rivolba [pseudonym of Fernando Bolívar]. *Recuerdos y reminiscencias del primer tercio de la vida de Rivolba.* Paris: Imprenta Americana de Rouge, Dunon y Fresné, 1873.

Rodríguez, Simón. *Cartas.* Caracas: UNESR, 2001.

Rodríguez Villa, Antonio. *El teniente general don Pablo Morillo: Primer conde de Cartagena.* 4 vols. Madrid: Fortanet, 1908.

Rojas, Armando. *Bolívar y Santa Cruz, epistolario.* Caracas: Gobierno de Venezuela, 1975.

San Martín, José de. *Documentos del archivo de San Martín.* 12 vols. Buenos Aires: Museo Mitre, 1910.

———. *San Martín, su correspondencia.* Madrid: Editorial-América, 1919.

Santander, Francisco de Paula. *Apuntiamentos para las memorias sobre Colombia y la Nueva Granada.* Bogotá: Lorenzo M. Lleras, 1838.

———. *El General Simón Bolívar en la campaña de la Nueva Granada de 1819.* Santafé de Bogotá, 1820.

———. *Escritos autobiográficos, 1820–1840.* Ed. Guillermo Hernández de Alba. Bogotá: Fundación para la Conmemoración del Bicentenario, 1988.

Semple, Robert. *Sketch of the Present State of Caracas.* London: Robert Baldwin, 1812.

Sucre, Antonio José de. *De mi propia mano, 1812–1830.* Caracas: Biblioteca Ayacucho, 1981.

Tristan, Flora. *Peregrinations of a Pariah.* Boston: Beacon, 1986.

Urdaneta, General Rafael. *Memorias del General Rafael Urdaneta.* Caracas: Imprenta Litografía del Gobierno Nacional, 1888.

Urquinaona y Pardo, Pedro. *Relación documentada del origen y progreso del trastorno de las provincias de Venezuela hasta la exoneración del Capitán General Don Domingo Monteverde, hecha en el mes de diciembre de 1813 por la guarnición de la plaza de Puerto Cabello.* Madrid: La Imprenta Nueva, 1820.

Vásconez Hurtado, Gustavo. *Cartas de Bolívar al General Juan José Flores: Historia y anti-historia.* Quito: Editorial Casa de la Cultura Ecuatoriana, 1976.

Villalba, Jorge, *Manuela Sáenz: Epistolario.* Quito: Banco Central de Ecuador, 1986.

Viscardo y Guzmán, Juan Pablo. *Letter to the Spanish Americans.* A facsimile of the second English edition (London, 1810), with an introduction by D. A. Brading. John Carter Brown Library. Providence, Rhode Island, 2002.

Vowell, Richard Longeville. *Campaigns and Cruises in Venezuela and New Grenada [sic], and in the Pacific Ocean.* London: Longman and Co., 1831.

Yanes, Francisco Javier. *Relación documentada de los últimos sucesos ocurridos en Venezuela.* 2 vols. Caracas: Editorial Elite, 1943.

SECONDARY SOURCES

Alvarez Saá, C. *Manuela: Sus diarios perdidos y otros papeles.* Quito: Imprenta Mariscal, 1995.

Adams, Randolph Greenfield. *A History of the Foreign Policy of the United States.* New York: Macmillan, 1924.

Adelman, J. *Sovereignty and Revolution in the Iberian Atlantic.* Princeton: Princeton University Press, 2006.

Aguilar Paredes, Jaime. *Las grandes batallas del Libertador.* Quito: Editorial Casa de la Cultura Ecuatoriana, 1980.

Amunátegui, Miguel Luis. *Vida de Don Andrés Bello.* Santiago de Chile: P. G. Ramírez, 1882.

Angell, Hildegarde. *Simón Bolívar: South American Liberator.* New York: W. W. Norton, 1930.

Archer, Christon I., ed. *The Wars of Independence in Spanish America.* Jaguar Books on Latin America, no. 20. Wilmington: SR Books, 2000.

Arciniegas, Germán. *América magica I: Los hombres y los meses.* Buenos Aires: Editorial Sudamericana, 1959.

———. *América mágica II: Las mujeres y las horas.* Buenos Aires: Editorial Sudamericana, 1961.

———. *Bolívar y la revolución.* Bogotá: Planeta, 1984.

Azpurúa, Ramón. *Biografías de hombres notables de Hispano-América.* 4 vols. Caracas: Imprenta Nacional, 1877.

Barros Arana, Diego. *Compendio elemental de historia de América.* Buenos Aires: Cabaut y Cía., 1904.

Barthèlemy, Rodolfo G. *Ascendencia gallega de Simón Bolívar.* Coruña: Edicios do Castro, 2004.

Basadre, Jorge. *Historia de la república del Perú,* 5 vols. Lima: Editorial Cultura Antártica, 1946.

Beals, Carleton. *Eagles of the Andes: South American Struggles for Independence.* Philadelphia: Chilton Books, 1963.

Becerra, Ricardo. *Ensayo histórico documentado de la vida de don Francisco de Miranda.* 2 vols. Caracas: Imprenta Colón, 1896.

Belaunde, Víctor Andrés. *Bolívar and the Political Thought of the Spanish American Revolution.* Baltimore: Johns Hopkins University Press, 1938.

Bernal Medina, Rafael. *Ruta de Bolívar*. Caracas: Ediciones de la Presidencia de la República, 1977.

Bethell, Leslie, ed. *The Cambridge History of Latin America: From Independence to c. 1870*. III. Cambridge: Cambridge University Press, 1985.

Bingham, Hiram. "On the Route of Bolívar's Great March: Caracas to Bogotá via Arauca and the Paramo of Pisva." *The Geographical Journal*, 32, no. 4 (Oct. 1908): 329–47.

Blanchard, Peter. *Under the Flags of Freedom: Slave Soldiers and the Wars of Independence in Spanish South America*. Pittsburgh: University of Pittsburgh Press, 2008.

Blanco, Eduardo. *Venezuela heroica*. Caracas: Imprenta Bolívar, 1883.

Blanco-Fombona, Rufino. *Bolívar y la guerra a muerte*. Caracas: Impresores Unidos, 1942.

———. *Ensayos históricos*. Caracas: Biblioteca Ayacucho, 1981.

———. *Mocedades de Bolívar: El héroe antes del heroísmo*. Lima: Ediciones Nuevo Mundo, 1960.

Borges, Jorge Luis. "Guayaquil." Short story in *Obras completas*. Buenos Aires: Emecé Editores, 1970.

Boulton, Alfredo. *Bolívar de Carabobo*. Caracas: Ediciones Macanao, 1992.

———. *El arquetipo iconográfico de Bolívar*. Caracas: Ediciones Macanao, 1984.

———. *El rostro de Bolívar*. Caracas: Ediciones Macanao, 1988.

———. *Iconografía del Libertador*. Caracas: Ediciones Macanao, 1992.

———. *Los retratos de Bolívar*. Caracas: Ediciones Macanao, 1964.

Bowman, Charles H., Jr. "The Activities of Manuel Torres as Purchasing Agent, 1820–1821." *The Hispanic American Historical Review*, 48, no. 2 (May 1968): 234–46.

Brewster, Claire. "Women and the Spanish-American Wars of Independence." *Feminist Review*, no. 79, Latin America: History, War and Independence (2005): 20–35.

Bulnes, Gonzalo. *Ultimas campañas de la independencia del Perú*. Santiago: Encuadernación Barcelona, 1897.

Bushnell, David. *The Santander Regime in Gran Colombia*. Newark: University of Delaware Press, 1954.

———. *Simón Bolívar: Liberation and Disappointment*. New York: Pearson Longman, 2004.

Bushnell, David, and Lester D. Langley, eds. *Simón Bolívar: Essays on the Life and Legacy of the Liberator*. Lanham, MD: Rowman & Littlefield, 2008.

Carlyle, Thomas. "Dr. Francia, 1843." In *Critical and Miscellaneous Essays*. London: Chapman & Hall, 1888.

Carnicelli, Americo. *La masonería en la independencia de América (1810–1830)*. 2 vols. Bogotá: Published by the Author, 40 copies, 1970.

Chasteen, John Charles. *Americanos: Latin America's Struggle for Independence*. New York: Oxford University Press, 2008.

Chumbita, Hugo. "El otro San Martín." www.argenpress.info.

———. *El secreto de Yapeyú: El origen mestizo de San Martín*. Buenos Aires: Emecé Editores, 2001.

Clayton, Lawrence. *The Bolívarian Nations of Latin America*. Arlington, IL: Forum Press, 1984.

Cochrane, Capt. Charles Stuart. *Journal of a Residence and Travels in Colombia, During the Years 1823 and 1824*. 2 vols. London: Henry Colburn, 1825.

Colombres Marmol, Eduardo L. *San Martín y Bolívar en la entrevista de Guayaquil: A la luz de nuevos documentos definitivos*. Buenos Aires: Casa Editora Coni, 1940.

de la Cruz, Ernesto. *La entrevista de Guayaquil: Ensayo histórico*. Santiago de Chile: Imprenta Universitaria, 1912.

de la Cruz Herrera, José. *Don Simón de Bolívar, O la formación de un Libertador*. Buenos Aires: Editorial Atlantida, 1947.

Delgado Nieto, Carlos. *Hermógenes Maza*. Bogotá: Instituto Colombiano de Cultura, 1972.

Encina, Francisco. *La primera república de Venezuela: Bosquejo psicológico de Bolívar*. Santiago: Editorial Nascimento, 1958.

Falcón Briceño, Marcos. *Teresa: La confidente de Bolívar*. Caracas: Imprenta Nacional, 1955.

Ferry, Robert J. *The Colonial Elite of Early Caracas*. Berkeley: University of California Press, 1989.

Fuentes, Julían. *Historia general de Venezuela: La emancipación del Ecuador, Tomo I, El Libertador y Sucre en el sur*. Caracas: Gráficas Herpa, 1974.

Gaitán de Paris, Blanca. *La mujer en la vida del Libertador*. Bogotá: Cooperativa Nacional de Artes Gráficas, 1980.

Galasso, Norberto. *Séamos libres y lo de más no importa nada: Vida de San Martín*. Buenos Aires: Colihue, 2000.

García Márquez, Gabriel. *El general en su laberinto*. Bogotá: Oveja Negra, 1989.

Gil Fortoul, José. *Historia constitucional de Venezuela*. 3 vols. Berlin: Carl Heymann, 1907.

Gómez Botero, Carlos. *La infancia del Libertador y la negra Hipólita*. Medellín: Municipal, 1988.

Gould, Robert Freke. *A Library of Freemasonry*. IV. Philadelphia: John C. Yorston Publishing Company, 1906.

Graham, R. B. Cunninghame. *José Antonio Páez*. New York: Cooper Square, 1970.

Groot, José Manuel. *Historia eclesiástica y civil de Nueva Granada*. 5 vols. Bogotá: Don Medardo Rivas, 1889.

Guerra, José Joaquin. *La convención de Ocaña*. Facsimile of the 1908 edition. Cali: Biblioteca Banco Popular, 1978.

Guevara, Arturo. *Boyacá, el genio militar del Libertador*. Caracas: Biblioteca de la Sociedad Bolívariana de Venezuela, 1993.

Hanke, Lewis. "Baptis Irvine's Reports on Simón Bolívar." *The Hispanic American Historical Review*, 16, no. 3 (Aug. 1936): 360–73.

Harrison, Margaret Haynes. *Captain of the Andes*. New York: Richard R. Smith, 1943.

Helz, Aline. "Simon Bolívar and the Spectre of Pardocracia: José Padilla in Post-Independence Cartagena," *Journal of Latin American Studies*, 35, no. 3 (Aug. 2003): 447–71.

Hildebrandt, Martha. *La lengua de Bolívar*. Caracas: Universidad Central, 1961.

Hoskins, Halford L. "The Hispanic American Policy of Henry Clay, 1816–1828." *The Hispanic American Historical Review*, 7, no. 4 (Nov. 1927): 460–78.

Humbert, Jules. *Les origines vénézuéliennes*. Paris: Albert Fontemoing, 1905.

Humphreys, R. A., and John Lynch, eds. *The Origins of the Latin American Revolutions, 1808–1826*. New York: Alfred A. Knopf, 1966.

Ibáñez Sánchez, José Roberto. *Campaña del sur: 1822, Bomboná–Pichincha*. Bogotá: Imprenta de las Fuerzas Militares, 1972.

Jaramillo, Juan Diego. *Bolívar y Canning: 1820–1827.* Bogotá: Banco de la República, Biblioteca Luis-Angel Arango, 1983.

Langley, Lester D. *Simón Bolívar: Venezuelan Rebel, American Revolutionary.* Lanham, MD: Rowman & Littlefield, 2009.

Lasso, Marixa. *Myths of Harmony: Race and Republicanism During the Age of Revolution, Colombia, 1795–1831.* Pittsburgh: University of Pittsburgh Press, 2007.

Lecuna, Vicente. "Adolescencia y juventud de Bolívar." *Boletín de la Academia Nacional de la Historia (BANH),* no. 52, Caracas, 1930.

———. "Bolívar and San Martín at Guayaquil." *The Hispanic American Historical Review,* 31, no. 3 (Aug. 1951): 369–93.

———. *Catálogo de errores y calumnias en la historia de Bolívar.* 3 vols. New York: Colonial Press, 1956.

———. *Crónica razonada de las guerras de Bolívar.* 3 vols. New York: Colonial Press, 1950.

———. *Documentos inéditos para la historia de Bolívar.* Caracas: Boletín de la Academia Nacional de Historia, 1937.

———. *En defensa de Bolívar: Refutación y mentis.* Caracas: Publicación de la Sociedad Bolívariana de Venezuela, 1942.

———. *La entrevista de Guayaquil: Restablecimiento de la verdad histórica.* Caracas: Academia Nacional de la Historia de Venezuela, 1948.

Lewis, William F. "Simón Bolívar and Xavier Mina: A Rendezvous in Haiti." *Journal of Inter-American Studies,* 11, no. 3 (July 1969): 458–65.

The Liberator Simón Bolívar in New York: Addresses Delivered on the Occasion of the Unveiling of the Statue of the Liberator Simón Bolívar. New York: American Association for International Conciliation, 1921.

Liévano Aguirre, Indalecio. *Bolívar.* Caracas: Academia Nacional de Historia, 1988.

Lockey, Joseph Byrne. *Pan-Americanism: Its Beginnings.* New York: Macmillan, 1920.

Lombardi, John V. *People and Places in Colonial Venezuela.* Bloomington: Indiana University Press, 1976.

Ludwig, Emil. *Bolívar: The Life of an Idealist.* London: W. H. Allen, 1947.

Lynch, John. "Bolívar and the Caudillos." *The Hispanic American Historical Review,* 63, no. 1 (Feb. 1983): 3–35.

———. *Caudillos in Spanish America.* New York: Oxford University Press, 1992.

———. *Simón Bolívar: A Life.* New Haven: Yale University Press, 2006.

———. *The Spanish American Revolutions: 1808–1826.* New York: W. W. Norton, 1986.

Madariaga, Salvador de. *Bolívar.* London: Hollis & Carter, 1952.

Mancini, Jules. *Bolívar y la emancipación de las colonias españolas desde los orígenes hasta 1815.* 2 vols. Traducción de Carlos Docteur. Bogotá: Biblioteca Popular de Cultura Colombiana, 1944.

Manning, William R. *The Independence of the Latin American Nations.* 3 vols. New York: Oxford University Press, 1925.

Marcucci Vera, César R. *Bolívar, 1783–1830–1980, y la mujer costeña en la independencia.* Bogotá: Editorial ABC. 1980.

Masur, Gerhard. "The Conference of Guayaquil." *The Hispanic American Historical Review,* 31, no. 2 (May 1951): 189–229.

————. *Simón Bolívar*. Albuquerque: University of New Mexico Press, 1948.

Maya, Antonio. *Jeanette Hart, la novia norteamericana de Simón Bolívar*. Caracas: Gráficas Bierzo, 1974.

McGann, Thomas F. "The Assassination of Sucre and Its Significance in Colombian History, 1828–1848." *The Hispanic American Historical Review*, 30, no. 3 (Aug. 1950): 269–89.

McKinley, M. *Pre-Revolutionary Caracas*. Cambridge: Cambridge University Press, 1985.

Mejía Gutiérrez, Carlos. *Bolívar en Paris*. Medellín: Academia Antioqueña de Historia, 1986.

Mijares, Augusto. *The Liberator*. Caracas: North American Association of Venezuela, 1991.

Mitre, Bartolomé. *Emancipation of South America*. Trans. William Pilling. London: Champan & Hall, 1893.

————. *Historia de San Martín y de la emancipación sud-americana*. 6 vols. Buenos Aires: Edición del diario "La Nación," 1950.

Molano, Enrique Santos. *Nariño: Filósofo revolucionario*. Bogotá: Planeta, 1999.

Monsalve, José D. *El ideal político del Libertador Simón Bolívar*. Madrid: Editorial América, 1916.

————. *Mujeres de la independencia*. Bogotá: Imprenta Nacional, 1926.

Morner, Magnus. *Race Mixture in the History of Latin America*. Boston: Little, Brown, 1967.

Morote, Herbert. *Bolívar: Libertador y enemigo no. 1 del Perú*. Lima: Jaime Campodonico, 2007.

Mulhall, Marion McMurrough, *Explorers in the New World Before and After Columbus*. London: Longmans, Green, 1909.

Murray, Pamela S. *For Glory and Bolívar: The Remarkable Life of Manuela Sáenz, 1797–1856*. Austin: University of Texas Press, 2008.

————. " 'Loca' or 'Libertadora'?: Manuela Sáenz in the Eyes of History and Historians, 1900–c. 1990." *Journal of Latin American Studies*, 33, no. 2 (May 2001): 291–310.

Niles, John M. *A View of South-America and México, by a Citizen of the United States*. New York: H. Huntington, Jr., 1825.

Olazábal, Ramón M. Jáuregui. *Vida y obra de Don Simón Rodríguez*. Mérida: Universidad de los Andes, 1991.

Ospina, William. *En busca de Bolívar*. Bogotá: Editorial Norma, 2010.

Palma, Ricardo. "Pan, queso y raspadura," from *Tradiciones peruanas*. Barcelona: Casa Maucci, 1906.

————. *Tradiciones peruanas completas*. Barcelona: Editorial Maucci, 1906.

Parra-Pérez, Caracciolo. *Historia de la primera república de Venezuela*. 2 vols. Caracas: Academia Nacional de la Historia, 1959.

————. *Mariño y la independencia*. Madrid: Ediciones Cultura Hispánica, 1954.

Paz Soldán, Mariano Felipe. *Historia del Perú independiente*. 2 vols. Buenos Aíres: Instituto Nacional Sanmartiniano, 1962. (Facsimile of 1868 Lima edition.)

Peñuela, Cayo Leonidas. *Album de Boyacá. Homenaje de la Comisión Asesora del Gobierno Nacional para la Conmemoración de la Campaña Libertadora de 1819*. 2 vols. Bogotá, 1919.

Pereyra, Carlos. *La juventud legendaria de Bolívar*. Madrid: M. Aguilar, 1932.

Pérez Silva, Vicente. *Bolívar, de Cartagena a Santa Marta*. (Text by Germán Arciniegas, Guillermo Hernández de Alba, and Eduardo Lemaitre.) Bogotá: Litografía Arco, 1980.

Pérez Vila, Manuel. *La formación intelectual del Libertador*. Caracas: Ministerio de Educación, 1971.

Petre, F. Loraine. *Simón Bolívar, "El Libertador."* London: John Lane Company, 1910.

Perico Ramírez, Mario H. *El héroe maldito*. Bogotá: Editorial Cosmos, 1976.

Polanco Alcántara, Tomás. *Simón Bolívar*. Caracas: Editorial Melvin, 1994.

Prago, Albert. *The Revolutions in Spanish America*. New York: Macmillan, 1970.

Puyo Vasco, Fabio, and Eugenio Gutiérrez Cely. *Bolívar día a día*. 3 vols. Bogota: Procultura S.A., 1983.

Racine, Karen. *Francisco de Miranda: A Transatlantic Life in the Age of Revolution*. Wilmington: Scholarly Resources, 2003.

Rama, Carlos M. *La imagen de los Estados Unidos en la América Latina: De Simón Bolívar a Salvador Allende*. México City: SEP, 1975.

Restrepo de Martínez, Rosa. *Así era Bolívar*. Bogotá: Editorial Cosmos, 1980.

Rippy, J. Fred. "Bolívar as Viewed by Contemporary Diplomats of the United States." *The Hispanic American Historical Review*, 15, no. 3 (Aug. 1935): 287–97.

———. *Rivalry of the United States and Great Britain over Latin America (1808–1830)*. New York: Octagon Books, 1964.

Rippy, J. Fred, and E. R. Brann. "Alexander von Humboldt and Simón Bolívar." *The Hispanic American Historical Review*, 52, no. 4 (July 1974): 697–703.

Robertson, William Spence. *Francisco de Miranda and the Revolutionizing of Spanish America*. American Historical Association. Washington, DC: Government Printing Office, 1909.

———. *Hispanic-American Relations*. New York: Oxford University Press, 1923.

———. "The Recognition of the Hispanic American Nations by the United States." *The Hispanic American Historical Review*, 1, no. 3 (Aug. 1918): 239–69.

———. *The Rise of the Spanish American Republics: As Told in the Lives of Their Liberators*. New York: D. Appleton-Century, 1918.

Rojas, Arístides. *Estudios históricos: Orígenes venezolanos*. Caracas: Imprenta y Litografia del Gobierno Nacional, 1891.

———. *Historia patria: Leyendas historicas de Venezuela*. 2 vols. Caracas: Imprenta de la Patria, 1890.

———. *Obras escojidas*. Paris: Garnier, 1907.

Rojas, José María, El Marqués de. *Simón Bolívar*. Paris: Librería de Garnier Hermanos, 1883.

Rojas, Ricardo. *San Martin: Knight of the Andes*. Trans. H. Brickell and C. Videla. New York: Cooper Square, 1967.

Rourke, Thomas. *Bolívar: El hombre de la gloria*. Buenos Aires: Editorial Claridad, 1942.

Rumazo González, Alfonso. *Manuela Sáenz, la Libertadora del Libertador*. Caracas: Edime, 1962.

Salcedo-Bastardo, J. L. *Bolívar: A Continent and Its Destiny*. Ed. and trans. Annella McDermott. Richmond, Surrey: Richmond Publishing Co., 1977.

———. *Historia fundamental de Venezuela*. Caracas: Universidad Central de Venezuela, 1970.

———. *Visión y revisión de Bolívar*. Caracas: Monte Avila, 1981.

Saurat, Gilette. *Bolívar, le Libertador*. Paris: Editions Jean-Claude Lattes, 1979.

Shepherd, William R. "Bolívar and the United States." *The Hispanic American Historical Review*, 1, no. 3 (Aug. 1918): 270–98.

Sherwell, Guillermo A. *Simón Bolívar: The Liberator*. Fullbooks.com, http://www.fullbooks.com/Simon-Bolívar-the-Liberator1.html, Parts 1–3.

Sinclair, David. *The Land That Never Was: Sir Gregor MacGregor and the Most Audacious Fraud in History.* Cambridge, MA: Da Capo, 2003.

Slatta, Richard, and Jane Lucas de Grummond. *Simón Bolívar's Quest for Glory.* College Station: Texas A&M University Press, 2003.

Sobrevilla Perea, Natalia. *The Caudillo of the Andes: Andrés de Santa Cruz.* New York: Cambridge University Press, 2011.

Sullivan, Francis Patrick, ed. *Indian Freedom.* Kansas City: Sheed & Ward, 1995.

Trend, J. B. *Bolívar and the Independence of Spanish America.* New York: Macmillan, 1948.

Tristan, Flora. "Cartas de Bolívar," in Marcos Falcón Briseño, *Teresa: La confidente de Bolívar.* Caracas: Imprenta Nacional, 1955.

Tucker, George Fox. *The Monroe Doctrine.* Boston: Rockwell & Churchill, 1903.

Unamuno y Jugo, Miguel de, ed. *Simón Bolívar: Libertador de la América del Sur, por los más grandes escritores americanos.* Madrid and Buenos Aires: Renacimiento, 1914.

Urdaneta, Ramón. *Los amores de Simón Bolívar y sus hijos secretos.* Caracas: Historia y Tradición Grupo Editorial, 2003.

Valdivieso Montaño, Acisclo. *Tomás Boves.* Oviedo: Grupo Editorial Asturiano, 1990.

Villanueva, Carlos A. *Bolívar y el general San Martín.* Paris: Ollendorff, 1912.

Villa-Urrutia, Marqués W. R. de. *La reina María Luisa y Bolívar.* Madrid: Francisco Beltrán, 1930.

Von Hagen, Víctor W. *The Four Seasons of Manuela: A Biography (The Love Story of Manuela Sáenz and Simón Bolívar).* Boston: Little, Brown, 1952.

Werlich, David P. *Peru: A Short History.* Carbondale: Southern Illinois University Press, 1941.

Whitaker, Arthur P. *The United States and the Independence of Latin America, 1800–1830.* New York: Russell & Russell, 1962.

Winsor, Justin, ed. *Narrative and Critical History of America.* 8 vols. (especially VIII, chap. V, by Clements R. Markham). Cambridge, MA: Houghton Mifflin, 1889.

Wood, Gordon. *Empire of Liberty.* New York: Oxford University Press, 2009.

Wright, Winthrop R. *Café con Leche: Race, Class, and National Image in Venezuela.* Austin: University of Texas Press, 1990.

Wu, Celia. *Generals and Diplomats: Great Britain and Peru, 1820–40.* Cambridge, MA: Center of Latin American Studies, 1991.

Index